The Offender in the Community

Second Edition

TODD R. CLEAR
John Jay College of Criminal Justice

HARRY R. DAMMER
University of Scranton

THOMSON

──────★──────™

WADSWORTH

Australia • Canada • Mexico • Singapore • Spain • United Kingdom • United States

Executive Editor: *Sabra Horne*
Editorial Assistant: *Paul Massicotte*
Technology Project Manager: *Susan Devanna*
Marketing Manager: *Dory Schaefer*
Project Manager, Editorial Production:
  Belinda Krohmer
Print/Media Buyer: *Doreen Suruki*

Permissions Editor: *Bob Kauser*
Production Service: *Matrix Productions Inc.*
Copy Editor: *Jan McDearmon*
Cover Designer: *Bill Stanton*
Cover Printer: *Phoenix Color Corp*
Compositor: *TSI Graphics*
Printer: *Maple–Vail/Binghampton*

Printed in Canada
1 2 3 4 5 6 7 06 05 04 03 02

For more information about our products, contact us at:
  Thomson Learning Academic Resource Center
  1-800-423-0563

For permission to use material from this text, contact us by:
  Phone: 1-800-730-2214
  Fax: 1-800-730-2215
  Web: http://www.thomsonrights.com

Wadsworth/Thomson Learning
10 Davis Drive
Belmont, CA 94002-3098
USA

Asia
Thomson Learning
5 Shenton Way #01-01
UIC Building
Singapore 068808

Australia
Nelson Thomson Learning
102 Dodds Street
South Melbourne, Victoria 3205
Australia

Canada
Nelson Thomson Learning
1120 Birchmount Road
Toronto, Ontario M1K 5G4
Canada

Europe/Middle East/Africa
Thomson Learning
High Holborn House
50/51 Bedford Row
London WC1R 4LR
United Kingdom

Latin America
Thomson Learning
Seneca, 53
Colonia Polanco
11560 Mexico D.F.
Mexico

Spain
Paraninfo Thomson Learning
Calle/Magallanes, 25
28015 Madrid, Spain

Library of Congress Cataloging-in-Publication Data

Clear, Todd R.
  The offender in the community / Todd R. Clear, Harry R.
  Dammer.—2nd ed.
    p. cm.
  Includes bibliographical references and index.
  ISBN 0-534-59526-X
    1. Community-based corrections. 2. Parole. 3. Probation.
  4. Alternatives to imprisonment. 5. Criminals—Classification.
  6. Criminals—Rehabilitation. I. Dammer, Harry R., 1957–
  II. Title.

HV9279 .C54 2002
364.6'8—dc21

2002028633

Contents

PART 2

The Implementation of Community Corrections 156

Preface

We decided to write *The Offender in the Community* because the study of offenders under community-based correctional supervision is neglected and very often misunderstood. When students think of offenders under community sanctions, they too often think of extremes. They may believe that people placed on probation have "gotten off" when they should have been put in prison or jail, or that offenders under parole supervision are there for "counseling and rehabilitation." Today, teaching the subject focuses on traditional agencies such as probation, parole, and diversion, even though many offenders under community sanctions are no longer handled in these traditional ways. In writing this book, we have described how the extreme views that most people take toward offenders in the community are often not backed up by the facts. We also stress how the traditional agencies have, in recent years, changed their philosophies in important ways and upgraded their technical capacities as well. The result is an issues-oriented text that stresses both the innovations in the field and the important challenges facing those who do this kind of work.

This book provides a thoroughly modern approach to community-based corrections. It is comprehensive and logically organized and presents in a balanced fashion all the alternatives to institutionalization, including electronic monitoring, house arrest, day treatment, boot camps, and drug courts. The book also emphasizes the human aspects of this growing field. It is intended for courses on community-based corrections or probation and parole for students in departments of criminal justice and sociology in two- and four-year schools. After reading this book, students should understand that the development of community corrections is essential for the future of the criminal justice system. We hope that our concern and interest in the topic of community corrections has been reflected in the book.

Key Features

The major features of this text are the following:

- Balanced coverage of the wide range of community-based corrections emphasizing much more than probation and parole; also included are the wide range of alternative sanctions and risk assessment.
- A thoroughly researched book that includes the most recent findings on policy, research, and application.
- A forward-thinking approach to community corrections: more on alternative sanctions such as electronic monitoring, house arrest, day treatment, boot camps, and fines than found in other books.
- Extensive pedagogical aids: chapter outlines, boldfaced key terms, chapter summaries, suggested readings, and Internet sites.
- Sections on comparative correctional systems that illustrate how other nations deal with offenders under community supervision.
- Descriptions of "key perspectives of community corrections." This feature describes the system, people, bureaucracy, and evidence perspectives for the main forms of community corrections programs.

We believe our partnership brings a unique blend to this book. Todd Clear, a distinguished professor at John Jay College of Criminal Justice, is a leading authority on community corrections and former president of the Academy of Criminal Justice Sciences. Harry Dammer, professor of Sociology and Criminal Justice at the University of Scranton, has written widely on correctional issues and is an accomplished undergraduate classroom instructor. Together, we hope to provide the reader with a blend of topical accuracy, together with readability and interest, so that the text effectively portrays our excitement about the topic and its importance as an aspect of the correctional function.

Organization

The book is divided into two parts. Part I is composed of five chapters that provide background material for the study of the offender in the community. In this part, we cover the history of community corrections, define the main terms and concepts of the field, and explain the growing topic of community corrections acts. We also discuss the problem of classification and the issues of managing and reducing risk. Part II covers the implementation of community corrections through the discussion of the different kinds of correctional agencies: diversion, intermediate sanctions, probation, parole, and so forth. Our coverage shows that in recent years these agencies have changed dramatically—there is no longer a clear line of distinction among them or their functions. The book concludes with chapters that cover "special kinds of offenders" including those with substance abuse issues, mental health problems, and juvenile offenders. By organizing the book in this way, we hope to have minimized overlap in our coverage while providing a comprehensive review of what is known about the field.

The chapter titles are as follows: (1) The Foundations of Community Corrections, (2) Offenders in the Community Through History, (3) The Classification of Crimes and Criminals, (4) Building Community Corrections, (5) Managing and Reducing Risk in Community Corrections, (6) Offenders Under Diversion, (7) Intermediate Sanctions, (8) Probation, (9) Promoting Justice in the Community, (10) Parole, (11) Special Offenders in the Community, (12) The Juvenile Offender in the Community, and (13) The Future of the Offender in the Community. We think this book has several advantages to recommend its use:

Coverage

Nowhere is corrections changing more rapidly than in its community-based applications. These changes, brought on by a history of failure and public pressure for more effective community strategies, involve every aspect of community correctional work, from everyday supervision strategies to broad philosophical shifts. Change also crosses agency boundaries, affecting multiple agencies. In Part II, we show how shifts in the goals of community corrections have translated into practical changes in action.

The Real World

This is not just a book about theory. "Real world" concerns are dominant aspects of everyday work in community supervision functions. As we discuss the agencies in Part II, we make certain to bring attention to the problems that workers and managers face in doing their jobs; we also describe how the agency's actions affect the life of the offender, trying to make it.

Evidence

Because so many new ideas in correctional work turn out to fail, we look for hard evidence to support or dispute the practices we describe. We find, too often, that evidence fails to support many of the most cherished ideas in the field, and many of the most common practices. This book includes the most recent research that discusses the effectiveness of the different community corrections programs.

Values

In the end, the field of corrections is a field in which values matter. What we believe in—the ethics and moral standards we apply to the work of our government—nowhere play a more important role than in correctional policy applied to offenders in the community. Throughout this book, we remind the reader of the values, controversies, and conundrums that must be addressed in developing effective correctional policy.

Supplements

Wadsworth/Thomson Learning offers a number of supporting materials for use by those who adopt this text. Among them are the following:

- **Instructor's Resource Manual**   053425375X
  Includes chapter outlines, objectives, key terms, suggested readings, discussion questions, and a comprehensive test bank of multiple-choice, true/false, fill-in, and essay questions.
- **Thomson World Class Learning Testing Tools**
  (Macintosh) 0534253768, (Windows) 0534253776
  This fully integrated suite of test creation, delivery, and classroom management tools includes Thomson World Class Test, Test Online, and World Class Management software. Thomson World Class Testing Tools allows professors to deliver tests via print, floppy, hard drive, LAN, or Internet. With these tools, professors can create cross-platform exam files from publisher files or existing WESTest 3.2 test banks, edit questions, create questions, and provide their own feedback to objective test questions—enabling the system to work as a tutorial or an examination. In addition, professors can create tests that include multiple-choice, true/false, or matching questions. Professors can also track the progress of an entire class or an individual student. Testing and tutorial results can be integrated into the class management tool, which offers scoring, gradebook, and reporting capabilities. Call-in testing is also available.
- **Criminal Justice Video List.** Qualified adopters can select from a variety of videos including exclusive CNN videos for Introduction to Criminal Justice, Criminology, and Juvenile Delinquency, which are tied to chapters of selected texts; an exclusive Introduction to Criminal Justice video from *Films for the Humanities;* eight dynamic *Court TV* videos profiling some of the most famous and current cases in the judicial system; and videos from the *A&E American Justice* Series, ABC News, MPI Home Video, *Films for the Humanities,* and the National Institute of Justice.
- **InfoTrac College Edition:** A Wadsworth exclusive. Students receive four months of real-time access to InfoTrac College Edition's online database of continuously updated, full-length articles from hundreds of journals and periodicals. By doing a simple keyword search, users can quickly generate a powerful list of related articles from thousands of possibilities, then select relevant articles to explore and/or print out for reference or further study.
  For professors, InfoTrac College Edition articles offer opportunities to ignite discussions or augment their lectures with the latest developments in the discipline. For students, InfoTrac College Edition's virtual library

allows Internet access to sources that extend their learning far beyond the pages of a book. Available packaged with the text.

- *The Internet Investigator II* 0534547265
  This colorful tri-fold brochure lists the most popular Internet addresses for criminal justice–related Web sites. Includes URLs for corrections, victimization, crime prevention, high-tech crime, policing, courts, investigations, juvenile justice, research, and fun sites.

- *Internet Guide for Criminal Justice* 0534527167
  Intended for the novice user, the first half of this 80-page booklet explains the background and vocabulary necessary for navigating the Web while the second half is customized for criminal justice–related Web sites as well as Internet project ideas.

- **Crime Scenes CD-ROM** (bundle) 0534214177, (stand alone) 0534214193
  An interactive CD-ROM featuring six vignettes that allow students to play various roles as they explore all aspects of the criminal justice system, such as policing/investigation, courts, sentencing, and corrections. Awarded the gold medal in higher education and silver medal for video interface by *New Media Magazine*'s Envision Awards.

- **Careers in Criminal Justice Interactive CD-ROM**
  This engaging self-exploration provides an interactive discovery of careers in criminal justice. Students can take an assessment test to learn what career might best suit them based on their personality, research careers from job descriptions, see videos of practicing criminal professionals, and learn about how to get a job from helpful tips on working resumes, cover letters, and more.

- **The CJ Resource Center at** http://cj.wadsworth.com
  This exceptional Criminal Justice resource Web site contains links to over 3,000 popular criminal justice sites, grants/funding, jobs, news, listservs, convention information, instructor resources, and other fun links.

- *Seeking Employment in Criminal Justice and Related Fields,* 3/e 0534521568
  This book is designed to help students develop a job search strategy through resumes, cover letters, and interview techniques; it also provides extensive information on various criminal justice professions (includes Careers in Criminal Justice Interactive CD-ROM).

Acknowledgments

In writing this book, we were greatly assisted by numerous people who merit special recognition. We acknowledge the work and support of Sabra Horne and her competent staff at Wadsworth/Thomson Learning. Many of our student assistants often provided valuable assistance with the text, most notably Janet McMahon from Niagara University.

As with many of our past and current projects, we are grateful for the assistance of Phyllis Schultze, librarian of the Rutgers University–NCCD Collection. We acknowledge the valuable contributions of numerous reviewers who provided essential advice for the second edition of this book: Joan Crowley, New Mexico State University; Darrel DeGraw, Delta State University; Donald Gilbert, Hudson Valley Community College; James Jengleski, Shippensburg University; William D. Kroman, Kent State University; Jess Maghan, University of Illinois at Chicago; Elizabeth McConnell, Charleston Southern University; Susan McGuire, San Jacinto College; Reid Montgomery, University of South Carolina; Linda J. O'Daniel, Mountain View College; Dennis J. Palumbo, Arizona State University; Robert W. Peetz, Midland College; Gary Perlstein, Portland State University; Gregory Petrakis, University of Missouri, Kansas City; Robert Sigler, University of Alabama; John R. Stratton, University of Iowa; and Thomas Sullenberger, Southeastern Louisiana University.

We would also like to acknowledge and thank Dina Rose and Eileen Sulzbach-Dammer for their love, patience, understanding, and support. We would like to dedicate this book to the "two new women" in our lives: Jaeli Rose and Katherine Dammer. You have brought us immeasurable pleasure, and we treasure every moment we spend in your presence.

Todd R. Clear and Harry R. Dammer

For the Instructor

Instructor's Resource Manual

This revised and updated *Instructor's Resource Manual* includes the following for every text chapter: chapter objectives, key terms, chapter outlines, suggested readings, Web links, student activities and discussion questions, and a test bank. The revised test bank features a minimum of 40 percent new questions in multiple-choice, true/false, fill-in-the-blank, and short answer formats as well as never-before-included essay questions.

CNN® Today: Criminal Justice Video Series

Now you can integrate the up-to-the-minute programming power of CNN and its affiliate networks right into your course. These videos feature short, high-interest clips perfect for launching your lectures. A current new volume is available to adopters each year. Ask your Wadsworth/Thomson Learning representative about our video policy by adoption size.

- **Corrections:** Vol. I: 0-534-52154-1. Vol. II: 0-534-52163-0. Vol. III: 0-534-52171-1.

Customized Criminal Justice Videos

Produced by Wadsworth and *Films for the Humanities,* these videos include short five- to ten-minute segments that encourage classroom discussion. Topics include: white collar crime, domestic violence, forensics, suicide and the police officer, the court process, the history of corrections, prison society, and juvenile justice. Vol. I: 0-534-52528-5. Vol. II: 0-534-57335-5

The Wadsworth Criminal Justice Video Library

So many exciting, new videos . . . so many great ways to enrich your lectures and spark discussion of the material in this text! Your Wadsworth/Thomson

Learning representative will be happy to provide details on our video policy by adoption size. The library includes these selections and many others:

- *Court TV Videos* . . . one-hour videos presenting seminal and high-profile court cases
- *Plus* videos from the *A & E American Justice Series, Films for the Humanities,* and the *National Institute of Justice Crime File Videos*

For the Student

Study Guide

Completely revised for this new edition, each chapter of this helpful guide contains learning objectives, detailed chapter outlines, chapter summaries, key terms and concepts, study tips, a practice test, and an answer key. The practice test questions include twenty-five multiple choice, fifteen true/false, and fifteen fill-in-the-blank, as well as 1–2 critical thinking activity worksheets.

Internet Activities for Criminal Justice, Second Edition This completely updated booklet shows how to best utilize the Internet for research through fun and informative exercises, searches, and activities.

Internet Guide for Criminal Justice, Second Edition Intended for the less-experienced Internet user, the first part of this completely revised booklet explains the background and vocabulary necessary for navigating the Internet while the second part focuses on Internet applications in criminal justice, doing criminal justice research online, and criminal justice career information on the Web.

The Criminal Justice Internet Investigator, Third Edition This colorful tri-fold brochure lists some of the most popular Internet addresses for criminal justice-related Web sites.

Internet-Based Supplements

The new book-specific Web site . . . so many great tools to enhance learning:

- Tutorial quizzing activities for every chapter of the text
- Relevant Web links
- Internet activities
- Flashcards
- A fun Concentration game that helps students test their knowledge of key text topics

It's easily accessible from Wadsworth's full-service Criminal Justice Resource Center at http://www.cj.wadsworth.com. This Web site provides instructors and students alike with a wealth of FREE information and resources, such as:

- The Criminal Justice Timeline
- What Americans Think
- BookFinder
- Terrorism: An Interdisciplinary Perspective
- National Criminal Justice Reference Service Calendar of Events

And so much more!

Chapter 1

The Offender in the Community

⊣ **OBJECTIVES** ⊢

The reader should be able to

1. Give reasons why the view that offenders should remain out of the community does not reflect reality.

2. Discuss ways offenders in the community differ from the average community member and draw implications from those differences.

3. Define recidivism and explain its importance.

4. Discuss how corrections and community corrections are a system within the criminal justice system.

5. Discuss the main objectives of corrections and community corrections.

6. Describe types of sentencing structures developed in the legislative phase of criminal justice.

7. Explain how community corrections can serve as punishment for offenders.

8. Analyze whether community corrections economically benefits the justice system.

9. Explain the implementation of restoration in the criminal justice system.

10. Explore four perspectives to understand the function of community corrections—system, evidence, bureaucratic, and people perspectives.

CRIMINALS IN OUR MIDST

Perhaps no other issue dominates today's public attention as does the presence of criminals in our communities. Citizens are distressed about crime, and they want something done about it. In the current political climate, "doing something" about crime usually stands for taking a tough stance against criminals—locking them up for a long term, getting the criminals in our midst away from us somehow.

That is why it surprises most people to learn how normal it is to have criminals living among us. It is "normal" to have criminals living in the community for two main reasons. The first is obvious: Everyone who commits a crime has at one time been free in the community where the crime was committed. The second reason is less obvious and less well known: By far, most offenders are punished by correctional programs that keep them living in the community. In fact, for every offender in prison or jail, there are nearly four offenders on the street.

Most books about crime and justice deal with offenders before they get caught. They study the causes of crime and the conditions under which criminal behavior flourishes. This book is about offenders after they have been caught and convicted. With only a handful of exceptions, these convicted criminals will return to the streets.[1] Many—in some states a majority—will walk out of the courtroom directly into some form of community-based corrections: probation or its equivalent. Of those who go to prison, nearly all

Photo: Manuel Santiago, right talks to workers from the Youth Violence Reduction Partnership Program in Philadelphia. Santiago faced a long prison sentence after a carjacking but instead the judge placed him in the experimental probation program for violent young offenders. The program provides mentoring, supervision, drug, vocational, and educational counseling. AP/Wide World Photos

will eventually be released back to the streets. In fact, the practice of maintaining offenders in the community is so ordinary that while the public thinks about the prison as punishment, most correctional professionals focus on the streets.

What are we to make of this? Is it bad or good that "known offenders"—known by virtue of their prior conviction—are walking the streets? When people think of what to do with offenders, when they think about corrections or punishment, they often think of prisons and jails. Perhaps this is understandable—the United States imprisons more of its citizens than any other Western nation; over 1.9 million adults were in prison or jail in 2000.

The penal imagery of prisons and jails is understandable, for in the common perception they stand as the most visible "fortresses against crime," and incarceration is typically thought of as the cornerstone of corrections. This common view is wrong.

Five million Americans are under some form of correctional control. Four-fifths of them are *not* in prison or jail; they are on probation or parole or in another community program. We refer to nonincarcerative programs for offenders as **community corrections.** Also called community-based corrections, these programs comprise the various ways in which an offender may be allowed to reside in the community while a criminal sentence is being served. When studying community corrections, we must keep in mind that it is entirely normal and usual that offenders reside among us, as well as the importance of characteristics of the offenders and how they behave in the community.

OFFENDERS AMONG US: AN ENTIRELY NORMAL CIRCUMSTANCE

Nationwide, about 1 in 47 adults is under some form of community corrections: 1 in 27 men, 1 in 160 women. Look around you—chances are that somebody you know, have met, or have passed on the street is currently under correctional supervision. This fact underscores how entirely normal it is that an offender under sentence should be walking the streets of our communities.

There are several ways to show the normalcy of offenders in our midst. In 1996, there were 15 million arrests. It is estimated that nearly two-thirds were released while awaiting trial,[2] a time period that was often six months or longer.[3] Of the almost 980,000 convicted felons in 1998, 32 percent received sentences straight to probation.[4] On average, 94 percent of all offenders in correctional institutions will eventually be released to the community, most under some form of supervision. Jailed offenders nearly always return to the community within a few months, many with probation terms left to be served. In short, large numbers of offenders are processed by the justice system every year, and by far most of them are dealt with at one time or another while living in the community.

Another way of looking at offenders in the community is to think about the ordinariness of criminal behavior. **Self-report studies** conducted through the years indicate that up to 90 percent of adults admit to having committed an undetected criminal offense within the last two years.[5] Although most of this criminality is what some would consider "minor"—illicit drug use and insignificant thievery—some of the crimes are less trivial, such as driving while intoxicated or even sexual or other assaults.

That criminal behavior is common is also supported by studies of birth cohorts (persons born in the same year) in the United States and England. Thirty-seven percent of Farrington and West's[6] London adult cohort experienced a conviction before the age of thirty-two; 47 percent of Wolfgang, Thornberry, and Figlio's[7] Philadelphia adult cohort were arrested by the age of thirty.

Finally, there is the obvious point that everyone who has ever committed a crime was, at some time or another, living in the community. Thus, the study of community corrections begins by recognizing that the presence of offenders in "regular" society is not unusual, but is common and to be expected. By normalizing the existence of offenders in our communities, we attack the myth that offenders who are not in prison are somehow getting a "break." In fact, doing time outside prison walls is typical in the American correctional system.

Judges sentencing offenders tend to select the most serious ones for incarceration, but it does not follow that the offenders on the streets are all minor offenders. On any given day, offenders convicted of a violent offense who are on probation or parole outnumber those in prison by nearly three to one.[8] This comes about because a percentage of violent offenders are sentenced to probation in the first instance—28 percent of assault convictions result in a probation term, for example—and over 80 percent of all violent offenders released from prison experience some form of community supervision.[9]

In short, when we study the supervision of offenders in the community, we address the largest aspect of the corrections system. Offenders on probation and parole outnumber those in prison by nearly three to one, those in jails by over seven to one. For a graphic description of the number of persons supervised in the community, as well as the growth in the correctional population over the last twenty years, see Figure 1.1. In recognizing the prominence of offenders living in the community, we acknowledge that it is neither improper nor inappropriate for offenders to serve their sentences under community supervision. We also accept that a full understanding of corrections is not possible without understanding the problems and issues involved with offenders in the community.

FIGURE 1.1 GROWTH IN CORRECTIONAL POPULATION, 1980–2000

All types of correctional functions have grown dramatically since 1980, but probation and parole combined have by far the most offenders.

Source: U.S. Department of Justice, Bureau of Justice Statistics.

www.ojp.usdoj.gov/bjs (October 8, 2001).

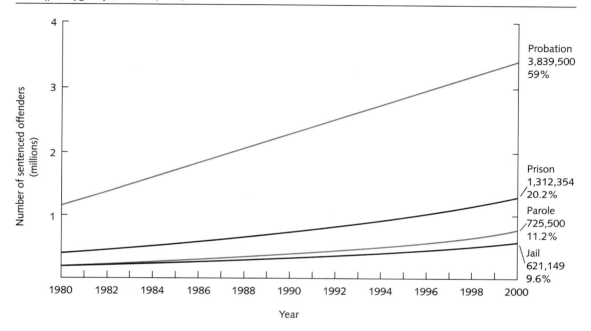

HOW OFFENDERS IN THE COMMUNITY BEHAVE

As we might expect, prison contains a higher percentage of violent offenders, and probation has a larger proportion of public-order offenses (driving while intoxicated, weapons offenses, and so forth). Parolees fall somewhere in the middle. In 2000, women made up about 22 percent of the nation's probationers and 12 percent of the parolees. Approximately 64 percent of the adults on probation were white, and 34 percent were black. Fifty-five percent of parolees were white, 44 percent black. Hispanics, who may be of any race, represented 16 percent of probationers and 21 percent of parolees.[10] That offenders under community supervision do not look like a random sample of citizens, but instead are likely to be young males of color, is a critical concern. There are practical problems that stem from a profile of offenders, some of which are discussed below. But there is also an important socially symbolic issue: Community supervision tends to concern itself with marginalized citizens, those who may feel left out of the mainstream of American social, political, and economic life. We shall return to this point in later chapters of this text.

How do these offenders behave under supervision? Answers to this question are controversial because different studies (and different ways of measuring behavior) produce different results. Clearly, the behavior most citizens are concerned about is new criminality. On this measure, results vary from place to place. A recent survey by Geerken and Hayes[11] found that rates of rearrest for new crimes—the most common way to measure **recidivism**—vary from a low of 18 percent to a high of 61 percent. In places where more serious offenders are placed under community supervision, and in studies using longer periods of follow-up to measure supervision, rates of new arrests are higher. A recent study by the Bureau of Justice found that 42 percent of state parole discharges in 1999 successfully completed their term of supervision, a figure relatively unchanged since 1990. Forty-three percent were returned to jail or prison, and 10 percent absconded.[12]

Other studies find arrest rates that are less extreme. A federal study of parolees[13] (those with the highest arrest probabilities, due to their age) found that these offenders accounted for about 6 percent of felony arrests during the period following their release. The federal study can be compared to a Louisiana study[14] which found that that state's probationers and parolees of all risk levels collectively accounted for about 10 percent of armed robbery and burglary arrests, and about 7 percent of all index arrests. Index arrests can be called serious or Part I offenses. They are the eight types of Part I offenses reported by the FBI but collected by local law enforcement: willful homicide, arson, forcible rape, robbery, burglary, aggravated assault, larceny, and motor vehicle theft. Finally, a Florida study looking only at parolees found they were responsible for 15,000 violent and property offenses during 1987–1991, but this was only about 1 percent of all such arrests in the state during that period.[15]

What does all of this mean? Offenders under community supervision commit more than their share of crimes, and this underscores how important it is to improve the effectiveness of community-based programs wherever possible. But in the larger scheme of things, these offenders are not solely responsible for the crime problem, as some might think. Because of their small numbers, they are only a modest part of the overall crime picture, even though they are a major part of the correctional system and a vital portion of correctional activity.

Still, some might suggest that we ought to try to suppress crime by removing these offenders from the community. It would be costly. At $20,000 per year in housing costs and $100,000 per offender in construction costs, the crime suppression policy applied to 3 million offenders in the community would cost us $360 billion more than we now spend on corrections in the first year, and $60 billion additional per year thereafter.[16] Would the crime reduction benefits resulting from removing all offenders from the streets be enough to justify doing so?

The Foundations of Community Corrections

We must also recognize that crimes are not the only types of behavior these offenders engage in. Almost one third (30 percent) of offenders pay some form of **restitution** to the victim, and 41 percent attend drug treatment programs, for example. These requirements are **conditions of supervision,** with which the offender must comply or the community supervision status may be revoked. Probationers and parolees are required to engage in a wide range of activities to make restitution to victims, decrease their risk of reoffending, and improve their social functioning.

In addition to these supervision conditions, offenders in the community engage in all manner of ordinary, everyday activities. They go to work, they pick up their children after school, they meet with friends, pay taxes, and buy goods and services. In many respects, most offenders are no different from other young and disadvantaged Americans; they want to live a satisfying and meaningful life, and they are trying to solve their problems so they can have such a life.

In this chapter, we explore how community corrections functions as a part of two larger systems in which it is embedded: the corrections system and the criminal justice system. We describe the role the community corrections agencies are expected to play in those systems. We define the major strategies that are used to develop community corrections programs. Finally, we provide a variety of ways to study community corrections.

COMMUNITY CORRECTIONS AND THE CRIMINAL JUSTICE SYSTEM

Much has been written about understanding crime and criminal justice within a "systems" concept. The term **criminal justice system** became common in the late 1960s as a term used to explain and understand all of the agencies whose goal it is to control crime. The criminal justice system consists of police, courts, and corrections agencies that act as **subsystems** within the larger system. The primary emphasis of the criminal justice system concept is that these subsystems are interrelated, work together, and have similar goals. Police investigate and arrest suspects, courts prosecute those accused of crimes, and the corrections system is responsible for punishment of offenders.

Corrections is a subsystem of the larger system that includes the various programs, services, and facilities responsible for the management of individuals who have been accused or convicted of criminal offenses. Today the American corrections system employs more than half a million administrators, psychologists, officers, counselors, social workers, and others. Authorized by the laws of the federal government, fifty states, over three thousand counties, and uncounted municipalities, corrections is administered by public and private organizations.

The three main components of corrections are jails, prisons, and community correctional services. **Jails** are facilities authorized to hold pretrial detainees, those awaiting transfer to another institution, and offenders sentenced as misdemeanants for periods usually no longer than one year. **Prisons** are institutions reserved for the incarceration of persons convicted of serious crimes.

Community corrections functions as a part of two larger systems in which it is embedded: the corrections system and the criminal justice system. Community corrections, also called community-based corrections, is more formally defined as a method of managing criminals that attempts to reduce institutional confinement in favor of supervising offenders in the community.

There are literally thousands of community corrections agencies operating in the United States, and even dozens of *types* of agencies and programs. A single agency, such as a probation service, may itself operate a dozen or more special programs. Providing a comprehensive description of community corrections programs is indeed a complicated task, and we devote all of Part II of this book to that end. One of the reasons community corrections is so complicated is that it often operates as a *local* function, under county or even municipal jurisdiction. When this is true, different counties tailor their programs to fit their particular needs and existing government structures. Community corrections, therefore, can be operated by a variety of agencies, but four common organizational strategies illustrate the ways services may be established:

- Specialized diversion programs can be administered by sheriffs who run local jails.
- Traditional probation services and special probation programs can be operated by court systems.
- Stand-alone organizations provide services to offenders under state contract.
- Community corrections services can be provided as a statewide function, such as parole.

In most states, most or all of these approaches exist. Coordinating them within the larger criminal justice system can be a complicated task.

Although there is some question about whether a criminal justice or correctional "system" really exists, using this terminology to understand the myriad of agencies and processes that are involved with crime serves us well. For our purposes, it is important to understand that the criminal justice system has four phases of activity, each acting as a filter into the corrections system.

The Legislative Phase of Criminal Justice

The first phase of the justice system, often neglected among criminologists, is the legislative phase. This stage is not always recognized, because it is not a formal part of the criminal justice system. Yet in some ways, this is the most important phase of criminal justice, since the establishment of a law is necessary before a person can be brought into the system. This may seem obvious, but the implications are enormous for corrections. Imagine, for example, that one of the states legalized narcotic use. How would that affect the correctional system in that state? The legislature also affects corrections by the way it structures its sentencing system. The sentencing structure constrains the choices available to judges and correctional administrators. There are two main types of sentencing systems: indeterminate and determinate sentencing. Each system poses different problems and opportunities for the correctional system.

From the 1930s until the mid-1970s most states, the federal government, and the District of Columbia maintained the indeterminate sentencing model. Under **indeterminate sentencing** systems, the judge imposes a penalty range, but the offender is eligible for parole. After a specified minimum amount of time served (determined either by statute or by the judge), the offender may apply for release, and a parole board decides if release is appropriate. Indeterminate sentencing is based on the assumption that correctional personnel must be given the discretion to release an offender after successful treatment. At the time of sentencing, the offender knows the range and recognizes that he or she will probably be eligible for parole at some point after the minimum term (minus good time) has been served. **Good time** allows inmates to subtract time from their maximum sentence by behaving well in prison.

The legislature also determines the balance of discretion held by judges and correctional officials. Three variations of indeterminate sentencing are discretionary, presumptive, and guidelines sentencing structures. *Discretionary* sentencing systems give the judge wide latitude to choose between a probation and a prison sentence, and to choose the length of the sentence. *Presumptive* sentencing systems give the judge an "ordinary" sentence that will be imposed in all but the most unusual cases, where there is a specific finding of special aggravating or mitigating factors that call for a stiffer or more lenient sentence. A hybrid of these two systems is a *guidelines* system, which gives the judge a "suggested" sentence from which he or she may depart only when the reasons are recorded in the judgment record.

Under **determinate sentencing** systems, the penalty to be served by the offender is "fixed" at the time of sentencing, based on the penalty imposed by the judge. Growing dissatisfaction with the rehabilitative goal and support for the concept of deserved punishment led to the push for determinate sentences.

In this sentencing structure, inmates receive fixed periods of incarceration (two years, five years, ten years), and at the end of this term, minus credited good time (time earned for good behavior), the prisoner is automatically freed. The amount of good time that can be earned varies from five to fifteen days a month. The amounts are written into the penal codes of some states and stipulated in department of corrections policy directives in others.

In some states, when ninety days of good time are earned, they are vested; that is, they cannot be taken away because of future misbehavior. Prisoners who then violate the rules risk losing only days not vested. In determinate sentencing, release is not tied to participation in treatment programs or to judgment by a parole board on the offender's likelihood of returning to criminal activities.

As states have moved toward determinate sentences, some have adopted penal codes that stipulate a specific term for each crime category; others still allow the judge to choose from a range of times to be served. Some states emphasize a *determinate presumptive sentence,* with specific terms based on a time range (six months to a year, four to six years) into which most cases should fall. Only in special circumstances can judges deviate from the presumptive sentence. Whichever variant is used, however, the offender knows at sentencing the amount of time to be served. One result of determinate sentencing is that, by reducing the discretion of the judiciary, legislatures have tended to limit sentencing disparities and ensure that terms will correspond to those deemed appropriate by the elected body.

A variation of determinate sentencing is **mandatory sentencing.** All but two states now require mandatory sentences, stipulating some minimum period of incarceration that must be served by persons convicted of selected crimes. No regard may be given to the circumstances of the offense or to the background of the individual; the judge has no discretion and is not allowed to suspend the sentence. Mandatory prison terms are most often specified for violent crimes, habitual offenders, drug violations, and crimes in which a firearm is used.

A recent report to the U.S. Department of Justice states that as of 1999 we have no standard approach to sentencing in the United States. More than thirty states still retain some form of indeterminate sentencing. Five states have statutory determinate sentencing. Most states retain good time but have reduced its use. At least eight states have adopted presumptive sentencing, another eight to ten have discretionary guidelines, and one has mandatory guidelines. All states are affected in some way by three-strikes, mandatory minimums, or truth-in-sentencing laws.[17]

The Role of Discretion in Sentencing. In indeterminate sentencing structures, the judge determines the type and length of sanction for an offender. The judge will make the necessary decisions based on his or her own discretion.

Discretion—the opportunity to make a personal decision—is a necessary yet problematic feature of the American criminal justice system. Throughout the system, from arrest to parole, individuals make decisions about the fate of people accused of crime. The purpose in allowing judicial discretion is to enable judges to take into account differences in the degree of guilt. Before sentencing, judges can account for, among other things, the intention of the criminal, the amount of harm inflicted on the victim, the victim's part in the crime, the background of the offender, and potential for rehabilitation. The problem with discretion on the judicial level is **sentence disparity**—when divergent penalties are given to offenders with similar backgrounds, who have committed the same offense, with no clear justification. Sentence disparity is the major motivation for the development of sentencing guidelines.

Research on Discretion in Sentencing. Despite our attempts to keep sentencing fair, there is some rather compelling evidence that links discretion with sentence disparity. Many studies have found that defendants with a higher employment status, economic status, and level of education receive less severe sentences than those without such resources.[18] Samuel Walker and his colleagues surveyed the research addressing these questions. They found that some studies show that members of racial/ethnic minorities are treated more harshly due to discrimination; other research has attributed sentencing disparities to the seriousness of the offenses and prior criminal record of the offenders; and a third set of studies points to economic or indirect discrimination as the main factor. They summarized by noting: "Although a number of studies have uncovered evidence of racial discrimination in sentencing, others have found either that there are no significant racial differences, or that blacks are sentenced more leniently than whites."[19]

Current Trends in Sentencing. Legislators have responded to the increase in the fear of crime and in what are seen as disparities in justice by passing laws that would deal with these issues. Three such laws are three strikes, truth in sentencing, and sentencing guidelines.

Three-Strikes Laws. In some states and in the federal government, a unique form of mandatory sentencing has been adopted—"three strikes and you're out" laws under which offenders with three felony convictions are sentenced to life without parole. The first implementation of three-strikes legislation was passed into law in the state of Washington in 1993. Soon thereafter, California passed its own version in March 1994. As of 1996, at least twenty-two states and the federal government had passed some form of three-strikes law.[20]

There is considerable variation in the kinds of three-strikes laws that have been passed throughout the United States. Some states require two of the convictions to be felonies; some mandate violent felonies. The federal government equivalent requires life imprisonment for three violent felonies or drug offenses. Whatever the form, three strikes is a policy with serious implications for the criminal justice system. Advocates claim that it is a policy whose time has come. Criminologist John J. DiIulio argues that society has a right not only to protect itself from convicted criminals, but also to express moral outrage at their acts by, among other things, keeping them behind bars.[21]

A double-digit drop in homicides in California during the first nine months of 1994 was attributed to the implementation of its three-strikes law. But an equal number of critics state that the policy will create problems for the criminal justice system. Samuel Walker has stated emphatically that "three strikes and you're out laws are a terrible crime policy."[22] One problem is the cost associated with incarcerating criminals for life. One estimate by the RAND Corporation stated that if California fully implements the law, it will cost the state an extra $5.5 billion a year over the next twenty-five years.[23]

There are also predictions of a dramatic increase in criminal trials. As a result, "getting tough on crime may result in getting softer" because prosecutors may dismiss more cases or reclassify crimes that they feel do not warrant life imprisonment.[24] It is "early in the game," but it appears the news of "three strikes" is less than promising.

Truth in Sentencing. During the last ten years, there has been a movement in both the federal and state systems to provide more honesty in the sentencing of offenders. The objective of this movement is to make offenders serve the sentence they actually receive rather than a sentence greatly reduced by good behavior and parole. The "truth in sentencing" idea was first conceived by the federal government in 1984 when the Comprehensive Crime Control Act nearly eliminated all kinds of good-time credits and aimed to eliminate parole by 1992 (later extended to 1997). It was strengthened by the 1994 Federal Violent Crime Control Act, which set aside $4 billion in federal funds for states that adopted truth-in-sentencing laws. To receive the money, the laws must specify that certain violent offenders serve 85 percent of their sentence. A number of states have started to develop laws and policies that adhere to truth in sentencing, and more are currently in the legislative stages.

Sentencing Guidelines. **Sentencing guidelines** were first developed in 1978 in the federal courts and seventeen states and have since been developed in five other states.[25] These guidelines are designed to reduce the sentencing discretion of judges so that there is less variation among sentences for offenders with similar charges and criminal histories. After experimentation in several courts during the 1970s, Minnesota led the way by adopting guidelines and forming a commission to implement them in 1980.[26] (See Figure 1.2.)

Sentencing guidelines are an attempt to direct judges to more specific actions. Sentence ranges provided for most offenders are based on the seriousness of the crime and the criminal history of the offender. The guidelines specify the presumptive sentence; some jurisdictions require that judges explain the special circumstances of a case that led them to impose a sanction out of the expected range. With sentencing guidelines, a grid is constructed on the basis of two scores, one related to the seriousness of the offense, the other to characteristics of the offender that indicate the likelihood of recidivism. The offender score is tabulated by adding the points allocated for the number of juvenile, adult misdemeanor, and adult felony convictions; the number of times incarcerated; probation or parole status; escape from confinement at the time of last offense; and employment status or educational achievement. The judge locates the recommended sentence by finding the appropriate cell. The hope behind sentencing guidelines is to eliminate sentencing disparity and thereby bring more "justice" into the criminal justice system.

FIGURE 1.2 MINNESOTA SENTENCING GRID

Severity levels of conviction offense		Criminal history score						
		0	**1**	**2**	**3**	**4**	**5**	**6 or more**
Unauthorized use of motor vehicle Possession of marijuana	I	12*	12*	12*	15	18	21	24
Theft-related crimes ($150–$2,500) Sale of marijuana	II	12*	12*	14	17	20	23	27 25–29
Theft crimes ($150–$2,500)	III	12*	13	16	19	22 21–23	27 25–29	32 30–34
Burglary—felony intent Receiving stolen goods ($150–$2,500)	IV	12*	15	18	21	25 24–26	32 30–34	41 37–45
Simple robbery	V	18	23	27	30 29–31	38 36–40	46 43–49	54 50–58
Assault, 2nd degree	VI	21	26	30	34 33–35	44 42–46	54 50–58	65 60–70
Aggravated robbery	VII	24 23–25	32 30–34	41 38–44	49 45–53	65 60–70	81 75–87	98 90–104
Assault, 1st degree Criminal sexual conduct, 1st degree	VIII	43 41–45	54 50–58	65 60–70	76 71–81	95 89–101	113 106–120	132 124–140
Murder, 3rd degree	IX	97 94–100	119 116–122	127 124–130	149 143–155	176 168–184	205 195–215	230 218–242
Murder, 2nd degree	X	116 111–121	140 133–147	162 153–171	203 192–214	243 231–255	284 270–298	324 309–339

Note: The left-hand column ranks the seriousness of the offense according to ten categories. The upper rows provide a seven-category criminal history score, calculated by summing the points allocated to such factors as the number of previous convictions, the total times incarcerated, whether the offender was on probation or parole, employment status or educational achievement, and the offender's history of drug and/or alcohol abuse. After calculating the offense severity ranking and the criminal history score, the judge determines the recommended sentence by finding the cell of the sentencing grid in the applicable row and column. The cells above the bold line call for sentences other than imprisonment; these numbers specify months of supervision. The cells below the bold line contain the guideline sentence expressed in months of imprisonment. The single number is the recommended sentence. The range extends plus or minus 5 to 8 percent from the guideline sentence. By law, first-degree murder is excluded from the guidelines and continues to have a mandatory life sentence.

*One year and one day.

Source: Minnesota Sentencing Guidelines Commission, 1981, p. 23.

The Apprehension Phase

The second phase of criminal justice is the apprehension phase, often called "law enforcement." In this phase, police are deployed to look for crimes, they encounter and arrest suspects, and they develop cases against them. The importance of the apprehension phase is obvious. A person cannot be convicted of a crime until first accused of a crime.

We know that police are not deployed evenly in every location. Most police officers spend their time in squad cars cruising streets of lower-class neighborhoods and areas of commerce where many people come and go all day. It should not surprise us, then, that most offenders under correctional control come from poor neighborhoods and that most have committed street crime, since the police are deployed in ways that tend to encounter these types of people. Although crime is not uncommon in the boardrooms of business and the hallways of government, the police do not spend their time in routine patrol of these localities. The police patrol the streets, looking for street crime, and that is what they find.

The Adjudication Phase

The third phase occurs in the courts, and the main actors are lawyers, victims, and witnesses. In this phase, an accused person's guilt is established, and a penalty is assigned by a judge. As we saw in the legislative phase, the judge and the courtroom lawyers work within an arena of discretion. In some respects, the legislature, by writing the penal code, determines how discretion is allocated among those parties.

In presumptive determinate systems, for example, every crime has an established penalty the judge must impose; judges may exercise very limited discretion only in extreme cases. This means that the charges the prosecutor selects determine the penalty that will eventually be chosen by the judge, should guilt be proven. Since most cases are decided by a guilty plea, the prosecutor has enormous discretion in these cases. Offenders are forced to negotiate their guilty pleas on the basis of the charges the prosecutor might be willing to drop or reduce.

In indeterminate discretionary sentencing systems, everybody—even the parole board when cases go to prison—has some discretion over the amount of time eventually to be served. Here, each party attempts to guess how the other will act, and adjusts decisions accordingly. Prosecutors press for long minimum terms, in case the parole board wants to parole the case too early.

Judges try to anticipate the parole decision and select sentences that will lead to an "appropriate" penalty in light of the crime. Parole boards try to understand the reasoning of the judge and prosecutor in deciding whether to release a person from prison.

The Correctional Phase

Corrections has some determination over its own workload. It often has the responsibility to assign *good time.* The amount of good time a prisoner gets generally depends upon the law, but there is usually a range of good time available, and the corrections officials may refuse to award it if the prisoner is misbehaving. Low levels of good time can be as little as one day per week—a seven-year sentence becomes in effect a six-year sentence. Some systems allow for up to "day-for-day" good time, essentially allowing a sentence to be cut in half.

Correctional officials—normally the parole board—also decide when to release a person in indeterminate sentencing systems. They may be constrained by law in certain cases, and increasing emphasis on sentencing severity has left many parole officers reticent to take risks. After all, it only takes one dramatic case of recidivism to publicly call into question the entire rationale for parole and for release of prisoners.

A final way in which the corrections phase determines, in part, its own work, is through the strictness with which it enforces the requirements of the law upon correctional offenders in the community. When probation and parole officers return offenders to court after the slightest provocation, there will be a large number of "technical" failures of probation and parole. When they work with the offender, trying to solve problems and overlook the petty problem, failures will be less frequent.

COMMUNITY CORRECTIONS: DEFINING THE MAJOR STRATEGIES

There are five main types of community corrections strategies. These strategies will be implemented in different ways by different agencies in different locations across the United States. Yet despite these differences, the strategies remain central for all of community corrections. Here, we offer basic definitions of the main community corrections strategies.

Probation

Probation is both a sentence and a status. As a sentence, probation means that a person who is guilty of a crime is allowed to continue to reside in the community, having been publicly warned to refrain from any further crimes. Probation sentences may also provide for the offender to pay restitution to the victim or provide free services to the community to compensate for the crime. It is also common for the probationer to be ordered to attend treatment programs to deal with problems that led to criminal involvement. Probation, as a status, is a kind of correctional limbo. Frequently, a sentence to prison has been suspended while the offender is allowed to prove he or she can live a crime-free lifestyle in the community. Always, the person is subject to official oversight—a probationer must obtain official approval of where and with whom he or she lives, and all life decisions, from taking a job to taking a vacation, must be reviewed and okayed by a correctional official.

Intermediate Sanctions

Most people believe that the choice between prison and probation is too extreme. Many offenders, it is argued, do not require the expensive and severe penalty of prison, yet traditional probation is wholly inadequate to protect the public or express public rebuke. Norval Morris and Michael Tonry[27] have made an impassioned and persuasive case for using a variety of **intermediate sanctions** that fall in severity between probation and prison. Intermediate sanctions are a variety of punishments that are more restrictive than traditional probation but less stringent and less costly than incarceration.

Some of these sanctions are fairly common. Fines, restitution, and community service are impositions upon the offender, but they cost far less than prison and have the possibility of helping offenders live as better citizens in the future. Other sanctions are fairly new—electronic monitoring and day reporting reflect the belief that offenders deserve to have restrictions on their freedoms, even if they do not deserve prison.

Early Release

The average first-time prisoner spends thirty-one months in prison.[28] With prisons crowded to a historically unprecedented degree, many people wonder if it would not be wise to allow a few, selected offenders to leave prison early under specially constructed programs of surveillance and treatment. To date, **early release** programs of one type or another operate in most states that have crowded prison systems. There are various types of early release programs. They include shock probation, shock incarceration, split sentencing, mixed sentencing, and pardons. Each of these will be discussed in more detail later in this book.

Parole

Parole is the original early release program, and it is now the form of release of 28 percent of all offenders leaving prison.[29] Parole is actually two different concepts. The first is the *release* concept, in which parole boards select certain offenders for release to the community prior to the completion of their sentences. The second is the *supervision* function, in which parole officers provide surveillance and service to recently released offenders. These are different functions deserving separate treatment, for some people who object to early release of offenders believe all people leaving prison should be subject to supervision, such as by a parole officer.

Parole release and supervision have always been controversial, but they are especially so today. Many critics of parole say that offenders who are released represent too much of a risk to the community, and they should have been kept in prison instead. Others may wonder if parole officers lack the ability to effectively supervise the offenders to whom they are assigned. Since the mid-1970s, at least thirteen states have abolished or severely limited parole, although some have decided to reinstate it and all retain some form of post-release supervision of offenders.

Diversion

Diversion is a strategy that seeks to avoid formal processing of the offender by the criminal justice system. Diversion operates when a person has been accused of a crime, but officials decide to forego either the prosecution or punishment of that offender.

Officials might decide to waive the formal processing of an offender for several reasons, but usually this happens when it is believed that both the offender and the community would be better off without taking the case through the formal system. It has been argued that diversion is not a community corrections strategy because, technically, it tries to prevent the immersion of the offender into the criminal justice and corrections systems. However, we chose to include it in the discussion of community corrections because it provides a solid option for administrators to reduce jail and prison crowding and keep offenders in the community with some supervision.

Our description of the main strategies of community corrections leaves us with a series of unanswered questions. Why do community corrections organizations exist? What is their function in the larger justice system? What objectives does community corrections embrace? To answer these questions we must first explore the goals of corrections in general, for it is here that the objectives of community corrections begin to surface.

THE OBJECTIVES OF CORRECTIONS

The main objectives of corrections are punishment of offenders and prevention of crime.

The Punishment Function

Society expects criminals to be punished for their crimes. This is a very basic idea, first explored by philosopher Emmanuel Kant, and more recently by sociologist Émile Durkheim. Their writings have helped us see that punishment is both a moral and a social imperative.

The moral basis for punishment is simple: It is only through the imposition of a penalty that a society declares the act forbidden. For Kant, this moral position is so important he has warned that a society that fails to punish its offenders is guilty of participating in their crimes. For it is by punishment that those who obey the law disclaim the lawbreaker and affirm the morality of their own compliance with the law.

Societies need punishment for more practical reasons, argues Durkheim. In a classic study of punishment in Puritan society, Kai Erikson[30] showed how the public penalties of early American societies defined moral conduct and played an essential role in establishing the social solidarity those communities needed to survive and prosper. When communities come together to punish deviant members, a sense of shared values and togetherness becomes a part of that community's identity. Durkheim called this the **conscience collective**— a collective social sentiment in favor of community norms and values.

Because punishment is important morally and socially, citizens are troubled when they feel some offenders are not punished for their crimes. Yet in modern societies, where the penal system is not a public activity but an isolated, secluded act carried out by professionals, it may be harder for the ordinary citizen to know when punishments actually occur. Most people are surprised to learn, for example, that the average time served for homicide offenders is about twenty-three years.[31] One of the reasons many people support chain gangs and capital punishment, despite repeated studies that question the effectiveness of these forms of punishment, is that they are very visible to the public.

This observation helps us understand that while punishment may be a moral and social necessity, the *form* and *degree* of punishment are open to dispute.

Compared to the United States, Western European nations routinely impose less severe punishments, while Arabic-speaking countries and Indonesia are routinely more harsh with offenders. Japan and Australia make extensive use of "shaming" approaches, especially with young offenders, which rely more on appealing to the offenders' sense of conscience than on their fear of punishment,[32] while in Germany and France, fines are often imposed on felony offenders.[33] In the United States, many people wonder if the *form* of our usual penalties—jail, prison, and traditional probation—is the best way to meet our moral and social obligation to punish criminals.

The Crime Prevention Function

We hope that whatever punishments we impose will leave us a safer society. In fact, one of the reasons we think of punishment as an important function is that its threat serves as a general deterrent, convincing citizens to obey the law. Yet for those who are not deterred by punishment, we want our correctional system to choose techniques that will prevent crime. There are three common crime prevention tactics employed in corrections: **incapacitation, rehabilitation,** and **restoration.** Later in the book, we review the evidence regarding these functions; our purpose here is to define them and explain their importance.

Incapacitation prevents crime by placing controls upon the offender that make it physically less possible for the offender to reoffend. The usual method of incapacitation is incarceration, but that is not the only way to control offenders. A range of techniques, from electronic monitoring (which controls whereabouts) to drugs such as antabuse (which makes a person violently sick when consumed with alcohol), are also chosen because they promise some incapacitative benefit.

There are two practical problems with incapacitation. Sometimes, an incapacitative method such as prison is chosen when the offender would otherwise not be a recidivist. This is not only a waste of costly prison resources; it also has the possibility of *increasing* public risk because the prison experience may lead to a bitter, angry parolee where there might otherwise have been a probationer who adjusted to the community. The second type of problem is the opposite, where the incapacitation fails, either because the offender is mistakenly thought to be a good risk for a probation sentence or because the offender persists in criminality despite the incapacitation—some people under electronic or drug controls will offend anyway, and some prisoners escape prison.

Rehabilitation prevents crime not by controlling the offender, but by changing his or her motivation for criminality through some form of treatment. There are numerous strategies of rehabilitation, each based on a different theory of what motivates offenders to commit crimes. Some programs try to provide opportunities such as jobs or education, assuming that offenders have too few choices for legitimate lifestyles. Other programs work on the offender's thoughts, emotions, and reasoning, based on the idea that the decision to commit crimes is based on patterns of reasoning and feeling that can be changed. Still other approaches attempt to be severely painful, based on a theory that crimes occur when they provide more in the way of pleasure and rewards than the penalty provides in the way of pain.

For most of correctional history, we have been engaged in a "search for the magic bullet." Experts assumed that we could find a single type of correctional rehabilitation program that worked for everybody. More recent correctional theory takes a more complex view, based on the idea of *salience of treatments*.[34] This approach asks not, "What works?" but instead asks, "What works with whom under what conditions?"

Restoration is in some ways the oldest correctional method, but it is also the most recent trend. The idea of restoration has its roots in Judeo-Christian religious thought, going back to Middle Eastern civilization. Religious traditions taught that those who offended against their neighbors could atone for their offenses and be restored to community life, if they made reparation for their misdeeds and promised to never repeat them. In fact, penitence, expiation, and forgiveness are central underlying concepts of Judeo-Christian morality. There is an active modern movement to resurrect these ideals. Called **restorative justice** (or sometimes, "community justice"), this approach calls upon offenders, victims, and community members to work together to define ways the offender may repay the victim and society for the crime. One of the most active versions of this approach is used by community justice panels in

WHAT IS RESTORATIVE JUSTICE?

Restorative justice is the term used to describe a plethora of community-based alternative programs that have been attempted worldwide. The three basic elements fundamental to restorative justice definition and practice are as follows:

1. Crime is viewed primarily as a conflict between individuals that results in injuries to victims, communities, and the state.
2. The aim of the process should be to create peace in communities by reconciling the parties and repairing the injuries caused by the dispute.
3. The criminal justice process should facilitate active participation by victims, offenders, and their communities in order to find solutions to the conflict.

Source: Burt Galway and Joe Hudson, eds., *Restorative Justice: International Perspectives* (Monsey, NY: Criminal Justice Press, 1996).

Vermont, where offenders propose to the board ways they will provide restitution to communities and to victims.

The restorative ideal is a form of crime prevention that seeks to make for stronger integration between offenders and their communities. Based on the belief that crime occurs less often when citizens have strong links to their communities, restoration seeks to reestablish peaceful, productive relationships among neighbors.

THE OBJECTIVES OF COMMUNITY CORRECTIONS

The main objectives of community corrections are punishment, cost savings, and reintegration of the offender.

Punishment

Advocates of community corrections are often asked to explain how this form of corrections performs satisfactorily as a punishment for crimes. To many observers, community corrections is a lenient sanction, and some even believe that community sentences are so lenient they undercut the credibility of the law. This is a shortsighted view of community corrections, for all the needs of corrections can be met by a community-based correctional program—in some cases, they are better met by a community sentence.

Community corrections is first and foremost a sanction. Offenders under community supervision are not free to do whatever they wish. They have more freedom than a prisoner, but their choices can be significantly restricted, should the community corrections official so desire. Among the limits commonly placed upon offenders in the community are numerous restrictions of freedoms the rest of us take for granted:

- Nightly curfews
- Weekend lockup
- Weekly drug testing
- Monthly (or more) reporting to an office
- Restrictions on travel, associations, living situations, and romantic involvements
- Financial penalties and restitution
- Unpaid community service
- Regular submission to searches
- Unannounced visits from correctional officials
- Family and friends subject to correctional system involvement
- Employer reporting to corrections on work effectiveness
- Required attendance at drug and other treatment programs
- Restrictions on ownership of weapons

This type of listing indicates that an offender under community supervision is certainly not "free," as the nonoffender experiences freedom. Moreover, this offender is subject to immediate revocation for misbehavior—the prison and jail stand over his or her head continuously. The point is made: A person who offends and receives a community sentence occupies a lesser status than the law-abiding citizen, and the reduced status is a public fact.

It may be that this symbolic sanction is less severe than prison or jail. But studies show prisoners do not always think so: A sample of 415 male and female inmates serving brief prison terms for nonviolent offenses indicated that inmates perceive alternative sanctions as more punitive than imprisonment.[35] The reason? Community restrictions are seen by offenders as more onerous to live with than the relatively easy shorter stay in a correctional facility.

If community corrections can serve as a symbol of the wrongfulness of the conduct, how well does it work as a crime prevention method? Even though there has been a growth in the kinds of chemical and mechanical controls that enable community corrections to improve its incapacitative ability with offenders, most experts acknowledge that community corrections is not a strong incapacitative method. As long as community corrections leaves offenders free to walk the streets, even with significant restrictions, its role as an incapacitation system will be limited, compared to prison.

Where does community corrections stand out in regard to the other crime prevention strategies, rehabilitation and restoration? Studies routinely find that most treatment programs work better when they are applied to offenders who live in the community.[36] This makes sense—prisons are artificial environments where offenders have trouble translating what they learn in treatment programs into real life. Obviously, it is difficult for an offender to restore the victim or the community while sitting in a prison cell. Thus, most experts agree that rehabilitation and restoration aims of corrections are aided by a sentence to community corrections. Thus, when it comes to crime prevention, most people think that the choice of strategy depends upon the objective: Incapacitation suggests an incarcerative term, while rehabilitation and restoration suggest community corrections as a priority.

Cost Savings

There is one thing community corrections is thought to do better than imprisonment, which few people dispute: Community corrections saves money.

This belief is based on the average-per-offender costs of correctional programs. Around the United States, correctional systems spend between $15,000 and $25,000 per year on each offender in prison; jail costs are half those amounts or more. By contrast, $500 to $1,000 is spent providing traditional supervision to a probationer for a year; intensive or special programs might be three times more expensive. Looking at these figures, community corrections seems to be a bargain. For more information about the cost differential between community supervision and incarceration, see the box on the next page.

It is certainly true that sentencing an offender to a community corrections penalty instead of prison will cost far fewer taxpayer dollars. This fact has led to a renewal of interest in intermediate sanctions, penalties that fall between prison and probation. Financially strapped state and local governments are searching for cost-effective ways to punish offenders and prevent crimes, and the community corrections alternative seems attractive. If dollars can be saved on safe alternatives to institutional corrections, it seems prudent to take advantage of the fact.

In actuality, it is not easy to save money simply by adding new programs to the correctional system. Implementation of the programs costs money. Moreover, when offenders fail in these new programs, they end up going into expensive prisons and jails anyway, wiping out the potential savings.

Critics also say that crime has extensive social costs that need to be factored into the equation. If a correctional program in the community saves tax dollars but increases victimizations in the community, some say it actually is *more* expensive than prison.[37]

Advocates respond that community-based crime prevention programs are more effective at crime control than incapacitation strategies because they prevent crime in the long term. These crime prevention effects can save both tax dollars and social costs, it is argued. The interest in correctional costs is relatively

COSTS OF INCARCERATION VERSUS COSTS OF PROBATION/PAROLE

Incarceration

- The average building cost of one minimum security prison bed is $43,000.
- The average building cost of one medium security prison bed is $53,000.
- The average building cost of one maximum security prison bed is $80,000.

In the state of New York, the average cost to build one maximum security bed is $100,000 with finance charges on interest rising to about $300,000. The correctional budget for the state of New York for fiscal year 2000 was $1,983,067,000. The average adult correctional agency budget for fiscal year 2000 in the United States was $696,291,450.

Ongoing operational costs—food, clothing, health care, corrections personnel, maintenance, utilities, and insurance—average $20,000 a year per prison bed. The yearly cost for housing inmates over age 60 is estimated at $69,000 due to higher health care costs associated with older inmates.

Probation/Parole

- The average yearly cost for regular probation/parole supervision is $1,222.75. For special probation/parole supervision, the average cost per year is $3,285.00.
- The average state probation and parole budget for the United States was $56,805,018 for fiscal year 2000.

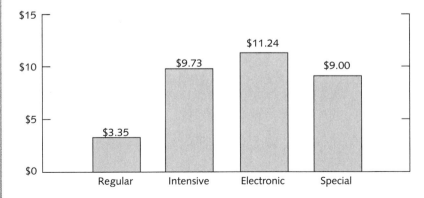

Sources: *The 1996 and 2000 Corrections Yearbook* (Middletown, CT: Criminal Justice Institute, 1997/2000) and Wm. M. DiMascio, *Seeking Justice: Crime and Punishment in America* (New York: Edna McConnell Clark Foundation, 1997).

new. It reflects the political reality that the growth in tax revenues has not kept pace with the growth in corrections costs. Officials seek to minimize the fiscal impact of growing corrections, since every new dollar spent on corrections has to be taken from a competing government function, such as health care, roads, or schools. Any role community corrections can play in becoming a fiscally responsible reaction to crime is very welcome.

Reintegration

A final objective of community corrections is to assist in the **reintegration** of the offender into the community. Reintegration is a model that emphasizes the maintenance of the offender's ties to family and the community as a method of reform, in recognition of the fact that the offender will eventually be returning to the community.

Reintegration is linked to the structures and goals of community corrections, and it is also supported in some correctional institutions that emphasize maintenance of the offender's ties to family and the community with the goal of reform. The idea is that although an offender is confined in a prison, that experience is pointed toward return to society. Prisons that have adopted this model gradually give inmates greater freedom and responsibility during their confinement and move them to a halfway house, work release program, or community corrections center before releasing them to supervision. The entire focus of this approach is on resumption of a normal life.

When reintegration is practiced on the community level, offenders are encouraged to live in an environment that fits their needs. These needs may include living in their own home, obtaining education or counseling, resuming the "normal" roles as a citizen and family member, and attending to the general day-to-day tasks of living life in free society.

THE STUDY OF COMMUNITY CORRECTIONS

As you just read, the field of community corrections includes a complicated variety of topics. This is true in part because offenders in the community are themselves so varied, but it is also true because communities differ so greatly from one place to the next. How can we usefully organize our investigation of community corrections?

First, we describe the foundations of community corrections including the historical background of the subject, the classification and assessment of offenders, and the development of community corrections policies and programs. Then we consider the main versions of community corrections in existence today: diversion, intermediate sanctions, probation, and parole. Finally, we discuss some of the unique problems of offenders in community corrections. Before we begin our exploration of the foundations of community corrections activities, we provide four perspectives that will help us gain the best understanding of the community corrections function. These four perspectives will be referred to often throughout the book to provide the reader with a unique understanding of this complicated and interesting subject.

The Systems Perspective

Corrections is a system—a set of interconnected components working toward a set of interrelated goals. After a person is arrested, he or she may be sent to jail to await trial, sentenced to probation, revoked and sent to prison, and later placed on parole in a halfway house. While it would be unusual for a single offender to experience all these aspects of the system in response to a single offense, the fact that it can occur shows how tightly intertwined correctional agencies have become.

If any subpart of the system changes, it can affect all other parts of the system. For instance, if a probation department increases its urine testing, it will find more rule violators, and this may lead to a larger number of probationers going to jail or prison, following revocation. If parole boards refuse to parole drug-addicted offenders except into drug treatment programs, these programs will quickly become filled, and addicted inmates will stack up awaiting a parole date when space becomes available.

As mentioned earlier, corrections is a system within a system—the criminal justice system. What judges, police, and even elected officials do in carrying out their jobs will affect the corrections system directly. In turn, the correctional worker's role performance will have impact on the entire criminal justice system's effectiveness.

Using a systems perspective, we look for the ripple effects that inevitably occur when one part of the system changes. We ask how one correctional agency's approach will influence the rest of the corrections system; we know that one of the roles every correctional agency must play is to support the needs of other criminal justice functions.

The Evidence Perspective

One of the major questions posed of community corrections, by its advocates and opponents alike, is "Does it work?" It will be important to retain this question in our thinking as we consider the various practices and approaches in community corrections functions.

Although the question sounds elementary, its simplicity masks a range of complexities that are important to bear in mind. For example, community corrections is expected to serve numerous goals—surveillance, treatment, and punishment among them. A given correctional program could be effective at one of these but ineffective at another.

There is also the implied retort, "compared to what?" For example, we know that offenders on probation sometimes commit crimes, but that does not mean probation "doesn't work." To understand probation's effectiveness, we must compare it to other alternatives—if the person had gone to jail for six months and then been released, would the result have been *more* crimes (or more serious crimes) after jail?

The "evidence" perspective makes us look past ideas or programs that may look good (or not so good) and ask for "hard facts" about them. Boot camps, where young offenders learn discipline and are treated to harsh regimen, may seem like a good idea; but before we get too enthusiastic about them, we should do a study or two to see how they actually work out. A lot of ideas that seem new, it turns out, have been tried before and discarded because they were thought to have failed—consider the history of chain gangs.

The Bureaucratic Perspective

Corrections agencies operate as bureaucracies. That means they are subject to the often perplexing habits of organizational life: Routines are established, paperwork is needed for seemingly every decision, and much of the work is about keeping the organization going, with meetings and planning and reports.

Because community correctional operations are bureaucracies, certain "rules" apply. The place is operated on the basis of information and authority—the person who knows the most or has the best position in the organizational structure will carry the most influence over what gets done. People tend to specialize their work, carve out special "turf," and may even become jealous of others' prerogatives.

Bureaucracies are notorious for resisting change. We will see as we study corrections that the famous old saying applies, at least somewhat: "The more things change, the more they remain the same." We will also see how tradition is an important part of correctional organizational life, and how patterns tend to develop in the field that become repeated across various jurisdictions. We will see that correctional systems are faced with all the problems of any bureaucracy and, in cases where it exists, all the benefits of organizational spirit as well.

The People Perspective

In the end, we must recognize that corrections is a "people" business, no matter how bureaucratic. It is concerned with processing people—offenders—and it is carried out by people—professional staff.

Being a human operation is what makes community corrections so interesting, because it gives the organizations a human face. The offenders who come into the corrections system face many of the same concerns as everyone else:

They have aspirations to live a good life, they care about their families and their friends, and they want to make sense out of an often puzzling world.

The human qualities of correctional staff are also important. Many who come into the corrections profession do so because they are committed to helping those who are in trouble. They feel compassion for less fortunate fellow citizens, and they feel a duty to help make our communities safer. Correctional staff, by bringing a human dimension to their work, help make corrections an interesting topic of study.

Corrections activity can be thought of as processes involving people in interaction with one another around problems of crime. It is thus important to include in our study a picture of the faces of victims of crime. They, by their suffering, help us to see why the business of corrections, performed by people, is so important.

SUMMARY

Most offenders are not in prisons or in jail, but are on the streets under the supervision of community corrections agencies. This is entirely natural and normal. To do otherwise would be unnecessary and inordinately expensive. Offenders under community supervision do commit crimes, of course. However, there is disagreement over the degree to which this group is responsible for the crime problem.

The criminal justice system has four phases of activity: legislative, apprehension, adjudication, and correctional, and each acts as a filter into the corrections system. The most important but least understood of these phases is the legislative phase. This phase develops the policies that deal with offenders through the passage of sentencing laws. Although indeterminate sentencing in its various forms is still present in most jurisdictions, other kinds of sentencing structures are gaining in popularity.

Community corrections is composed of several main strategies by which offenders are maintained in the community instead of being placed in prisons or jails: diversion, probation, intermediate sanctions, early release programs, and parole. Corrections and community corrections operate as a part of the larger criminal justice system, and they are affected by the way that system operates. The two main functions of corrections—punishing offenders and preventing crime—are also served by community corrections, but with a different emphasis than the prison and jail systems. Community corrections recognizes punishment as a legitimate goal and crime prevention as something to be achieved through the reintegration function. Reducing cost is also very important for community corrections. Learning about the systems, evidence, bureaucracy, and people perspectives improves our understanding of community corrections.

1. Respond to the statement that "jails and prisons are the cornerstone of our corrections system and they deserve our full attention."
2. How effective is supervision of offenders in the community? In light of that effectiveness, discuss the rationality of increasing incarceration and limiting community corrections.
3. To begin your exploration into community corrections, make a list of the different kinds of sentences that are available for correctional offenders in your state. Which of them are used most frequently?
4. What criteria do you believe should be used to determine the success of a community corrections program? Be specific in your response.
5. The main objectives of corrections are punishment of offenders and prevention of crime. How do these objectives compare with the objectives of community corrections?
6. How would your characterize the kind of sentencing system that is currently in use in your state?

—————| **SUGGESTED READINGS** |—————

Clear, Todd R. *Harm in American Penology.* Albany: State University of New York Press, 1994. Analyzes the sources and results of the severe increase in the U.S. prison population since 1970. Author argues that the expansion of penal harm cannot be justified.

Gest, Ted. *Crime and Politics: Big Government's Erratic Campaign for Law and Order.* New York: Oxford University Press, 2001. Inside view of how crime policy is formulated within the Washington beltway and state capitals.

Lauen, Roger. *Positive Approaches to Corrections: Research, Policy and Practice.* Lanham, MD: American Corrections Association, 1997. Analyzes contemporary policy problems in corrections and suggests policy options supported by the best available research.

Lerman, Paul. *Community Treatment and Social Control.* Chicago: University of Chicago Press, 1975. A classic evaluation of the problems in community corrections strategies.

Walker, Samuel. *Sense and Nonsense About Crime: A Policy Guide,* 5th ed. Belmont, CA: Wadsworth, 2001. Examines crime control practices that don't work and those that have some potential for success.

Zimring, Franklin E., and Hawkins, Gordon. *Incapacitation.* New York: Oxford University Press, 1995. Examines the theoretical issues surrounding incapacitation and its use to justify imprisonment today.

—————| **WEB SITES** |—————

Web site for major source of criminal justice data by the Bureau of Justice Statistics
www.ojp.usdoj.gov/bjs/dtdata.htm

Web site for numerous publications about community corrections by the American Correctional Association
www.corrections.com/aca/publications/index.html

Web site for National Institute of Corrections community corrections information
www.nicic.org

Web site for the U.S. Sentencing Commission, whose purpose is to establish sentencing guidelines
www.ussc.gov

Web site for a correctional chat room
www.corrections.com/cornet/center.html

NOTES

1. Some offenders receive life sentences; others are sentenced to death. Yet even among these, most (over 94 percent) eventually will be back on the streets, though usually after very lengthy sentences.
2. U.S. Department of Justice, *Pre-trial Release of Felony Defendants, 1996* (Washington, DC: U.S. Department of Justice, November 1998), p. 2.
3. U.S. Department of Justice, *Felony Sentences in State Courts, 1994* (Washington, DC: U.S. Department of Justice, January 1997), p. 10.
4. U.S. Department of Justice, *Felony Sentences in State Courts, 1996* (Washington, DC: U.S. Department of Justice, May 1999), pp. 2–3.
5. The first and still most famous study on this topic was James Wallerstein and Clement Wylie, "Our Law-Abiding Law-Breakers," *Probation* 35 (April 1947): 107–119.
6. David P. Farrington and Donald J. West, "The Cambridge Study in Youth Development: A Long-Term Follow-Up Study of 411 London Males," in *Criminality: Personality, Behavior and Life History,* ed. H. J. Kerner and G. Kaiser (Berlin: Springer-Verlag, 1990), pp. 115–138.
7. Marvin Wolfgang, Terrence P. Thornberry, and Robert M. Figlio, *From Boy to Man, From Delinquency to Crime* (Chicago: University of Chicago Press, 1987), p. 20.
8. Joan Petersilia, "A Crime Control Rationale for Reinvesting in Community Corrections," *Prison Journal* 75:4 (December 1995): 479–496.
9. U.S. Department of Justice, *Correctional Population in the United States, 1993* (Washington, DC: U.S. Department of Justice, 1995), table 5–13.
10. U.S. Department of Justice, *Probation and Parole Statistics, 2000* (Washington, DC: U.S. Department of Justice, October 2001), Summary Statistics: www.ojp.usdoj.gov/bjs/pandp.htm
11. Michael R. Geerken and Hennessey D. Hayes, "Probation and Parole: Public Risks and the Future of Incarceration Alternatives," *Criminology* 31:4 (November 1993): 549–564.
12. U.S. Department of Justice, *Probation and Parole Statistics, 2000.*
13. U.S. Department of Justice, *Recidivism of Young Parolees* (Washington, DC: U.S. Department of Justice, 1987)
14. Geerken and Hayes, "Probation and Parole."
15. Florida Department of Corrections, *SAC Notes: Study Examines Inmate Recidivism* (Tallahassee: Florida Statistical Analysis Center, 1993).
16. By comparison, we spend $30 billion in total on corrections (anticipated 1999 adult correctional annual budget), and in 1995 there was an increase in prison construction (up $926 million to $2.6 billion); university construction funding dropped by a nearly identical amount ($945 million to $2.5 billion). Source: www.prisonactivist.org
17. Michael Tonry, "The Fragmentation of Sentencing and Corrections in America," *Sentencing and Corrections Issues for the 21st Century,* No. 1 (Washington, DC: U.S. Department of Justice, September 1999).
18. Wm. J. Chambliss and Robert B. Seidman, *Law, Order, and Power* (Reading, MA: Addison-Wesley, 1971).
19. Samuel Walker, Cassia Spohn, and Miriam DeLone, *The Color of Justice: Race and Crime in America* (Belmont, CA: Wadsworth, 1995), chap. 6.
20. D. Shichor and D. K. Sechrest, eds., *Three Strikes and You're Out: Vengence as Social Policy* (Thousand Oaks, CA: Sage, 1996).
21. John J. Dilulio, "Instant Replay," *American Prospect* 18 (Summer 1994): 12–18.
22. Samuel Walker, *Sense and Nonsense about Crime and Drugs: A Policy Guide,* 4th ed. (Belmont, CA: West/Wadsworth, 1998).
23. P. Greenwood, C. P. Rydell, A. F. Abrahmse, J. P. Caukins, J. Chiesa, K. E. Model, and S. P. Klien, *Three Strikes and You're Out: Estimated Benefits and Costs of California's New Mandatory Sentencing Law* (Santa Monica, CA: RAND Corporation, 1994).
24. P. J. Benekos and A. V. Merlo, "Three Strikes and You're Out! The Political Sentencing Game," *Federal Probation* 59 (1995): 6.

The Offender in the Community **29**

25. Richard S. Frase, "State Sentencing Guidelines: Still Going Strong," *Judicature* 78 (January/ February 1995): 176.

26. Michael Tonry, "Sentencing Commissions and Their Guidelines," in *Crime and Justice: An Annual Review of Research,* vol. 17, ed. Michael Tonry (Chicago: University of Chicago Press, 1993), pp. 140–141.

27. Norval Morris and Michael Tonry, *Between Prison and Probation: Intermediate Punishments in a Rational Sentencing System* (New York: Oxford University Press, 1991).

28. Bureau of Justice Statistics, *Felony Sentences in the United States, 1994* (Washington, DC: U.S. Department of Justice, July 1997).

29. Joan Petersilia, "Parole and Prisoner Reentry in the United States," in *Crime and Justice: An Annual Review of Research,* ed. Michael Tonry (Chicago: University of Chicago Press, 1999).

30. Kai Erikson, *Wayward Puritans* (New York: Wiley, 1966).

31. Bureau of Justice Statistics, *State Court Sentencing of Convicted Felons* (Washington, DC: U.S. Department of Justice, 1994), p. 11.

32. John Braithwaite, *Crime Shame and Reintegration* (New York: Cambridge University Press, May 1989).

33. Sally T. Hillsman, "Fines and Day Fines," *Crime and Justice: An Annual Review of Research,* vol. 12, ed. Michael Tonry (Chicago: University of Chicago Press, 1990), pp. 49–98.

34. Ted Palmer, *A Profile of Correctional Effectiveness and New Directions for Research* (Albany: SUNY Press, 1994).

35. Peter B. Wood and Harold G. Grasmick, "Towards the Development of Punishment Equivalencies: Male and Female Inmates Rate the Severity of Alternative Sanctions Compared to Prison," *Justice Quarterly* 16:1 (March 1999): 19–50.

36. James Maguire, *What Works: Reducing Reoffending* (New York: Wiley, 1995).

37. John DiIulio and Anne M. Piehl, "Does Prison Pay?" *Brookings Journal* (Fall 1991).

Chapter 2

Offenders in the Community Through History

—| OBJECTIVES |—

The reader should be able to

1. Define the cycle of correctional reform and give three examples of it throughout history.

2. Identify three ways in which the removal of offenders from the community for their crimes has changed throughout history.

3. Describe early forms of parole, and explain how they have evolved into today's parole.

4. Describe early forms of probation, and explain how they have evolved into today's probation.

5. Identify the different societal forces that have influenced the different eras of correctional thought.

6. Give the background for the emergence of intermediate sanctions.

7. Examine the three eras that have influenced community corrections: reform, rehabilitation, and reintegration.

8. Analyze how the "war on crime" changed how we view criminal offenders.

9. Explain how the "war on drugs" has impacted society and the criminal justice system.

Few topics provoke a more heated discussion than that of offenders in the community. A vocal, popular majority expresses outrage whenever it becomes apparent that an offender is being released to the community or allowed to remain there. A smaller, equally vehement opinion is backed by institutionalized government programs that ensure that large numbers of offenders—the vast majority—are allowed new opportunities for community life. For every public outcry demanding restrictions on the practice of retaining offenders in the community, there is a quiet, determined effort on the part of officials and other citizen reformers to find new, more effective ways to keep offenders from being expelled.

Thus, there is a paradox: Powerful forces continually voice concern over the presence of offenders in the community; equally powerful forces make certain that offenders have access to community life. Regardless of the public fear of crime and the resulting demands for removal of offenders, the dual realities of basic fairness to offenders on the one hand, and the costs of wholesale removal on the other cannot be denied. Thus, penal policy is delicately balanced between a call for severity in handling offenders and pressures for restraint.

These countervailing pressures exist today, and they have been around for more than a quarter of a millennium. The history of offenders in the community is a history of social ambivalence and cycles of reform. The ambivalence is reflected in the amount of controversy that surrounds any proposal to change offenders' access to community life—either by reducing access, such as through longer and more certain incarceration terms, or by increasing it by mechanisms such as early release or expanded probation. The cycle of reform, then, runs a predictable course in response to this social equivocation. When efforts to restrict offenders' access to the community succeed, they are always followed by pressures to find new avenues for access; when a reform places more offenders in the community, it leads to public pressures for greater confinement of offenders.

Photo: Stocks, used for punishment in England, circa 1735.
© The Image Works Archives

Social conflict about the wisdom of allowing offenders to live in the community is caused by the structure of the social problem. When offenders reside in the community, there is always the potential for a repeat offense. When these offenses occur, they provoke an outraged public to call for restrictive policies toward identified offenders. Restrictions, however, are inevitably expensive and typically apply more broadly than is intended or is fair. In their most extreme forms, they contradict some of the basic tenets of democratic political life by a suggestion of totalitarian and authoritarian state controls. So authorities then seek ways to rationalize or overcome the effects of expensive, overbroad restrictions.

This cycle has defined correctional thought since the advent of democracy, and it has produced the major innovations in correctional practice. In the discussion that follows, we review the development of correctional practice over the last three hundred years. We begin by describing corrections before the advent of democracy. We then describe the processes by which three innovations became institutional in democratic correctional practices: release from prison, probation sentences, and intermediate sanctions. We show how each of these innovations developed in order to soften harsh correctional practices of the day, and we describe the backlash each produced. We also show how each of the innovations was couched in the preeminent correctional language of the era in which it arose.

PREDEMOCRATIC CORRECTIONAL PRACTICE

During the Middle Ages, the **secular law** of England and the Continent was organized according to the feudal system of the times, under authority of landed lordships. Where there was no strong central government, crimes among neighbors took on the character of war: The public peace was endangered as one feudal lord attempted to avenge the transgression of another. The main aim of criminal law was thus to maintain public order among people of equal status and wealth. Formal punishments did not exist, but the practice of **wergild** in England required offenders to recompense the families of their victims, and thus it helped reduce the amount of violent, retaliatory bloodshed.

The church, as the dominant institution of the Middle Ages, maintained its own system of ecclesiastical punishments, which had a great impact on society as a whole. Especially during the Inquisition of the fourteenth and fifteenth centuries, the church zealously punished those who violated its laws with torture and execution. At the same time, it gave refuge from prosecution to those who could claim "benefit of clergy," in which the accused would seek to repent of the crime and claim the protection of the church. In time, **benefit of clergy** was extended to all literate persons, and its tie to the ecclesiastical courts lessened. Given the parties involved, the main criminal punishments during this period were penance and the payment of fines or restitution. Lower-class offenders without money received physical punishment at the hands of their masters.

Both cases—the church and nobles—demonstrate this historic tension between community intolerance of offending and the desire to offer offenders second chances. The expected price of criminality was the ultimate—the offender paid with his life. But on a large scale, this was counterproductive, because the family of the offender would themselves be forced to a vow of vengeance, and the spectre of widespread revenge of the all-powerful on the poor peon of a citizen fed resentment of the wealthy noble classes and the clergy. In the end, only by extending the soft hand of compassion could the awesome power of the autocracy be sustained.

In later years, after the emergence of strong monarchies in England, France, and elsewhere, the full authority of the Crown permeated all law. In fact, in Victorian England, violations of the law were thought of as offenses against the Crown—violations of "the King's Peace." The criminal law system more fully developed. With the rise of trade, the breakdown of the feudal order, and the emergence of a middle class, other punishments appropriate to the existing conditions were developed. In addition to fines, five punishments were common in Europe prior to the nineteenth century: galley slavery, imprisonment, transportation, corporal punishment, and death.

It is important to recognize that no police force or other centralized instruments of order existed until the eighteenth century. Deterrence was therefore the dominant purpose of the criminal sanction. It was thought that one of the best ways to keep order was to torture the convicted person in public so that the entire population might see what lay in store for lawbreakers. Yet corporal punishment was the only available punishment that routinely offered the possibility of allowing the offender to remain in the community. All other penalties removed offenders from society, one way or another. Public torture was such a brutal public spectacle that by the end of the eighteenth century, many began to doubt its effectiveness in maintaining public order.

Galley slavery forced men to power ships by rowing. Often associated with ancient Rome or Greece, the practice was not formally abolished throughout Europe until the latter part of the eighteenth century. It had, however, begun to wane by the sixteenth century, with the advent of heavy sailing ships. Originally the exclusive function of slaves or men captured in battle, galley slavery came to be the lot of some convicts, often as a reprieve from the gallows. According to a proclamation of Queen Elizabeth I in 1602, the galleys were considered more merciful than ordinary civil punishments, even though the oarsmen might be chained in bondage for life.[1]

Imprisonment meant jail, and until the eighteenth century, it was used primarily to detain people awaiting trial. It is true that some sentenced political criminals and lower-class persons who could not pay their fines or debts were also imprisoned, but these groups represented a small proportion of all those under penal sanction.

The conditions of jail were appalling. Men, women, and children, healthy and sick, were all mixed together; the strong preyed on the weak, sanitation was nonexistent, and disease was epidemic. Further, the authorities made no provision for the inmates' upkeep. Often the warden viewed his job as a business proposition; he sold food and accommodations to his charges. The poor thus had to rely for survival on alms given by charitable persons and religious groups.

Attempts to reform prisons began in various European countries in the sixteenth century. With the disintegration of feudalism, political power became more centralized, and economies began to shift from agriculture to the production of goods. Without links to the feudal landlords, the rural poor wandered about the countryside or drifted to the cities. The emphasis of the Protestant Reformation on the duty to labor and the sinfulness of sloth stirred English reformers to urge that some means be found to provide work for the idle poor. It was out of these concerns that the house of correction was born.

In 1553, London's Bishop Nicholas Ridley persuaded Edward VI to donate Bridewell Palace as the first house of correction. The inmates, primarily prostitutes, beggars, minor criminals, and the idle poor, were to be disciplined and set to work. Given the nature of its population, the house of correction combined the major elements of a workhouse, poorhouse, and penal institution. In 1576, Elizabeth I promulgated a law providing for the establishment of a similar institution in every county. By providing employment for people who were not contributing to the economy through socially useful work, these institutions were expected to instill the habits of industry and prepare the inmates to be productive upon their release. The products made in the house of correction were to be sold on the market, so that it would be self-sufficient and not need government subsidy.[2]

Transportation was originally offered to English prisoners in place of the gallows or the whipping post. The Vagrancy Act of 1597, however, prescribed transportation for the first time. By 1606, with the settlement of Virginia, the transportation of convicts to North America became economically important for the colonial companies for whom they labored for the remainder of their terms. It also helped relieve the overcrowded prisons of England.

Transportation seemed such a successful policy that in 1717 a statute was passed allowing convicts to be given over to private contractors, who then shipped them to the colonies and sold their services. Any prisoners who returned to England before their terms expired were to be executed. Transportation was the standard sanction during this period for about 90 percent of convicted felons. It is estimated that from 1596 to 1776 up to two thousand convicts a year were shipped to the American colonies.[3]

With the onset of the American Revolution, transportation from England came to a halt. By this time, questions had been raised about the policy. Some critics argued that it was not just to send convicts to live in a country where their lives would be easier than at home. But perhaps more important, by the beginning of the eighteenth century American planters had discovered that African slaves were better workers and economically more viable than English convicts. The importation of black slaves increased dramatically, the prisons of England again became overcrowded, and large numbers of convicts were assigned to live in hulks (abandoned ships) along the banks of the Thames.

Transportation began again in 1787 to different locales. In the next eighty years, 160,000 prisoners were transported from Great Britain and Ireland to New South Wales and other parts of Australia. As discussed by historian Robert Hughes in *The Fatal Shore,* "Every convict faced the same social prospects. He or she served the Crown or, on the Crown's behalf, some private person, for a given span of years. Then came a pardon or a ticket-of-leave, either of which permitted him to sell his labor freely and choose his place of work."[4]

But in 1837 a select committee of Parliament studied transportation and reported that, far from reforming criminals, it created thoroughly depraved societies. Critics of transportation argued that the Crown was forcing Englishmen to be slaves. The committee recommended that transportation be abolished and that a penitentiary system with confinement and hard labor be substituted. This recommendation was only partially adopted; it was not until 1868 that all transportation from England ceased.

Although **capital punishment** and **corporal punishment** have been used throughout history, the sixteenth through the eighteenth centuries in Great Britain and Europe were particularly brutal in these respects. Punishments were carried out in the market square for all to see and were thus considered useful instruments of deterrence. The punishments themselves were harsh: Whipping, mutilation, and branding were used extensively, and death became the common sentence for a host of felonies. It is recorded that 72,000 people were hanged during the reign of Henry VIII (1509–1547), and that during the Elizabethan period (1558–1603) vagabonds were strung up in rows of 300–400 at a time.[5] Today's equivalent would be 15,000–23,000 Americans strung up at once. Those criminals who were not hanged were subjected to various forms of mutilation so that they could be publicly identified. Removing a hand or finger, slitting the nostrils, severing an ear, or branding usually made it impossible for the marked individual to find honest employment. Almost every imaginable torture was used in the name of **retribution, deterrence,** the sovereignty of the authorities, and the public good. Further, the mob of spectators often added its own punishment, throwing rocks or other objects at the offender. The number of crimes for which the English authorized the death penalty swelled from 50 in 1688 to 160 in 1765, and reached 225 by 1800. Some of the new statutes made capital crimes of offenses that had previously been treated more lightly; other laws made certain activities criminal for the first time. But the criminal law, popularly known as the "Bloody Code," was less rigid than it seemed; it allowed for judicial discretion, and lesser punishments were often given.[6]

London and other cities doubled in population from 1600 to 1700, while the entire population of England and Wales rose by only 25 percent. As might be expected, the incidence of crime in the cities ballooned. It has been estimated that in London, for example, from 1805 to 1833 there was a 540 percent increase in the number of convictions.[7] The crime wave was undoubtedly related to the desperate poverty and the overwhelming increase in the city's population.

THE DEVELOPMENT OF THE DEMOCRATIC IDEAL

Simultaneously with the development of the urban industrial economy of the eighteenth century came a revolution in political thought known as "democracy." The idea of democracy, with its staunch advocates in the American colonies, called for a completely new relationship between state authority and private citizens. Under monarchy, the Crown claimed total authority over citizens and maintained this authority by a monopoly over punishment and benevolence. Democracy, however, viewed private citizens as imbued with important political rights that could not be taken away by government. The democratic state was not seen as replacing the awesome authority of the Crown, but as transforming it from autocracy to self-rule.

The seeds of democratic thought had already been sown in England by the early days of American colonial life. The triumph of William of Orange in the Glorious Revolution of 1688 gave new power to the English Parliament as a representation of the people. In 1690, John Locke's treatises on government defined the concept of liberty and described the ideal of liberal society. Similar works by French intellectuals Montesquieu and Voltaire signaled a European call for individual liberty and just governments of popular authority.

The emerging democratic ideal carried a powerful set of implications for the penal system. Three forces are particularly deserving of comment: distrust of repression, belief in the reformability of the human spirit, and a call for a science of penal methods.

Distrust of repression was understandable. As resistance to the Crown grew in England and later in France, the imperial classes grew ever more brutal in their modes of repression. The common classes were subjected to public displays of torture and death; the political opponents were imprisoned, exiled, or executed. The power of the law represented the claims of imperial omnipotence, and reformers sought to contradict this claim by rationalizing the law and tempering its greatest excesses. A criminal law without regard for anything but suppression was reminiscent of the very regimes of power the democratic reformers sought to replace. What better way to illustrate the differences in vision than through a rational, intentional system of rights under law? In place of an all-powerful Crown, reformers sought a state operating under consent of the governed, using limited powers to administer a "social contract" in which citizens could expect to pursue their personal happiness and fulfillment.

Belief in the reformability of the human spirit went hand in hand with the ideal of democratization of the state. A faith in the underlying goodness of humanity was necessary to support a call for representative government drawn from the voices of the citizenry. Perhaps nobody more powerfully reflected this belief than prison reformer John Howard, who first exposed the brutal inhumanities of British prisons. It is hard to overstate the depravity of the prison system Howard sought to expose: Overcrowded and chaotic, prisoners faced hunger, exploitation, and the dreadful possibility of death from the rampant illness called "prison fever." In the 1770s, Howard wrote in exhaustive detail about these conditions, and he called for an upgrading of the conditions of confinement as a way to allow the confined to reform.

The ideal of reforming even the most corrupted of society was an exciting prospect that fascinated the advocates of democracy. The prison system they invented was filled with a relentless hope for reforming the aberrant and was so impressive that Alexis deToqueville, the French intellectual who visited America in the early days of the Republic, was captivated by what he saw, writing effusively about the great new penal experiment as embodied by the Walnut Street Jail in Philadelphia.

The call for a science of penal methods was consistent with the overall positivism of the Enlightenment. The new penal science held that a perfectly effective method of dealing with offenders was discoverable through trial and error. In 1764, Cesare Beccaria wrote *Essays on Crimes and Punishments* in which he described a regime designed to prevent crime by making its consequences less desirable than its benefits. He argued that as long as there existed no reasonable link between the gravity of offenses and the severity of punishments, no headway would be possible against crime. In place of the system of brutalizing punishments motivated by a desire for revenge, Beccaria argued for a public system operating under rational law in which punishments were tailored to the crime.

Beccaria's sentiments were taken to even more precise scientific detail by Jeremy Bentham, whose 1789 book *Introduction to the Principles of Morals and Legislation* developed the idea of "utilitarianism" to its logical extreme. Utilitarianism holds that the aim of democratic government action should be "the greatest happiness for the greatest number." When it came to crime, Bentham saw offenders as motivated by a "hedonistic calculus" in which they engaged in crime because of the pleasures derived from the criminal acts. The criminal law should be designed to impose pains upon the offenders that exceed the pleasures derived from criminality, thus altering the balance of the reasoned calculation in choosing crime. His most elaborate contribution to this ideal was a detailed depiction of the "panopticon," a prison designed to implement penalties in the most effective, behavior-shaping manner.

THE ORIGINS OF PAROLE

The prison was thus a reform intended to improve upon prevailing penal practices by helping to perfect the human spirit and confirm the goodness of the democratic citizen by changing criminals into productive citizens. No sooner was the prison invented, though, than it seemed to find itself faced with critics. The original American prisons were truly "penitentiaries": Prisoners were held in solitary cells, surrounded in silence, without human contact, and were provided with a Bible and instructions to meditate on their sins. Some critics felt that this allowed an unduly luxurious life for convicts, while others bemoaned the cruelty of solitary confinement.

The debate in the United States centered on how best to reform the criminal. The "soft" ideal was urged by Quakers, who invented the separate confinement methods and felt with devotion that prisoners who are given a chance to consider their behavior and pray to their God will repent and reform. The "hard" ideal was advanced by advocates of the silent, congregate system of confinement. They saw the need to "break" the corrupt wills of the criminal mind and subdue the beast in the man. To this end, they isolated prisoners only at night, allowing them daytime assembly for group labor under absolute silence.

In the end, both systems left something to be desired. The isolation system proved wildly expensive—prisoners could produce little of market value to defray the costs of their confinement. Isolated prisoners also suffered from the strains of the seclusion, including depression and mental illness. The congregate system was less costly, but efforts to maintain order in the face of a determined inmate population bred resentment and active resistance. Neither system seemed to promote the reentry of ex-offenders who were better equipped to live lawfully—return to prison was frequent under both systems.

According to many critics of the prison system of the 1800s, the main problem was that prisoners had little hope under either system, and thus they had little incentive to learn to obey social rules or plan and invest in the possibilities of the future. Reformers began to search for ways to soften the impact of confinement on the long-term prospects of convicts, almost all of whom would eventually be back on the streets. One of the most popular solutions involved offering the offender an opportunity for early release through parole.

Parole in the United States evolved during the nineteenth century out of such English, Australian, and Irish practices as conditional pardon, apprenticeship by indenture, and "tickets-of-leave" or licenses. These methods have as their common denominator the movement of criminals out of prison (usually in response to overcrowding), the need for labor, and the cost of incarceration rather than any reason linked to the goal of the criminal sanction.

In the development of parole, two individuals stand out: Captain Alexander Maconochie and Sir Walter Crofton. Maconochie criticized lengthy, fixed prison terms and developed a system of rewards for good conduct, labor, and study. Through a classification procedure he called a **mark system,** prisoners could enter upon stages of increasing responsibility that led to freedom. These stages were (1) strict imprisonment, (2) labor on government chain gangs, (3) freedom within a limited area, (4) a **ticket-of-leave** or parole resulting in a conditional pardon, and (5) full restoration of liberty. He reasoned, "When a man keeps the key of his own prison, he is soon persuaded to fit it to the lock."[8] Maconochie's ideas did not, however, sit well with the colonists in Australia, where the discharged felons would be released.

It was in Ireland that Maconochie's mark system was realized and linked to a ticket-of-leave, thanks to Crofton, who developed what became known as the Irish or intermediate system. After a period of strict imprisonment, offenders were transferred to an intermediate prison where they could accumulate marks based on work performance, behavior, and educational improvement. Eventually, they would be given tickets-of-leave and released under supervision. Parolees were required to submit monthly reports to the police, and an inspector helped them find jobs and generally oversaw their activities. One study of 559 prisoners showed that only seventeen licenses had to be revoked. The concepts of the intermediate prison, assistance, and supervision were Crofton's contributions to the modern system of parole.

The effects of the English and Irish developments were felt across the Atlantic. Conditional pardons and reductions for good time had been a part of American corrections since the beginning of the nineteenth century, but offenders whose terms were shortened in this manner were released without supervision. During a visit to Ireland in 1863, Gaylord Hubbell, warden of Sing Sing, was impressed by Crofton's innovations and urged that graded institutions and the mark system be made a part of New York's correctional arrangements. Franklin Sanborn, secretary of the State Board of Charities for Massachusetts, championed the Irish system. At the Cincinnati meeting of the National Prison Association in 1870, specific references to the Irish system were incorporated into the Declaration of Principles, along with such other reforms as the indeterminate sentence and classification based on a mark system.[9]

With New York's adoption of an indeterminate sentence law in 1876, Zebulon Brockway, superintendent of Elmira Reformatory, began to release prisoners on parole when he believed they were ready to return to society. Initially, the New York system did not require supervision by the police, as in Ireland, because parolees were placed in the care of private reform groups. As their numbers increased, the state replaced the volunteer supervisors with correctional employees.

The extension of the parole idea in the United States was linked to the indeterminate sentence. As states adopted indeterminate sentencing, parole followed. By 1900, twenty states had parole systems, but it was not until the 1920s that parole really caught on. From 1910, each federal prison had its own board made up of the warden, the medical officer, and the superintendent of prisons of the Department of Justice. The boards made release suggestions to the attorney general. The U.S. Board of Parole was created by Congress in 1930. Thus by 1932, forty-four states and the federal government had put this release mechanism in place. Today all jurisdictions have some mechanism for release of felons into the community under supervision. As we noted earlier, however, the shift to determinate sentencing has severed the connection between release on parole and performance in prison treatment programs. In states that have the determinate sentence, inmates must be released at the completion of their terms minus good time and other reductions. They nevertheless must remain under supervision for a time.

Parole has been controversial throughout its history. When an offender who has committed a particularly heinous crime, such as Charles Manson, becomes eligible for parole or when someone on parole has again raped, robbed, or murdered, the public is outraged. During the recent debate on rehabilitation, both parole and the indeterminate sentence were criticized on the grounds that release was tied to treatment success, that parole boards were abusing their discretion, and that inmates were being held in suspended animation—one more pain of imprisonment.

THE HISTORY AND DEVELOPMENT OF PROBATION

Just as some reformers sought to soften the impact of harsh prison terms through parole, others felt that avoiding incarceration altogether would be a useful option for minor offenders. They believed that prison was often a brutalizing experience that left offenders bitter and less capable of adjusting to society than before they were incarcerated. Their hope that some offenders could avoid incarceration led to the development of probation.

Probation is basically the idea that in lieu of imprisonment, the offender is given the chance to remain within the community and demonstrate a willingness to abide by its laws. In this country, probation began with the innovative work of **John Augustus,** a Boston bootmaker who was the first to stand bail for defendants under authority of the Boston Police Court. But the roots of probation lie in earlier attempts, primarily in England, to mitigate the harshness of the criminal law.

Benefit of Clergy

From the thirteenth century until the practice was abolished by statute in 1827, persons accused of serious offenses in England could appeal to the judge for leniency by reading in court the text of the Fifty-first Psalm. The original purpose of this practice was to protect persons who were under church authority, such as monks and nuns, from the awesome punitive power of the state represented by the king's law. Because this benefit was gradually extended to protect ordinary citizens from capital punishment—the predominant sanction for serious offenses under English law in those days—the Fifty-first Psalm came to be known as the "neck verse."

Originally, the invocation of the Fifty-first Psalm required that the person be able to read, and thus it discriminated in favor of the upper social classes. Eventually, common thugs memorized the verse so they could pretend to read it before the court and avail themselves of its protection. Consequently, judges became arbitrary in their application of the benefit.

For a short period the benefit of clergy was practiced in the United States, but it eventually fell into disrepute because of its unequal application and confused legal character. Criticisms once leveled against it—arbitrariness and invidious favoritism—are often directed today at probation. Probation's detractors assert that the cynical penance of the privileged and socially advantaged affords them a leniency denied to lower-class and less reputable offenders.

Judicial Reprieve

The statutes written by legislatures are often based on an image of the offender as evil or dangerous. But in reality, many offenders are neither. Most are more or less ordinary individuals whose problems or circumstances have led to confrontations with the law. Judges have long understood the need for leniency with some offenders, and they regularly seek avenues of punishment that deflect the full punitive force of the law.

In England, a common law practice called **judicial reprieve** became widespread in the nineteenth century. If a convicted offender requested, the judge could elect to suspend either the imposition or execution of a sentence for a specified length of time, on condition of good behavior. At the expiration of that time, the offender could apply to the Crown for a pardon.

In the United States, judicial reprieve took a different form and led to a series of legal controversies. Rather than limiting the duration of the reprieve, many judges suspended imposition of punishment indefinitely, so long as the offender's behavior remained satisfactory. The idea was that the reprieved offender who remained crime-free need not fear the power of the court; the offender who committed another crime, however, was subject to punishment for both crimes.

The discretionary use of such indefinite reprieves was declared unconstitutional by the Supreme Court in 1916.[10] The Court recognized the occasional need to suspend a sentence temporarily because of appeals and other circumstances, but it found that indefinite suspension impinged on the powers of the legislative and executive branches to write and enforce laws. With this opinion, the practices of probation became subject to the provisions of the states' penal codes.

The uneasy balance between the legislature and the judiciary in selective mitigation of the harshness of the law continues today. While the judiciary seeks discretion to avoid imposing the full sentences specified by law on all defendants, legislatures increasingly pass mandatory penalties that make probation unavailable to certain offenders. The innovation of judicial reprieve, which essentially forgave offenders on condition of good behavior, no longer seems a legitimate sentencing alternative.

Recognizance

In a search for alternative means to exercise leniency in sentencing, judges began to experiment with extralegal forms of release. Much of this innovation occurred among the Massachusetts judiciary, whose influence on modern probation was enormous.

One of the most famous trailblazers was Boston Municipal Court Judge Peter Oxenbridge Thatcher, the originator of the practice of recognizance. In 1830 Thatcher sentenced Jerusha Chase "upon her own recognizance for her appearance in this court whenever she was called for."[11] The idea of recognizance with monetary sureties was made law in Massachusetts in 1837. What made recognizance important was the implied supervision of the court—the fact that the whereabouts and actions of the offender were subject to court involvement.

The main thrust of reprieve and recognizance was to humanize the criminal law and mitigate the law's harshness. They foreshadowed the movement toward individualized punishment that would dominate corrections a century later. All the major justifications for probation—the need for flexibility in sentencing and individualized punishment—already had strong support. Yet an institutionalized way of performing recognizance functions was still needed. This formalization of court leniency is the main contribution of John Augustus.

John Augustus

Virtually every basic practice of probation was originally conceived by John Augustus, the first probation officer. He was the first person to use the term *probation,* and he developed the ideas of the presentence investigation, supervision conditions, social casework, reports to the court, and revocation of probation.

Augustus's story is one of admirable humanitarianism combined with reformist zeal. He was a man of substantial financial resources, and he had the intent of putting into practice the principles of philanthropy espoused by the nationwide temperance movement. Over several years' work, the methods used by Augustus came to parallel those of modern probation. He was careful to screen his cases "to ascertain whether the prisoners were promising subjects for probation, and to this end it was necessary to take into consideration the previous character of the person, his age, and the influences by which he would in future be likely to be surrounded."[12] His supervision methods were analogous to today's casework strategies: He obtained the convict's confidence and friendship, and by helping the offender obtain a job or aiding the family in various ways, he helped the offender to reform.

Do not assume, however, that Augustus's work received uniform support from his fellow Bostonians. The public and officials of the court were skeptical of and even hostile to much of his work. Since the local correctional officer received seventy-five cents for each prisoner, some of the objections were due to finances. Eventually, Augustus extended his work to the municipal court, where the supportiveness of the judiciary made his probation practice a little easier.

INFLUENCES ON THE OFFENDER IN THE COMMUNITY THROUGH HISTORY

As we have seen from the foregoing discussion, modern corrections grew out of a shift in state power from feudal society to democracy. The arrival of democracy shifted the role of the civilian in society from subject of the king to citizen of the state. Citizenship was inherently valuable, and the idea of democracy was that the "free citizen" was the building block of society. The invention of the prison had two philosophical foundations. First, democracy created the idea of personal freedom, and because freedom was seen as so valuable, taking it away was an appropriate symbol enforcing the social contract. Under monarchies, the king was the source of all beneficence, so it was appropriate for the king to be the potential source of pain for those who violated the king's law. Under democracy, citizens were imbued with freedoms as a right of birth, which the democratic powers could retract upon failure to abide by the legal restrictions of citizenship.

The second idea was that good citizenship should be the aim of correctional efforts. Debate ensued among penologists and reformers about the best method of developing productive citizens. Pennsylvania's Quakers led in advocating a "soft" (penitentiary) penology of lengthy, self-reflective meditation. By contrast, followers of New York's congregate (reformatory) system held that strict discipline and hard work were necessary to reform the criminal element. In the end, the demands of the new capitalism were too powerful, and the New York model prevailed. Not only was the system of isolation more expensive, but the image it suggested—"thoughtful" ex-convicts—was far less appealing to the public than the image promoted by the reformatory model of disciplined workers ready for full participation in the industrial era.

If experience showed that the prison seemed disquietingly incapable of producing such a citizen, the reformers turned toward corrections in the community. Parole and, later, probation were offered as the better way to reform offenders by working with them in their community settings. From the mid-1800s through the mid-1900s, these two forms of community corrections were the primary alternatives to imprisonment for those who felt incarceration failed to provide society with a chance to change offenders for the better. During this time, three successive ideals dominated thought about the best ways to deal with offenders in the community. Vincent O'Leary and David Duffee[13] have referred to these ideals as three distinctive eras: reform, rehabilitation, and reintegration.

The Reform Era

The earliest orientation toward community corrections was based upon a view of offenders as morally flawed individuals. The predominant idea in the "reform" era was to remold offenders into productive citizens—the model citizen was based on the Protestant ethic. Thus, the corrections system was designed to produce willing laborers, good fathers, and clean-living Christian men.

Community-based correctional workers—probation and parole officers—were supposed to be authoritarian and paternalistic in style. They saw themselves as representatives of community moral and ethical standards, and their job was to inculcate within the offender the disciplines and attitudes consonant with community values. Offenders in the community were required to work, support their families, attend church, and make their children available to the involvement of correctional officials. It was commonly required that offenders live "upright and virtuous" lives, and what would today be considered minor violations, such as drinking or violating a curfew, would result in serious consequences, even return to prison.

Under the "reform" philosophy, the offender needed not only to obey the law, but to show evidence of a compliant lifestyle through a good family, a good job, and good neighborly relations. The probation and parole officers were drawn from two major professions—clergy and law enforcement. Each represented a kind of moral authority as a role model, and the roles of the probation or parole officer were often performed by volunteers who saw this as an opportunity to contribute to the betterment of community life. When departments finally developed paid, full-time jobs in probation or parole, it was common for employers to fill vacancies with retired policemen or ministers who operated as watchmen and missionaries to the criminal classes.

Correctional work took place in the homes and residential areas of the offenders. Officers would visit offenders and their families in their homes, talk to employers and the local clergy, and visit with neighbors and other significant community members to determine whether the offender's adjustment and lifestyle were acceptable. Field visits were made at all hours of the day, often unannounced, in order to make sure the offender's compliant conduct was not feigned. On the whole, the job involved a kind of mentoring, advising, cajoling, and when necessary, threatening—anything to make certain the offender would become a reformed member of the community to make the correctional worker proud.

The reform approach was popular, but it was not without its detractors. The cultural ideal of the "good Christian" may have seemed attractive, but it was often badly at odds with the real impediments of poverty and discrimination faced by the immigrant poor of the mid-1800s. The image of a "firm but fair" parole officer haranguing the illiterate, unskilled lower-class citizenry into a cultural lifestyle that mirrored the "everyday Joe" was so inappropriate that it made the experienced penologist cringe. Most offenders needed a job, not a role model.

The Rehabilitation Era

The reform era dominated community correctional thought from the mid-1800s until the 1930s, when it began to be replaced by a professional orientation adopting the language and techniques of the new science of the psyche. The work of Sigmund Freud, exploring the anatomy of emotional functioning, was a powerful new idea in the early 1900s, and it led to the development of psychotherapy and the field of psychology. Penologists began to attribute criminal behavior to defective mental and emotional functioning, and the "medical model" of corrections was the result.

In the prison setting, the medical model turned confinement from a punishment for crime into a treatment for crime. Carl Menninger, in his classic *The Crime of Punishment*,[14] argued that it was folly to lock offenders up without paying heed to the psychosocial inadequacies they suffered from—and that caused their criminality. A new correctional system was envisioned in which people were not punished, but rather received treatment for the problems that caused their criminality.

The medical model asked correctional workers to approach offenders as suffering from mental illness. In place of the volunteer and paraprofessional ideal of the reform era, under the rehabilitation ideal, correctional staff were to be professionals skilled in the methods of mental health treatment. The primary technique to be used was interpersonal counseling. Probation and parole officers abandoned field visits and family and employer contacts, and established themselves in professional offices, seeing offenders (called "clients") by appointment.

The counseling sessions became wide-ranging excursions into the motives and insights of the offender, trying to determine the underlying reasons for criminal conduct and help the offender overcome the urges that produce the misbehavior. Sometimes the probation or parole officer would investigate the early childhood experiences of the offender to look for clues about the antecedents of criminality. Other times, the emotions and reasoning of the offender would be deciphered in pursuit of the mental aberrations that made crime occur. The end result sought by the probation or parole officer as counselor was to promote the offender's "insight" into the criminality, and thus to break its hold on the psyche.

The problem with the rehabilitation ethic was twofold: Not all offenders were mentally ill, and not all community corrections workers were skilled as psychotherapists. Many "treated" offenders continued to offend, even after treatment. And many correctional employees practiced a brand of "treatment" that bore little relationship to the grand ideas of Freud and his followers. The full level of funding a medical model never occurred.

The Reintegration Era

There could be no question that poverty and crime were linked. The idea that mental illness afflicted the poor but left the wealthy unaffected seemed weak at best, specious at worst. By the 1960s, sociologists began to discuss the way in which access to society gave one a stake in society's rules, and alienation from social benefits meant one had no reason to obey the rules of the game. In place of simply trying to increase an offender's mental health, penologists thought of increasing the legitimate ties of the offender to mainstream society as a correctional approach of promise. In 1967, when President Lyndon Johnson's Commission on Law Enforcement and Administration of Justice considered the ideal corrections system, it reported that "crime and delinquency are symptoms of failures and disorganization of the community. . . . The task of corrections, therefore, includes building or rebuilding social ties, obtaining employment and education, securing in the larger senses a place for the offender in the routine functioning of society."[15] This analysis was consistent with the views of advocates of community corrections who felt that the goal of the criminal justice system should be the reintegration of offenders into the community.

The reintegration ideal was consistent with Johnson's "Great Society" programs of the 1960s, which sought to end poverty and discrimination. The correctional version of the great society involved job-training programs for ex-offenders, creation of special employment opportunities, and an emphasis on community-based programs. A wide variety of programs existed, all seemingly based on a view of offenders who commit crimes because noncriminal choices eluded them due to lives of poverty and social alienation. The point of these programs was to strengthen the offender's social skills, especially those related to employment, and thereby help offenders find legitimate roles in society.

The most important change of the reintegration era was the primacy of non-prison correctional alternatives for handling offenders. Probation and parole became the chief methods in the correctional arsenal, and a few correctional leaders began to think of the prison as a failed experiment, obsolete as a correctional technique.

One major event that aided the move toward reintegration and community corrections was the inmate riot and hostage taking at New York State's Attica Correctional Facility. On Monday morning, September 13, 1971, after four days of negotiations, a helicopter began dropping CS gas (an incapacitating agent) on the inmates milling around in the prison yard. Following the gassing, there was a rain of bullets from state police guns that hit 128 men and killed 39, 29 inmates and 10 hostages. With the exception of the Native Americans massacred in the late nineteenth century, it was the "bloodiest one-day encounter between Americans since the Civil War."[16] The hostilities at Attica were viewed by many as evidence that prisons are counterproductive and unjust. They urged that decarceration through community corrections should be the goal and pressed greater use of alternatives to incarceration such as probation, halfway houses, and community service. The fact that three-quarters of offenders were under supervision in the community was seen as a good thing, a number that needed to be increased.

Reintegration and community corrections called for a radical departure from the medical model's emphasis on treatment in prison. Instead, prisons were to be avoided because they were artificial institutions that interfered with the offender's ability to develop a crime-free lifestyle. Proponents argued that corrections should turn away from psychological treatment in favor of programs that would increase offenders' opportunities to become successful citizens. Probation would be the sentence of choice for nonviolent offenders so that they could engage in vocational and educational programs that increased their chances of adjusting to society. For the small portion of offenders who had to be incarcerated, the amount of time in prison would be only a short interval until release on parole. To further the goal of reintegration, correctional workers would serve as advocates for offenders as they dealt with governmental agencies providing employment counseling, medical treatment, and financial assistance.

The reintegration idea was dominant in corrections for about a decade, until the late 1970s. Advocates of reintegration claim, as did advocates of previous reforms, that the idea was never adequately tested. The community corrections ideal remains one of the significant ideas and practices in the recent history of corrections.

In the remaining sections of this chapter, we will explain three major crime policy ideas that have developed since the early 1970s. Each has helped to shape the face of corrections and will continue to influence it as we proceed into the twenty-first century.

The War on Crime

Although many correctional officials were convinced that the route to a more effective correctional system lay in slow and steady expansion of and improvements in the community-based strategies of probation and parole, the **war on crime** eliminated any vestiges of hope for serious change in the penal system. The war on crime, a slogan used by politicians since the 1960s, employed "get tough" rhetoric and imagery that carried far more dramatic effect with the general public than "treatment" programs. The war on crime was the most important development in criminal justice over the last thirty years, and its approach toward crime and criminals proved a political gold mine. Electoral politics provided a platform for the candidates to show they took public fears and the rising crime rate seriously.

Attacks upon the leniency of corrections had been heard sporadically for years, of course. But the "war" rhetoric and the public response galvanized a dramatic shift away from the reintegrative ideal toward a system that sought to effectively restrain today's offenders from repeat criminality and deter potential offenders from starting a life of crime. The attacks on correctional programming were aided by rising crime rates and a growing sense that correctional programs had failed to rehabilitate offenders—a belief that was supported by Robert Martinson's landmark study in 1975: "What Works?—Questions and Answers About Prison Reform."[17] Martinson reviewed the results of over 250 correctional program evaluations to find no evidence that any approach was "consistently effective" at reducing recidivism.

A disorganized coalition of liberal and conservative intellectuals emerged attacking the traditional correctional methods based on offender treatment and reintegration. Conservatives such as Ernest Van den Haag[18] and James Q. Wilson[19] argued that the restorative aspects of penology were flawed both technically and morally. They called for a new penology based on concepts of **deterrence** and **incapacitation.** Liberal reformers such as David Fogel[20] and David T. Stanley[21] argued that the system of coercive correctional treatment and parole had dehumanized offenders and resulted in inexcusable abuses of power by authorities.

In the 1970s, both probation and parole came under attack by both ends of the political spectrum. Probation was faulted by the right as a too-lenient and ineffectual slap on the wrist, and by the left as paternalistically intrusive and disrespectful of offenders' legal rights. Parole was attacked by the right as a form of undue reduction in punitiveness that put the public at risk, and by the left as an arbitrary and capricious form of penal treatment. It sometimes seemed that no defenders of the current system existed to counter the attacks from all directions.

Faced with this heat, the penal system changed in many ways. In 1976, the U.S. Supreme Court opened the way for the states to reenact the death penalty, and within a few years a majority of states had followed. Probation was limited and parole eliminated in a number of states. This was the heritage of the war on crime of the 1970s, a conflict that continued through the 1990s. It was also during this time period that the United States embarked on a new model that paralleled the war on crime—the crime control model.

Offenders in the Community Through History

The Crime Control Model

Faced with high crime rates and information about the "failure" of rehabilitation, legislators, judges, and correctional officials in the late 1970s responded with a renewed emphasis on a **crime control model** of corrections. First presented by Herbert Packer as a framework to understand the "two models of the criminal process,"[22] the term *crime control model* has come to be used in a more general way to describe how we deal with crime and criminals. The crime control model is based on the assumption that criminal behavior can be controlled by more incarceration and other forms of strict supervision in the community. It has led to many changes in the criminal justice system and has contributed to the "get tough" attitude toward crime and the punishment of offenders. This mentality has called for new determinate sentencing laws designed to incarcerate violent offenders and career criminals for longer periods of time and for the elimination of rehabilitation programs in prisons. Changes have been made in the detention without bail of accused persons thought to present a danger to the community, reinstitution of the death penalty in thirty-seven states, and the requirement that judges impose mandatory penalties for persons convicted of certain offenses or having extensive criminal records. In community corrections, changes in the sentencing structures in some states led to the abolition of parole release. Most states developed programs that required intensive supervision of probationers. By the end of the century, the effect of these "get tough" policies was evidenced by the record numbers of prisoners, the longer sentences being served, and the increase in the size of the probation population.

In addition to the war on crime and the crime control model, the **war on drugs** has surfaced as another crime policy with the intent of being "tough on crime." Crusades against the use of drugs have been a recurring theme of American politics since the late 1800s. The latest manifestation began in 1982 when President Ronald Reagan declared another "war on drugs" and asked Congress to set aside more money for drug enforcement personnel and for prison space. This came at a time when the country was scared by the advent of crack cocaine, which ravaged many communities and resulted in an increased murder rate. In 1987, Congress imposed stiff mandatory minimum sentences for federal drug law violations, laws that were copied by many states.

The drug war reached its peak in 1988 when President George H. W. Bush created the Office of National Drug Control Policy and declared drugs to be the "gravest domestic threat facing our nation today."[23] It has succeeded in each administration, with each president urging Congress to appropriate billions of dollars for an all-out law enforcement campaign against drugs.

The "war on drugs" has succeeded on one front by packing the nation's prisons with drug law offenders, but many scholars believe that is about all it has achieved. Research on the impact of the war on drugs has shown that drug enforcement has had little impact on the level of drug use or the crime rate.[24]

But the drug war has led directly to an increase in arrests, convictions, and long prison sentences. With additional resources and pressures for enforcement, the number of people sentenced to prison for drug offenses has increased steadily. In 1980, only 19,000 or about 6 percent of state prisoners had been convicted of a drug offense; by 2000 this number had risen to 251,200. Today, 21 percent of state prisoners are incarcerated for drug offenses, and the percentage in federal prisons is even higher, at almost 60 percent. Furthermore, the average state drug sentence has increased from thirteen months in 1985 to forty-seven months in 1998.[25]

Critics of the war on drugs have argued that in addition to the minimal reduction in drug use and increased system cost, another major problem with the war on drugs is that it has been waged primarily against black men. Research supporting this view states that although African Americans make up 13 percent of the population and only 15 percent of illegal drug users, 35 percent of all people arrested for drug offenses, 55 percent of those convicted, and 74 percent of those sentenced to prison for drugs are black.[26] Noted criminologist Jerome Miller has characterized the war on drugs as a "search and destroy" mission directed at young African American men.[27] Although the war on drugs has had a significant impact on American society and on the minority community, it is unsure whether we can say it has been effective at reducing drug use and serious crime.

The impact of the war on crime, the crime control model, and the war on drugs has been significant for community corrections. For instance, there have been calls to drastically change the way probation and parole are delivered. Between the years 1972, the year of Nixon's second election, and 1992, every state passed laws restricting the availability of probation and parole, and several states abolished parole altogether. At the same time, as discussed in Chapter 1, since 1973 there has been an unprecedented growth in the use of all forms of corrections. As a result, there has been a call to develop new ways to work with offenders in the community. The final sections of this chapter will address some of these ideas.

CURRENT TRENDS IN COMMUNITY CORRECTIONS

As the United States enters a new century, it is an exciting time for community corrections policy and practice. Because the financial and human costs of the crime control policies of the 1990s have taken their toll, many of those policies are now in question. A major concern raised is whether we can achieve justice—punish offenders for their crimes—while still limiting costs and maintaining community safety. Two community corrections strategies have recently surfaced with the hope that they can address these and other concerns of a troubled corrections system—intermediate sanctions and restorative justice. Each of these will be discussed in more detail in later chapters, but they are briefly mentioned here because they comport with our immediate discussion about the background of community corrections.

The Development of Intermediate Sanctions

The growth of corrections from the 1970s through the 1990s fit well with a public mood intolerant of crime, but it was troubling to many experts. Most observers recognized that the growing financial commitment to the prison was a fiscal and strategic mistake. But they equally realized that traditional probation methods were outmatched by the growing seriousness of repeat offenders in the penal system. Some began to call for development of an array of correctional methods falling between probation and prison—intermediate sanctions. As we explained in Chapter 1, intermediate sanctions are any number of punishments that fall between probation and prison. Most of these sanctions would operate in community contexts, but they would contain considerable increases in the level of restrictiveness and controls placed on offenders subjected to these sanctions.

The most comprehensive explanation of the need for intermediate sanctions has been provided by Norval Morris and Michael Tonry in their book *Intermediate Punishments.*[28] They argue in favor of a "rational, principled sentencing system," which would incorporate intermediate sanctions as a regular form of criminal penalties for offenders whose crimes are of medium seriousness. Thus, they provide for graduated levels of control and punishment severity, depending upon the crime. They call their system "principled" because it fits the punishment to the crime; they call it "rational" because it incorporates a range of sanctions beyond the traditional extremes of probation and prison.

Intermediate sanctions that represent forms of correctional supervision that are tougher than probation, but less drastic than prison, began to become much more common in the late 1980s. Among the more popular intermediate sanctions are these:

- Residential drug treatment facilities
- Boot camps
- Intensive supervision
- Electronic monitoring
- Home confinement

The closing years of the twentieth century have very much been the years of intermediate sanctions. Current evaluations, however, seem to find only limited support at best for their effectiveness (see Chapter 7). Yet they continue to flourish because they hold promise of being so much less expensive and less intrusive than prison, without the weaknesses of probation.

The Restorative Justice Movement

Restorative justice is the recent movement to resurrect an old idea that is rooted in indigenous cultures and Judeo-Christian religious thought. As briefly mentioned in Chapter 1, restorative justice calls for the offender, the victim, and the community to work together to deal with the problems and solutions of crime. Restorative justice is unique in that it borrows from two other correctional philosophies—retribution and community reintegration. It is linked to **retribution** by the principle of reciprocity and through paying restitution to the community and victim for harms committed. At the same time, it calls for the offender to remain in the community and to regain status as a functional member of society.

There are at least three reasons why the restorative justice movement has found a new home in American corrections. First, because the traditional correctional approaches of rehabilitation and punishment have proven to be relatively ineffective in the reduction and prevention of crime, new approaches are necessary for dealing with crime and its prevention. Second, the success of community-oriented policing in the reduction of everyday disorder has caused other sectors of the justice system to take notice of what can be accomplished when the problems of crime are dealt with on the community level.[29] Community prosecution courts, drug courts, and on the corrections level, community restoration boards have all formed a new breed of justice programs. Finally, the restorative justice ideal is also related to another important criminal justice issue of our times—the victims' rights movement. The victims' rights movement, first initiated in the 1970s, has recently led to the development of interventions that force offenders to deal with the consequences of their crimes. Victim–offender mediation and conciliation, restorative group conferencing, and community sentencing boards are just a few of the programs that have been born from the marriage of victims' rights and restorative justice.[30]

It appears that restorative justice has gained considerable support from both sides of the political spectrum. Restorative justice holds the criminal responsible for his or her crime while it promotes positive reintegration into the community. It can reduce serious correctional intervention (incarceration) and also provide for victim compensation. For reasons such as these, restorative justice has invigorated those who work and study in the field, and it provides hope for the future of community corrections.

FORCES THAT DRIVE CORRECTIONAL CHANGE

In our discussion about the historical development of community corrections, one of the underlying themes has been the various societal forces that helped to create correctional change. In the predemocratic era, feudalism and the church influenced policy to harshly deal with offenders. Early democratic times saw the philosophical call for a science of rationality that could link the gravity of the offense and the severity of the punishment. Offenders were believed to be able to discern right and wrong based on the amount of pain brought by punishment. The advent of the American penitentiary and later parole and probation were rooted in the belief that reform was possible, especially if the offender was willing to accept the societal norms of family, work, religion, and citizenship. The hope of rehabilitation for offenders in prison and the community was the result of the birth of the science of the psyche.

In the last years of the twentieth century, correctional policy was formed by political forces that were acutely aware of the rising crime rate and the even higher fear-of-crime rate. Fear of crime has been exacerbated by the constant depictions of crime and justice issues in the media. The media, especially television, has become the way in which most people learn about crime and justice, and politicians have learned to respond to their concerns. Victims' groups, law enforcement and correctional union workers, and senior citizens are three of the more successful groups that lobbied long and loud for politicians to respond to their needs and to "get tough on crime." The call has been heard loud and clear.

However, society has started to feel the financial and social impact of "get tough" crime strategies. Those in power have started to search for cost-effective strategies that "do justice" and prevent crime. As a result, community-based strategies have resurfaced as alternatives to the traditional approaches to the treatment and punishment of offenders.

However, in spite of the growth and support of these movements, it is difficult to speculate what forces will surface to help form the central paradigm of corrections in the next decade and beyond.

SUMMARY

From the invention of the prison in the 1700s until the present day, the practice of placing offenders in the community has been encased within a cycle of reforms. These reforms can be seen as something of a hopeless search for a corrections system that symbolizes the public alarm and disgust about crime, yet also gives promise of returning to us ex-offenders prepared to live within the limits of the law.

The original prison was a reform designed as a more humane form of punishment than torture, execution, and banishment—something that would give offenders a chance to amend their ways. Flaws in the results of the prison approach led to the invention of nonprison alternatives: First, what today is known as parole was added as a release option; soon after, probation was added as a way to avoid confinement altogether. Years after, the operations of probation and parole were scrutinized and found by some to be insufficiently punitive and by others inadequate to assist offenders in becoming crime-free. A prison expansion spree followed, with a historically unprecedented growth in imprisonment in the United States. While concerns about offenders in our midst has led to a call for toughness and their removal from society, experiences with toughness soon produce their own pressures for innovation that returns offenders to community life. This has been a pattern for nearly three hundred years. Alarm at the social and fiscal costs of the burgeoning prison system, together with doubts about the effectiveness of prison in preventing crime in the long run, have now led to the development of an array of intermediate sanctions and a call to restore offenders, victims, and the community to their previous condition.

This search for a perfect system may be "hopeless," because the desires are contradictory. "Tough" approaches sound good to people who are upset about crime and want action. But tough programs are largely irrelevant to the causes of crime and, in the end, can never fully suppress crime. They may not have much impact on crime, but they certainly challenge a free society's self-image. The more repressive the penal system, the more uncomfortable a democratic people become. By the same token, there is no 100 percent safe way to maintain offenders in the community. As long as some offenders are living among us, there will be stories of some percentage who return to crime. And these stories will produce a pressure to clamp down on crime.

┤ DISCUSSION QUESTIONS ├

1. What are some of the social forces that led to changes in correctional systems during the 1800s? Do any of these factors currently affect correctional policy?
2. What was the rationale behind the development of parole in the United States?
3. What has been the effect of the "war on crime" and the "war on drugs" on the crime rate, the correctional system, and criminal offenders?

4. Discuss the basic premise behind the intermediate sanctions movement, and explain how it compares with the current trend to treat criminals more harshly.
5. How do you think offenders will be punished in the United States in the future? What philosophical and technical developments would buttress the approaches you foresee?

┤ SUGGESTED READINGS ├

Christianson, Scott. *With Liberty for Some.* Boston: Northeastern University Press, 1998. Examines the paradox of a country that prides itself as the citadel of individual liberty, yet has maintained five centuries of imprisonment.

Freidman, Lawrence M. *Crime and Punishment in American History.* New York: Basic Books, 1993. Gives an excellent historical overview of the American criminal justice system.

Garland, David. *The Control Society.* Chicago: University of Chicago Press, 2001. Describes the growth in all forms of social control since the 1970s and analyzes the causes of this trend.

Mauer, Marc. *Race to Incarcerate.* New York: New Press, 1999. Explores the intersection of race and class that underpins policies that have expanded incarceration.

Menninger, Karl. *The Crime of Punishment.* New York: Viking Press, 1969. Time-tested book explores the way we punish criminals in America, arguing that vengeance, arbitrariness, and lack of compassion have done more damage than good in dealing with those who have committed crime.

Reiman, J. H. *The Rich Get Richer and the Poor Get Prison: Ideology, Class, and Criminal Justice.* 5th ed. Boston: Allyn & Bacon, 1998. An important book that describes the inequities of justice and punishment in the United States.

Sullivan, Larry E. *The Prison Reform Movement: Forlorn Hope.* Boston: Twayne, 1990. A concise history of American penology from the eighteenth century to the present.

WEB SITES

Web site with NCJRS article on History of Community Corrections and Intermediate Sanctions
www.ncjrs.org/txtfiles/bcamps06.txt

Web site of the Federal Bureau of Prisons
www.bop.gov

Web site on early history of American prisons
www.notfrisco.com/prisonhistory/origins/index.html

Web site that provides information about Jeremy Bentham
www.ucl.ac.uk/Bentham-Project/index.htm

Web site that provides excellent links on a variety of criminal justice topics
http://arapaho.nsuok.edu/~dreveskr/cjr.html-ssi

NOTES

1. See George Ives, *A History of Penal Methods* (Montclair, NJ: Patterson Smith, 1970).
2. Adam J. Hircsh, *The Rise of the Penitentiary* (New Haven, CT: Yale University Press, 1992).
3. Thorsten Sellin, *Slavery and the Penal System* (New York: Elsivier, 1976), p. 94.
4. Robert Hughes, *The Fatal Shore* (New York: Knopf, 1987), p. 282.
5. Georg Rusche and Otto Kirchheimer, *Punishment and Social Structure* (New York: Russell and Russell, [1939] 1968), p. 19.
6. Michael Ignatieff, *A Just Measure of Pain* (New York: Pantheon Books, 1978), p. 27.
7. Ignatieff, *A Just Measure of Pain.*
8. David T. Stanley, *Prisoners Among Us* (Washington, DC: Brookings Institution, 1976), p. 2.
9. Harry Barnes and Negley G. Teeters, *New Horizons in Criminology* (Englewood Cliffs, NJ: Prentice Hall, 1944), pp. 550, 553.
10. *Ex Parte United States* 242 US 27 (1916), often referred to as *Killits.*
11. John Augustus, *A Report of the Labors of John Augustus, for the Last Ten Years, in Aid of the Unfortunate* (Boston: Wright and Hasty, 1852). Reprinted as John Augustus, *First Probation Officer* (New York: Probation Association, 1939), p. 26.
12. Augustus, *First Probation Officer,* p. 34.
13. Vincent O'Leary and David Duffee, *Correctional Policy Inventory: A Classification of Goals for Change* (Hackensack, NJ: National Council on Crime and Delinquency, 1975).
14. Carl Menninger, *The Crime of Punishment* (New York: Viking Press, 1969).
15. President's Commission on Law Enforcement and Administration of Justice, *The Challenge of Crime in a Free Society* (Washington, DC: U.S. Government Printing Office, 1967), p. 7.
16. New York State Special Commission on Attica, *Attica: The Official Report of the New York State Special Commission on Attica* (New York: Bantam Books, 1972), p. xi.
17. Robert Martinson, "What Works? Questions and Answers About Prison Reform," *Public Interest* 35 (1974): 22–54.

18. Ernest Van den Haag, *Punishing Criminals: Concerning a Very Old and Painful Question* (Lanham, MD: University Press of America, 1975).

19. James Q. Wilson, *Thinking About Crime* (New York: Random House, 1985).

20. David Fogel, *We Are the Living Proof: The Justice Model for Corrections,* 2nd ed. (Cincinnati, OH: Anderson, 1979).

21. David T. Stanley, *Prisoners Among Us* (Washington, DC: Brookings Institution, 1976).

22. Herbert L. Packer, "Two Models of the Criminal Process," in *The Limits of the Criminal Sanction* (Stanford, CA: Stanford University Press, 1968), chap. 8.

23. *New York Times* (September 6, 1989).

24. Peter Reuter, John Haaga, Patrick Murphy, and Amy Praskac, *Drug Use Programs in the Washington Metropolitan Area* (Santa Monica, CA: RAND Corporation, 1988).

25. U.S. Department of Justice, Bureau of Justice Statistics, *Bulletin* (August 2001), p. 9.

26. Marc Mauer and Tracy Huling, *Young Black Americans and the Criminal Justice System: Five Years Later* (Washington, DC: The Sentencing Project, 1995).

27. Jerome G. Miller, *Search and Destroy: African American Males in the Criminal Justice System* (New York: Cambridge University Press, 1996).

28. Norval Morris and Michael Tonry, *Between Prison and Probation: Intermediate Punishments: Toward a Rational Sentencing System* (Chicago: University of Chicago Press, 1990).

29. Todd R. Clear, "Societal Responses to the President's Crime Commission: A Thirty Year Retrospective," in *The Challenge of Crime in a Free Society: Looking Back, Looking Forward.* (Washington, DC: U.S Department of Justice, June 19–21, 1997), p. 148.

30. Clear, *The Challenge of Crime in a Free Society,* p. 149.

Chapter 3

The Classification of Crimes and Criminals

──────────────── ┤ KEY TERMS AND CONCEPTS ├────────────────

assessment process | false positives | risk management

classification system | needs criteria | risk criteria

criminogenic needs | probabilistic classification | seriousness scales

criteria of eligibility | program salience | stakes

false negatives | risk assessments

All of us classify people around us. We think, John is a Democrat, Nancy is a nice person, Tim is untrustworthy, and so on. We classify people because we have ideas of what they are like based on the way they have behaved in the past or on their personality and attitudes. But when we classify those around us, we keep in mind that our judgments may not be airtight. We realize that the terms we use to define people do not fully describe those persons but serve only as rough labels that help us to gauge how they may behave or think in a given situation. In reality, we know that on some occasions John may sound like a Republican, Nancy may be grumpy, and Tim may keep his word. A person's behavior may be characterized by certain tendencies, but it is seldom fixed.

The variability of human behavior makes it critically important to understand offender classification as a rough way of grouping people. It is equally important to be precise about the criteria used for grouping. If we can classify offenders accurately, we can better anticipate how they will behave, and thus we can manage them more effectively in correctional programs. Thus, in corrections, one of the first complicated issues is to determine the offender's *classification*. Many experts argue that this is the single most important decision made about an offender, after the conviction. Classification is often used in jails and prisons to help assign inmates to different types of custody levels and treatment. However, our discussion will concentrate on the use of classification in community corrections.

THE IMPORTANCE OF CLASSIFICATION

The classification decision involves assigning the offender to a category of offenders, such as "low risk" or "nonviolent," and this category will be the basis for how that offender is processed through the justice system. For example, when prosecutors decide to designate a defendant as a "career criminal," they assign this offender to a special track of prosecution designed to increase the chances of conviction and the severity of the punishment.

Photo: Rap Star Eminem, left, whose real name is Marshall Bruce Mathers III, reacts to his sentence in court, April 10, 2001 in Mount Clemens, Mich. Mathers was sentenced to two years probation for carrying a concealed weapon. At right is attorney Brian Legghio. AP/Wide World Photos

Classification is particularly important to community corrections, because the classification decision frequently determines the offender's eligibility for certain programs within the community corrections system—or whether a community corrections sentence will be selected in the first place. It is common for a community corrections program to restrict eligibility for offenders determined to be "high risk" or "violent." These terms are placed in quotation marks because many classification decisions are discretionary judgments made by professionals, and they involve subjective evaluations of the offender.

At first glance, classification decisions appear to be "naming" decisions. They seem to be ways we decide what offenders are "like," how we identify who they "are" according to their most important characteristics. Thus, we have different images of offenders when they are referred to as "drug offenders" or "first-time offenders." These images may be true in a general sense, but they are always simply that—a generalization about a complex human being.

Another way to understand classification is that rather than saying what an offender is like, we are simply assigning the offender to a category or group, and we will use that assignment to help us decide which programs the offender will receive in a correctional setting and how we will deal with him or her in those programs. A person gets assigned to a group called "first-time offenders" upon receiving a first conviction for a crime, but the people who are placed in that group will vary dramatically in the criminality that precedes their first conviction. Similarly, people placed in the group "sex offenders" will differ in the level of their commitment to illegal sexual conduct; "drug offenders" will vary in the drugs they use and the degree of their involvement in drug-related crime.

In fact, it may turn out sometimes that the group to which a person is assigned is potentially misleading. A woman may commit a homicide, calling for her to be treated as one of many "violent" offenders, but a closer inspection reveals she was the victim of extreme spousal abuse and exploded in reaction, killing her abuser. Or a person convicted of "receiving stolen property" may be addicted to drugs, and even may appear to have a history of assaultive offenses for which no charges have yet been filed.

This explains why so often we will need to go past the classification in taking effective, appropriate action with a given offender. An offender is placed in a group *not* because that tells us everything we need to know, but because we group offenders to make our own work easier. It is simply inconceivable to act as though each new offender is a blank page on which we must rewrite a brand-new correctional program. Rather, we inspect offenders for cues and other indications as to which program is their most appropriate assignment from among the programs we have available. We group offenders for our own convenience.

Nowhere is this more true than in community corrections. A classification system determines how closely the offender will be supervised in the community and which special services the offender may be eligible to receive—and even whether the offender will be allowed in a community program in the first place. This is done in three steps. First, community programs establish **criteria of eligibility,** which indicate the types of offenders who will be allowed into (or, more commonly, excluded from) the program. Second, programs develop **assessment processes** in which offenders' current situations and past behavior are inspected for indications of their suitability for various programs. Often, these classification processes involve the use of **classification systems,** or standardized sets of criteria for evaluating every community corrections offender (see below for a more detailed description). Third, the offender is subjected to the classification process in order to arrive at a final classification, and this is then used to place the offender in a suitable program.

Classification systems can be grouped into two general approaches—those that assess offender characteristics, seeking homogeneous offender groupings based upon those characteristics; and those that assess characteristics of the offense, seeking homogeneous groups based on the current offense. There is some overlap between these two approaches, but their fundamental aims are different. Offense groupings are used to establish sanctioning strategies, ensuring that offenders are not subjected to penalties less (or more) severe than are called for by the seriousness of the crime.

Offender classifications are used to create groupings, so that offenders will be assigned to the right type of treatment and surveillance approaches. Offense and offender classifications also assist correctional officials in determining the amount of resources that should be allocated based on the risk represented by correctional clients. This concept, called **risk management,** is discussed in detail in Chapter 5, but it is introduced here because of its importance to understanding classification.

We continue by reviewing three commonly used offender classification approaches: risk, needs, and program salience. In describing each, we define the types of programs these classifications are used to support, and we indicate some of the common problems encountered in using each approach. We then investigate the uses of offense-based classifications for community corrections. We conclude our discussion of classification with a few cautions about classification in community corrections.

CLASSIFYING THE OFFENDER

Human behavior may be impossible to predict, but we can certainly make educated guesses about a person's likely future behaviors. Thus, a five-time check forger is likely to commit a similar offense again, just as a first-time offender is unlikely to do so. We know, of course, that the check forger may stop offending after the fifth time, just as the first-time offender may continue. But, on average, our educated guesses will more often than not be right. This is often thought of as a probabilistic approach to classification.

Recent classification systems have included probabilistic concepts. Officials try to see what offender characteristics are associated with reinvolvement in crime. The approach is similar to that used by automobile insurance companies, whose actuaries recognize that even though many teenagers do not have accidents, teenagers as a group have much higher accident rates than adult drivers. Therefore, teenagers pay higher premiums because they represent a greater risk.

Similarly, offenders who have characteristics associated with higher risk can be classified as more likely to pose a threat and so can be required to pay a penological "premium": higher bail or no bail, closer supervision on probation or parole, tighter security in institutions, and so on. Therefore, even though most offenders will not commit more offenses, **probabilistic classification** serves the action needs of corrections.

Three general kinds of criteria are used to classify offenders in community corrections: (1) **risk criteria** classify offenders as to the probability of future criminal conduct, (2) **needs criteria** classify offenders according to their crime-related problems, and (3) **program salience** criteria classify offenders as to whether a particular correctional treatment is appropriate or suitable to the person's needs and situation. These criteria are used to assign offenders to different programs that supervise offenders, but they operate in different ways. Our discussion below defines how these classification approaches work, and how they are used to make programming decisions more effectively.

In examining the offender classification process, it is helpful to understand the concept of classification systems. All classification decisions are judgments, in that the final classification assignment is always a choice made by a professional of one assignment out of several possibilities. In every instance, however, more than one classification outcome will have some merit. In fact, two classification agents, looking at the same offender, might reasonably arrive at different classification assignments for that offender: Where one person sees "high" risk, another thinks the risk is only "moderate." Where one rater sees the offender as "resistant to change," another will find evidence of glimmers of desire for a different lifestyle. Classification is not a firm science, and considerable disparity exits in classification judgments.

This disparity is a problem for several reasons. First, it is unfair for two offenders who are very much alike to be treated differently simply because two professionals assess them differently. Basic justice requires that all professionals use the same criteria in assessing offenders, since the assessment will determine the correctional programs they will be experiencing. Second, programs suffer when clients are assigned inappropriately. It is a correctional manager's nightmare to design and operate a program for one kind of offender, and yet receive quite different offenders for the program because of others' inadequate classification decisions. Finally, correctional effectiveness suffers when programs are applied to offenders who are not well suited to benefit from them.

In order to obtain more consistency in classifications, correctional administrators have increasingly relied upon classification "systems" as an aid to classification determinations by staff. These systems make use of a set of standard, objective criteria for classification assignments. For example, it may be that in order for a person to be rated as "high" risk, that offender must have at least three felony arrests previous to the current offense. Or it may be that eligibility for a "boot camp" is restricted to military-age offenders, eighteen to twenty-two. Classification systems typically make use of a list of such criteria, called "factors," and provide for a simple way to "score" the factors, thus arriving at a suggested classification decision based on those factors. If the professional does not agree with the classification suggested by the "system," a different decision may be imposed, but it must be justified in writing to a supervisor.

Classification systems differ with regard to the three main offender-based approaches—risk, needs, and program salience. They are also used in support of correctional pursuit of different goals. In Chapter 5, we illustrate some of the more common classification systems and show how they are used to achieve correctional goals in the community.

Risk

Perhaps the most pressing question we all ask when confronted with a convicted offender is this: Will it happen again? Risk-based classifications are designed to rate the offender's likelihood of committing a new offense. Obviously, offenders who are more likely to reoffend will be subjected to much tighter scrutiny under community corrections than those less likely to do so.

Risk assessments are a type of prediction, but they differ from traditional predictions in several important respects. A prediction is a statement about what *will* occur in the future—we say that we predict this offender will commit a new offense, but some other will not do so. Risk assessments do not predict what an offender will do; instead, they are designed to indicate how likely the offender is to reoffend, given the offender's characteristics. No firm predictions are made; rather, offenders are rank-ordered according to their likelihood of causing new trouble—some offenders are seen as "high" risk, and others as "low" risk.

Thus, risk assessments are different from the usual predictions we make because the risk assessment places the offender in a group of similar offenders, while a prediction applies to the specific offender and nobody else. Predictions are subject to errors. **False positives** occur when a person is predicted to be a recidivist, but is not. **False negatives** occur when a person is thought to be a nonrepeater, but later commits a new offense. We discuss the implications of these types of errors for correctional programming in Chapter 5.

Risk assessments do not have the problem of prediction errors, because the classifications are based on "probable" behaviors, not "absolutes." It is known, for example, that some offenders who fall into the "high" risk category will never reoffend, while some of those who are placed in the "low" risk group will do so. Risk assessments are merely groupings of offenders into homogenous groups—it is expected that offenders in the "high" group will have a substantially greater failure rate than those in the "low" group.

Classification systems that assess risk are usually composed of a set of factors known to be characteristics of offenders who recidivate: long criminal histories, early involvement in crime, substance abuse, and unstable employment and living situations. The more of these risk indicators in an offender's situation, the greater the risk of recidivism.

The implication of a risk assessment is evident—offenders who are higher risk will require a greater degree of attention and resources than offenders whose profiles suggest less risk. For the highest-risk offenders, the basic correctional strategy will require attention to effective risk control methods, based on restriction and surveillance. Most experts agree that the focus of correctional effort is best spent on the higher-risk offenders, because of the crime prevention benefits that potentially derive from working with these offenders. Chapter 5 addresses risk control programs based on risk assessment classifications.

Needs

All of us have needs, and the nature of these needs vary. Some of us need help with school, some need to be surrounded by friends, some need medical assistance with chronic problems, some need more time in solitude. Needs are, according to psychologists, the deficits that motivate our behavior.[1] People who "need" security will be motivated to achieve it; people who "need" friends will be motivated to seek friendship.

Correctional programs make a distinction between the everyday needs of all humans and the particular types of needs that motivate a person toward criminal behavior. The latter are referred to as **criminogenic needs**—their presence in a person motivates that person to commit crimes. Although various forms of social services might help people ameliorate certain needs, correctional services specialize in criminogenic needs.

Some researchers have been working to document systematically the nature of criminogenic needs and how they are best approached in correctional programming. Psychologists Don Andrews and James Bonta[2] have shown that certain types of needs, once alleviated, are consistently associated with reductions in criminal behavior. Primary among these needs are the following:

- Antisocial/delinquent associates
- Antisocial/procriminal attitudes
- Family conflict/violence
- Poor adult supervision
- Psychological disadvantage in school

- Impulsivity/poor problem solving
- Thrill-seeking behavior
- Early school problems in performance and behavior
- Below average verbal intelligence
- Interpersonal conflicts
- Risky leisure activities

Classification systems that seek to assess offenders' needs usually provide a list of criminogenic needs and ask the classification professional to determine which of those needs are present and how serious they are for the offender in question. Some offenders have so many needs that priorities must be established for addressing them. Usually, this is done in a supervision plan that indicates what the corrections agency and offender will be doing to overcome the needs.

The reason for a needs assessment is that no correctional program is capable of meeting all the common offender needs. By the same token, correctional programs are expensive, and it is wasteful (and counterproductive) to assign offenders to programs that are designed to deal with needs the offender does not necessarily have. Moreover, when offenders are assigned to treatment programs inappropriately, it makes these programs less effective for the clients appropriately assigned to them.

Therefore, it is important to be certain that the correctional program to which an offender is assigned is capable of meeting the primary needs that offender faces. Thus, needs assessments are designed to guide risk reduction efforts, in which interventions in treatment programs alter the offender's current situation such that more conforming behavior will ensue by the offender's own volition. They do this primarily by overcoming deficits in the offender's life, such as lack of job skills, or by altering the way the offender thinks about and reacts to the events that happen in the normal course of living.

Suitability for Treatment

A final approach to offender classification is to assess the offender's suitability for a given treatment strategy. This is usually two separate questions: (a) Does the offender fit a profile of the types of persons the intervention program seeks as its clients, and (b) is the offender motivated to take advantage of the program?

Program eligibility profiles are written to restrict the program to offenders thought to be likely to benefit from the program. For example, boot camps might be restricted to young males who are first-time offenders, while intensive supervision programs might be made available only for those who have failed under regular supervision. It is through the eligibility criteria that program administrators seek to ensure the clients they receive will be manageable under their program's operations. This typically is done by publishing a checklist of the criteria the program requires and making certain that classification officers have completed the checklist before making a referral to the program.

One of the problems with program eligibility requirements is that many programs seek the same type of offender—young, first-time offenders with good verbal skills. There are simply not enough of these offenders to go around. A second problem has already been mentioned: When a new program is restricted to the least-serious offenders, it may have little chance of making a difference, because these offenders are likely to do well even without the program.

Program "readiness" is a relatively new concept in classification, although experienced professionals agree that it has always been an important component of an offender's response to a community corrections program. Recently, a few psychologists have developed self-completion questionnaires that offenders complete and that can be scored to indicate the offender's readiness for change.[3] For those who are motivated, immediate entry into the program is possible. For those who express less motivation to change, preprogram strategies can address the offender's reluctance to change and what is feared.

THE AIM OF OFFENDER-BASED CLASSIFICATIONS: THE CRIME PREVENTION FUNCTION

Offender-based classifications aide correctional officials in risk management because they are designed as tools to help plan supervision and treatment strategies for offenders who reside in the community. Specifically, they have three main benefits for risk management.

- Risk assessments help identify those offenders who need to be considered for strict risk control programs, as well as those whose limited risk makes them suitable for minimally intrusive risk control approaches.
- Needs classifications assist correctional managers in assigning offenders to programs that will reduce their risk of rearrest, and, taken across a sample of offenders, they help managers construct an inventory of the repertoire of risk reduction programs they need in order to meet the many needs of their clientele.
- Program criteria protect the integrity of risk management functions, ensuring that programs targeted for low-risk offenders do not receive a problematic clientele, and vice versa. They also help ensure that effective programs or popular ones do not get overloaded with so many clients that they are unable to function effectively.

Thus, offender classifications are closely associated with the community corrections' "crime prevention" function. They are employed to reorganize a heterogenous set of offenders who are candidates for community corrections into a concentrated group of assignments to particular programs that are appropriate to their risk and needs. The success of any classification system, then, is based on its ability to sort people accurately and assist in their suitable assignment.

This introduces a final point. Classification is unnecessary if every offender is to be treated the same. In localities whose only community program is traditional probation, offenders are seen once a month in the probation office. But if localities desire a more complex array of community programs—and most local areas want this—then classification is necessary to determine who goes where, and why.

[handwritten: have diff level of punishment depending on the crime committed]

THE AIM OF OFFENSE-BASED CLASSIFICATIONS: THE PUNISHMENT FUNCTION

We classify offenses because we want to treat some crimes as more serious than others, and we want to do so purposefully and with consistency. Thus, the underlying reason for offense classifications is to assist corrections in carrying out the punishment function. This is often defined as the need to rank-order crimes so that the severity of the penalty can fit the seriousness of the crime. Because we know that crimes are legal categories that sometimes cover a range of actions, offense classifications become more sophisticated when they take into account the particulars of a given offense, not simply the legal category of the offense: Did this offender intend grievous harm in the manner of the offense, or was there a benign quality to the threats of harm? Was the victim a contributor to the crime? Has the victim's suffering been disproportionate to the offense; was the victim from a particularly vulnerable class such as children or senior citizens?

When we use offense classifications to establish a picture of the seriousness of the crime, we in effect set upper and lower limits on the appropriate penalty. The correctional punishment function not only requires that offenders experience a sanction, it also requires that serious crimes receive more severe sanctions and less serious crimes be treated with more leniency. With regard to community corrections, the implication is plain: Some crimes are thought too serious to merit a community sanction, while others are thought too minor to deserve confinement. The cases falling in the middle are more complicated—both a strict community sentence and a short custodial term seem appropriate in terms of punishment. How is the sentence selected?

CLASSIFYING THE OFFENSE

It is natural to want to characterize a crime in general terms, such as "violent" and "heinous," or "minor" and "insignificant." But these and other types of broad generalizations about a crime can be misleading. For example, an angry dispute between spouses in which one threatens another is a crime that seems insignificant, but many people point out that this kind of conduct often presages an extremely violent crime. At the other extreme, the crime "assault" is clearly violent in nature, but two friends may have an argument that gets out of hand and degenerates into an assault, even though both are remorseful later and remain friends.

We want to classify crimes because we want to know how serious they are. That is, all crimes are serious, but some are more serious than others. We want our response to a crime to reflect how serious the crime is, and so we need to understand how serious the crime is, compared to other offenses. When we try to characterize a criminal act in a word or two, we run the risk of oversimplifying a complicated event, and we run the risk of failing to account for important distinguishing characteristics that might make two events that come under the same title quite different in terms of their seriousness. For example, using a machine gun to rob a store and using a squirt gun for the same purpose are both "armed robbery" and are both very serious, but we might reasonably decide to treat the crimes differently in terms of how much they alarm us and how much punishment they deserve.

Most people think that serious crimes deserve more severe punishments, and at some point a crime becomes too serious to merit consideration of a community penalty. It is in this way that we stand to make errors if we allow our offense classifications to be too general. Some crimes may carry a serious-sounding title, like simple assault, but a community penalty may be entirely appropriate under the circumstances. Others—such as illegal sexual contact—may point to very serious underlying behavior, even if the crime is only moderately severe.

Offense Seriousness Scales

Interest in the comparative seriousness of crimes has led some researchers to construct crime **seriousness scales** in such a way that the rankings indicate not only which crimes are seen as more serious than others, but also *how much* more serious those crimes are felt to be. Crime seriousness scales are usually constructed mathematically, with a sample of respondents comparing every crime to each other crime, in a list of pairs of offenses. The relative seriousness of an offense is determined by how many times a given offense is rated the more severe of the two, across all the pairs. Table 3.1 is a listing of the results of one such study.

In some ways this list seems obvious, and it gives few surprises. Nearly everyone agrees that murder is more serious than burglary, theft less serious than sexual assault. This research indicates that a broad social consensus exists about the relative seriousness of crimes, and that fact is useful in thinking about eligibility for less severe penalties in the community.

But a consensus about crimes is not the same as a consensus about penalties. We may agree that the average fraud is less serious than the average breaking and entering. But one person might adamantly believe that both criminals should be eligible for probation, while someone else might just as strongly

TABLE 3.1 THE NATIONAL SURVEY OF CRIME SEVERITY: HOW PEOPLE RANK THE SEVERITY OF CRIME[a]

Severity Score	Offense
72.1	A person plants a bomb in a public building. (highest score)
52.8	A man forcibly rapes a woman. As a result of physical injury, she dies.
47.8	A parent beats his young child with his fists. As a result, the child dies.
33.8	A person runs a narcotics ring.
30.0	A man forcibly rapes a woman. Her physical injuries require hospitalization.
21.2	A person kidnaps a victim.
18.3	A man beats his wife with his fists. She requires hospitalization.
16.9	A legislator takes a bribe of $10,000 from a company to vote for a law favoring the company.
14.6	A person, using force, robs a victim of $10. The victim is hurt and requires hospitalization.
9.0	A person, armed with a lead pipe, robs a victim of $1,000. No physical harm occurs.
6.2	An employee embezzles $1,000 from his/her employer.
3.1	A person breaks into a home and steals $100.
1.6	A person is a customer in a house of prostitution.
0.8	A person under 16 years old runs away from home.
0.8	A person is drunk in public.
0.5	A person takes part in a dice game.
0.2	A person under 16 years old plays hooky from school.

[a]This represents only a selection of the 204 items rated.

Source: Marvin E. Wolfgang et al., *The National Survey of Crime Severity* (Washington, DC: U.S. Department of Justice, 1985), pp. vi–x.

object to a probation sentence in either case. This lack of consensus about appropriate penalties is less applicable to crimes at the extremes—few would send shoplifters to prison or place murderers on traditional probation—but it plagues community corrections policymakers on middle-seriousness offenses. As a result, these managers tend to develop offense shorthands to describe who is and is not eligible for community penalties. These often compare violent offenders to nonviolent, and they create special categories for drug offenders and sex offenders.

Violent Crimes Versus Nonviolent Crimes

One approach to community corrections sanctions is to draw a line—to say that a person convicted of any crime more serious than, say, a burglary is ineligible for a direct sentence to a community penalty. The idea is often to restrict community penalties to "nonviolent" crimes and to punish violent offenders more severely. This sounds like a reasonable idea, but it is fraught with potential problems.

The Classification of Crimes and Criminals **69**

Earlier we pointed out that a one-word characterization of an offense can conceal a range of pertinent facts about the crime itself. Just because a particular type of crime is typically too serious (or not) for a community sanction does not mean *every* crime of that type will necessarily look like the typical offense. People may believe that all offenders convicted of a violent offense are poor candidates for a community program, but it is not hard to think of exceptions to this general rule. Here are a few illustrations:

- A woman who pleaded guilty to hitting her young child out of frustrated anger could benefit from being enrolled in a parenting program that focuses on helping parents deal with the frustrations of child misconduct rather than spending a term in jail.
- A man whose drinking problem has led him into altercations and who eventually was convicted of assault for wielding a broken bottle after starting a fight in a bar could do better attending Alcoholics Anonymous while on probation as compared to a prison or jail term.
- A homeless woman of limited intelligence who was arrested for robbing a convenience store using a plastic gun might be better off placed in a residential center as a condition of probation, compared to a term in a women's prison.
- A young man who has never been in trouble before but ends up pleading guilty in a group's carjacking episode, in which he was neither the instigator nor the ringleader, might do better in an intensive supervision program with group treatment than in reform school.

These scenarios involve serious offenses—assault on a child, aggravated assault, armed robbery, and carjacking. They also illustrate a key point about offense classifications: Descriptions of the crime alone do not always tell us a great deal about the offender who committed the crime. Each of these situations, for example, includes a mitigating fact—a fact that tends to reduce the seriousness of an otherwise serious crime. From the point of view of community corrections, the mere fact of a "violent" offense may not mean that the offender should automatically be excluded from eligibility. A person could argue that no violent offenders deserve a break, but that ignores the reality that violent episodes sometimes happen in a person's life in ways that many of us could understand—and for which a community penalty might seem appropriate.

There is one further reason to be careful about overgeneralizing the unsuitability of community sanctions for violent offenders. Treatment programs for violence—anger management and cognitive restructuring—are proven to be effective in reducing violence, and they operate very successfully in community contexts.[4] It may be good to consider assigning violent offenders to these programs when there are mitigating factors in their offenses or personal circumstances.

It is also true that an automatic eligibility requirement based on property offenses may seem sensible, but it may often be wise to deny a community penalty for a nonviolent offender. Research shows that people convicted of a current nonviolent crime may have property crimes in their past criminal histories. Moreover, few offenders specialize, and this suggests that some offenders currently convicted of nonviolent crimes will eventually be arrested for violence.[5]

Nevertheless, it offends our sensibilities to think that people who commit violent offenses—those who show a capacity to injure their fellow citizens—would be allowed to continue to live in free society, even if under correctional authority. For this reason, authorities are usually hesitant to allow offenders convicted of violent acts to remain in the community without having served any time in confinement. It may not always be an effective use of correctional resources to deny these offenders a community sentence, but it is usually good public relations to impose at least some confinement, given the seriousness of their crimes. A good offense classification system is necessary to differentiate the heinous personal offenses that arouse public outcry from incidents that, while explicitly violent crimes, are not the kinds of acts we are so alarmed about.

Drug Offenses

Drug offenders represent a difficult issue for correctional administrators and policymakers. In recent years, concern about drug use in America has led to a new decisiveness about dealing with drug crimes. In many states, drug law reform has toughened penalties, with potentially powerful impact:

- New Jersey led the way by making possession of a drug within 1,000 feet of a school a serious felony with a mandatory three-year sentence. Many states have adopted versions of the safe-school-zone law.
- In Delaware, possession of 3 grams of any illegal drug results in a mandatory three years in prison.
- In California, a third conviction of a felony drug offense makes a person eligible for enhanced penalties—up to forty years in prison.
- In the federal jurisdiction, possession of an amount of drugs deemed to suggest a drug dealer can lead to a mandatory sentence to prison that exceeds the term for bank robbery.

These illustrations demonstrate a trend: Sentencing of drug offenders has become much more severe over the years. This trend is best illustrated in federal prisoner data: In 1970, 16 percent of prisoners were doing time for drug offenses; by 2001 that percentage had grown to 56.3 percent. In raw numbers, the increase is stunning: 3,384 incarcerated federal drug offenders in 1973, and almost 65,000 in 2001.[6]

Between 1986 and 1999, average prison terms imposed on drug offenders increased from 62 months to 74 months. The average term drug offenders entering prison could expect to serve rose from 30 months to 66 months. During 1999, the longest prison terms were imposed on drug offenders involved with crack cocaine (114 months), drug offenders who possessed firearms (133 months), and drug defendants with extensive prior records (125 months).[7]

Studies have found that addicted offenders who are in secure drug treatment (typically a therapeutic community in a prison setting) for six months or longer appear to do better than those who receive outpatient or shorter residential programs.[8] This research supports the value of confinement with drug offenders who are addicted. But we must be cautious not to overextend this argument. Many offenders convicted of drug offenses are not true addicts, and they may be inappropriate for these drug treatment approaches. For those who need treatment, studies show that programs are not available—less than half of the offenders with drug problems receive drug treatment while incarcerated, and only a fraction of that number experience the intensive approaches known to work.

Drug treatment in the community, thus, will remain a critical element of drug policy, because it is more realistic to treat offenders early in their drug histories in the community than to wait until they are immersed in the drug world. In Chapter 11 we assess the effectiveness of community-based drug treatments.

The reality is that there are many kinds of drug offenders, and this requires a variety of drug treatment approaches. Youngsters who are experimenting in drugs require one approach; dealers whose livelihoods are dependent upon drug markets require another; the drug-dependent still another. Without an array of approaches, it is likely that drug policy will continue its disappointing results.

Classification systems tailored to drug offenders are used to place drug offenders into the most appropriate treatment approaches. Specialized drug use classification systems have been developed that are based upon how the offender's patterns of drug involvement indicate the nature and degree of drug dependency.[9] These classification approaches place offenders into drug use categories that look beyond the specific offense and seek to classify the offender in terms of broader behavior with drugs; in this way, they are a hybrid of offense- and offender-based classification approaches, attempting to obtain the benefits of each.

Sex Offenses

A second type of specialized classification applies to sex offenders, who are of increasing concern to criminal justice professionals and the general public. The indication of concerns can be illustrated by two new legislative initiatives:

- After a released former child sex-offender raped and killed tiny Megan Kanka in New Jersey, many states passed sex offender notification laws that require authorities to notify neighbors when a former sex offender moved into their community.
- Faced with increases in pregnancies of teenage girls with older males, Florida imposed a prison term for men over twenty-one whose sexuality with girls under eighteen results in a pregnancy.

These two examples highlight the broad range of offenses that come under the heading "sex offense." Compare, for example, the items on this listing of crimes:

- Soliciting prostitution
- Unwanted sexual touching during a date
- Fondling a child
- Sex with a minor
- Selling pornographic sexual material

When most of us think about a "sex offender," we think of a person who assaults innocent strangers in the dead of night or a person who lures trusting children into their homes and deceives them into sexual behavior. But many types of illegal sexuality exist, and to group them all under a simple heading, "sex offenses," is to miss important differences in the motives and seriousness of the conduct. After all, we are sexual beings, and the diversity of sexual appetites is a valuable aspect of human experience. There is an important difference between deviance and victimization, though often the distinction becomes fuzzy.

Classification systems applied to sex offenders attempt to evaluate the degree of compulsivity of the actions and the amount of violence the offender exhibits. They assess the age and sex appropriateness of sexual victims, and they evaluate the degree of repetitiveness of the conduct. As for classifications of drug offenders, they are a hybrid of offense- and offender-based classification approaches, attempting to uncover distinctions between the serious sex offender and the more trivial sexual deviant.

Many forms of sexual misconduct can be effectively managed in the community, and nearly all sex offenders will return to the community some day, despite the seriousness of their offenses. Thus, community corrections has a deep interest in classifying and managing sexual misbehavior and the propensity of some sex offenders to repeat their crimes. We will return to the subject of drug and sex offenders in the community in Chapter 11.

PLACING THE OFFENDER IN COMMUNITY CORRECTIONS

Ordinarily, combinations of classification criteria are used to decide who gets assigned to a community corrections program. Offender classification systems are often combinations of risk and needs assessments, and program eligibility is often determined partly by the current offense. The best classification systems are often multifocused and assess several dimensions of the correctional programming decision, to be certain that offenders who have different correctional characteristics do not get the same correctional consequences. Many offenders who committed serious crimes are not likely to do so again, and many offenders who have few treatment needs still represent a risk to the community. Correctional systems need to use a range of classification systems to determine the most appropriate way to manage any given offender. The most important issue is usually not who is eligible, but who is *ineligible:* who cannot be placed on probation or in a community corrections center, and why. Inevitably, ineligibility stems from one of three criteria—offense type, offender characteristics, or program requirements.

Exclusions Based on Offense

Many community corrections programs state that "violent offenders" are not eligible. Some of these programs go on to indicate what is meant by "violent" offenses, listing the crimes that will not be considered. Other programs are satisfied that a general prohibition against violent offenders will eliminate consideration of inappropriate offenders.

The usual rationale given for restricting community programs to nonviolent offenders is community protection—officials want to reassure the public that offenders in the community will not put them at undue risk. As we have seen, there are at least three problems with this rationale. First, a significant number of violent offenders do well under community supervision, and perhaps because their violent offenses resulted from special circumstances, they represent a small risk to the community. Second, for the vast majority of violent offenders who are sentenced to confinement, either in jail or prison, return to the community is simply a matter of time—months or years—and the community risk question will have to be faced sooner or later. Finally, studies show that most offenders do not specialize in violent or nonviolent crimes. A person currently convicted of a nonviolent crime may well have been arrested for a violent offense in the past—or may experience such an arrest in the future. There are no guarantees.

The insistence that offenders in most community sanctions be "nonviolent" is less a community risk issue than it is a program **stakes** issue. That is, no program wants to put the community at risk of new crimes, but every program administrator knows what can happen to a program when a new crime gets caught up in public scrutiny—the very survival of the program may be at stake. Noted criminologist Don Gottfredson illustrates the distinction between risk and stakes by pointing out that most people would willingly bet $1 on a 10 percent chance of winning $10, but few would bet $1,000 on the same chance of winning $10,000—the odds (risk) are the same, but the stakes (losses) are too much to risk. In the face of a publicized violent crime, a beleaguered program administrator can explain to an angry public why it was worth taking a chance on a nonviolent offender, but when a new, vicious crime is committed by someone who already was known to be capable of violence, no answers seem sufficient. Experienced program administrators know that no matter how good the program, eventually there will be a new, serious crime to explain to an anxious public. Excluding violent offenders from program consideration helps make the explanations easier.

Public alarm about recidivists in community corrections has led policy-makers to establish legally binding exclusions of violent offenders. Called "mandatory sentences," these restrictions are codified in law, making probation and sometimes even parole unavailable for offenders convicted of certain offenses. Studies have shown that mandatory penalties are not very effective—they clog up the courts with trials, give excessive power to prosecutors who control access to community corrections through the charges they impose on offenders, and in the end they often keep good candidates for community corrections in confinement.[10] To avoid legislative restrictions with these undesirable consequences, program administrators often will voluntarily exclude offenders convicted of violent offenses.

Another frequent exclusion is for drug offenders. The reason for forcing drug offenders into confinement is often to "send a message" that drug crime is considered serious. Drug crimes are typically nonviolent, and when a drug offender is incarcerated, another young person comes along to take the vacated role in the drug trade; thus, few crimes can be prevented by incapacitation. And many point out that prison-based drug treatment is more expensive than any other form. Nonetheless, most states now have mandatory sentences that restrict eligibility for community corrections for some types of drug offenders.

Exclusions Based on Offender Characteristics

When program managers are concerned about inappropriate offenders in their programs, they will establish requirements that offenders have certain profiles to be eligible for admission. For example, administrators concerned that their program may not provide very close surveillance will restrict offenders whose long criminal history indicates they are a poor risk. By contrast, programs that provide intensive services and surveillance may exclude first-time offenders, who are unlikely to need that much involvement in their lives.

Risk assessment systems play a role in determining these sorts of eligibilities. By taking account of the offender's criminal history and current problems, a risk assessment will help determine which level of correctional supervision an offender most requires. The same problems of stakes apply to risk assessment systems—it is one thing to take a chance on an offender thought to be low risk, but when the classification comes out high risk, program managers become concerned that a dramatic failure will come back to haunt them. So even though a given program may be suitable for high-risk offenders because it provides intensive treatment and close surveillance, program managers will still try to steer away from the most problematic of high-risk offenders.

Risk assessments, because they are based on "probabilities" of misconduct, inevitably have misclassifications, as we said earlier. But some forms of misclassification are more visible than others—a low-risk offender who commits a new crime while in a community program draws the attention of everybody in the corrections system and may even provoke a public outcry. But a high-risk offender who does well is overlooked. Thus, there is an inevitable pressure on programs to avoid the possibility of low-risk failures, even when they are relatively rare events. Program brochures may advertise that they are built to be tough with high-risk offenders, but an inspection of the assessment process will often reveal that program managers work hard to keep out offenders whose past behavior indicates trouble.

Exclusions Based on Program Salience (Responsivity)

A recent trend in correctional programming is referred to as *saliency*—to ensure that offenders admitted to the program have characteristics that suggest they can benefit from the program's treatment approach. Programs with good salience for their offenders are said to be *responsive* to offenders' needs and problems, and this is often referred to by treatment providers as the "responsivity" principle of effective programming. For example, a group counseling approach will restrict itself to offenders who are of a similar age group and will exclude nonverbal types who are unlikely to participate fully in the counseling. Likewise, an approach based on rigorous, outdoor experiences will not be made available to older offenders or the infirm, or a job-training program will not accept people who have not yet overcome the drug dependence that makes them irresponsible workers.

In Chapter 5 we investigate more fully some of the principles of program design for treatment interventions. At this point, it is sufficient to recognize three points about program salience:

- First, every risk reduction program bases its interventions on concepts about why its clients are involved in crime and what it will take to reduce that involvement. Program salience requires that eligibility be limited to offenders who fit these assumptions.
- Second, the same problems of risks and stakes apply to treatment programming in other correctional settings, so these programs face pressure to be conservative in the offenders they admit.
- Third, the knowledge base for effective correctional program design may be growing, but it is still limited. Even the best correctional treatment programs work in a context of uncertainty about their methods and their clients.

PROBLEMS IN CLASSIFYING OFFENDERS

We have already considered some of the most significant problems in classifying offenders for correctional programs. Most of these problems stem from the fact that offenders are people, and people are by nature complex and somewhat unpredictable. This unpredictability can be good. For example, we all benefit when a long-term offender eventually decides to go straight. But for correctional administrators, unpredictability of offender behavior is the bane of daily existence. At any time, a problem can arise with an offender that, in retrospect, makes decisions made about that offender seem obviously unwise. Yet at the time, the decisions seemed reasonable. This form of second-guessing, often with very high stakes, sustains an environment of caution in all decision making in corrections. Classification systems prevent the worst of the problems, but they are not perfect. Here we present some of the general problems associated with classifying offenders.

Overlap and Ambiguity in Classification Systems

Some sex offenders may also be alcoholics; some situational offenders may have emotional problems (perhaps even stemming from their new status as offender); some career criminals may be addicts. A classification system that has so much overlap can furnish correctional decision makers with little guidance as to appropriate treatment. Should an addicted multiple burglar be treated as a career criminal or as an addict?

To combat overlap and ambiguities in classification, correctional administrators have used classification systems to apply set objective criteria to all inmates in order to arrive at an appropriate classification. The criteria usually include such factors as current and prior offense histories, previous experiences in the justice system, and substance abuse patterns. By using objective criteria, these systems reduce the unreliability of the offender's classification, and by limiting the criteria to a few relevant facts, overlap can be minimized.

Sociopolitical Pressures and Classification

One of the most frustrating aspects of offender classification is that the public response to crime frequently makes classification a highly charged emotional issue. As a result, corrections is often forced to respond to changing public demands in its management of offenders.

Over the years, different types of offenders have been subjected to intense public hostility. In the 1940s and 1950s, public outrage over the use of narcotics led to the establishment of stiff penalties for their sale and the establishment of addiction hospitals in several regions across the United States. Public attention to the "psychopath" in the 1950s and 1960s led to the establishment of long-term treatment facilities just for the "dangerous" offender, such as Maryland's famous Patuxent Institution. A recent version of this recurrent theme has been the attention drawn to "high-rate" offenders and the resulting policies oriented toward selective incapacitation of recidivists and "three strikes" legislation.

In each of these cases, public alarm about crime has produced a labeling response on the part of the criminal justice system, with special handling given to all those who fit the label. The difficulty is that the labels are often broadly applied (partly because of the overlap in any classification system) and the handling is ordinarily more severe than necessary. Those who object to the frequent "reform" movements in corrections recognize that great harm can be done by the misapplication of labels. Yet in many instances, the accuracy of the label and the appropriateness of the new offender-management method the label calls for are of little concern to correctional policymakers, who face a more severe problem in the public demand for "action" to "crack down" on some type of crime or another. The problem is more political than penological.

Distinctions in the Needs of Offenders

The composition of the correctional population has a direct influence on the programs and treatment approaches employed. Many of corrections' clients are undereducated, underskilled, and ill prepared for legitimate lifestyles. Educational programs often must be designed for people who have only minimal reading skills. Job training must be undertaken at the most rudimentary level. Since offenders come predominantly from the underclass, many of them bring little preparation to the programs offered to them.

In some respects, every offender assigned to corrections is unique; no two offenders are exactly alike. In writing about "types" of offenders, we may then group individuals because they share an important characteristic (such as type of offense) while differing in some other vital characteristic (such as prior record or intelligence). Any attempt to describe groups of offenders is a decision to generalize about people at the potential cost of specific accuracy. Thus when we talk about groups of offenders, we are really talking about individuals who, although unique, share some characteristic, even though we know quite well that not all persons in that group are alike.

When offenders are discussed, however, this point is too often forgotten. We tend to talk about "sex offenders" or "professional criminals" as though they all behaved in the past (and will behave in the future) in the same way. This approach simplifies policymaking and correctional programming, but it bears little resemblance to reality. Therein lies the peril of grouping offenders. We forget that the grouping is done only to enable correctional officials to take action, and that groupings in some respects inevitably offer distorted portraits of the individual offenders.

To be honest then, our discussion of criminal classifications will contain inaccurate statements about groups of offenders with whom corrections must work. Keep this in mind as you learn about offenders. Whether situational offender or career criminal, some individuals will fit in a group nicely; others are more difficult to place, and all individuals within a group will vary in some respects. The groupings are made for our convenience, to help us understand the types of clients corrections manages and the way their characteristics influence the work of community corrections.

SUMMARY

Classification decisions are among the most important made in corrections. These decisions often determine whether an offender will be permitted to receive a community corrections sentence or will be required to experience confinement as a penalty. Because classification decisions involve judgments about offenders, in recent years correctional authorities have adopted classification systems to improve the accuracy and consistency of decision making. Two general approaches to classification are used. Offender classification systems are concerned with the person's risk, needs, and sutiability for treatment, and they attempt to ensure that the most effective crime prevention approach is implemented for that offender. Offense classification approaches attempt to rank offenders in terms of the seriousness of their crimes, and they seek to ensure that offenders' punishments are appropriate to their offenses. For the most part, classification approaches are used to exclude some offenders from consideration for sentences to community corrections. Among those that may be excluded are very serious offenders, offenders with long criminal histories, and those that are resistant to treatment. Classfication of offenders is less than an exact science. Because community correctional decision making operates in an environment of volatile public opinion, and because it suffers from the inevitability of error, decisions tend to be conservative, avoiding risk and keeping stakes to a minimum.

--------| DISCUSSION QUESTIONS |--------

1. If you were the person making the decisions for classifying offenders in your jurisdiction, what criteria would you use? How are your ideas similar to or different from how classification is typically done in corrections?
2. How can an effective classification process benefit the public, the corrections system, and the offender?
3. What are three problems with restricting community corrections programs to nonviolent offenders?
4. What types of community corrections programs may be viable for drug offenders? Sex offenders?
5. What are the major problems associated with classifying offenders? What are some solutions?

--------| SUGGESTED READINGS |--------

Gottfredson, D. M., and Tonry, M. (eds.). *Prediction and Classification: Criminal Justice Decision Making.* Chicago: University of Chicago Press, 1987. A collection of essays by distinguished international scholars.

Schwartz, B. K., and Cellini, Henry P. *The Sex Offender: Corrections, Treatment, and Legal Practice.* Kingston, NY: Civil Research Institute, 1995. A collection of articles dealing with all aspects of sex offenders in corrections, from psychodynamics to treatment and management in the community.

Van Voorhis, Patricia. "An Overview of Offender Classification Systems," in *Correctional Counseling and Rehabilitation,* 3rd ed., by P. Van Voorhis, M. Braswell, and D. Lester. Cincinnati, OH: Anderson, 1997. Edited book that contains thirteen chapters covering a range of correctional counseling topics: background, assessment, theory, and intervention strategies.

⊣ WEB SITES ⊢

Web site providing links to resources relating to behavior analysis, including those related to community corrections
www.coedu.usf.edu/behavior/behavior.html

Information on screening and assessment tools along with cognitive and behavioral interventions
www.tyc.state.tx.us

Web site for the Institute for Reliability and Risk Analysis (IRRA), which focuses on the develop-ment and application of methodology in addressing and solving practical problems
www.seas.gwu.edu/irra/Irra_files/irra_institute.html

Web site for the Oregon Department of Correction Classification and Training Unit
www.doc.state.or.us/institutions/class/welcome.htm

⊣ NOTES ⊢

1. Abraham Maslow, *Eupsychian Management,* (New York: Wiley, 1962).

2. Don Andrews and James Bonta, *The Psychology of Criminal Conduct* (Cincinnati, OH: Anderson, 1998). List is from Don Andrews, "Recidivism Is Predictable and Can Be Influenced: Using Risk Assessments to Reduce Recidivism," *Forum on Correctional Research* 1:2 (1989): 11–18.

3. W. R. Miller and S. Rollnick, *Motivational Interviewing: Preparing People to Change Addictive Behavior* (New York: Guilford Press, 1991).

4. Ted Palmer, *A Profile of Correctional Effectiveness and New Directions for Research* (Albany: State University of New York Press, 1994).

5. Griffin B. Bell and William J. Bennett, *The State of Violent Crime in America,* First Report of the Council on Crime in America, Washington, DC, January 1996.

6. United States Department of Justice, U.S. Federal Bureau of Prisons. http://bop.gov/fact0598.html

7. "Federal Drug Offenders, 1999, with Trends 1984–99" (NCJ-187285) by John Scalia, Bureau of Justice Statistics, Washington, DC.

8. James A. Inciardi, Dorothy Lockwood, and Robert M. Hoper, "Delaware Treatment Program Provides Promising Results," *Corrections Today* (February 1994): 34–40.

9. Gregory P. Falkin, Michael Prendergast, and M. Douglas Anglin, "Drug Treatment in the Criminal Justice System," *Federal Probation* 58:3 (1994): 31–40.

10. L. L. Motuik, "Where Are We in Our Ability to Assess Risk?" *Forum on Correctional Research* 5 (1993): 14–19.

Chapter 4

Building Community Corrections

⊣ OBJECTIVES ⊢

The reader should be able to

1. Describe the initial development and purpose of community corrections acts (CCAs).

2. Assess the financial implications for community corrections acts.

3. Explain the four elements that underlie the development and functioning of community corrections acts.

4. Describe the problems associated with community corrections acts.

5. Understand the two general approaches used to determine whether an offender should participate in a CCA program.

6. Discuss the process for reimbursement under CCA programs.

7. Summarize the initiatives that have been brought forth by the federal government to promote community corrections.

Imagine you are a judge. Standing before you is a young man, William J. James, twenty-three years old, just having been convicted of a residential burglary. It is his second burglary conviction in the last three years. You must sentence him.

The victim, one Anna Stephens, is in the courtroom, sitting front and center. A single mother who lost about $500 worth of property and cannot afford to replace it, she reports that her grade-school children cannot sleep at night from fear of another break-in. In the front row, on the far side of the courtroom, sits the offender's mother, quietly crying. She is holding James's two-year-old son, Latham, for whom she is now the primary caretaker. James has lived with his mother and Latham, providing some support to both through odd jobs—and, apparently, fencing stolen goods. He has been without a dependable job for the last two years, ever since he was laid off by the delivery company he worked for since high school—they have a policy not to employ felons, and he was fired when they found out about his conviction. That is when he started using drugs more than just occasionally.

The prosecutor has argued for the maximum sentence—five years in the state prison, of which at least three would be served. He has said that the defendant is responsible not only for this burglary, but for another dozen assorted crimes, none of them violent. ("Yet," he says.) The defense has urged probation with drug treatment, but the presentence report says that James was already on probation, and there will not be an opening in the drug treatment program for at least six months.

What do you decide?

In the back of your mind is another factor. James stole $500 during his burglary. If he serves the entire three years urged by the prosecutor, his sentence will cost the state's taxpayers, your constituents, over $60,000. Even taking into account the pain and suffering of James's past (and perhaps future) victims, the cost benefits do not seem to add up very clearly.

Obviously, none of these choices is attractive. James certainly deserves to be punished. You could send him to prison, but that will do little to deal with his drug or employment problem. Going to prison will also reduce financial

Photo: Roslyn Morgan, of the State Probation & Parole office, speaks to other state workers and supporters at a rally to protest proposed budget cuts in August 2001 in St. Louis.
AP/Wide World Photos

and personal support for Latham, and it will do nothing to help the victim deal with her losses. To top it off, you realize, he'll eventually have to face the same problems he has now, after he is released. On the other hand, another probation term seems as unlikely to work as the one he has just violated. You also know that two burglary felony convictions are a significant indication of risk of more criminality. If only you had other choices.

At its broadest level, the concept of community corrections is best understood as a goal: to reduce reliance on traditional maximum security prisons in the punishment of offenders. In pursuit of this goal, community corrections embraces a wide spectrum of alternatives to incarceration among which judges and other officials may choose when offenders come before them. Community corrections is about creating choices in situations such as this one—and the many other similar cases that wind their way through our courts.

Community corrections begins with the unhappy recognition that the choices available to most sentencing judges do not inspire much confidence. To this problem is added the financial dilemma that the most publicly popular choice—prison—is inordinately expensive. The community corrections approach seeks to capture some of the money that is usually spent on incarceration and to reassign it to the community, creating more options for sentencing offenders to tough, effective community penalties.

In this chapter we explore the concept of community corrections as an attempt to create tough, effective, and less expensive sanctions in the community. This is usually done through the enactment of a community corrections act. **Community corrections acts (CCAs)** are laws that provide states with opportunities to return some of their revenues to local correctional authorities if they elect to keep offenders locally rather than sentence them to state prison. Just over half of the states have such acts (see Figure 4.1). But even those states without specific CCA legislation face the same issues of creating vibrant, local sentencing alternatives from which sentencing authorities may choose.

THE ENABLING LEGISLATION OF COMMUNITY CORRECTIONS ACTS

In the late 1960s and early 1970s, several states considered legislation that would establish financial and programmatic incentives for community corrections. In 1965, California passed the Probation Subsidy Act, which sought to reimburse counties for maintaining offenders in the local corrections system, especially probation, instead of sending them to state facilities. Minnesota developed the first formal CCA when in 1973 it passed what was

Building Community Corrections **83**

FIGURE 4.1 STATES WITH COMMUNITY CORRECTIONS LEGISLATION, JANUARY 1996

Sources: M. Kay Harris, "Key Differences Among Community Corrections Acts in the United States: An Overview," *Prison Journal* (June 1996); Margot Lindsay in *Partnerships in Corrections: Six Perspectives* (Washington, DC: Center for Community Corrections, June 1999), p. 23; and Mary K. Shilton, "Community Corrections Acts May Be RX Systems Need," *Corrections Today* 57:1 (February 1995): 32–37.

called the Community Corrections Act. The Act provided funding of local correctional systems with money saved by state corrections when individuals were not sent to state facilities. It is believed that the Minnesota CCA was developed by persons who had studied the California Subsidy Act and a successful local services program in Des Moines, Iowa. Soon after, the states of Iowa and Colorado crafted their own version of the CCA using the Minnesota model as a framework. By reviewing the first three CCAs (Minnesota, Iowa, and Colorado), we can trace the formation of subsequent CCAs. For an example of the laws contained in a CCA, see the box.

Professor Mary Kay Harris has described the key similiarites and differences among CCAs. She proposes that there are really four general CCA models. The first three, the Minnesota, Iowa, and Colorado models, are based on the basic ideas developed in those three states. The fourth, called the "Southern model," is a hybrid based on a combination of models and has been adopted by Tennesee, Alabama, Florida, and Kentucky. Harris has identified the shared characteristics that are present in CCAs as well as those that create distinctions among CCAs. They are as follows:

MINNESOTA DEPARTMENT OF CORRECTIONS

Community Corrections Act: Chapter 2905

2905.0100	Definitions.
2905.0200	Introduction.
2905.0300	Application for participation.
2905.0400	Development of comprehensive plan.
2905.0500	Changes in comprehensive plan and budget.
2905.0600	Information systems and evaluation.
2905.0700	Training and education.
2905.0800	Fiscal management.
2905.0900	County assumption of state probation, parole, and supervised release cases.
2905.1000	Use of existing community resources.
2905.1100	Program relevance to correctional objectives.
2905.1200	Local programs and services.

2905.0200 INTRODUCTION.

Subpart 1. **Authority.** Minnesota Statutes, section 401.03 provides that the commissioner of corrections promulgate rules for the implementation of Minnesota Statutes, sections 401.01 to 401.16. This chapter is intended to meet that requirement.

Subp. 2. **Purpose.** The purpose of this chapter is to provide a framework within which services will be delivered and coordinated in the various areas of the state where the Community Corrections Act is operational.

Subp. 3. **Responsibility for planning.** The Community Corrections Act places responsibility for correctional planning and implementation at the local level of government. This chapter is intended to ensure that the various planning efforts are compatible with one another and with the basic requirements of the state's correctional system.

Source: www.revisor.leg.state.mn.us/arule/2905

Shared characteristics of CCAs

- CCAs are legislatively authorized: Statutes provide the framework and authority for the other defining features of CCAs.
- CCAs are authorized statewide: CCAs mandate or authorize all localities, individually or in combination, to take advantage of the funds and authority granted.

- CCAs provide for citizen participation: CCAs provide for citizen involvement and specify roles that citizens may play.
- CCAs define an intergovernmental structure: CCAs delineate the roles to be performed and the power and authority to be exercised by involved state and local agencies or units of government.
- CCAs require local planning: CCAs provide that local planning will precede and serve as the basis for the development, implementation, and modification of local correctional sanctions and services.
- CCAs provide for state funding: CCAs provide for state subsidies to support local correctional programs and services.
- CCAs call for decentralized program design and delivery: CCAs provide for local control of the processes employed to assess local needs, to establish local priorities, and to plan local programs.
- CCAs endorse locally determined sanctions and services: CCAs provide resources and authority for sanctions and services to be developed and delivered at the local level.

Distinctions among CCAs

- The extent of decentralization of correctional services: Some CCA programs are administered by the state and others by local units of government.
- The nature of citizen participation: CCA citizen participation can range from simply soliciting views to allowing citizens to make decisions on offenders who participate in programs.
- The emphasis on deinstitutionalization: States differ in the intensity in which they support regulating the use of correctional facilites.
- The level of focus on rehabilitation of offenders within the community approaches used: CCAs vary in the way they promote rehabilitation, restoration, and dealing with the core problems that create crime.[1]

The experience of the original states in developing community corrections acts has been positive enough that since 1995, over half of the states have passed similar legislation. Although support varies considerably for their development and administration, they seem to be a positive step toward providing alternatives to incarceration, reducing state correctional costs, and motivating local communites to become more involved in the correctional system.

THE FISCAL POLITICS OF COMMUNITY CORRECTIONS

Community corrections is born from the powerful forces of money and politics.

The fiscal side of community corrections is fairly straightforward: It costs between twenty and fifty times more to incarcerate a person for a year than to place the person under community supervision for a year.

For example, in New York it can cost over $32,000 to house an inmate for one year in a correctional facility but slightly more than $3,000 to place the offender on parole. In an average year, between seventeen and twenty thousand people are sentenced to prison.[2] If an incentive can be created to sentence some of those offenders to community penalties instead of prison, the savings will be potentially quite high.

The political force behind community corrections has to do with who decides the sentence and who pays for its costs. Prison systems are operated by state-level government, paid out of state revenues generated by state income taxes or sales taxes. By contrast, most sentencing authorities are selected in local elections, and many of their salaries are paid for locally. Those who are accountable to local sentiments have little incentive to use community penalties: They are typically paid for by local revenues, and using them makes the sentencing judge vulnerable to backlash when the sentence does not work out. Thus, local officials are "encouraged" by the politics of the situation to use prison sentences more heavily, with the consequence of repeatedly using prison sentences that cost so much more than community penalties.

Economists tell us that this kind of incentive structure will spur decision makers to use prison, even when another sanction might make just as much sense. State government officials know that this situation can get very expensive. In 2000, the average total budget for state correctional agencies in the United States was almost $700 million, with a high of $4.5 billion in California and a low of $20.9 million in North Dakota. In these states, almost 90 percent of the funds goes to prisons. On average, states spend only 15 percent of their correctional budgets on community corrections. However, in strong CCA states like Minnesota and Iowa, the community corrections budget often receives over 20 percent.

But these statistics do not tell the entire political story. What makes this situation troubling to state officials is not the fate of the offenders who end up in prison, but the way the prison system keeps eating up more and more dollars that could be used for other purposes. In many states, the prison budget grows annually, while other state agencies such as education, health, or transportation struggle just to keep from being cut. Correctional budgets in many states are the fastest growing part of the state government.[3] As long as the incentives remain for local authorities to spend state revenues, these economics will continue.

Community corrections strategies attempt to change this incentive structure. Through partial state funding of local correctional initiatives, usually in the form of a community corrections act, they attempt to provide financial incentives for local sentencing officials to manage offenders locally. They also try to provide political incentives for local correctional functions to develop as meaningful alternatives to the state prison system. Thus, CCAs are legislative attempts to manage the disjunction between a state's fiscal needs and its judges' sentencing practices. Here is how they work.

LOCAL ALTERNATIVES TO IMPRISONMENT

The plan of the CCAs is to fund the local development of correctional programs that will be so effective and so appropriate that sentencing judges will be persuaded to use these programs instead of sentencing the offender to prison. Earlier CCAs made the money available to existing local correctional authorities—jails and probation. Some of the more recent legislative acts allow the local government to contract with private, nonprofit agencies to develop these programs for offenders. In these states, halfway houses, drug treatment programs, and other forms of correctional strategies can be established by private individuals who enter into contracts with the local government to deal with selected offenders. Obviously, new programs cost money. How can these programs be funded?

THE TARGET GROUP AND THE PAYBACK FORMULA

The funding strategy undertaken by these CCAs is to identify a group of offenders currently being sent to prison, and to target them for the community corrections programs. CCAs develop a formula to determine how much the state might spend on incarcerating these offenders, and a portion of those costs are designated for return to the localities for keeping offenders from those target groups in local programs. The total amount a locality receives depends upon the number of offenders it retains locally. This figure is based on a "payback formula" that estimates the number of offenders being kept locally, under the law's provisions.

The rest of the funding is left to the localities. It is the responsibility of the local authorities to make the CCA work by designing local programs that serve as attractive alternatives to incarceration, and by managing these programs in ways that inspire the confidence of local decision makers. This all sounds straightforward, but it is not as easy as it seems. A more complete understanding of the community corrections approach can be developed by looking in detail at the workings of the four main elements of community corrections acts.

EXPLORING THE ASSUMPTIONS OF COMMUNITY CORRECTIONS

Four main elements underlie the development and functioning of community corrections acts:

1. Target group
2. Funding source
3. Programming level
4. Accountability

Each of these elements is based upon assumptions about how community corrections systems will operate, in practice. But each element also encounters practical problems in making CCAs work. In the sections that follow, we explain these elements, investigate the practical problems community corrections acts face regarding each of the elements, and explore how CCA advocates attempt to resolve these problems.

Target Group

Some offenders now sentenced to prison could be managed more cost-effectively by local correctional programs, if those programs were to be created. The most important tactical problem faced in the design of CCAs is the establishment of the **target group.** This term refers to a set of offenders who meet specified criteria—usually offense and prior record—that would ordinarily lead them to be sentenced to state prison, but that make state officials want them to be kept locally. Just who could these offenders be?

Defining a target group to be diverted from prison into local correctional programs is not an easy task. Some of the reasons are political. Most offenders who go to prison either have been convicted of a serious offense or have had several convictions for less serious felonies. Neither type of offender looks like a good prospect for diversion from prison, at least on paper. Most everyday citizens would look at these offenders and think they belong in prison. When it comes time to sentence an offender who has engaged in repeated crimes or a single serious offense, most sentencing authorities are hesitant to take a chance on them.

This is a classic problem of stakes. It doesn't matter how many offenders will do well in a program; a single, dramatic failure can cancel everything else out. Most correctional managers can imagine the headlines: "Felon enrolled in special diversion program shoots liquor store owner during holdup." Such instances inherently endanger entire programs. It is understandable that the mere thought of this kind of news story is enough to make any program manager conservative in establishing eligibility criteria for these programs. So when it comes to the criteria for eligibility for prison diversion, the presence of any serious prior offense involving violence tends to exclude a person, as does a long prior record.

Conservatism about the prison diversion target group is ironic, however. Despite public qualms about them, corrections professionals know that some of these offenders can do quite well under close supervision in the community. With proper treatment programs and strict surveillance, an offender with extensive experience in the justice system can be gradually shaped into a successful community adjustment, and failure rates in community corrections programs can be kept under 25 percent, even with offenders who have failed under previous probation or parole terms. Or, in comparison, an offender convicted of a violent offense might have faced a situation that, when remedied, leaves little risk of a new crime—interpersonal conflicts often fit this description. Thus, when community corrections diversion programs operate under stringent eligibility rules, it is often the case that otherwise suitable candidates are made ineligible by those rules.

There is another problem with narrowly drawn eligibility criteria—sometimes only a handful of cases meet them. Most first-time felons already receive a probation term, unless their crime is serious enough to be legally ineligible for probation. The advent of "three strikes" laws, which force lengthy prison terms on repeat felons, makes these offenders ineligible, even when the new crimes are themselves not very serious. In many states, the remaining pool of offenders is very small indeed, and this makes it difficult for diversion programs to accept sufficient numbers of offenders to remain viable.

Excluding repeat felons and those convicted of violent offenses—as most CCAs do—leaves a small pool of eligibles mostly filled with drug offenders who would be unlikely prison candidates in the first place. Among drug offenders, those who might be prison-bound are either dealers, for whom community corrections programs are not very well suited, or heavy drug users who can be treated in the community but must be classified as "high risk" of recidivism, even under the best of circumstances. Put succinctly, the CCA target group problem is this: Among prison-bound offenders, there is little political support for allowing violent offenders or repeat felons into the community programs, and of the remaining offenders, many have personal problems that make them risky to include in the program.

How can these issues be resolved?

The usual technique is to define a pool of eligible offenders that includes "borderline" cases—offenders who might go to probation or prison, depending upon a large number of factors. The CCA then rewards local correctional authorities for attempting to design such programs by offering "payback" funds to the localities for every offender who meets these criteria who is placed in the program.

The box "Sentencing Reform Guidelines" shows how the system works in North Carolina. A sentencing guideline is established for all felonies that takes into account the seriousness of the crime and the length of the prior record. The most serious cases all receive prison terms, and the most minor cases are slated for regular community sanctions such as probation. The middle-range cases are eligible for special community corrections programs, and localities may receive payback fees for keeping these offenders locally instead of sending them to the state prison.

The North Carolina model is typical of the newest CCA structures in that it identifies a group of offenders who might not all go to prison, but some will. The legislation then creates an incentive for local authorities to design programs that convince the local sentencing authorities to choose community corrections instead of state prison. The overall strategy of the law is to balance the sentencing incentives by making creative, local programs cost-effective for local correctional professionals.

SENTENCING REFORM GUIDELINES
IN NORTH CAROLINA

In 1993 North Carolina reformed the state's sentencing and corrections policies. Changes were made based on the recommendations of the North Carolina Sentencing and Policy Advisory Commission. The guidelines and policies that were developed actually were derived from guidelines developed in other states (MN, WA, OR, KS, PA). After January 1, 1995, all crimes committed are sentenced following a new set of guidelines that establish new community corrections strategies, abolish parole release, and change good-time laws. The goal is to hold the prison population within a planned capacity range. Four key elements of the legislation include:

Presumptive Sentencing Guidelines

The guidelines group offenders by reference to their convictions, offenses, and criminal histories, and then establish presumptions concerning whether offenders should be imprisoned and for how long. They create three applicable ranges of presumptive sentence for each offender—standard range, aggravated range, and mitigated range. The standard range normally applies, but the court can apply aggravated or mitigated depending on circumstances and may sentence within those ranges.

   The guidelines recognize three levels of sentences—active, intermediate, and community—and specify the kind of sentence within each guideline cell. As the figure on the next page indicates, for example, an offender with a modest criminal record (category II) convicted of an E Class offense could be sentenced to either a custodial or an intermediate punishment. For more serious offenses, only custodial sentences are authorized unless the judge finds "extraordinary mitigation," a finding the state may appeal.

Parole

Parole release is abolished for felons and misdemeanants. Felons in Classes B–E are subject to six months postrelease supervision and can be returned to prison for up to nine months. There is no postrelease supervision for misdemeanants.

Good Time

Judges set the duration of the minimum custodial sentences. The maximum is an automatic multiple of the minimum. Existing good and gain time have been eliminated and replaced by an earned-time system that can reduce the maximum but not the minimum sentence. Earned time accrues for good behavior, work, and program participation.

Community Corrections

The State-County Criminal Justice Partnership Act encourages counties to develop community-based programs. The Department of Corrections will provide technical assistance, review local plans, and establish program standards. The department will provide funds to participating counties for new programs.

			PRIOR RECORD LEVEL				
		I 0 Pts	**II** 1–4 Pts	**III** 5–8 Pts	**IV** 9–14 Pts	**V** 15–18 Pts	**VI** 19+ Pts
	A	Mandatory Life or Death as Established by Statute					
	B	A *135–169* **108–135** *81–108*	A *163–204* **130–163** *98–130*	A *190–238* **152–190** *114–152*	A *216–270* **173–216** *130–173*	A *243–304* **194–243** *146–194*	A *270–338* **216–270** *162–216*
	C	A *63–79* **50–63** *38–50*	A *86–108* **69–86** *52–69*	A *100–125* **80–100** *60–80*	A *115–144* **92–115** *69–92*	A *130–162* **104–130** *78–104*	A *145–181* **116–145** *87–116*
	D	A *55–69* **44–55** *33–44*	A *66–82* **53–66** *40–53*	A *89–111* **71–89** *53–71*	A *101–126* **81–101** *61–81*	A *115–144* **92–115** *69–92*	A *126–158* **101–126** *76–101*
	E	I/A *25–31* **20–25** *15–20*	I/A *29–36* **23–29** *17–23*	A *34–42* **27–34** *20–27*	A *46–58* **37–46** *28–37*	A *53–66* **42–53** *32–42*	A *59–74* **47–59** *35–47*
	F	I/A *16–20* **13–16** *10–13*	I/A *19–24* **15–19** *11–15*	I/A *21–26* **17–21** *13–17*	A *25–31* **20–25** *15–20*	A *34–42* **27–34** *20–27*	A *39–49* **31–39** *23–31*
	G	I/A *13–16* **10–13** *8–10*	I/A *15–19* **12–15** *9–12*	I/A *16–20* **13–16** *10–13*	I/A *20–25* **16–20** *12–16*	A *21–26* **17–21** *13–17*	A *29–36* **23–29** *17–23*
	H	C/I *6–8* **5–6** *4–5*	I *8–10* **6–8** *4–6*	I/A *10–12* **8–10** *6–8*	I/A *11–14* **9–11** *7–9*	I/A *15–19* **12–15** *9–12*	A *20–25* **16–20** *12–16*
	I	C/I *6–8* **4–6** *3–4*	C/I *6–8* **4–6** *3–4*	I *6–8* **5–6** *4–5*	I/A *8–10* **6–8** *4–6*	I/A *9–11* **7–9** *5–7*	I/A *10–12* **8–10** *6–8*

Disposition for class B row: Aggravated Range / **PRESUMPTIVE RANGE** / Mitigated Range

OFFENSE CLASS (vertical label at left)

North Carolina Felony Punishment Chart (numbers shown are in months).

Notes: A = Active Punishment; I = Intermediate Punishment; C = Community Punishment.

Source: North Carolina Sentencing and Policy Advisory Commission (1994).

Source: Stan C. Proband, *North Carolina Legislature Adopts Guidelines in Sentencing Reform in Overcrowded Times: A Comparative Perspective,* ed. Michael Tonry and Kathleen Hatlestad (New York: Oxford University Press, 1997), p. 77.

Funding Source

Fiscal incentives are needed to fund local correctional options and to encourage local sentencing authorities to use them in preference to state prison. The cost-effectiveness of community corrections depends upon the all-important **payback formula.** The formula is based on a calculation of how much is "saved" when an offender is kept locally rather than sentenced to prison. Ideally, the logic is as follows: It costs $20,000 a year in state funds to maintain a person in prison, one-tenth that if the person is kept locally. For each person who is not sent to prison, then, the state will reimburse the local authority $10,000, and both the state and the local authority will benefit.

This seems logical, but as we shall see, there are several problems with the strategy. The two most critical issues are these: How do we know the person is a true diversion from prison? And how much is the right amount to pay to the locals for the diversion?

True Diversions. The discussion above should give an indication of how difficult it is to know whether an offender is truly being diverted. We can think of this in terms of "probabilities" of going to prison. Some offenders are almost certain to be sentenced to prison—murderers, rapists, drug dealers, and most violent felons. They are generally ineligible for community corrections. At the other end of the spectrum are those offenders who rarely go to prison: first-time property offenders, drug possession offenders, and so on. It makes little sense to reimburse localities for new programs that accept these offenders, since the localities would be taking them anyway without the CCA, and so the state is saving no prison funds through those programs. In the middle are the "borderline" offenders—for the sake of argument, let us say that about half of these offenders go to prison without the CCA, and half do not.

The question is, how do we know whether any given "borderline" offender accepted into a CCA program would have gone to prison? After all, the offender in a borderline category has an equal chance of prison or not.

There are two general approaches that are taken, the case-by-case approach and the aggregate approach. The **case-by-case assessment approach** asks sentencing authorities to decide whether they would have used prison for a given case, had the CCA program been unavailable. When they say that the existence of the CCA program was the only reason they chose not to sentence the offender to prison, then the state agrees to reimburse the local CCA program for taking that offender. The case-by-case approach has the obvious weakness of encouraging local decision makers to "fudge" their opinions about a case, saying that the person was prison-bound without the CCA, so that the CCA program gets the money—even when the offender would likely have never gone to prison.

The **aggregate assessment approach** is more difficult to fudge. It takes into account a local jurisdiction's sentencing history and/or current practice to determine the amount a local jurisdiction will be reimbursed for its CCA programs. The "historical" approach is a common method, in which the state gathers data about the number of offenders sent to state prison from a given local jurisdiction in a previous, "base rate" year, and then "pays back" the jurisdiction for staying below that number in subsequent years. The "current practice" approach compares the jurisdiction's performance to the past state average: If the state average before the CCA was that 50 percent of the target group was sent to prison, then the jurisdiction gets reimbursed only for the number of offenders over the 50 percent state average kept in local CCA programs.

There is no perfect way to know the number of **true diversions** a local jurisdiction is able to keep locally. Each system invites a different form of "fudging," and any system based on historical data benefits the local jurisdictions that were the worst at keeping local offenders locally before the CCA, since they will find it easiest to identify offenders to divert. Local areas that had very strong local correctional programs before the CCA will already have been keeping a large number of borderline cases, and so they will find it more difficult to show they are saving the state money by increasing diversion rates after the CCA is enacted.

Most CCAs resolve the diversion problem by identifying as specific a pool of offenders as possible, one for which a sentence to incarceration is typical. To help ensure that CCA programs have sufficient numbers of offenders to be viable, they allow other offenders to be sentenced to those programs. But they only provide payback funds for the target group, from whom the bulk would be in prison without the CCA-supported program.

Payback Rate. How much should the state reimburse the counties for CCA cases? The rate of reimbursement is a sensitive issue. The state wishes to establish a payback rate that enables it to save some of the money that might have been spent on the prison system. The counties want to receive sufficient funds that innovative local programs may be run for diverted offenders without needing support from local revenues. With such a wide gap between the per-offender costs to the state and to the locals, $20,000 per year in prison versus $1,000 per year or less for probation, it seems that there is ample leeway within which to work. Some amount between those extremes should save funds for each party.

It does not always work that way. For one thing, community corrections programs tend to be far more expensive than traditional probation—often as much as five times the probation costs. If too little money is provided by the payback formula, it will not cover the costs of the programs, and counties will be the loser. On the other hand, under just about any formula, the state will end up reimbursing for specific cases that would not have gone to prison, without the CCA. If this number gets large enough, then the state will lose money because of the large number of "fudge factor" cases it is paying for.

There are political problems, as well. The payback system has to establish some formula for determining what baseline prison commitment rates would be without the financial incentive provided by the legislation, and the same formula has to apply to all the state's jurisdictions. Local corrections systems do not contribute equally to overincarceration of offenders; for example, urban and rural areas are bound to contribute differently. The funding formula, then, is likely to result in some serious inequities.

For example, California's original Probation Subsidy Act formula did not adjust for counties that had traditionally restricted their use of incarceration; as a consequence, subsidies given to so-called progressive counties were not equal to those given to more "conservative" counties. Further, California's original rate of payback ($4,000 per offender) was not adjusted for inflation, and by 1975 this amount was worth less than $2,500 per offender. In contrast, Minnesota's formula included an inflation factor and permitted adjustments for a locality's crime rate and the capacity of its corrections system. Yet it was criticized for providing lesser financial incentives to cities, which had more offenders and correspondingly larger corrections systems.

CCA advocates agree that there is no completely satisfactory formula for reimbursement. Over time, however, it appears that acceptable practices develop from trial and error. While the payback system receives the bulk of the attention when CCAs are first enacted, experience shows that these issues can be resolved, and they are eventually replaced by programming and evaluation concerns.

Programming Level

Each locality has a different set of local correctional needs, and so the responsibility for the design and operation of these programs ought to be local. If CCAs are to work, they must lead to an array of creative and successful programs operated at the community level. What kinds of programs do local communities develop for offenders? This is one of the secrets of the community corrections approach: whatever the local community believes is important.

Corrections in the United States has always had a community focus. In Puritan society, the public, punitive use of the stock and the pillory was a direct reflection of community values that were intolerant of religious and behavioral differences. When William Penn and his Quaker followers contemplated the tragedy of moral failure among fellow citizens of Philadelphia, their manifest aim was a deep reflection of Quaker religious beliefs: to construct facilities run by religious volunteers where the fallen might go to do penance and be reformed.

COMMUNITY CORRECTIONS IN CANADA

As of 1995, there were 15 Canadian Community Correctional Centres (CCCs) and 160 Canadian Residential Facilities (CRFs) operating in Canada. The following is an example of one CRF in Canada.

Edmonton John Howard Society's 101 Street Apartments offers a Community Reintegration Program, a basic living skills program in which participants meet on a daily basis prior to and after release. The goals of the program include enhancing the quality of participants' lives, allowing participants to manage their mental illness, and preventing future hospitalization or incarceration.

The reintegration program consists of four treatment steps or components that begin in the correctional facility and progress to follow-up in the community. The first component, conducted in-house at Fort Saskatchewan Correctional Centre, teaches bachelor survival skills, leisure planning, and basic job skills over a six-week period. The second component runs for two weeks and is conducted at Edmonton John Howard Society's 101 Street Apartments. This treatment phase focuses on teaching living skills including nutrition, hygiene, budgeting, communication, anger management, victim empathy, and medication effects within a group setting. Three to five weeks following the second component, the focus of treatment turns to specific, individual needs that were identified in prior group sessions. Treatment sessions take place within 101 Street Apartments and in the community. The final component assists clients in the community as they establish themselves on their own, specifically to help them assimilate skills and knowledge learned at 101 Street Apartments into their own daily routines. The pattern of follow-up is based on client visitations on a weekly basis for the first two weeks, then every two weeks for six weeks followed by monthly phone calls until no longer needed.

The Community Reintegration Program is innovative in that it provides treatment before and after release from an institution. Furthermore, the program also conducts follow-up in the community after an offender's stay at the community residential facility. Providing pre-release, in-house, and follow-up care greatly increases the program's ability to rehabilitate and reintegrate an offender into the community.

Source: John Howard Society of Alberta, Canada, "Community Correctional Centres and Residential Facilities." ACJNET Publication, 1997.

Even today, correctional systems that are but a few miles apart can vary dramatically in philosophy and practice because of differences in community values and interests. For instance, a person who crosses the border from Minnesota to Wisconsin leaves a state with one of the lowest incarceration rates in the United States and enters a state with one of the highest, even though the crime rates of the two states are nearly the same. Going from Washington to Oregon or from Kansas to Oklahoma is a similar trip from one kind of corrections system to another.

The differences in style and philosophy of correctional programs in different communities reflect a very basic truth about law and order: Beliefs about right and wrong, and values about how to deal with wrongdoers, change from one community to the next. Throughout the years, the concept of community corrections has had many themes, but the core idea is that communities know best how to deal with their own crime problems. To implement this idea, CCAs have three programmatic themes: local mission, community advice, and local offender-based programming.

While different community corrections agencies handle their particular program in different ways, they all emphasize local programming as their main contribution to the correctional agenda. The first way they do this is to develop a local mission statement that specifies the values and objectives of local community corrections, and how those values and objectives are special to the local area. The development of a local mission statement is usually achieved through a process of consultation with the community. All community corrections systems operate under some form of community advice, usually with a community advisory board composed of influential citizens and leaders of associated social service agencies. These boards can be a powerful influence on CCA practices, from establishing priorities for treatment programs and community sanction initiatives to speaking about community corrections concerns to important constituencies in the local area. In addition to community advisory boards, many CCA programs survey the community through city hall–type open meetings and by attending other community organizations' meetings. Finally, CCA programs will conduct needs assessments of offenders to determine the types of programs most needed by those offenders in the target group for community corrections.

The result is a unique package of offender management programs that fits the specific philosophy and needs of the community. It is this community-level focus that makes CCA programs so attractive to local sentencing authorities—typically, these authorities were involved in the design of the programs and have a stake in making them work.

This is an attractive idea, but the practical problem is that there are only so many types of programs available to be designed. All CCAs must provide programs that include surveillance, drug treatment, restitution, job training, and education. Local authorities will differ in the way they offer these programs—some in conjunction with jail terms or other residential facilities, others by established correctional services such as probation, under contract to local CCA authorities. In addition to these basic programs offered by all CCAs will be a variety of special programs, such as counseling and treatment, victim–offender mediation, and so on. But these additional programs will not be the core approaches that most sentencing authorities need to have confidence in the sanction.

Because the services CCAs provide often bear a resemblance to operational agencies in the local areas, there is sometimes a programmatic tension between standard correctional services, such as probation, and specially funded CCA programs. Probation administrators sometimes wonder why a different organization is made eligible for funds to support running programs that are virtually identical to the ones probation has been operating for years. In many jurisdictions, for example, the CCA programs are not run as governmental agencies with line-item budgets, but operate as private nonprofit organizations under contract to the local government for the services on a per-case basis.

This kind of arrangement can feed the understandable tension between old-line agencies and new community corrections operations that get special funds. Advocates of the private contract approach argue that this strategy leads to improved accountability for services and the capacity for rapid change. They also say that private programs provide better-quality services and take less of a bureaucratic point of view. Whether this is supported by firm studies of CCAs is open to debate.

Accountability

To be most effective, local correctional programs should operate under contractual accountability to an oversight agency run by the state. The community corrections acts set an ambitious agenda: to shift sentencing priorities toward greater use of local correctional programs by creating fiscal incentives for the design and use of those programs. Significant amounts of money are transferred from state coffers to these local initiatives. State governments that engage in these transfers seek some accountability for the use of the funds.

Accountability systems take two different forms: offender diversion evaluations and program outcome evaluations. They are designed to measure the two most important aspects of community corrections programs, whether they are diverting offenders from prison and whether they are effectively managing offenders in the community.

Evaluations of the diversionary impact of California's Probation Subsidy Act were carried out in the 1970s.[4] They found that the availability of probation subsidies resulted in several policy shifts and compensatory decisions on the part of local decision makers. Commitments to state facilities for adults and juveniles decreased immediately following the enactment of the probation subsidy. These early findings led supporters of the subsidy to conclude that it was extremely effective at reducing commitments. Closer inspection raised questions about whether the reduction in commitments reduced the overall level of control of offenders. In the local justice systems for both adults and juveniles, the general intrusiveness of corrections was increased. More offenders were given jail terms; more offenders received closer control through commitment to local drug treatment and mental health facilities. The overall effect of the subsidy was to transfer the incarceration of offenders from state-funded prisons to state-subsidized local corrections—hardly a resounding victory for community corrections. Later evaluations of the diversion effects of CCAs produced similar findings.[5]

Why do some programs fail? The answer to this question depends on what is meant by the word *fail*. Every CCA seems to divert some offenders from the state level of corrections to local correctional systems. What evaluations raise about this diversion is that the numbers may not be large enough to save much state money in the long run. There are no claims that CCAs have led to closing a prison due to fewer prisoners—every state in the United States, whether it has a CCA or not, has experienced prison growth for over two decades. The best that can be claimed—and this would be quite a positive outcome if it is true—is that CCA states have had slower growth, building fewer new prisons. These claims appear to have the greatest credibility in Minnesota and Georgia, though even the results in those states are inconclusive.

For those who wish to use the CCA as a technique to reduce the overall level of social control, however, the evaluation results are even more distressing. Those offenders who are diverted to local correctional systems do not consistently experience a more user-friendly correctional process. Many spend time in jail—often about as much time as they would have in prison. Most experience a level of community control that exceeds what would have happened upon release from a prison sentence.

These controls come as a part of overall community corrections operations that attempt to provide treatment, not just punishment and surveillance. How well do these programs work at reducing risk through treatment? In part, this is a question about the effectiveness of risk reduction programs generally. We cover this topic in some detail in Chapter 5. However, our concern here is whether treatment programs offered by community corrections agencies are any better or worse, on average, than those same programs offered by other agencies.

The answer is that according to studies of program setting, treatment programs provided in community corrections settings seem to work somewhat better than when they are offered in confinement settings.[6] There may be several reasons for this. Treatment programs rely, for their effectiveness, upon a degree of motivation for change on the part of the offender. Being able to stay on the streets is one form of motivation that community corrections can bring that prisons do not have available. Moreover, the inherently coercive nature of prison life is believed, by some, to decrease the effectiveness of prison treatments in comparison with the less coercive community corrections setting.

By far, the most persuasive explanation of the greater effectiveness of treatment in community settings is that these programs take place in the same setting where their results are being displayed—the community. That is, offenders who are enrolled in community corrections programs are receiving treatment in the same setting where they are expected to show improvement. It gives them an opportunity to test what is learned in treatment, and they can receive support while the treatment progresses.

A final argument community corrections managers give in support of their programs is that their programming options are, ironically, more flexible than are those of other correctional operations. Mainstream correctional agencies have to have their budgets approved on a line-item basis, and it is easy for funding sources to cut treatment line items to keep the budgets trimmed. By contrast, CCA-funded agencies receive each year a budgetary sum for which there is wider flexibility in developing a spending plan. So long as the plan is consistent with state-established guidelines, and the local advisory board approves the plan, it can be put into action. For CCAs, it is comparatively easy to devise a plan that includes a heavy emphasis on successful programs, since that is typically what the advisory board wants to see.

There is recent research available that projects a positive light on the benefits of CCA and community corrections programs. In 1989, colleagues at the National Council on Crime and Delinquency (NCCD) completed an evaluation of Ohio's CCA programs and two community-based correctional facilities. They concluded that the community corrections programs in Ohio did divert offenders from prison and that the program should be expanded.[7] An update of the NCCD study was completed by researchers at the University of Cincinnati in February 1997. That study concluded that the revenues and savings generated by the CCA and other community-based programs are considerable, and that returning offenders to the community did not "appreciably increase the risk of victimization to the public."[8] Results of this kind provide some hope for those who support the growth of CCAs and community-based corrections programs.

WHY COMMUNITY CORRECTIONS IS A GROWING IDEA

As we mentioned earlier, the first community corrections act was passed by California in 1965, but the modern forerunner of the community corrections act was developed and passed in Minnesota in the early 1970s. Since then, over half the states have passed CCA legislation in one form or another. Why is the CCA so popular?

The most important reason has to do with the economics of punishment. Imprisonment is expensive. While tough punishment is good politics, it comes with a price tag that makes the state elected officials uneasy. It is one thing to

MEASURING COMMUNITY CORRECTIONS

In 1993, the National Institute of Justice (NIJ) sponsored a project by the American Probation and Parole Association (APPA) to develop a model process for devising and implementing alternative outcome measures that could be used by community corrections agencies to evaluate staff and over-all agency performance. The following is a summary of the process and the expected benefits.

Key findings: The APPA model is based on a five-step process:

1. Clarify values.
2. Define agency mission.
3. Develop organizational goals.
4. Implement activities to meet agency goals.
5. Evaluate performance.

Expected benefits of this process for community corrections agencies include the following:

1. Better assessment of activities (e.g., treatment and services, surveillance, enforcement) that define the profession.
2. Clear differentiation between long-term goals (such as reduced recidivism) and short-term objectives (such as increased probation completion rate).
3. "Results-oriented management" through establishment of benchmarks and standards on which to base organizational improvement and judge success or failure.
4. Creation of a learning environment that contributes to organizational growth through structured feedback and continuous monitoring and evaluation.
5. Ability to successfully compete for limited public funds by demonstrating agency value.

Source: Harry N. Boone and Betsy A. Fulton, "Implementing Performance-Based Measures in Community Corrections." National Institute of Justice: Research in Brief, June 1996.

be in favor of handing out tough, uncompromising prison terms. But when this comes at the expense of having to reduce funding for schools, roads, economic development, health care, and other priorities, many elected officials begin to wonder if too much money is going to the prison system.

But the politics of crime policy are complicated. Any elected official who seems to be less than tough runs the risk of being defeated at the polls. Elected officials who would like to see a waning emphasis on spending for prisons at the expense of other government priorities see the community corrections act as a way out of the bind, because if there is any tradition in American politics that is more deeply ingrained than getting tough on crime, it is letting people deal with their problems locally rather than centrally. CCAs provide for a shift in emphasis from state-operated penal processes to locally managed correctional programs. When these options are considered, powerful forces arise locally to support them. After all, local officials are unlikely to turn down the opportunity for funds to run local initiatives.

So community corrections, like any successful reform in American politics, fills a need for several constituencies. It provides state officials with a set of incentives for shifting penalties from expensive state prisons to cost-effective local corrections. It supports local incentives to develop local programs and new technologies to keep local offenders under local control. It enables correctional authorities to provide renewed emphasis on treatment and other forms of offender programming. And it provides an opportunity for citizens to become educated and involved in correctional policy and practice. With all these backers, it is not hard to see why the idea of community corrections acts has such support.

PROBLEMS FACED BY THE COMMUNITY CORRECTIONS APPROACH

Community corrections faces problems as well. At its broadest level, the concept of community corrections is best understood as a goal: to reduce reliance on traditional maximum security prisons in the punishment of offenders. In pursuit of this goal, community corrections embraces a wide spectrum of alternatives to incarceration among which judges and other officials may choose when offenders come before them. There are at least four recurrent problems that must be addressed by all those who support these programs:

1. Can the goals of community corrections be clarified? No program can operate successfully for long if its goals are not clearly defined. The goals espoused by most programs today are vague generalizations: reduction of overcrowding, rehabilitation, protecting the community, reintegration, cost-effectiveness, and so on. Although no legitimate government operation can reject any of these considerations, some ordering of priorities must occur before these new forms of correctional functions can take their rightful place as core operations in the overall system.

2. Can CCAs and community corrections programs achieve their stated goals? Nobody can deny that CCAs make big promises. They promise, on the one hand, a less expensive correctional system, with more offenders being retained in local correctional programs that cost far less than state prison systems. On the other hand, they promise greater effectiveness with offenders by providing programs designed to reduce the offenders' recidivism and increase their positive adjustment to the community. Any program that is both cheaper and more effective is indeed a good investment. But as we might expect, it is not as easy as that. As we discussed earlier, it is not easy to determine whether CCAs and community corrections programs do in fact save money. Measuring recidivism is another stumbling block. Clearly, when an offender is released into the community and then commits another serious crime, recidivism is present. But what if an offender stays away from criminal behavior for five or ten years and then commits a relatively nonserious crime? Or if an offender commits a less serious crime, one far less serious than he previously committed on a regular basis, was the corrections program a failure?

Also, the politics of penal reform tend to reinforce a measure of conservatism about allowing offenders to remain in the community, and so there tend to be strict restrictions on who is made eligible for community corrections in CCA legislation. And when it comes to programs for offenders, there are no magic bullets. CCAs are forced to work with a relatively well established array of programs, most of which work moderately well for some offenders but not for all. It is in this gap between promises and practical realities that community corrections programs strain for credibility.

Ultimately, community corrections legislation has at least two aims: to reduce the rate and number of persons sentenced to state correctional facilities and to reduce the revenues spent on corrections by transferring both the costs and the funding to less expensive local correctional facilities.

Have these aims been achieved? What is the evidence? As we have seen, the answer is complicated.

Certainly, it must be recognized that community corrections has not been a panacea. The desire to reduce the penetration of offenders into the system must be supported by procedures to control the manner in which offenders are handled in local programs. The community corrections movement has had limited impact on prison populations in most states that have enacted such legislation. Generally, the prisons in CCA states remain extremely crowded after the law has been passed. As a surefire way to control prison overcrowding, CCAs have not been a proven solution.

Then has community corrections legislation failed? The results are not entirely conclusive. All studies of community corrections have found that some offenders were shifted to local corrections, and this is encouraging. The problem is how to control local correctional programs to ensure that the penalties are actually reduced under the new policies as the legislation intended. The community corrections acts that allow the local government to contract with private, nonprofit businesses that provide services to offenders claim they create private jobs while reducing commitments to prison, and this aspect of community corrections acts may be a benefit to all concerned. And most observers agree that community corrections agencies are able to develop and operate programs for offenders that are often better and more creative than those offered by the standard prison-probation-parole system.

These twin results of limited impact on prison populations but demonstrably more effective programming may explain why the trend in recent CCA legislation is to underplay the prison diversion objectives in favor of greater emphasis on more effective offender handling in the community. This trend suggests that CCAs are here to stay, most likely as ways to shore up local correctional programs and to make local correctional options more attractive to sentencing authorities.

3. How will community corrections deal with the issue of bias in decision making?
Entry into community corrections programs is almost always discretionary on the part of program officials. Where there is discretion, there is the possibility of abuse of decision-making authority. Judges, parole boards, and program administrators are human. When they consider an offender for a community program in place of incarceration, they are looking for attributes that give reason to believe the offender will succeed in that program. It is not difficult to imagine that some of those attributes might be correlated with social statuses we think are not permissible for them to use.

The most significant problems have to do with race and ethnicity. The criminal justice system already has a significant overrepresentation of African Americans and Latinos, and the explanations of this fact are both controversial and troubling.[9] Black Americans involved in the criminal justice system are more likely to be unemployed, undereducated, unskilled, very young, and with a more serious criminal history than their white counterparts—each of these issues is sometimes used as a criterion against admission to discretionary programs. The outcome may be that programs operate with a kind of understandable partiality that results in unanticipated biases in selecting clients.

A different problem occurs with respect to gender discrimination. In order to be affordable, community corrections programs need to admit a sufficient number of clients to be cost-effective. At the same time, research shows that female offenders have a different set of needs—and pose a different set of case management problems—than their male counterparts.[10] This means that community corrections programs often cater to a male clientele. For example, staff might focus on surveillance and risk control, when female offenders often benefit more from support services. The problem is that community corrections programs, especially the special new intermediate sanctions programs that stand as alternatives to traditional probation, may feel more comfortable admitting men than women, and their surveillance strategies may set women up to fail.

A final type of potential bias in community corrections relates to the offender's social class. The same problems of program admission criteria that raise concerns about potential racial and ethnic bias apply to problems of social class: Middle-class offenders tend to look better on paper than socially disadvantaged offenders, and offenders with means and strong family ties have reasons to stay in the community and pay restitution that isolated, underclass offenders cannot claim. In trying to admit a clientele that can succeed, community corrections programs may not work well on the behalf of the underclass.

4. Can people's perception of community corrections be changed and can adequate support for community corrections be garnered? One major problem is the perception of most of the general public—and many within the justice system—that community corrections is a lenient sanction, perhaps too lenient for most offenders. Probation is "a slap on the wrist," a halfway house is "a break," and parole is "early release." Observers seldom think about the fact that offenders are placed into these programs for important justice and system reasons; often, they just think the offender is getting away with something.

All it takes is one dramatic public failure in the program to drive the point home. The news media and elected officials will ask why the crime was not prevented, why the offender was allowed to remain on the streets, in short, why "something wasn't done." Compared to prison, the community program will seem to operate at the expense of community safety, not in behalf of it. The fact that numerous offenders who leave prison do not reoffend will be lost on an alarmed public. The fact that many offenders in the program succeed quite well is not as visible as the single, sensational case that fails.

When an offender recidivates, gaining support for CCAs and community corrections becomes more difficult. Citizens fear living among offenders. Active measures must be taken to allay those fears, to help citizens become comfortable with the mission of community corrections, which recognizes a wide array of programs other than incarceration-based punishments. Offenders who live in the community require supervision and rehabilitation services. They obtain these services through regular visits to various government and private agencies, or they reside in a community-based correctional facility. These facilities, also referred to as **community corrections centers,** usually require offenders to live on the premises while working in the community. They usually provide counseling and drug treatment, and they impose strict curfews on residents when they are not working. Many of these facilities are renovated private homes or small hotels, permitting a less institutional atmosphere. Individual rooms, along with group dining and recreation areas, help these facilities achieve a homelike character. By obeying the rules and maintaining good behavior in the facility, residents gradually earn a reduction in restrictions—for instance, the ability to spend some free time in the community. The idea is to provide treatment support to the offender while promoting the step-by-step adjustment to community life.

Community corrections centers face problems, however. With very high staff–resident ratios, they are relatively expensive to operate; they represent a real savings in costs only when they enable a jurisdiction to avoid construction of a new prison. Studies also show that some centers have high failure rates—one-third or more of the residents may be rearrested in a year. But the main problems with these centers are political. Misbehavior by residents makes them unpopular with the local community. Just one serious offense can result in a strong public backlash.

As a result of these problems, citizens often complain about the building and managing of community corrections centers in their neighborhoods. This mindset is generally referred to as **NIMBY,** which stands for "Not In My Back Yard." For years, NIMBY was a regular call from citizens who rejected the building of prisons in their communities. But the loss of industry and the serious reduction in the number of private farms in many rural areas have changed the public view of prison building. Now prisons are highly sought as a "clean" industry that provides jobs to areas previously troubled by economic downturn. However, community corrections has not gained this level of public support. Citizens feel that having offenders living in the community is dangerous and may lower property values. There are no guarantees in community corrections. It is possible that offenders who live in the community may victimize innocent people. However, the rising costs related to incarceration, and the reality that most offenders will eventually be released from jail or prison, makes it imperative that we reconsider the development and managing of CCAs and their related programs.

COMMUNITY CORRECTIONS AND THE FEDERAL JUSTICE SYSTEM

Under the auspices of the Office of the Federal Bureau of Prisons Community Corrections and Detention Division, the federal government also develops, implements, and manages community corrections programs throughout the United States and its territories. The nearly 600 programs are organized from the central office in Washington, D.C., and administered by thirty-three community corrections offices spread throughout the United States. Each of the community corrections offices has a manager who is responsible for the administration of programs within his or her geographic area. State, county, and city governments as well as private agencies work with the bureau under a contractual basis to provide the community corrections services. The services include prerelease programs, home confinement programs, detention programs, electronic monitoring programs, work camps, and drug abuse treatment programs.

Federal initiatives have also been developed to respond to prison and jail crowding, offender recidivism, and issues related to offender reentry. These initiatives are in the form of program development, grant funding, and managing various kinds of community corrections programs and facilities. One of the first steps made in this direction was the the formation of the Corrections Programs Office (CPO). The CPO was established by the U.S. Department of Justice in 1995 to implement the correctional grants program created by the 1994 Violent Crime Conrol and Law Enforcement Act. The CPO primarily serves to administer grants related to institutional corrections. For example, it may provide financial support for states that develop truth-in-sentening legislation, or to Indian territories that agree to build jails or prisons within their jurisdictions. However, the CPO also serves community corrections through developing, funding, and administering programs for inmates who are soon to be released into the community.

One CPO program, called the Serious and Violent Offender Reentry Initiative, provides funding to develop, implement, enhance, and evaluate reentry strategies that will "ensure the safety of the community and the reduction of serious, violent crime through the preparation of targeted offenders to successfully return to their communities after having served a significant period of secure confinement in a State training school, juvenile or adult correctional facility, or other secure institution." This initiative represents an innovative approach to supporting community-based reentry and is designed to protect the community from returning offenders who pose the greatest risk of recidivating or revictimizing society. Selected communities are asked to take part in the program through developing reentry strategies that will fit community needs and resources.[11]

Another program developed by the CPO, called the Reentry Partnership Initiative, is a federal effort to assist jurisdictions in facing the challenges presented by the return of offenders from prison to the community. The goal of the program is to improve risk management of released offenders by enhancing surveillance and monitoring, strengthening individual and community support systems, and repairing the harm done to victims. Participating states include Florida, Maryland, Massachusetts, Missouri, Nevada, South Carolina, Vermont, and Washington.

SUMMARY

Community corrections has as its main goal to divert offenders from traditional prison to community-based correctional programs. In doing so, community corrections can save money, reduce the need and impact of incarceration, and involve the community in the corrections system. Some states have enacted legislation to promote community corrections. In the 1960s the California Probation Subsidy Act was passed to encourage counties to maintain offenders in the community rather than send them to state correctional facilities. Colorado, Minnesota, and Oregon, among others, have passed similar legislation. Now called community corrections acts, more than half the states have adopted variations of the founding three models. Each of these models calls for the targeting of a population to service, developing of funding sources, developing of community programs, and evaluation of those programs.

Advocates of intermediate sanctions and community corrections have argued that they are cheaper than incarceration. This consideration has proved a powerful incentive to adopt this orientation. At the same time, those who support CCAs and community corrections must be aware of the problems that can surface. These problems include goal clarification and achievement, bias in offender selection, and the gaining of community support. Recently, the federal government has made an attempt to support the development, funding, and administration of community corrections programs.

DISCUSSION QUESTIONS

1. What do you see as the benefits of community corrections acts? What are some of the reasons why community corrections acts might be a "hard sell" to local leaders and the public?
2. How can we assess whether the target offender chosen for a CCA program would have in fact been sent to prison?
3. Does your state have a CCA? If so, how does it compare with the similarities and differences explained in this chapter?
4. In your view, what is the best way to judge the effectiveness of CCA programs?
5. What issues must be dealt with to improve the viability of CCA programs?
6. Do you believe the federal government should get involved in the business of community corrections?

SUGGESTED READINGS

Anderson, David. *Sensible Justice: Alternatives to Prison.* New York: New Press, 1998. Provides a comprehensive review of the argument for alternatives to incarceration and develops a politically feasible case for expanded use of alternatives.

DiMascio, W. M. *Seeking Justice: Crime and Punishment in America.* New York: The Edna McConnell Clark Foundation, 1997. This booklet consists of succinct and current information on a variety of correctional topics including cost of incarceration, trends in sentencing, and public attitudes toward punishment.

Petersilia, Joan. *Community Corrections: Probation, Parole and Intermediate Sanctions.* New York: Oxford University Press, 1998. This edited book is a collection of readings on the current context, implementation, and impact of community-based corrections.

"Programs in Correctional Settings: Innovative State and Local Programs." NCJ-170088. Washington, DC: U.S. Department of Justice and Bureau of Justice Assistance, June 1998. This monograph describes the goal and objectives, program components, results, and impact of twenty-one state correctional programs in state and local settings.

WEB SITES

Web site for information on measuring the performance of community corrections
www.bja.evaluationwebsite.org

Web site for the U.S. Department of Justice and its offender reentry initiative
www.ojp.usdoj.gov/reentry

Web site for information on legislation enacted by Congress based on topics including community corrections
http://thomas.loc.gov/home/thomas.html

Web site for State of Minnesota Community Corrections Act
www.revisor.leg.state.mn.us/arule/2905

Web site for State of Ohio Community Corrections Act Programs
www.drc.state.oh.us/web/CCA.htm

NOTES

1. M. Kay Harris, "Key Differences Among Community Corrections Acts in the United States: An Overview," *Prison Journal* 76:2 (June 1996): 192.

2. Personal correspondence with Martin Cirincione, Executive Director of Parole, New York State Department of Corrections, Albany, NY (February 14, 2002).

3. Stan C. Proband, "State Corrections Budgets up 5.1 Percent," *Overcrowded Times* 9 (April 1998): 2.

4. Paul Lerman, *Community Treatment and Social Control* (Chicago: University of Chicago Press, 1975).

5. Edwin Lemert and F. Dill, *Offenders in the Community* (Lexington, MA: Lexington Books, 1978).

6. Don Andrews, Ivan Zinger, Robert D. Hoge, James Bonta, Paul Gendreau, and Francis T. Cullen, "Does Treatment Work? A Clinically Relevant and Psychologically Informed Meta-Analysis," *Criminology* 28 (1990): 369–404.

7. J. Austin, P. Quigley, and S. Cuvelier, "Evaluating the Impact of Ohio's Community Corrections Programs, Public Safety and Costs: Final Report" (San Francisco: National Council on Crime and Delinquency, 1989).

8. E. J. Latessa, L. F. Travis, and A. Holsinger, "Evaluation of Ohio's Community Corrections Act Programs and Community Based Corrections Facilities: Final Report." Department of Criminal Justice, University of Cincinnati, OH. February 1997.

9. Michael Tonry, *Race Matters* (Chicago: Oxford University Press, 1996).

10. Merry Morash, Robin N. Haar, and Lilian Rucker, "A Comparison of Programming for Women and Men in the U.S. Prisons in the 1980s," *Crime and Delinquency* 40 (April 1994): 197–221.

11. www.ojp.usdoj.gov/reentry/field_tested_programs.htm

Chapter 5

Managing and Reducing Risk in Community Corrections

There is no problem more important to administrators of corrections in the community than the constant realization that some offenders assigned to their care will commit new crimes. Experienced correctional officials know that new arrests are inevitable, for at least some of the offenders they supervise.

Almost no good comes of a new arrest. Every arrest is yet another indication that the community corrections agency has not succeeded. After a few years of what seems like too many clients getting arrested, staff can begin to doubt their own effectiveness. Dramatic rearrests can also make news headlines, and further erode public confidence in corrections. Administrators know that when a client is arrested, there arises the potential for a hostile demand from public officials that the failure to prevent the crime be explained—and often this is not an easy task, for it can turn into a highly charged accusation played out in newspaper stories.

When the arrest has merit—when the offender is actually guilty of the crime—there is often an even more somber reality: another victim. The fact that a fellow citizen suffers the losses stemming from a new crime is always a chilling reminder of how serious are the responsibilities of community corrections for public quality of life. Few experiences are more sobering for a correctional worker than to face the victim of a crime committed by a client for whose supervision that professional worker was responsible.

For these political and human reasons, correctional administrators are concerned about the risk represented by the clients. As we pointed out in the opening chapter, most clients of the community corrections system complete their terms under supervision without a new arrest. That fortunate fact does not detract from the seriousness of the failures when they occur, but it does prove they are not inevitable for every offender under supervision. Correctional officials want to be certain that they focus their efforts upon the offenders who are most likely to be involved in new crimes, and that they organize their efforts to make those crimes less likely.

Photo: Death row inmate Anthony Porter lifts Northwestern University journalism professor David Protess after being released from prison in Chicago on February 5, 1999. Protess and some of his students were instrumental in getting Porter released. AP/Wide World Photos

In this chapter, we describe how community corrections approaches the problem that the clients of the system represent a special risk to the community. We describe what is meant by "risk" and how it is managed, then we describe approaches taken by corrections to reduce the risk of reoffending. We also develop a central theme of corrections: More than any other issue, the accurate assessment, management, and reduction of risk is the highest responsibility of community corrections.

THE RISK MANAGEMENT FUNCTION

Risk management is the philosophy that correctional officials must allocate correctional resources according to the risk represented by correctional clients. This ordinarily means that the higher-risk clients get more time and attention from correctional staff than lower-risk offenders. The idea of risk management is important in community corrections, especially for caseload management in probation and parole. As we shall see, a strong case can be made that focusing correctional resources on the highest-risk cases pays off.

This idea seems little more than common sense, but in practice, the management of risk is a complicated idea. It involves first clarifying the concept of risk, and then articulating a procedure for measuring risk and developing a system for allocating resources to reflect the different levels of risk. In this section, the concepts of risk management are described in more detail.

BACKGROUND OF RISK ASSESSMENT

Statistical methods have been used to assess and classify offenders in the correctional setting since the 1920s, but the application of risk assessment and management in community corrections is a relatively new idea. In the early 1970s, Vincent O'Leary and his colleagues at State University of New York, Albany, developed the Salient Factor Score instrument for federal parole officials to help determine who should be released on parole. Later that decade, Christopher Baird and others at the Wisconsin Department of Corrections developed assessment tools for adult offenders based on the degree of risk posed by the offender and the amount of assistance the offender requires while under community supervision. The Wisconsin model has been adopted by the National Institute of Corrections (NIC) as a model system of probation risk assessment and supervision.

In the mid-1980s James Bonta, Donald Andrews, and others used previous research of hundreds of studies to develop a risk and needs assessment instrument called the Level of Supervision Inventory—Revised (LSI-R). The LSI-R has been highly recommended because of its high validity (ability to measure correctly) and ease of use in a variety of criminal justice settings.[1] More specifically, the LSI-R is a quantitative survey of attributes of offenders and their situations that is calculated to determine decisions related to the kind and level of service offenders need. There are actually two kinds of LSI-R surveys, but the one most often used by correctional agencies is the fifty-four-item survey, where items are answered in a "yes-no" format or in a "0–3" rating format based on level of satisfaction. After the offender completes the survey, it is totalled and compared with a profile sheet that provides interpretation of the final score. In the box "Excerpts from the LSI-R," is a list of the categories of questions and examples of specific questions within six of those categories.

EXCERPTS FROM THE LSI-R: THE LEVEL OF SERVICE INVENTORY

Categories of questions:

1. Criminal History
   Example question: Yes   No   Do you have any record of assault/ violence?

2. Educational/Employment
   Example question: Yes   No   Were you ever fired?

3. Financial Situation
   Example question: Yes   No   Are you reliant on social assistance?

4. Family/Marital
   Example question: 3 2 1 0   How rewarding is your situation with your parents?

5. Accomodation
   Example question: Yes   No   Have you had three or more address changes in the last year?

6. Leisure/Recreation
   Example question: 3 2 1 0   Could you make better use of your time?

7. Companions

8. Alcohol/Drug Use

9. Emotional/Personal Situation

10. Attitudes/Orientation

Developed from LSI-R: The Level of Service Inventory by D. A. Andrews and J. L. Bonta. Copyright 1995; used with permission from Multi-Health Systems, Inc., N. Tonawanda, NY.

THE CONCEPT OF RISK

What is meant by the term *risk*? Obviously, to be concerned about risk means to be concerned about the chances that some particular event will occur in the future. For example, the chance that an earthquake will occur is thought of as the risk of an earthquake, and the chance that a person will get cancer is thought of as risk of cancer.

Four important points are immediately apparent from this idea of risk. First, it refers to an event that *might* happen, not something that *will* happen. Since everyone will someday die, for example, it makes no sense to discuss a person's risk of death, but it is reasonable to estimate a person's risk of dying prior to the age of, say, seventy, because some people will live past that age. In this sense, we use risk to refer to a *probability* that something will happen when we cannot be certain that it will, or will not, occur.

Second, the actual risk of an event depends upon certain variables. For example, risk that a person will die before age seventy increases if the person is a smoker, is overweight, and has high cholesterol. The variables that tend to increase risk are known as *risk factors,* and the more there are present in a given case, the higher the risk of the event. But the fact that risk factors are present does not guarantee the event will occur, just that it is more likely to occur. For example, a study might show that 80 percent of overweight smokers with high blood pressure died before their seventieth birthday, but clearly it also shows that some of the people with those same risk factors lived into their seventies and perhaps beyond.

Third, risk assessments are really statements about a person's *risk grouping* or the group that they belong to with similar characteristics. To use our hypothetical example, we would not say that "an overweight smoker with high blood pressure has an 80 percent chance of dying before reaching seventy," because this is nonsensical. Every individual will either die or not before reaching the seventieth birthday, but those who smoke, are overweight, and have high blood pressure will show a higher rate by that age. Thus, the estimated risk level for an individual is really a *group rate,* based on characteristics of the individuals in the group. The technical meaning would be "This person comes from a group of whom 80 percent will not reach their seventieth birthday." Whether this particular person will reach seventy remains an unknown until that time.

Fourth, because we use the group rate as an estimate of the individual's risk, and because that risk is a probability and not a certainty, our risk assessments inevitably have errors. Some who are high risk (overweight smokers with high blood pressure) live much longer than we expect. We make them pay more for their life insurance than low-risk people, because on average their high-risk group costs more to insure—but it turns out we were wrong to charge them so much. For reasons that we may not ever understand, they beat the odds. Our assessment turns out to be wrong.

In corrections, we are interested in the risk of a person committing a new offense. We identify risk factors and develop risk groups based upon those factors, and then we deal with offenders according to the risk grouping to which they belong. Sometimes, it turns out that our risk assessments were wrong, since the simple fact that a person has risk factors does not mean he or she will certainly reoffend.

THE THEORY OF RISK MANAGEMENT

The theory of risk management in corrections is an *actuarial* concept; it is based on statistical analysis of past behavior to predict future chances of the same behavior. This concept is very much like the theory of risk management in the insurance industry. The idea is to break down the population of offenders into subgroups with very different rates of risk, and to deal with the different groups depending upon their risk. Insurance companies require higher-risk people to pay a greater premium; corrections requires higher-risk offenders to be subjected to closer supervision.

Insurance companies make money by charging high enough premiums for the higher-risk cases so that they can afford the high costs of misfortune—auto accidents, illnesses, and the like. Corrections is not in the risk management business to make money, but to control rearrests. The theory of risk management is that by knowing which cases are higher risk, correctional officials will be capable of taking actions that reduce or prevent the offenses from occurring. Thus, the risk management theory has two components:

- **Risk control** is the application of restrictions such that the offender is less likely to be able to engage in criminal behavior.
- **Risk reduction** is the use of treatment programs to change the offender's basic level of risk, resulting in a lower overall probability of new offenses among high-risk offenders.

These two ideas are related strategies, but they have a different intent. Risk control strategies attempt to alter the offender's immediate environment, usually through the use of restrictions on the offender's movement but also by using medication. Under risk controls, the offender's motivation for crime is not meant to be affected directly. Risk reduction, by contrast, attempts to change the offender's thought and emotions, leading the offender to choose to obey the law. We first discuss issues related to risk control and then devote the remainder of the chapter to the strategy of risk reduction.

MEASURING RISK

Risk is measured by the presence (or absence) of risk factors. These, in turn, are identified by *recidivism studies.* A recidivism study follows a sample of offenders through a period of time while they are under correctional supervision in the community. Some are involved in new offenses, others are not; nationally it appears that far less than half are rearrested while on probation.[2] The question asked by recidivism studies is, "What is the difference between those who fail and those who succeed?"

Probationers who fail are different from those who succeed on a number of issues: They have longer criminal histories, they abuse alcohol and drugs, and they live in unstable circumstances. These characteristics are designated as **recidivism risk factors.** Offenders under community supervision who have these risk factors are at greater risk of recidivism; those without them pose a lesser risk.

Even though the methods for identifying risk factors are fairly straightforward, the measurement of risk involves a number of important problems. Some of these are technical: What type of statistic should be chosen to measure risk? How should the sample be drawn? How long should offenders be followed? Questions such as these are frequently discussed by researchers, and various approaches are tried and debated.[3] A detailed discussion of them is not needed here; however, some of the issues have policy implications, and to understand risk assessment approaches we need to be aware of these issues. Three of the most important are the criterion problem, bias, and generalizability.

The *criterion problem* means "risk of what?" Risk studies have focused on different risks, among them risk of rearrest for any offense, risk of rearrest for violence, and risk of a new felony conviction. Each of these risks is a different "criterion," and the factors associated with different criteria vary. It makes sense that this would be so. The factors that might lead an offender to commit a violent crime can be different from those that lead to a property offense. When it comes to risk of a new conviction, a wide range of factors get added to the puzzle—prosecutorial policies, strength of the case, and credibility of witnesses, to name a few.

Because risk factors vary from one criterion to the next, risk management policies require that the program manager be aware of precisely which risk type is being managed. New violent offenses are sufficiently rare—they occur less that 10 percent of the time, usually—that they turn out to be harder to predict than arrests for any new crime. Assessing risk of a new conviction may seem more fair, but the muddy water created by differences in prosecution and trial practices can make these risk assessments problematic, for they measure criminal justice system behavior nearly as much as they measure offender behavior. For these reasons, most risk assessment systems are based on a criterion of "any new arrest."

Obviously, *bias* can enter into the measurement of these risk factors. To the extent that police are attuned to closer surveillance of ex-offenders, young males, and people of color, reliance upon arrests alone to determine risk factors can give more weight to these characteristics than they deserve. To the extent that the criminal justice system is broadly biased against the poor and racial minorities—a point that has been heatedly debated—these biases will show up in risk assessment systems. Since risk assessment systems are themselves used to justify policy and practices with individual cases, experts fear that a biased risk approach will further intensify and solidify the disadvantages suffered by certain groups at the hands of the criminal justice system.

It is also the case that female offenders have very different risk profiles than males, and on average demonstrate a much lower level of risk, even in the face of the presence of known risk factors. To treat women as representing the same level of risk as men is to systematically overestimate their risk. Yet some women will be a greater risk than some men; that is, it is not the case that all men are higher risk than all women. This complicates the need for risk factors to be counted for women in a way that doesn't overestimate the true risk they represent.

A related problem is the reluctance of judges and probation officers to fully utilize risk scales. What sometimes happens is that other factors impact risk decisions. Factors such as the offender's demeanor during hearings or his or her race can determine the level of "dangerousness" that the offender poses and the kind of supervision he or she will receive.

Although a perfectly unbiased risk management system may not be possible to design, in part due to the larger problem of inequality in American society, advocates of risk assessment approaches have developed ways to minimize the impact of racial and social bias in the systems they use. Joan Petersilia has shown how through employing special statistical techniques, the possibility of racial bias can be reduced.[4]

A final concern has to do with *generalizability,* which is the idea that any set of risk factors proven to work on one sample of offenders can be expected to work on any sample (or all samples) of offenders. It seems this would be true, but it turns out that when recidivism studies are repeated across different offender samples, they turn out differently, usually mildly but sometimes quite significantly. The most important difference across samples is in the overall failure rate, known as the **base rate,** which can be as low as 20 percent or less for some Midwestern samples of probationers and as high as 60 percent for some serious offender samples (probationers and parolees) in California. Obviously, knowing the base rate is an important part of effective risk management—the stakes get higher as the risks increase. Base rates are also important in understanding errors in classification.

Table 5.1 demonstrates this with hypothetical illustrations of how a validation study of the same classification risk factors might turn out on three different offender samples from three different agencies around the country.

TABLE 5.1

Example A (Base rate = 50%)

Risk Level	Percent Fail	Percent Succeed
High	55%	45%
Moderate	50%	50%
Low	45%	55%

Example B (Base rate = 33%)

Risk Level	Percent Fail	Percent Succeed
High	50%	50%
Moderate	33%	67%
Low	17%	83%

Example C (Base rate = 12%)

Risk Level	Percent Fail	Percent Succeed
High	25%	75%
Moderate	12%	88%
Low	7%	93%

(Although these examples are hypothetical, they mirror results that have occurred from various actual studies.[5]) Example A shows the results of an invalid risk classification system. Even though there are differences between the risk groups in the percentage of cases who fail, the differences are too small to be important, and so it makes little sense to rely on the classification system to treat offenders differently. This contrasts with example B, in which the failure rates in the risk groups are quite different. The base rate in example B is 33 percent, meaning that one-third of the total sample will be expected to fail. In the high-risk group, one-half will fail; in the low-risk group, about one in six will fail (17 percent). These differences are large enough to matter, for it makes intuitively good sense for us to deal with two groups of offenders differently when we know that in one about half will fail, and in the other about one in six will fail. Example C shows how a valid risk assessment can produce a different result when the base rate is different. In this case, a much lower base rate exists, so while the differences are also important in example C (one-fourth the high-risk cases fail compared to fewer than one in ten of the low risk), the lower base rate results in an anomaly: Cases accurately referred to as "low risk" in example B turn out to be almost the same threat as those called "moderate risk" in example C.

This illustrates one of the most important aspects of the meaning of the term *risk:* It is a comparative term, signifying "risk compared to X." That is, there is no objective "truth" to the term *high risk,* for all it means is "higher risk than other groups." As a result of this and other issues, even though some risk factors seem to occur repeatedly in studies across multiple samples, most experts agree that it is important to validate on the offenders in question any risk management approach relying on risk factors. This is accomplished by applying the risk factors to a sample of offenders and seeing if it works on them.

TYPE I AND TYPE II ERRORS

Classification errors can be obscured by the fact that risk assessment is different from prediction. In prediction, an outcome is foretold for each individual. Errors in prediction are obvious, since the predicted outcome either occurs or does not. But as we saw above, risk assessments place individuals into risk groupings. Some of the individuals in each group will fail, some will succeed. If the rates of failure within these groups are sufficiently different, then the risk classification system is itself successful. But this success in grouping individuals according to their risk should not be taken as an indication that individuals have been successfully predicted. Some individuals placed into risk groups will behave differently than expected. In a sense, then, these individuals are "classification errors," for they behave differently than the rest of their group.

We expect to encounter two types of classification errors:

- **Type I error** occurs when we classify a case as low risk of failure, and the person turns out to fail.
- **Type II error** occurs when we classify a case as high risk of failure, and the person turns out to succeed.

Although each of these errors is a classification problem, they are not equivalent, for they impose different costs and carry important political and practical differences for the agency seeking to manage its clients' risks. Type I error is by far the more visible, for a case that was treated with a low priority ended up getting involved in trouble. When this occurs, the public loses confidence in corrections, and in particularly dramatic cases, political leaders and the public media may start calling for "reform" of the corrections system. Type II error is often called "invisible," for everyday citizens seldom hear about the cases in which high-risk offenders successfully complete their terms of community supervision. The costs of these errors are also less severe, since the main expense is simply that the program of closer supervision and control may have been erroneously applied to these clients. On the basis of costs alone, administrators are generally more concerned about avoiding Type I error than Type II error.

Returning to Table 5.1, we can see what the classification errors are in the examples. In example B, the high-risk cases have a fifty-fifty chance of failure, indicating that the Type II error rate will be about 50 percent. Among the low-risk cases, 17 percent will fail, and that is the Type I error rate. In example C, the Type II error rate is 75 percent (the rate of high-risk cases who do not fail), much higher than that of example B, because the latter's base rate is so much higher. Example C's rate of Type I error for low risk is only 7 percent, for the same reason. Another way to compare these two examples is to compare the *ratio* of Type II to Type I error. Example B makes about three Type II errors for every Type I error, while example C makes about nine Type II errors for every Type I error.

Which example is to be preferred? There is no easy answer to that question. Obviously, the risk classification seeks to minimize both types of error, though neither type will ever be eliminated. (To eliminate error would require perfect predictions of the future for every offender, and that is simply not possible.) The errors in example C seem preferable, but they are made possible primarily because the base rate for that example is so low. In the end, the decision of how many errors can be tolerated of which type is a judgment call that correctional administrators have to make.

Knowledge of the base rate is a first step in understanding classification errors and how they might be managed. When the base rate is high, it will be difficult to keep Type I errors to a small number in the low-risk group. This means that no matter how many offenders come out low risk, when there are numerous errors in that group the administrator will have to devote some level of resources to them in order to try to reduce the number who get rearrested. Since resources in terms of time and staff are fixed by the agency's budget, the decision to devote some resources to the low-risk cases reduces the amount of staff and programmatic attention available for the high-risk clients. So agencies who suffer from a high base rate of failure face a difficult dilemma: They would like to concentrate their attention on the highest-risk cases, because there are so many failures in that group, but they cannot afford to ignore the lowest-risk cases, for the same reason.

MANAGING RISK

Having discussed the theory behind risk and the ways to measure it, we now turn to the issue of managing risk. The question of managing risk is the question of allocating a finite amount of resources among a group of clients, based upon the risk of those clients. Managing risk means treating the higher-risk clients differently than the lower-risk clients in order to try, overall, to avoid the most failure. Agencies approach this through three strategies: They develop a plan for different levels of involvement in a case, they place these levels of involvement into a continuum of supervision, and then they structure their enforcement accordingly.

Supervision Levels

Supervision levels are based upon the number and type of contacts with clients. The main types of contacts are the following:

- Direct contacts with clients, which can be in person or over the phone
- Face-to-face, in which clients are seen personally
- Field contacts, which occur in the client's home, neighborhood, or workplace
- Office contacts, which occur in the agency workplace
- Collateral contacts, which take place with someone other than the client, such as a family member or employer

The theory of the supervision contact is that it provides an opportunity to learn about the client's progress in the community and to reinforce the requirement that the client remain law-abiding. Higher supervision levels call for more frequent and more varied contacts. The typical community supervision agency will establish four levels of supervision and indicate contact requirements that go with each. The actual contact requirements will depend upon the agency's "workload," or the capacity of supervision staff and number of clients. Table 5.2 shows how this works. Each of the agencies has four supervision levels, and the names of the levels are the same. However, the

TABLE 5.2

	Agency A	Agency B
Intensive supervision	3 face-to-face per week	1 face-to-face per week
	1 in the field per month	$\frac{1}{2}$ in the field per month
	3 collateral per week	2 collateral per week
	3 urine tests per week	1 urine test per week
Maximum supervision	1 face-to-face per week	2 face-to-face per month
	$\frac{1}{2}$ in the field per month	1 in the field per month
	1 collateral per week	2 collateral per month
	2 urine tests per month	1 urine test per month
Medium supervision	2 face-to-face per month	1 face-to-face per month
	1 in the field per month	Office only
	1 collateral per month	1 collateral per month
	1 urine test per month	1 urine test per month
Minimum supervision	1 face-to-face per month	1 face-to-face per quarter
	1 urine test per month	1 urine test per quarter
Caseload ratio	40 clients per worker	75 clients per worker

contact requirements in agency A are considerably higher than in agency B, and this is allowed because it has a better workload, as indicated by its ratio of staff to clients.

Some agencies would add a fifth level of supervision, in which the contacts are by mail or telephone only, and occur once per month. Such a supervision level, often called **paper reporting,** is reserved for the lowest-risk offender and is used in order to provide supervision to the lowest-risk cases with a minimal requirement of resources.

Supervision Continuum

The idea of the **supervision continuum** is that, as we have seen, a range of supervision levels is established, and offenders are classified to begin at a level appropriate to their risk, and move upward or downward depending upon their behavior. When an offender is classified, say, as medium risk, that offender would begin under a medium level of supervision for a specified period of time, say twelve months. If that offender were to complete the year without any problems, meeting all the supervision conditions fully and showing no dirty urine tests, then the supervision level would be reduced to "minimum" for an additional six months, and eventually to paper reporting. Cases that have problems are moved up a level on the continuum—so, for example, a failure to keep a curfew or a failure to appear for a scheduled office appointment might move a person up to a maximum level of supervision for a brief period, say six months, before the offender is allowed to try medium supervision again.

The concept of the continuum is based upon three related ideas. First, it attempts to match the level of agency contact to the degree of offender risk. Second, it recognizes that risk may oscillate upward and downward over the duration of the sentence, as events change and the offender progresses. Third, it seeks to reinforce offender compliance by imposing stronger controls when the offender disobeys and relaxing controls when the offender complies with the rules.

Not only is the continuum idea sensible on its face, but it fits the experience of many offenders under supervision. For most offenders, successful completion of the sentence in the community is not easy. It can involve false starts and mistakes; after weeks or months of compliance with the rules, an offender can have a "slip" and get drunk or violate a curfew, miss work or fail to keep an office appointment. Experienced correctional workers know that this kind of minor misbehavior is often a "signal" that the offender is drifting back into previous types of conduct. A rapid, but measured response can mark the system's seriousness about full compliance with the law, but do so without overreacting to the misbehavior. The continuum also gives the correctional worker a straightforward way to explain the way supervision works:

"As long as you obey the rules, you will be fine. If you want to get out from under the requirements, cooperate. After you have shown that you can stay in compliance, the amount of control will gradually be reduced. Whether or not that happens is in your hands, not mine."

Structured Enforcement

Central to a risk management system is a structured, predictable way to enforce the rules of supervision. As we have seen, that is essentially the purpose of the continuum of sanctions idea. But often the offender's misbehavior gets more serious than the typical rules violation. For example, if the offender turns in a dirty urine, it certainly makes sense to increase the level of contact. But, depending on the circumstances, an even more strict response may be called for. Some loss of freedom may be desired, and a formal hearing might be useful to call the offender's attention to the seriousness of the misconduct.

The problem is that revocation hearings are expensive, time-consuming, and often occur only after some period of delay, which could defeat the symbolic purpose. The result of a revocation hearing is problematic also, for frequently the misconduct is not serious enough to warrant return to prison and serving the full sentence. Rather than a quasi-judicial procedure, administrators want an immediate response that they can control and implement without involving outsiders. To accomplish this, some agencies have arranged a structured system of enforcement that allows for the immediate imposition of restrictions, but falls short of the full revocation and return to prison.

A typical **structured enforcement** system will empower the agency administrator to order intermediate restrictions in accelerated fashion, to support the enforcement of the rules. For example, repeated failure to keep office appointments might result in a weekend of detention, and the first instance of a dirty urine (positive drug test) might have the same result. Often, a structured enforcement system has several levels of restrictions that might be imposed, and a full revocation hearing is scheduled only if the offender continually disobeys the rules. In practice, an offender might receive structured enforcement responses for up to three or four violations before a full revocation hearing is scheduled before a sentencing authority. Examples of the structured enforcement restrictions, and how they can be stepped up, are as follows:

- Curfew at 7 P.M. for one month
- Weekend detention
- Multiple detention over consecutive weekends
- Detention and community service

The purpose of this range of restrictions is to create some flexibility in the responses of the system to both enforce the rules of conduct and conserve the valuable time of staff and administrators for the most serious violations.

By authorizing graduated sanctions as agency policy, decision-making officials and administrators can empower staff to impose sanctions rapidly yet with consistency and appropriate severity.

CASE MANAGEMENT SYSTEMS

To a certain extent, community corrections officials have always practiced some form of risk management. Practitioners have recognized that their profession would not long survive if they appeared unconcerned with the safety of the citizens who paid their salaries. They also knew, from experience, how painful it could be for fellow citizens when they failed to give enough importance to the risk their clients represented.

For most of recent history, the effective management of risk was left to individual staff members responsible for the supervision of offenders. Each staff member would apply whatever standards of reporting and surveillance was felt necessary to the cases assigned, the caseload. Obviously, this allowed substantial differences to develop in the way cases were handled. Some staff members cultivated reputations as "tough" supervisors of offenders, with regular surveillance and strict enforcement of the rules. Others were more lax, giving offenders leeway as long as they cooperated and stayed crime-free. In this sense, supervision of offenders in the community was said to be idiosyncratic, reflecting the values and orientations of the staff person involved. At one time, remarking that there were 250 parole officers in California operating under very individual standards and approaches, Elliot Studt indicated that instead of one parole agency, there were really 250 of them.[6]

In recent years, critics have wondered whether this extreme discretion is the best way to approach managing offenders in the community. They point out that such discretion promotes wide disparity in treatment of offenders. It also allows the least-skilled staff or those with the poorest judgment to do whatever they like with their cases, often to the detriment of the offender, the agency, or the community.

To remedy this situation, **case management** systems have been developed that attempt to standardize the supervision practices of all staff in a given agency. First designed by the National Institute of Corrections (a division of the United States Bureau of Prisons), in its Model Probation and Parole Management System Project beginning in 1981, the case management systems approach included five main elements (see the box "National Institute of Corrections"). Since that project, the case management systems approach has been implemented in nearly every adult community corrections agency, and most juvenile agencies as well. The three elements described in more detail in the next sections are classification/risk and needs assessment, supervision planning, and workload accounting.

NATIONAL INSTITUTE OF CORRECTIONS CASE MANAGEMENT SYSTEM

Case management systems have been developed to focus the supervision effort of probation officers on clients' problems, identified using a standardized assessment of probationer risk and needs. In 1980, the National Institute of Corrections (a division of the Federal Bureau of Prisons) developed what it referred to as a "model system" of case management. This model has five principal components—statistical risk assessment, systematic needs assessment, contact supervision standards, case planning, and workload accounting—each of which is designed to increase the effectiveness of probation supervision.

1. *Statistical risk assessment:* Since fully accurate predictions are impossible, there is pressure to be conservative when assessing risk, considering the client a risk even when the evidence is ambiguous. This tendency to overpredict (estimating that a person's chance of being arrested is greater than it actually is) means officers will spend their time with clients who really need very little supervision. The use of statistically developed risk assessment instruments reduces overprediction and improves the accuracy of risk classifications.

2. *Systematic needs assessments:* Subjective assessments of clients' needs often suffer from lack of information and even biases on the part of the probation officer. Systematic needs assessment, which requires an evaluation of the client on a list of potential needs areas, is a more comprehensive way to determine what problems the probation officer should address.

3. *Contact supervision standards:* Probation officers have an understandable tendency to avoid "problem" clients and spend more time with the ones who cooperate with supervision. In terms of the aims of probation, however, more time should be focused on the cases with the greatest risk and needs. Using the assessments, offenders are classified into supervision "levels." Each level has a minimum supervision contact requirement; those of the highest risk or need receive the most supervision.

4. *Case planning:* The broad discretion given probation officers to supervise their clients leads to idiosyncrasies in approaches. By having the probation officer indicate the supervision plan in writing, a better fit is created between the client's problems and the officer's supervision strategy, and the officer's work is more easily evaluated.

5. *Workload accounting:* Since cases pose very different issues in the supervision they need, simply counting cases can misrepresent the overall workload of an agency. A better system for staffing the agency is provided by

using time studies to estimate the number of staff needed to carry out the supervision policies.

The model has enjoyed widespread support from probation and parole administrators. The model has been adopted in a number of countries and is now considered standard practice in virtually every large probation agency in the United States. Structured case management systems also help the probation staff to determine more reliably which clients need intensive supervision, special services, or traditional probation monitoring.

Source: National Institute of Corrections, Model Probation and Parole Case Management System (Washington, DC: National Institute of Corrections, 1982).

CLASSIFICATION: RISK AND NEEDS ASSESSMENT

Using standardized risk assessment forms described earlier in this chapter, the risk of an offender is assessed by measuring the presence of risk factors. Several risk assessment devices are used, but they all have the same types of factors and they all have the same result: The offender is placed in a risk category such as "high," "moderate," or "low."

Rehabilitation workers have identified a number of areas in which offenders commonly have needs for treatment programming. These are referred to as "needs" factors, and they are assessed in a similar fashion to risk factors for every offender. Depending on the number and seriousness of needs in the case, the resulting designation may be "high," "moderate," or "low" needs.

The final classification decision is in reality a programming decision more than it is a description of the offender, for it answers the question "How much supervision shall this offender receive?" The eventual amount of supervision an offender receives depends upon the risk/needs classification. Cases scoring high on *either* instrument are assigned to maximum supervision; cases assigned to low on *both* instruments are designated for minimum supervision. The remaining cases receive moderate supervision. A minimum frequency of supervision contacts is prescribed for each of these supervision levels. Table 5.2 illustrates the frequency of contact that might accompany a typical classification system.

The use of these classification systems ensures some predictability and rationality in the amount of attention offenders receive from the staff assigned to supervise them. Instead of haphazard rates and levels of reporting, the offender can expect to be supervised according to a system that applies to everyone the same way.

Supervision Planning

The supervision plan is the description of the goals to be sought and the activities to be carried out during the supervision process. It is different from the supervision levels, which merely define a minimum number of contacts to be kept between the agency and the offender, in that the supervision plan defines the content of those contacts—what will be discussed when the offender meets the staff member and what results are expected from those discussions. Thus, while classifications systems are standard for all offenders under a given agency, supervision plans are specialized to reflect the particularities of every given case in the agency.

Most supervision plans make a distinction between the goals of the supervision process and the tasks of the offender and the officer. For example, one offender's goal might be to remain free of alcohol use during supervision. The task for that offender might be to maintain regular weekly attendance at Alcoholics Anonymous meetings. The idea is that if the offender is successful at the tasks, the goals will eventually be achieved.

Some case-planning systems also provide for a listing of the staff member's tasks during supervision. In these approaches to case planning, the staff member can be made accountable for carrying out the tasks of the supervision plan. Agencies do this because it separates the client's performance from that of the staff member. In other words, experienced correctional officials know that clients sometimes fail to obey the rules or get rearrested, even when the staff member has done an excellent job with the tasks of supervision regarding the case. The reverse is also true: An offender can successfully complete supervision despite an inadequate job by the correctional worker. Thus, agencies seek to hold staff members accountable only for *their* tasks, and not for how the offender behaves.

Three kinds of goals are generally established for cases. *Risk* goals are designed to alleviate significant problems in a case—typically, they are designed to reduce or control the effects of a risk factor or needs factor on an offender's adjustment to the community. *Punitive* goals are designed to impose some penalty or restriction, which symbolizes the community's claim that the criminal behavior is unacceptable. Community service, fines, and restitution are common punitive goals, but home confinement, curfews, and other restrictions are also used. *Management* goals are designed to maintain the case's effective supervision, and they include regular reporting, keeping a job, and maintaining a suitable living situation.

Workload Accounting

In most community corrections agencies, workload has always been measured by the size of a staff member's assigned caseload—the offenders under his or her direct supervision. For years, correctional officials sought smaller caseloads for their workers, in the understandable and commonsense belief that this would enable them to be more effective. Nobody knew the "best" caseload size, but most people believed workers should not be asked to supervise more than sixty offenders or so. Because, in most areas of the country, actual caseloads ran much higher than these "desired" levels, some researchers sought to test the importance of caseload size.

There were actually several studies of the effects of caseload size, and in all of them the effectiveness of supervision of smaller caseloads was compared to that of larger caseloads by comparing rates of new arrests and other types of failure by clients. The results were virtually unanimous: The size of the caseload made no difference in an offender's likelihood of being rearrested. Offenders on large caseloads appeared to do about as well—in some studies even better—than those on small caseloads.[7] These results proved consternatious to community corrections professionals who were committed to the idea that smaller caseloads were preferable, and so they began looking for reasons why this might be so.

One reason had to do with clients. While it is said that "a rose is a rose is a rose," in community corrections, a client is not necessarily a client. Depending on the degree of risk and nature and extent of problems, two clients can require very different levels of time and attention. This is one of the reasons that measures of caseload size seem so unimportant to casework effectiveness. The new classification systems developed in the 1980s showed the importance of differences among clients in their risk factors and need factors.

It is equally true that a staff member is not a staff member. In fact, differences in work styles among staff members explain more of the differences in supervision outcomes than does the size of the caseload. Even with small caseloads, it turns out, some staff spend little time with clients, preferring to concentrate on paperwork and other duties. Obviously, giving such a staff member a smaller caseload only frees up time for paperwork and related office duties; it does not necessarily result in better supervision.

Systematic case management systems have changed all that. With standard reporting requirements for cases based upon classification results, differences among offenders tend to produce differences in supervision by all staff, regardless of their philosophy of the job. This is the concept of **structured differential supervision,** that different offenders receive different types of supervision from staff, based upon the problems they represent. In contrast to the disappointing studies of caseload size, studies of structured differential supervision find that this approach often does result in lower rates of rearrest by clients, especially those who are at highest risk.[8]

Workload systems are designed to make certain that staff have sufficient time available to carry out structured differential supervision of their cases. They contrast with caseload-based systems because they do not rely on the number of clients, but rather on the amount of time a given client's supervision will require, given the classification results.

To establish the workload accounting system requires two steps. In the first step, the amount of time a staff member has available for supervision is calculated. For example, while a typical staff member may be paid for a forty-hour week, not all of that time is available for casework. Vacations, sick time, and holidays must be subtracted, as well as time spent in noncasework activities such as staff meetings and training programs. In the end, as much as 30 percent of the forty hours per week may be spent on tasks unrelated to direct supervision of clients (paperwork is counted as case-related work, even though it does not involve supervision).

The second requirement is to learn how much time a case might require. To estimate time requirements, a time study is done on a sample of actual cases from the different supervision-level requirements, noting how much time is required on average for each supervision level.

The workload accounting system then is very simple. The total time required for all cases in the agency is calculated by summing the amount of time for each classification level and multiplying by the number of cases in that level. The total time required is then compared to the total staff time available to supervise them—the number of staff multiplied by the number of hours each staff member can devote to the job. The result is a **workload formula,** which represents the agency's estimate of whether its staff resources are sufficient to carry out its case management system.

Agencies that calculate a workload formula often find out that the time available to supervise cases is insufficient to meet the time required by their cases. When this happens, a workload adjustment must be made. This means that either the number of cases in the most time-consuming categories is reduced by changing classification standards, or more staff are hired.

RISK MANAGEMENT AND PUBLIC ACCOUNTABILITY

One of the main aims of a risk management system for community corrections is to be accountable to the public for the way an offender is supervised while living in the community. The accountability is threefold. First, the agency is accountable to the public for designing and carrying out a carefully planned supervision program based upon a realistic understanding of the offender's risk. Second, the agency is accountable to staff to be certain that they are provided with sufficient time and resources to do their jobs. Third, the agency is accountable to offenders for having an objective, equitable system to justify the requirements placed upon them.

Accountability of public agencies was an important new development in the 1990s. With a growing disregard for public agencies and their effectiveness, and a general cynicism about government that became stronger in the 1980s under Ronald Reagan, public agencies sought to strengthen their image with a dubious American public. In corrections, this meant to accept the fact that offenders under supervision in the community represented to the public a serious concern, and the correctional system was responsible for developing programs and approaches that lessened those concerns. The idea of risk management based on principles of case management systems is like a public commitment by the government to provide quality services to the citizenry.

ISSUES IN THE RISK MANAGEMENT FUNCTION

It is clear that managing the risk offenders represent to the community is now and will remain one of the most important functions of community supervision. Yet even though we expect community supervision to concern itself with community safety by managing offenders effectively, the concept of risk management has its controversies. Some of the issues in offender management have to do with the overall effectiveness of the techniques we use to deal with offenders in the community, the inevitability that some offenders may fail in the community, and the very idea of social control in community settings. We deal with each of these in the following section, but first we describe the different ways we control offenders in the community.

Human Surveillance

When it comes to surveillance, no approach can fully supplant the basic strategy of increasing the offender's contact with an experienced correctional worker. Unlike other techniques, personal contact allows the correctional worker to process an array of subtle information—body language, attitudes, odors, and so forth.

Intensive supervision systems have been used to increase both the frequency and the diversity of this surveillance contact. The frequency is increased by reduced caseloads and minimum contact requirements for every offender under supervision. Typically, these offenders are seen at least weekly and sometimes more often than that. What makes the surveillance effective is not just how much contact there is, but where and when it occurs. Offenders are seen at the office, in their homes, and at work; they are seen at regular intervals and in "surprise" visits without prior notification. The dominant effect is an aura of surveillance in which no aspect of the offender's life is totally free of potential observation.

In short, through routine, random contacts, the correctional officer is able to observe a wide range of the offender's behavior in a broad array of situations, which yields a deeper understanding of the offender's compliance with the law.

Controls on Freedom of Movement

Increasingly, offenders under community supervision have their freedom of movement restricted. This often takes the form of a curfew, but it can also include restrictions in associations, access to schools and playgrounds, and ability to visit places that sell alcohol. Often, these restrictions are imposed by the court, but compliance is left to the offender. Sometimes, however, as offender management programs grow weary of offenders' unwillingness to abide by the restrictions, electronic surveillance is used to increase obedience with these requirements.

Perhaps the dominant penal innovation of the 1980s was electronic monitoring. The idea of electronic monitoring has much to recommend it: It represents "high-tech" corrections, and it costs less than prison. Since its initial application in the early 1980s, electronic monitoring has become a major industry, and thousands of offenders now are monitored each day.

The electronic age also has provided other forms of surveillance technology. For example, the technology now exists for visual monitoring via telephone lines. Therefore, video screens could be used to ensure that the offender is actually at home during the phone call. The probation officer could simply call the offender on the phone and then conduct a face-to-face interview without ever leaving the office.

Also possible is routine, random video surveillance without the telephone hookup. Under this system, the probation officer could activate a video camera in the offender's home at any time and obtain direct, unbiased information about the offender's behavior and compliance with the law.

As another level of surveillance, consider the technology of the "electric fence" that is now used to confine some dogs. It establishes a perimeter (usually the yard) outside of which the dog may not venture without triggering an electric shock. This technology might be easily adapted to keep certain offenders away from schools, bars, or other areas. In theory, at least, it could allow extensive freedom within the necessary restrictions. The box "Update on Electronic Monitoring" describes efforts at electronic monitoring in England and the United States.

Chemical Controls

It is perhaps ironic that in a society so concerned about drug abuse, one of the main strategies for controlling human behavior is the use of chemicals. Yet a long tradition of prescribing drugs for precisely this purpose exists in the United States. Here we describe only a few such drugs, but the extent of their use underscores the importance of **chemical controls.**

- Antabuse is frequently given to alcohol abusers, because when combined with alcohol, it makes a person become violently nauseated and therefore suppresses the desire for alcohol.

UPDATE ON ELECTRONIC MONITORING:
"THE BAG" BEATS "THE TAG"

The English are not wild about "tagging offenders"—the way they refer to electronic monitoring. But their prison population has risen so drastically—by 10,000 offenders in two years to a total of more than 62,000—that some are beginning to consider the idea.

Of course, by American standards, their alarm seems misplaced. We house almost 20 times as many offenders in our prison systems, and incarcerate our citizens at 5 times the rate they do. But still, when it comes to the discipline of the incarcerated world, it is all what you are used to. Americans may not understand the English unease at their present prison circumstances, but a host of electronic monitoring executives from this country have made it their business to visit England and with "aggressive marketing" convince them it is time to get into the business of tagging offenders to deal with prison growth.

In 1989, the British Home Office, the policy arm of the government, conducted an experiment with tagging as a condition of bail. The results were widely seen as a fiasco—more than half the tagged offenders violated their conditions or were rearrested while under monitoring, and the program cost the equivalent of about $20,000 per offender. But that did not deter the government from undertaking a plan to use tagging on a field-test basis with curfew orders on probationers—typically unemployed men in their 20s and 30s, convicted of a repeat drunkenness-related offense, such as brawling.

The Home Office evaluation of the new project is under way, and early results are only a bit more positive than the first round. Magistrates (English lower-court judges) are loathe to assign the tag as a condition, and offenders are resistant to its use—only 83 offenders were sentenced to tagging in the first 12 months. Although the majority of cases did well, and the scheme cost less than $1,500 per person overall, the results are still meager. The Chief Probation Officers Association has written an official policy statement that tagging "does not add anything that cannot already be achieved through existing community penalties." Everyone acknowledges that tagging cannot work unless it is part of a support, service-oriented probation approach.

Meanwhile, in the United States, the brave new world of electronic monitoring gets braver.

Disaffected with the limitations of telephone-based systems, there is new experimentation with Global Positioning Systems (GPS). The weakness of the traditional system includes the fact that once the offender has left the property, his or her whereabouts are undetermined—all that is known is that the offender is not home. This means that the offender is monitored when under curfew, but at other times is free to be anywhere—even places that are prohibited.

The GPS system solves that. It requires the offender to carry a "bag" (some systems use a box) at all times. The bag transmits a signal to the satellite system developed by the U.S. military for surveillance purposes, which routes the information back to central control. What is actually being tracked is the device in the bag, but the bag has the ability to inform central control if the offender's bracelet (and presumably the offender) has ceased to be within a short distance—say, 20 feet—of the bag. It means that the central control officer is able to know at all times where the bag is and whether the offender is nearby: 24-hour, worldwide electronic surveillance.

The companies that produce the technology charge $18/day—about half the cost of jail. The marketers also indicate that their accuracy is far superior to the traditional systems, and with additional gadgetry, the accuracy can be enhanced even more. The prospect of being able to monitor any offender all the time is no longer mere science fiction.

Sources: Prison Reform Trust, "Electronic Tagging: Monitoring in the U.K. and Europe," *Journal of Offender Monitoring* 11 (Winter 1998): 13–19; and Marc Renzema, "Satellite Monitoring of Offenders: A Report from the Field," *Journal of Offender Monitoring* 11:2 (Spring 1998): 5–11.

- Sometimes called "chemical castration," the drug Depo-Provera has the effect of constraining the male sexual response. It is used to reduce or eliminate the sex drive of men convicted of certain sex offenses.
- Thorazine is a very strong drug that is used to suppress agitation and thought disorders. Some have labeled it a chemical lobotomy because it creates a lethargic mood in its users and, by diminishing the capacity for excitement and expressive emotions, reduces the likelihood of violence.
- For offenders who suffer from depression, the drug Prozac is often prescribed to decrease the low, sad feelings that accompany depression.

Some of these drugs have negative side effects: Antabuse reduces sexual drive, and Thorazine reduces emotional response. At the same time, none of these drugs is 100 percent effective at preventing crime. There are well-documented cases of crimes committed while drinking under Antabuse (often accompanied by retching and vomiting) and of Depo-Provera takers committing sexual assault. These incidents confirm that drugs do not always control behavior, and that the wellsprings of criminal conduct are substantially social and not primarily chemical.

Programmatic Controls

The most widely used techniques of surveillance and control are implemented through the established elements of treatment programs. Drug testing is a good example. In these programs, urine samples are routinely taken to test for potential drug use. Normally, the offender is required to submit a urine sample (with a correctional worker watching as it is "produced" to ensure that it is truly the offender's urine and not a substitute), which is then sent to a lab for testing.

Not only is this procedure awkward and invasive, it is untimely, involving substantial delay between the time of surveillance (the actual urine evaluation) and subsequent arrest and revocation if the urine proves "dirty." Recently, on-the-spot tests have been developed, usually involving a drug-sensitive strip of paper. Some are used with urine samples; others are performed on saliva samples. In addition, because some drugs leave no traces of their presence in the urine and saliva within hours of their use, some programs have adopted the expensive alternative of hair testing. Traces of some illegal drugs can be detected in human hair for a year or more after the drug's ingestion.

Programs also sometimes provide for systems of surveillance and control. The most famous example is Vermont's "Relapse Prevention Program" for sex offenders. This program trains the offender to be aware of potential signs indicating a reversion to deviant sexual behavior. These signals include sudden changes in mood, renewed drinking, loss of a job, depression, and so forth. What makes this program unusual, however, is that selected individuals living in the offender's community—family, friends, therapists, and coworkers—also are taught to look for the same signs. In effect, these people become additional eyes and ears for the correctional worker, who contacts them on a regular basis to see if the offender is exhibiting evidence of a behavior change that should concern the authorities. The community thus augments the system by providing additional surveillance

The Effectiveness of Risk Control

Just how effective are all these various methods at actually controlling risk? It depends on the methods being evaluated. There is little evidence that ever greater levels of surveillance in supervision programs actually result in fewer rearrests—indeed, some evidence suggests that greater surveillance results in higher levels of rearrest, not lower, probably due to a greater possibility of detection through the increased surveillance.

This general pattern of findings—that closer monitoring does not automatically translate into greater success—is an important caution to those who would develop community supervision programs. It also illustrates a significant irony in offender management programs: The potential for a good idea to backfire must always be considered. For example, electronically monitored restrictions on movement pose their own problems. They cannot ensure crime-free behavior, because some types of crime—drug use and spousal assault, for example—are easily committed in the offender's home. Moreover, the close surveillance of this type of restriction is bound to turn up high rates of noncompliance, and this provides still another reason to find an offender in violation of the rules of supervision. And as we discussed earlier in this section, the use of chemical controls does not always control criminal behavior. These examples teach us that even the best intentions cannot guarantee success.

The Inevitability of Error

Recognizing the problem of **inevitability of error** is crucial to understanding the limits of offender management. There is simply no strategy that will guarantee success in handling offenders in the community. The relative costs of crime, compared to unnecessary intervention into an offender's life, always leave the balance seeming to favor the latter. As a consequence, case managers tend to become conservative over time, willing to apply a restriction and enforce it whenever there is a small suspicion that the offender might be headed for problems.

This act runs contrary to common perception. Many people think that community supervision workers—probation officers and parole agents—are by nature lenient. They think that the profession attracts people who want to give offenders a break, and always offer the offender the benefit of the doubt. Even if this is the case, the professional case worker soon learns that always being willing to give the offender rope can have publicly disastrous and professionally damaging consequences. All it takes is one offender who commits a serious crime because the caseworker decided to "take a chance" and not impose a restriction, and the lesson will be learned: When in doubt, establish a control on behavior.

The irony is that no control is guaranteed to work. So over the years, the caseworker will have numerous experiences in which there were controls imposed that did not prevent the crime, and these will tend to reinforce ever more conservative thinking about imposing greater controls whenever there is a problem. When there is no repetition of the problem behavior, the caseworker will tend to conclude that the control "worked." But, of course, there is no way for the caseworker to find out if the same thing would have happened without the controls that were imposed. Thus, there is something of a system that tends to justify a practice of ever-increasing controls being placed on offenders, only to have the inevitable few of them not work.

Control: A Double-Edged Sword

Many of us might initially regard the idea of tighter surveillance of offenders as a good thing. Various forms of surveillance are common in modern society—and they are not necessarily bad. Parents put listening devices in infants' rooms so they can hear when the baby wakes up; banks put video monitors in their ATMs to take photos of people who withdraw money; airports X-ray all bags to check for weapons; businesses and stores run checks on credit cards before a purchase to be certain they are valid. With the advent of the information age, surveillance has become a more likely option for preventing problems than ever before.

Yet Americans also have a tradition of respect for individual privacy—and unquestionably surveillance invades privacy. We are especially suspicious of any invasion of the home, no matter what its benefits might be; thus, the increase in community surveillance comes at a price. The main cost is civil liberty. Just as studies have shown that families suffer from a member's incarceration, they also show that house arrest, electronic monitoring, and intensive supervision place stress on the family. Sometimes these measures infringe directly on the privacy of innocent people. Can you imagine the annoyance of an offender's wife whenever the phone rings in the middle of the night? Or the sense of personal violation provoked by the surreptitious video monitoring?

Tony Fabelo, who is director of the Texas Criminal Justice Policy Council, has expressed grave concerns about the growth of the use of technological forces by the correctional system. He analyzes the increased reliance of correctional officials on pharmacological and electronic controls of offender behavior as a troubling new development in the field. He especially deplores "the incentives it offers to expand the net of state control in order to deal with social and behavioral problems in the name of public safety.[9]

Critics of the new community surveillance argue that, historically, whenever government is allowed to intervene into citizens' lives without restraint, tyranny results. Unless we jealously protect our civil liberties from intrusion by the state, freedom will inevitably and continually erode. To support their case, these critics point out that airport metal detectors were supposed to be a temporary measure when they were first developed and that the social security number was supposed to have no official use other than keeping track of social security benefits.

The advocates of control concede these points. But they also note that airplane hijackings have decreased in frequency and that life is more convenient now that we have social security numbers. Moreover, surveillance is almost always less restrictive than prison (suggesting that convicted criminals' rights to privacy are not strong); and the right to privacy might be deemed less important than the need to prevent crime.

Admittedly, however, when new technologies are developed for corrections, it is difficult to stop them from spreading, for they quickly become quite popular. Who can argue against electronic fences for criminals if it can be shown that they work? Already, some city streets are blocked off to prevent drug sales. The image of a future society in which whole sections of town are cordoned off from certain people for legal reasons may not be far-fetched.

Thus the new surveillance and control emphasis of corrections is a major change, not just for the field but also for the community at large. We must recognize that the advocacy of technological surveillance and control changes our communities, perhaps in some ways we would not choose. And we must also acknowledge that the debate about freedom and control is a very old one, one that cannot be resolved in a few pages.

THE PROFESSIONAL ROLE OF THE CASE MANAGER

What does it mean to have the person who handles an offender in the community adopt the role of "case manager"? Not too many years ago, the profession of probation officer or parole officer was one that provided to the individual worker a great deal of latitude in how to do the job. Indeed, some would say that one of the great sources of job satisfaction for the individual worker was this ability to control one's own style of work and approach to the job. Case management strategies change some of that, by imposing a supervision structure that seems to standardize the job by removing discretion. Does this make the job less satisfying?

On this question, arguments may be made both ways. On the one hand, something all of us want in a job is latitude, and any changes that reduce professional latitude can also be seen as reducing some of what makes the job satisfying. On the other hand, one of the great frustrations of working with offenders in the community is the propensity for second-guessing. Whenever a problem comes up, it is easy for an outsider to see actions the caseworker might have taken to avoid the problem (even though, as we know, there are never any strategies that would guarantee success). The case management approach may structure some of the caseworker's discretion, but it also provides a policy for action that enables the caseworker to avoid second-guessing in the face of a problem.

Feeley and Simon[10] have been critical of the risk management idea in corrections for a different reason. They see it as one more step in a general trend of dehumanizing the face of corrections: Offenders are not people, they are "cases", and their treatment depends upon the risk group to which they are assigned by the classification forms that are filled out. In the end, those who agree with this criticism see corrections under the "risk regime" as no longer an optimistic profession dedicated to assisting offenders in improving their lives, but rather a managerial profession dedicated to controlling the "dangerous classes" in society.

NEW AND EMERGING CASE MANAGEMENT APPROACHES

Case management appears to be here to stay. Now, as we begin a new century, almost every community supervision agency uses some form of a standardized classification process to assess its clients and apply supervision standards, and some form of differential supervision is in operation nearly everywhere. The question is, where is case management headed in the future? Whatever happens in the case management system, the dominant forces that shape case management in the future will be information technology and intervention theory.

Information technology will shape case management by increasing the use of computerized systems for organizing the community supervision workload. Computers will assist in the classification of offenders, the preparation of documentation about their behavior under supervision, and even the supervision itself. Already, for example, reports from probationers are being taken by ATM-like electronic machines in New York City street locations, and probation officers in Maricopa County, Arizona, carry laptops with them when they make field visits.

In some ways, the more interesting innovations of the future will have to do with intervention theory, and they will seek to answer the question "What supervision methods work best with which types of offenders?" These innovations already take the form of cognitive-based treatment programs, relapse prevention systems, and so on. As new supervision strategies are evaluated, the results will begin to influence the supervision process in ways that attempt to reduce risk rather than just manage it—this is the topic to which we now turn.

THE RISK REDUCTION FUNCTION

The question seems like a no-brainer: "Should correctional programs seek to reduce the risk their clients represent to the community?" After all, what could seem more natural than to ask of community corrections that it change the offenders under its supervision?

Yet in recent correctional thought, the question of risk reduction as a priority has been hotly debated. Critics have charged that correctional treatment programs designed to reduce risk are ineffectual at best, abusive at worst. They point to a litany of studies finding that correctional rehabilitation programs fail to reduce the recidivism rates of those who enter the programs. To this is added the complaint that coercive treatments in corrections violate the human dignity of the offender. Supporters of risk reduction reply that the critics misread the evidence on program effectiveness; in fact, they say, these programs often work if they are well designed and well implemented. By definition, they assert, a risk reduction program that works adds to the dignity of everyone involved in the program, especially the offenders themselves.

Who is right? Do treatments work? Are they abusive? Should we require offenders to undergo correctional treatment programming? The answers to these questions are not obvious. The remainer of this chapter will address these and related issues about risk reduction. But before we can understand the role of risk reduction for offenders under community supervision, we must consider both the values underlying the criminal law and the large body of evidence provided by the social sciences.

THE DEBATE ABOUT RISK REDUCTION

For most of the history of corrections, it was simply assumed that the purpose of correctional work was to change offenders for the better. In the 1870 American Congress on Corrections (now the American Correctional Association), for example, reforming the offender was identified as the central priority of the correctional system. Indeed, the term *corrections* asserts the importance of the idea that offenders will emerge from their sentence as better people, more responsible citizens. The idea that corrections was a "people-changing" enterprise was hardly questioned until the second half of this century.

Then a debate surfaced. The initial criticisms came as published research began showing that correctional programs were not working. The social science community became skeptical of the entire enterprise of correctional rehabilitation. Civil libertarians, who had long been pressing for an increase in prisoners' rights, began to press for an end to parole systems that were based on the flawed rehabilitation model. To this chorus of skepticism eventually was added the qualms of political conservatives, who observed that ineffectual correctional policy left law-abiding citizens exposed to ever-increasing levels of crime.

ARGUMENTS AGAINST THE TREATMENT IDEAL

Correctional Treatments Do Not Work

The most famous example of this claim was Robert Martinson's 1974 paper in *The Public Interest,* entitled "What Works?—Questions and Answers About Prison Reform."[11] This article reviewed over 200 studies of treatment programs and concluded that no program was "consistently effective" at reducing recidivism. Although Martinson's work drew widespread media attention and was popular with the public, it was not the first scientific treatise exposing the ineffectiveness of treatment. Several earlier papers had made similar points, beginning with a powerful summary of 100 treatment studies written by Walter Bailey in 1966, a decade earlier.[12] Martinson's paper, however, was the first to attract the attention of a wide audience, and it is usually cited as defining the failure of treatment programs.

Because Martinson's article came out at a time when the crime rate and the fear of crime were very high, politicians siezed the opportunity to utilize the research to promote their own political agendas. Although Martinson never specifically stated that "Nothing works" relative to correctional treatment, this phrase was adopted by those who had issues with the rehabilitative ideal. It has since been used repeatedly to describe the failure of rehabilitation and in support of "get tough" crime measures. Additional support for "Nothing works" came later in the 1970s, when other research efforts found that Martinson's findings were essentially correct.[13]

The arrival of a stream of research studies questioning the effectiveness of treatment hit the field of corrections like a ton of bricks. Correctional treatment programs had always faced the daunting onslaught of conservatives who did not like the way treatment programs "coddled" criminals. These studies provided them with new ammunition to argue that treatment was a hollow idea, and the field should embrace punishments instead. Within a few years, the doubts of the effectiveness of treatments had become a pervasive undercurrent in correctional thought, and efforts to sustain the treatment agenda, at least in the United States, reached a low point in correctional history.

Correctional Treatments Coercively Violate Human Rights

The image of powerful mind-altering experiences, possibly involving shock treatments and strange drugs, may have been placed in the public mind by movies such as Stanley Kubrick's *A Clockwork Orange* and Jack Nicholson's vivid character in *One Flew Over the Cuckoo's Nest.* Scholarly support to these images was provided by researchers such as Jessica Mitford, who in 1973 wrote *Kind and Usual Punishment,* a blasting critique of the ethics of coercive treatment programs. When, in 1971, the prison revolt at Attica brought national attention to prisoners' dissatisfaction with correctional programming and especially the parole system, a liberal consensus began to emerge that understood compulsory treatment programming as a violation of the offender's dignity. Legal scholar Nicholas Kittrie wrote the most blistering critique of the treatment ideology, in a book arguing that offenders and others ought to have the right to refuse treatment.

In today's callousness toward offenders and their interests, it is hard to imagine the popularity of an argument that offenders should have the right to refuse help. But in the 1970s, parole was not seen as an "early release" mechanism, as it is today, but instead was regarded as a system for keeping prisoners locked up who deserved to be released. Liberals called for the abolition of parole release, and this occurred in major penal code reforms in Maine, Indiana, California, and Connecticut. The rationale for parole abolition was an argument of "fairness" in punishments. An offender's response to treatment, it was argued, had no place in determining the release date from prison.

Correctional Treatments Make the Crime Problem Worse

The classic complaint against treatment was provided by James Q. Wilson in *Thinking About Crime,* published in 1977,[14] arguing for tougher measures against crime and a devaluation of treatment strategies as failed and counterproductive. Wilson's book had been preceded two years earlier by an equally strongly worded (if less readable) call for rethinking penal theory written by Ernest Van Den Haag, entitled simply *Punishing Criminals.*[15] These and similar works gave respectable voice to conservative calls for a new emphasis on getting tough on crime and criminals through programs of deterrence and incapacitation.

The conservative call for an end to rehabilitation was not merely based on its purported lack of effectiveness. It came because the emphasis on rehabilitation detracted from what conservatives thought the corrections system should be doing instead—punishment. They argued that stern punishments would send a signal to potential offenders that the law will not tolerate criminal behavior, and prison terms would incapacitate those offenders who have proven so difficult to change through rehabilitation programs.

These arguments, then, collected around the failure of the rehabilitation model, carried much weight with policymakers. Between 1974 and 1982, nearly every state in the union undertook sentencing reform that lengthened sentences, restricted release on parole, restricted granting probation—or all three. This trend has remained dominant for twenty years.

While legislatures rewrote their penal codes as a dramatic gesture to allay public discontent about crime, within the corrections system a much more striking set of changes was under way: Correctional treatment programs were dwindling in number and variety. Convinced that the public mood was decidedly antirehabilitation—and faced with fiscal demands to expand prison cells with strained budgets—correctional authorities downplayed the treatment agenda, turning instead to an offender-management rationale. Determinate sentences and long prison terms made treatment programs obsolete, and in the community, expanding programs made treatment programming unmanageable. The programs simply became too large to adequately supervise the number of participating clients. By the mid-1980s, most correctional systems had only a vestige of their previous commitment to changing offender behavior through programs. Even the programs that remained seemed to operate under a cloud—most people felt they did not work.

PROBLEMS WITH THE DEVALUATION OF TREATMENT

About most reforms of public policy, history informs. And it has been no different for the end to rehabilitation. Time has taught us that two of the more cherished ideals underlying the reforms of the 1970s, the divestment of rehabilitation programs and tougher punishments, have neither made streets safer nor made confinement less coercive or intrusive. This point has been made convincingly by Francis Cullen and Karen Gilbert in their book *Reaffirming Rehabilitation*.[16] But the main reason rehabilitation came under attack in the first place remains an issue—correctional programs face an enormous literature suggesting they are not effective in changing criminals' minds about crime.

Or so it seems. In the last few years, a series of new studies have emerged questioning the wisdom of those original studies about correctional treatment. These new studies reflect a shift in the mentality about correctional rehabilitation called "What works." This phrase is a response to the earlier "Nothing works" mentality that dominated correctional literature for over twenty years. Using a new methodology borrowed from the medical sciences—**meta-analysis**—these new studies suggest that not only can treatments prove effective in correctional settings, but it is possible to learn lessons about how to design and implement correctional treatment to ensure that they will have the best chance of working. The implementation of methodological methods like meta-analysis has resulted in the growing body of literature referred to as "What works." Before turning to our discussion about meta-analysis, we briefly summarize the evolution of the "What works" literature.

FROM "NOTHING WORKS" TO "WHAT WORKS"

Much controversy has surrounded Robert Martinson and his work that helped to formulate the "Nothing works" mentality about correctional rehabilitation. Although Martinson's work—which rebuked rehabilitation—gained much support in the 1970s, from the start many claimed that the Martinson research contained serious methodological flaws. Among the criticisms were that most of the 231 program evaluations studied were rejected because they contained unreliable measures of success, they failed to clearly determine the treatment modality used, they neglected to implement control groups, and they drew questionnable conclusions from the data.[17] Even Martinson appeared to contradict himself and retract his negative remarks about rehabilitation when in 1979 he stated that some treatment programs do have an effect on recidivism and that the "critical fact seems to be the conditions under which the program is delivered."[18]

But probably the best contradictory evidence against the "Nothing works" position has been the approximately two dozen reviews of "What works" literature that have surfaced in the last fifteen years. These meta-analysis studies have produced data of approximately 500 control group studies of offender treatment programs. It has been concluded that such programs have reduced recidivism in the range of 25–60 percent.[19] There are several factors common to programs that reduce recidivism. Those factors are discussed in the meta-analysis outcomes section of this chapter.

The "What works" agenda has been broadened and strengthened by the "Maryland Report," which was published in 1997.[20] Named after the researchers' affiliation (University of Maryland), the report was commissioned by the National Institute of Justice to determine how effectively Justice Department funds (nearly $4 billion a year) have been used and to locate and evaluate crime prevention programs. The final 500-plus-page report provides analysis of crime prevention programs that work, don't work, might work, and others that may need more analysis. Chapter 9 of the report deals specifically with correctional programs, and the author (Doris Layton MacKenzie) concludes that some corrections programs can be effective if they properly match the offender with the correct program. Problems surface if the offenders are not held accountable for their behavior, if the progam is not held responsible for expected outcomes, and if the system fails to sanction offenders who neglect to follow program requirements.[21] The most central finding of the Maryland Report—that crime prevention programs can work if they are focused on particular places and simultaneously address a range of different problems—comports well with the goals of community corrections discussed throughout this book.

HOW META-ANALYSIS WORKS

Let us say you are running a treatment program—call it jump rope therapy—in a small community residential facility, and you want to know whether it is working. You divide your population of twenty residents into two groups, purely at random, and give the treatment to only half; they are taught to jump rope, the rest are not.

You then follow up your subjects for a year, and find that four of the "treatment" group have been rearrested, compared to five of the "control" (untreated) group. What do you conclude? Does your treatment work? After all, your treatment group fails at a 20 percent lower rate!

From a statistical standpoint, you will conclude that "the evidence that the treatment program works is too small to be significant." In other words, you will fail to conclude that jump rope therapy "works," even though fewer of the subjects given the treatment fail in your study. Why? Because the difference between the groups in terms of raw numbers is too small to be "statistically significant." A difference such as this could very easily have occurred just by chance alone, and is therefore not reliable.

But let us say that you read the literature and find that there are 100 studies of jump rope therapy, each involving 20 subjects, and they all turn out the same. In each, 40 percent of the treated group—which now numbers 2,000 subjects total—fail, compared to 50 percent of the nontreated. Would you be able to conclude that jump rope therapy "works," at least in the statistical sense? It makes sense to say yes.

That is essentially how meta-analysis works. It adds together a large number of diverse studies, each of which might be too small to justify firm conclusions, and then it searches through the aggregate for statistical patterns. For example, if, on average, treatments reduce recidivism for the experimental group by, say, 25 percent compared to the control group across numerous small studies, then the meta-analysis would conclude that treatment has an "effect size" of 0.25, or 25 percent reduction. Of course, it is never the case that multiple examples of identical studies are added together to form a single meta-analysis. Instead, different types of treatments are being applied to different types of offenders in different ways—critics of meta-analysis say this is the main fault of the technique, "adding apples and oranges." But the advocates of the technique say that when there are enough studies in the analysis, the variety of studies actually enables researchers to investigate the effects of different kinds of treatment with different types of offenders in different settings.

The early reviews of treatment studies investigated reasonably large numbers of studies, often as many as 200 studies in a given review. But they did not "add them up" the way meta-analysis does. For example, if someone were to take the 100 jump rope therapy studies in our hypothetical example and analyze them from the point of view of 100 individual studies and their results, the conclusion would be very powerful: Out of 100 studies of jump rope therapy, *not one* finds a statistically significant difference between the experimental and control; therefore, it must not work. By contrast, meta-analysis would add all the studies together, finding a consistent, medium-range, and statistically significant effect: a 20 percent reduction in recidivism. Consider also that meta-analyses use far more studies—at least 400 and some more than 500— and it becomes apparent why the technique and its findings have drawn so much attention.

Which approach should we believe? It is partly a matter of taste. Traditionalists argue that in order to learn from a study, it must be carefully designed, taking into account the size of the sample needed to draw meaningful conclusions. They say meta-analysis is sloppy science. But the meta-analysts reply that for many types of studies, it is simply not feasible to obtain large sample sizes. Even more important, they argue, small treatment programs may be even more effective than large programs, and so it is important to allow the study to proceed with small numbers. Finally, to try to base public policy on a strategy of single-issue studies, one at a time, is simply impossible. That is why meta-analysis has been a favorite design for medical studies, because small samples are very common in medicine, and repetitive studies of small samples have been used to instruct us about important medical advances.

WHAT THE META-ANALYSES TELL US

Meta-analyses have been focused upon two general questions: What are the correlates of offenders' risk of failure? and What are the characteristics of programs that reduce offenders' risk of failure? In the first set of studies, researchers study clients in treatment programs, and they try to identify the factors that repeatedly come up as important indicators that a person will fail. In the second set of studies, programs are investigated to see which types of programs work better. We will investigate these topics in more detail in the following sections.

The Meta-Analysis of Risk Indicators

Gendreau and his colleagues reported a meta-analysis of risk studies in 1996.[22] They analyzed a total of over 1,000 studies of risk involving different offender populations, different legal systems, different outcome measures, and different follow-up periods. The meta-analytic technique collapsed these into a single study and determined which factors are associated with failure. The box "Meta-Analysis of Risk" provides a list of those factors.

The box lists two types of risk indicators. **Static risk factors** cannot be changed by external forces. **Dynamic risk factors** are those that can be changed by planned and sustained programs. The box indicates that both static and dynamic factors are important as risk indicators. The static indicators are not surprising: age, IQ, sex, criminal history, and assorted family factors. The dynamic factors are **criminogenic needs,** that is, offender needs that, if unresolved, might tend to lead toward more criminality. Taken together, the dynamic factors turn out to be slightly more important than the static ones in assessing risk.

This distinction turns out to be very important for correctional programming. Static factors, because they cannot be changed, can never be targeted by a correctional program. It is difficult to try to increase a person's IQ or change the offender's current age. Dynamic factors, on the other hand, are frequently the targets of correctional programs: Offenders are given training and helped to find jobs; they are exposed to counseling that attempts to alter the way they think about crime and victims of crime.

This suggests the three major ways that corrections can change the risk factors of offenders:

- A static risk factor can change naturally—an offender can *age out* of the crime-prone years.
- A dynamic risk factor can change due to an event in the offender's life—marriage, birth of a child, a new job.
- A dynamic risk factor can change due to purposeful correctional programs—the offender can develop a less antisocial attitude and resolve to stay away from antisocial associates.

META-ANALYSIS OF RISK

The following predictor domains have been determined by prior research to be significant predictors of recidivism.

Static Factors

- Age
- Criminal History: Adult
- History of Antisocial Behavior: Preadult
- Family Criminality
- Family Rearing Practices
- Family Structure
- Gender
- Race

Dynamic Factors

- Intellectual Functioning
- Socioeconomic Status
- Antisocial Personality
- Companions
- Criminogenic Needs
- Interpersonal Conflict
- Personal Distress
- Social Achievement
- Substance Abuses

Source: Paul Gendreau, Tracy Little, and Claire Goggin, "A Meta-Analysis of the Predictors of Adult Offender Recidivism: What Works!" *Criminology* 34:4 (November 1996).

It is in this latter area that programmatic meta-analyses are useful: Looking across a wide range of correctional programs, what seems to work, for whom, and why?

Meta-Analyses of Treatment Programs and Their Outcomes

Meta-analyses in corrections have all been published in the last decade, and most of them only very recently.[23] Most of today's meta-analyses take the following approach:

- All published studies of correctional treatments are coded for a series of variables, such as nature of treatment, strength of research design, type of client, setting of treatment, and so forth. The result usually numbers near or above 500 total studies.
- Statistical analysis proceeds by using characteristics of the study to explain study outcome; that is, study design, client characteristics, and so forth, are correlated with the size of the difference, if any, in recidivism outcomes.

Results are typically reported in two ways: overall "effect size" of treatments, and the manner in which certain attributes alter the effect size. For example, a meta-analysis might show that the overall effect of a given treatment is 25 percent (indicating the treated group is 25 percent less likely to reoffend than the nontreated group) and that this effect is increased to 35 percent when subjects were males under the age of twenty-five. In order to do several such comparisons of effect sizes, there obviously must be a large number of studies in the analysis for each factor being investigated.

Andrews and his colleagues[24] have summarized the meta-analytic literature as leading to a series of main conclusions, some of which have to do with specialized issues in the field. Four of his conclusions deserve exploration, because they have considerable importance in the design of successful treatment programs.

The Risk Principle: Target Offenders of Higher, Not Lower Risk. The first principle may be the most counterintuitive: Design treatment programs for higher-risk offenders. The reason this is counterintuitive is twofold. First, many practitioners feel that they are more successful when they work with offenders who are "motivated to change." Second, whenever we establish a program for high-risk offenders, our experience is that the subjects have high failure rates, which makes us think the program does not work. In fact, these go together, on an everyday basis—high-risk cases fail frequently (as would be expected) while lower-risk cases do well (as expected) in our programs, making us think we should concentrate on the lower-risk offenders.

But the question is not how well the offenders are doing in the program, but how well they do compared to not being in the program. Upon a more careful consideration, we would expect high rates of failure from the difficult cases and low rates from the easy ones. The question is, how does the program experience change rearrest rates compared to what would otherwise have been expected? Looking at the problem this way, it soon becomes clear that we have a better chance to succeed with higher-risk cases. For example, a fancy new program will have trouble showing any improvement with low-risk cases, of whom only, say, 8 percent are going to be arrested without the program—the program is "wasted" on 92 percent of the cases. By comparison, even a moderately powerful program might stand a chance with the "high risk" group, of whom, say, 75 percent are going to be rearrested without the treatment. Table 5.1 illustrates this point.

The meta-analytic statistics bear this out. Of programs targeting higher-risk cases, effect sizes are overall moderate (in the 15–20 percent recidivism reduction range) in strength. In those programs targeting lower-risk offenders, effects are near zero or even negative (indicating a potential *increase* in recidivism.)

Because the risk principle is so counterintuitive, we fail to take it into account in designing our programs. We think we want to give new programs a chance to succeed on "good" cases, and so we target first-time property offenders—by definition, low-risk cases. Then some evaluator comes along, does a controlled study, and finds "no significant difference" in the way our first-time property offenders perform with and without the program. In other words, they do well regardless! Should we be surprised?

The risk principle is also useful to us as a matter of public safety. It says we are most likely to be effective in preventing return to crime for cases having a high probability of return to crime! This is good news, indeed.

The Setting Principle: Maximize Treatments in the Community. Meta-analytic studies find that treatment programs operating in community settings are superior in effects to those operating in institutional settings. This finding is consistent with arguments made for decades: Whenever possible, provide services to offenders in the community rather than in prison.

This principle makes sense from the point of view of logic. The treatment agenda is behavior change, and this requires the opportunity for the offender to test the behavior in the real-life place it will occur. Prisons are artificial environments, in which behavior is so controlled that offenders have little opportunity to choose their new action strategies in realistic situations. Seen from this perspective, a prison sentence is not a treatment; rather, it delays using the best treatment settings for the offender.

Again, this is contrary to practice. In the United States, the sentence to prison or jail is becoming increasingly the likely response to a conviction. While the meta-analyses show that treatment provided in these settings can be effective under some circumstances, the effect size is far smaller than equivalent treatments provided in the community. This confirms the idea that community-based correctional authorities ought not to be content with merely watching offenders more closely; they ought to be designing positive programs for behavior change, because they are in the best situation to deliver such programs.

The setting principle is also very good news for community corrections. It suggests that offenders who are likely to benefit from treatment are best dealt with in the community. Rather than a weak setting for treatments, a community supervision sanction turns out to be quite an appropriate choice.

The Sanction Principle: Increase Services, Not Penalties. Programs that seek to change behavior through the threat of increased sanctions do not show very sizable effects—in fact, under some circumstances, they lead to worse recidivism rates. Our natural expectation is that if we can make failure costly enough for offenders, we will convince them not to fail. As sensible as this seems to us, it does not pan out in the studies. When a program has a "tougher sanction" as its main treatment component, it produces failures at a higher rate than programs that try to provide services that support behavior change.

This finding helps explain why summary studies of boot camps such as that reported by MacKenzie and others[25] have found little evidence in support of reduced reoffending in these cases. Indeed, where there are effects, they appear to be due to the services provided during and after the boot camp experience, rather than the boot camp itself. Those programs that are based upon a threatening infrastructure appear to have found plenty of opportunities to deliver on the threat, but with little evidence of intended results.

Why do "get tough" measures fare so poorly in the meta-analyses? It is not easy to answer this question. Some observers speculate that this result ties in with a general principle of human behavior: People change their behavior more readily for a positive goal (to attain something they desire) than a negative one (to avoid something bad). In any event, this finding is disquieting, in the face of current policy initiatives that seem so fond of tough rhetoric and even tougher action with offenders. These approaches may be counterproductively emphasizing the negative and ignoring potential positives for behavior change.

The Need/Responsivity Principle: Target Criminogenic Needs in Proven Ways. One of the more controversial—and elusive—findings of meta-analysis is the way it instructs us on the types of programs we ought to favor. This has two components, often discussed separately: need and responsivity. "Need" refers to the problem that is leading to criminality; "responsivity" refers to the strategy of the treatment program. Obviously, the idea is to design a program that tries to alter the criminogenic need and does so in ways that fit known successful program strategies.

Among the most important criminogenic needs are the following:

- *Antisocial thinking* including attitudes, beliefs, and rationalizations
- *Antisocial supports* such as gangs, friends, and cocriminal associates
- *Antisocial behavior* such as hostility, rule avoidance, and problems in anger and arousal control

It can be seen that these are fairly specific targets for change programs rather than general "attitude counseling" approaches, which often are designed. As a consequence, three kinds of treatment strategies are designed to address these needs:

- *Social learning and cognitive programs* that focus on teaching new behaviors in place of prior, criminogenic behaviors
- *Constructive interaction* that uses modeling, concrete problem solving, and supportive relationships in which the use of authority is fair
- *Multimodal strategies* that take into account the multiple needs of the offender, including the current level of motivation for change

Today's approach to correctional treatment is often inconsistent with these results. There is often a reliance on general counseling or group-based insight counseling (which meta-analyses find result in net negative effects on post-treatment behavior). Moreover, the professional involvement with clients that is assumed in these approaches is not often possible with heavy workloads in treatment agencies.

RELIABILITY OF THE NEW META-ANALYSES OF TREATMENTS

These four elements of correctional treatment programs—risk, setting, sanction, and need/responsivity—when present in the programs subjected to meta-analysis, increased dramatically the effect size of the treatment programs to a 40 percent reduction in rearrests or more. This is a considerable impact, one that has obvious implications for community safety, crime prevention, and even long-term cost savings.

But the new meta-analyses are not without critics. Lab and Whitehead[26] have wondered whether the coding schemes in the data analysis and the categories used to classify programs are clear enough to justify conclusions that are drawn. They suggest that their own findings, which support a more limited confidence in treatment, are more conservative and ought to give policymakers more than what they view as wildly optimistic results of other studies. Perhaps this is so. But even under rules of due caution, the new meta-analyses call our attention to the ways in which we might increase the impact of correctional programming.

In the end, however, the new research on corrections provides a powerful incentive to develop new treatment interventions in corrections. These interventions will involve a kind of teaching of offenders of ways to think about and react to the pressures and dynamics that lead toward crime. These programs will involve staff who model appropriate types of thinking and behavior, and they will give the offender opportunities to try out those new ways of behaving. This approach has often been called a "social learning" approach to correctional treatment, because it is based on "cognitive" therapies that target the offender's thoughts rather than feelings, the offender's responses to situations that occur rather than the resources that offenders have to work on their problems. **Cognitive therapies** are general therapies that deal with the broad spectrum of offenders under correctional supervision. When they are used correctly—when they are directed toward the higher-risk cases and delivered in the community—these programs have shown a powerful potential to reduce risk.

One of the advantages of these cognitive approaches is that they can be offered in a classroom-style format to groups of offenders. They involve "lessons" about thinking patterns and problematic reactions to situations, and they use role-playing and other techniques to instill new behavioral skills in the "students." There is "homework"—specific problem-solving tasks that the offender must undertake in his or her place of residence, neighborhood, or work setting to solve specific problem situations that are occurring there. The use of groups moves this kind of correctional programming away from "individualized counseling" approaches that have proven ineffective, time and again, and led to the original devaluation of treatment in the 1970s. Whether the promise of these programs will continue to hold will become apparent in the coming years. To date, the widespread adoption of cognitive strategies is too new to permit a conclusive evaluation of their effectiveness.

THE FUTURE OF RISK REDUCTION

It is not conceivable that risk reduction will ever be eliminated as a concern of agencies that manage offenders in the community. The public expects correctional agencies to try to reduce the risk its clients represent to the community—especially when they reside in the community. Reducing an offender's risk is the most efficient and least intrusive way to prevent crime, without recourse to imprisonment. The question is, what kinds of risk reduction strategies will be used in the future?

There is a growing consensus that attempts to change behavior through general counseling have proven to be of extremely limited success. It is likely that risk reduction strategies that simply attempt to talk to offenders about their adjustment to the community will become of dwindling importance. Talking, by itself, does not seem to do much.

On the other hand, evidence is mounting that more active strategies have much more notable effects. These strategies seem to be based, in one way or another, on actually teaching offenders how to cope with their problems without resort to criminal behavior. They follow different strategies, depending on the problems: providing alternative ways to achieve a goal, training the offender to be sensitive to precursors to failure, modeling more successful strategies of problem solving, and so forth. These are cognitive methods, and they combine well-established principles about the ways adults learn with knowledge about the circumstances that offenders must avoid (or embrace) in order to prevent return to crime.

It is likely, as well, that these training types of risk reduction strategies will be coupled with better surveillance and control methods while the offender is under supervision and treatment. This ensures that as offenders are receiving reinforcement of their behavioral change, they will also be under strict observation to make certain the training is having its desired effect. The combination of training and control is one of the ways that community corrections workers strengthen the effects of both of these methods.

Thus, in the future, professionals in community corrections will likely become more proficient in cognitive methods of risk reduction to be used in tandem with established techniques of risk control. There is no good reason to expect any new, powerful breakthroughs in risk reduction, however. The sources of criminal behavior are as old as the behavior itself, and although progress is being made in dealing with offenders so that their risk of return to crime is reduced, this will be a steady process of improving the professional skills of workers, not a dramatic new discovery of a treatment technique heretofore unknown.

SUMMARY

The ever-present risk of new crimes by offenders in the community is a central concern of administrators of community supervision agencies. Risk management as a philosophy of community supervision is built around (1) a suitable, systematic assessment of the offender's risk of a new offense, (2) the development of a meaningful supervision plan to deal with that risk, and (3) the establishment of workload standards that ensure the supervision plan will be carried out. Regardless of the quality of the supervision plan, there is the inevitability that error will occur in the classification process, and the supervision plan will sometimes overestimate and sometimes underestimate the risk of recidivism. The problem of error is dealt with by structured supervision standards, structured processes of enforcement of community supervision conditions, and supervision quality control. The development of the case management model of community supervision has been controversial, because it reduces the discretion of community supervision workers and focuses their attention on standardized tasks rather than human interaction. Future innovations in case management will incorporate technical advances in information systems as well as improvements in our understanding of effective interventions to reduce risk.

Although the goal of rehabilitation (and reducing risk) would seem to be essential in corrections, it has not gained much support in the correctional literature over the past thirty years. Only recently has a new wave of studies called meta-analysis revived the hope that some forms of treatment can reduce the risk of crime for some offenders. These studies have reported that if certain conditions are followed, offenders can be controlled and rehabilitated in the community. Additional attention must be given to offenders with special problems because traditional case management supervision does not attend to the criminogenic issues of these offenders. What rehabilitation and risk reduction will look like in twenty years is unknown, but with research like meta-analysis and emphasis on new cognitive therapies, the future is promising.

1. For years, the common response to rehabilitation has been that "Nothing works." From what we know now about the topic, is this statement still valid?

2. How has meta-analysis changed the way we view the research on correctional effectiveness?

3. According to Andrews and his research on recidivism, why should we concentrate our treatment efforts on high-risk offenders?

4. Why is it difficult to measure and assess risk?

5. What are some risk factors that are highly associated with criminal recidivism? Which do you believe are the best predictors, and why?

6. Discuss how Type I and Type II errors can be problematic to community corrections.

7. As a community corrections worker who has discretion to reward or punish offenders, what criteria would you use to move an offender forward or backward on the supervision continuum?

SUGGESTED READINGS

Andrews, Don A., and Bonta, James. *The Psychology of Criminal Conduct.* Cincinnati: Anderson, 1994. Discusses the theory and practice of offender rehabilitation.

Clear, Todd R., and O'Leary, Vincent. *Controlling the Offender in the Community.* Lexington, MA: Lexington Books, 1981. Presents the argument for risk management methods in probation supervision.

Cullen, F., and Gilbert, K. *Reaffirming Rehabilitation.* Cincinnati: Anderson, 1982. Argues that correctional treatment is more humane than incarceration and can be effective if implemented effectively.

Lauren, R. J. *Positive Approaches to Corrections: Research, Policy, and Practice.* Lanham, MD: American Correctional Association, 1997. Provides positive insights that support the use of psychology in treating offenders.

Palmer, Ted. *A Profile of Correctional Effectiveness and New Directions for Research.* Albany: State University of New York Press, 1994. A description and analysis of the most effective strategies for offender treatment.

Sechrest, Lee, White, Susan O., and Brown, Elizabeth (eds.). *The Rehabilitation of Offenders: Problems and Prospects.* Washington, DC: National Academy of Sciences, 1979. Up to 1979, the most comprehensive review of correctional treatment and its effects.

Weibush, R. C., Baird, C., Krisberg, B., and Onek, D. *Risk Assessment and Classification for Serious, Violent, and Chronic Juvenile Offenders.* San Francisco, CA: National Council on Crime and Delinquency, 1994. Essential text in offender assessment that provides risk/needs scales and addresses risk factors for offenders.

WEB SITES

Web site to learn more about corrections technology
www.ctmmag.com

Web site for Rand Corporation research on risk reduction
www.rand.org

Web site for information on case management and risk assessment in community-based corrections
www.justiceconcepts.com

Web site for Justice Concepts Incorporated, which provides articles and information on case management and risk assessment in community-based corrections
www.justiceconcepts.com

Web site for information on case management at Utah Department of Human Services Youth Corrections
www.hsdyc.state.ut.us

Web site for information on assessment and treatment of the offender in the community
http://transport.com/~comklly/assesst.html

Web site to read summary of Maryland Report
www.ncjrs.org/pdffiles/171676.pdf

| NOTES |

1. R. J. Lauren, *Positive Approaches to Corrections: Research, Policy, and Practice* (Lanham: American Correctional Association, 1997).

2. Michael R. Geerken and Hennessey D. Hayes, "Probation and Parole: Public Risks and the Future of Incarceration Alternatives," *Criminology* 31:4 (November 1993): 549–564.

3. See Michael Maltz, *Recidivism* (Chicago: University of Chicago Press, 1979).

4. Joan Petersilia, *Racial Disparities in the Criminal Justice System* (Santa Monica: Rand Corporation, 1983).

5. See Paul Gendreau, Tracey Little, and Claire Goggin, "A Meta-Analysis of the Predictors of Adult Offender Recidivism: What Works!" *Criminology* 34:4 (1996): 575–608.

6. Elliot Studt, *Service and Surveillance in Parole Supervision* (Los Angeles: UCLA Press, 1967).

7. Todd R. Clear and Vincent O'Leary, *Controlling the Offender in the Community* (Lexington: Lexington Books, 1983).

8. Don Andrews, Ivan Zinger, Robert Hoge, James Bonta, Paul Gendreau, and Francis T. Cullen, "Does Correctional Treatment Work? A Clinically Relevant and Psychologically Informed Meta-Analysis," *Criminology* 3 (1990): 369–404.

9. Tony Fabelo, "Technocorrections: The Promise of Uncertain Treats," in *Sentencing and Corrections Issues for the 21st Century,* Papers from the Executive Sessions on Sentencing and Corrections, no. 5 (Washington, DC: U.S. Department of Justice, May 2000).

10. Malcolm Feeley and Jonathon Simon, "The New Penology: Notes on the Emerging Strategy of Corrections and Its Implications," *Criminology* 30:3 (1992): 449–474.

11. Robert Martinson, "What Works?—Questions and Answers About Prison Reform," *The Public Interest* 35 (1974): 22–54.

12. Walter Bailey, "Correctional Outcome: An Evaluation of 100 Reports," *Journal of Criminal Law, Criminology, and Police Science* 57 (1966): 137–260.

13. D. F. Greenberg, "The Correctional Effects of Corrections: A Survey of Evaluations," in *Corrections and Punishment,* ed. D. F. Greenberg (Beverly Hills, CA: Sage, 1977), pp. 111–148.

14. James Q. Wilson, *Thinking About Crime* (New York: Basic Books, 1977).

15. Ernest Van Den Haag, *Punishing Criminals: On an Old and Painful Question* (New York: Basic Books, 1975).

16. Francis Cullen and Karen Gilbert, *Reaffirming Rehabilitation* (Cincinnati, OH: Anderson, 1982).

17. Douglas Lipton, Robert Martinson, and Judith Wilkes, *The Effectiveness of Correctional Treatment* (New York: Praeger, 1975)

18. Robert Martinson, "Symposium on Sentencing: Part II," *Hofstra Law Review* 7:2 (1979): 248–258.

19. Paul Gendreau and Mario Paparozzi, "Examining What Works in Community Corrections," *Corrections Today* 57:1 (February 1995): 28–32.

20. University of Maryland, *Preventing Crime: What Works, What Doesn't and What's Promising* (Washington, DC: Government Printing Office, 1997).

21. Doris Layton MacKenzie, "Criminal Justice and Crime Prevention," in *Preventing Crime: What Works, What Doesn't and What's Promising* (Washington, DC: Government Printing Office, 1997) pp. 9-1–9-76.

22. Paul Gendreau, Tracy Little, and Claire Goggin, "Meta-Analysis of the Predictors of Adult Offender Recidivism: What Works!" *Criminology* 34:4 (1996): 575–608.

23. For a review of recent studies using meta-analysis, see James McGuire, ed., *What Works: Reducing Reoffending* (Chichester: Wiley, 1995).

24. Don Andrews, Ivan Zinger, Robert D. Hoge, James Bonta, Paul Gendreau, and Francis T. Cullen, "Does Correctional Treatment Work? A Psychologically Informed Meta-Analysis," *Criminology* 28:3 (1990): 369–404.

25. Doris MacKenzie and Eugene Hebert, *Correctional Boot Camps: A Tough Intermediate Sanc-tion* (Washington, DC: U.S. Department of Justice, 1996).

26. S. P. Lab and J. T. Whitehead, "From 'Nothing Works' to 'Appropriate Works': The Latest Stop in the Search for the Secular Grail," *Criminology* 28 (1990): 405–417.

Chapter 6

Offenders Under Diversion

Imagine that you are arrested.

Perhaps you were driving home from a party, where you had too much to drink. Or an argument with a roommate got out of hand, erupting into violence, and now you find yourself facing assault charges. Or you were out for the night with two friends, and it turns out one of them was carrying illegal drugs, for which you have all been charged.

What goes through your mind? You may be ashamed of yourself, shocked at what has happened. Undoubtedly you are worried about what this arrest will mean for you: Are you going to jail? Will you lose your job? Will everybody find out?

Being processed by the justice system is one of the most humiliating experiences a person can have. It makes you feel powerless: Strangers have complete say over what you must do, where you must go. People you will never meet determine what is going to happen to you. A label—"defendant"—is attached to your name, and it may seem that everything about you dissolves and only that label matters.

One of the most understandable feelings would be to want the whole thing to stop. You "made a mistake," and you not only regret it, but you have suddenly learned how important it is to avoid mistakes like this in the future. You might think, "If only I could have another chance. . . ." You might very well be right. Your life and the lives of those around you might truly be better if the criminal justice process did not proceed with your case.

THE PHILOSOPHY OF DIVERSION

In an informal sense, **diversion** merely means officially exercising discretion at any point in the criminal justice process. This happens every second of the day in the world of criminal justice. Diversion can involve the police deciding not to arrest a husband involved in a domestic dispute. It can mean involving offenders in treatment programs or some form of community service imposed in lieu of the regular justice process. These are just two of the many examples of the use of diversion. It is often made available to lesser offenders, juveniles, first-time offenders, or offenders who repeat minor

Photo: Offenders in Hillside, NJ, complete their community service at a nonprofit community food bank.
© Jeff Greenberg/The Image Works

offenses because of problems the regular criminal justice process can do very little about. More formally, diversion usually includes the suspension of the criminal process in favor of some noncriminal disposition. That is what diversion is all about—stopping the justice system so that a person can have another chance. Under diversion, the regular processes of the justice system are interrupted.

According to the National Advisory Commission on Criminal Justice Standards and Goals, diversion is "activities formally acknowledged and organized to utilize alternatives to initial or continued processing into the justice system. To qualify as diversion, efforts to find alternatives should be undertaken prior to adjudication and after a legally proscribed action has occurred."[1]

This points to an important distinction—the difference between informal and formal diversion strategies. Informal diversion occurs when an official in the justice system decides, using appropriate discretion, not to take a case any further into the justice system. Such diversion decisions occur every day—when a police officer decides to warn a citizen rather than make an arrest and booking; when a victim decides not to press charges; when a prosecutor decides not to prosecute a defendant. When informal diversion is used, the justice official decides, for whatever reason, that the case would be better kept out of the justice system. Formal diversion is different in that there is typically a program for the accused to enter and complete, set up as a condition of diversion. In formal diversion decisions, the offender is offered some form of treatment or voluntary sanction that, once completed, justifies the closing of the original case. These two kinds of diversion are important to bear in mind, because even when a formal program is not available to the defendant, informal diversion can be used if the official thinks it is called for by the circumstances of the case.

Although diversion is generally used as a way to initially divert persons away from the formal functioning of the justice system, it is also related to the community corrections aspects of the criminal justice system. This happens in at least three ways. First, those accused of crimes are allowed to enter a program and, in exchange, the charges against them will be dropped. While attending the program, the accused is supervised and in this way is involved in a form of preconviction probation. If the person fails to meet the requirements of the specified program, he or she is then formally processed into the system. Second, through various pretrial release practices the accused is allowed to remain in the community while his or her case is pending. During this period, the person may or may not be under the direct supervision of the court. Prerelease practices serve to reduce jail populations and allow the accused to remain employed while awaiting trial. A third way diversion is broadly related to corrections is through the formal sentencing of an offender to probation or some other intermediate sanction. If an offender is found guilty and sentenced to some form of community service or restitution and is allowed to remain in the community, he or she is in fact diverted from incarceration. These kinds of diversion applications will be discussed in more detail later in this chapter.

HISTORICAL BACKGROUND OF DIVERSION

The idea of diversion, or keeping the offender out of the criminal justice system, is probably as old as the system itself. Police officers and court officials have always exercised their discretion so as to prevent the formal processing of offenders. During colonial times, a cobbler from Boston named John Augustus developed an idea that would keep diverted offenders out of the criminal justice system. This idea was called probation. More recently, the formalized practice of diversion, the use of diversion as an acknowledged and acceptable activity of the justice system, originated in 1965 in Genesee County, Michigan. In 1967, the U.S. Department of Labor began to fund pretrial diversion programs for offenders. Soon thereafter, the Law Enforcement Assistance Administration funded experimental alcohol detoxification programs. With the support of the 1967 President's Commission on Law Enforcement and the Administration of Justice and the 1973 National Advisory Commission on Criminal Standards and Goals, diversion programs during the 1970s prospered. During the decade, over 1,200 diversion programs were established at a cost of over $112 million.[2] Although federal funding for formal diversion programs waned in the 1980s, many diversion programs still exist. In most cases, state and local governments have assumed the costs of implementation of diversion programs.

GOALS AND BENEFITS OF DIVERSION

The main goal of diversion is to provide services or treatment for offenders in lieu of their becoming involved in the criminal justice system. In this way, diversion is intended to rehabilitate offenders. According to Samuel Walker, rehabilitation can occur through diversion in three ways. First, by keeping offenders out of jail or prison, diversion helps them establish a normal lifestyle away from the negative effects of incarceration. Correctional institutions have been viewed as "colleges of crime" where offenders learn to become better criminals and part of a criminal subculture.

Second, diversion can promote rehabilitation by eliminating the stigmatization effect of the criminal process. The justice system can do a great deal of damage to a person. A criminal record can stand as a permanent bar against certain professions, and a stretch in prison can leave a person embittered toward the system and might wipe out any lessons learned from being arrested in the first place. The criminological theory called "labeling" argues that if a person is coined "criminal," he or she will proceed to act out the role and commit more crime. Many experts believe that the best option for some offenders is to avoid all this by diverting the person from these consequences.

Third, diversion programs can rehabilitate because they provide essential social services that can address the offender's real problems. Alcohol, drug, or family counseling is what many offenders need, not a stint in jail or prison.

There are a number of other possible benefits for diversion aside from rehabilitation. For one, diversion may be much cheaper than getting someone involved in the criminal justice system. For example, placing someone in a treatment or counseling program would be much less expensive than processing that person through the court system and then locking him or her up in jail or prison for a year or more.[3]

Diversion is also much less costly for the offender in a number of ways. If a person is officially charged with a crime, he or she would need to be represented by legal counsel. If the person is indigent, a public defender will be provided by the local court. However, many people accused of crime choose to hire their own legal counsel. And personal legal counsel costs money. Although the cost of legal counsel varies considerably, it is usually in the range of $75–$100 per hour.

Another financial benefit is that an offender who obtains diversion can retain his or her job in the community. Incarceration, even for a short period of time, can be reason for a boss to terminate employment. This may cause the offender more difficulties, especially if the job is needed to pay for counseling, restitution, fines, or court costs. Persons who have been incarcerated also may have difficulty acquiring future loans for housing or educational purposes.

PROBLEMS WITH DIVERSION

As sensible as diversion programs seem at first glance, they are often surrounded with controversy. Among the criticisms of diversion are that such programs are seen as lenient, they neglect victims' needs, they may be more costly in the long run, they promote net widening, and individual rights may be compromised.

The successful diversion programs appear to save tax dollars, improve life circumstances for offenders, satisfy victims, and provide services to the community. Yet even these programs are faced with severe criticism as unduly lenient with criminal offenders. Diversion provides for an offender to stay out of the system and to be sanctioned in a manner that is unconventional to many Americans. In the United States, many people feel that if an offender is not incarcerated for his or her crime, then the punishment is not severe enough, and justice has not been served. There are many reasons for this line of thinking. For one, many people are fearful of crime and criminals in America. This is understandable considering that crime is a major social problem and the face of crime is brought out every day in numerous television and newspaper stories. As a result, they do not want criminals to be living among them.

THE USE OF DIVERSION IN THE FEDERAL CRIMINAL JUSTICE SYSTEM

Under the law Title 18, S.S.C. Section 3152 (b), pretrial diversion court services have been established in U.S. federal districts and are administered by the chief pretrial service officer. Pretrial diversion programs are available on the federal level of criminal justice in almost every district in the country. As on the state level, federal pretrial diversion looks to divert certain offenders from traditional criminal justice processing into a program of community supervision administered by a pretrial services agency or probation office. The U.S. Justice Department has listed three main objectives for the pretrial diversion program: to prevent future criminal activity among certain offenders against whom prosecutable cases exist by diverting them from traditional processing into community supervision and services; to save prosecutive and judicial resources for concentration on major, serious cases; and to provide, where appropriate, a vehicle for restitution to communities and victims of crime.

Source: George F. Moriarty, Jr., "Pretrial Services Include Diversion," *Federal Probation* (March 1993).

Another reason people see diversion as lenient is that this country has a long history of imprisonment and strict punishment for offenders and very little experience with alternatives to incarceration such as diversion. The average citizen is unfamiliar with the benefits of such programs and is less likely to support their implementation.

In a related issue, some argue that diversion focuses on the offender and neglects the victims of crime. Because diversion often looks at the needs of the offender and the savings to the criminal justice system, it may be true that little consideration is given to the victims' needs and feelings about the crime. But this problem can be solved without eliminating diversion programs. One idea would be to involve the victim in the diversion process. Victims can be allowed to be present at hearings to give their opinion about whether offenders should be given diversion. Allowing for victims to be active in the diversion process can change their attitudes about diversion and about harsher punishment in general. They may be able to better understand the reasons behind crime, and that will help them psychologically adjust to being the victim of a crime. Those who commit crimes may also benefit from meeting with victims. By having offenders meet face-to-face with victims, those who offend may better learn to appreciate the results of their illegal behavior.

Diversion may also be problematic because of the unfortunate reality that not all programs are successful. Some offenders fail to meet the requirements of diversion. This may entail failing to attend counseling sessions, neglect of restitution payments, and even future criminality. The actual administration of diversion programs may be a problem. Perhaps those who work in diversion programs will neglect to supervise offender caseloads in a conscientious manner. When diversion programs fail, individuals suffer and the results can be troubling. They cost tax dollars, increase victimization, and lead to a lack of credibility for the system. In some cases, diversion can be more expensive than "normal" entry into the system because offenders who fail in these programs later have to be processed through the system and then incarcerated.

A common criticism of programs like diversion is the concept of **net widening.** Net widening is when some program or form of social control is given to an individual who otherwise would not be part of the system. To explain in a different way, if a person commits a minor offense and is placed in a diversion program, and had the diversion program been unavailable the person would probably have been released without sanction, then net widening is present. Net widening is a problem for diversion because it is in direct conflict with the goal of diversion—to keep a person out of the criminal justice system and process. Through net widening, diversion programs may actually result in more severe treatment of offenders, rather than the lesser severity they claim. This can happen when an offender in a diversion fails to comply with the minimal conditions of the program (e.g., counseling) and as a consequence receives probation or even incarceration when typically the case would have been dropped or solved without criminal justice intervention. Evaluations of net widening have shown that it can actually increase the number of people in the criminal justice system.[4]

Diversion programs can also create some problems related to the legal rights and treatment of those who are accused of illegal acts. When an offender chooses diversion over formal processing, he or she gives up certain due process guarantees that the formally prosecuted offender receives. These include the following:

1. The right to plead not guilty
2. The right to a speedy trial
3. The right to a trial by jury
4. The right to confront his or her accusers
5. The privilege against self-incrimination

In some cases, diversion can be used to force treatment upon people who have committed no crime. For instance, if a person has the choice of being processed into the criminal justice system with probation and even the possibility of incarceration, or of being placed in a diversion program, he or she may choose the latter. The person may in fact not be guilty, but because of the hassle of being involved with the system, he or she chooses the "lesser of two evils."

A similar scenario can develop for offenders who are given the option of some form of treatment or formal involvement in the system. In most cases, offenders would choose treatment or counseling over the possibility of receiving probation or incarceration. In this case, police or prosecutors may coerce treatment when a crime has been committed but evidence is insufficient to obtain a conviction. In this way, diversion may be used to cover up inappropriate or careless police procedures that produce evidence that is inadmissible in court.

Finally, it is possible that the application of diversion can be discriminatory. Diversion may be applied differently among jurisdictions. Socioeconomic status, race or ethnicity, or gender may influence whether diversion is used or the offender is processed and prosecuted. For example, a person in an affluent suburb may be more likely to receive the benefits of diversion than someone in the inner city because of the person's standing in the community or because of the greater number of social programs available to the accused.

DIVERSION AT VARIOUS STAGES OF THE JUSTICE SYSTEM

Diversion is not unusual in the justice system. In fact, the twin rationales of diversion—to avoid the human and financial costs of justice processing and to provide services outside the justice system—are used to justify diversion at every stage of criminal justice. Experts recognize that the justice system is expensive and sometimes ineffectual, and that it should always be possible to avoid the full force of the law when circumstances warrant.

Diversion issues and diversion programs differ at each new stage of the justice process. As the defendant is taken into deeper stages of the justice system—past arrest into prosecution and even incarceration—the stakes change regarding the diversion decision. The kinds of diversion methods available to professionals and the offenders they are processing also change. For one thing, diversion decisions made later in the process—after conviction or even after some confinement—are far more visible to the public. As a result, public officials are often more careful when approaching diversion options later in the process.

In the section below, we consider diversion questions as they are faced at each successive stage of the justice system. We describe the types of diversion programs and services available, and we discuss the issues system officials encounter concerning the diversion option. In the box "Current Uses of Diversion," we list some examples of different kinds of diversion programs that are available throughout the United States. They represent what diversion has to offer to a range of criminal offenders.

Diversion from Arrest

The most common diversion decision occurs when the police officer decides not to arrest a suspect of a crime, even when there is considerable evidence an offense has occurred. Police will consider diverting a suspect when the offense

CURRENT USES OF DIVERSION
ACROSS THE UNITED STATES

In Multnomah County, Oregon, prosecutors have diversion programs that include first-offense DWI charges, drug charges, and diversion for some domestic violence cases.

The prosecutor in King County, Washington, diverts first-time defendants accused of a variety of nonviolent property and public disorder offenses to a 30-day program. An eligible defendant is sent a hearing summons with an offer to participate in the diversion program. The requirements of the program include payment of $75 or completion of 15 days of community service.

In Marion County, Indiana, a panel that includes a prosecutor, public defense counsel, and a mental health professional identifies and screens mentally ill persons within 72 hours of their arrest to determine their eligibility for a court-monitored mental health treatment program. The team devises a treatment plan that must be approved by the court. The court holds a bimonthly hearing in each case diverted to monitor compliance with the treatment plan. Persons in the program who complete treatment requirements and are not arrested for a new offense for a specified period, usually 6 to 12 months, have their criminal charges dismissed.

In Quincy, Massachusetts, first- and second-time DWI offenders may be placed on probation as an alternative to jail and ordered to a certified drunk driving treatment program. In this 26-week program, offenders are required to attend weekly group counseling sessions and Alcoholics Anonymous meetings. Offenders are required to remain abstinent, and many may be required to undergo random drug testing. The program is reported to be an effective jail crowding countermeasure while yielding high rehabilitative success rates.

One alcohol diversion program is the Alcoholism and Drug Services Center in San Diego County, California, which is operated by Volunteers of America and law enforcement officers. One of the five programs that the center offers is its around-the-clock Inebriate Reception Center, which provides a police diversion plan, detoxification and survival referrals, basic needs assessment, and minimal care 24 hours a day. The police take publicly intoxicated individuals to the center. Clients who agree to stay for a minimum of 4 hours are not arrested. San Diego County claims success in relieving jail crowding through this process.

The Shisler Sobering Center in King County, Washington, provides a 60-bed facility for inebriates brought into the center by law enforcement officers in lieu of arrest.

Under a new program instituted by the San Francisco, California, mayor's office in 1999, chronic inebriates (persons arrested three times within a 60-

day period) are ordered to treatment programs in the city. Those who refuse are sent to jail.

In San Diego, California, the police department's Psychiatric Emergency Response Team (PERT) pairs licensed mental health professionals with police officers who are responding to situations that involve people with mental disorders. The team receives 80 hours of training over a 4-week period. Since it began operations in 1996, PERT has handled more than 3,000 cases, only 1 percent of which have resulted in incarceration. Individuals in the remaining cases were assisted through county mental health facilities or transferred to outpatient clinics. When the PERT teams are not responding to calls, they are following up on prior cases. The PERT program started with eight clinicians who were paid by the San Diego Alliance for the Mentally Ill, with funding from a federal grant and the Vista Hill Foundation.

In 1998, the Atlanta, Georgia, Police Department launched a pilot program aimed at diverting mentally ill persons who violate city ordinances. Under this initiative, the police department trains officers to recognize signs of mental illness and then call the Fulton County Mobile Crisis Unit rather than make an arrest. The unit includes a social worker and a psychiatric nurse who are authorized to commit a suspect at the scene and take the person to one of two participating hospitals.

Source: A Second Look at Alleviating Jail Crowding: A Systems Perspective. Bureau of Justice Assistance Monograph, October 2000. www.ncjrs.org/txtfiles1/bja/182507.txt

is very minor—for example, a traffic violation or a disturbing of the peace—and they will consider it when the suspect's demeanor is calm and shows deference. Police diversion does not necessarily reduce the workload of the police, but these programs can reduce the costs of jail detention and prosecution.

Police diversion becomes controversial when the suspected crime involves a threat of harm to the victim. This is the case with domestic disputes, in which one spouse has behaved with such a threat (or open violence) that the police have been called to the scene. For many years, many police believed that the most important thing to do was to calm the angry spouse and mediate the argument. Police might take a man for a walk around the block or drive him to a friend's house for the night—anything to break the tension and separate the couple. Some police believed that such fights were "normal" for most couples, and that with a little time, tensions would simmer down.

Women's advocates have recently disputed this approach. They point out that police indifference to the battered woman's fears and complaints encourages the batterer and sets the stage for an escalation in violence when the police officer leaves the scene. Studies have supported this view, showing that men who are violent toward their female partners on one occasion are quite likely to repeat these acts not once or twice, but with frequency. People concerned about violence toward women use these findings to claim that men who are abusive to their spouses should never be diverted from arrest, since diversion tends to confirm to the abuser that the violent behavior is acceptable. But this claim runs contrary to other studies that show that arrest actually exacerbates spousal violence in some domestic situations, such as when the husband is unemployed.

These critics received support when one famous police experiment found that repeat violence was significantly lower following a policy of mandatory arrest of abusers than when the police used their discretion to divert cases seeming to be minor.[5] Following the study, many police departments revised their policies to require an arrest in all domestic disputes as a way of declaring the importance of the problem and reducing repeat violence. Conclusions about the value of mandatory arrest policies have been complicated by later studies that find far less support for their impact on reducing violence, and at least one study finds that arrests work only when the batterer receives mandatory counseling services on how to reduce domestic violence.

The same kinds of issues involved in spousal assault arise in other arrest diversion decisions. If a police officer fails to make an arrest in the face of criminal conduct, does this inevitably denigrate the seriousness of the misconduct, thus indirectly contributing to tolerance of the behavior? If the officer makes an arrest, will services be available to help prevent repeat criminality? Or is the arrest simply going to invoke the first stage of a revolving door, in which the criminal behavior occurs again and again? In the end, will the arrest simply result in problems for the citizen arrested—loss of a job, social disapproval, alienation from family and friends—that distance the offender from the supports of law-abiding community life and push him or her further into a criminal lifestyle?

Diversion from Prosecution

The value of the arrest is that it gives formal criminal justice control over the person accused of a crime. This control can often be used as a threat to get the accused into a social service program that ordinarily would not have been available without the arrest. This approach, diversion from prosecution, is based on the idea that many people get into trouble with the law because of personal problems that, if solved, would prevent reoccurrence of the crime. Primary among the problems seen in this framework are substance abuse, uncontrollable anger, and inability to earn a legitimate living. For offenders suffering from these deficits, prosecutors will often forego formal prosecution of the crime if the defendant enrolls in a treatment program for the problem— especially when the person is a first-time offender.

Diversion of this type is also called pretrial diversion or court diversion. When pretrial release is tied into particpation with some program, it is some-

---

THE PRETRIAL DIVERSION "PROCESS"

1. Court staff (probation department and prosecutor's office) review records and interview defendant to see if he or she is a good candidate for the program. (Key issues: Is person amenable to treatment? How serious is offense? Prior criminal history?)
2. Defendant must waive right to trial, and must volunteer for program.
3. Agreement is sought between defendant, diversion program, and prosecutor or judge. (Key issues: What will offender do during diversion period to improve and to avoid future criminality?)
4. Defendant enters a program either in the community or while living in a residential setting.
5. Progress is monitored by diversion program staff.
6. After completion of the program, the defendant is brought before the court to determine the final outcome of the case. Options: Legal case dropped, program extended, full prosecution continued, or reduced to a lesser charge.

---

times called *conditional release*. In all of these programs, the offenders have been arrested but not convicted of their criminal charges.

Pretrial diversion can occur at any stage of the system after arrest and prior to adjudication. When a person receives diversion from prosecution, the legal case of the offender will be continued for a period of time after which one of three dispositions will be chosen: (1) dismiss pending charges if the offender has shown satisfactory progress and self-improvement, (2) extend the period of time for the offender to participate in the program, or (3) return the case to normal court processing because of unsatisfactory performance in the program. Most often, pretrial diversion release officers or community agencies report back to the court (prosecutor's office) to verify whether an offender has fulfilled the program's objectives. When release and subsequent adjudication is connected with some participation in a program, then it is called conditional pretrial release.

Diversion from Jail

Unlike prosecution diversion programs, jail diversion typically has a very simple aim—to allow the offender to avoid confinement awaiting trial. The benefits of avoiding confinement are considerable. A pretrial jail term, even if only a few weeks, can mean loss of a job and disruption of family life and other social ties. Being locked up also makes it harder for the defendant to assist counsel in the preparation of the legal defense. Some jail diversion programs operate a little like the prosecution diversion programs described above, but most simply seek to find a way to allow the defendant to avoid jail while fighting the charges.

Jail diversion frequently is an option exercised by the police officer making the arrest. In cases of a minor offense, a *summons* can be given on the spot, indicating a date and time for the accused to be in court and face the charges. The summons operates much like a traffic ticket does—the accused is technically being arrested and the officer will later "book" the arrest, but the accused is free to go after receiving the summons and agreeing to its court appearance date. Because of fears a summons may underplay the seriousness of criminal accusation, its use is restricted to only the least serious misdemeanors. The three most common diversion-from-jail programs are release on own recognizance, bail, and pretrial release.

Release on Own Recognizance. A more frequent jail diversion approach, which occurs after the suspect has been brought to the station house and booked on the arrest charges, is called **release on own recognizance (ROR).** Another less used term to describe recognizance release is *promise to appear* (PTA). Under ROR, the accused promises to appear in court on a specified date in exchange for release from custody. No cash or property bond is required. Two types of ROR programs exist. The most common programs simply provide for a release if the defendant promises (a) to appear for the scheduled court hearings and (b) to obey the law in the meantime. Sometimes more elaborate ROR programs allow for the defendant's release so long as a list of conditions are met. These conditions can be fairly extensive, including, for example, attending treatment programs, submitting to drug tests, or meeting regularly with an officer of the court, such as a probation officer.

ROR is not available to everyone, but even some defendants accused of serious crime can qualify. Whether ROR will be offered is usually determined by an interview of the accused immediately after station house booking or the initial entry into the jail. The interview will delve into the defendant's ties to the community—family, employment status, living situation—because it is known that the greater the ties to the community, the more likely the defendant will be to appear at trial. The relationship between community ties and appearance at trial makes sense, because citizens who have more stake in their community relationships are less likely to flee when faced with criminal charges.

Research on ROR finds consistently high rates of court appearance for those granted such release—on the order of 50 percent in many jurisdictions. The program has thus been thought a real winner on all counts, since the defendant avoids the hardships of jail while the state avoids the costs of pretrial detention. Yet ROR has recently come under attack by conservatives who claim that far too many defendants are released under no supervision, only to commit more crimes against the public. This viewpoint has been most forcefully pressed by John DiIulio, who says that about twenty crimes each year are committed by each person on the streets awaiting trial.[6]

Criticisms of ROR have led to a tightening of the requirements of this form of release. It is now more common for offenders to be required to undergo a certain amount of surveillance, abide by a curfew, and even take regularly scheduled drug tests in order to remain under release. A defendant who fails to meet any of these conditions is immediately subject to having the ROR status revoked and being jailed on the original charges.

Bail. The majority of defendants who appear in court are not likely to escape or injure others before coming to trial. When the judge feels this is the case, he or she may release the defendant prior to trial with a personal or financial guarantee of court appearance. This is known as **bail.** Bail, which comes from the French word *bailer* and means "to hand over or deliver," is a pretrial release program that can be traced back to medieval England, when those accused of crime were held in jail until the traveling magistrate arrived in their jurisdiction. Because jailers did not enjoy this task, they were willing to hand over the defendant for money to a third party who would be legally liable for the conduct and court appearance of the defendant. If the defendant failed to appear, the third party would lose the money or be imprisoned himself. In the early nineteenth century, the commercial or bail bondsman became the vehicle for many to buy their freedom. If a defendant could not find the money needed for bail, he could hire a bail bondsman who would pay the bail fee. The bondsman provided this service in return for a nonrefundable fee.[7]

Bail serves two purposes: (1) it helps ensure reappearance of the accused, and (2) it prevents unconvicted persons from suffering from imprisonment unnecessarily. There are two major problems with bail administration. The first is that many defendants simply cannot afford it. In 1973, a report by the National Advisory Commission on Criminal Justice Standards and Goals found that as many as 93 percent of felony defendants were unable to make bail.[8] In recent years, many jurisdictions have adopted state operated pretrial service agencies that eliminate the need for for-profit bail bond businesses. And a number of states have enacted laws that provide alternatives to the traditional cash bond system[9] and make bail more available to a greater proportion of nondangerous arrestees. These alternatives include the use of property bonds, unsecured bonds, and signature bonds. With property bonds, the accused's possessions—such as land, house, cars, and stocks—are held as collateral. Similarly, but more like a credit card, with unsecured bonds the accused agrees in writing to appear in court or he or she will forfeit a predetermined amount of money. The money can eventually be obtained through seizures of land, personal property, or bank accounts. Signature bonds, in which the offender simply agrees in writing to appear before the court, are used in less serious cases such as traffic or petty drug cases.

Another problem is related to the setting of bail. Just who should receive bail and how much money should it cost? In the early history of bail, the local sheriffs determined who would receive bail and for what price. This led to abuses of bail. Fortunately, however, in recent times laws have been made that have changed the way bail is administered. Judges are now responsible for determining who should receive bail. And although the amount of bail to be set for certain offenses has not been structured by law, safeguards have been developed such as the United States Constitution, which specifically states that "Excessive bail shall not be required. . . ." In an attempt to reduce judicial discretion and improve equity, guidelines have been developed to assist judges in pretrial and bail release decisions.[10]

Pretrial Release. Another kind of diversion program that can occur in lieu of jail time is called a **pretrial release** program. The idea of pretrial release is not a new one. The history can be traced back to medieval England. At that time, the detained suspects would have to wait in jail until the traveling magistrate arrived in their town to hear their case. Because this wait often took months, and the local sheriff did not have the resources or interest to watch over them, a new system developed. The sheriff would allow a third party to have custody if this person would agree to become legally liable for the conduct of the accused and for his or her appearance before the magistrate.[11] As noted above, when pretrial release involves financial obligation, it is called bail.

One of the first and most famous pretrial release programs was developed in New York City. In 1960, Louis Schweitzer, who was a retired chemical engineer, visited the Brooklyn House of Detention. As a young immigrant Russian boy, he had once lived a few blocks from where the jail stood. What he saw during his jail visit appalled him. He found that nonconvicted inmates were treated like convicted criminals. Most were too poor to obtain bail; many were later given suspended sentences or even acquitted after a time in jail. After his experience, he established and funded the Vera Foundation (named after his mother) and the Manhattan Bail Project. The original purpose of the Vera Foundation was to assist judges in identifying who could safely be released on their own recognizance prior to trial. The Manhattan Bail Project staff would provide judges with information about whether defendants were good candidates for release prior to trial. Based on carefully monitored evaluation procedures, the Manhattan Bail Project was judged a success, and as a result, many other cities across the United States adopted similar programs.[12]

Pretrial release, like ROR and bail, tries to ensure that the defendant will appear at the trial and at the same time protect the community. In many cases, pretrial release programs require defendants to be under some form of court supervision.

Typical conditions imposed on defendants include (1) regular reporting to a pretrial agency, (2) maintaining a stable residence, (3) finding and maintaining employment, (4) having a third party (relative or friend) that is willing to

---

A DOMESTIC VIOLENCE DIVERSION PROGRAM IN CALIFORNIA

Tarzana Treatment Centers of California have developed a Domestic Violence Diversion Program that is a minimum twenty-week education program for men who have been referred by the courts for domestic-violence-related offenses. The weekly meetings include educational presentations, group discussions, individual assignments, and using videotaped vignettes and group discussions on the Internet. The program gives men concrete tools to more appropriately deal with feelings and thoughts that in the past resulted in abusive behavior. The program and services are provided by staff who are certified in the intervention, counseling, and educational aspects of domestic violence.

Source: www.intros.com/ttc/drg_div.htm

---

accept custody of the defendant, and (5) other probationary conditions such as obeying curfew, staying away from complaining witnesses, refraining from criminal activity, and participating in drug- or alcohol-related treatment.

Releasing the accused prior to trial is common practice in the United States. Studies show that approximately 85 percent of all state-level defendants and 82 percent of federal defendants are released prior to trial. Sixty-two percent of all state-level and federal felony defendants are released.[13] ROR is the most common form of nonfinancial release.

Diversion from Imprisonment

Once convicted, the offender faces the bench for sentencing. For most felony crimes, the judge may impose a term of incarceration in jail or prison. Most offenders will not serve the full term of incarceration provided by law; they will be considered good candidates for one or another form of diversion— either a term on probation or some form of release prior to the completion of the sentence. In subsequent chapters, we discuss in detail the three major forms of diversion from incarceration: probation (Chapter 8), parole and early release (Chapter 10), and intermediate sanctions (Chapter 7), as well as the specific kinds of programs that they support. We need not discuss these forms of diversion here.

It is worth noting, however, that the controversies surrounding prison diversion programs, issues we discuss in the remaining chapters, often are presented as though diversion from incarceration reflects some sort of unusual undercutting of the penal system. In fact, at every stage of justice processing, from arrest to imprisonment, policymakers have seen fit to provide for alternative routes that allow the offender and the system to avoid the full consequences of the penal law. This arrangement mirrors the history of penal sanctions described in Chapter 2, in which harsh sanctions come to be seen as so ominous that they produce a pressure for the availability of less severe forms of sanctions. The criticisms of prison diversion programs may have merit, but to the degree they are based on a claim that every offender should face the full impact of the penal law, they are contrary to history and practice.

BASIC ELEMENTS OF DIVERSION

Diversion programs typically have three elements: treatment, sanction, and enforcement. The *treatment* component of diversion is a counseling intervention designed to help the offender overcome the problem leading to the offense. Usually, the program involves a series of group counseling sessions, in which basic information is presented and participants are given a chance to learn new skills and hone them in interaction with other group members. The most common programs are the following:

- *Drug awareness programs* that teach young people facing drug possession charges the dangers of drug abuse and show them ways to resist drug use
- *Family-strengthening programs* that teach parents how to deal with their children without physical violence and teach couples how to resolve disputes without aggressive acts
- *Anger management programs* that help those accused of assault learn techniques for controlling their tempers and avoiding violence
- *Job readiness programs* that teach basic skills in job hunting to the chronically unemployed

The *sanction* component of diversion programs involves some form of community service by the accused—for example, doing volunteer work in a hospital or cleaning a public park. The rationale for the sanction component is that people who commit offenses owe a debt to society, and diversion from prosecution should not leave that debt unpaid. Sanction aspects of diversion programs are controversial, because critics point out that they impose punishments on citizens who have not been convicted of a crime. Proponents respond that diverted offenders face far less in the way of community service under diversion than what they might be forced to do after a conviction.

The *enforcement* component of diversion is simple: Diversion agencies make certain the accused abide by diversion requirements—attend all treatment program sessions or complete the designated community service—or else the recommended prosecution will commence. Enforcement is a way to make certain that diversion programs have "teeth." The threat of full prosecution will be lifted only after the offender has completed the diversion program and been arrest-free for a reasonable period, such as six months.

Diversion programs differ in whether they commence before or after a formal charge has been filed. The advantage of diversion before formal charging is that the arrested offender can avoid the negative impact of the indictment. When offenders avoid formal prosecution, there is always some form of informal fact-finding prior to admission to the program to determine whether there is sufficient evidence against the defendant to warrant charges. This avoids the problem of placing citizens in diversion programs when they would never have faced formal charges in the first place.

It is more common to begin the diversion process after the defendant has been formally charged. This gives the prosecutor a carrot and a stick with which to manage the diversion process: The "stick" is the threat of prosecution on existing charges should the defendant fail during the diversion process; the "carrot" is the promise to drop the charges once the program has been successfully completed.

RESTITUTION AND COMMUNITY SERVICE

In many diversion programs, the offender is provided with the option to pay restitution and/or perform some kind of community service rather than be processed through the criminal justice system. When restitution and community service are used as a diversion program, they usually occur within a specified time period immediately after court intervention (six months to one year), after which the court will dismiss the charges against the offender. Restitution and community service are also commonly used not only as a diversion option, but as an alternative sentence for convicted offenders and even as a requirement of parole supervision. The following section discusses restitution and community service generally, as both a diversion and a sentencing option.

Restitution is technically when the offender is required or volunteers to participate in service designed to make reparation for harm resulting from a criminal offense. In most cases, restitution is used in crimes related to economic offenses such as theft or damage to property. Money or possessions taken from victims and damage done to property are more easily restored through the financial payment of restitution. Restitution is rarely used for diversion with offenders who commit violent crimes, due to the serious nature of such crimes. In most of those cases, diversion is not an option.

It is important to mention here that restitution is not victim compensation. In victim compensation programs, the government makes payments to crime victims. Over the past fifteen years there has been an increase in victim compensation programs. Many states now earmark funds for payment to victims for crimes perpetrated against them. Some states have programs that pay victims even when the offender is not apprehended. With restitution, payment is made by the offender and eventually it is received by the victim.

Community service, also an attempt to repair past wrongs, requires the offender to spend some time working for a community agency. It is unpaid service to the public to symbolically atone for the harm done by the crime. In community service, the offender repays the community he or she offended by performing some work for it, rather than by making monetary reparation. It might consist of working for the local Kiwanis Club, the YMCA, or a library, or removing litter from local parks and roadsides. Community service is like

RESTITUTION ON THE FEDERAL LEVEL

In the early 1980s, Congress attempted to address the unmet needs of crime victims by enacting the Victim and Witness Protection Act of 1982 (VWPA). One of the concerns addressed in this legislation was victim restitution. In this connection, Congress recognized that

> [t]he principle of restitution is an integral part of virtually every formal system of criminal justice, of every culture and every time. It holds that, whatever else the sanctioning power of society does to punish its wrongdoers, it should also insure that the wrongdoer is required to the degree possible to restore the victim to his or her prior state of well-being.

Despite the importance of restitution as a criminal justice sanction in principle, Congress acknowledged that restitution had "lost its priority status in the sentencing procedures of our federal courts long ago." Under federal law prior to the VWPA, there was only limited authorization for the restitution sanction. Moreover, in practice, the sanction was "infrequently used and indifferently enforced . . . , reducing restitution from being an inevitable if not exclusive sanction to being an occasional after-thought." In enacting the VWPA's restitution provisions, Congress attempted to "restore restitution to its proper place in [federal] criminal law" by expanding the scope of the federal restitution sanction, encouraging its increased imposition, and fostering improved monitoring and enforcement procedures.

A review of the expanded right to restitution in federal criminal cases during the last decade indicates that while the statutory and interpretive framework for an expanded restitution sanction have been established, the use and enforcement of the sanction must be further increased before restitution can be considered restored to "its proper place" in the federal criminal justice system, as Congress intended.

Source: Peggy M. Tobolowsky, "Restitution in the Federal Criminal Justice System," *Judicature* 77:2 (Sept./Oct. 1993).

restitution in that it is both punitive and rehabilitative—punitive in that the offender must pay for his or her crime in time and effort, and rehabilitative in that it can provide a vehicle for the offender to do something positive and to increase self-esteem.

Background of Restitution

The idea of paying for loss, damage, or injury to crime victims is an ancient idea. In the Old Testament of the Bible and the 4,000-year-old Code of Hammurabi, it was stated that the offender must repay in kind or extent to crime victims. Our current idea about restitution has developed over centuries. Initially, people acted on their own to punish others for transgressions against them. But as people began living in large tribes, blood feuds between the different groups developed for the purpose of administering punishment. To solve the sometimes violent feuds between tribes, the crime victims or their families were given compensation for the crimes committed against them. Over time, the families' role in the compensation process withered, and by the thirteenth century the state (or reigning king) became the offended party in criminal offenses. With this development, the state became responsible for punishing offenders and collecting fines. As time passed, the victim became less and less involved in the punishment process. In eighteenth-century England, restitution resurfaced when Jeremy Bentham, a philosopher, thought that payment of monetary fines was essential to his ideas that punishment should equal the crime.[14]

In the early years of the United States, imprisonment and fines paid to the government became the chief punitive sentencing measures, and restitution to victims played only a minor role in the range of sentencing options used by American courts. By the late 1800s and early 1900s, restitution fell into disuse. In the 1930s and 1940s restitution was resuscitated, but it was not until the "victims' rights movement" of the 1970s that restitution became a frequently used method of punishment in the United States. During that time, there was a resurgence of concern about the victim's role in the American criminal justice system as well as interest in making offenders more accountable for their crimes. These interests provided impetus for the development of mechanisms in the criminal justice system to require offenders to make restitution to their victims for losses suffered as a result of their crimes. During the next decade, many states expanded their authorization and use of restitution.

Currently, twenty-nine states require a court to order restitution to the victim, or to state on the record the reasons for failing to order restitution. Ordinarily, before restitution can be ordered a finding or plea of guilty must be made. However, this does not apply to cases involving restitution ordered during the pretrial diversion process. Courts are allowed to specify the amount, payment plan, and other conditions of the sentence, probation order, or pretrial diversion order.

AN EXAMPLE OF A COMMUNITY SERVICE PROGRAM

Alexander Killens with a pointy stick, picking up trash or shelving books at the library? Could be, according to the people who run the state's Community Service Work Program. The former state commissioner of motor vehicles, who pleaded guilty Monday to a misdemeanor charge of obstructing justice and was sentenced to 125 hours of community service, joins a burgeoning force of nonviolent offenders paying their debt to society with a little sweat and elbow grease.

The program, established in 1983, began as part of a crackdown on drunken drivers. Even today, nearly a third of all people given community service sentences get them as part of their punishment for driving while impaired. But these days, the program also enlists the labor of all sorts of other people—even some convicted of felonies.

And because of the structured-sentencing rules imposed on the courts in 1994, their numbers are going to rise. Last year, more than 73,000 people were sentenced to a total of 2.3 million community service hours, according to the state Division of Victim and Justice Services. Gregg Stahl, assistant secretary for the Department of Correction, said the growth of community service is more evidence of a philosophical shift toward restitution and punishment as the primary goals of the criminal justice system. "Let's say you get caught with a DWI," he said. "You haven't caused an accident, but you've done something to put the community at risk. By doing the hours of community service, you are restoring the community in some way, and it's also punishment because you're giving up your evenings or weekends."

Rob Lubitz, the director of the Governor's Crime Commission, said the program also has a rehabilitative effect. "Community service is a way for the offender to pay back," Lubitz said. "In some ways, it also restores the offender by allowing him to make reparations for his crime, to pay his debt."

Steve Clarke, a professor of public law and government at the Institute of Government at UNC-Chapel Hill, has found in his research that offenders in the community service program have significantly lower recidivism rates than other offenders. In a study beginning in 1998, Clarke followed 38,000 offenders on probation or released from prison, many of them felons, to see whether they had been arrested again over the next 30 months. He found that recidivism was six percentage points lower among those whose sentences included community-service work. "If you take two offenders with similar backgrounds, the one on community service would have a significantly lower chance of being arrested for a new crime," said Clarke.

A similar analysis, presented to the General Assembly this year by Kitty Herrin, associate director of the N.C. Sentencing and Advisory Commission, also found a correlation between community service and lower recidivism for people on probation. Herrin found no such correlation, however, for offenders released from prison on parole. Those who performed community service work were as likely as other criminals to be arrested again.

Neither Clarke's study nor Herrin's included offenders on unsupervised probation. In other words, most people convicted of misdemeanors or drunken driving were not factored into their findings. But Stahl, of the Department of Correction, notes that the vast majority of DWI offenders are "middle class with middle-class values" and unlikely to commit new crimes.

Clarke's analysis did not stop at recidivism. He and an assistant also looked at the cost of the program and found it to be extremely low—about 70 cents an hour in overhead and administrative costs for every hour of community service performed. But Clarke and his assistant also offered up one criticism of community service. In their study, they found that many of the community-service hours sentenced are not actually served. A report from the Division of Victim and Justice Services bears that out. Of the nearly 69,000 cases "terminated" in fiscal year 1994–95, the report states, 22,403 were terminated unsuccessfully, many of them because the offenders did not show up to finish their hours.

Sylvia Wiggins, who heads the Helping Hand missions of Wake County and is otherwise a big fan of community service, said she sees it all the time. "Not showing up?" she said. "Yes."

A common view of community service is that it is a cushy way for white-collar criminals to avoid time behind bars. Some criminals undoubtedly do get easy work assignments, but generalizations are difficult. Program participants do a wide array of nonprofit and governmental jobs, from building bridges and clearing out parks to donating legal services or providing medical care. For example, Kevin Fowler, 19, is putting in 25 hours at Wiggins' Raleigh mission. "It teaches me respect," he said. "I have to be on time."

Susan Katzenelson, the new executive director of the sentencing commission, noted that many offenders now ordered to perform community service might simply have been fined or put on probation before the state's structured-sentencing system was put in place in 1994—people such as Killens, who was convicted of obstructing; real estate broker Charlie Grady, convicted in June on a conflict-of-interest charge; and former UNC law professor Barry Nakell, who admitted shoplifting. "Some people will say, 'Let's lock them all up,'" she said. "But is that what we really want to do?"

Katzenelson thinks that community service plays an important role in the system, but she warns against unrealistic expectations. "It's almost unfair to expect that any program will completely change you," she said. "There will be some people who are committed to changing. But if all your life has led you to crime, a few hours of community service is not likely to change that."

And to Frances Battle, manager of the Community Services Work Program in Wake County, reforming offenders is just icing on the cake. "I have never felt [that] my purpose is to rehabilitate," Battle said. "If that happens, that is wonderful. I view our work as a way to handle people who had historically been a burden to the community, taking up space and money in the jail and courts. Now they're paying something back."

For the nonprofit organizations that use the workers, the community service program is welcome. Jill Staton Bullard, director of the Interfaith Food Shuttle, says community service workers provide the "brawn" for her operation, which serves the hungry. Wiggins says she relies on the workers for a host of tasks at her missions—from dishing up food to picking up and delivering clothes. "We've been in the program for years," she said. "Knowing you have somebody to count on is wonderful."

Source: "Community Service Helps Society—and Some Offenders," *News and Observer* (Raleigh, NC), September 21, 1997.

A COMMUNITY SERVICE/RESTITUTION PROGRAM IN NEW YORK CITY

The Center for Alternative Sentencing and Employment Services was established in 1989 when the Court Employment Project and the Community Service Sentencing Project—originally demonstration projects designed and managed by the Vera Institute of Justice—were gathered under the umbrella of a single, independent nonprofit corporation. Today, with a staff of 180 and an annual budget of $12 million, CASES provides services and supervision for almost 4,500 offenders a year.

The mission of CASES is to increase the understanding and use of community sanctions that are fair, affordable, and consistent with public safety. For more than 30 years, CASES has worked with the justice system to find sentencing alternatives that respond to justice system needs. By addressing the factors that underlie criminal behavior, such as poor education, lack of community support, inability to get and keep a job, substance abuse, and low self-esteem, CASES's programs help young and adult offenders re-integrate into society. It offers structured alternatives that are more substantial than probation, but less costly and intrusive than jail or prison. CASES and its programs contribute to safer streets and save taxpayer dollars each year.

Source: www.cases.org

Benefits of Restitution

Restitution can provide a number of constructive benefits for society, the criminal justice system, the victim, and the offender. Because restitution is perceived as making amends for wrongdoing, the need for vengeance in society is reduced. Individuals, or families of those who have been harmed, will not feel the need to take criminal law into their own hands. This is important on a societal level because if people decide to punish offenders on their own, uncontrolled vigilantism is soon to follow. For the criminal justice system, restitution provides a more easily administered sanction. Most restitution is ordered by the judge in the sentencing phase of the system. But restitution can be ordered much earlier by preliminary hearing judges, probation departments, and even citizen review boards that are set up in local communities to handle less serious criminal cases. By keeping the offender from deeply penetrating the system, court and correctional resources will be saved. Restitution aids the offender, and it integrates the punitive and rehabilitative purposes of criminal law.

In less serious cases, restitution relates punishment to the extent of damage done. For example, if an offender steals or damages the property of another, he or she must make amends by repayment of the loss. In this way, restitution provides redress for crime victims. For the offender, restitution provides a less severe and more humane sanction. This kind of sanction is especially good for minor offenders and juveniles. Restitution also allows the offender a sense of accomplishment when the task is completed, and it provides a concrete way of expressing guilt and atoning for offenses.[15]

Related to restitution is an important set of issues regarding payment. The first is how much the offender should be ordered to pay and what happens if his or her ability to pay is limited. The determination of how much an offender should repay the victim is usually based on the damage caused by the offender. In some states, however, the "total damage caused" or what the offender should pay is separated from the actual "total amount of restitution ordered." That is because if an offender is forced to pay for restitution beyond his or her means, or within a time frame that is unrealistic, the offender is sure to falter in his or her payment. In most court jurisdictions, the court is only allowed to order restitution when it is "reasonable" or "appropriate" after considering an offender's ability to pay. Common sense and flexibility are needed by judges in determining how much and over what time period an offender must pay.

Also at issue is the nature of the offender–victim relationship during the period of restitution. Should the offender pay the restitution directly to the victim or through a probation agency? Some feel it is valuable for the offender to pay directly to the victim. It is hoped that direct payment can foster offender responsibility toward the victim, can help the victim deal with hostile feelings toward the offender, and can save court administration costs. However, problems can arise when the relationship between the offender and the victim is strained or if the offender misses payments. And, if the offender does not pay the agreed-upon restitution, the issue arises as to how the court should enforce payment. Who is responsible for action that will return the offender to court for failure to pay? The victim? The local probation department? And if the offender continues to be negligent in payment, how should he or she be sanctioned? What impact might additional sanctions (e.g., more fines or incarceration) have on the offender and the criminal justice system?

In most cases when an offender fails to pay restitution, the probation department is granted the power to temporarily incarcerate to "get the attention" of the offender and to issue a warning or reprimand. If this does not help, the offender in diversion cases may be returned to court for formal processing. If the offender is on probation, his or her probation may be revoked after a formal proceeding. It has been ruled by the court in *Beardon v. Georgia*, 461 U.S. 60 (1983) that to revoke an offender for failure to pay restitution it must be shown that the offender intentionally neglected payment and did not make a good-faith effort to obtain means to repay. If the probation or diversion status is rescinded by the court, a number of options can result for the offender. The most obvious, and most costly, is incarceration. The court may rule to amend the restitution because of the offender's inability to pay. In this case, the court may reduce the total amount of restitution ordered, adjust the payment schedule, or suspend payment until the offender can acquire a new or better job. In some states, courts can "encourage" payments of restitution through the garnish of wages, bank accounts, and financial holdings. This option is also used in states that have passed laws that automatically convert restitution orders—although initiated in criminal court—to civil court orders. Finally, the original sentencing court can extend the probationary or parole supervision status for offenders who fail to pay restitution in a timely manner.[16]

INTERNATIONAL FACTS ABOUT COMMUNITY SERVICE

- In the Netherlands, 240 hours of community service is equivalent to 6 months imprisonment.[17]
- In England, community service has been used extensively for over twenty-five years. In 1972 the Criminal Justice Act authorized courts to order offenders to complete 40–240 hours of unpaid community service as punishments for imprisonable offenses.
- By the late 1970s, community service programs flourished in the United States, United Kingdom, Canada, Australia, and New Zealand.
- In the 1980s, programs were implemented in Denmark, Germany, France, the Netherlands, Norway, and Portugal.[18]

EVALUATIONS OF COMMUNITY SERVICE IN ENGLAND, SCOTLAND, AND NEW YORK CITY

Community service was carefully evaluated by the Home Office of England in the early 1980s. The evaluations concluded that recidivism rates for offenders sentenced to community service were neither better nor worse than for offenders receiving other sentences. They also concluded that community service was applied equally to offenders who would otherwise be incarcerated and to others who would normally receive probation. Because some offenders who would normally be given probation now receive community service, there is evidence that net widening is present.[19]

Community service in Scotland was introduced on an experimental basis in 1977 and currently exists throughout the country. The Scottish model resembles the approach developed by England in the early 1970s. The program permits offenders convicted of offenses punishable by imprisonment to be ordered to perform between 40 and 240 hours of community service. A comprehensive evaluation of the program has shown that offenders sentenced to community service in Scotland have no worse recidivism rates than comparable imprisoned offenders and that some of those in the program exhibit greatly reduced subsequent property offenses. Further, offenders, social service agencies, judges, and service recipients tend to believe the program is worthwhile and the services provided valuable.[20]

In the 1980s, the use of community service in New York City was evaluated by the Vera Institute of Justice. The evaluation examined the various costs and benefits of community service orders. It was found that offenders in community service programs were rearrested at the same rate as similar persons sent to jail for short terms and then released.[21]

Background of Community Service

In community service, an offender is asked to personally "pay back" in time and effort through performing a set number of unpaid hours of work for a not-for-profit agency. Community service mixes two historical traditions: ordering offenders to make reparation for crimes and requiring unpaid labor as punishment. Community service as part of restitution can probably be traced back to ancient times when Babylonian, Greek, Roman, and Jewish law all contained provisions for compensation to be paid by offenders. In the early seventeenth century, offenders in England would be "persuaded" to join the Royal Navy in exchange for more formal punishment. In some cases, they were transferred to English colonies to act as servants to free settlers.[22]

Community service as we know it today, as a sanction independent of a custodial sentence, was not ordered by an American court until 1966 in Alameda County, California. The program was originally developed for female traffic offenders, many of whom could not afford a fine but for whom a jail sentence would have been a hardship and unnecessarily burdensome to the criminal justice system. But it was in England in the early 1970s that community service programs were first fully implemented. After a recommendation by the Advisory Council on the Penal System in 1970, courts in England were authorized to order offenders to complete 40 to 240 hours of unpaid service as punishment for imprisonable offenses. By the late 1970s, community service programs were accepted correctional practice throughout the United Kingdom, as well as in Canada, Australia, New Zealand, and the United States.

Currently, community service in the United States and Great Britain has become a regular sanction, used both as an alternative to incarceration and as a supplement to probation. In many cases, community service is used as a sentence in lower and misdemeanor courts. Traffic, DWI, and juvenile cases are common instances where community service is implemented. Community service has also been presented as part of the larger restorative justice movement.[23] Restorative justice, discussed in more detail in Chapter 9, tries to impress upon the offender his or her obligation to the community when a crime is committed, and to involve the victim and local community in doing justice and in reintegration of the offender.

Benefits of Community Service

Community service, like restitution programs, provides a number of benefits to the criminal justice system, the community, and the offender. Community service provides additional sentencing options for judges. Judges can implement community service as an alternative to no sanction, probation, or incarceration. If the judge chooses to keep the offender out of the formal processing of the system, as is done with many nonserious and juvenile cases, community service is a cost-saving alternative. By diverting offenders from the system, or by choosing community service rather than jail time, the criminal justice system can save financial resources.

The use of community service is evidence to the public that something is being done with offenders who commit crime. Whether it is picking up roadside trash or painting community youth centers, offenders working in the community present visual evidence to the community that offenders are receiving punishment. If offenders are working on projects with other citizens, community service serves to connect the community with offenders and the workings of the criminal justice system. This provides for more community involvement and a better understanding of the criminal justice system. A secondary benefit of community interaction with offenders is that such activity will "humanize" offenders in the eyes of the public. The public will learn that criminal offenders are very often decent people who have made a mistake or have some serious personal problems. This kind of process can do much to reduce the punitive attitudes of the general public toward criminal offenders.

The community also benefits through receiving the free labor that community service programs provide. Offenders do work that many local communities cannot afford to include in budgets of public works departments. With this work, money is saved and the community appearance is enhanced. In short, offenders can make a positive contribution to society rather than becoming a financial burden to the taxpayers.

For offenders, community service reduces the intrusiveness of the criminal justice system. In diversion cases, community service can prevent the offender from being officially processed into the criminal justice system. Officially processing can increase the stigma attached to being an offender and can increase legal fees. In locales where community service is not available, and short-term incarceration is the only alternative, such a sentence can cost an offender his or her means of employment and separation from family responsibilities. In cases where the offender has personal problems (drug addiction, illiteracy), community service work can allow him or her the opportunity to receive needed assistance while remaining in the community. Finally, community service serves an important function in that offenders are forced to take responsibility for their actions. By working in the community—paying back the community in a symbolic fashion—the offender is acknowledging wrongfulness and (it is hoped) learning from past misdeeds.

Community services programs are not without controversy. Three issues that should be addressed when discussing the issue are qualifications for participation, type and length of participation, and the "success" of the programs.

What kind of offender should receive community service? Should community service be reserved for misdemeanor crimes? For the most part, these questions are unanswered. The sanction of community service is used by court systems in a variety of ways. Some jurisdictions order community service primarily for juvenile offenders and white-collar criminals who have committed nonviolent crimes. Others use community service for first-time violation of drinking and driving laws. Community service has also been used for celebrities that come in contact with the law (see the box "Who's Who List"). Always a major concern is whether those conducting community service are dangerous to public safety. This becomes an issue when community service is extended to include drug offenders and anyone accused of any violent offense. Supporters would argue that the offender has shown the courts and correctional officials that he or she is ready for community reintegration. Those against may feel that even the slightest chance of repeat behavior should preclude program participation. In most cases, community service is used as a primary sanction for less serious or nonviolent crimes, or as a parole requirement after serving time in a correctional facility. For example, Mike Tyson, the boxer, was required to serve 100 hours of community service after completing his prison sentence for rape.

＋ 𝍩𝍩𝍩𝍩 ＋

WHO'S WHO LIST OF COMMUNITY SERVICE PARTICIPANTS

Darryl Strawberry (baseball player) crime: tax evasion—100 hours community service

Jose Canseco (baseball player) crime: possession of a loaded gun—80 hours

Zsa Zsa Gabor (actress) crime: assault on police officer—120 hours

Michael Milken (securities) crime: selling junk bonds—1,800 hours

Mike Tyson (boxing) crime: rape—100 hours

(Not included here is any time spent in jail or prison as part of sentence.)

Source: USA Today, July 6, 1995.

There is also very little consensus about what service should be performed and how long community service sentences should be. The former is easier to determine because courts and probation departments can often match the offenders' skills with community needs. For example, a sports figure can often give clinics to youngsters in a public setting. But how long the community sentence should be is a much tougher decision. How many hours are equivalent to a day in jail? For example, in Washington State it has been decided that one day of confinement equals three days of community service. In states where community service is used in lieu of a fine, how many hours equals how much money in fines? In some jurisdictions, a certain number of community service days (at eight hours per day) equals a certain number of days incarcerated. Others determine community service hours based on the income of the offender. At least in the United States, little uniformity has been shown in giving community service sanctions. In other countries, the *day fine* concept has provided some structure to determining equitable sanctions. Under this idea, an offender is sentenced to a fine of his or her earnings for a given number of days, so that the amount of money owed is equal to the size of earnings.[24] (Day fines are discussed in Chapter 7.)

Another important issue is related to the "success" of the community service sanction. To most of the public, and especially politicians, the bottom line is "Does community service save money?" On face value, it appears that community service can be a tremendous cost savings to the criminal justice system and the community. This can be calculated by determining the value of services provided by the offender based on what it would cost the community to provide an equal service. Also, economic resources are apparently saved when an offender receives community service instead of being placed in a correctional facility. Other benefits, albeit more difficult to measure, such as public opinions about "justice being served" and increase in the self-worth of the offender for accomplishing a task, can also be added to the "success" equation. However, measuring success is never that simple, at least not in criminal justice. What happens to "success" if the offender fails to complete his or her community service hours? If failure occurs, how do we compute the costs of reprocessing the offender back into the system? If an offender commits an offense while doing community service, how do we measure the cost of the loss of trust in the system by local citizens? Again, there are no easy answers to these questions. Costs vary greatly depending on the magnitude of the community service programs and the kinds of offenders that participate. Nevertheless, the questions posed here must be considered when considering the "success" and true costs of community service programs.

There is no concrete evidence to show that restitution or community service reduces crime or recidivism. However, these programs remain in many communities because they serve at least two functions: They provide some victims or the community with compensation, and they provide an alternative for judges that is somewhat punitive and far less expensive than jail or prison time.

DIVERSION OF DRUG OFFENDERS

Probably the most serious problem facing the criminal justice system today is the large number of drug offenders that are brought into the system. Drug offenders create a backup of cases in the courts, exacerbate jail crowding, overload probation departments, and provide motivation for the building of more and larger correctional facilities.

In the last ten to fifteen years local, state, and federal authorities have realized that the problem has reached serious proportions, and they have looked for ways to lessen the strain of drug offenders on the system. One of the developments has been an attempt to deal with the drug offender as a "community" problem. As an alternative to sending a drug offender immediately to jail or prison, an effort is being made to deal with the offender and the problems of addiction prior to incarceration. The result has been the development of hundreds of community drug programs that serve as a form of diversion for those involved with drug offenses. Because of the importance of drug offenders to community corrections, we will address this issue in more detail in Chapter 11.

DIVERSION AND COMMUNITY CORRECTIONS

In a sense, then, every offender in the community is there because of some form of diversion. If every arrest were prosecuted to the full extent of the law, and every conviction punished to the full extent of available penalties, there would still be a large number of offenders in the community. They would all be *former* offenders, however, having been punished as fully as the law allows, and they would be free citizens. Instead, many of the offenders in the community are under some form of diversion authority—pretrial services, probation, parole, or community corrections. The existence of community corrections is thus a way of sustaining correctional control over offenders who live among us in our communities. Its advocates claim this is how community corrections serves as a way to protect the community from crime.

Diversion is central to the larger practices of the justice process. In this section, we return to three of the themes described earlier in the chapter and discuss the way they play out as a part of diversion programs.

How Diversion Serves the System

It may seem that the main advantages of diversion apply to offenders, who get to avoid the most severe consequences of their acts. But diversion not only benefits offenders; it also carries important benefits for the system. It is these benefits that ensure the continuation of diversion practices in the face of a chorus of detractors—the system needs diversion. In fact, within the justice system, the most vocal critics of diversion—often these are prosecutors who want to enjoy a public posture of toughness—are often those who rely most upon the existence of diversion to support their own activities.

Penalties for crimes in the United States are extreme—the most extreme in the Western world. They are also expensive. The most obvious benefit of diversion programs is that they provide a way to avoid the expense and harshness of the full operation of the criminal law. The fact that almost all offenders experience a taste of diversion in their criminal careers (many experience some form of diversion even when they repeat offenses) is an indication of how central the diversionary system is to the overall penal system. There are not enough police to arrest every offender, not enough prosecutors to give everyone a trial, not enough prisons and jails to fulfill the full threat of the law. Diversion makes our current justice system possible, fiscally and strategically.

Diversion also influences the balance of power among system officials. This has been described elsewhere as the principle of *exchange relationships:* Every role in the court system has needs that can be met only if other officials cooperate. Judges need to avoid the time-consuming jury trial, which means that offenders must be willing to plead guilty (or accept a bench trial). Prosecutors want convictions and defensible penalties, and these are also made most likely by guilty pleas with few promised concessions. The defense wants to control and limit the severity of the penalty, which requires cooperation of both the court and the prosecution. The idea of exchange is that each actor will be willing to give up something the other needs in exchange for some of its own needs being met. Thus, the defense may offer to plead guilty if the prosecutor will agree not to object to the court's consideration of a probation sentence.

The key element of diversion programs is that they increase the options of the justice system, to enable justice officials to tailor penalties more to the details of the case. This increase in discretion allows the justice officials some room to maneuver as they try to balance the case and the demands of justice.

Diversion has become so important to the corrections system that almost all correctional agencies operate some form of diversion strategy. Jails have work programs, for example, and probation departments have alternatives to revocation. Even prison systems allow for some cases to be sent to less secure facilities or to be "housed" outside the walls in community-based centers.

Increasingly, however, the trend is for diversion programs to be run by organizations that are separate from existing correctional agencies. This strategy calls for the creation of a new agency—usually a nonprofit organization—that will supervise diverted offenders. These organizations typically work under contract with the criminal justice system and receive a fee for each offender that is supervised.

People disagree about whether it is better to place diversion entities within existing correctional organizations or to house them in new organizations. The advantage of using existing agencies is that these groups already have well-established relationships with service delivery systems that work with offenders, and they have long-term working relationships with other criminal justice agencies, such as the police. Critics say, however, that diversion programs operated by traditional correctional agencies tend to work harder to meet the needs of the agency than to meet the needs of the offender. Whenever financial pressures are encountered, the broader responsibilities of the correctional agency often receive more emphasis than the diversion programs, which are seen as of secondary importance. As a result, diversion programs run by existing correctional organizations are often seen as weaker than they ought to be.

By contrast, specialized diversion agencies give their entire attention to working with diverted offenders. The contracting system means that they can be held financially accountable for the effectiveness of the work they do, and staff know that they are supposed to give the highest priority to the diversion function. Critics of this approach point out, however, that specialized diversion agencies have no incentive to take difficult cases and little incentive to work with problems that arise in their cases; thus, these programs may focus on "easy" clients—and merely widen the net, either by taking those who were not incarceration-bound or by revoking diversion status too easily.

Diversion Bureaucracies

The entry into diversion programs is always a matter of discretion—an authority with power to open the door to the diversion program will determine who gets in and who does not. This control of access to diversion gives its owner power over offenders and other officials, and it affects the balance of exchange relationships in the system's day-to-day practices. The power over the offender comes because the offender wants to be eligible for the diversion program, and so must meet the discretionary eligibility criteria of the decision maker. The power over other officials comes from the control of the "faucet"—officials such as diversion program managers and defense attorneys want access to diversion for their clients, and so they have to meet the needs of those who have their hand on the handle.

Usually, the discretion over entry into the diversion program is held by law enforcement officials—police, prosecutors, and judges—not correctional officials. In fact, most diversion programs are actually housed within prosecution, courts, or sheriffs' offices, and so they are built to serve the needs of those organizations. The correctional managers who run those programs, in order to obtain any clients at all, must not only be sensitive to the aims of law enforcement but also actually facilitate those objectives in the design and operation of their programs.

Thus, ROR programs will work hard to coordinate recommendations with judicial priorities and keep the court well informed about ROR compliance. Jail diversion programs will exclude offenders who might otherwise be good candidates but whose charges are serious enough that their acceptance into the program would undermine a prosecutor's stance on penalties. The operation of a program of summonses will be built to integrate well into the day-to-day practices of street policing.

The control over the entry into diversion programs also gives law enforcement a carrot to hold out to offenders: "Cooperate with your case and we will consider you for XYZ Diversion Program." This acts as a way to enhance the hand of the law enforcement aspect of the system as it pursues it objectives, so offenders have an incentive to cooperate when otherwise the best strategy would be resistance. The existence of diversion programs may seem to complicate the system, but they actually tend to add oil to the cogs in the machinery of justice. The first consequence when diversion programs are closed down—as occurs with restrictions on access to probation in mandatory penalties—is usually a slowing down of the system.

Evidence About Diversion Programs

Determining the number of persons placed on diversion is a very difficult task. This is primarily because when diversion is done correctly, it serves to prevent immersion into the criminal justice system. As a result, many persons who would be counted as a "statistic" are diverted out of the system. Although one source has indicated that diversion statistics for the year 1999 reflect that 5,115 persons were formally involved in an adult diversion program,[25] there is good evidence that the numbers may be larger. For example, it is estimated that in a year when there are nearly 3 million index crime arrests, there will be less than 900,000 felony convictions and less than 500,000 felons sentenced to prison. Some of this drop-off in numbers reflects cases that are too weak to obtain a conviction, but by far most of this is due to the concept of diversion operating at each stage of the criminal justice process, including sentences to probation that are seen as diverting offenders from prison. For many offenders, if not most, diversion will be the first consideration of officials as they decide how to proceed on a case. How well do diversion programs work? The answer to this question depends a great deal on what they are expected to do. Typically, two main goals are expressed for diversion programs:

- To improve justice by avoiding the full power of the law when circumstances require it
- To increase public safety by helping offenders avoid repeat criminality

These are quite different aims, and they deserve separate analysis. Surprisingly, with all the proliferation of diversion programs there has as yet been only limited study of their effectiveness. Earlier we mentioned that an evaluation of the Manhattan Bail Project proclaimed their program a success with a recidivism rate half that of offenders without the program or from a control group. However, a later evaluation of the Manhattan Bail Project reached very different conclusions. The evaluation revealed that the project did not reduce recidivism and had no effect on the employment record of the clients.[26] Two other evaluations of diversion reflect similar negative results. Thomas Blomberg found in his review of juvenile diversion that net widening was a major problem in fifteen California diversion programs. Similarly, evaluations of an adult program in Iowa found that the program had little impact in reducing recidivism.[27]

So it appears that diversion programs have an uneven history. As sensible as these programs seem at first glance, many are surrounded with controversy. The successful diversion programs appear to save tax dollars, improve life circumstances for offenders, satisfy victims, and provide services to the community. Yet even these programs are faced with severe criticism as unduly lenient with criminal offenders. The unsuccessful programs are troubling in their results. They cost tax dollars, increase victimization, and lead to a lack of credibility for the system. Through net widening, they may actually result in more severe treatment of offenders, rather than the lesser severity they claim.

PERSPECTIVES ON DIVERSION

In this chapter, we investigate programs whose purpose is to help offenders avoid going to prison or jail. These programs can be thought of as "what if" programs because they ask, "What if we had a special option available to do "X" . . . would it help divert some offenders from an expected term of incarceration?" The typical diversion program, then, is a change program in that it changes the services available in the system as a way of trying to change the way the system works. If diversion programs are successful, people who ordinarily would have been processed into jails or prisons will instead be supervised in the community. We can look at diversion programs through the four perspectives of community corrections: systems, evidence, bureaucrasy, and people.

Systems

Diversion programs are classic systems-related programs. The core principle underlying the systems concept is that a change in one part of the correctional system will inevitably lead to changes in other aspects of the system. Since we have already argued that diversion programs are system change programs, what we are really saying is that diversion programs attempt to become a force in one part of the corrections system that changes the way the rest of the system operates.

For example, a diversion program that operates as a drug court will try to make an array of valuable treatment programs available to drug offenders so that the judge will see placing offenders in those programs as more desirable than incarceration. The new option, it is hoped, will change the way all the preexisting options are evaluated.

The systems principle means that the existence of the new diversion option will also affect the way the other programs operate, because they will come to compensate for the existence of the new choice—sometimes in ways that are unanticipated. This is a key problem for diversion programs, as we will see. For instance, it may seem wise to offer a special camp for serious delinquents as an alternative to training school placement, but it may turn out that judges use the new camp for delinquents who otherwise would have gotten regular probation terms, because they were worried that probation would not be stern enough.

Whenever a diversion program is proposed, we will be faced with systems-related concerns: Where will the diversion program get its clients? How will the new option affect the way the other choices are evaluated? If this program proves attractive, what changes will it force other programs to consider? How will the system change to compensate for the advent of this new diversion strategy?

Evidence

Diversion programs are, in fact, evidentiary claims. Whenever a diversion program opens its doors, it justifies itself by saying, "We will take cases that otherwise would be handled more severely, should we not exist." Whether or not the program delivers on this promise is a question of evidence.

As we will see, it is hard to show that diversion programs really take cases that otherwise would have been in a jail or a prison. One reason is that some people who go to jail look a lot like some people who go to probation, and so it is not easy to know where the person actually would have ended up if the diversion program had not been in place. It is easy enough to show that every person in a given program deserves to be in that program, of course, but that does not mean the program is getting those people from a more intrusive alternative. One of the themes of this chapter is that diversion programs regularly fail to prove their value as true alternatives to incarceration; instead, they merely serve to "widen the net of social control." Hard, irrefutable evidence that a diversion program really succeeds in diverting cases from confinement is hard to come by.

There is another evidence question that plagues the diversion approach: public safety. All programs have failures, of course, a point that is central to understanding the way corrections works. But diversion programs are under closer scrutiny to have low failure rates. Because they claim to take offenders from behind bars and place them in community settings, public safety is always a concern that diversion programs face. Not only are they required to develop evidence that they work, but they also have to satisfy a worried public that they do not leave people at risk of crime.

Bureaucracy

Diversion programs are typically new and innovative, and as a result they often avoid some of the more problematic tendencies of bureaucratization. The typical diversion program is able to attract motivated staff, provides a vision of services for clients, and operates outside the usual bureaucratic umbrella of corrections organizations. Because diversion programs compete with traditional correctional agencies for clients, they seldom are a part of those agencies; instead, they often stand alone or exist as part of a noncorrectional organization.

But that does not negate the need for rules, procedures, and regular expectations. No matter how new or innovative, diversion programs eventually become routinized. And in the end, they face the same dilemmas any organization faces when developing traditions, procedures, operating habits, and so forth. As diversion programs become more bureaucratic, we will have to ask whether this alters their overall effectiveness. We will have to consider whether the dictates of bureaucracy are compatible with the aims of diversion.

People

Diversion workers are often seen as having a different philosophy from that of the standard correctional professional. When they are committed to their jobs, diversion workers labor under a belief that prison is not always a good option and that keeping offenders from having to experience incarceration is beneficial. Because these programs have this flavor, they often develop an offender-centered ethic; that is, they come to see themselves as oriented toward supporting offenders and meeting their needs rather than controlling offenders and making sure they are punished. For all these reasons, staff who are attracted to positions in diversion agencies tend to have a different orientation to their work than does the typical criminal justice official. Many people see them as "pro-offender" (though, in practice, that is not the view that most offenders develop of these staff).

It also can be important that many offenders that are taken into diversion programs are selected by the program itself. They are handpicked, in a way. This means that the typical array of offenders entering the corrections system does not end up in diversion, but rather a subgroup that, for whatever reason, is seen as suitable for these programs. The selectivity of the diversion population can lead to a higher-than-usual motivation level among the clientele.

Even so, the population is not always an easy one. Convicted offenders can be a problem group, even when they are handpicked. So diversion programs face all the dilemmas of working with divergent personalities in effective ways that any human service organization has to confront. When we look at a diversion program, we ask: What types of staff are working here, and what do the offenders look like who end up here? How are they different? What motivates them; what problems do they encounter? How does the inevitable need for bureaucracy make service delivery more difficult, and how do the inevitable human frailties make the diversion program harder to run? These are questions still to be answered.

THE FUTURE OF DIVERSION

As the costs of incarceration continue to increase, local, state, and federal officials will likely see an increase in diversion as a lower-cost punishment and treatment alternative. It is probable that as technology in corrections becomes more common and cheaper, it will be used to augment diversion programs. In addition to its use with minor offenders and drug offenders, it is possible that diversion can be used to serve other offender populations. In cases involving domestic violence, offenders can receive individual and family counseling while continuing to reside and work in the community. For those accused of driving while intoxicated (DWI), programs can be provided for offenders to deal with alcohol addiction. Deadbeat dads, men who are charged with the failure to financially support their families, can prevent detention and at the same time be "persuaded" to pay child support. In collaboration with mental health agencies, diversion can be used to serve offenders who have been categorized as mentally ill. The topic of dealing with mentally ill offenders will be addressed in Chapter 11.

SUMMARY

Diversion occurs in all the steps of the criminal justice system, but nowhere is it more valuable to the system than in the area of community corrections. Among the benefits of diversion are providing rehabilitation opportunities, overcoming stigmatization, significant cost savings, and providing much-needed services for the offender. Some of the challenges include overcoming issues relative to diversion as a "lenient" punishment, that it neglects victims, that it has limited effectiveness, and that it may lead to net widening. Diversion programs are implemented by police, prosecutors, jails, and even long-term imprisonment facilities. Other examples of diversion programs for offenders include restitution, community service, and drug offender programs.

Diversion serves the corrections system in a variety of ways, and it is also part of a larger bureaucracy—that of the criminal justice system. As a result, decisions made about diversion programs and offenders are often made for reasons removed from the justice process. Although there is limited research that can verify the efficacy of diversion programs, there is little doubt that diversion programs will continue to be an important option for offenders as correctional populations soar and correctional budgets swell.

⊢ DISCUSSION QUESTIONS ⊢

1. How do diversion programs contribute to net widening in criminal justice?
2. Why is it controversial for diversion programs to sanction offenders before they are convicted of a crime?
3. What are the benefits and problems associated with restitution and community service programs?
4. With what kinds of offenders might diversion programs be most effective? Why?
5. How might diversion programs benefit the criminal justice system?
6. How would you summarize the findings about the effectiveness of diversion programs?
7. If you were the director of Criminal Justice of a state with jail and prison overcrowding, how might you use diversion to help mitigate the problem?

⊢ SUGGESTED READINGS ⊢

Champion, Dean, J. *Diversion and Standard and Intensive Supervised Probation Programs in Corrections in the United States: A Contempory Perspective,* 3rd ed., pp. 359–409. Paramus, NJ: Prentice Hall, 2001.

Fields, Charles (ed.). *Innovative Trends and Specialized Strategies in Community-Based Corrections.*

New York: Garland, 1994. An anthology of twelve previously unpublished articles describing innovative programs in contemporary community corrections, including new models for community supervision.

Performance Standards and Goals for Pretrial Release and Diversion. Washington, DC: National

Association of Pretrial Services Agencies, 1995. Offers performance standards and goals for pretrial release and diversion programs throughout the United States.

Satisfying Justice: A Compendium of Initiatives, Programs, and Legislative Measures. Ottawa, Canada: Church Council on Justice and Corrections, 1996. A manual of nearly 100 worldwide community programs and legislative measures used to reduce the use or length of imprisonment.

Tonry, Michael, and Hamilton, Kate (eds.). *Intermediate Sanctions in Overcrowded Times.* Evanston, IL: Northwestern University Press, 1995. An extensive collection of readings about a range of punishments including restitution, fines, and community service.

⊢ WEB SITES ⊢

Web site for State of Minnesota's 2001 Statutes that define and outline pretrial diversion programming www.revisor.leg.state.mn.us/stats/401/065.html

Web site that provides an extensive list of publications about new community corrections programs nationwide www.corrections.com

Web site that provides an eighty-six-page document that addresses diversion practices at all stages of the system and gives examples of programs and practices in various cities www.ncjrs.org/txtfiles1/bja/182507.txt

---

⊢ NOTES ⊢

1. National Advisory Commission on Criminal Justice Standards and Goals, *Corrections* (Washington, DC: Government Printing Office, 1973).

2. James Austin and Barry Krisberg, "Wider, Stronger and Different Nets: The Dialectics of Criminal Justice Reform," *Journal of Research on Crime and Delinquency* (January 1981): 165–196.

3. Samuel Walker, *Sense and Nonsense about Crime and Drugs,* 3rd ed. (Belmont, CA: Wadsworth, 1994).

4. Thomas G. Blomberg, "Widening the Net: An Anomaly in the Evaluation of Diversion Programs," in *Handbook of Criminal Justice Evaluation,* ed. Malcom W. Klien and K. D. Teilman (Beverly Hills, CA: Sage, 1980), pp. 572–592.

5. Lawrence W. Sherman, *Political Domestic Violence: Experiments and Dilemmas* (New York: Free Press, 1992).

6. John DiIulio and Anne Piehl, *Does Prison Pay?* (Washington, DC: Brookings Institution, Fall, 1991).

7. National Advisory Commission on Criminal Justice Standards and Goals, *Corrections* (Washington, DC: Government Printing Office, 1973).

8. Frank Schmalleger, *Criminal Justice Today,* 4th ed. (Upper Saddle River, NJ: Prentice Hall, 1997), p. 304.

9. J. S. Goldkamp, M. R. Gottfredson, P. R. Jones, and D. Wieland, *Personal Liberty and Community Safety: Pretrial Release in Criminal Court* (New York/London: Plenum Press, 1995).

10. Belinda McCarthy and Bernard McCarthy, *Community-Based Corrections,* 2nd ed. (Belmont, CA: Wadsworth, 1991), p. 80.

11. National Center for State Courts, *An Evaluation of Policy Related Research on the Effectiveness of Pretrial Release Programs* (Denver, CO: National Center for State Courts, 1975), p. 5.

12. Belinda McCarthy, Bernard McCarthy, and Matthew Leone, *Community-Based Corrections,* 4th ed. (Belmont, CA: Wadsworth, 2001).

13. Brian A. Reeves, *Felony Defendants in Large Urban Counties, 1994,* NCJ 164616 (Washington, DC: Bureau of Justice Statistics, 1998);

and Brian A. Reeves, *Pretrial Release of Federal Felony Defendants* (Washington, DC: Bureau of Justice Statistics, February 1994).

14. J. Hudson and B. Galaway, *Considering the Victim* (Springfield, IL: Thomas, 1975), pp. xix–xx.

15. Burt Galaway, "The Use of Restitution," *Crime and Delinquency* 23:1 (1977).

16. INFOLINK: A program of the National Victim Center, No. 62, 1995. www.nvc.org/ddir/info62.htm

17. J. Hudson and B. Galaway, "Community Service: Toward Program Definition," *Federal Probation* 54:2 (June 1990): 3–10.

18. Hans-Horg Albrecht and Wolfram Schadler, eds., *Community Service: A New Option in Punishing Offenders in Europe* (Freiburg: Max Planck Institute for Foreign and International Penal Law, 1986).

19. Ken Pease, "Community Service Orders," in *Crime and Justice: An Annual Review of Research,* vol. 6, ed. Michael Tonry and Norval Morris (Chicago: University of Chicago Press, 1985).

20. Gill McIlvor, "Community Service by Offenders: Agency Experiences and Attitudes," *Research of Social Work Practice* 3:1 (January 1993): 66.

21. Douglas C. McDonald, "Community Service Sentences," in *Intermediate Sanctions in Overcrowded Times,* ed. M. Tonry and K. Hamilton (Boston: Northeastern University Press, 1995).

22. Douglas C. McDonald, "Punishing Labor: Unpaid Community Service as a Criminal Sentence," in *Smart Sentencing: The Emergence of Intermediate Sanctions,* ed. J. M. Byrne, A. J. Lurigio, and J. Petersilia (Newbury Park, CA: Sage, 1992).

23. G. Bazemore and D. Maloney, "Rehabilitating Community Service: Toward Restorative Service Sanctions in a Balanced Justice System," *Federal Probation* 58:1 (1994): 24–35.

24. R. M. Carter, J. Cocks, and D. Glaser, "Community Service: A Review of Basic Issues," in *Contemporary Community Corrections,* ed. Thomas Ellsworth (Prospect Heights, IL: Waveland Press, 1996), pp. 266–278.

25. Camile Graham Camp and George M. Camp, *The Corrections Yearbook 2000* (Middletown, CT: Criminal Justice Institute, 2000).

26. U.S. Department of Justice, *Diversion of Felony Arrests: An Experiment in Pretrial Intervention* (Washington, DC: Government Printing Office, 1981).

27. Thomas G. Blomberg, "Widening the Net: An Anomaly in the Evaluation of Diversion Programs," in *Handbook of Criminal Justice Evaluation,* ed. Malcolm W. Klein and K. S. Teilman (Beverly Hills, CA: Sage, 1980), pp. 572–592.

Chapter 7

Intermediate Sanctions

boot camp   intermediate sanctions

continuous signaling device   mixed sentence

continuum of sanctions   principle of interchangeability

day fine   programmed contact device

day reporting centers (DRCs)   shock incarceration

electronic monitoring (EM)   split sentence

halfway house   tourniquet sentencing

house arrest/home confinement   unit fine

intensive probation supervision (IPS)

Put yourself in the judge's shoes. When you are getting ready to impose a sentence, how adequate are the available choices?

It is easy to think about the best way to sentence offenders whose crimes and backgrounds place them at the extremes. Imposing a prison term on a murderer, a rapist, or someone who engages in gratuitous violence makes sense to just about everyone. And for the first-time offender whose crime is neither violent nor unusual, and who has a solid link to the community such as a good job, most of us would feel comfortable with a probation term. But the cases you will face will seldom be violent crimes, and the true first-time, nonviolent felon will also be unusual. The far more likely case will have complexities that make choosing a sentence a problem.

Usually the offense you must consider is not the first crime in which the defendant has been involved. Probation or some other sanction has been tried before, and it may have worked well for a while, but the person now returns to stand before the bench, ready for another judgment. The crime will be serious enough, of course, but not alarming: The person was caught once again using drugs, or was implicated in another theft, or was caught with an illegal handgun, or got drunk and got in a fight. Yet under what circumstances would you want to try another term of probation? What message does that send?

However, a prison term makes little sense. At over $20,000 a year in taxpayer costs, the eighteen months or so your sentence will require—$30,000—seem a bit expensive in view of the minor costs of the crime itself. And what will prison accomplish? You have seen plenty of cases fresh from incarceration, seemingly damaged by the experience, standing in front of you with glazed eyes, having pleaded guilty to yet another crime. What will prison teach the average case?

There are other considerations. The typical, middle-range case standing before you has dependents—a spouse and children—and you wonder what will happen to them. If you send to prison the felon standing before you, you

Photo: Mike Quintata, who has campaigned to clean up graffiti in Denver, stands in front of a graffiti-covered wall in southeast Denver. He was convicted of misdemeanor assault for spray painting the face of a teenager caught painting graffiti on the outside of a gym, sentenced to 40 hours of community service, and fined $27. AP/Wide World Photos

will make a hard life harder for some innocents who deserve better and pile disadvantages onto a person who started life out with one strike against him or her. It doesn't help that they all seem to be poor—too often, people of color—and face hard enough times as it is.

You look into the eyes of the self-admitted, repeat, second-rate felon, and search for something: remorse, or a promise to reform. If you could wave a magic wand, the person standing before you would feel immense contrition and would promise to pay the victim restitution, make reparation to the community, get into a treatment program, get a job, and more. These are all routes you hope for when you impose a probation term, but with probation officer caseloads in excess of 100, what can you realistically expect?

You wish you had some choice between probation and prison—some intermediate sanction. As you mentally express this desire, you join thousands of other judges in feeling dispirited about the traditional sentencing options available for the vast majority of cases. As the judge, what do you decide?

Many people believe that history will define the last years of the twentieth century as the beginning of the correctional era of intermediate sanctions. This move stems from a desire to find effective and fair ways to respond to criminal conduct that are less onerous than prison but more controlling than traditional probation.

The case for intermediate sanctions can be made on several grounds, but Norval Morris and Michael Tonry put it best: "Prison is used excessively; probation is used even more excessively; between the two is a near vacuum of purposive and enforced punishments."[1] **Intermediate sanctions** are a variety of punishments that are more restrictive than traditional probation but less severe and less costly than incarceration.

This chapter analyzes what might be called the modern intermediate sanctions movement. We call it the modern movement because in the history of correctional reform there have been other times when leaders have called for similar changes. Since history never repeats itself exactly, we first present the main arguments for this approach in their contemporary context. We then explore the different forms of intermediate sanctions that have developed in corrections over the last fifty years.

HISTORICAL BACKGROUND OF INTERMEDIATE SANCTIONS

The idea of having some form of punishment between incarceration and total release back into the community is not a new idea. There is evidence that in sixth-century Europe, religious groups provided temporary food and shelter to prisoners who were released early from their sentence but who could not yet return to their communities.[2] In the United States, the earliest **halfway houses** were formed by the Quakers in the 1840s to assist those released from prison. In the twentieth century, the state of Wisconsin developed the first formal work release program in 1914. Different forms of intensive probation supervision were developed as early as the 1950s, and in the mid-1980s the movement began toward other supervision programs such as boot camps, electronic monitoring, day reporting, and house arrest.

Interestingly, the programs started in the 1980s were first called intermediate punishments, not intermediate sanctions. This terminology better served the needs of politicians who wanted the programs to be "tougher" than traditional probation. Tougher meant more control and a stronger emphasis on the concept of "just desert." Even though the programs were administered within the community setting, proponents did not necessarily support the rehabilitation ideal. Over the last twenty years, the term has evolved to *intermediate sanctions,* and the underlying ideals of control and desert have remained paramount.

THE CASE FOR INTERMEDIATE SANCTIONS

The realization that there is a need for correctional strategies that fall between probation and imprisonment is based on four related ideas: Imprisonment is an unnecessary and overly restrictive sanction for many offenders, traditional probation is ineffective with most offenders, justice is well served by having options between prison and probation, and incarceration is not cost effective. Let us now explore these arguments in more detail.

Unnecessary Imprisonment

By virtue of history and tradition, those in the United States tend to think of prison as equivalent to punishment. When offenders receive sentences other than prison, many are tempted to think they "got off." When a short prison sentence is imposed, many think that the offender "got a break." Yet to treat prison as though it is the primary means of punishment is wrong on two grounds.

First, most sanctions imposed in the United States and in other Western democracies do not involve imprisonment.[3] In the United States, probation is the most commonly imposed sanction: Three offenders are on probation or parole for every one in prison or jail. In reality, prison is not the centerpiece of American practice. In fact, most offenders experience quite different correctional sanctions. In research conducted on inmates currently incarcerated, it was found that the majority of inmates preferred prison to probation and that the preference is especially strong for inmates who are older and have more experience with the criminal justice system.[4]

In most countries, the fine is the most common noncustodial sanction imposed on criminal offenders. Fines are used in as many as 95 percent of cases in Japan and in more than 70 percent in most of Western Europe.[5] Community service orders are seen as the option of choice for most property

COSTS OF COMMUNITY CORRECTIONS

A 1994 survey[7] of correctional costs in Colorado, North Carolina, Ohio, and Virginia found the average annual cost of operations per offender in the following programs:

Community service	$ 2,759	House arrest	$ 402
Probation	$ 869	Halfway house	$12,494
IPS	$ 2,292	Boot camp	$23,707
EM	$ 2,759	Jail	$14,363
Day reporting	$ 2,781	Prison	$17,794

offenders in England.[6] In Sweden, The Netherlands, France, Austria—and virtually every other Common Market country—sanctions other than prison are used far more than incarceration. Since nonprison sanctions are a worldwide phenomenon, it makes little sense to think of them as nonpunishment.

There is a second reason why an inordinate focus on prison as punishment is unwise: Prison as punishment is not very effective. One expectation we have for punishment is that the offender will learn something from it and reject the life of crime. But considerable evidence shows that this does not happen for many offenders. One study suggests that only 42 percent of all state parole discharges from prison in 1999 successfully completed their parole.[8] Another study found that prisoners have a higher rearrest rate than do similar offenders sentenced to probation.[9] The point is that prison punishes but does not educate or necessarily change the offender.

If prison is neither the most common nor the most effective sanction, why does it dominate our thinking when it comes to punishment? Perhaps it is time to recognize that corrections can and should develop nonincarcerative sanctions that fill the gap between prison and probation.

Limitations of Probation

Many believe that probation has proved ineffective with many offenders. There is a good basis for this concern, especially if an offender is a serious or repeat offender. In most jurisdictions, caseloads are too large to allow meaningful probation supervision. With 100 or more offenders per officer, the average probationer can get no more than 15 minutes of contact per week, hardly what we would consider to be meaningful supervision. Such minimal supervision is especially problematic with serious repeat offenders who have historically required higher levels of supervision. Even in less serious cases, what happens between the probation officer and the offender is not very relevant to the offender's special problems. The probation officer may check the client's pay stubs; a urine sample may be taken to test for drug use. But in the limited time available, little may happen to help the probationer achieve a change in lifestyle.

Intermediate sanctions can improve on traditional probation supervision in two ways. First, they often can intensify the supervision of the offender. If the offender is classified as a serious or repeat offender, he or she can receive more attention from the court and be asked to more closely follow supervision rules. Second, intermediate sanctions can provide for specialized programs that are better suited to address the offender's needs. If the offender has a special problem (e.g., vocational limitations), then the intermediate sanction can specifically address the problem area. Other problems associated with probation are described in Chapter 8, but at this point it will suffice to state that plain probation as administered in most jurisdictions is not for everyone. It is limited in its scope and effectiveness. Probation that is supplemented with other forms of intermediate sanctions has an improved chance of success.

Improving Justice

Judges sometimes complain that their sentencing choices are too limited. They say they find themselves confronted with an offender whose crime does not warrant prison, but for whom probation seems inadequate as well. The development of an array of sanctions between these two extremes enables judges to better fit the sentence to the crime's seriousness.

A similar problem occurs when an offender fails to abide by the rules of probation or parole supervision. Some response is needed to maintain the credibility of the rules, but to send the rule violator to prison for behavior that is not otherwise criminal seems unwarranted.

Intermediate sanctions may also provide alternatives to the court when the probation supervision levels, jails, and prisons have reached maximum capacity. When a judge is able to select an intermediate alternative rather than overloading probation caseloads or having inmates in the jails and prisons sleep on temporary cots in the gym, they will most likely choose that alternative. Such choices can save money, prevent legal difficulties created by overcrowded facilities, increase the effectiveness of probation supervision, and still provide justice for those who commit crime.

Finally, intermediate sanctions allow a closer tailoring of the punishment to the offender's situation. In this way, intermediate sanctions provide a more fair and fitted level of "just deserts" for those who have committed crime. Many offenders can be adequately punished by a fine. Others may be equally well punished by being required to complete a drug treatment program. Still others can be subjected to a period of house arrest. It is argued that intermediate sanctions, tailored to fit the offender's circumstances, can be more just. This may be one reason why public opinion surveys so consistently find support for intermediate sanctions as alternatives to prison and traditional probation.[10]

Cost

To save taxpayers money by providing cost-effective alternatives to incarceration for those who will be sent to jail or prison is probably the most common reason for the adoption of intermediate sanctions. This issue will be discussed throughout this chapter when we detail the different forms of intermediate sanctions. The difference in the cost of imprisonment versus a community sanction may be obvious, but another related but sometimes overlooked reason for intermediate sanctions is to keep the offender in the community because of the social costs associated with incarceration. The social costs of removing an offender from his or her family, and the long-term stigmatization that comes with incarceration, are often underestimated. There is a growing body of literature that supports this line of thinking.

Dina R. Rose and Todd R. Clear have argued that high levels of incarceration, concentrated in poor and disadvantaged communities, can backfire, leading to more crime. In some neighborhoods, as many as one-fourth of the parenting-age men are locked up on any given day, and as many as 12 percent are removed to go to prison or jail each year. This high volume of "coercive mobility" has a destabilizing effect on the community's capacity for informal social control—families, neighbors, financial security, civic participation, and so forth—and leads to a diminished neighborhood capacity. The result, they argue, is more crime despite high rates of community crime control.[11]

THE CONTINUUM OF SANCTIONS CONCEPT

One way to establish intermediate sanctions is to use the **continuum of sanctions** approach. Continuum of sanctions refers to a range of correctional strategies that vary in terms of level of intrusiveness and control. Offenders are initially assigned to one of the levels based on the seriousness of their offense and their prior record. Offenders then may move to a less restrictive or a more restrictive level, depending on their conduct and their response to supervision. When the sentencing judge increases and tightens the amount and conditions of punishment based on offender performance, it is referred to as **tourniquet sentencing.**[12]

Delaware's sentencing accountability approach illustrates this idea. Under Delaware's model, all offenders are graded regarding risk of a new offense and seriousness of current offense. Their movement through the corrections system depends on their performance at each level of sentencing accountability. See Figure 7.1 for a diagram that explains the use of intermediate sanctions in Delaware.

FIGURE 7.1 CONTINUUM OF SANCTIONS

Judges may use a range of intermediate sanctions, from those in which the offender requires a low level of control to those in which the offender requires a high level of control.

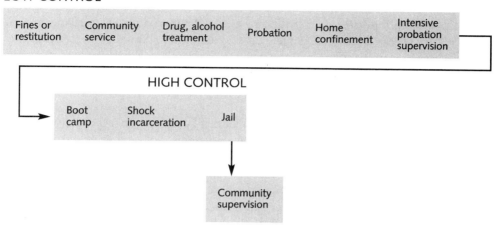

LOW CONTROL

| Fines or restitution | Community service | Drug, alcohol treatment | Probation | Home confinement | Intensive probation supervision |

HIGH CONTROL

| Boot camp | Shock incarceration | Jail |

Community supervision

Many jurisdictions have made an effort to develop a continuum of sanctions, and the advantages of this approach now seem plain. First, it makes the correctional system's capacity much more flexible. As the more costly and less elastic custodial portions of the corrections system become crowded, selected offenders can be moved to less restrictive options. For instance, jailed inmates can be placed in an electronic monitoring program. Second, it allows a more responsive management of individual offenders, based on the needs of the corrections system. For example, if a person on regular probation is not reporting, a brief period of house arrest can be imposed, followed by a return to probation.

The continuum-of-sanctions idea is flexible enough that it can operate at both the state and the county level. It can be codified into law, or it can be operated as a practice agreed to by the various agencies responsible for correctional programs. For instance, in Maricopa County, Arizona, the combined resources of multiple agencies—the jail, treatment centers, and probation—are used to rationalize the punishment system along a continuum of sanctions. This approach accomplishes the same aims as Delaware's sentencing accountability system, but it is not a part of penal law, nor is it operated by a single state agency.

PROBLEMS WITH INTERMEDIATE SANCTIONS

Despite the growing range of available alternatives, all is not well with the intermediate sanctions movement. There are problems in the selection of agencies and offenders: which agencies should operate the process and which offenders should receive intermediate sanctions. Further, intermediate sanctions often bring up the issue of widening the net.

Agencies

Administrators of such traditional agencies as probation, parole, and institutional corrections often argue that they should be allowed to operate intermediate sanctions. They have the staff and the experience to design new programs to meet the requirements of special subgroups of offenders, they say, and if the system is to have programmatic coherence, they ought to operate all correctional processes.

Critics of this point of view say that new agencies, public and private, ought to be charged with operating the new programs. Since traditional correctional organizations must give highest priority to traditional operations, it is argued, they cannot give the attention or support to a mid-range alternatives movement that is necessary to make it succeed.

Inevitably, critics believe, intermediate sanctions programs will be controlled by the currently dominant probation and prison systems—especially as these systems need intermediate sanctions to resolve problems of overcrowding of caseloads and cells.

Offenders

A second issue has to do with the selection of appropriate offenders for alternative programs. One school of thought emphasizes the seriousness of the offense; the other concentrates on the problems of the offender. A focus on the offense usually results in the elimination of some crime categories from consideration for intermediate sanctions. It is often argued that violent or personal offenses and drug-marketing offenses are so abhorrent that a nonincarcerative program is not an appropriate form of punishment for such offenders. Yet these offenders are often the best able to adjust to these programs. Moreover, to the degree that these programs are needed to reduce prison overcrowding, they must include more serious offenders.

In practice, both the crime and the criminal are taken into consideration. Certain offenses are so serious that the public would not long tolerate intermediate punishments for them (even though numerous instances of successful community-based control of murderers and other serious offenders exist). Likewise, judges want programs to respond to the needs of the offenders they sentence.

Underlying this issue is the thorny problem of stakes.[13] The concept of stakes is easily illustrated. Most of us would be willing to bet $1 on a one-in-ten chance of winning $10, yet few of us would be willing to bet $1,000 on a one-in-ten chance of winning $10,000. The odds are the same, but we stand to lose so much more that the bet may be unwise. In the same way, intermediate sanctions officials are often unwilling to accept offenders convicted of serious crimes, particularly violent crimes, even though the chances of the offenders' successfully completing a program may be quite good. If those offenders commit serious new crimes, the damage to the community and—through negative publicity—to the corrections system can be substantial. With some offenders, the stakes are simply too high, regardless of the amount of risk.

Widening the Net

Ambivalence about the appropriate selection of offenders for intermediate sanctions has led to the third major problem of the movement: net widening. In some ways, this problem is potentially the most damaging because it strikes at the very core of the intermediate sanctions concept. Critics argue that instead of reducing the control exerted over offenders' lives, the new programs have in fact increased it. We can readily see how this might be so. The existence of an alternative at each point in the system makes it possible for the decision maker to impose a more intrusive option than ordinarily would have been imposed—rather than a less intrusive one. Community service, for instance, can be added to probation; shock incarceration can be substituted for the straight probation that might otherwise have been imposed.

Available evidence reveals that intermediate sanctions have created the following:

1. *Wider nets:* Reforms increase the proportion of individuals in society whose behavior is regulated or controlled by the state.
2. *Stronger nets:* Reforms augment the state's capacity to control individuals through intensification of the state's intervention powers.
3. *Different nets:* Reforms transfer or create jurisdictional authority from one agency or control system to another.[14]

One of the main factors that control net widening is the person who determines whether an offender will be put into an intermediate sanction program or not. If a judge makes the decision, and the offender would not have been sent to prison if the intermediate sanction did not exist, then net widening is present. If the decision to release to an intermediate sanction program is made by the Department of Corrections, it is clear that there will be less net widening.

VARIETIES OF INTERMEDIATE SANCTIONS

There are many different types of intermediate sanctions, and it is important to know that how the programs are administered usually depends upon the jurisdiction running them. In one county, for example, intensive supervision can be used in lieu of a sentence to jail, whereas in another system it may be devoted to probation violators. In other jurisdictions, intermediate sanctions can overlap.

Offenders receiving electronic monitoring may also be assigned to intensive probation supervision. Shock incarceration offenders may later be confined to their homes. When a judge decides to include both time in an institution and a period of time in the community under supervision, it is called a **split sentence.** Defendants who receive split sentencing are often ordered to serve time in a local jail, for example ninety days, and then are released to probation supervision. Split sentencing is often used with minor drug offenses and sometimes with DWI infractions. It is not uncommon for an offender to receive a split sentence of some kind. In 1995, it was estimated that at least 15 percent of adults on probation from state or federal courts were on split sentencing.[15]

Another similar option is to require an offender to serve some period of time in a correctional facility while being on probation supervision in the community. This is called a **mixed sentence.** With the mixed sentence, inmates usually serve their sentence from Friday evening to Monday morning, although another option would allow them to serve from 8A.M. to 4P.M. on Saturday and Sunday.

These are just a few examples of the many variations of intermediate sanctions. Table 7.1 provides an overview of the variety of intermediate sanctions that were being used in probation and parole agencies throughout the United States as of January 2000.

For a general understanding of intermediate sanctions, we have organized our description based on the agencies generally running the programs—the judiciary, probation departments, and corrections departments. Additional detailed descriptions of some forms of intermediate sanctions are discussed in other chapters of this book. Nevertheless, they are also mentioned here to show their place in the schema of intermediate sanctions. Finally, it is important to mention that the intermediate sanctions described in this chapter and in this book do not represent all the different varieties of intermediate sanctions practiced throughout the United States and abroad. Individual programs may vary considerably depending on a number of factors such as the kind of offender served within the program, the qualifications of the staff, and the resources provided to run the program.

Sanctions Administered Primarily by the Judiciary

The need for intermediate sanctions is often driven by judges' dissatisfaction with the choices they have available. In courts that have managerial authority over probation, this discontent has translated into the kinds of new probation programs we describe later in this section. Other courts have sought to expand their sentencing options by greater reliance on programs they can operate under their own auspices. Three of these are pretrial diversion, fines, and forfeiture. The aim of these programs is clearly to reduce the trial caseload, especially focusing upon the less serious offenders who ought not to tie up the court system.

TABLE 7.1 PROGRAMS AVAILABLE IN PROBATION & PAROLE AGENCIES ON 1/1/00

Probation	Restitution Comp.	Parenting Classes	DWI Programs	Group Homes	Halfway Houses	Supv. Home Rel.	Intens. Supv.	Cmty. Svc.	Shock Prob.	Other Progs.
Arizona[1]	✓	✓	✓	✓	✓	✓	✓	✓		✓
Colorado	✓	✓	✓			✓	✓	✓		
Connecticut	✓	✓	✓	✓	✓	✓	✓	✓		✓
Dist. of Col.	✓		✓					✓		
Georgia[2]	✓						✓	✓		✓
Hawaii[3]							✓			✓
Illinois	✓		✓			✓	✓	✓		
Kansas	✓		✓			✓	✓	✓		
Massachusetts	✓	✓	✓	✓	✓	✓		✓		✓
Nebraska	✓					✓	✓	✓		
New Jersey[4]	✓					✓	✓	✓	✓	
New York[5]	✓		✓			✓	✓	✓	✓	✓
South Dakota	✓	✓	✓			✓	✓	✓		
Tennessee	✓				✓	✓	✓	✓	✓	✓
Texas[6]	✓	✓	✓	✓	✓	✓	✓	✓	✓	✓
West Virginia	✓						✓			
Federal[7]	✓	✓		✓	✓	✓	✓	✓		✓
Total	**16**	**7**	**10**	**5**	**6**	**13**	**15**	**15**	**4**	**10**

Parole	Restitution Comp.	Parenting Classes	DWI Programs	Group Homes	Halfway Houses	Supv. Home Rel.	Intens. Supv.	Cmty. Svc.	Shock Prob.	Other Progs.
Arizona						✓		✓		
California[8]	✓	✓			✓		✓	✓		✓
Colorado	✓					✓	✓			
Connecticut[9]			✓	✓	✓		✓	✓		✓
Dist. of Col.					✓		✓			
Georgia[10]	✓	✓					✓	✓		✓
Hawaii	✓	✓			✓		✓			
Illinois[11]		✓				✓	✓			✓
Indiana[12]							✓			✓
Kansas	✓				✓			✓		
Massachusetts[13]							✓			✓
Nebraska						✓	✓			
New Jersey[14]	✓	✓			✓	✓	✓	✓		✓
New York[15]								✓		✓
South Dakota	✓							✓		
Tennessee				✓			✓			
Texas[16]	✓									✓
West Virginia	✓	✓	✓	✓	✓			✓		
Federal						✓	✓			
Total	**9**	**7**	**2**	**3**	**9**	**6**	**14**	**10**		**9**

Probation and Parole	Restitution Comp.	Parenting Classes	DWI Programs	Group Homes	Halfway Houses	Supv. Home Rel.	Intens. Supv.	Cmty. Svc.	Shock Prob.	Other Progs.
Alabama	✓					✓	✓	✓		
Alaska[17]					✓	✓	✓	✓		✓
Arkansas	✓	✓	✓			✓	✓	✓		
Delaware[18]					✓	✓	✓	✓		✓
Florida	✓					✓	✓	✓		
Idaho	✓	✓	✓			✓	✓	✓		
Iowa[19]	✓		✓		✓	✓	✓	✓		✓
Kentucky					✓	✓	✓	✓	✓	
Louisiana	✓						✓	✓		✓
Maine	✓							✓		
Maryland						✓	✓	✓		

(Continued on next page.)

TABLE 7.1 (CONTINUED)

Probation and Parole	Restitution Comp.	Parenting Classes	DWI Programs	Group Homes	Halfway Houses	Supv. Home Rel.	Intens. Supv.	Cmty. Svc.	Shock Prob.	Other Progs.
Minnesota	✔					✔				
Mississippi	✔	✔	✔			✔	✔	✔	✔	
Missouri	✔	✔	✔		✔	✔	✔	✔	✔	
Montana	✔				✔		✔	✔		
Nevada	✔					✔	✔	✔		
New Hampshire[20]	✔				✔	✔	✔	✔	✔	✔
New Mexico					✔		✔			
North Carolina		✔				✔	✔			
North Dakota	✔				✔	✔	✔	✔		
Ohio					✔	✔			✔	
Oklahoma	✔	✔			✔		✔	✔		
Oregon	✔	✔	✔			✔	✔	✔		
Pennsylvania	✔					✔				
Rhode Island							✔			
South Carolina	✔					✔	✔		✔	✔
Utah	✔	✔			✔		✔			
Vermont[21]										
Virginia[22]	✔	✔			✔	✔	✔	✔	✔	✔
Washington[23]	✔					✔		✔		✔
Wisconsin	✔	✔	✔	✔	✔	✔	✔	✔		
Wyoming	✔				✔	✔	✔	✔		
Total	**23**	**9**	**8**	**1**	**15**	**24**	**26**	**24**	**8**	**7**

Totals	Restitution Comp.	Parenting Classes	DWI Programs	Group Homes	Halfway Houses	Supv. Home Rel.	Intens. Supv.	Cmty. Svc.	Shock Prob.	Other Progs.
Probation	16	7	10	5	6	13	15	15	4	10
Parole	9	7	2	3	9	6	14	10	NA	9
P&P	23	9	8	1	15	24	26	24	8	7
Total	**48**	**23**	**20**	**9**	**30**	**43**	**55**	**49**	**12**	**26**

[1]Other includes day reporting centers, drug courts, and literacy programs only.   [2]Other includes Gripp, Toppstep, and drug courts.   [3]Other includes drug court.   [4]Other includes a pretrial intervention (PTI) program for felony offenders diverted in Superior Court; Conditional Discharge (CD) is a program for misdemeanant drug offenders diverted in Municipal Court.   [5]Division of Probation and Correctional Alternatives (DPCA) is a state regulatory agency that administers funds and provides training and technical assistance to 58 local probation departments.   [6]Other includes a felony diversion program.   [6]State of Texas provides funds to local departments that provide all these services. Other includes pretrial.   [7]Other includes pretrial diversion.   [8]Other includes literacy programs, domestic violence, and transitional case management.   [9]Other includes sex offender and mental health programs.   [10]Other includes cognitive skills.   [11]Other includes community drug intervention and day reporting.   [12]Other includes temporary confinement for drug users.   [13]Other includes a MassCAPP Program for developmentally disadvantaged parolees.   [14]Other includes day reporting centers.   [15]The division does not operate a separate intensive supervision program. We do, however, supervise new parolees more intensively and on smaller caseloads during their first 12 months of supervision. This supervision technique is a part of the division's model of caseload management, referred to as differential supervision. In this model, individuals are assigned to caseloads with a ratio of 40 parolees per parole officer. These case loads were designed to provide parole officers with time for the service delivery and surveillance necessary for this at-risk population. Upon completion of the required period of time under intensive supervision, parolees are moved to supervision caseloads with a ratio of 100 parolees per parole officer, which reflects their reduced threat to the community. Other includes relapse prevention, community based residential programs, and employment programs.   [16]Other includes sex offender treatment; mentally retarded/impaired and special needs; cognitive skills; education; employment; superintensive supervision; prison industry enhancement; family support; and volunteer.   [17]Other includes victim impact, cognitive skills, and mental health diversion program.   [18]Other includes retrial supervision/diversion and Safe Streets.   [19]Other includes violator program, sex offender program, BEP, TASC, and Drug Court.   [20]Other includes an academy.   [21]Data is as of 1/1/99.   [22]Other includes nine day reporting centers, six diversion centers, five detention centers, and three drug court programs (within day reporting centers).   [23]Other is work crews.

Source: The 2000 Corrections Yearbook (Middletown, CT: Criminal Justice Institute, 2000).

Pretrial Diversion. The functions of pretrial diversion as an alternative to jail, prosecution, and imprisonment are laid out in Chapter 6. But it is relevant to mention here that pretrial diversion programs are often used by the courts as a form of intermediate sanction. This has occurred because although the courts have extremely broad discretion when it comes to pretrial matters, some have recently sought to expand the uses of this discretion to a broader range of cases and offenders.

Commonly, these new programs target petty drug offenders. A new strategy in Wayne County (Detroit), Michigan, exemplifies this idea. First-time arrestees for drug possession are "fast-tracked" into drug treatment programs within twenty-four hours of their arrest. They are promised that if they successfully complete the drug treatment program, the charges against them will be dropped. This kind of treatment-based diversion program is based on cooperation between the court and the prosecution. Judges indicate a willingness to delay trial under the condition that prosecutors are willing to drop charges on minor offenders who show changes in their lives.

Fines. According to estimates, over $1 billion in fines is collected annually in the United States. Yet when compared with other Western democracies, the United States makes little use of fines. For example, Germany imposes fines on two-thirds of its property offenders, and in England the figure approaches one-half. When judges do use fines in this country, it is typically as an add-on to another sanction, such as probation. For example, it is not unusual for a judge to impose two years of probation and a $500 fine. Many judges cite the difficulty of collecting and enforcing fines as the reason that they do not make greater use of this punishment. They say that offenders tend to be poor, and many judges fear that fines would be paid from the proceeds of additional illegal acts. Other judges are concerned that reliance on fines as an alternative to incarceration would mean that the affluent would be able to "buy" their way out of jail and that the poor would have to serve time.

There are two ways that fines can be determined. One is the *fixed-sum* rate system. In this system, specific offenses are allocated a certain value and dollar amount. Then each offender is fined according to the offense he or she commits. This method appears easy to administer and rather equitable. However, the problem with the fixed-sum method is that not all offenders are able to pay the fines assessed for their crime. What can happen is that those with better economic resources are able to pay the fines while poorer offenders find themselves in violation of the court's order. This can lead to further legal difficulties. A second fine-setting method is called the *day fine* (or structured fine). This method will be discussed in some detail later in this chapter.

Advantages and Disadvantages of Fines. Fines can serve many benefits for the criminal justice system and for society in general. When used as an alternative to incarceration, fines can lower the numbers of persons in jails and prisons and thus save taxpayers money. At the same time, because fines are inexpensive to administer by the court system and also bring in money to the system, government coffers gain economic benefit from fines. In Texas, for example, it has been estimated that 50 percent of the probation office budget comes from the collection of fines.[16]

To illustrate the point of how increasing fines can reduce the number of those going to prison, we turn to the case of Germany. In 1970, the German legislature enacted a law stating the courts could impose an incarceration sentence of less than six months only under exceptional circumstances, such as rehabilitation or protection to the community. As a result of this law, sentences of six months or less dropped from 184,000 in 1968 to 48,000 in 1989.[17] This example reflects that if judges are asked to seriously consider whether six months of imprisonment is really necessary, they will most likely choose an alternative sentence.

In addition to the economic benefits, fines can serve the correctional purposes of rehabilitation and desert. When offenders are required to pay fines, they can learn to be more financially responsible. Fines can serve as the "just desert" for many crimes motivated by economic benefit. If, for example, an offender is found guilty of theft or some form of embezzlement, then an economic sanction would be a very appropriate punishment.

At the same time, offender fines do have some limitations. Many offenders find it very difficult to pay any fines, while others will have little economic hardship in doing so. In this way, fines are discriminatory against those with few economic resources. For those who are concerned with offenders living in the community, fines appear to be too lenient a sentence. Especially amid the call to "get tough on crime" and in times of high incarceration rates, fines seem to be the "soft" approach on crime and offenders. Another criticism of fines is they are often very difficult to collect. Ex-offenders may have problems finding work, may lose their jobs during tough economic times, or may be disabled. Many change residences. One could also argue that those who usually are in charge of collecting fines, probation and parole officers, have more important things to do than be collection agents.

Some jurisdictions have come up with some clever methods to aid in the collection of fines. One idea is using a positive strategy based on incentives for those who are paying rather than negative sanctions for those who do not. Another is the use of amnesty days, where on certain days an offender can pay the original fine without any back penalty. The development of computer-based tracking systems and credit-card payment plans have also been implemented. A most prudent approach is to prevent the beginning of delinquent fines by developing a plan to encourage payment. That plan should be flexible to the ability of the offender to pay, keep the time for payment short, and promote cooperation by the offender by having him or her agree to the terms of payment. Those who have studied collection of offender fees have found that collection is most successful when the collection agency has incentives to collect fees, procedures and sanctions are developed for nonpayment, non-professional staff collect the money, and the entire process is monitored by computerization.

DAY FINES IN GERMANY: COULD THE CONCEPT WORK HERE?

Modern implementation of fines related to the income of the offender began with creation of the day fine system in Finland in 1921, followed by its development in Sweden (1931) and Denmark (1939). The Federal Republic of Germany instituted day fines in 1975. Since then there has been a major change in punishments, so that now more than 80 percent of those convicted receive a fine-alone sentence.

Judges determine the amount of the day fine through a two-stage process. First, judges relate the crime to offense guidelines, which have established the minimum and maximum number of day fine units for each offense. For example, according to the guidelines, theft may be punished by a day fine within the range of 10 to 50 units. Judges choose the number of units by considering the culpability of the offender and by examining the offender's motivation and the circumstances surrounding the crime. Second, the value of these units is determined. The German day fine is calculated as the cost of a day of freedom: the amount of income an offender would have forfeited if incarcerated for a day. One day fine unit is equal to the offender's average net daily income (considering salary, pensions, welfare benefits, interests, and so on), without deductions for family maintenance, as long as the offender and his or her dependents have a minimal standard of living. Finally, the law calls for publishing the number of units and their value for each day fine set by the court so that the sentencing judgment is publicly known.

For example, say a judge faces two defendants, separately convicted of theft. One defendant is a truck driver who earns an average of DM100 per day and the other is a business manager whose earnings average DM300 per day. The judge decides that according to the guidelines, the circumstances of the theft and the criminal record of each offender are the same. He decides that each should be assessed 40 day fine units. Multiplying these units by the average daily income for each, the truck driver's fine is DM4,000 and the manager's fine is DM12,000.

Since the day fine system was introduced in Germany the use of fines has increased and short-term incarceration has decreased. The sizes of fines have also increased, showing that affluent offenders are now being punished at levels corresponding to their wealth. Fines for poor offenders have remained low. These fines have not increased the default rate.

Some Americans believe day fines would be more equitable than the current system of low fines for all regardless of wealth. Others believe that to levy higher fines against rich people than poor people is unjust, because the wealthy person is being penalized for working hard for a high income. What do you think?

Source: T. R. Clear and G. F. Cole, *American Corrections*, 5th ed., p. 205 (Belmont, CA: West Wadsworth, 2000).

Day Fines. In many countries, fines are enforced and are normally the sole sanction for a wide range of crimes. The amounts are geared to the severity of the offense and the resources of the offender. To deal with the concern that fines exact a heavier toll on the poor than on the wealthy, Northern European countries have developed the **day fine** (also called structured fine), which is a criminal penalty that is based on the amount of income an offender earns for a day's work. Day fines take into account the differing economic circumstances of offenders who have committed the same crime. The amount of the fine is determined in a two-stage process. First, the number of units of punishment is determined according to the seriousness of the offense and such elements as the offender's prior record. Second, the monetary value of each unit of punishment is established in light of the offender's financial circumstances.

Thus, the total penalty—the degree of punishment—should cause an equivalent level of economic burden to offenders of differing means who are convicted of similar offenses. For example, a person making $36,500 a year and sentenced to ten units of punishment would pay $3,650; a person making $3,650 and receiving the same penalty would pay $365. The day fine concept is currently being adapted to the U.S. system and tested in seven jurisdictions in Arizona, Connecticut, Iowa, New York, Wisconsin, Oregon, and Washington. In 1988, in Staten Island, New York, day fines were implemented and evaluated, and it was determined that the day fine was an "attractive, workable sentencing option that has some advantages over the fixed fines traditionally imposed by the American courts."[18]

Day fines seem to serve at least two advantages. First, they provide a balance to the crime committed and the offender's ability to pay for his or her crime. Offenders are required to literally "pay for their crimes," but not beyond what is possible for them, to fulfill their legal obligation. This reduces discrimination of the sentence and increases the likelihood of payment. Second, the day fine provides courts and correctional officials with another alternative to incarceration, one that is more punitive than probation supervision and less harsh than jail or prison.

The U.S Department of Justice, in a monograph produced in 1996,[19] outlined a number of potential benefits of day fines (structured fines). They are as follows:

1. *Offender accountability:* Day fines are unequivocally punitive, with the severity of the punishment (in terms of economic impact on the individual offender) varying with the gravity of the offense. The offender is, quite literally, made to pay his or her debt to society.

2. *Deterrence:* Structured fines provide an economic disincentive for criminal behavior. They enable courts to impose meaningful monetary consequences for conviction of a criminal offense.

3. *Fairness:* Judges and other criminal justice practitioners who have become familiar with structured fines are impressed by the essential equity of the concept. Although they may be simpler to use, tariff fines are inherently unfair because, all too often, the fine amounts are too low to be meaningful to affluent offenders but high enough to exceed the ability of some defendants to pay.

4. *Effective and efficient use of limited system resources:* Structured fines are relatively inexpensive to administer compared with most other types of intermediate sanctions—including intensive supervised probation, electronically monitored home confinement, day reporting centers, and residential or outpatient substance abuse treatment centers. Although staff and computer resources are required to establish payment plans, monitor compliance, and take follow-up action when necessary, the level of resources needed is far less than for virtually any other sanction. In addition, the use of structured fines frees scarce (and more expensive) prison, jail, and probation supervision resources for use with offenders who pose more of a risk to public safety.

5. *Revenue:* There is evidence that structured fines can be more effective than tariff fines in generating revenue. As a source of net revenue, structured fines are undoubtedly far more effective than sanctions involving incarceration or supervision.

6. *Credibility of the court:* In a well-designed structured fine system, the court has a good collections capability. Although payment may sometimes be difficult and require time, offenders pay in full in a very high proportion of cases. In the small proportion of cases where fines are not collected, the court imposes a backup sanction that is roughly equivalent to the structured fine in terms of punitive impact. When these conditions are present, the structured fine is a meaningful sanction, and the court's sentence has credibility with the offender and the community.

The problems with day fines are that they are difficult to calculate and enforce. Determining just how much an offender can afford and how much a certain crime is "worth" is a difficult process that is subjective and prone to error. After the fine amount is determined and the offender is released to the community, it is also very difficult to track down offenders and to insist they pay. Failure to pay could result in incarceration and a new set of criminal justice system costs.

Forfeiture. With passage of the Racketeer Influence and Corrupt Organizations Act (RICO) and the Continuing Criminal Enterprise Act (CCE) in 1970, Congress resurrected forfeiture, a criminal sanction that had lain dormant since the American Revolution. Through amendments in 1984 and 1986, Congress improved ways to implement the law.[20] Similar laws are now found in a number of states, particularly with respect to controlled substances and organized crime.

Forfeiture, in which the government seizes property derived from or used in criminal activity, can take both civil and criminal forms. Under civil law, property used in criminal activity (for example, equipment to manufacture illegal drugs, automobiles, boats) can be seized without a finding of guilt. Under criminal law, forfeiture is imposed as a consequence of conviction and requires that the offender relinquish various assets related to the crime. These assets can be considerable. For example, in 1990 state and federal officials confiscated an estimated $1 billion worth of assets from drug dealers.

However, forfeiture is controversial. Critics argue that confiscating property without a court hearing violates citizens' constitutional rights. In 1993, the U.S. Supreme Court restricted the use of summary forfeiture. Now the growth in this form of sanction has waned.[21]

Sanctions Administered in the Community

The basis for the intermediate sanctions movement rests a great deal on the argument that probation, as traditionally practiced, is inadequate for large numbers of offenders. Probation leaders have responded to this criticism by developing new programs and expanding old ones. New programs often rely on increases in surveillance and control. Old programs are often revamped to become more efficient and expanded to fit more probationers.

Community Service and Restitution. The concepts of community service and restitution are dealt with in detail in Chapter 6. But they are also mentioned in this chapter because recently, with the effects of prison overcrowding and with judges searching for efficient sentencing options, the interest in using them as intermediate sanctions has increased.

A community service condition requires the offender to provide a specified number of hours of free labor in some public service, such as street cleaning, repair of run-down housing, or hospital volunteer work. A restitution condition establishes a sum of money that must be paid by the offender, either to the victim or to a public fund for victims of crime.

COUNTRIES IN EUROPE USING DAY FINES AND YEAR OF INTRODUCTION (IF AVAILABLE)

Finland	1921
Sweden	1931
Denmark	1939
Germany	1975
France	1983
Hungary	
Greece	
Austria	
Portugal	
England	(In 1991 temporarily adopted use of **unit fines,** which are based on a week's income rather than a day's income.)

Source: Josine Junger-Tas, *Alternatives to Prison Sentences: Experiences and Developments* (New York: Kluger, for the Dutch Ministry of Justice, 1994).

Both alternatives rest on the assumption that the offender can atone for his or her offense with a personal or financial contribution to the victim or to society. They have been referred to as reparative alternatives because they seek to repair in part the harm done by the offender. These approaches have become popular because they force the offender to make a positive contribution to offset the damage inflicted, and thus they satisfy a common public desire that offenders not "get away" with their crimes. They are also advocated as ways to reduce correctional overcrowding.

The evidence on the effectiveness of these programs is mixed. Most studies seem to find that in the absence of such programs, the vast majority of offenders who were ordered to provide community service and restitution would have been punished with a traditional probation sentence—this bodes poorly for community service as a real solution for correctional crowding. Nor have community service and restitution programs proved especially effective at reducing the criminal behavior of their participants; in fact, studies have shown that they have somewhat higher failure rates than do the regular supervision cases.[22]

In sum, community service and restitution stand as excellent illustrations of the fact that simply implementing a so-called alternative does not always achieve the aims of intermediate sanctions. Careful attention must be paid to the selection of appropriate offenders so that the phenomenon of net widening is avoided. Judicial decision making must be controlled to ensure that persons who enter the programs are those who otherwise would have been incarcerated.

Probation Day Reporting (Treatment) Centers. As prisons became more and more crowded, judges grew reluctant to place probation violators in jail or prison except when the violation involved a new crime. The result was that probationers in some jurisdictions began to learn they could disregard probation rules, with little consequence. Probation administrators found the lack of credibility with clients to be a severe detriment to effective supervision.

The result has been the development of probation-run enforcement programs called **day reporting centers (DRCs).** In these centers, offenders on pretrial release, probation, or parole are required to appear at a certain location on a regular basis to receive supervision or participate in rehabilitation programs. Centers often require offenders to fully account for their daily schedule, call in by phone throughout the day, be receptive to frequent phone checks at home, and take random drug tests. The first DRCs were implemented in Great Britain in the early 1970s when correctional officials found that imprisonment and probation were ineffective for chronic but nonserious offenders. In 1985, the states of Massachusetts and Connecticut were the first in the United States to adopt the British idea of day centers. The purposes of the early DRCs were to provide a high degree of supervision and reduce prison crowding by providing early release for moderately serious felons. Both of these states still employ DRCs, but in Connecticut they are now used to reduce pretrial confinement and as a sentencing option for newly convicted felons. The number of DRCs in the United States has grown from 13 in 1990 to over 114 in 22 different states in 1995.[23]

The types of DRCs vary widely, but all have in common the desire to provide a credible option for probation agencies to enforce their conditions, when prisons are too overcrowded to accept probation violators.[24] Most DRCs incorporate a potpourri of common correctional methods. For example, in some, the treatment regime is comparable to that of a halfway house—but without the problems of visiting a residential facility. Others "provide contact levels equal to or greater than intensive supervision programs, in effect, creating a community equivalent to confinement."[25] The goals of DRCs are also quite diverse. According to a comprehensive survey of the 114 DRCs located in the United States, the primary goal of most centers was to provide offenders with access to treatment or services. These services vary and include job-seeking skills, drug abuse education and treatment, counseling, and life-skills training. A secondary goal of DRCs was shown to be reduction of prison crowding.

There have been a limited number of evaluations of DRCs in the United States, and when they are conducted they look at only one or a few programs. An evaluation of a DRC for drug-using offenders in Chicago, Illinois, revealed that the centers were an effective means to reduce drug use, and that program participants found the DRC to be supportive of the program and the staff members.[26]

In an evaluation of four DRCs, it was determined that 78 percent of the participants successfully completed the program, with 20 percent being returned to jail for program violations and 2 percent failing due to committing a new crime or escape.[27] One study of New York City's program found that its stiff eligibility requirements resulted in very small numbers of cases entering the program, a problem common to newly established intermediate sanctions programs.[28] Evaluation of DRCs in Britain has determined that 63 percent of offenders ($n = 606$) were reconvicted of another offense at least once within twenty-four months of being ordered to attend a day center.

Taking into account the high-risk offenders who were in the day centers, and the wide variation of results among the thirty-eight centers, evaluators felt that the reconviction rates were not unacceptable.[29] The real test of these programs will involve two issues: How much do they improve probation's credibility as a sanction, and how well do they combat jail and prison crowding? These questions remain unanswered.

Intensive Supervision. Although **intensive probation supervision (IPS)** is often viewed as a "new idea" in community corrections, the fact is different kinds of IPS were initiated in probation and parole on both the state and federal levels over thirty years ago. For example, from 1954 until 1964 a Special Intensive Parole Unit experiment was implemented in California, during which caseload sizes varied from fifteen to thirty-five. Probation and parole departments have used IPS programs to better manage caseloads of offenders who were high-risk recidivism cases or in need of special rehabilitation services. When evaluations of these early programs were conducted, they commonly found that smaller (IPS) caseloads did little except to generate more technical violations.

However, in the last fifteen years the United States has seen a significant increase in the number of IPS programs. Outside of regular probation supervision, IPS is the most commonly used intermediate sanction today. By 1990, over 70,000 offenders were under intensive supervision in the community, and at least one jurisdiction in every state had implemented IPS.[30]

Although traditional probation caseloads vary greatly from state to state, with some probation officers having as many as 300 cases, IPS average caseload is 29 offenders for each probation officer.[31]

As intensive probation supervision programs have sprung up around the country, they seem ideally suited to the pressures facing corrections today. Because they target offenders who are subject to incarceration, they should help to alleviate crowding; because they involve strict and close supervision, they are responsive to community pressures to control offenders. These two aims—reduction of jail and prison crowding and community protection—are the main objectives of most IPS programs. IPS is also used with offenders who have special needs, such as those with substance abuse issues.

What constitutes intensive supervision? In IPS, offenders are allowed to live at home but severe restrictions are placed on their behavior. The offenders are required to work, attend school or training programs, obtain treatment for addictions, submit to drug testing, and meet with a probation officer on a regular basis—ranging from once a day to weekly. Whatever the restrictions placed on the offender, the primary emphasis is on strict supervision and enforcement of probation conditions. When the offender violates one of the conditions, he or she may receive more restrictions (e.g., more frequent visits) or be removed from the community and incarcerated. Even the most ambitious programs require only once-a-day meetings between officers and offenders. Such meetings, which may last ten minutes or less, can never take up more than a minuscule portion of the offender's waking hours. So, no matter how intensive the supervision, a substantial element of trust must still be placed in the probationer.

Although there are many variations of IPS, they can generally be categorized as one of three types: probation enhancements IPS, institutional diversion, and early release IPS programs. Probation enhancements IPS, also called the case management approach, diverts offenders from traditional probation sentences. In most cases, offenders who have committed offenses that are too serious for traditional supervision are selected for this type. The goal is to enhance regular probation supervision. Institutional diversion programs (also called "front-end" IPS) are used for low-risk offenders who may be incarcerated but, because of the nonserious nature of their offense, can be released to IPS as a substitute for a prison term. The goal is to limit the number of offenders entering prison. The third type, early release (also called "backend" IPS), provides a mechanism for releasing offenders already in prison. The goal of this type of IPS is to conserve prison resources and save money.

Evaluation of IPS Programs. Evaluations of programs in Georgia, New York, and Texas found evidence that intensive supervision can cut into the rearrests of probationers. The Georgia program, in particular, reported that the first thousand participants engaged in fewer than twenty-five serious offenses; by its sixth year, the program had saved the state millions of dollars in corrections costs.[32] Similarly, research of IPS programs in Ohio have concluded that the programs were saving the state more than the cost of incarceration.[33]

Nevertheless, these programs are not without controversy. For one thing, the impact on rearrests comes at a cost. All evaluations of intensive supervision find that, probably because of the closer contact with the clients, probation officers uncover a larger number of rules violations than occur in regular probation. Therefore, these programs often have higher failure rates than regular probation, even though their clients produce fewer arrests.

This was precisely what Rand researchers found in a series of experiments testing the effectiveness of intensive probation supervision. Offenders were randomly assigned to IPS versus regular probation. Results indicated no differences in overall arrest rates but substantial differences in probation failure rates. IPS clients did much worse under the stricter rules—possibly because IPS makes detecting rules violations easier.[34] The result was that these programs not only failed to reduce crime but actually cost the public more than if the programs had not been started in the first place. In a recent article summarizing the research available on IPS programs, the following was determined to be generally true about IPS programs:

- IPS programs have failed to alleviate prison crowding.
- Most IPS research fails to show significant differences in the recidivism of IPS offenders versus comparison groups.
- If IPS participants are in treatment and employment programs, their likelihood of success is greater.
- IPS programs are more effective in meeting offenders' needs than regular probation.
- IPS does serve as an intermediate sanction.
- IPS is less expensive than prison but more expensive than first thought.[35]

Despite questions about the effectiveness of IPS, the approach has enjoyed wide support from corrections administrators, judges, and even prosecutors. The close supervision has revitalized the reputation of probation in the criminal justice system. It has also demonstrated probation's ability to enforce strict rules, ensure employment, support treatment programs, and so forth. Given the good public relations, it is likely that IPS is here to stay.

Much as intensive supervision may satisfy public demands for control measures, probationers continue to need various forms of assistance. Many offenders are buffeted by serious personal problems—unemployment, emotional and family crises, substance abuse—that cannot be addressed effectively without some form of service or treatment. So officers still have to juggle the roles of helper and controller. In intensive supervision programs the conflicts between these roles may seem less extreme on paper, but in practice they may well continue and perhaps be exacerbated by the mixed messages of the programs.

The Future of IPS. It appears that with the current need in corrections to reduce jail and prison crowding, along with the call to increase punitiveness, intensive probation supervision is likely to flourish. This is not surprising since it placates both the liberal and conservative crime ideologies. For liberals, IPS serves as a less serious punishment and as an alternative to incarceration.

For conservatives, IPS functions as a more stringent form of probation supervision. If IPS will be a common correctional program much into the future, it may be wise to consider how we can make it a more effective correctional alternative. Arthur Lurigio and Joan Petersilia[36] have provided the following framework for improving the quality of IPS programs:

1. *Better selection of who is to receive IPS:* We now know enough about offenders to know which ones are more or less likely to recidivate and more likely to benefit from what kind of treatment modality. We need to match more effectively the kind of inmate that can succeed with IPS with the program. Some have argued that it may be advisable to limit the kinds of offenders that receive IPS to those who have a lower risk of recidivism, such as older property felons or even first-time violent offenders.

2. *Community collaboration:* IPS programs must work with other community agencies to enhance the chance of offender success. Drug treatment programs, family counseling centers, and even church leaders can all assist in the supervision of offenders.

3. *Reconsider the emphasis of IPS supervision:* Many who supervise IPS offenders spend much time and energy trying to catch and revoke them for technical violations. This kind of supervision is based on the assumption that technical violations, if ignored, will lead to more serious criminal behavior. This assumption is accepted in spite of the research indicating that IPS offenders with technical violations are no more likely to have new arrests than offenders without violations.[37] It may be time to refocus IPS supervision on preventing and detecting serious offenses.

4. *Rethink the criteria for "success of IPS":* When an IPS offender is arrested for a new offense or technical violation, one can view this action as a sign of IPS program "success" versus "failure." If the public wants the objective of IPS to be "public safety," then maybe an arrest is a sign of program effectiveness. If correctional administrators hope to reduce jail or prison crowding, then expanding IPS supervision to additional offender populations may be advisable.

House Arrest. The use of **house arrest,** also called **home confinement** or home detention, is far from being a new form of punishment. Throughout history, many persons have been confined to their homes for violating laws of the land. Some of the more famous include Galileo, who was confined to his home for making scientific statements contrary to the Roman Catholic Church. More recently, Lech Walesa in Poland and Winnie Mandela in South Africa have received this sentence.

House arrest is basically a simple concept: Offenders are sentenced to terms of incarceration, but they serve those terms in their own homes. Some offenders might, after a time, be allowed to venture out to work or for restricted periods of the day. Others might be allowed to maintain their employment for the entire duration of their sentence. Whatever the details, the concept has as its basic thrust the use of the offender's residence as the place of punishment. In many cases, house arrest is combined with electronic monitoring as a correctional sanction. Electronic monitoring will be discussed in the following section.

There are at least three kinds of house arrest, which can best be understood in terms of levels of restrictiveness. The lowest level is a simple curfew—when an offender is required to be home after a certain hour. A second, more restrictive level is when an offender is allowed to be away from home during certain hours of the day for work, school, religious reasons, or counseling sessions. This kind of punishment is often called home confinement. A third form of house arrest, called home incarceration, is the most punitive and restricts a person to home at all times unless a special situation arises, such as a medical or legal appointment.[38]

On the surface, there is much to recommend the idea of house arrest. It costs the state nothing to house the offender; lodging, subsistence, and often even the cost of an electronic monitor are covered by the offender's own resources. House arrest is also very flexible, allowing an offender to attend work, school, or counseling programs. More important, significant community ties—to family, friends (restricted visitation is ordinarily allowed), employers, and community groups—can be maintained. The punishment is more visible to the community than if the person were sent away to prison. In a sense, the goals of reintegration, deterrence, and financial responsibility are simultaneously served.

The arguments against house arrest are at least three. Some feel that allowing offenders into the community will endanger public safety. Although the offenders who receive house arrest are usually nonviolent offenders, the public may fear future incidences of criminality. Another criticism is the possibility of net widening. Offenders who receive house arrest may best be handled by less punitive measures such as fines, diversion, and mental health programs, or even no correctional sanction. Finally, some opponents view house arrest as a possible source of violation of the constitutional right to privacy in one's own home. Of course, the opposing argument will always be that the offender has given up his or her right to privacy by committing a criminal offense.

Evaluations of house arrest provide a few impressions of how the program works. One survey concluded that "most offenders placed in home confinement [i.e., house arrest] appear to be more similar to incarcerated offenders than to probationers and [it] does genuinely divert from incarceration at least half, and sometimes a much higher proportion, of those who receive it."[39]

Anecdotal evidence suggests the effectiveness of house arrest seems to wear off after a few months; it is increasingly difficult to enforce detention conditions as the sentence rounds into its second half-year. (This should come as no surprise: The impact of imprisonment on the offender seems to stabilize after about the same length of time.) The program appears to be best suited to low-risk offenders who have relatively stable residences in which to be detained.

Probably the most ambitious house arrest program in the United States is in Florida. The Florida Community Control Program includes thousands of offenders who are restricted to their homes and receive unannounced visits by officers of the court. Offenders are allowed to leave only for work, rehabilitation programs, or community service. Offenders agree to certain conditions including payment of restitution, family support, and community supervision expenses.

Electronic Monitoring. One of the most popular approaches to probation supervision is the use of electronic monitors to expand the surveillance capacity of supervision. **Electronic monitoring (EM)** was initially developed in 1964 by a Harvard University researcher, Ralph Schwitzgebel. The original goals of EM were to reduce criminal offenses, to promote a therapeutic relationship with clients, and to provide a humane alternative to incarceration.

The current use of EM can be traced to 1983 when a New Mexico judge, inspired by the "Spiderman" comic strip, placed a probation violator on EM for one month. Other states soon adopted the idea, and by January 1, 2000, an estimated 63,000 people were being monitored in all 50 states. At least 1,800 federal offenders add to that total.[40]

Electronic monitoring is ordinarily combined with house arrest and is used to enforce its restrictions. However, there are many other ways that EM has been used in corrections. In Los Angeles County, EM has been used for IPS programs, work furlough–home detention programs, temporary detention of juveniles, gang drug supervision, narcotic surveillance, and traditional home detention.[41] Other uses include supervision of parolees and pretrial defendants.

The electronic monitor is a small mechanical device that emits an electronic signal. There are a number of types of electronic monitoring devices, and the technology is constantly changing. Two of the most common are programmed contact devices and continuous signaling devices.

The **programmed contact device** is a passive monitor that responds only to inquiries. Most commonly, the offender receives an automated telephone call from the probation office or via the computer. The offender then must verify his or her identity. This is done either through voice verification, a wrist device that transmits a code into the telephone, or a mechanism attached to the offender's arm that is inserted into a special box attached to the telephone. **Continuous signaling devices** are active in that they send continuous signals that are picked up by a receiver. If a break in the signal is noted by the receiver, a computer compares the data received with an offender's curfew and restrictions schedule and alerts authorities about the infraction.

Advocates of EM point out that it is cheaper than incarceration (especially since the offender often pays to use the system). EM costs about $5,000 to $6,000 per year, which is inexpensive compared to the average cost of incarceration per year ($25,000–30,000). Other estimates place the average cost of EM between $5 and $25 per day as compared to the $50 per day it costs to keep an offender in the detention center.[42] Because EM limits the daily freedom of the offender, it is also apparently tougher than traditional probation. Although EM programs are undoubtedly intrusive, they appear to be more humane than prison or jail. An important advantage of EM is that the offenders are able to remain in the community, which means they can keep their jobs and stay with their families. This can help to ease the financial burden of many families and keep the offenders in contact with family members. The importance of being at home with family, especially young children, cannot be overestimated. Our prisons are full of young men who were raised by one guardian or by a guardian who was too busy with work or other children to attend to their supervision. Finally, being in the community allows for the rehabilitation of the offender. Offenders can attend school, training programs, and individual or family counseling. In the long run, this will help the offenders and their families more than incarceration.

Some are more skeptical about EM. The apparent cost savings that can be gained from the implementation of EM can be easily undermined if costs are viewed more closely. Unless EM programs recover costs through user fees, reduce the need to build new correctional facilities, and prevent recidivism, additional revenues will be needed. It is also possible that EM can result in net widening—including offenders in the program that would otherwise receive either no sanction or less serious punishment such as traditional probation. It can be argued that EM may be economically discriminatory. This can occur if EM is provided only for those offenders who own telephones and can afford the $25 to $100 per week to rent the system.

Recent problems have arisen with the reliability of EM devices. Some offenders have figured out how to remove the monitors without detection; others have been found in violation of the house arrest when they were arrested at the scene of a crime—even though the monitoring system indicated they were safely at home. Studies also suggest that the monitors have a significant negative side effect—they can intrude on the privacy of the family and may be demanding and stressful for the offender's family members.[43]

Moreover, a major reason why some fear the increase in the use of home confinement with EM is that confinement to the home, even with an electronic device, is no guarantee that crimes will not occur. Many crimes—child abuse, drug sales, and assaults, to name a few—commonly occur in offenders' residences.

There has been limited research reviewing the success of EM programs. In one of the few large-scale evaluations of EM, a National Institute of Justice survey revealed that some administrators of EM programs reported that few participants failed to complete the program while others reported that up to half of the participants failed to comply with EM program requirements. Most of the program failures were for technical violations, such as breaking curfew and using drugs or alcohol.[44]

Most of the evaluative research about EM deals with effectiveness of the program when it is combined with home confinement (HC). Some of those studies found it to be cost-effective,[45] while others found EM/HC to be too expensive and not to reduce jail overcrowding,[46] or at least to be susceptible to net widening.[47] Some good news about EM when combined with HC can be found if we review the research that studies the effects on certain kinds of offenders. More specifically, there is good evidence that EM/HC is relatively successful when trying to deter DUI (driving while under the influence) offenders.[48]

Despite its limits, and the minimal research that supports its effectiveness, the growth of electronic monitoring seems a safe bet. Jail and prison populations continue to increase beyond capacity while citizens clamor for strict punishment of offenders. Research has indicated that citizens support the use of EM in certain conditions—that is, if offender seriousness is taken into account.[49]

The recent development of global positioning systems (GPS) has also created new opportunities for EM. GPS is a network of satellites that are used by the U.S. Department of Defense to pinpoint targets and guide bombs. The satellites have a variety of uses including telling time, helping persons determine their physical location, and helping law enforcement officials track stolen vehicles. Lately, GPS has been used to more easily track offenders on probation or parole. With GPS, a probation officer can track an offender on a computer screen and can determine the street location of the offender. It can also be used to determine whether an offender is avoiding certain trouble spots, can help determine if the offender was around an area when a specific crime was committed, and can assist in apprehension. The GPS tracking device can be programmed to specify "inclusion zones" or areas where offenders are allowed to be while also emitting information about "exclusion zones" or "hot zones" where an offender is not allowed. For example, this technology can be used to keep an offender away from his partner in a domestic violence case.[50]

Correctional systems throughout the United States have begun to develop, test, and use GPS in probation and parole supervision. However, the technology is not without fault. It is possible to lose the signal of the offender if there is battery failure, if the offender enters certain buildings, or if other equipment failure occurs. Also, it is more expensive than regular electronic monitoring in that it can cost an average of $30 to $40 a day. As the GPS technology continues to improve, EM will be a likely choice for helping to deal with offenders in the next century.

Sanctions Administered in Institutions and the Community

Corrections agencies have been the hardest hit by problems of overcrowding. They have tried to develop intermediate sanctions as ways to manage a burgeoning load of offenders. While some corrections agencies rely on electronic monitoring to support an early release program, the three most common versions of corrections programs are shock incarceration, boot camps, and halfway houses.

Shock Incarceration. The fact that the deterrent effect of incarceration wears off after a very short term of imprisonment has led to experimentation with **shock incarceration,** in which the offender is sentenced to a term in jail or prison, then, after the offender has been incarcerated thirty to ninety days, the judge reduces the sentence. When a period of shock incarceration is followed by a period of probation, then the sentence is called *shock probation.* The assumption behind shock incarceration or probation is that the offender will find the jail experience so distasteful that he or she will be motivated to work harder at staying free of crime.

Shock incarceration is a controversial program. Its critics argue that it combines the undesirable aspects of both probation and imprisonment. Offenders who are incarcerated lose their jobs, have their community relationships disrupted, and are exposed to the labeling and brutalizing experiences of the institution. The release to probation reinforces the idea that the system is arbitrary in its decision making and that probation is a "break" rather than a truly individualized supervision program. It is hard to see how this kind of treatment avoids demeaning and embittering offenders.

Yet studies of shock incarceration find that it has little effect one way or the other on the offender's adjustment in the community. A major study of Ohio's shock program found little or no difference in the performance of "shocked" probationers, regular probationers, and incarcerated offenders, suggesting that shock incarceration is of minimal effectiveness. This finding echoes those of other studies of programs designed to shock or scare offenders into complying with the law: At best they seem to have no effect; at worst they sometimes increase misbehavior.[51] Although research shows little reduction in recidivism rates for such programs, the interest in them has remained high and has led to a new form of the shock technique called boot camps. In most of the correctional literature, shock incarceration is synonymous with the term *boot camp.*

Boot Camps. A variation on the idea of shock incarceration is the **boot camp.** It is a short-term institutional sentence, usually followed by probation, that puts the offender through a physical regimen designed to develop discipline and respect for authority. Boot camps differ from shock incarceration in that inmates are separated from others and receive a strong dose of military training. Most boot camps limit participation to young, nonviolent offenders. Many prefer offenders who have not been previously incarcerated.

The first boot camps were opened in Oklahoma and Georgia in 1983. The boot camps were similar to earlier shock probation and parole programs that released offenders to probation or parole after a short time in prison. On January 1, 2000, there were 6,983 offenders in 51 adult boot camp programs in 30 states plus the federal government, with 7.8 percent ($n = 545$) female offenders. The length of boot camp programs ranges from three to six months, with the average stay being four months.[52] Most boot camps serve adults, but some serve juveniles.

The main characteristic common to all boot camps is rigorous military discipline. The daily routine includes strenuous workouts, marching, military drills, and hard physical labor. Although all boot camps require some form of physical discipline, the amount and intensity vary. The number and quality of rehabilitation programs in boot camps also varies considerably. For example, in Georgia, most of the inmates' time is spent in physical training, drills, and work, whereas in New York, inmates spend a large amount of their time in rehabilitation programs such as education and substance abuse counseling. Other boot camps provide additional rehabilitative services such as anger management training, health and wellness courses, financial management, literacy training, and often high school equivalency (GED) courses.

There is also variation in the way boot camp participants are selected. In some states judges sentence directly to boot camps, whereas in others, such as New York, correctional officials select participants. In some states, boot camps are voluntary; in others they are mandatory. Also, the kind of aftercare that an offender receives after incarceration may be different. Upon release, some inmates are placed in intensive probation supervision programs, some in electronic monitoring, and some in both. Inmates in programs may or may not receive aftercare rehabilitation programs such as drug therapy or academic education.[53]

Although state correctional systems run most of the boot camps, the federal government and private companies also have gotten into the act. The Federal Bureau of Prisons has two shock incarceration facilities called intensive confinement centers (ICC). One, located in Lewisburg, Pennsylvania, is a male facility and the other, in Bryan, Texas, is for females. Federal ICCs are different from the state-run facilities in that they contain a slightly older population, they do not allow summary punishments by staff, they emphasize nonmilitary rehabilitative activities, and they do not reduce the sentences of boot camp participants if they do well in the program.[54]

BOOT CAMP DAILY SCHEDULE

Typical daily schedule of boot camp participants in New York state:

5:30 A.M.	Wake-up call and standing count
5:45 A.M.	Calisthenics and drills
6:30–7:00 A.M.	Run
7:00–8:00 A.M.	Breakfast and cleanup
8:15 A.M.	Standing count
8:30–11:55 A.M.	Work/school
12:00 noon	Lunch and standing count
12:30–3:30 P.M.	Afternoon work/school
3:30–4:00 P.M.	Shower
4:00–4:45 P.M.	Network community meeting
4:45–5:45 P.M.	Dinner, prepare for evening
6:00–9:00 P.M.	School, group counseling, drug counseling, prerelease counseling, decision-making classes
8:00 P.M.	Count while in programs
9:15 P.M.	Squad bay, prepare for bed
9:30 P.M.	Standing count, lights out

Source: C. L. Clark, D. W. Aziz, and D. L. MacKenzie, "Shock Incarceration in New York: Focus on Treatment." National Institute of Justice Program Focus, 1994. http://ncjrs:71/0/4/1/pubs/nyshock.txt

Proponents of the boot camp argue that many young offenders get involved in crime because they lack self-respect and are unable to order their lives. Consequently, the boot camp model targets young first offenders whose initial crimes seem to suggest a future of sustained criminality.

Evaluations do show that offenders may experience improvements in self-esteem, and some studies have been able to demonstrate that boot camps can lead to a change in offender attitudes. More specifically, successful boot camp participants have more prosocial attitudes than those who drop out, have more prosocial attitudes than regular prison inmates, and develop more positive attitudes about the program, especially if it was devoted to offender rehabilitation.[55] Other research has shown that boot camps that are carefully designed, target the right offenders, and provide them rehabilitative services are likely to save money and reduce recidivism.[56] Table 7.2 provides an overview of boot camps and the costs per inmate for those that are in operation in the United States.

TABLE 7.2   BOOT CAMPS IN OPERATION AND COST PER INMATE PER DAY

	Year First Opened	Boot Camps	Program Length (mos.)	Daily Cost Per Inmate	Planned for 2000
Alabama[1]	1988	1	4.5	$16.37	0
Arkansas	1990	1	4	$38.31	0
Colorado	1991	1	3	$64.93	0
Delaware	1997	1	6	$38.71	0
Florida[2]	1987	2	4		0
Georgia	1991	6	3	$42.42	0
Idaho	1971	1	4	$34.42	0
Illinois	1990	3	4		0
Kansas	1991	1	6	$51.08	1
Kentucky[3]	1993	1		$38.10	0
Louisiana[4]	1987	1	6		0
Maryland	1990	1	6	$68.18	0
Massachusetts	1992	1	4	$69.42	0
Michigan[5]	1988	1	3.1	$68.74	0
Minnesota	1992	1	6	$103.27	0
Mississippi	1985	3	4	$30.10	0
Missouri	1994	1	3		0
Montana[6]	1984	1	3	$118.55	0
Nevada	1991	1	6	$45.32	0
New Jersey	1997	1	6	$96.00	0
New York	1987	4	6	$64.25	0
North Carolina[7]	1989	2	4	$60.00	0
Ohio[8]	1991	2	3	$77.85	0
Oklahoma[9]	1984	2	4		0
Pennsylvania[10]	1992	1	6	$104.85	0
South Carolina	1987	2	3	$29.58	0
Tennessee[11]	1989	1	3.5	$42.30	0
Texas	1989	2	3	$62.56	0
Washington[12]	1993	1	4	$76.00	0
Wyoming	1990	1	4		0
Federal	1990	3	6	$47.39	0
Average/Total		**51**	**4**	**$59.55**	**1**

Source: The Corrections Yearbook (Middletown, CT: Criminal Justice Institute, 2000).

[1]Program length is based on a range of three to six months. [2]The minimum program length is four months. [3]Program length is 126 days. [4]Program length is six months at a minimum; the boot camp does not have a separate budget. [5]Length of program is 13 weeks. [6]Program length of 12 to 17 weeks plus up to 90 days aftercare; daily cost per inmate includes outside medical and administrative overhead. [7]The program is known informally as a boot camp; the actual program name is IMPACT. IMPACT was an in-prison program into calendar year 1999; it is now a probation and parole program. The program length is three to four months. [8]SCI costs $77.85 per inmate per day; ORW costs $53.27 per inmate per day. [9]Program length is four months for males and twelve months for females. [10]No new boot camps are planned; however, 400 beds have been added to the existing boot camp. [11]Program length is three to four months. [12]Daily cost per inmate is approximate.

But critics of boot camps argue that military-style physical training and the harshness of the boot camp experience do little to overcome the problems that get inner-city offenders in trouble with the law in the first place. In fact, studies of traditional boot camp graduates show they do no better than other offenders after release from the program.[57] When it comes to whether boot camps reduce prison crowding, it appears that they have little impact. Boot camps can reduce crowding if the offenders are let out early from prison or can earn their way out of prison. However, it appears that because net widening often occurs—inmates who would otherwise receive probation get boot camp—the possible reduction of crowding is negated. In this instance, the only result is the need for more prison beds. Perhaps job training, drug treatment, and education would be better than physical training. The intentionally harsh tactics of boot camp may seem brutal, especially for young offenders who are impressionable. Some critics have even argued that boot camps may violate the Eighth Amendment against cruel and unusual punishment. The verbal confrontations and summary punishments meted out by correctional staff can sometimes cross the line into emotional and/or physical abuse. Reports of physical and mental injuries are not uncommon. Nevertheless, boot camps have proven to be very popular with a public searching for new ways to handle offenders.

Females in Boot Camps. As mentioned earlier, there are over 500 women in the United States that are currently participating in boot camp–style programs. Because of the relatively small numbers of women who are sent to boot camps, some states integrate the female inmates with male boot camp inmates. In studies conducted of females participants, it has been found that they often encounter problems that are different from male offenders. For one, women in boot camps often have difficulty meeting the physical demands of the program. This is because the physical standards of boot camps were originally designed to meet the average male's strength and stamina levels.[58] Also, research has determined that female boot camp participants experience more emotional stress than male participants. This stress is more apparent when the female inmates are integrated with the male inmates. One of the specific problems is created by the confrontational nature of drill instructors in the boot camp programs. Women offenders have reported that being in these boot camps, with the constant verbal abuse and physical demands, is sometimes a reminder of past abusive relationships.[59]

Halfway House. The last form of intermediate sanction to be discussed may be the oldest form of community corrections program—the halfway house. The halfway house, also called the community treatment center, is an agency-administered or contract facility located in the community designed to transition inmates nearing the end of their sentences from prison life to community living.

As mentioned in the beginning of this chapter, the halfway house can be traced back to sixth-century Europe and over 150 years ago in the United States. Originally, the halfway house provided housing for homeless men. In the past 100 years, the halfway house correctional systems have used these facilities to gradually allow offenders to gain more independence and to slowly adjust to living in free society. Offenders who live there usually leave during part of the day to either work, attend school, or participate in some rehabilitation program. Most recently, halfway houses have evolved into multipurpose facilities that serve a variety of roles including the supervision and provision of services for those awaiting trial, probationers, abused women, drug and alcohol offenders, mentally ill offenders, and in many cases juveniles. As of January 2000, nearly 27,000 inmates were in 72 halfway houses in the United States, up from 19,000 in 1995. Almost 7,000 of the total are under the control of the Federal Bureau of Prisons.[60] While most halfway houses are administered by federal, state, or county correctional agencies, in recent years the private sector has begun to fund and staff these facilities. The halfway house or community treatment center has become a viable intermediate sanction because, while being a supplement to probation and parole, it increases severity of punishment and adds to public safety.

EVALUATION OF INTERMEDIATE SANCTIONS

A very interesting barometer of just how well intermediate sanctions work may be the offender self-report research on the effects of the sanctions. Three recent studies shed some light on this issue. Offenders in Minnesota were surveyed to determine their perceptions on sanctions severity. The findings indicated that some punishments, like jail and prison, are more severe than others but that intermediate sanctions such as intensive probation supervision, electronic monitoring, and house arrest can be as severe as incarceration, depending on duration and level of supervision.[61]

In Texas, 128 recently convicted offenders were asked to rate the severity of twenty-six felony punishments ranging from six months of probation through a variety of intermediate sanctions to five years in prison.[62] In Oklahoma, a survey of 415 male and female inmates serving brief prison terms for nonviolent offenses rated the punitiveness of several alternative sanctions.[63] The findings from both Texas and Oklahoma indicated that intermediate sanctions sometimes are more punitive than incarceration, they can provide a true continuum of sanctions, and there is the possibility of some interchangeability among punishments. In short, what these studies reflect is that there are sentencing options that exist between probation and prison and that they can serve the dual purposes of deterrence and cost savings (see Figure 7.1).

Because of the relatively recent development of intermediate sanctions programs (ISPs), the number and quality of evaluations are limited. The evidence

FIGURE 7.2 COMMUNITY CORRECTIONS COST PER DAY
IN OREGON

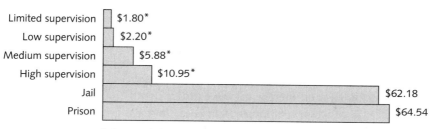

*These include supervision, sanctions, and services.

Source: www.doc.state.or.us/community_corrections/whatiscc/whatiscc.shtml

that is available is quite mixed. The Maryland Report, mentioned earlier, summarized a number of intermediate sanctions evaluations and reported that except in a few instances, there is no evidence that ISPs are effective in reducing crime.[64]

Another recent study that reviewed fifteen years of evaluations of ISPs concluded that relative to program costs, recidivism, and prison crowding three major findings are consistent. First, ISP participants that were sentenced by judges were not prison-bound offenders but rather high-risk probationers. Because of this finding, we can say that prison space and costs were not saved even though the ISP sentence did provide better supervision and accountability for felony probationers. Second, ISP offenders were watched more closely, but the supervision did not necessarily decrease arrests or overall justice system costs. In addition, technical violations were more likely to surface during ISP supervision. Third, and probably the most important finding, was that recidivism rates were more likely to fall if strict supervision was combined with drug treatment participation.[65] This finding is similar to an older meta-analysis study by Canadian researchers Paul Gendreau and Tracy Little that found supervision of probationers and parolees can reduce recidivism if it is structured, maintains firm accountability for program participation, and connects the offender with treatment and other prosocial activities.[66]

One of the problems that surfaces with evaluations of intermediate sanctions is that ISPs often profess lofty goals: improve justice, save money, and prevent crime. Any correctional strategy that can produce these results surely deserves broad support. Yet the limited record on intermediate sanctions suggests that these goals are not always accomplished. For intermediate sanctions to work, they must be carefully planned and implemented—and even then, there will be challenges to overcome if they are to be effective. In the following sections, we discuss some of the issues that these programs must resolve if they are to reach their potential as correctional approaches. These issues are sentencing, selection of offenders, surveillance and control, and personnel issues.

Sentencing Issues

The most important issues concerning use of intermediate sanctions have to do with the sentencing philosophy and practice. In recent years, there has been a trend toward the emphasis of deserved punishment in sentencing philosophy: Offenders convicted of similar offenses ought to be subjected to penalties of corresponding severity. Since intermediate sanctions fall between imprisonment and probation, they could potentially increase the number of mid-range severe punishments and thereby improve justice.

Yet advocates of deserved punishment argue that it is not automatically evident how intermediate sanctions compare with either prison or probation, in terms of severity, nor is it clear how they compare with each other.[67] For example, it may violate the equal punishment rationale of just deserts to allow one offender to be placed on intensive probation, while another is ordered to pay an extensive fine.

When intermediate sanctions are used to reduce prison crowding, the problem becomes even more serious. Using intermediate sanctions as sentencing alternatives for some offenders may raise serious concerns about equity. Is it fair for some offenders to receive prison terms while others receive the intermediate alternative?

For intermediate sanctions to be effective, exchange rates consistent with the principle of interchangeability must be developed so that one form can be substituted for or added to another form. The **principle of interchangeability** states that different forms of intermediate sanctions can be calibrated to make them equivalent as punishments despite their differences in approach. For example, two weeks of jail might be considered as equal to thirty days of intermittent confinement or two months of house arrest or a hundred hours of community service or one month's salary.

Advocates say that a short prison sentence can be roughly equivalent to some intensive supervision programs or residential drug treatment, in terms of intrusiveness, and that various forms of intermediate sanctions can be made roughly equivalent to each other. Studies of intensive supervision support this contention when they find that some offenders would rather be in prison than be placed on the tough intermediate sanctions.[68] Thus, it is possible to design intermediate sanctions so that they equate with incarceration in terms of intrusion, and they therefore do not violate principles of deserved punishment.

In practice, some have tried to structure this principle of interchangeability by describing punishment in terms of units: A month in prison might count as thirty units; a month on intensive supervision might count as ten. Thus, a year on IPS would be about the same as a four-month prison stay. To date, no one has designed a full-blown system of interchangeability, although both the Federal Sentencing Guidelines and those in the state of Oregon embrace the punishment units concept. It is likely that future years will see attempts to create interchangeability, using strategies that provide for equivalence in punishments.

Selection of Offenders

If intermediate sanctions are to work, they must be reserved for appropriate offenders. Which offenders are appropriate for a given program depends upon the program's goals. Regardless of the program's goals, however, the availability of intermediate sanctions should not be biased against anyone because of race, sex, or age.

The Target Group. There are two general goals of intermediate sanctions: to serve as a less costly alternative to prison and to serve as a more effective alternative to probation. To meet these two goals, intermediate sanctions managers search for appropriate offenders for their staff to supervise. It is not always easy to identify appropriate offenders and move them into these programs.

Prison alternatives are designed for offenders who would otherwise be sentenced to prison. But it is difficult to be certain that an offender given an alternative sanction would have otherwise been sentenced to prison. In most jurisdictions, a person who is sentenced to probation is legally eligible for a prison sentence. Research shows that even though many offenders who are sentenced to intermediate sanctions are eligible for prison, most—if not all—would actually have been on probation instead. Because of judges' reluctance to divert offenders from prison, many intermediate sanctions programs billed as prison alternatives actually serve as probation alternatives. As an example, consider boot camp programs, which are usually restricted to first-time property offenders who are sixteen to twenty-five years old. Boot camp, then, cannot be considered an effective prison alternative, since young, first-time property offenders seldom go to prison.

Probation alternatives (often called probation enhancements) face a similar problem. In theory, they should be restricted to the greatest risks on probation, those needing the most surveillance and control. Typically, however, the natural conservatism that accompanies new programs means that the true high-risk offender is made ineligible for the program, which is instead afforded to better risks on probation.

It should be clear that when intermediate sanctions are applied to the wrong target group, they cannot achieve their goals. When prison alternatives are applied to nonprison cases, they cannot save money; when probation enhancement programs are provided to low-risk clients, they cannot reduce much crime. One of the solutions advanced by some scholars is to use intermediate sanctions as backups for clients who fail on regular probation or parole. This makes it more likely that the target group is composed of high-risk, prison-bound offenders.

Problems of Bias. Race, sex, or age bias is a concern anywhere in the justice system, but it is a particular concern for intermediate sanctions. Since getting assigned to an intermediate sanction is usually a matter of official (usually judicial) discretion, the concern is that officials will be more likely to want to take a chance on white, middle-class offenders than on others. Many programs have found that nonwhites are more likely to stay in prison rather than receive alternative sanctions, and minorities are more likely to be subjected to tougher supervision instead of regular probation.

Alternative sanctions also tend to be designed for men, not for women. The understandable reason for this is that men make up over 80 percent of the corrections population. But if the result is that special programs are available to men but not to women, this is patently unfair. Moreover, the design of intermediate sanctions, which is often based on tough supervision, is questioned by some experts on female offenders. They are concerned that toughness may be inappropriate for many women offenders, whose problems require more of an emphasis on social services.

The solution to problems of bias is neither obvious nor uncontroversial. Most observers recognize that some discretion is necessary to place offenders in specialized programs. They believe that without the confidence of program officials, offenders are likely to fail. This means that automatic eligibility for these programs may not be a good idea. It may be necessary to recognize the potential for bias and to control for it by designing programs especially for women, making certain that cultural factors are taken into account in selecting offenders for them.

Surveillance and Control

The new intermediate sanctions have, for the most part, been developed during a period in which correctional policy has been enmeshed in the politics of "getting tough on crime." It is not surprising, then, that most of these alternatives tend to emphasize, at least in their public relations, their toughness. Boot camps are described as providing no-nonsense discipline; intensive supervision is expressly designed to incorporate surveillance and control as primary strategies with offenders.

Certainly this rhetoric is useful in obtaining public support for the programs. But do the programs themselves benefit from being so unabashedly tough? James Finckenauer's classic evaluation of the "scared straight" program in Rahway Prison provides a good illustration. When popular actor Peter Falk served as narrator in describing the program's main tenet—prisoners serving life in Rahway would use threatening and confrontational techniques with first-time juvenile offenders, literally to try to scare them into giving up petty crime—the public was impressed. Finckenauer's evaluation found, however, that scare tactics may backfire: The juveniles who went through the program were actually arrested more than a matched sample not sent to the program.[69]

There is growing evidence that the tough aspects of intermediate sanctions may not be totally positive. As we've seen, when both the requirements of supervision and the surveillance of offenders are increased, more violations occur. Whether it is in the interest of the system to increase violations by upgrading the supervision standards and their enforcement—by being tough—is an open question. If this tough approach has no impact on crime, but instead merely costs more money (through the need to process more violators), what is the benefit?

In many jurisdictions, violators are a serious management problem. In Oregon, recently, over 60 percent of new prison admissions were probation or parole violators, many of whom had not been accused of a new crime.[70] In other states, such as California and New York, if the rate of violations could be reduced, the costs of the equivalent of an entire prison's population could be saved. The increase in violations has been in part a product of more stringent enforcement and in part a result of improved surveillance, especially drug testing. Some people wonder whether the benefits of these changes have outweighed the costs.

The New Corrections Professional

Without a doubt, the advent of intermediate sanctions has changed the work world of the professional in corrections. The long-standing choice between prison and probation has been expanded to include community and residential options that run the gamut from tough, surveillance-oriented operations to supportive, treatment-based programs. The kind of professional needed to staff these programs varies from recent college graduates to experienced and well-trained mental health clinicians. Central to this growth, however, are two major shifts in the working environment of the new corrections professional.

First, organizations that are not governmental agencies have emerged to administer community corrections programs. Hundreds of nonprofit organizations now dot the correctional landscape. These organizations contract with agencies of probation and parole to provide services to clients in the community.

Second, there is an increased emphasis on accountability. The individualistic and discretionary work of past eras no longer exists. Instead, professionals use their discretion within boundaries, often defined as guidelines, that provide a set of rules for choosing actions with a case. For instance, a staff member may be told that each offender must be seen twice a month in the office and once a month in the community, and that in each contact, a urine sample must be taken. Rules such as these not only constrain discretion but also provide a basis for holding staff accountable for the way they handle offenders.

Third, the relationship between the professional and the client has become less important than the principles of criminal justice that underlie that relationship. Instead of training in psychology and counseling, for instance, the new corrections worker receives training in law and criminal justice decision making. This means that the sources of job satisfaction have shifted from helping offenders with their problems toward managing offenders through the system.

Thus, the new corrections professional is more accountable for decision making and is more oriented toward the system in carrying out agency policy. This has significant implications for motivation and training of staff, but it also means that in the traditional three-way balance between offender, staff, and agency, the latter has grown in importance.

PERSPECTIVES ON INTERMEDIATE SANCTIONS

Systems

Intermediate sanctions programs try to "fit into" the corrections system. That is, these sanctions have a true systems rationale in that they try to fill a gap in the array of penalties currently available, making for a more complete system of penalties. If they work correctly, intermediate sanctions will affect the work of every part of the corrections system. They will receive some of their cases from probation, where offenders were not likely to receive the level of supervision and control that they need. And they will receive some of their cases from institutional corrections, where the level of intervention is too extreme for the offender or the offense.

It is easy, then, to think of intermediate sanctions programs as attempts to assist other parts of the system in achieving their aims, but siphoning off inappropriate cases. But we can also see how intermediate sanctions programs could create pressure on these other parts of the system. By taking some of the "easier" cases from institutional corrections, they might then leave those prisons and jails with a more difficult population to manage overall. If this is the case, the job for institutional correctional administrators might get a bit harder, not easier. Likewise, if the tougher cases are taken from probation settings, then it may become harder for probation leaders to justify their budget requests, since the caseload is both smaller and less problematic. How the implementation of any intermediate sanction will impact the system cannot be predicted, so a certain amount of flexibility is necessary. Program administrators and budget managers may be directly affected. However it goes, we must recognize that the basic reason for intermediate sanctions is to change the system.

Evidence

There are two evidence questions directed toward intermediate sanctions: Do they get the right offenders? and Do they handle those offenders effectively?

Getting the right offenders is much more difficult than it seems. Intermediate sanctions programs are a kind of "diversion" program, and so they face all the pressures of any diversion approach. They also face a pressure of status quo for the offenders who have been going to older programs. These pressures make it hard, sometimes, for intermediate sanctions programs to attract the cases they were created to take.

Thus, a probation department will create an intensive probation supervision with the idea that it will supervise offenders who otherwise would go to prison or jail. However, the judges and prosecutors make ceratin that the IPS cases are not jail-bound, but instead the worst of the probation-bound offenders. But the usual "net widening" problem that correctional innovation must be concerned about does not apply to intermediate sanctions in the same way it does to other programs. Intermediate sanctions programs actually seek to widen the net—at least for some cases. If they get the "right kind" of clientele, some offenders who would have gotten probation will get the more stringent intermediate program, instead. Others who would have gone to a cell will also get the program.

Obviously, this presents a complex picture. How much of a mix is needed for the intermediate sanction approach to have the "right" cases? If 80 percent are diverted from probation, and only 20 percent from prison, is this good enough? The answer lies in the program itself—what was it built to do and who was it created to serve? For some programs, this kind of a mix will be good, for others it will not.

People

Intermediate sanctions programs are a "hybrid" in corrections: close to a kind of confinement, but also incorporating a certain degree of liberty. For this reason, they tend to attract a kind of "hybrid" correctional professional. It takes a special kind of person to want to work in these programs—a "hybrid" correctional employee.

Because these employees are asked to work with offenders who might have been incarcerated, there is often a sense that they need to be "tough." Yet at the same time, most intermediate sanctions programs place a premium on working effectively with offenders, so merely being tough is not enough. There is a need to incorporate strategies that will work in the longer term—strategies in which correctional professionals provide support, mentor clients, and serve as good behavioral models for change.

This brief summary illustrates the problem facing those who work in the field of intermediate sanctions: They are asked to be extremely versatile. This is a source of both job satisfaction and frustration. It is satisfying to be able to exercise judgement about how to handle the offenders placed under supervision, but it can be stressful when the technique required in one case is not right for the next.

Bureaucracy

Because the main problem facing intermediate sanctions programs is getting the "right" offenders, these approaches tend to develop rules—sometimes elaborate rules—for who is eligible. Most of these programs have requirements related to an offender's risk and current offense. Low-risk offenders who seem to be suitable for probation become eligible only if their offense is serious enough that closer supervision is warranted. By contrast, higher-risk offenders may be accepted into the program, so long as the current offense is not so serious as to suggest a term of incarceration.

The development of these eligibility rules lends a kind of "bureaucratic" quality to many intermediate sanctions programs, even when the programs are new and still have an innovative style. Sometimes, elaborate forms have to be completed by intake staff to determine if an offender can be accepted into an intermediate sanctions program. Other times, eligibility comes only when other correctional approaches have already failed. In either case, the bureaucratic feel of these programs can be that they are a bit "exclusive," and this can lead to conflict with other bureaucracies that have less control over which clients they are given to supervise.

THE FUTURE OF INTERMEDIATE SANCTIONS

What does the future hold for intermediate sanctions and community corrections? Without a crystal ball it is impossible to tell, but certainly three recurrent problems must be addressed by all those who support these programs.

First, some way must be found to overcome the seemingly immutable tendency of the criminal justice system to resist placing offenders in less restrictive options and instead keep increasing the level of corrections. As we have seen, studies of nonprison alternatives find that even the most successful programs enroll only a minority of offenders who would otherwise have been incarcerated. The usual pattern is to place offenders in prison first, then release them to the community. New alternative programs are filled with persons who formerly would have been placed on regular probation. Nonprison programs, whether they be intermediate sanctions or community corrections programs, must improve their ability to attract the kinds of offenders for which they are intended. It is possible that the improvements in technology, especially the use of satellites, will assist in the growth of intermediate sanctions.

Second, the purposes of these sanctions must be clarified. No program can operate successfully for long if its goals are not clearly defined. The goals espoused by most programs today are vague generalizations: reduction of overcrowding, rehabilitation, protecting the community, reintegration, cost effectiveness, and so on. Although no legitimate government operation can reject any of these considerations, some ordering of priorities must occur before these new forms of correctional functions can take their rightful place as core operations in the overall system.

Third, community support for these programs must become a central concern. Too often, citizens fear the offenders in their midst. Active measures must be taken to allay those fears, to help citizens become comfortable with a corrections mission that recognizes a wide array of programs other than incarceration-based punishments. This problem is especially important if there is to be an increase in the long-term development and implementation of intermediate sanctions. Without public support, the policymakers will continue to promote the "get tough" agenda that has proven to be politically beneficial for the last twenty years. If the public become more aware of the long-term financial and social benefits of intermediate sanctions, they may be more likely to withdraw their political support for candidates who promote institutional corrections as the best and only cure for crime in the United States.

SUMMARY

Intermediate sanctions is a new movement that seeks to establish correctional programs falling between standard probation and prison. Although a core argument for intermediate sanctions is that prisons are overcrowded, a second reason for this strategy is to improve justice by increasing sentencing options. Many jurisdictions have tried to develop a continuum of sanctions as a way of responding to the need for greater sentencing options.

Some intermediate sanctions programs are operated by the courts; others are operated by probation and by corrections agencies. The main forms of intermediate sanctions are fines, community service, restitution, intensive supervision, house arrest, electronic monitoring, day fines, shock incarceration, and boot camps. These innovations have not been widely studied, and little can be said definitively about how well they work.

If intermediate sanctions are to reach their potential, there are some key issues that must be addressed. These issues are sentencing, selection of offenders, surveillance and control, and personnel issues. In spite of mixed results, intermediate sanctions will probably be a vibrant part of corrections in the future because they meet two important goals: They provide more rational punishment alternatives and save correctional resources. In these two ways, intermediate sanctions reduce the need for either probation or incarceration.

┤ DISCUSSION QUESTIONS ├

1. Are intermediate sanctions better as a way to improve on probation or to avoid the negatives of imprisonment? Support your answer.
2. Should intermediate sanctions be run by traditional probation and prison systems, or by new agencies seeking to serve as alternatives to them?
3. If you were to develop a continuum of sanctions for your local county, what sanctions would

you include, and in what order? Describe your rationale.
4. Do you think that intermediate sanctions are acceptable to the general public in the current political climate?
5. What intermediate sanctions do you believe will survive well into the twenty-first century? Explain your position.

SUGGESTED READINGS

American Corrections Association. *Community Corrections.* Lanham, MD: ACA, 1996. A series of twenty-one papers on various aspects of intermediate sanctions, discussed from the point of view of the program administrator.

Anderson, David. *Sensible Justice: Alternatives to Prison.* New York: New Press, 1998. Specially written for an informed lay audience, the book provides a comprehensive review of the argument for alternatives to incarceration, and develops a politically feasible case for expanded use of alternatives.

Byrne, James M., Lurigio, Arthur J., and Petersilia, Joan. *Smart Sentencing: The Emergence of Intermediate Sanctions.* Newbury Park, CA: Sage, 1992. Explores various issues in the design and implementation of intermediate sanctions programs.

DiMascio, W. M. *Seeking Justice: Crime and Punishment in America.* New York: Edna McConnell Clark Foundation, 1997. Document produced by private foundation that covers a wide range of current topics in corrections with the goal of dispelling myths of crime and punishment in the United States.

Mair, George. *Evaluating the Effectiveness of Community Penalties.* London: Avebury Press, 1995. Evaluates electronic monitoring, intensive supervision, and community service, among other types of probation programs.

McGarry, Peggy, and Carter, Madeliene M. (eds.). *The Intermediate Sanctions Handbook: Experiences and Tools for Practitioners.* Washington, DC: National Institute of Corrections, 1993. Provides exercises and "how-to" advice for the successful design and implementation of intermediate sanctions programs.

Morris, Norval, and Tonry, Michael. *Between Prison and Probation: Intermediate Punishments in a Rational Sentencing System.* Oxford: Oxford University Press, 1990. Urges development of a range of intermediate punishments that can be used to sanction offenders more severely than nominal probation but less severely than incarceration.

WEB SITES

Web site for learning more about the use of community corrections alternatives worldwide
www.iccaweb.org

Web site for an overview of findings on intermediate sanctions programs in the state of Pennsylvania
www.pccd.state.pa.us

Web site for learning more about the history of community corrections and intermediate sanctions
www.ncjrs.org/txtfiles/bcamps06.txt

Web site from the National Institute of Corrections concerning community corrections and intermediate sanctions
www.nicic.org/about/divisions/comm_corr.htm

Web site that describes the use of global positioning systems (GPS) to track offenders
www.sierrawireless.com/solutions/protech.html

Web site that provides links to additional resources in corrections
www.ncjrs.org/corrwww.html

NOTES

1. Norval Morris and Michael Tonry, *Between Prison and Probation: Intermediate Punishments in a Rational Sentencing System* (New York: Oxford University Press, 1990), p. 3.

2. J. T. James, "The Halfway House Movement," in *Alternatives to Prison: Community Based Corrections,* ed. G. R. Perlstein and T. R. Phelps (Pacific Palisades, CA: Goodyear, 1975).

3. Erika Fairchild and Harry R. Dammer, *Comparative Criminal Justice* (Belmont, CA: Wadsworth–Thompson Press, 2000) p. 214.

4. E. Apospori and G. Alpert, "Research Note: The Role of Differential Experience with the Criminal Justice System in Changes in Perception of Severity of Legal Sanctions over Time," *Crime and Delinquency* 39:2 (1993): 184–194; see also B. M. Couch, "Is Incarceration Really Worse? Analysis of Offenders' Preferences for Prison over Probation," *Justice Quarterly* 10:1 (1993): 67–88.

5. U. Zvekic, "International Trends in Non-Custodial Sanctions," in *Promoting Probation Internationally,* ed. R. Ville, U. Zvekic, and J. F. Klau, Proceedings of the International Training Workshop on Probation, July 1997, Valletta, Malta (Rome/London: United Nations Interregional Crime and Justice Research Institute, Publication No. 58).

6. Ken Pease, "Community Service Orders," in *Crime and Justice: A Review of Research,* vol. 6, ed. Michael Tonry and Norval Morris (Chicago: University of Chicago Press, 1985), pp. 36–80.

7. M. Shilton, International Association of Residential and Community Services, Survey of Selected States, 1994.

8. U.S. Department of Justice, "Probation and Parole Statistics," February 2002. www.ojp.usdoj.gov/bjs/pandp.htm

9. Joan Petersilia, Susan Turner, and James Kahan, *Prison vs. Probation in California: Public Choices and Alternatives* (Santa Monica, CA: Rand Corporation, 1987).

10. Michael G. Turner, Francis T. Cullen, Jody L. Sundt, and Brandon K. Applegate, "Public Tolerance for Community-Based Sanctions," *The Prison Journal* 77:1 (March 1997): 6–26.

11. D. Rose and T. Clear, "Incarceration, Social Capital and Crime: Examining the Unintended Consequences of Incarceration." *Criminology* 36:3 (August 1998), pp. 441–479.

12. James M. Byrne, Arthur J. Lurigio, and Joan Petersilia, *Smart Sentencing: The Emergence of Intermediate Sanctions* (Newbury Park, CA: Sage, 1992).

13. Don M. Gottfredson and Stephen D. Gottfredson, "Studies and Risk: Assessing the Potential for Criminal Violence," Report of the Justice Policy Research Corporation, Sacramento, CA, August 1988.

14. James Austin and Barry Krisberg, "The Unmet Promise of Alternatives to Incarceration," *Crime and Delinquency* 28 (1982): 374–409.

15. Bureau of Justice Statistics, *Correctional Populations in the United States, 1996* (Washington, DC: U.S. Department of Justice), pp. 40–41.

16. George Cole, "Innovations in Collecting and Enforcing Fines," *National Institute of Justice Research in Action* 215 (July/August 1989): 2–6.

17. Thomas Weigend, "Fines Reduce Use of Prison Sentences in Germany," in *Intermediate Sanctions in Overcrowded Times,* ed. M. Tonry and K. Hamilton (Boston: Northeastern University Press, 1995), p. 43.

18. S. T. Hillsman, "Day Fines," in *Between Prison and Probation: Intermediate Punishments in a Rational Sentencing System* by N. Morris and M. Tonry (New York: Oxford University Press, 1990), p. 19.

19. "How to Use Structured Fines (Day Fines) as an Intermediate Sanction," written by the Bureau of Justice Assistance and the Vera Institute of Justice, Monograph NCJ 156242, November 1996.

20. Karla R. Spaulding, "Hit Them Where It Hurts: RICO Criminal Forfeitures and White-Collar Crime," *Journal of Criminal Law and Criminology* 80 (1989): 197–198.

21. *Austin v. United States,* 61 Lw. 4811 (1993).

22. Joe Hudson and Steven Chesney, "Research on Restitution: A Review and Assessment," in *Offender Restitution in Theory and Action,* ed. Burt Galaway and J. Hudson (Lexington, MA: Lexington Books, 1978), pp. 131–148; and K. Pease, S. Billingham, and I. Earnshaw, *Community Service Assessed in 1976* (London: Home Office Research Unit, 1977).

23. D. Parent, J. Byrne, V. Tsarfaty, L. Valade, and J. Esselman, *Day Reporting Centers,* vol. 1 (Washington, DC: National Institute of Justice, 1995).

24. Jack McDevitt and Robyn Miliane, "Day Reporting Centers: An Innovative Concept in Intermediate Sanctions," in *Smart Sentencing,* ed. Byrne, Lurigio, and Petersilia, p. 153.

25. Dale G. Parent, *Day Reporting Centers for Criminal Offenders: A Descriptive Analysis of Existing Programs* (Washington, DC: National Institute of Justice, 1990), p. 1.

26. D. C. McBride and C. VanderWaal, "Day Reporting Centers as an Alternative for Drug Using Offenders," *Journal of Drug Issues* 27:2 (Spring 1997): 379–398.

27. E. L. Curtin and J. McDevitt, *Massachusetts Day Reporting Centers Task Force: Final Report* (Boston: Massachusetts Executive Office of Human Services, 1990).

28. Peter Jones and Alan Harland, "Edgecombe: A Preliminary Analysis" (paper presented to the American Probation and Parole Association, St. Louis, MO, September 1, 1992).

29. G. Mair and C. Nee, "Day Centre Reconviction Rates," *British Journal of Criminology* 32:3 (Summer 1992).

30. W. M. DiMascio, *Seeking Justice: Crime and Punishment in America* (New York: Edna McConnell Clark Foundation, 1997).

31. Camille G. Camp and George M. Camp. *The 2000 Corrections Yearbook: Adult Corrections* (Middletown, CT: Criminal Justice Institute, 2000), p. 176.

32. Billie S. Erwin, *Evaluation of Intensive Probation Supervision in Georgia* (Atlanta: Georgia Department of Corrections, 1987).

33. E. Latessa, L. F. Travis, A. Holsinger, and J. Hartman. *Evaluation of Ohio's Community Corrections Act Program and Community Based Correctional Facilities: Final Report* (Cincinnati, OH: Division of Criminal Justice, University of Cincinnati, 1997).

34. Joan Petersilia and Susan Turner, *Intensive Supervision for High-Risk Offenders: Findings from Three California Experiments* (Santa Monica, CA: Rand Corporation, 1990).

35. B. Fulton, E. J. Latessa, A. Stichman, and L. F. Travis, "The State of ISP: Research and Policy Implications," *Federal Probation* 61:4 (1997) 65–75.

36. A. J. Lurigio and J. Petersilia, "The Emergence of Intensive Probation Programs in the United States," in *Smart Sentencing*, ed. Byrne, Lurigio, and Petersilia.

37. Petersilia and Turner, *Intensive Supervision Probation for High-Risk Offenders.*

38. P. J. Hofer and B. S. Meierhofer, *Home Confinement* (Washington, DC: Federal Judicial Center, 1988).

39. Marc Renzema, "Home Confinement Programs, Development, Implementation, and Impact," in *Smart Sentencing,* ed. Byrne, Lurigio, and Petersilia, p. 47.

40. Camille G. Camp and George M. Camp, *The 2000 Corrections Yearbook: Adult Corrections* (Middletown, CT: Criminal Justice Institute, 2000), p. 170; and J. R. Lilly, "Electronic Monitoring in the United States," in *Intermediate Sanctions in Overcrowded Times,* ed. M. Tonry and K. Hamilton (Boston: Northeastern University Press, 1995), pp. 112–120.

41. S. X. Zhang, R. Polakow, and B. J. Nidorf, "Varied Uses of Electronic Monitoring: The Los Angeles County Experience," in *Intermediate Sanctions: Sentencing in the 1990s,* ed. J. Smykla and W. Selke (Cincinnati, OH: Anderson, 1994).

42. National Law Enforcement and Corrections Technology Center, "Keeping Track of Electronic Monitoring" (Rockville, MD, October 1999), p. 1.

43. Terry L. Baumer and Robert I. Mendelsohn, *The Electronic Monitoring of Non-Violent Convicted Felons; An Experiment in Home Detention,* final report of grant no. 86-IJ-CX 0041 (Indianapolis: Indiana University School of Public and Environmental Affairs, 1990).

44. A. K. Schmidt, "Electronic Monitoring Offenders Increases," NIJ Report (NCJ 116750) (Washington, DC: National Institute of Justice, 1988), pp. 2–5.

45. J. R. Lilly, R. A. Ball, G. D. Curry, and R. C. Smith, "The Pride Inc. Program: An Evaluation of Five Years of Electronic Monitoring," *Federal Probation* 56:4 (1992): 42–47.

46. R. A. Ball, R. C. Huff, and J. R. Lilly, *House Arrest and Correctional Policy: Doing Time at Home* (Newbury Park, CA: Sage, 1988).

47. T. Forgach, "Cost Effectiveness and the Use of House Arrest with Electronic Monitoring in Pima County, Arizona," *Journal of Offender Monitoring* 5:2 (1992).

48. K. C. Courtwright, B. L. Berg, and R. J. Mutchnick, "Effects of House Arrest with Electronic Monitoring on DUI Offenders," *Journal of Offender Rehabilitation* 24:3/4 (1997): 35–51.

49. M. P. Brown and E. Preston, "Electronic House Arrest: An Examination of Citizen Attitudes," *Crime and Delinquency* 41:3 (July 1995): 332–346.

50. National Law Enforcement and Corrections Technology Center, "Keeping Track of Electronic Monitoring," p. 5.

51. See A. Waldron and N. R. Angelino, "Shock Probation: A Natural Experiment on the Effect of a Short Period of Incarceration" (paper presented to National Conference on Criminal Justice Evaluation, Washington, DC, February 22, 1977).

52. Camp and Camp, *The 2000 Corrections Yearbook*, p. 120.

53. D. L. MacKenzie, "Boot Camps," in *Encyclopedia of American Prisons,* ed. M. D. McShane and F. P. Williams (New York: Garland, 1996), pp. 61–65.

54. Jody Klein-Saffran, "Bureau of Prisons: Expanding Intermediate Sanctions Through Intensive Confinement Centers," February 5, 2000. www.kci.org/publication/bootcamp/docs/nij/Correctional_Boot_Camps/chpt6.htm

55. D. L. MacKenzie and C. C. Souryal, "Inmates' Attitude Change During Incarceration: A Comparison of Boot Camp with Traditional Prison," *Justice Quarterly* 12:2 (June 1995).

56. D. L. MacKenzie and A. Piquero, "The Impact of Shock Incarceration Programs on Prison Crowding," *Crime and Delinquency* 40:2 (April 1994): 222–249.

57. R. C. Cronin, *Boot Camps for Adults and Juvenile Offenders: An Overview and Update* (Washington, DC: U.S. Department of Justice, 1994).

58. Doris L. MacKenzie and H. Donaldson, "Boot Camp Prisons for Women Offenders," *Criminal Justice Review,* 21:1, 21–43.

59. A. Gover, G. J. Styver and D. L. MacKenzie, "Boot Camps and Traditional Correctional Facilities for Juveniles: A Comparison of the Participants, The Daily Activities, and Environments." *Journal of Criminal Justice* 28:1, 53–68.

60. Camp and Camp, *The 2000 Corrections Yearbook,* p. 125.

61. Petersilia and Turner, "Intensive Supervision Probation for High-Risk Offenders."

62. W. Spelman, "The Severity of Intermediate Sanctions," *Journal of Research in Crime and Delinquency* 32:2 (May 1995): 107–136.

63. Peter B. Wood, Harold G. Grasmick, "Towards the Development of Punishment Equivalencies: Male and Female Inmates Rate the Severity of Alternative Sanctions Compared to Prison," *Justice Quarterly* 16:1 (March 1999).

64. Lawrence Sherman et al., University of Maryland, *Preventing Crime: What Works, What Doesn't and What's Promising* (Washington, DC: Government Printing Office, 1997). See especially chap. 9, pp. 9-1–9-76, by Doris L. MacKenzie.

65. Joan Petersilia, "A Decade of Experimenting with Intermediate Sanctions: What Have We Learned?" *Federal Probation* 62:2 (1998): 3–9.

66. Paul Gendreau and Tracy Little, "A Meta-analysis of the Effectiveness of Sanctions on Offender Recidivism," unpublished manuscript, University of New Brunswick, St. John, B.C., 1993.

67. Andrew von Hirsch, Martin Wasik, and Judith Greene, "Punishment in the Community and the Principles of Dessert," *Rutgers Law Journal* 20 (1989): 595–618.

68. Joan Petersilia and Susan Turner, "An Evaluation of Intensive Probation in California," *Journal of Criminal Law and Criminology* 82:3 (1991): 610–658.

69. James O. Finckenauer, *Scared Straight and the Panacea Phenomenon* (Englewood Cliffs, NJ: Prentice Hall, 1982).

70. Annual Report of the Oregon Sentencing Commission (Salem, OR: Oregon Sentencing Commission, 1992), p. 23.

Chapter 8

Probation

The New York City Probation Department is one of the most overworked and underappreciated organizations in the nation's largest city. Probation officers in New York say they have, for years, felt their efforts are poorly understood and badly supported by the city that pays their salaries. With caseloads approaching 200 felons per officer, workload relief seems a financial impossibility in a city that grapples with perennial financial strains along with growing numbers in the city's court system, most of whom end up on probation. An improvement in public perception of probation seems an even more Herculean task, given the general public indifference (or worse, antagonism) toward probation.

A few years ago, to combat the unwieldy caseloads, the probation department undertook what the *New York Times* called "a bold experiment," setting up a two-tier system of supervision: Violent offenders were to be seen intensively in individual and group counseling sessions; nonviolent offenders would not see a probation officer but would report electronically to kiosks—banklike ATM machines—that use laser techniques to read their fingerprints.[1] This new system had the desired result of easing the workload of probation officers, allowing them to focus their attention on the most serious cases. But it did nothing about the poor public appraisal of the value of probation in the first place. In fact, the idea that convicted felons would be monitored by machines seemed to give further support to a general public distrust of probation in New York City.

So the probation officials in the city have decided to take a new, even more radical step: They are closing down some of their downtown offices and taking the probation supervision function out into the community. In a new project called Neighborhood Shield, probation officials have moved some of their most effective staff away from their downtown offices out into decentralized locations in some of New York City's toughest, most troubled neighborhoods.[2]

The plan has two aims. First, using partnerships with community groups and law enforcement, the probation department hopes to provide more effective supervision of the offenders who live in those neighborhoods and thus help improve public safety. Second, and just as important, probation wants to

Photo: A probation officer counsels a young offender in Los Angeles.
© A. Ramey/Stock Boston

improve its image with the public, and it is beginning this work in the neighborhoods where the probation caseload lives.

These two innovations speak volumes about modern probation. Instead of dealing with petty offenders, today's probation departments are increasingly called on to deal with tough, even violent offenders. Yet they are asked to handle this more difficult workload under decreasing levels of funding. In New York City, probation officials are trying to forge a new way out of this dilemma. If the experiment works, probation in New York and other big cities will never be the same.

Probation is by far the most extensively used form of corrections in the United States. Nearly 65 percent of all adults under correctional authority are serving probation sentences. On December 31, 2000, state and local probation agencies supervised more than 3.8 million adult U.S. residents. (See Table 8.1.)

TABLE 8.1 ADULTS ON PROBATION, 2000

Region and jurisdiction	Probation population 1/1/00	Probation population 12/31/00	Percent change during 2000	Number on probation on 12/31/00 per 100,000 adult residents
U.S. total	3,779,922	3,839,532	1.6	1,836
Federal	32,843	31,539	−4.0	15
State	3,747,079	3,807,993	1.6	1,821
Northeast	574,264	587,601	2.3	1,449
Connecticut[a]	55,070	55,070	—	2,148
Maine	7,524	7,788	3.5	800
Massachusetts	46,267	45,233	−2.2	933
New Hampshire[a,b]	3,629	3,629	—	392
New Jersey	128,984	130,610	1.3	2,064
New York	183,068	191,970	4.9	1,344
Pennsylvania[b]	118,770	121,034	1.9	1,293
Rhode Island	21,753	22,964	5.6	2,869
Vermont	9,199	9,303	1.1	2,017
Midwest	876,139	899,597	2.7	1,884
Illinois	134,270	139,029	3.5	1,515
Indiana	105,071	107,673	2.5	2,390
Iowa	19,675	21,147	7.5	964
Kansas	16,785	15,996	−4.7	810
Michigan[b]	170,041	173,676	2.1	2,365
Minnesota	113,265	114,468	1.1	3,151
Missouri	52,493	49,975	−4.8	1,199
Nebraska	20,462	21,483	5.0	1,704
North Dakota	2,783	2,789	0.2	579
Ohio[b]	184,246	194,875	5.8	2,302
South Dakota	3,790	4,214	11.2	763
Wisconsin	53,258	54,272	1.9	1,359

TABLE 8.1   (CONTINUED)

Region and jurisdiction	Probation population 1/1/00	Probation population 12/31/00	Percent change during 2000	Number on probation on 12/31/00 per 100,000 adult residents
South	1,556,545	1,564,576	0.5	2,095
Alabama[b]	40,595	40,627	0.1	1,222
Arkansas	28,505	30,353	6.5	1,523
Delaware	20,976	20,052	−4.4	3,404
District of Columbia	12,129	12,061	−0.6	2,639
Florida[b]	291,631	294,786	1.1	2,390
Georgia[b]	307,686	308,344	0.2	5,124
Kentucky	18,988	20,610	8.5	676
Louisiana	35,118	35,854	2.1	1,103
Maryland	81,286	83,852	3.2	2,128
Mississippi	13,427	15,118	12.6	731
North Carolina	105,095	105,949	0.8	1,741
Oklahoma[b]	28,075	30,994	10.4	1,212
South Carolina	48,585	42,883	−11.7	1,428
Tennessee	39,596	40,829	3.1	952
Texas	446,685	442,251	−1.0	2,955
Virginia	32,098	33,955	5.8	636
West Virginia[b]	6,070	6,058	−0.2	431
West	740,131	756,219	2.2	1,638
Alaska	4,547	4,760	4.7	1,091
Arizona[b]	56,960	60,751	6.7	1,614
California	332,414	343,145	3.2	1,394
Colorado[b]	48,733	47,084	−3.4	1,471
Hawaii	15,707	15,525	−1.2	1,695
Idaho[c]	36,436	35,091	—	3,794
Montana[b]	5,906	6,043	2.3	899
Nevada	11,787	12,189	3.4	820
New Mexico	9,878	10,512	6.4	802
Oregon	44,777	46,199	3.2	1,794
Utah	9,397	9,828	4.6	649
Washington[b]	159,748	160,977	0.8	3,675
Wyoming	3,841	4,115	7.1	1,128

Note: Because of nonresponse or incomplete data, the probation population for some jurisdictions on December 31, 2000, does not equal the population on January 1, 2000, plus entries, minus exits.

—Not calculated.

[a]All data were estimated.

[b]Data for entries and exits were estimated for nonreporting agencies.

[c]Data include estimates for misdemeanors based on admissions.

Source: www.ojp.usdoj.gov/bjs/pandp.htm

These figures reflect that there are over three times more adults on probation than in all penal institutions combined. Even though it is the escalating prison growth that gets the public's attention, since 1990 the nation's probation population has grown an average of 3 percent per year.[3] Since 1985, this population has actually grown at a faster rate than the incarcerated population.

Despite the wide use of probation, it is frequently given short shrift by media critics, who tend to portray it as "a slap on the wrist." In everyday conversation, the word is often used with a sense of derision: "I bet that offender will get *probation*"—almost as if the word itself is distasteful to the tongue. This notion is so widespread that a well-known scholarly work on correctional policy once referred to probation as "a kind of standing joke."[4] These views sharply contrast with official policies. For example, government devoted over a quarter of a billion dollars in federal funds to improve and expand probation in the past decade alone, and supervision in the community is being used as the sanction for more and more offenders. Further, advocates of intermediate sanctions point to probation as the base on which more severe punishments can be built.

Although probation may well deserve some criticism, people's common perceptions of it are almost always based on a simplistic idea of what it is and how it works. As it turns out, probation is one of the most successful forms of criminal sanctions. It is widely used and, usually, the most cost-effective sentencing strategy available to a judge. It is unfortunate that probation is so often misunderstood, because not only is it an important and useful correctional function, but it can also be a deeply satisfying professional career.

In this chapter, we explore the complicated ideas and practices that constitute modern probation. The formal definition of probation is a sentence the offender serves in the community while under supervision. But, in fact, we see that probation is many things to many people, with three quite separable functions representing three very different client groups. To the judge, probation constitutes an information service to help select a sentence. To the offender, probation is a temporary status that must be survived. To the corrections system, probation is a bureaucracy, an agency that handles much of the work of the entire corrections process. Since its earliest days, probation leaders have struggled to balance their obligations to the court, to the offender, and to sister correctional agencies.

In recent years, it has become increasingly clear that probation must also respect a further obligation—to the community in which the system operates. Probation is responsible for a sensitivity to victims of crime and for a willingness to consider community safety in the actions taken with offenders on probation. Probation must also help neighbors adjust to the presence of an offender in their midst, even as it seeks to help the offender adjust in the community.

To be successful, probation must balance these different roles and integrate them into an overall work strategy. Probation must be accessible to the court

JOHN AUGUSTUS (1785–1859)

John Augustus was a Boston bootmaker who became a self-appointed probation officer, thereby developing the concept of probation as an alternative to incarceration. His initial probation effort occurred in the Boston Police Court in 1841 when he posted bail for a man charged with being a common drunkard. Because his philanthropic activities made Augustus a frequent observer in the courts, the judge was willing to defer sentencing for three weeks and release the man into Augustus's custody. At the end of this brief probationary period, the man convinced the judge that he had reformed and therefore received a nominal fine. The concept of probation had been born.

Continuing his interest in criminal justice reform, Augustus was frequently present in Boston courts, acting as counsel and furnishing bail. He found homes for juvenile offenders and frequently obtained lodging and employment for adults accused or convicted of violating Boston's vice or temperance laws. Between 1842 and 1858 he bailed out 1,152 men and 794 women, making himself liable for $243,235 and preventing these individuals from being held in jail to await trial. He reported great success with his charges—of the first 1,100 offenders he discussed in his autobiography, he claimed only one had forfeited bond—and asserted that, with help, most of them eventually led upright lives. Since Augustus belonged to no charitable or philanthropic society, his primary sources of financial support were his own business and voluntary contributions. He never received a salary from any organization.

As a result of Augustus's efforts, criminal justice gained a new practice that has since become commonplace.

for information about offenders, and it must be sensitive to judicial priorities for sentencing. Once an offender is placed on probation, there must be an effective and appropriate supervision plan to maintain the offender in the community. This plan must be carried out with a recognition of the role of probation in the larger corrections system, which includes a recognition of the impact of probation decisions on other corrections agencies and on the broader community.

Many of the complaints about probation are in reality complaints about one or another of these functions. To some extent, the problems probation confronts stem from rather natural conflicts in carrying out the mission: Time spent serving the information needs of the court must be taken from that available to assist and monitor the offender and work with community groups. Support given to the offender's adjustment often requires taking calculated risks about community safety. The needs of the corrections bureaucracy impede innovation and imagination in other functions. It is not surprising that, with so many competing "customers" to please, the probation business sometimes comes under such heat.

Despite the obvious importance of probation, its work is carried out in an atmosphere of social and political ambivalence about punishment. This ambivalence, together with uncertainty about treatment methods, leaves probation in a quandary: We ordinarily rely heavily on it in sentencing offenders, but we seem to have limited confidence in its corrective capacities.

Modern probation seeks to address this ambivalence through a new clarity about its complicated mission. Indeed, probation is no longer exclusively a sentence imposed in lieu of prison. In various jurisdictions, one or more of the following probation approaches apply:

- *Split sentence:* The court specifies a period of incarceration to be followed by a period of probation.
- *Modification of sentence:* The original sentencing court may reconsider an offender's prison sentence within a limited time and modify it to probation.
- *Shock incarceration:* An offender sentenced to incarceration is released after a period of time in confinement (the shock) and resentenced to probation.
- *Intermittent incarceration:* An offender on probation may spend weekends or nights in a local jail.
- *Shock probation:* The practice of sentencing offenders to prison, allowing them to apply for probationary release, and then resentencing them to probation. The term *shock* is used because release supposedly comes as a surprise to the offender.

THE ORGANIZATION OF PROBATION TODAY

Probation originated in a court, and the first probation agencies were units of the judicial branches of city and county governments, primarily in the eastern United States. As the idea of probation caught on and moved westward, variations in its organization were attempted. Probation has been placed in the executive branch, it has been subjected to statewide unification, and it has been consolidated with parole.

Three general issues are involved in the organization of probation: (1) whether it should be centralized or decentralized, (2) whether it should be administered by the judiciary or the executive branch, and (3) whether it should be combined with parole services.

Should Probation Be Centralized or Decentralized?

The centralization issue concerns the location of authority to administer probation services. Proponents of decentralization argue that an agency administered by a city or county instead of a state is smaller, more flexible, and better able to respond to the unique problems of the community. Because decentralized probation draws its support from the community and from its city or county governments, it can offer more appropriate supervision for its clients and make better use of existing community resources.

In contrast, centralization places authority for a state's probation activities in a single statewide administrative body. Proponents of this approach assert that local probation has been characterized by a lack of professionalism and a tendency to follow outdated practices. State agencies, they argue, are larger, can train staff to take a variety of roles, and can implement broader programs with greater equality in supervision and services.

Who Should Administer Probation?

Although the recent trend has been away from judicially administered probation, many observers (especially those who seek greater accountability in probation) believe that the probation function rightfully belongs under the judiciary. See Figure 8.1 for a description of the seven jurisdictional patterns of probation. The usual claim is that under judicial administration probation is more responsive to the desires of the sentencing judge, who is more likely to scrutinize supervision when it is performed by judicial employees. Also, probation officers' morale is believed to be higher when they work closely with judges.

Proponents of placing probation under the executive branch argue that the judiciary is ill prepared to manage a human services operation. To coordinate and upgrade the quality of a human services operation like probation requires the full attention of professional public administrators. As the National Advisory Commission noted, placing probation under the executive branch would result in better allocation of probation services, increased interaction and administrative coordination between corrections and allied human services, increased access to the legislature and the budgeting process, and more appropriate service priorities.[5]

Should Probation Be Combined with Parole?

Probation and parole are analogous services in that both supervise offenders who are serving portions of their sentences in the community. Indeed, the growth in the use of split sentences and shock probation means that probation often begins after a jail or even prison term—just as with parole.

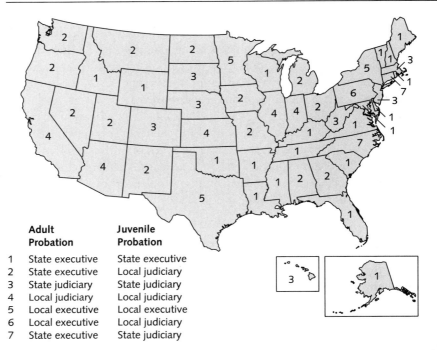

FIGURE 8.1 THE SEVEN JURISDICTIONAL ARRANGEMENTS FOR PROBATION, BY STATE

	Adult Probation	Juvenile Probation
1	State executive	State executive
2	State executive	Local judiciary
3	State judiciary	State judiciary
4	Local judiciary	Local judiciary
5	Local executive	Local executive
6	Local executive	Local judiciary
7	State executive	State judiciary

Source: American Correctional Association, *ACA Directory 1995* (College Park, MD: American Correctional Association, 1995).

Because of these similarities, many states have combined probation and parole functions into a single agency, which promotes more efficient hiring and training practices. Arguably, the professionalization of community supervision officers also is promoted by such comprehensive community correctional approaches.

There are, however, subtle but important distinctions between probationers and parolees that some experts suggest are hard to sustain in a unified system. Probation clients ordinarily are less deeply involved in criminal lifestyles, and parole clients always face the serious problems involved in reentering the community after longer periods of incarceration. These differences call for different handling, which some people believe can best be accomplished by separate agencies.

No solution to the problem of how to organize probation is at hand. Rather than searching for a single "best" way to organize probation, it may be more fruitful to look at how criminal justice services are generally operated in a state or region. In jurisdictions with a tradition of strong local government, decentralized probation under the executive branch may be the best alternative. In states that typically have provided services through centralized, large-scale bureaucracies, perhaps probation should be a part of such services. Likewise, a strong judiciary with a history of administrative competence may be the optimal site for probation authority.

THE TWO FUNCTIONS OF PROBATION: INVESTIGATION AND SUPERVISION

Even with the increasing complication of probation work, there are still two main functions performed by all probation systems: investigation and supervision. No matter the specifics of a given probation agency's structure or practices, certain aspects of investigation and supervision are uniform. In this section, we define and explore these two functions.

Investigation involves the preparation of a **presentence investigation (PSI)** report to be used by the judge in sentencing an offender. Typically, the PSI is ordered by the court following the offender's conviction (often on a guilty plea). A date is set for sentencing the offender, and in the interim the probation officer conducts the investigation and prepares a report.

The PSI process usually begins with an interview of the newly convicted offender to obtain basic background information. The probation officer then seeks to verify, clarify, and explore the information derived from (or left out of) the initial interview. The final PSI document is a summary of what has been learned and an evaluation of the offender, often with a sentence recommendation.

Supervision begins once an offender is sentenced to probation. There is no standard way to describe the supervision process, because the policies and practices vary greatly from agency to agency. In general, supervision involves three steps:

1. A relationship is established with the offender, and the roles of officer and offender are defined.
2. Certain supervision aims are pursued to help the offender comply with conditions established by the court (often directed at helping the offender confront significant needs or problems in his or her life).
3. On the basis of the offender's response to supervision, a decision is made on how to terminate probation. This decision may be early termination based on satisfactory adjustment, termination because the sentence has expired, or revocation because of a new conviction or violation of probation conditions set by the judge or probation officer.

This description of supervision is, of course, very general. As we point out later in this chapter, the leeway typically given officers in carrying out supervision makes management of this function very difficult. For this reason, many probation administrators have recently begun to require officers to use standardized offender classification and supervision techniques.

Investigation and supervision are divergent functions. In investigating the client and preparing a PSI report, the probation officer is working primarily with other human service professionals—teachers, officials, psychologists, and so forth. There is often a sense of partnership with the judge: Both parties seek the best sentence and therefore value useful, accurate information on which to base the disposition. The investigation will also be used by other correctional agencies to help classify the offender after sentencing and to perform research on program effectiveness. The professional relationships the probation officer establishes in performing investigations reinforce self-esteem and job satisfaction. Moreover, the tangible product—the report—can be a well-written, high-quality piece of work. Thus, the investigation function places the probation officer in the service of two of the primary clients of probation—the judge and the corrections bureaucracy.

Supervision, by contrast, is fraught with uncertainty and error. There are no standard solutions to the problems faced by most probationers, and the daily interactions with clients, many of whom are troubled and hard to manage, may provide little sense of worthwhile accomplishment. Further, there is seldom a tangible product; instead, work consists of a series of tasks loosely connected to eventual rehabilitative results. Often the main "customers" of this part of the job, the offender and the community, harbor resentments and suspicions about the probation officer and are resistant to the task requirements the officer faces.

This difference in the task structures of the two functions often puts informal pressure on probation officers to give investigation a higher priority than supervision. The quality of the investigation is more visible to superiors than the quality of supervision; in effect, then, "producing a sound, professionally appealing report has become more important than serving the client who is the subject of that report."[6]

To circumvent this problem, large probation departments "specialize" their staff—they assign some officers exclusively to supervision and others to investigation. Although there are some obvious efficiencies in this approach, there are inefficiencies as well. The officer who supervises a client must learn much of the information that has already been discovered by the presentence officer. Similarly, when probationers are convicted of new offenses, it is easier for the supervision officer to write a PSI report, given his or her familiarity with the case. Ironically, specialization does not necessarily protect the supervision function: Many times the best staff members are assigned to the PSI units and top priority is given to maintaining an adequate PSI workforce, even in the face of unwieldy supervision caseloads. This happens in agencies that place their highest priority on maintaining a satisfied judiciary.

Nevertheless, it is much easier to manage a probation system whose workers are specialized. Accountability for the timeliness and accuracy of PSIs is enhanced, while the operation of supervision routines according to agency policies can be more easily ensured. Therefore, the trend is toward specialization of these functions, almost as if they were two different jobs.

THE INVESTIGATION FUNCTION

We first examine the PSI—its purpose and content—and discuss its typical uses. The primary presentence investigation helps the judge select an appropriate sentence. Among its secondary purposes are to help with eventual classification decisions regarding probation, institutions, and parole agencies that may encounter the offender; to aid in treatment planning; to aid parole decisions; and to serve as a document for systematic research.

Purpose

Despite its many other uses, the true value of the PSI lies in its role in the sentencing process. Its importance is compounded by the fact that there are no uniformly accepted guidelines or rationales for sentencing. Individual judges, even those in the same court system, may vary in the weight they give to factors in the case. The PSI must therefore be comprehensive enough to meet the information needs of judges with a variety of sentencing perspectives.

For most of this century, judges needed a great deal of information for sentencing decisions. For most crimes and in most circumstances, judges had a great deal of latitude in selecting a sentence. They could place an offender in prison or instead try probation for most offenses, and the length of the sentence was also a matter of judicial discretion. Given such broad latitude, judges needed information to assist them in arriving at a decision: Has this offender been given probation before? Does the offender show an interest in treatment programs? Can the offender benefit from drug treatment? Questions such as these would help the judge choose from among a variety of sanctions the one approach that best fit the circumstances of the case.

Beginning in the mid-1970s and continuing throughout the last twenty-five years, attacks on judicial discretion at sentencing led to numerous revisions in state and federal penal codes. Judges' freedom to select sentences and sentence lengths became severely constrained. Increasingly, the penal code itself dictated whether probation was available as a sentence and, if not, the presumed prison sentence the judge would impose. In cases where the court was given discretion, the factors to be considered in selecting the actual sentence were carefully spelled out. As a consequence, judicial information is now less of a necessity for deciding a sentence. The result is that in those states where sentencing is determined by law, the PSI has become less important as part of the sentencing process.

Some observers regret this change. They argue that judges need a certain amount of discretion in choosing a sentence, because no two cases are the same. Circumstances of the crime and the situation of the offender can both vary dramatically, and a sentence that makes sense in one case may not apply well to another, even though both involve the same law violation. Many judges say they feel this loss of authority, and they are often placed in the position of pronouncing sentences with which they disagree, solely because no other choices are allowed under the law.

Others disagree. They say that the devaluation of the PSI has improved justice by making sentencing decisions more objective and more reliable. The attitudes of probation officers who write PSIs should, they argue, never have been a part of selecting a legal penalty. Moreover, the selection of a correct sentence is not a function of the court; rather, it is appropriately a function of the legislature, which best represents the opinions of the people.

Not only is the PSI less important as a result of the recent trend toward more structured sentencing decisions, but even when a penal code allows judges some discretion, the PSI writer has to confront the reality that most convictions come about as a result of plea bargaining. When the eventual sentence has already been proposed in the process of negotiation between the prosecutor and the defense attorney, the role of the PSI is altered. It no longer serves as the basis of the judge's decision but is used instead to determine whether the negotiated agreement is appropriate. To counter this problem, some probation officials argue that PSIs should be written before the defendant's plea. Although support exists for this innovation, it is unclear whether in the long run pre–plea bargain PSIs would be feasible for most cases.[7] The limits of the PSI have long meant that some observers feel its importance is vastly overestimated. Much of the time, they say, the sentence is determined by facts about the case—the offense, the plea agreement—that are far more obvious than anything the PSI can uncover. Others argue that the traditional PSI is a relic of a long-past era of the "medical model" of corrections, when judges relied on clinical assessments of defendants awaiting sentencing.[8] Small wonder some studies have shown that judges and other users of the PSI rely upon only a small amount of its information, and rather than read all of it, scan for a few relevant facts so they can make sure their intended decision makes sense.[9]

The reduced role of the presentence report should not be taken to mean it has no legitimate purpose in today's sentencing process. Even the most tightly structured sentencing systems call upon the judge to weigh aggravating and mitigating circumstances of both the crime and the offender when considering the sentencing decision, and the PSI is the most unbiased source of information about this. Moreover, the PSI is an essential third-party way to evaluate the appropriateness of a negotiated plea agreement, before the court accepts the plea. And when the judge has some influence on the terms of probation or on access to a treatment program in a penal facility, knowing the nature of an offender's problems, based on a thorough presentence evaluation, can be extremely helpful.

Contents

For many years, the ideal PSI was thought to be a lengthy narrative description of the offense and offender, culminating in a recommendation in regard to the sentence and a justification of that recommendation. Early manuals for the writing of PSIs stressed length and breadth of coverage. Now, however, people are questioning the assumption that more is better. While long PSIs make interesting reading and may be relatively satisfying to prepare, information theory suggests PSIs that are short and to the point are not necessarily less useful.

A large body of research on human processing of information suggests that the number of information items (facts or data) a person can normally consider simultaneously in making a decision varies from five to nine, depending on the person and the problem. When this number of items is exceeded and so much information is included in a message that it interferes with the recipient's ability to process it, the person undergoes information overload. Information overload seems to be associated with both a decrease in the accuracy of judgments made and, interestingly, increased confidence in them. Under conditions of overload, apparently the decision maker perceives redundant information (information that simply repeats facts presented earlier) as new information and gives it more weight than it deserves. In addition, noise (information unrelated to the problem, although it may appear to be important) is not distinguished from relevant information. The implication is ominous: No judge is able to take all of the information contained in a lengthy, detailed PSI into consideration when determining a sentence. So different judges are likely to consider different information and assign inappropriate importance to some facts in the PSI. Further, a judge may have unwarranted confidence in the sentencing decision.

Information theory is supported by the experiences of probation officers who have seen the judges skim through the long PSIs they prepared. The judges search for a few pertinent items and then read the sentencing recommendation. In effect, judges knew that much of the information in the PSI was irrelevant to the sentencing decision, and so they avoided wasting time by sorting through it.

The recent trend has been toward a shortened, directed, and standardized PSI format. This approach may seem less professional, but in practice it places even greater responsibility on the probation officer. It requires the probation officer to know the case and the penal code well enough to know precisely what information the judge requires to evaluate the sentencing options available.

Often, the penal code will specify what must go into the PSI. For example, nearly every state mandates a **victim impact statement,** which requires the probation officer to interview the victim and determine, in the victim's own words, the damage caused by the crime. This also makes it necessary to provide a detailed description of the offense itself. Victims' advocates claim that adding these statements to the PSI would let the judge better appraise the seriousness of the crime and choose a sentence that best serves both the offender and the victim. Critics worry that the judge would be unfairly prejudiced by articulate victims and those who overestimate their true losses. However, studies have shown that the addition of victim impact statements to PSIs neither increases officials' consideration of harm to victims nor results in generally harsher sentencing decisions.[10]

Recent interest in the relationship between drug abuse and crime has meant that an assessment of the offender's drug involvement and alcohol use patterns is a standard part of the presentence investigation. Every sentencing statute requires the court to consider prior involvement in the criminal justice system, and so a criminal history will be necessary as well. Once these elements of the PSI are provided, a fairly complete picture of the crime and the offender has been painted—at least for sentencing under most penal codes. The tendency, then, is to build the PSI around these requirements and add little more extraneous information. Sometimes, a description will be provided of the offender's education and employment history, and current circumstances will also be described. But these factors typically have little impact on the sentence.

Reliability and Validity

PSIs are not very useful unless the information they contain is valid and reliable. Although the terms have more precise meanings in the social sciences, for our purposes we may think of *validity* as the degree to which information is an accurate representation of the reality of the situation and of *reliability* as the degree to which other investigators would come to the same conclusion about the facts (or the degree to which the same investigator would make the same sorts of observations and reach the same conclusions in similar cases).

Two techniques improve validity and reliability: verification and objectivity. Verification occurs when PSI information is cross-checked with some other source for accuracy. If the offender states during the PSI interview that he or she has no problem with drinking, for example, the investigator questions the offender's family, companions, and employer before writing "No apparent problem" in the PSI. Objectivity is aided by avoiding vague conclusions about the case. For instance, rather than describe the offender as immature (a term that is subject to various interpretations and thus is of doubtful reliability), the PSI writer might describe the offender's observed behaviors that suggest immaturity: poor attendance at work, lack of understanding of the seriousness of the offense, and so forth.

PRESENTENCE INVESTIGATION REPORT

Date: May 13, 1997
Name: Matthew Martin
Address: Metropolis, Jefferson
County: Jefferson
Court Number: 1775-1
Offense: Burglary I
Class: Felony A
Custody Status: Jail
Maximum Penalty: 20 years/$2,500
Detainers or Pending Charges: None known
Judge: Wilson Morgan
D.A.: Paula Harrison
Counsel: David Acorn
Plea: Not Guilty
Verdict: Guilty
Birth Date: 8/19/69
Height: 5'11"
Eyes: Brown
Age: 27
Weight: 198
Hair: Red
Race: White
Sex: Male
Marital Status: Single
Education: 3 years college
Citizenship: U.S.A.
Employment Status: Temporary leave
Concerned Agencies: None known
Place of Birth: Delta, Louisiana
Marks: Tattoo, right arm: "Born to Raise Hell"
No. of Dependents: None

Report Submitted by: Leslie Blue

Jefferson County Probation Department
State of Jefferson

The Honorable Wilson Morgan
May 13, 1997

Jefferson County Circuit Court
Court Number 1775–1
10 Main Avenue
Metropolis, Jefferson 99999

Dear Judge Morgan:

The following is the presentence report on Matthew Martin that you ordered on April 15, 1997.

Offense Summary

On February 13, 1997, Jefferson Police arrested Matthew Martin at the scene of a burglary. He was subsequently charged with Burglary I. On April 15, 1997, Jefferson County Circuit Court Jury found Mr. Martin guilty of the charge. He is in custody and sentencing is set for May 20, 1997, at 9:00 A.M.

Plea Bargain/Negotiations and Stipulations

N.A.

Official Version

On February 13, 1997, at approximately 7:09 P.M. Jefferson Police responded to a silent alarm at Petcare Animal Clinic, located at 17 Maybelle Dr. Upon arrival, the responding officers discovered Mr. Martin and Arthur James on the roof of the building. Mr. Martin had a pair of gloves, a screwdriver, and a pocketknife. The defendant refused to answer any questions without his attorney present. Mr. Martin and Mr. James were taken into custody.

Further investigation revealed that entry was made through a plastic-covered window. The plastic was cut away from the window frame. Drawers and cabinets had been rummaged through, a wooden box had been pried open, and numerous burnt matches were found on the floor.

During an interview, Mr. Martin reported that he burglarized the veterinarian clinic to obtain records on his cat. He explained that he had brought his cat to the clinic a couple of weeks ago and did not have the money to pay the bill. It was his intention to remove the records on his cat, but he found the bookkeeping system to be very extensive and he was unable to find the file. He admitted to gaining entry by cutting the plastic on the window but refused to answer any further questioning. The police confirmed the fact that Mr. Martin's cat was treated at the Petcare Animal Clinic from 2/2/97 to 2/4/97.

Defendant's Version

Mr. Martin admitted to breaking into the animal clinic, but explained that he became "petrified" and decided to leave the building. At that point, the police came and he stated that he lay down and waited for them. The defendant related that he had been unemployed and was behind in rent. His cat acquired a respiratory disease and he took her to the veterinarian. Mr. Martin indicated that he gave the clinic $10 and was to pay them $40 at a later date. One evening, he and Mr. James were sitting around "chewing the fat" and he came up with the idea to break in the office and get the records. He admitted to entering the animal clinic by ripping the plastic-covered window.

Mr. Martin expressed his remorse and stated, "I don't blame anyone but myself." He related that he did not take the stand at his court hearing upon his attorney's suggestion and feels that this may jeopardize his position at the time of sentencing.

Accomplices/Codefendants

Criminal Circuit Court records indicate that on 4/10/97 Judge Carey issued a bench warrant for Mr. James's arrest. As of 5/8/97, the Court had not received a return of services.

Victim's Statement/Damages

Dale Rector, the receptionist at Petcare Animal Clinic, reported that although the office was badly vandalized, no items were noted to be missing with the exception of a screwdriver.

Prior Record

Conviction Summary

Juvenile:
1. 11/3/83: Metropolis, Jefferson—Incorrigible, Beyond Parental Control—Committed to Danville School for Boys.
2. 6/27/86: Metropolis, Jefferson—Child Molesting—Returned to Danville School for Boys. The defendant had a five-year-old girl's clothes off and was fondling her genitals.
3. 8/29/88: Metropolis, Jefferson—Runaway, Burglary I—Returned to Danville School for Boys. Mr. Martin had run away from Danville and committed burglary.
4. 4/5/89: Bequinta, California—Carrying a Concealed Weapon and Runaway—Returned to School for Boys. Mr. Martin went to California and was picked up by police for carrying a concealed weapon.

Adult:
1. 1/5/89: Metropolis, Jefferson—Resisting Arrest, Theft II—The defendant indicated that he received ten days County Jail time.
2. 2/11/91: Metropolis, Jefferson—Burglary I—Pled guilty to Burglary II, sentenced to five years jail. Records reveal that Mr. Martin broke into the Rialto Theater, took $900, and flew to Texas with the stolen money.
3. 3/15/94: Metropolis, Jefferson—Sodomy I—The defendant was sentenced to ten years jail to run concurrently with item number 2. The defendant

engaged in sexual intercourse with a seven-year-old boy while he was released on recognizance for his burglary charge.

4. 3/25/94: Metropolis, Jefferson—Theft II, Menacing with a Knife. The defendant was found guilty of Theft II and sentenced to nine days County Jail time.

5. 2/13/97: Metropolis, Jefferson—Burglary I—Present offense, disposition pending.

Arrests Not Resulting in Conviction

Juvenile:

1. 5/9/87: Metropolis, Jefferson—Vandalism and Burglary in a School—Disposition unknown.

2. 12/26/87: Metropolis, Jefferson—Shoplifting—No complaint.

3. 1/21/88: Metropolis, Jefferson—Unauthorized Use of a Vehicle—Released.

Adult:

1. 2/12/92: Metropolis, Jefferson—Theft II—Dismissed.

2. 10/26/93: Metropolis, Jefferson—Schedule IV Drug Possession—No misdemeanor complaint.

Driving Record

Division of Motor Vehicle records reveal that Mr. Martin's driver's license is currently invalid. His license was suspended for Failure to Appear at a Hearing. He incurred citations for Expired Registration, No Driver's License, and Failure to Obey Traffic Control Device.

Prior Parole, Probation, and Institutional Performance

Mr. Martin was committed to Danville School for Boys 11/3/86 for Incorrigibility and Beyond Parental Control. During the five years he spent at Danville School for Boys, he had at least two runaways and incurred new charges each time.

Mr. Martin was received at Jefferson State Correctional Institution on 4/11/94 and again on 6/27/94, for a period of five years and ten years concurrent on charges of Burglary II and Sodomy I. He was paroled to Washington County on 10/5/95 with conditions. On 2/13/96, his parole officer, Larry Prouse, submitted a special report to the Parole Board informing them that Mr. Martin was arrested and charged with Theft II. The charges were later dismissed. The defendant's parole was continued on February 28, 1996. The defendant had been receiving mental health treatment with Dr. Cathart. Through Dr. Cathart's recommendation, Mr. Martin reported to the State Hospital on 3/8/96. The hospital would not admit the defendant, and he was subsequently referred to the Division of Mental Health. During his parole supervision he was enrolled as a student at Metropolis Community College.

On 3/25/96, Mr. Martin was again arrested. He was charged with Theft II and Menacing with a Knife. A special report was again submitted by his probation officer, and Mr. Martin's parole program evaluation was considered as "poor." Washington County detectives indicated that Mr. Martin was involved in at least twenty-five burglaries and thefts in Lincoln and Washington counties. His former parole officer, Larry Prouse, recommends that Mr. Martin be sent back to the penitentiary. While Mr. Martin was incarcerated, he was involved in the sex offender group. Dr. Williams, psychiatrist, indicated that Mr. Martin "has learned some insight, and through some college classes in psychology and sexual education and school, he has learned that he is pretty much like everyone else except for his acting out with pedophilia. Apparently he has made a great deal of growth in this institution, especially in the last eight months."

Family History

Father: Bernard Martin died in 1977 from chronic alcoholism. The defendant related that his father was in the United States Army for twenty-eight years.
Stepfather: Willie Olsen, age unknown, is currently unemployed. The defendant related that his stepfather and his mother had been living together since 1982 and were divorced only recently.
Mother: Bernice Olsen, 51, lives in Delbarten, Jefferson, and is employed as a waitress. The defendant indicated that she and his natural father were divorced when he was very young.
Sister: Lucy Daly, 30, lives in Wilson, Jefferson. She is employed as a secretary. She is divorced and has three children.
Sister: Dettie Conwald, 28, also lives in Wilson, Jefferson. She is a housewife and has a part-time job with a dentist. She is married and has three children.
Brother: Barry Martin, 26, lives in Jefferson; address and employment are unknown to the defendant. The defendant related that his brother is married and has one child.
Brother: David Martin, 20, lives in Metropolis, Jefferson. The defendant related that he is employed as a painter, is single, and has no children.
Stepsister: Melissa Olsen, 12, lives with her mother in Wilson, Jefferson. She attends junior high school.
The Defendant: Matthew Martin was born to the union of Bernard Martin and Bernice Cathwall in Delta, Louisiana, on August 19, 1969. His parents were divorced when he was approximately five years old, and the defendant remained with his mother. The defendant's mother married Willie Olsen when the defendant was twelve years old. His stepfather was described as a "strict disciplinarian" and his mother as an "extremely permissive, indulgent person." Correctional files indicate that Mr. Martin's deviant behavior began at the age

of twelve. State Prison files report that Mr. Martin had been kidnapped and sexually molested for three days when he was six years old. The defendant related that this "messed up" his sexual orientations since that time. He indicated that he does not remember this episode, which he learned of from his psychologist.

Mr. Martin moved to Metropolis in 1977 and indicates that he has lived within the area in various residences since that time.

Marital History

Mr. Martin has never been married.

Education

The defendant reports that he has received forty-four college credit hours, being registered in educational courses at Jefferson State Prison and college courses at Metropolis Community College subsequent to his release. He relates that he was enrolled in General Studies courses. He related that, prior to his college credits, he received his high school diploma while incarcerated at State Prison.

Health

Physical: The defendant related that his physical health is good and that he suffers from no handicaps. He stated that he is allergic to penicillin.

Mental: A psychiatric evaluation stated, "He does not appear to be psychologically ill, only anxious, and has a grossly immoral character." Another psychological report indicated that "Matthew does not belong in Danville School for Boys. He is certainly much more a candidate for State Hospital." Mr. Martin was involved in the Sexual Offenders Program while incarcerated. He related that his psychologists gave him a "clean bill of health." He related that he saw Dr. Cathart for nine months while he was incarcerated and two months subsequent to his release. Dr. Cathart believes that Mr. Martin no longer needs mental health treatment.

Alcohol: The defendant related that he began alcohol consumption at the age of seventeen. He related that he drinks once a week "at the most." He stated that he has never had an alcohol problem and has never received any alcohol abuse counseling.

Drugs: The defendant related that he began experimenting with drugs at the age of seventeen. He indicated that he received drug abuse counseling while he was incarcerated and explained that his attorney told him to admit to a drug abuse problem to get him into a treatment program. He indicated that this did not work out the way he wanted it, since he had no drug abuse problem. Mr. Martin denies any current usage of illicit drugs.

Employment

October 15, 1995 to Present (Approximately two and one-half years, inter-mittently)—Paint Contractor. The defendant related that he and his brother-in-law are painting subcontractors. He related that when he is working, he earns $5.00 per hour working 55 hours a week. We were unable to verify employment information at the time of this writing. His parole officer related that this job was only part-time and described it as "fishy."

June 1995 to August 1995 (Approximately three months)—Camp Counselor. The defendant related that he was a youth camp counselor for the summer, earning $800.00 per month. This information was verified on 5/11/97.

October 1994 to January 1995 (Approximately four months)—Nurse's Aide. His employer indicated that he was employed as a nurse's aide, earning $3.25 per hour. The defendant indicated that he quit subsequent to being accused of stealing a purse. Employment verification was made on 5/11/97.

Military Service

Mr. Martin has never been in the military.

Financial Condition

Mr. Martin reported that his income averages between $400.00 and $600.00 per month. He related that he pays $250.00 per month in rent and $80.00 per month in utilities. He indicated that he has no car and stated that he has no other assets nor outstanding debts.

Current Situation

Mr. Martin lives by himself but also spends a great deal of time with his girl-friend, Sheila Vettor. He says that they are considering marriage but that the prospect is unsettling to him. He reports he has few regular friends.

Psychological Evaluation

This twenty-five-year-old white male was interviewed and administered a battery of psychological tests in the Jefferson County Jail on May 12, 1997. During the psychological evaluation, he was initially somewhat sleepy, dis-tracted, and wary. As the interview progressed, Mr. Martin became quite articulate, intelligent, and extraordinarily alert.

There is a high level of vigilance and distrust in this man's overt behavior that would be highly suggestive of underlying emotional or psychological problems. This perhaps is exemplified by the fact that Mr. Martin refused to complete any formal psychological tests presented to him by this examiner. He said he didn't trust psychologists and he didn't trust the criminal justice system; he believes the type of questions and procedures that psychologists offered were stupid and of little value. He said he had taken many psychological tests in the past, and no one ever seemed to give him any help following these tests. He insisted that it was a waste of time.

Mr. Martin went on to say that he really didn't care what happened as the result of this refusing to take the tests. He noted, "I'm unique. I don't want to be categorized. I just want to be left alone. I never want to see another cop or another judge or another psychologist again. I hate tests. I am a unique individual. People may believe I am institutionalized. I am not institutionalized. I am not a criminal. Lots of things have changed in my life. I have stayed out of trouble for three years. I have a girlfriend. I don't hang around with the same kind of people I used to. I have taken all of the psychological tests before, and I refuse to be categorized."

Mr. Martin also indicated that he received an extended amount of psychotherapy from Dr. Cathart regarding some underlying sexual problems, and he signed a release indicating that I could talk to Dr. Cathart about his treatment. This examiner was unable to reach Dr. Cathart prior to the dictation of this report.

Mr. Martin was able to discuss some of his history. He explained that he was born in Delta, Louisiana, but traveled all over the country because his father was in the service. In 1974 he came to Metropolis and subsequently spent some time in Danville. He reported that he had a "nervous breakdown" in 1983 or 1984 when he was at Danville. According to his account, he was told by a staff member that he would never again return home. As the result of this information, he became extremely hysterical and in spite of injections of tranquilizing medication, they were unable to calm him and so he was transferred to the State Hospital where he spent some time. Mr. Martin also openly admitted that he spent much of a five-year sentence in the State Prison as the result of a burglary and sodomy conviction. He noted that while there, he participated in their sex offender program for about a year and then followed up with about four months of psychotherapy with Dr. Williams in the community.

This examiner's impression is that Mr. Martin is a stubborn, control-avoidant, and paranoid individual. It was also indicated that he probably has above-average intellectual abilities and he has taught himself to be highly tuned to the slightest intrusion upon his sense of independence and autonomy. Even though some of his suspicions and distrust of the mental health and criminal justice system may be justified, he seems unable to escape from the sweeping generalization that everybody that he meets is going to assume a persecutory role. He did indicate that he did have a considerable amount of trust in Dr. Cathart and that he would allow Dr. Cathart to report openly regarding his course in treatment.

Mr. Martin is the type of person who tends to provoke the most unsympathetic types of sentiments from people in the criminal justice system. As long as he remains in the system, neither he nor the system will have much relief from that antagonism. In many ways, Mr. Martin's desired outcome of being free from contact with the system is the most desirable one for the system as well. Unfortunately, the way in which he goes about trying to avoid the system is highly ineffective.

Diagnosis: Borderline personality

Prognosis: Guarded

CASE SUPERVISION PLAN

Supervising Officer: Leslie Blue   **Client's Name: Matthew Martin**

Date: 6/12/97

Supervision Level _X_ Intensive ___ Regular ___ Minimal

Client's Supervision Objectives	Target Date	Resource
1. To obtain full-time employment	6/30/97	Probation Officer; Metropolis Employment Center
2. To enroll in college on a part-time basis; at least one course per semester	9/1/97	Probation Officer; Metropolis Junior College
3. To have no contact with Arthur James while on probation	N.A.	Probation Officer
4. To discuss with girlfriend the nature of their relationship in order to clarify whether to marry	N.A.	Metropolis Community Mental Health Center

Special Conditions:

1. Probationer will seek and cooperate with mental health treatment.
2. Probationer will make $500 restitution to victim.

Sentencing Recommendations

Sentencing recommendations are a controversial aspect of the PSI because a person without authority to sentence the offender is nevertheless suggesting what the sentence should be. For this reason, not all probation systems include a recommendation in the PSI. With sentencing reform placing increased restrictions on the judge's sentencing options, PSI recommendations are not as important as they once were. Yet there is a well-established tradition of sentence recommendations by nonjudicial court actors; normally, the judge solicits recommendations from the defense and prosecution. The probation officer's recommendation is but one of many that the judge routinely accepts. But what the probation officer says may carry extra weight because it is a presumably unbiased evaluation of the offender. Moreover, the judge may be hesitant to place an offender on probation without confirmation that the sentence is supported by the probation department.

Studies of the congruence of the PSI recommendation and the judicial sentence find a range of agreement from 70 percent to over 90 percent.[11] Of course, it is hard to know whether judges are following the officers or whether the officers' experience has given them the ability to come up with recommendations the judges will select. If the reason for the congruence between the probation officer's recommendation and the sentence imposed is the judge's confidence in the officer's analysis, that confidence may be misplaced. One evaluation found that "in only a few instances did the offenders they recommended for probation behave significantly better than those they recommended for prison."[12]

JAPAN'S PROBATION AND PAROLE MODELS

To bring America's crime explosion under control, new prisons and longer sentences will not be enough. Most criminals are eventually released, and many return to a life of crime. In addition to tougher law enforcement, we need to find ways to turn former criminals into law-abiding citizens. Perhaps here, Americans can learn from the success of volunteer probation and parole officers in Japan.

In the United States, each of the nation's 35,000 probation and parole officers supervise up to 100 convicts. With so many charges, the typical officer is lucky if he can find his parolees or probationers, let alone monitor their movements. "Most state probation and parole systems have a serious problem with case overload," says Steve Varnum, the Executive Director of Justice Fellowship at Prison Fellowship Ministries. "This leads to a high percentage of parole and probation violations, with many offenders returning to prison."

Japan, by contrast, has fewer than 1,000 full-time professional probation and parole officers. These officers are recruited and trained as professionals in counseling, but with an average of 100,000 new qualifying convicts each year, they are too few to counsel clients individually. Their real work is to assign cases to approximately 48,000 volunteer probation and parole officers throughout the country.

Each volunteer on average supervises only two convicts, and his primary responsibility is to help them rejoin their families and neighborhoods as well as to monitor their movements. These volunteers-cum-social workers are clearly getting the job done: Fewer that 4 percent of Japanese criminals who have been assigned to a volunteer office will commit another crime within a year of their release on parole or probation.

What is the Japanese secret in dealing so effectively with criminal offenders? Part of the answer is the selection process for parole and probation. To qualify for probation or parole in Japan, an offender must show remorse for his crime and meet certain criteria that prevent the release of serious or habitual criminals.

In Japan, acceptance by one's family is often the most important factor in an offender's rehabilitation, for the concept of shame is still alive and well in this society. A volunteer officer visits the offender's home to help his family overcome the shame of having a relative convicted of a crime. If family reunification is deemed impossible, the volunteer finds the offender a place at a halfway house or with friends.

The next step is to help the offender find stable employment, so he may again become a functional member of his community. This is also considered essential to rehabilitation, as the importance of societal acceptance is second only to that of acceptance by one's family. After a residence and a job have been secured, the volunteer officer continues to meet with his charge once or twice a month to provide counsel and to monitor his progress.

An appointment as a volunteer probation or parole officer requires no special training or background; candidates must simply be respected and financially stable. Volunteers come from a range of occupations, but more than half are fishermen or farmers, religious leaders, housewives, and retired people. Ninety percent of the volunteers are at least 50 years old and 80 percent are men.

Once appointed by the Ministry of Justice, a volunteer's term of service is two years, but most are reappointed several times. Almost half serve at least 10 years.

Japan formally authorized its system of suspended prosecution in 1924, and codified the network of volunteers upon which it depended in 1950. Research conducted by Japan's Ministry of Justice shows that the success of volunteer probation officers lies in the individual attention they are able to give each offender; they are often seen as friends or mentors rather than authority figures. Many convicts, moved by the fact that someone has taken an interest in their well-being, feel an obligation to work toward rehabilitation.

Could such a system work in the United States? America would need more that 1.75 million volunteers to achieve the same 2:1 ratio as Japan. Still, small caseload ratios are key to the successful supervision of offenders. "Most criminal activity is preceded by a progression of inappropriate behaviors," Varnum says. "If an agent spends time with an offender and sees the environment the offender lives in, it will be much easier for the agent to recognize the inappropriate behaviors that may lead to the offender's participation in further criminal activity. The Japanese parole model serves that purpose of real time supervision."

It's true that Japanese society, particularly the role of the family, is quite different from that in the United States. Sharing in the public control of behavior, of course, is not unique to Japan. Many U.S. cities have volunteer organizations whose members patrol their communities or teach conflict resolution and job skills. Churches and mosques have begun to welcome and find employment for former criminals. It's time to go further, and experiment with the Japanese volunteer model.

Source: Leslie Gardner, *Policy Review* 75 (Jan./Feb. 1996): 17.

Disclosure

In view of the importance of the PSI to the sentencing decision, one would think that the defendant would have a right to see it. After all, it may contain inadvertent irrelevancies or inaccuracies that the defense would want to dispute at the sentencing hearing. Nevertheless, in many states the defense does not receive a copy of the report. The case most often cited in this regard is *Williams* v. *New York,*[13] in which the judge imposed a death sentence on the basis of evidence in the confidential PSI despite the jury's recommendation of a life sentence. The Supreme Court upheld the judge's decision to deny the defense access to the report, although without such access the defense was incapable of challenging its contents at the sentencing hearing.

Cases and state law since 1949 have reduced the original restrictive impact of *Williams.* At least one circuit court has held, for example, that illegally seized evidence excluded from a trial cannot be referred to in the PSI.[14] And legislation in sixteen states requires full disclosure of the PSI. In the other states, the practice is generally to "cleanse" the report and then disclose it. Cleansing involves the deletion of two kinds of statements: (1) confidential comments from a private citizen that, if known to the offender, might result in danger to the citizen, and (2) clinical statements or evaluations that might be damaging to the offender if disclosed. Moreover, many judges allow the defense to present a written challenge of any disclosed contents of the PSI.

Private PSIs

Private investigative firms have recently begun to provide judges with presentence investigation reports. These firms work in one of two ways. Some contract with defendants to conduct comprehensive background checks and provide judges with creative sentencing options as alternatives to incarceration. In this approach, often called client-specific planning, the agency serves as an advocate for the defendant at the sentencing stage. In the second approach, the court contracts directly with a private investigator to provide a neutral PSI in lieu of the traditional version prepared by a probation officer. This is often justified by a desire not to add to the heavy workloads of the existing probation office. Advocates also point out that traditional PSIs tend to be developed in a bureaucratic setting with little imagination or insight into the particulars of the case.[15]

Privately conducted PSIs have sparked controversy. Because client-specific planning is paid for by the defendant, many people view it as an advantage for upper- and middle-class offenders who can afford the special consideration the advocacy report provides. Often it is the white-collar offender who can make the best case for creative sentences. (Richard Nixon's convicted former aide John Ehrlichman offered to do free legal work with Native Americans in place of going to prison, but his suggestion was rejected.) Their concerns are well taken; the advocates of private PSIs point out that their reports often result in less severe sentences for their clients.

The neutral PSI also raises serious issues. Advocates say that private investigators do what the probation department does—only better.[16] Yet critics question whether private firms ought to be involved in the quasi-judicial function of making sentence recommendations. Moreover, the liability of private investigators for the accuracy and relevance of the information they provide to government agencies such as courts is unclear. It is also likely that private PSIs, when purchased by the court, cost the taxpayer more than the traditional public alternative.

USE OF PRIVATE PSIs IN LOS ANGELES COUNTY

In budget-strapped and crime-infested areas like Los Angeles County, enforcement of probationers can be a nightmare. If budget cuts go through, each probation officer will juggle 5,000 cases vs. the 1,000 they currently supervise.

"A lot of programs are or can be subject to abuse," says Barry Nidorf, chief probation officer for LA County. "Clearly we don't have someone supervising everyone doing community service. But my gut feeling is that perception of abuse is far, far greater than the reality."

Indirectly, money can make a big difference in convincing judges to hand down a sentence of probation and community service.

In Los Angeles County, for example, most indigent offenders have to rely on overworked probation officers to draft a pre-sentencing report to give the judge an objective appraisal of whether probation should be considered. If budget cuts go through, the department will no longer draft reports for misdemeanor offenses.

Defendants can spend up to $5,000 to hire private groups, known as sentencing advocates, to put together pre-sentencing reports to impress judges. The reports are supposed to be neutral evaluations but they include thorough character references, psychological evaluations and a tailor-made community service plan. A 1994 Sentencing Project Study of 22,000 cases shows that judges adopt 70% of those recommendations.

Source: USA Today, July 6, 1995.

Getting Probation

For most offenders, the best possible result of the sentencing decision is to receive a sentence of probation. All penal codes restrict the availability of probation to certain types of offenses and certain offenders—usually first- or second-time felons convicted of property crimes or violent offenses involving impulsive, unarmed acts of aggression. Legislation that provides for probation specifies the conditions under which the judge "may" impose a term of probation. These laws never compel the decision by indicating specific offenses or offenders for which the judge "shall" choose probation. Instead, sentencing law allows probation only when the court arrives at certain conclusions about the case. Typically, these conclusions involve judicial judgments such as the following:

- The offender does not represent an undue risk to community safety.
- A term of probation will not be inappropriate given the seriousness of the offense.
- The offender's circumstances are such that a term of probation offers the best opportunity for an eventual successful adjustment to crime-free community life.

Most penal codes do specify offenses for which a probation term is prohibited, and in this way they restrict judicial discretion. Being placed on probation is thus seen as a discretionary privilege offered by the court, not a right of the offender who meets the criteria for probation. Thus, the decision to deny probation is generally unreviewable, and the judicial processes by which the court concludes probation is appropriate to a given case involve the full panoply of recommendations by the prosecution, the defense, interested citizens, and the review provided by the PSI. In the end, however, the decision to grant probation is a final bastion of judicial discretion.

Intensive Probation Supervision

In many states, judges now can sentence an offender to **intensive probation supervision (IPS).** With IPS, the offender receives probation as an alternative to incarceration under the conditions of strict reporting and frequent face-to-face contacts with a probation officer who has a limited caseload. The background and implementation of IPS were discussed in more detail in Chapter 7.

Felony Probation

Although probation has traditionally been given to offenders found guilty of misdemeanors and nonviolent crimes, jail and prison crowding has forced correctional administrators to expand the use of probation for convicted felons. When probation is used for serious offenders, it is called **felony probation.**

DEALING WITH TECHNICAL VIOLATORS

In the last several years many probation agencies have begun to explore options to increase probation compliance and reduce violations. Some of the mechanisms that have been developed to deal with this issue include the following:

- Rating noncompliant behavior—Because all noncompliant behavior does not merit the same attention, violations can be categorized on the basis of the offense and the risk imposed. For example, Category A violations would require a warrant or citation by some hearing officer. Violations would include convictions for a new offense, possession of a weapon, and refusal to pay financial penalties. Category B violations would require placing the offender in another intermediate sanction program or referring the case to a hearing officer. Such would be the case in instances where the offender is unwilling to cooperate with general conditions of probation such as drug or alcohol use. Category C violations would be minor and could be resolved at the probation supervision level.
- Administrative hearings—To provide a formal structure for responding to noncompliant behavior, some jurisdictions such as South Carolina have developed a system of guidelines that deal with handling technical violations. Such systems formulate guidelines for probation officers, develop violation categories, provide additional sanctions for noncompliant behavior, and implement hearing officers to address behavior.
- Graduated sanctions—Some jurisdictions use various forms of intermediate sanctions such as day fines, electronic monitoring, day reporting, halfway houses, and restitution centers instead of incarceration for technical violators of probation.
- Special court dockets—Rather than squeeze violation of probation hearings into an already crowded court docket, jurisdictions such as Maricopa County (Arizona) have established a special court docket to respond more quickly to probation violators. As a result, the percentage of offenders reinstated to probation without any additional conditions decreased sharply.

Source: Fay S. Taxman, "Dealing with Technical Violators," *Corrections Today* 57:1 (February 1, 1995): 46–53.

Proponents of felony probation argue that it is a viable alternative to incarceration.[17] However, opponents feel that it poses a serious threat to public safety and is administered in an inconsistent fashion.[18] Their concern is supported by the fact that during 2000 it was determined that 52 percent of offenders on probation had been convicted of a felony.[19] Even with the problems associated with recidivism, there is little doubt that as prison populations and costs continue to rise, felony probation will remain as a viable alternative to incarceration for many offenders.

Federal Probation

Although the use of probation on the state level began in the early 1840s, its use on the federal level was not formally accepted as an alternative to incarceration until 1925. In that year Congress passed the Federal Probation Act, authorizing the use of probation in federal courts.[20] The decision to authorize probation for federal crimes was motivated by federal prison crowding created by Prohibition legislation. Unlike the federal parole system, which is in the process of being abolished, federal probation has flourished. This is not surprising in light of the serious crowding problems in the federal correctional facilities, which during the early 1990s were operating at 125 percent of capacity due in great part to the escalating "war on drugs," which has created stiff laws and penalties for those involved in the use, possession, and sale of illicit drugs.

The federal probation system is reputed to be a well-run organization that employs competent and qualified professionals. The resources made available to federal probationers such as treatment for substance abuse, employment training, and job placement surpass those provided in state and local probation agencies. Training for federal probation officers is also more frequent and substantial than for state employees. Recent research has indicated that federal probation has been quite successful as compared to many state correctional systems when it comes to cost-efficiency and reducing recidivism.[21] The cost of supervising one offender under federal probation has been estimated to be under $2,400 per year as compared to the cost of incarceration at approximately $25,000 per year. Such data indicate why federal probation has become a common alternative to incarceration for those found guilty of federal crimes.

Fees in Probation

The collection of supervision fees from offenders on probation is a growing idea in community corrections supervision. Fees are collected for a variety of correctional services such as electronic monitoring, drug counseling, and regular probation supervision. As of January 2000, there are fifteen states that have only monthly probation fees, fourteen that utilize fees for parole supervision, and twenty-two that have adopted the practice for probation and parole. The lowest monthly cost is $10 (four states), and the highest is $85 in New Mexico.[22]

The fees collected help support the budgets of probation agencies and also can serve a rehabilitative function for offenders. Because they are forced to pay for supervision, they may be more likely to participate in programming and less likely to treat probation as a meaningless sanction.

Some are critical of the probation supervision fee idea. As with regular fines, it is believed that charging for such services is unequitable because some people under supervision may find it difficult to pay, whereas for others it is not a financial hardship. A related problem is the collection of fees by probation staff. Probably since the beginning of probation supervision, officers have been asked to act on behalf of the court to collect court cost, restitution, fines, and now supervision fees. But probation staff universally dislike this "bill collector role" because it is not viewed as part of their preferred roles as treament and supervision officers.

THE SUPERVISION FUNCTION

Defendants who are granted probation are placed under some form of supervision of the court, generally through the office of probation. Formally, the supervision process involves three components: the written conditions of probation, regular reporting, and the enforcement of the orders of the court. The legal basis of probation supervision derives from these three components, and the statutory powers of the probation officer are limited to these aspects of the job. Stated succinctly, the written conditions of probation define the scope of areas of the probationer's life in which the probation office has a legitimate interest; the regular reporting of the probationer to the probation office provides the basis for monitoring compliance with the conditions of probation; and the activities of the probation officer are limited to those necessary to enforce the conditions of probation.

We will discuss this formal understanding of probation supervision in some detail. However, we must recognize that to think the probation function is fully described by these formal components would be to misunderstand how probation works in practice. The formal aspects of probation constitute only one part of the probation supervision world. In truth, there is a vibrant and intricate informal aspect to probation supervision involving interactions among the officer, the client, and the organizational bureaucracy. Later we explore this informal aspect of the "real" probation supervision practice. For the probation officer and the client, this informal probation world is the everyday reality and in many ways is more important than the formal components of probation, because the probation supervision process emerges from informal understandings and interdependencies. Yet as important as this informal probation practice can be, its underpinnings are the formal, legal aspects of probation. And so we begin our discussion of probation supervision with the formal rules and requirements.

The Conditions of Probation

In assigning a term of probation, the sentencing judge will establish a set of "conditions" of probation. Probation conditions are the requirements for conduct that must be observed by the probationer in order to remain on probation. Two types of conditions are imposed—standard and "special." Standard probation conditions apply to all cases sentenced to probation, whereas **special conditions of probation** are applied to the particular case by the judge due to special circumstances of the offender. For example, every probationer might be prohibited from owning a handgun or from consuming alcoholic beverages, while another obvious condition will require defendants to obey all laws. On the other hand, a probationer with a substance abuse problem may be specially ordered to attend counseling sessions and provide urine samples for drug testing, or a defendant convicted of spouse assault may be ordered into a treatment program about marital violence. For a list of special conditions imposed on probations see Table 8.2.

Probation conditions are intended to accomplish different objectives. Standard conditions, which generally define limits on movement and other actions, are usually designed to help the probation department establish controls over the probationer so that the probation term can be effectively managed. For example, one of the usual standard conditions is that the probationer must "report as directed by the probation officer," a condition that establishes the basis for all supervision actions. Special conditions attempt to allow the probation officer to tailor the supervision to the particulars of the case, monitoring the probationer's progress in dealing with problems that lead to criminal conduct.

TABLE 8.2   SPECIAL CONDITIONS OF PROBATION

Conditions of Sentence	Percentage of Probationers
Supervision fees	61
Fines	56
Court costs	55
Employment	35
Mandatory drug testing	33
Restitution to victim	30
Alcohol abuse treatment	29
Community service	26
Drug abuse treatment	23
At least one condition	99

Source: Thomas Bonczar, *Characteristics of Adults on Probation* (Washington, DC: U.S. Department of Justice, Bureau of Justice Statistics, 1997), p. 7.

Reporting

The central aspect of probation is the "reporting requirement"—offenders on probation are required to meet with a probation officer, in the field or at the probation office, and discuss whatever topics the probation officer considers important to enable the progress on probation to be monitored. The reporting requirement is usually vaguely defined: The offender must report as directed. Whatever reporting the probation officer "directs" for any given offender turns out to be a major element in the actual requirements of probation for that offender.

For most of the history of probation, the decision as to how much reporting to require was left to the individual probation officer. Some officers were vigilant in their requirements, seeing offenders frequently in the office and in the "field" (at work or in the offender's home). Others were much less persistent, asking for occasional office visits for specific purposes. Nationwide, the unarticulated standard was to require a minimum of one report per month, more if circumstances required.

In recent years, this discretion over reporting standards has begun to disappear, and instead offices have established standardized practices for reporting requirements. These reporting standards are based upon formal, standardized classification systems, in which a set of factors is applied to every case to establish supervision priorities. The arrival of standard classification systems to establish reporting standards has been part of a general trend in probation supervision, in which the discretion of the probation officer has been gradually eroded by policies that establish standards for practice.

Probationer reporting occurs both in the office and in the field. Office reports, scheduled in advance, are the usual way probationers make themselves available for supervision. In an office visit, the probation officer will question the probationer about compliance with court-ordered conditions, including employment and general social adjustment. If a drug test has been ordered, the probationer will provide a urine sample. These office visits can be fairly perfunctory, taking ten minutes or less to complete. Most probationers and probation officers treat them as routine events in which the ordinary business of probation is transacted. Although they have been traditionally thought of as "counseling" sessions, in today's probation with growing caseloads and increasing demands for accountability, little counseling takes place during office visits.

Field reporting can be a different matter. Often, the probation officer will arrive at the probationer's home (or sometimes, at the workplace) without an appointment. This enables the probation officer to observe the probationer's life away from the office without warning—experienced probation officers tell tales of discovering drug use in progress, disorderly home life, heated marital conflicts, and the like. The unstructured nature of field contacts gives the officer a grounded idea of how the probationer is doing, and it opens the door to realistic counseling and problem solving when the problems are evident.

Enforcing the Terms of Probation

The fundamental responsibility of the probation system is to enforce the conditions of probation, as ordered by the sentencing judge. In theory, the sentencing court expects to hear of any violations of probation, and supervision is organized to detect any misbehavior regarding the court order.

There are two types of probation violations. The first is a **technical violation,** which is an infraction of one of the conditions of probation but not a violation of law. The second, called a **new offense violation,** is when the offender is involved with a new crime, which *is* a violation of the law.

Violations of the probation order can lead to a revocation hearing, in which the judge considers whether to rescind probation and send the offender to a term of prison or jail. Later we discuss the revocation process and its pressures, but the possibility of revocation makes rules violations—and the court hearings to consider the alleged violations—a major force in the probation process.

In practice, probation rules are broad enough and cover enough territory that minor violations are common, although few are brought before the sentencing judge. In fact, old-time probation officers know that any time they want to "file a violation" (inform the court in writing of a violation of a probation rule), they can find a basis for doing so. Judges know this, as well, and they generally let the probation department know that petty violations should not be turned into court hearings; if every probation violation made it to a judicial hearing, the judge would have no time for other court duties. This is significant in light of the research that shows that more than 50 percent of offenders are not in compliance with court orders sometime during their probation period. To elucidate further on the problem, figure with 3.1 million adult offenders on probation, if (only) 25 to 50 percent of probationers engage in behavior that requires court attention, this would equate to 750,000 to 1.5 million offenders requiring at least one court hearing during the probation period.[23] Adding up to 1 million hearings to the already crowded court dockets of America would spell disaster for the "Halls of Justice."

So the enforcement of conditions is always a balancing act—the probation officer has to decide which misbehaviors on the offender's part are important enough to justify involving the judge in the case. To assist probation departments in sorting out the importance of various violations, some probation departments have worked out a violation process that enables the probation system to handle minor violations without informing the court.

Two other factors that may influence whether a probation officer decides to enforce conditions of probation are the availability of alternatives to incarceration and the number of empty jail and prison beds. Officers may have tried a variety of ways to "motivate" the offender to behave with little success. If a more strict supervision method is available, then the tourniquet of sentencing may be tightened. However, if all else fails, short-term incarceration in jail or a longer stint in prison may be the only way to curtail criminal behavior. The problem is, however, that neither an intermediate sanction nor bed space may be readily available. Probation officers in jurisdictions that lack these resources may find their supervision enforcement choices quite limited.

Conditions, reporting, and enforcement are the skeleton of the probation process. But the flesh on the bones of probation consists of pressures and routines that dominate the probation system. To describe these, we analyze the forces stemming from the perspectives of the probation officer, the offender, and the probation bureaucracy.

The Probation Officer

The probation officer's supervision work world is defined by "the caseload." The caseload is the group of offenders assigned to the probation officer for supervision and enforcement. Whatever happens within the caseload—when a probationer is arrested, or whenever a violation is filed—becomes the basis by which the probation officer will be evaluated in job performance. The caseload is the engine of accountability, and keeping the caseload in "good order" is essential. This means that supervision contact requirements must be met, necessary paperwork filed, and court reports kept up-to-date. A "problem caseload" is one in which the paperwork is in disarray and the compliance of probationers unverified. Problem caseloads reflect negatively on the skills of the probation officer. The average number of inmates on a probation caseload varies greatly in the United States. In some states the number is as low as 10, for special offender populations such as those on electronic monitoring, and as high of over 400. Statistics show that during 1999 the average caseload per officer was 139 for regular probation supervision.[24]

The main tools the probation officer uses to keep the caseload in good order are interpersonal skills in the balanced use of power and authority. Power is the ability to force a person to do something he or she does not want to do. Authority is the ability to influence a person's actions in a desired direction without resort to force. Thus, a person who chooses to exercise power in a relationship can almost always be shown to lack authority.

The problem of power and authority is a thorny one for probation officers. Officers are expected to exercise the power of law in controlling offenders under their care. This is one reason that in many jurisdictions probation officers are legally classified as "peace officers," with the power of arrest. Yet the actual power of the role is less than it seems: Short of the formal power to arrest or hold probationers, there is normally little that probation officers can do to force compliance with the law.

The lack of substantive power explains why probation officers rely heavily on their authority in supervising offenders: It is a more efficient and ultimately more effective tool. The officer attempts to develop the offender's trust and confidence so that through a measure of authority, the offender will be guided to change patterns of living that tend to promote involvement in crime. Yet both parties know that the officer has raw power to be exercised should the offender falter. Often the point comes across as "let me help you—or else!" This kind of mixed message leads to manipulation by both the officer and the probationer and may make the supervision relationship seem inconsistent.

Complicating supervision styles is the fact that probation officers can be held legally accountable for any abridgment of the community's safety that occurs as a result of any error in the performance of their duties. In practice, this means that reasonable efforts must be made to monitor the behavior of clients and to show particular care with those whose backgrounds make them potential risks to the community. The most famous case that establishes this principle involved a probationer who had been convicted of sexual assault. His probation officer helped him get a job as a maintenance worker in an apartment complex, a position that gave him access to keys to various apartments. In placing the probationer, the officer withheld his client's past record from the employer. The probationer sexually assaulted several apartment residents, who later sued the probation officer for his cover-up of the probationer's record. The court held in favor of the victims, ruling probation officers liable for their conduct as government employees.[25]

The liability of probation officers (and parole officers as well) is a new area of law, one that is not yet well formulated. The chief significance of the emergence of this issue is that operational procedures in probation become even more important. To defend against possible allegations of misconduct, probation officers need more than ever to document in writing the actions they are taking with their clients so that they can meet a potential challenge of the reasonableness of the actions—and to keep their caseloads in "good order."

The Offender

Most probationers believe they have little influence on the supervision process. Although probation officers' power is limited, it often seems to offenders much greater than it actually is. Moreover, officers decide on the style of supervision—whether relatively supportive or controlling—and the offenders have few direct ways of influencing even this decision. Therefore, probationers often perceive themselves to be relatively impotent against the potentially arbitrary decisions of the officers.

It is not surprising, then, that probationers commonly resent their status, even when most people think they should be grateful for "another chance." Many probation officers try to blunt the indignity by involving the probationer in determining the goals and strategies of supervision. Rather than simply requiring the offender to seek assistance, the officer brings the client into a problem-solving process. Such strategies are aimed at reducing the perceived discrepancy between the power of the officer and the powerlessness of the client. They also help establish a more positive authority relationship between the officer and the probationer.

In the end, the probationer's attitude toward supervision and response to the officer's supervision style will have a major impact on the ultimate outcome of the probation term. Some researchers believe that differences in probationer responses to supervision are so important that the officer should tailor the style of supervision to the offender to take into account the probationer's response. One study of probationers' responses to supervision identified four supervision strategies based on the probationer's response to supervision:

1. Selective intervention strategies are designed to help clients cope with the temporary situational crisis that led to involvement in crime.
2. Environmental structure strategies attempt to develop daily living skills so that clients can reduce their associations with criminal peers.
3. Casework/control strategies attempt to overcome serious problems with stability, particularly in emotional, personal, and substance abuse areas.
4. Limit-setting strategies provide for close monitoring of conditions of probation and assertive enforcement of the requirements of supervision.[26]

This classification scheme underscores the importance of selecting appropriate ways to handle probationers. Consider, for example, how ineffective a supportive, nonaggressive selective intervention approach would be with an offender who needs the control implied by a limit-setting strategy. The most effective probation officers appear to be the ones who can "read" their cases' responses to their authority and tailor their supervision approaches accordingly.

The Bureaucracy

Three organizational pressures govern the bureaucratic world of probation supervision: case control, case management structure, and competence.[27]

Case control pressures emerge because judges, prosecutors, administrators, and community members all expect probation officers somehow to "make" probationers abide by the conditions and legal requirements of probation. But there is little the officer can do to "make" the offender cooperate, because real power (such as the threat of revocation) may be limited. Consequently, officers are forced to rely on their discretion and individualistic supervision style, often minimizing or deliberately ignoring formal requirements in order to persuade the offender to cooperate.

Similarly, the heavy caseloads of probationers and the unpredictability of the job produce a need for case management structure. It is achieved by means of paperwork documenting the officer's activities on cases and by such routines as scheduled reporting days (when offenders come for office visits) and field days (when officers make home visits). But the demands of the caseload do not always correspond to the case management routines, nor do documented activities always lead to positive results. And so the management of work through regular schedules and operating procedures limits the creativity, intensity, and responsiveness of the supervision effort.

The pressure for competence can be demoralizing for probation staff. It is simply not possible for officers to be effective with all their cases. There is no surefire approach to take with offenders. At best, the officer is faced with a variety of approaches that may or may not work. Add to these uncertainties the fact that the officer typically receives little feedback about successes but much about failures, and what you have is an unintentional but systematic attack on the officer's sense of competence. Many officers react with cynical, defensive stances: Probationers cannot be changed unless they want to be, probationers are losers, and so forth. When several probation officers within an office develop this kind of cynicism, their negativism can pervade the entire working atmosphere.

In sum, the informal world of supervision is best understood as a complex interaction between officers (who vary in style, knowledge, and philosophy) and offenders (who vary in responsiveness and need for supervision) in a bureaucratic organization that imposes significant formal and informal constraints on the work. In light of such complexity, it is not easy to assess the effectiveness of probation supervision.

Special Supervision Programs

The needs of probationers vary dramatically. Sex offenders require different supervision strategies than do cocaine addicts; mentally ill offenders must be handled differently than embezzlers. With caseloads often exceeding 100 probationers per officer, it is unrealistic to expect the probation officer to tailor the supervision effort to fit each person on the caseload. Instead, there has

PROBATION OFFICER STYLES: PAST VERSUS PRESENT

Past

In what has become a classic article in the area of probation, Carl B. Klockers described in 1972 what were the different probation officer roles. The four roles were the Law Enforcer, Therapeutic Agent, Time Server, and Synthetic Officer. More recently, probation supervision has been described by many to be based more on service delivery than law enforcement. Two service delivery strategies that have been described are the Casework approach and the Resource Brokerage approach. Learning these roles and strategies can help

The Implementation of Community Corrections

the reader develop a better understanding of how probation officers supervise correctional offenders in the community. If you were a probation officer, which of the following styles would you follow?

The Law Enforcer: Probation officers in this style stress their legal authority and law enforcement elements of their job. Primary concern is with enforcing the "letter of the law" or strictly enforcing the wishes of the court. Related concerns include the full execution of authority given by the court, public safety, and performing police-like tasks.

The Therapeutic Agent: In this role, the probation officer sees himself or herself as a person who has the responsibility of providing treatment and rehabilitative resources for the offender. Effort is made to understand the offender's personal problems and to seek solutions to those problems. Viewing the offenders as clients, applying the casework approach, and seeking professional advancement is not unusual for these probation officers.

The Time Server: These probation officers avoid following law enforcement or casework functions. They view their jobs as "just a job." They minimally meet job demands and avoid any form of professional improvement. Basically, the Time Server is putting in his or her time until retirement.

The Synthetic Officer: As the term suggests, these officers try to blend the law enforcement and therapeutic approaches. They attempt to be authoritarian or helping toward the offender, depending on the situation that arises.

(Summary developed from Carl B. Klockers, "A Theory of Probation Supervision" *Journal of Criminal Law, Criminology and Police Science* 63:4 (1972): 550–557.)

Present

The Caseworker Model: In this approach, the probation officer (also called a probation counselor) stresses treatment, counseling, and a one-to-one relationship with the offender. Effort is made to develop a positive relationship that will provide the impetus for personal change. The officer or counselor views himself or herself as a social worker who utilizes the individualized casework method to deal with offenders' problems.

The Resource Broker Model: The resource broker approach assumes that there is not enough time and there are too many offenders to help them all. The officer in this model evaluates the offender's needs, arranges for him or her to seek help in the community, and then supervises and evaluates the progress of the offender. This approach is rooted in the reintegration movement of the early 1970s, which held that offenders must develop strong ties to the community if they are to avoid future criminality.

been a growing emphasis on specializing probation caseloads. Specialization groups probationers with similar problems into a single caseload. It allows the probation officer to develop better expertise in handling that problem, and it promotes a concentrated supervision effort to deal with that problem.

Studies of specialized supervision show this approach has promise.[28] A program of employment counseling and support services failed to reduce recidivism, but it did have a positive effect on the employment status of its participants. Specialized treatment programs operated by probation agencies have reduced recidivism for sex offenders. In general, targeted, specialized services have been found to be more effective than traditional services.

Recent interest in the problem of substance abuse has increased the attention given to offenders on probation who have problems with drugs and alcohol. Several special programs have been tried to combat the use of drugs by probationers. These programs typically take advantage of new techniques for drug surveillance and treatment. For example, urinalysis is used to determine whether an offender is continuing to use drugs. Methadone is used to allow addicts to avoid withdrawal symptoms. These approaches are often combined with close surveillance to reinforce abstinence on the part of probationers. The difficulty with special supervision programs is what to do with the "ordinary" offender who is slated for traditional services. There is often a feeling that "regular" probation is a less attractive function, and conflict among the specialized units can become a serious management problem. As a consequence, specialized service programs in probation, even when successful, require extensive managerial support. In Chapter 11 we will delve further into the issues related to the needs of special offenders in community corrections.

Special Needs of Women Offenders

Women apparently are more likely to receive community-based sentences. There are at least two reasons why this is true. The first is what has been coined the "chivalry factor." It states that because women have been considered less capable than men in all spheres but the domestic, presumably they require greater legal protection than men and should be differentiated from them by the criminal justice system. Judges have said that when they sentence women, they feel compelled to treat them differently than they treat men, and not only because children are often involved. Analysts believe that this differential treatment arises from the fact that most jurists are men and have the attitudes typical of men: Women are weak and require gentle treatment; it is difficult for them to take women seriously. Perhaps they see their mothers or wives in front of them at the time of sentencing and just cannot imagine that women require severe punishment. The chivalry factor seems to be at work from the time a crime is committed until the offender is paroled. Police often officially ignore women suspected of drug use or shoplifting, the offenses for which they are most frequently arrested.[29] Women are more likely than men to be released on bail, have their cases dismissed, and receive suspended sentences or probation.

A second possible reason why women receive less serious sentences than men is the fact that women generally commit less serious crimes. As tabulated by the Uniform Crime Reports, females account for 22.2 percent of all arrests and 26.4 percent of all arrests for serious (index) crimes. The majority of crimes committed by women are larceny theft, followed by assaults and drug violations.[30] Although these are serious crimes that may warrant incarceration, they are less in number and mild in comparison to the number and quality of crimes committed by men.

Whatever the reasons, in the end a greater proportion of women offenders than men offenders are placed on probation. In 2000, women constituted 22 percent of the number of persons on probation, or twice as large a share as among the jail (11.4 percent) and parole (12 percent) populations and more than three times the share of women in prison (6.6 percent).[31] While on probation, female offenders have special problems and needs that must be addressed if the sentence is to be successful. Three special needs of women offenders are child responsibilities, economic independence, and substance abuse.

Over half of women offenders have children. Many women who are parents are also divorced or single and carry the burden of child care alone. As a result of these roles, many women lack the necessary resources for successful living. Education and training, child care, and meaningful employment are often unavailable to women—especially those of the lower economic classes. Some have personal, financial, or physical problems that preclude them from being able to function properly and to care for their children in a competent fashion. Many turn to family members or social programs to provide assistance. When financial resources are limited, the situation worsens and some turn to criminality or substance abuse to improve their plight, albeit for the short term.

Programs for Women Offenders

To improve the situation for female offenders, we must develop a community-based correctional system that deals with the special problems of women. The first step is to develop and strengthen community-based correctional programs—like probation—that allow female offenders to remain in the community and to live with their children. Unnecessarily removing children from their parent(s) can cause future harm to the fabric of society.

Once allowed to live in the community, female offenders need help to rebuild their lives. This is not an easy task, and it requires effort by the community and the female offender to ensure success. Programs need to be developed to assist female offenders and to act in support of probation supervision.

Some of these may include programs that first help to build the woman's confidence and enhance her ability to develop economic independence. Essential programs of this type would be those that center on financial aid for college education, vocational training, job readiness training, job placement, and follow-up services that provide women with individual counseling on job-related issues. Parenting programs that teach women the different needs of children at various stages of life, consistent discipline skills, and proper nutrition are needed. Also essential are programs that center on personal counseling—to assist the offender to deal with the deeper issues related to criminality. Many women suffer from poor self-esteem, dysfunctional backgrounds, victimization, discrimination, or poor decisions made in the past.

Finally, but not least important, substance abuse counseling is essential considering the number of women involved. Over 75 percent of female offenders need some form of substance abuse treatment. Research has shown that success of probation and parole increases if substance abuse treatment and aftercare are implemented. What is advocated here is dealing with the problems of female offenders on probation in a holistic fashion. Programs that promote the female offender's gaining personal independence through education, training, and employment are the best way to solve the long-term problems associated with criminality.

Performance-Based Supervision

Questions about the effectiveness of supervision have spawned a performance-based approach to community supervision. This approach elevated the importance of "results" in setting community supervision priorities and selecting community supervision activities. The focus on results becomes important both in the strategies of client supervision and in the priorities of the community supervision agency.

The **performance-based supervision** movement has called for a reshaping of the philosophy of probation with a new emphasis on the primacy of public safety.[32] Rather than an amorphous belief in offender rehabilitation, this new philosophy of probation squarely accepts responsibility for adopting approaches that help enhance the safety of the public. With clients, the focus on public safety results is expressed in two ways. First, supervision strategies are chosen that reflect what is known about the effectiveness of supervision. In most cases, this means providing the most attention to the highest-risk cases, emphasizing the reduction of the kinds of problems that most contribute to crime, and consistently reinforcing crime-free behaviors. Second, the organization that adopts a performance-based orientation sets goals for improved supervision outcomes with its clients. In Georgia, for example, the administration set goals for improvements in several key areas of overall client performance: a higher rate of successful terminations of supervision, more clients with full employment, fewer positive drug tests, more attendance in drug treatment programs, and so forth.[33]

The key idea in the performance movement is to shift the focus of supervision plans from the activities of supervision to the results of supervision. The plan is to invent a new conception of probation that de-emphasizes what probation officers do and values what they accomplish. The test of probation, in this circumstance, is how well the sentence turns out in the end.

Broken Windows Probation

One expression of the performance-based approach to community supervision is "broken windows probation." **Broken windows probation** is the adoption of a policy that probation should be responsible for doing everything it can—even dealing with problems of public disorder—in order to improve public safety. By accepting public safety as a primary aim, probation leaders recognize the critical role probation can play, not just in reducing crime, but in enriching the quality of community life by contributing to a sense of personal security and quality of life.[34] The "broken windows" idea enables probation to embrace new problem-solving and partnership strategies that have proved successful for law enforcement.

The broken windows probation model first surfaced in March 1997, when a group of probation administrators formed a Reinventing Probation Council and began meeting in New York City with the idea of developing a new approach to probation supervision. The group included several of the most prominent national spokespersons in the field and was led by prominent corrections critic John DiIulio, professor at the University of Pennsylvania. The result of their meetings, which occurred at regular intervals over a three-year period, was a call for a new vision for probation supervision—an approach they called "broken windows" probation. The term *broken windows* was adopted from a community policing approach developed by criminologists James Q. Wilson and George Kelling in the early 1980s. It was based on the premise that if police deal with social disorder crimes that are relatively small problems (figuratively, broken windows), then the problem will not deteriorate to a larger problem (more serious crime).

The new vision begins with a frank admission that traditional probation supervision has failed to protect the public because it has failed to hold probationers accountable for their conduct. The result is a system of probation that serves neither the public nor the victims of crime, and fails to provide what probationers need in order to comply with the law and reclaim their roles as citizens. To remedy this situation, the group called for seven new strategies to be adopted by probation supervision:

Strategy 1: *Place public safety first*—Adopt an organizational mission that gives primary importance to the safety of the community.

Strategy 2: *Supervise probations in the neighborhood, not in the office*—Take the work of the probation officer out of the office and into the field, where it will have more impact on probationer behavior.

Strategy 3: *Rationally allocate resources*—Provide more supervision to high-risk cases; provide special supervision to cases with special problems.

Strategy 4: *Provide for strong enforcement of probation conditions and a quick response to violations*—Make sure probationers comply with their conditions and do not let probation violators languish without attention.

Strategy 5: *Develop partners in the community*—Build good working relationships with the police, social services, and local community leaders such as clergy and neighborhood associations.

Strategy 6: *Establish performance-based initiatives*—Set individual organizational goals and evaluate whether they are accomplished.

Strategy 7: *Cultivate strong leadership*—Build the basis for a generation of new leaders in probation who share the vision for the future.[35]

The announcement of the broken windows probation model has received a great deal of fanfare in the profession—not to mention some criticism.[36] But the ideas promoted by the model are already gaining ground in probation departments around the country. The broken window probation model has been supported by a larger movement that calls for increased cooperation between law enforcement and correctional agencies. Advocates of this movement are finding that police–corrections partnerships have the potential to reshape the way policing and correctional services are performed. It is hoped that these partnerships can help to prevent crimes, reduce the demand for high-security confinement, and in the end save money. See the box "Operation Night Light" for an example of one of the first and longest-lasting partnerships between police and correctional agencies.

OPERATION NIGHT LIGHT, BOSTON, MASSACHUSETTS

Boston's Operation Night Light is one of the oldest corrections–police enhanced supervision partnerships. A partnership between the Boston Police Department and district court probation officers, Operation Night Light had its roots in a chance encounter in 1990 between probation officers and members of the police department's gang unit, during which they all noted that they often were dealing with the same offenders. This realization sparked a series of brainstorming ways they could work together more effectively. Using intelligence information from the police gang unit, probation officers began asking judges to include curfews and area restrictions as conditions of supervision when gang-involved offenders were placed on probation. Probation officers also began doing curfew checks and monitoring activity on the streets to ensure that probationers were complying with these conditions.

These precursor relationships became formalized as Operation Night Light in 1992 when probation officers and Boston police officers began joint patrols and curfew checks of probationers who, based on intelligence information, were thought to be criminally active. Night Light staff have since:

- Shared intelligence information on gang members and activity with local, state, and federal agencies such as the Drug Enforcement Administration (DEA); the Bureau of Alcohol, Tobacco, and Firearms (BATF); the Immigration and Naturalization Service (INS); and the Massachusetts Violent Fugitive Strike Force.
- Met with gangs to announce zero-tolerance policy for gang-related violence and to promise aggressive enforcement against gangs that engage in acts of violence.
- Cooperated with other agencies in efforts to "take down" gang leaders and break up gangs that continued to commit violent crimes.

Operation Night Light gives Boston police officers (not just members of the gang unit) information on who is on probation and what conditions they are required to obey. As a result, police officers on patrol in Boston reported that they acted as additional eyes and ears for probation around the clock. Because many gang leaders and members are on probation, technical violations of conditions of supervision can be grounds for removing them from the streets quickly, pending the outcome of legal proceedings related to alleged new crimes.

Since Operation Night Light began, police and probation officers have made more than 5,000 contacts with gang-involved probationers in the community. No evaluation has been done to determine the extent to which Night Light may have contributed to Boston's contemporaneous drop in serious crimes. Several other initiatives were under way in Boston to combat youth violence, and crime declined in many other cities throughout the United State during the same time period. Regardless, the number of homicides, homicides with firearms, and assaults with firearms all dropped sharply in Boston during the 1990s. In 1993, there were 93 homicides in Boston, compared to 39 between January 1 and November 30, 1997. Sixty-five of the homicides in 1993 involved firearms, compared to 21 in the first 11 of 1997. Assaults with firearms dropped from 799 in 1995 to 126 during the first 11 months of 1997. Between early 1995 and late 1997, Boston went $2^{1}/_{2}$ years without a juvenile homicide involving firearms. In the previous years $2^{1}/_{2}$ years, 26 Boston teens died from gunshots.

Officials report that Operation Night Light's efforts—joint patrols, curfew checks, and information sharing—have had a significant impact on gang members who are on probation because they have begun to take conditions of supervision much more seriously (although no data are readily available on changes in probation outcomes). In addition, police and probation officers reportedly have developed new respect for one another and recognize that they can use their formal powers in complementary ways in the pursuit of a common purpose.

Source: Dale Parent and Brad Snyder, "Police-Corrections Partnerships," U.S Department of Justice, National Institute of Justice, March 1999. www.ncjrs.org/txtfiles1/175047.txt

ADVANTAGES OF PROBATION

Lower Cost

The cost of placing an offender in a correctional institution is generally believed to be far greater than the cost of probation. For example, to incarcerate a single offender in most states exceeds $20,000 per year, while probation can be administered at an annual cost of between $1,000 and $3,000. There are approximately twice as many persons on probation as incarcerated. Probation is itself "big business," employing tens of thousands of people in the United States alone. And, as mentioned earlier, the collection of probation fees can help lower the cost of probation administration.

Maintains Community Ties

Offenders who are placed on probation continue to live in the community, and this serves a number of purposes that can be beneficial to society. While residing in the community, the offender may look for work or retain his or her job. If employed, probationers pay taxes, provide financial assistance to family, contribute to the local economy, and may be able to make restitution to victims.

Promotes Rehabilitation

Probation may provide an offender with the motivation and supervision he or she needs to find help with psychological problems, substance abuse, family issues, financial assistance, and job training. In the long run, these issues must be addressed if the offender is to remain free of crime.

Reduces Stigmatization

Being labeled an "ex-con" can stick with a person for a lifetime. After being released from incarceration, the ex-offender could experience various forms of discrimination while seeking employment or find it difficult to gain the support systems, such as friends, neighbors, and other community contacts, that prevent criminality.

Avoids Criminalization

Numerous authors have documented that being incarcerated is a very difficult psychological and physical experience, one that could lead to an offender becoming permanently socialized into the criminal lifestyle. Probation can help prevent this occurrence by keeping first-time offenders and those who commit nonserious crimes out of correctional institutions and away from the negative effects of prison.

Community Protection

The most recent call for the use of probation has been as a way to protect the community. Probation can protect the community in at least three ways. First, by developing the PSI, probation can assist judges in sentencing. Without this information, judges would be unable to make educated guesses about who can succeed on probation supervision. That same information can help those who supervise the needs and risk of offenders on their caseloads. Second, probation allows for a formal mechanism for supervising offenders while they reside in the community. Without any supervision, the offender is unchecked by the system. Finally, probation can protect the community by helping to prevent future criminality. This happens (it is hoped) as the result of monitoring the offender's participation in various rehabilitation programs.

DISADVANTAGES OF PROBATION

Protection of Community Compromised

The release of those convicted of crimes into the community undoubtedly increases the risk of future criminality. The quality of probation supervision—whether it really does what it is supposed to do—has always been in question. Recidivism in probation has been shown to be very high, with almost half of probationers being rearrested for a felony within three years of being placed on probation.[37]

Justice Concerns

Probation is often viewed as a nonsentence or without any punishment value. Some critics of probation feel that the sentence undermines the seriousness of the offense, especially in cases where the offender could receive a long prison sentence for a felony crime. In cases where probation is received as the result of a plea bargain, then the due process of the criminal justice system is weakened.

Possible Abuse of Discretion by Judges and Probation Officers

In states without mandatory imprisonment laws, judges may choose to place an offender on probation who in other states or circumstances would receive incarceration. The same judge may revoke probation simply because she does not like the "attitude" of the offender during the revocation hearing. The probation officer may choose not to file a technical violation on an offender because he feels the person deserves another chance. These are all examples of the use of discretion in probation and situations in which a person in power can possibly misuse his or her authority with the result being a loss of justice or personal damage to the offender involved.

RESEARCH ON PROBATION EFFECTIVENESS

When discussing probation effectiveness the first question that must be asked is, "What is the definition of effectiveness?" Probation effectiveness could mean when an offender is deterred from committing any future criminal offense. Or maybe it refers to abstaining from very serious crimes, not from those of a minor nature such as technical violations listed in the probation agreement. The determination of effectiveness is not an easy task. What is usually used as the criterion for probation effectiveness is measurement of recidivism—or return to criminal behavior. This seems logical since one of the proposed aims of a criminal sanction like probation is to deter future criminality. However, the actual measurement of recidivism is not so simple. **Recidivism in probation** can be measured in at least four different ways:

1. Violations of the conditions of probation
2. Arrests for new offenses committed by probationers
3. Convictions for new offenses
4. Revocations of probation

Any one of these or a combination may display some level of recidivism. The matter is further complicated by the large amount of discretion that is given to probation officers. If the officer deems the offender's behavior to be insignificant, such as a minor infraction of the probation contract, then none of the above will result in recidivism or revocation. Because of the difficulties of measuring probation effectiveness, the results of research on the issue vary considerably. According to most studies of probation revocation, from one-fifth to one-third of probationers fail to abide by the terms of their probation.[38] A widely publicized Rand Corporation study, however, which found much higher rates of violation, resulted in a sense of concern on the part of probation administrators. The Rand researchers studied a sample of probationers from two urban California counties who had been placed on probation for FBI index crimes, following them for forty months. More than one-third had been reincarcerated for technical violations or new offenses, 65 percent had been arrested for a felony or misdemeanor, and 51 percent were convicted of a crime. Many of these probation "failures" remained on probation after their convictions, even though the crimes were often serious. This study found that once a person is placed on probation, serious misbehavior does not necessarily result in removal from the community.[39]

The overall results of the Rand study have been supported by other follow-up studies of probationers. A three-year follow-up of over 12,000 Texas probationers found that one-third of that group ended up revoked and back in prison.[40] A similar study of a national sample of probationers found that 36 percent were incarcerated before successfully completing their terms.[41]

Replications of this type of follow-up study outside of "big-corrections states" such as California and Texas have found somewhat lower levels of serious misbehavior by probationers. In 1998, a national survey of probationers found that 59 percent of the adults released from probation successfully completed their sentences, while only 17 percent had been reincarcerated.[42]

Perhaps probation works well in some areas, but less well in others, depending partly on the nature of the person placed on probation. As it turns out, the kind of person placed on probation varies dramatically from place to place. One study of felony sentencing found that rates of probation sentences for robbers varied among fourteen cities from a low of less than 1 percent to a high of 13 percent, and probation sentences varied from 2 to 40 percent.[43] Probation agencies that supervise more serious offenders can be expected to have higher rates of revocation. In locations where probationers have serious criminal histories, some probation departments have begun to collaborate with police departments to improve the public safety effectiveness of both agencies.[44]

So then, what should we believe about the effectiveness of probation? It is difficult to say at this point. Probation does seem to work for some offenders in some jurisdictions depending on the level of competence and supervision provided. But it can be stated that because of the difficulty of measuring recidivism and the differences in probation supervision and administration, probation effectiveness is impossible to clearly assess at this juncture.

SUPERVISION EFFECTIVENESS

For many years, experts believed that supervision could be made more effective by reducing the size of the caseloads being managed by probation officers. They reasoned that smaller caseloads would allow the officers to devote more attention to each client, thus improving the services provided. Frequently cited standards called for caseloads of thirty-five to fifty persons, though such figures had never been justified by empirical study. During the 1960s and 1970s, dozens of experiments were conducted to find the most effective size of a caseload. Yet a review of those studies concluded that "caseload reduction alone does not significantly reduce recidivism in adult probationers."[45]

Why don't smaller caseloads improve the effectiveness of supervision? Perhaps the assumption that "more supervision is better supervision" is too simplistic, because it fails to take into account the significant elements of supervision. It seems that "the nature of the supervision experience, the classification of offenders, officers, and types of treatment, and the social systems of the corrections agency" have more impact than the size of the caseload.[46]

REVOCATION AND TERMINATION OF PROBATION

Probation status is ended in one of two ways: The person successfully completes the period of probation and is terminated, or the person's probationary status is revoked because of misbehavior. **Revocation** is when a person fails on probation (or parole) to fulfill the responsibilities of supervision and is returned to court for a new disposition. At this time, the sentencing judge may wish to continue supervision or impose incarceration. Revocation can result from a new arrest or conviction or from a rules violation—the probationer has failed to comply with a condition of probation. Rules violations that result in revocations are referred to as technical violations.

Revocations for technical violations are somewhat controversial, because behaviors that are not ordinarily illegal—changing one's residence without permission, failing to attend a therapy program, neglecting to report to the probation office, and so forth—result in incarceration. Some years ago, technical violations were common whenever probationers were uncooperative or resistant to supervision. Today, probation is revoked when the rules violation is persistent or poses a threat to the community. Otherwise, rules violations are handled by other means.

Although patterns vary across the country, the most common reason for a revocation is a new offense by the probationer. Sometimes the court will await conviction on the new offense before revoking probation, but if the offense is serious enough, probation is immediately revoked. In such a case, a technical violation is alleged, even though the real basis for revocation is the new offense.

Because the revocation of probation represents a serious change in the offender's status, the courts have ruled that the offender has several due process rights in the revocation procedure. The major case governing probationers was decided by the Supreme Court in 1967 in *Mempa* v. *Rhay*.[47] The suspension of Jerry Mempa's sentence for the offense of joyriding had been revoked after he admitted involvement in burglaries while on probation for the joyriding offense. The court ruled that sentences could not be imposed after a probation revocation without an attorney to represent the offender.

In a subsequent decision, *Gagnon* v. *Scarpelli* (1973), the Supreme Court further clarified the procedures for a revocation.[48] The approved practice is to handle the revocation in three stages.

1. In the first stage (sometimes waived), often called the preliminary hearing, the facts of the arrest are reviewed to determine if there is probable cause that a violation has occurred.
2. In the second stage, the facts of the allegation are heard and decided. The evidence to support the allegation is presented by the probation department, and the probationer has an opportunity to refute the evidence. The

probationer has the right to written notice of the charges and the disclosure of evidence of the violation; the right to testify and to present witnesses and evidence to contradict the allegations; the right to cross-examine adverse witnesses; the right to a neutral and detached hearing officer; and the right to a written statement of findings. Unless unusual grounds exist to deny counsel, the probationer also has a right to an attorney.

3. The third stage is the sentencing stage. With an attorney present, the judge decides whether to impose a term of incarceration and, if so, the duration of the term. The third stage is more than a technicality because probation will often be reinstated with greater restrictions following a minor violation.

For those who successfully complete probation, the sentence is terminated. Ordinarily the probationer is then a completely free citizen again, without obligation to the court or to the probation department.

PERSPECTIVES ON PROBATION

Systems

Probation is the corrections system's entry stage. This is true in two respects. First, probation is the most common sanction for first-time offenders, especially those who are convicted of less serious offenses. Second, probation officers write presentence investigation reports and make sentencing recommendations that help determine where offenders will be placed when they are sentenced by the court.

Because it occupies such an important entry location, a probation system will have ripple effects throughout the rest of the corrections system. When correctional officials and other criminal justice decision makers see their probation system as a strong and effective service, they will more readily defer to its strategies and they will accept probation as a meaningful sanction. But when probation is seen as weak or lacking credibility, the other actors in the criminal justice system will want to avoid using probation or discredit its recommendations.

Because probation is far cheaper than most other correctional strategies, it can also serve as a kind of correctional "dumping ground," taking cases that don't seem to fit well with any other alternative. When this becomes a common way of operating, probation work can lose some of its importance as a supervision or management tool, serving the needs of the system more than the requirements of offenders.

But in hard, cold facts, the correctional system could not operate without probation. The average probation officer accounts for as many as 100 cases or more. These offenders have to be managed by probation, because there is not enough room in jails or prisons to hold them. Probation is often the right sanction, but it is always needed as an available sanction.

People

Of all the correctional methods, probation is perhaps the most person-dependent: It is in practice a relationship between a probation officer and a person on probation. How this relationship develops over time will define what probation means, both for the offender and for the officer.

Probation officers and their clients are in a particularly interdependent relationship. Probationers have been given a "chance" by the court, and they may come to see that the probation officer is standing between them and complete freedom. Probation officers, on the other hand, face the reality of working with offenders under extreme constraints of time and other resources. This can create a tension between them.

However, when you ask probation officers what they like about their jobs, they almost always answer in part that they "like working with people." Likewise, when a probationer says probation was "good," it is usually attributed to the fairness, reasonableness, and assistance provided by the probation officer. Although they may only encounter one another for a few minutes a month, the way each will come to see the probation experience depends a lot on how the other acts.

Bureaucracy

Probation organizations have to run efficiently, because they face an enormous and demanding workload. Constrained by the requirements of the court for enforcement of rules, and practically limited by large and changing caseloads, probation must determine ways to become efficient.

That is why all probation departments develop classification systems, usually formally but sometimes informally, that determine which clients get the most attention and which get the bare minimum. It simply is not feasible for a probation agency to give all its clients the attention they need.

The presence of this bureaucratic need for efficiency in the context of an overwhelmingly interpersonal work creates a tension in the organization: Probation departments thrive on effective personal relationships, but they crave rules that structure the way these relationships emerge.

The bureaucracy, then, becomes a contingency that both clients and probation officers have to learn how to manage. For clients, the bureaucracy is a set of rules that have to be obeyed—or at least dealt with. For probation officers, there is a similar issue: The requirements of probation supervision operate to structure the way the probation officer has to approach his or her job, as well.

Evidence

Probation has not fared well from an evidence perspective. There have been numerous studies of probation effectiveness, and most of them seem to show that more intensive probation methods do not result in less revocation than less intensive probation activity. Most observers tend to interpret this pattern as suggesting that probation "does not work." But is that necessarily so?

Studies that investigate the effectiveness of probation by comparing "some" of it to "more" of it make the assumption that the benefits of probation "add up" like a bank account. But what if this is not the case? What if the benefits of probation mostly involve what it is *not*? That is, because probation's effectiveness has not been studied in comparison to *prison,* we really cannot say whether probation, per se, works. We have enough data to say that closer probation supervision is not necessarily better than "loose" probation supervision, but we cannot say how probation fares compared to confinement.

Most probation advocates would argue that this comparison—probation versus prison—is the more important one. But these advocates face a tough challenge. It is hard to conceive of a sanction that is more controlling than confinement, and so the questions about probation's effectiveness remain difficult. Yet for most of the history of probation, we have known that the success rates of offenders on probation are superior to those of offenders who have been to prison. Of course, a higher-risk offender is selected for prison. But what if some of the difference comes from the fact that the negative effects of prison are avoided through probation?

THE FUTURE OF PROBATION

As we enter the new century, there is evidence of dramatic change in probation. Caseloads of traditional probation are growing well beyond reasonable management: 200- and even 300-person caseloads are not unusual. In many locales, traditional probation has experienced a deterioration in the quality of supervision due to loss of staff and an increase in cases. Yet the importance of probation for public safety has never been greater: It was estimated that up to 17 percent of felony arrests in one sample of large urban counties were of people who were on probation at the time of their alleged offense.[49] As a result of the renewed emphasis on public safety, many agencies also experienced a resurgence of intensive and structured supervision for selected offenders.[50]

Since that first day in 1841 when John Augustus looked for a better way of working with criminals, probation has continued to grow. What was once known as an "alternative to incarceration" is now the number one sentencing option used by judges all across the United States.

During the last twenty years, probation has gone through some major changes, from an emphasis on rehabilitation to one of surveillance, and eventually to a concentration on risk management. Probation now finds itself on the brink of what could be another major directional change. More and more jurisdictions are indicating that probation must take responsibility for the desired behavioral changes in probationers.

This leaves us with two increasingly divergent probations of the future. One is largely a paper exercise. Whatever services are provided will be done through brokerage: The probation officer serves as a referral agent, involving the probationer in single-focus community service agencies (such as drug treatment programs) that work with a variety of community clients, not just with offenders. The remaining probationers—a minority of all offenders, to be sure—will be watched closely and will receive first-rate supervision and control from highly trained professionals working with reasonable levels of funding and programmatic support.[51]

The use of brokerage is not necessarily a bad idea. Its proponents argue that persons with special skills in any problem area can provide treatment superior to what a generalist probation officer can give and that the community ought to be providing such assistance to its offenders. Yet community agencies are not always quick to offer services to offenders; they prefer to work with voluntary clients, not those who must avail themselves of services under threat of law.

Probation administrators are also changing the way they want to be evaluated. Most of the time—and in most studies cited in this chapter—probation's effectiveness is determined by rearrest rates: High rates are seen as a sign of ineffective supervision. Yet administrators know that high rearrest rates can also mean that staff are watching high-risk clients vigilantly, something most citizens would applaud. From this viewpoint, recidivism rates are not the sole outcome criterion for a probation department. Instead, some feel probation should also be evaluated by a series of "performance indicators" that better reveal whether probation is doing its job. These indicators include numbers of community service projects performed by probationers, the amount of probation fees and restitution collected, days free of drug use, employment rates, and taxes paid.[52] However, detractors claim that even if these performance indicators are high, the public is interested in crime as a bottom line—and that means recidivism rates matter most.

In many respects, then, probation finds itself at a crossroads. While its credibility is probably as low as it has ever been, its workload is growing dramatically and, in view of the crowding in prisons and jails, will probably continue to do so. Under the strain of the workloads and on-again, off-again public support, probation faces a grave challenge: Can its methods of supervision and service be adapted to work effectively with high-risk offenders? There is no certain answer to this question, and trends are ambiguous. Many innovations are being attempted, but it is unclear whether such new programs actually strengthen probation or detract from it. Certainly, they expand the variety of probation sanctions, making them more applicable to more offenders. But do they strengthen the mainstream functions of probation—

investigation and supervision? These functions must be improved for probation to succeed in its current challenge.

SUMMARY

Probation is the most extensively used form of punishment in the correctional system. About two-thirds of all adults under correctional supervision are on probation. Probation can be used in combination with incarceration or other punishments, such as fines, restitution, and community service. Probation allows offenders to serve the terms imposed by the court in the community, under supervision.

Probation officers serve two major functions: investigation and supervision. The presentence investigation helps judges determine the appropriate punishment for the offender. The extensiveness of the investigation varies, but increasingly there is a trend toward short reports that focus on the issue of risk. Such organizational problems as unclear sentencing goals, plea bargaining, and heavy workloads limit the influence of the PSI on the sentencing decision.

The probation officer, required both to enforce the law and to help the offender, faces role conflict in virtually every aspect of the job. Because officers lack substantive power, they must rely heavily on their authority in supervising offenders. The offender's response to supervision greatly influences the nature and effectiveness of the relationship with the officer, as does the fact that all supervision activities take place in the context of the probation bureaucracy.

Three ideas that have recently come to be commonplace in correctional agencies are performance-based supervision, supervision fees, and police– corrections partnerships. Of growing concern to corrections agencies is the large number of offenders that can be called "special" because of the unique supervision and rehabilitation needs that they possess. Although a large majority of those on probation are men, women offenders on probation are growing in number. Women on probation often have different problems than do men, and these issues must be dealt with if we wish to improve probation effectiveness. There are a number of advantages and disadvantages of probation. Each must be explored to fully understand the complexity of probation supervision and implementation.

Probation may be revoked as the result of a new arrest or for violation of the conditions of community supervision. When an offender is charged with being in violation of probation, he or she is allowed certain legal procedures during the revocation process.

Results on probation effectiveness concentrate on recidivism. The research results on the topic are mixed. Most research reports that about a third of probationers do not complete probation successfully. A recent study in California, however, indicated a much higher rate.

DISCUSSION QUESTIONS

1. How does the use of probation affect the corrections system? Why is it used so extensively?
2. Of the three recent developments in probation (supervision fees, performance-based supervision, and broken windows probation), which do you think is the most helpful to correctional agencies? Explain why you think so.
3. Why might some probationers be kept in the community after a technical violation, rather than having their probation revoked?
4. Given the two major tasks of probation, how should officers spend their time? How *do* they spend their time?
5. What are some of the unique problems facing women offenders on probation? How can we mitigate these problems for women offenders?
6. If you were a leader in the corrections field, what would you do to improve the current status of probation supervision?

SUGGESTED READINGS

Augustus, John. *A Report of the Labors of John Augustus, for the Last Ten Years, in Aid of the Unfortunate.* Boston: Wright & Hasty, 1852. Reprinted as *John Augustus, First Probation Officer* (New York: Probation Association, 1939). Historical account of first probation officer.

Clear, Todd R., and O'Leary, Vincent. *Controlling the Offender in the Community.* Lexington, MA: Lexington Books, 1981. Presents the argument for risk management methods in probation.

Ditton, Jason, and Ford, Roslyn. *The Reality of Probation: A Formal Ethnography of Process and Practice.* London: Avebury Press, 1995. Uses interviews with judges, probation officers, and probationers to paint a picture of the operations of the probation system.

Petersilia, Joan, and Turner, Susan. *Granting Felons Probation: Public Risks and Alternatives.* Santa Monica, CA: Rand Corporation, 1985. Recounts the results of a study of probation for serious offenders in California.

Vass, Anthony A. *Alternatives to Prison: Punishment Custody and the Community.* Newbury Park, CA: Sage, 1990. Gives an up-to-date critique of imprisonment and defense of probation.

WEB SITES

Web site for probation and parole statistics with links to related sites
www.ojp.usdoj.gov/bjs/pandp.htm

Web site about the Reinventing Probation Council
http://web5.infotrac-college.com/wadsworth/session/916/498/18208498/15!xrn_31_0_A19548344

Web site for the American Probation and Parole Association
www.appa-net.org

Web site for Rand Corporation publications on probation
www.rand.org/crim

Web site to learn more about client-specific planning from the National Center on Institutions and Alternatives
www.ncianet.org/ncia

1. Marc Renzema, "Reporting Kiosks: A Logical Idea Meets Resistance," *Journal of Offender Monitoring* 11 (Summer 1998): 13–14.

2. Frank Domurad, "Neighborhood Shield," Presentation to the American Probation and Parole Association, Phoenix, AZ, July 2000.

3. U.S. Department of Justice, Bureau of Justice Statistics, Press Release, August 26, 2001.

4. Robert Martinson, "California Research at the Crossroads," *Crime and Delinquency* 22 (April 1976): 191.

5. National Advisory Commission on Criminal Justice Standards and Goals, *Standards Relating to Corrections* (Washington, DC: Government Printing Office, 1973).

6. F. Hussey and D. Duffee, *Probation, Parole, and Community Field Services* (New York: Harper & Row, 1980), p. 134.

7. Mark M. Lanier and Cloud Miller, "Attitudes and Practices of Federal Probation Officers Toward Pre-Plea/Trial Investigation Report Policy," *Crime and Delinquency* 4:3 (July 1995): 364–377.

8. Jeanne B. Stinchcombe and Darryl Hippensteel, "Presentence Investigation Reports: A Relevant Justice Model Tool or a Medical Model Relic," *Criminal Justice Policy Review,* 12:2, (June 2001): 164–177.

9. Michael D. Norman and Robert C. Waldman, "Utah Presentence Investigation Reports: User Group Perceptions of Quality and Effectiveness, *Federal Probation* 64:2 (2000): 7–12.

10. Robert C. Davis and Barbara E. Smith, "The Effects of Victim Impact Statements on Sentencing Decisions: A Test in an Urban Setting," *Justice Quarterly* 11:3 (September 1994): 453–470.

11. Comptroller General of the United States, *State and Local Probation: Systems in Crisis,* Report to Congress (Washington, DC: Government Printing Office, 1976).

12. Joan Petersilia, Susan Turner, James Kahan, and Joyce Peterson, *Granting Felons Probation: Public Risks and Alternatives* (Santa Monica, CA: Rand Corporation, 1985), p. 39.

13. *Williams v. New York,* 337 U.S. 241 (1949).

14. *Verdugo v. United States,* 402 F. Supp. 599 (1968).

15. John Rosencrans, "Maintaining the Myth of Individualized Justice: Probation Pre-Sentence Reports," *Justice Quarterly* 5 (1988): 235–256.

16. James S. Granelli, "Presentence Reports Go Private," *National Law Journal* (May 2, 1983): 9.

17. J. T. Whitehead, "The Effectiveness of Felony Probation: Results from an Eastern State," *Justice Quarterly* 8 (1991): 525–543.

18. Petersilia et al., *Granting Felons Probation,* p. 41.

19. Bureau of Justice Statistics, "Probation and Parole in the United States," August 2002, NCJ 18208. www.ojp.usdoj.gov/bjs/pandp.htm

20. Sanford Bates, "The Establishment and Early Years of the Federal Probation System," *Federal Probation* (June 1987): 4–9.

21. Loren A. N. Buddress, ed. "Federal Probation and Pre-trial Services—A Cost Effective and Successful Community Corrections System," *Federal Probation* 61:1 (March 1997): 5–13.

22. Camille G. Camp and George M. Camp, *The 2000 Corrections Yearbook: Adult Corrections* (Middletown, CT: Criminal Justice Institute, 2000), p. 192.

23. Fay S. Taxman, "Dealing with Technical Violators," *Corrections Today* 57:1 (February 1, 1995): 46–53.

24. Camp and Camp, *The 2000 Corrections Yearbook,* p. 176.

25. *Rieser v. District of Columbia,* 21 Cr. L. 2503 (1977).

26. Todd R. Clear and Vincent O'Leary, *Controlling the Offender in the Community* (Lexington, MA: Lexington Books, 1983), pp. 55–61.

27. Ibid.

28. *This Works! Community Sanctions and Services for Special Offenders* (La Crosse, WI: IARCA, 1994).

29. Meda Chesney-Lind, "Chivalry Reexamined: Women and the Criminal Justice System," in *Women, Crime and the Criminal,* ed. Lee H. Bowker (Lexington, MA: Lexington Books,

1978), cited in Sharon L. Fabian, "Women Prisoners: Challenge of the Future," in *Legal Rights of Prisoners*, ed. Geoffrey P. Alpert (Newbury Park, CA: Sage, 1980), p. 176.

30. U.S. Department of Justice, Bureau of Justice Statistics, *Crime in the United States, 2000.* www/fbi.gov/ucr/cius_ 00

31. Bureau of Justice Statistics, "Probation and Parole in the United States," August 2001, NCJ 18208; and Bureau of Justice Statistics, "Prisoners in 2000," August 2002. NCJ 188207. www.ojp.usdoj.gov/bjs/pandp.htm

32. William D. Burrell, "Probation and Public Safety: Using Performance Measures to Demonstrate Public Value," *Corrections Management Quarterly* 2:3 (Summer 1998): 61–69.

33. David Goff and Brian Owens, "Results Driven Supervision: Georgia Creates a Model for the Future," *Perspectives* 23:2 (Spring 1999): 25–27.

34. Michael E. Smith and Walter J. Dickey, "What If Corrections Were Serious About Public Safety," *Corrections Management Quarterly*, 2:3 (Summer 1998): 12–30.

35. The Reinventing Probation Council, *Transforming Probation Through Leadership: The "Broken Windows" Model* (New York: Center for Civic Innovation at the Manhattan Institute, 2000).

36. Faye Taxman and James Byrne, "Fixing Broken Windows Probation," *Perspectives* 25:2 (Spring 2001): 22–29.

37. P. A. Langan and M. A. Cunniff, *Recidivism of Felons on Probation, 1986–1989* (Washington, DC: Bureau of Justice Statistics, 1992).

38. Michael Geerken and Hennessey D. Hayes, "Probation and Parole: Public Risks and the Future of Incarceration Alternatives," *Criminology* 31:4 (November 1993): 549–564.

39. Petersilia et al., *Granting Felons Probation*, p. 39.

40. Bill Bryan, *Recidivism of Offenders in Community Corrections: The Record So Far* (Austin, TX: Criminal Justice Policy Council, May 1996).

41. Joan Petersilia, "Probation in the United States," in *Crime and Justice: A Review of Research,* vol. 22, ed. Michael Tonry (Chicago: University of Chicago, 1997), pp. 149–200.

42. U.S. Department of Justice, Bureau of Justice Statistics, *Bulletin* (August 1999): 4.

43. Stephen Klein, Patricia Ebener, Allan Abrahamse, and Nore Fitzgerald, *Predicting Criminal Justice Outcome: Measuring What Matters* (Santa Monica, CA: Rand Corporation, 1991).

44. Richard Faulkner, "Community Policing and Community Corrections," *Perspectives* (Summer 1997): 10.

45. Robert M. Carter and Leslie T. Wilkins, "Caseloads: Some Conceptual Models," in *Probation, Parole, and Community Corrections,* ed. Robert M. Carter and Leslie T. Wilkins, 2nd ed. (New York: Wiley, 1976), p. 394.

46. K. D. Morgan, "Factors Associated with Probation Outcome," *Journal of Criminal Justice* 22 (1994): 341–353; see also B. Shims and M. Jones, "Predicting Success or Failure on Probation: Factors Associated with Felony Probation Outcomes," *Crime and Delinquency* 43:3 (July 1997): 314–328.

47. *Mempa v. Rhay,* 389 U.S. 128 (1967).

48. *Gagnon v. Scarpelli,* 411 U.S. 778 (1973).

49. Brian A. Reaves and Pheny Z. Smith, *Felony Defendants in Large Urban Counties, 1992* (Washington, DC: Government Printing Office, 1995).

50. Joan Petersilia, "A Crime Control Rationale for Reinvesting in Community Corrections," *Prison Journal* 75:4 (1995): 479–496.

51. James M. Byrne, "The Future of Probation and the New Intermediate Sanctions," *Crime and Delinquency* 36 (1990): 6–14.

52. Harry N. Boone and Betsy Fulton, *Results-Driven Management: Implementing Performance-Based Measures in Community Corrections* (Lexington, KY: American Probation and Parole Association, 1995).

Chapter 9

Promoting Justice in the Community

⊢ **OBJECTIVES** ⊢

The reader should be able to

1. Explain the concept of community justice.

2. Describe the three necessary concepts of a just society.

3. Describe the three key elements of the community justice perspective.

4. Explain how community justice is at once a *philosophy* of justice, a *strategy* of justice, and a series of justice *programs.*

5. Discuss how unit sanctions and interchangeability can be implemented in a community-based sanctioning system.

6. Understand the two key components of problem solving in community justice: problem set and opportunity set.

7. Summarize the arguments for and against community justice.

Walter Harrison is a probation officer, on his way to work. But you wouldn't know it from the look of things: It is 7 P.M., and his destination is the local police precinct in Roxbury—a tough, inner-city neighborhood in Boston. There he will partner up with another probation officer and two police officers, members of the Gang Unit of the Boston Police Department assigned to police the gangs of Roxbury.

Their workday begins with a strategy session, in which the police–probation team reviews the files of twelve gang members they expect to see sometime throughout the evening. They know the names and faces well, but the review serves as a reminder. Each gang member has a criminal record—many include multiple arrests for violent crimes involving guns. And each gang member is on probation for a recent conviction, with an evening curfew as a condition of probation. The team's job is to make sure that the probationers are obeying the curfew. They also want to make sure that, whatever else, the young men they see are not carrying guns. This probation team wants the violence to stop.

The officers start their shift by setting priorities—who needs to be seen most; where might they expect to find problems; what new information has come to light about one of the probationers; what they have learned from recent forays into the field. After talking through their cases and setting objectives for the night's tour, they drive into the streets of Roxbury in an unmarked car. It is 8 P.M., the time by which every gang member on probation must be at home.

The first stop is a local park where youths congregate at night. They pull up near a small group of young people and look for the familiar faces of the gang members on probation. Although they recognize many of the youths—and adolescents signal that they recognize the unmarked car—there are no probationers there. One youth approaches the car; for a brief

Photo: Members of the South Burlington Community Sentencing/ Reparations Board discuss a case.
© Glenn Russell

time he and the officers engage in an almost friendly banter. The youth's older brother is on probation and is doing well, and Harrison asks about how things are with the family. After a few minutes, the team drives off. The interaction has been calm and even cordial—everybody seems to know what is going on.

The team pulls up to a three-story, run-down apartment building and makes the first curfew check. James Sampson, a sixteen-year-old on probation for illegal possession of a gun, lives here. The police officers check the area for safety issues, noting the area surrounding the home and any exits. The probation officers approach the front door. Sampson's mother meets them at the door and seems almost glad to see them. What proceeds is a fairly typical home visit, with routine questions about Sampson's activities, especially his new job. The officers make an effort to keep things cordial and relaxed, because they want to show respect for the probationer and his family. The visit goes well. As they leave, Sampson's mother thanks them and says with emotion that curfew means she no longer has to wonder if "my Jamie" will die on the streets in the middle of the night. It is a sentiment the team has heard before, even from the former gang members. The team heads on to its next stop. They are engaged in a new kind of correctional work in the community.

Some observers see a trend in what is going on in Boston and a number of other cities and states. In Milwaukee, for example, probation and police work together to deal with a variety of problems facing high-crime neighborhoods; in Portland, Oregon, prosecutors have moved into the highest-crime neighborhoods to begin dealing with the problems of everyday citizens who live there; in Phoenix, probation staff have opened up neighborhood centers where they run literacy programs for residents; in Vermont, citizens are a part of sanctioning boards called Reparative Panels, and they impose sanctions on offenders sent to the boards from the courts. Each of these is an example of a change in the way justice works—a change toward "community justice."[1]

JUSTICE, CRIME, AND SOCIETY

In a democratic society, there is no treasure more valuable than social justice.

We believe in equal treatment under the law, because a society without equal treatment would be unjust. We believe that each person should be allowed to pursue a personal vision of the good life, because to deny this would be unjust. Every major civil right and social ethic finds its germination in the profound declaration of American democracy, that each of us has an essential right to enjoy "life, liberty, and the pursuit of happiness." Social justice, then, is embodied in the guarantee of this democratic promise. Without social justice, there can be no hope for democratic society, nor pride in democratic institutions.

Crime is an injustice. But unlike a social injustice, such as inequality or discrimination, crime is a kind of personal injustice. It represents not simply a breaking of the law, but an acute taking of advantage by one person of another. A person who violates the law says, in a way, that "other people have to play by the rules, but the rules don't apply to me." They take unfair advantage of others who obey the law.

The criminal justice system responds to the injustice of crime by exacting punishment that holds law violators accountable for their misdeeds. The punishment imposes a cost upon the offender that counterbalances the advantage gained by the crime. From the point of view of moral philosophers, in works that date back to the 1700s, punishment is appropriate when it conveys a moral message that speaks to all, offender and nonoffender alike, of the wrongfulness of criminal conduct. This is referred to as the "moral education" function of punishment—that it teaches people the rightfulness of obeying the law. Advocates of this perspective point out that to fail to punish those who violate the law is akin to approving their conduct. They argue that justice is produced when the guilty receive appropriate punishments for their crimes.

In modern society, however, the desire for criminal justice is housed uneasily within a broader, more compelling interest in social justice. The criminal justice system is concerned with individual cases, but when it comes to social justice, we must be concerned about people in groups and communities.

From the perspective of social justice, it is notable that crime is concentrated among the poorest communities, and that people who are from these communities are the most likely to be victims and to be offenders. To anyone who has spent even a small amount of time in our major cities' courts or visited a state prison, it is apparent that the criminal justice system overwhelmingly involves itself in the lives of the most disadvantaged among us.

This is why there is a tension between criminal justice and social justice. Criminal justice achieves its aims by imposing a personal cost upon law violators—a penalty that, by restricting personal freedom and applying a stigmatizing label, intentionally reduces the offender's well-being and status in society. This response to a person's criminality seems entirely fair, on the one hand: It seems a simple, indisputable fact that those who break the law deserve to be punished. But when we think about how penalties work in practice, it is understandably troubling that they affect so many who start out facing the social disadvantages of poverty and inequality.

We know that of the many who are born into disadvantage, not all will end up in trouble with the law. To equate poverty-stricken birth with criminal behavior is not fair to those who fight through the paralyzing effects of poverty and other social obstacles without resorting to crime. Enough of those born poor are able to survive without lawbreaking that we know poverty and criminality are not synonymous. Yet we must recognize that the stories of those who overcome these obstacles are not the norm. For most young men who grow up under impoverished circumstances, the temptations of drugs, gangs, and illicit conduct far outweigh the realistic opportunities that flow from legitimate work.

In their study of gangs in St. Louis, Scott Decker and Barrick Van Winkle[2] point out how the protection of gang membership combined with the shortage of realistic alternatives to the gang makes gang membership a compelling choice for many of the young males in their study. Once they have joined the gang, the downward cycle of crime and violence inevitably brings these young men into contact with the criminal justice system and, eventually, jail or prison. What is true in St. Louis is true elsewhere, with devastating results: One study found that in many cities, over one-fourth of the men of color are incarcerated or under community supervision,[3] and another study estimated that in some of the hardest-hit neighborhoods in Washington, D.C., up to one-fourth of African American males between the ages of twenty and forty are locked up in jail or prison and close to 45 percent are under some form of criminal justice supervision.

In the areas hardest hit by crime, it is understandable that community members might feel that criminal justice and social justice collide. On the one hand, the heavy toll of crime borne by these areas calls for an increasing dose of criminal justice—police, prosecution, and punishment. Yet when the justice system comes into play, what is left is an even more desolate picture, with so many of the residents suffering *both* the consequences of crime and the costs of punishment. It is easy to see how the justice system comes to stand, for those who live in these areas, as just another hardship in a life filled with hardships. For a visual example of how hard incarceration can impact a neighborhood see Figure 9.1. The chart depicts the number of persons by neighborhood who went to prison or jail in 1998 in Brooklyn, New York.

This stark reality has led some reformers to try to imagine an alternative way to pursue justice in the community. An emerging vision of community justice has begun to interest professionals in the criminal justice system. The term **community justice** is used to describe the recent trend to include victims, the community, and the offender in the process of justice. The interest in community justice has emerged from the victims' rights movement and subsequent victim–offender mediation programs that began at the end of the 1970s and reached their peak in the 1980s.[4]

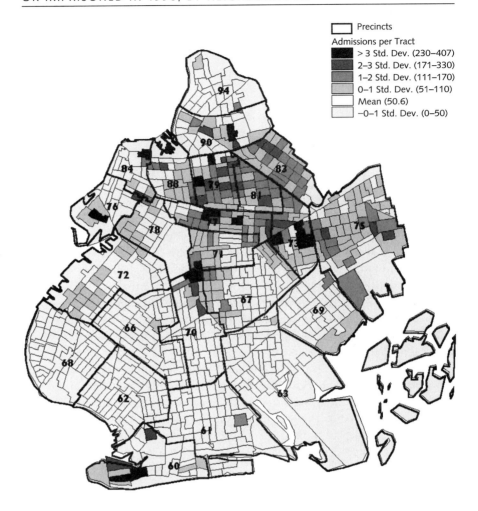

FIGURE 9.1 PERSONS FROM BROOKLYN, NY, WHO WERE JAILED OR IMPRISONED IN 1998, BY NEIGHBORHOOD

Precincts

Admissions per Tract
- > 3 Std. Dev. (230–407)
- 2–3 Std. Dev. (171–330)
- 1–2 Std. Dev. (111–170)
- 0–1 Std. Dev. (51–110)
- Mean (50.6)
- −0–1 Std. Dev. (0–50)

COMMUNITY JUSTICE DEFINED

The community justice approach can be more formally defined as an ethic that transforms the aims of the justice system into enhancing community life or sustaining community.[5] However, community justice is not a simple idea that can be explained in a single sentence. It is at once a *philosophy* of justice, a *strategy* of justice, and a series of justice *programs*.

A Philosophy of Justice

As a philosophy, community justice is based on a vision of justice that is more ambitious than the traditional three tasks of criminal justice—the apprehension, conviction, and punishment of offenders. In addition to these ordinary aspects of criminal justice, community justice recognizes that crime and the problems that result from crime are a central impediment to the quality of community life. Thus, the community justice approach not only seeks to respond to criminal events but also sets as a goal the improvement of quality of community life, especially for communities afflicted by high levels of crime. Robert Sampson of the University of Chicago and his colleagues have coined the term "collective efficacy" to denote the quality of life that communities need to reduce crime.[6]

A Strategy of Justice

The strategy of the community justice approach combines two contemporary justice innovations: community policing and environmental crime prevention. Both of these innovations have proved promising as a way of preventing crime and reviving community safety. **Community policing,** as briefly mentioned in Chapter 8, is the approach to law enforcement that employs problem-solving strategies to identify ways to prevent crimes by getting to root causes instead of relying on arrests as a way to respond to criminal events. Rather than reacting to 911 calls for service, community policing attempts to identify crime "hot spots" and change the dynamics of those places that seem to make crime possible. Rather than keeping citizens at arm's length, police officers actively seek to develop partnerships with residents and citizen groups in pursuit of safer streets. Rather than a hierarchical, paramilitary structure, community policing seeks to decentralize decision making to officers at the local areas, and seeks to design area-specific strategies for overcoming the crime.

By the end of the 1990s, the community policing movement had become enormously successful. Over 80 percent of police departments said they practiced some form of community policing, and most observers credited the approach as partly responsible for the drop in crime in the latter half of the decade.

Environmental crime prevention is a crime prevention approach that begins with an analysis of why crime tends to concentrate in certain locations and at certain times. "Hot spots" of crime exist and, in some cities, 70 percent of crimes occur in 20 percent of the city's locations. By analyzing the reasons for that pattern, this approach looks for ways to revise the physical environment of crime—houses, streets, and other public space—as a means of thwarting crime.

What is it about those places that produces such high concentrations of crime? And what can be done about those places?

These are the questions that occupy the attention of environmental crime prevention specialists. These new professionals make it their business to change the places crimes tend to occur in ways that reduce crime. They bring light to darkened street corners that otherwise attract gangs, establish procedures to keep elevators in repair so that people need not use isolated stairways to get to their apartments, change the traffic flow in streets that used to serve as drug markets, and restore open areas so that they serve as playgrounds rather than vacant lots.

A Series of Programs

Programs of community justice include a varied package of methods. A brief listing of a few illustrates the range and innovative nature of community justice:

- Crime mapping is used to identify where the problem of crime is most concentrated.
- Citizen advisory groups are used to help identify local crime problem priorities.
- Partnerships between justice agencies and citizen groups are used to improve the legitimacy of justice programs and to help justice officials tailor their strategies to make them fit local needs.
- Police, prosecutors, judges, and corrections officials are organized locally to enable them to develop local strategies of crime prevention.
- Citizens and victims are involved in sentencing decisions to increase their confidence in the wisdom of the sanctions.
- Offender community service is used to sanction offenders and restore victims and their communities.

Most of all, community justice is concerned with taking seriously the problems faced by people who live amid high levels of crime, some of whom are themselves involved in crime. When Walter Harrison, described at the beginning of this chapter, goes to work, he is practicing community justice in a way that is not any one of these particular programs, but that reflects them all. He is not out to arrest kids, but to help keep them safe. He is not saying, "I am a probation officer, not a policeman"; rather, he is trying to practice probation in a way that is relevant to the particular needs of the offenders, their families, and their neighbors, each of whom is concerned about being safe.

Community justice is also a broad extension of two similar ideas that recently flourished in criminal justice: balanced justice and restorative justice. **Balanced justice,** used primarily in the juvenile justice system, is based on the idea that justice is best served when the community, victim, and youth are viewed as equal participants in the system who all need attention and individualization.[7]

Restorative justice is an approach to sanctioning offenders that seeks to restore the victim, the offender, and the community to a level of functioning that existed prior to the criminal event. The restorative justice approach calls for offenders to admit what they have done and take steps to make restitution.[8]

There are four basic types of restorative justice strategies: victim–offender mediation, community reparative boards, family group conferencing, and circle sentencing. In all of these strategies, victims and offenders are often brought together to identify the steps that offenders may take to help victims recover from the crime. Then the offender gets involved in programs designed to help reduce the chances of reoffending. For a further explanation of the different types of restorative justice strategies, see the box "Varieties of Restorative Justice Practices."

Balanced and restorative justice approaches (when used together called BARJ) have been supported in the United States by the U.S. Department of Justice and the Office of Juvenile Justice and Delinquency Prevention through technical assistance and training for communities that wish to implement the concept. At least fourteen states have adopted BARJ as part of their juvenile code.[9] The idea has also been developed extensively in New Zealand and Australia, where the family and the community work closely to address crime issues with juveniles.[10]

Community justice, as well as balanced justice and restorative justice, all have as their focus two main objectives: first, to understand crime as being against individuals and communities rather than against the state; second, to develop responses to crime that not only promote public safety but also advance broader aims of social justice. The reasoning behind this reform movement begins with a reconsideration of the concept of justice, so that the personal dimensions of justice are emphasized. Before discussing in detail the concepts behind community justice, we first turn to an explanation of "justice" and how it connects with the community justice approach to dealing with offenders.

VARIETIES OF RESTORATIVE JUSTICE PRACTICES

- *Victim impact statements* provide an opportunity for victims to express their concerns to the prosecutors and the court. *Victim impact panels* provide victims an opportunity to confront groups of offenders—not necessarily the ones who committed their crimes—and to talk about the anger and hurt caused by the crime.

- *Victim–offender mediation* offers victims an opportunity to meet offenders in a safe setting and engage in a mediated discussion of the crime and solutions to repair harm and seek crime prevention solutions. (See the box "A Victim–Offender Mediation Program" for an example of such a program.)
- *Family group conferences* are an indigenous Maori approach recently being adapted to the majority culture in some areas of New Zealand, Australia, and the United States. These group victim–offender mediations include family members of both victims and offenders.[1]
- *Sentencing circles* are an American and Canadian Indian approach that is being revived. They involve a wide array of interested parties, including those closest to the victim and offender and others likely to affect their future. Saskatchewan is increasingly using sentencing circles.[2]
- The *Balanced and Restorative Justice (BARJ) project,* which is supported by the U.S. Department of Justice's Office of Juvenile Justice and Delinquency Prevention and is in place in several sites,[3] calls for every sanction involving juveniles to include consideration of public safety, accountability to victim and community, and the development of competency by offenders.
- Vermont uses *citizen reparative boards* to determine the nature and details of the conditions of probation for convicted offenders. Trained volunteers provide offenders with a clear understanding of the impact their crimes had on the community as well as appropriate and relevant assignments to repair the damage.
- *Restorative justice sentencing plans* are being developed in Winnipeg, Canada, as strategies that are individualized to the offender and victim and are cost-effective sanctions that help repair the harm.[4]

[1]McElrea, F. W. M., "Restorative Justice—The New Zealand Youth Court: A Model for Development in Other Courts?" *Journal of Judicial Administration* 4 (1994); and Immarigeon, Russ, "Family Conferences, Juvenile Offenders, and Accountability," *The New York State Child Advocate* 3 (Fall 1994).

[2]Stuart, Barry, "Circle Sentencing—Mediation and Consensus: Turning Swords into Ploughshares," *Accord* 14(1) (June 1995).

[3]Bazemore, Gordon, and Mark Umbreit, *Balanced and Restorative Justice Program Summary,* Washington, DC: U.S. Department of Justice, Office of Juvenile Justice and Delinquency Prevention, October 1994.

[4]The Restorative Resolutions Project in operation in Winnipeg, Canada, prepares client-specific plans based on restorative principles. See Galaway, Burt, and Gord Richardson, "Evaluation of the Restorative Resolutions Project of The John Howard Society of Manitoba, Final Report," Winnipeg, Canada: University of Manitoba, June 1995.

Source: Extracted from "Restorative Justice: An Interview with Visiting Fellow Thomas Quinn," in *National Institute of Justice Journal,* March 1998, p. 12. National Institute of Justice, U.S. Department of Justice.

A VICTIM–OFFENDER MEDIATION PROGRAM

The victim was a middle-aged woman. The offender, a 14-year-old neighbor of the victim, had broken into the victim's home and stolen a VCR. The mediation sessions took place in the basement of the victim's church.

In the presence of a mediator, the victim and offender talked for two hours. At times, their conversation was heated and emotional. When they finished, the mediator felt that they had heard each other's stories and learned something important about the impact of crime and about each other.

The participants agreed that the offender would pay $200 in restitution to cover the cost of the damages to the victim's home resulting from the break-in and $150 for the cost of the stolen VCR. They also worked out a payment schedule.

During the session, the offender made several apologies to the victim and agreed to complete community service hours working in a food bank sponsored by the victim's church. The victim said that she felt less angry and fearful after learning more about the offender and the details of the crime. She also thanked the mediator for allowing the session to be held at her church.

Source: Gordon Bazemore and Mark Umbreit, "A Comparison of Four Restorative Conferencing Models," Juvenile Justice Bulletin, U.S. Department of Justice, Office of Justice Programs, February 2001.

NEIGHBORS, VICTIMS, OFFENDERS COLLABORATE ON SENTENCING

MINNEAPOLIS—In the shadow of the city's downtown skyscrapers, a comfortable home sits on a quiet street, opposite a school and a park. It looks nothing like a court of law.

But as often as twice a week, it functions much like a courthouse. In the large living room, criminal offenders admit their guilt, and a punishment is determined and approved, even though no judge, jury, or police officers are present.

This is no kangaroo court. Instead, it's a social experiment by a state with a lengthy pedigree of reform. The aim is to reduce crime, strengthen community bonds, and reduce the caseload in the local criminal justice system, which has struggled in the last decade as Minneapolis began suffering from urban problems that used to plague only other cities.

The Aims of Community Corrections

The concept is called "circle sentencing," and is off to a promising start with support from local prosecutors, judges, and public defenders. Minnesota is the first state to try the idea, which originated among an aboriginal people deep in Canada's Yukon Territory and has now spread to Franklin County in Western Massachusetts.

The process works like this: When a person is convicted in court, a judge can decide to let the community sentence the offender. If the judge turns over the sentencing power to the community, a group of volunteers—anyone from the area can participate—gets together, along with the offender, and sometimes with the victim as well.

So far, several jurisdictions in Minnesota, plus the Mille Lacs band of Chippewa Indians, have used circle sentencing. Most of the cases involve younger offenders and relatively minor cases such as property crimes. Sitting in a circle, the group talks with the offender about the crime, each person explaining why the act is considered an affront to the community. Everyone has a chance to speak, including the offender and the victim, and members of the circle try to elicit an admission of guilt.

"We're trying to get the [offender] to see the light," said Oscar Reed, a volunteer in North Minneapolis, a high-crime area that began using circles this year to promote understanding.

The objective at this juncture, advocates for the circle concept said, is to promote healing and understanding for both the community and the offender. Members of the circle want the offender to know the behavior is intolerable, but they also make an effort to understand his or her motivation, whether it's anger, an alcohol or drug problem, or a lack of skills or self-esteem. They try to help the person, if they deem it possible.

"What it's really about is the whole community coming together to take care of its own," said Kay Prannis of the Minnesota Department of Corrections, who brought the concept to the state's attention. "It's very, very important work that has implications for democracy, for sort of re-creating a form of social control that's healthy." On an unseasonably warm Minneapolis night recently, circle volunteers met at the home-cum-courthouse to decide what should be done with a ten-year-old boy from North Minneapolis, who had been convicted in juvenile court of shooting a pellet gun in public. He has shot the gun at a stop sign, and later at his brother, participants said. The boy's parents also attended.

Volunteers were worried that the boy, who had been hanging out with a tough crowd, was on track to commit more-serious crimes as he moved into his teenage years.

Initially, the boy was sullen and withdrawn. Wearing an ankle bracelet to monitor his whereabouts, he sat on a sofa and wouldn't look anyone in the eye, nor would he admit he had done anything wrong.

"I didn't do it," the boy repeatedly said, looking only at the floor. But the dozen circle volunteers, many of whom came from the immediate neighborhood, gently probed and prodded him for more than an hour.

Gradually, the boy warmed to them and began to admit his guilt, a bit at a time, first admitting having the gun outside, although he insisted his escapade went unnoticed.

"No one saw me with it," he said.

"Then who called the police?" several volunteers wanted to know.

"I don't know," he replied.

After realizing someone had seen him with the gun outside, he confessed to shooting at a stop sign, before finally conceding he had shot at his younger brother, although he continued to insist that was an accident. By the end of the night, the boy was smiling and animated, and the circle volunteers had gained a measure of trust. Their main goal was not to punish him; they didn't see a juvenile lockup as the solution. Instead, they hoped he would understand why his conduct was unacceptable, and would begin to distance himself from the crowd with which he was associating.

"It's extremely helpful to realize that there are other ways to get to these kids without being punitive," said Alice Lynch, who runs a shelter for battered women and coordinates the North Minneapolis circle program. "We are focusing on the needs of young people and their families, which doesn't happen in the courtroom." But the process isn't only about understanding and rehabilitation. It's also about allowing the community to determine the appropriate punishment, a power that people across the country have sought in recent years. Offenders must agree.

If the initial circle is successful, another circle is scheduled for sentencing.

To arrive at a punishment, everyone involved must agree to the proposed sentence, including the offender. This prevents an angry or fearful community from going down the path of vigilantism.

If agreement is reached, the case returns to the judge, who typically approves the sentence. If consensus proves elusive, the community can ask the judge to take back control of the process and sentence the offender. Thus far, sentences have ranged from community service to jail time.

"You're pretty well protected from outrageous conclusions," Prannis said.

"If an offender agrees to something outrageous, I would expect the system people to say no."

In one case, an offender found the circle so beneficial, he attended another offender's circle. "One young man completed the circle," Lynch said, "and came to another young man's circle to offer assistance." A belief in the process.

Thus far, circles have been used on a small scale, and there are no statistics showing whether they prevent crime. But advocates believe that by connecting with offenders, providing them with support, and getting them help, frayed community bonds can be restored and crime can be reduced.

"We're not going to know about the kids who didn't commit a crime as a result of this process," said Don Johnson, a juvenile prosecutor in Hennepin County, which includes Minneapolis.

Franklin County, Massachusetts, has become the first U.S. area outside Minnesota to give the idea a try.

The county recently completed its first sentencing circle, for an offender from the poverty-stricken community of Orange. The man who was sentenced has benefited enormously from the process, said Lucinda Brown, who recently was hired as community relations coordinator for the county and will oversee the circle process there.

"It is an amazing change, the development we've seen already in his capacity to understand that everything we do has repercussions," she said.

But Brown said the best part is that while the sentence may be an end point for the traditional court system, it is only the beginning for the circle process.

The volunteers who spoke and listened and helped determine the sentence will continue to work with the offender, to help him reconstruct his life.

"I believe in this stuff," said Brown. "We're really making dramatic changes. We're making history."

Source: Stephen J. Siegel, *Boston Globe*, January 3, 1999.

WHAT IS JUSTICE?

Many a volume has been written about the meaning of justice. This might seem odd, since the concept of justice seems simple enough. In a democracy such as the United States, we think of "justice" as involving a straightforward formula: Allow each individual the freedom necessary to pursue that person's vision of "the good life," and enable each person to harvest the fruits—good and bad—of choices made along the way. Philosophers remind us that what seems simple on the surface is, on closer inspection, mired in a complexity of problems and dilemmas. There are two reasons that such a simple notion of justice turns out to be so complex. First, each of us has a different set of ideas about what constitutes "the good life." And second, each of us starts out with a different set of capacities for realizing our version of the good life.

This means that before the game of life begins, the deck is stacked. Some, those who aspire to the highest of achievements, face a daunting possibility of failure compared to those who set their sights lower. Because society places a value on ambition, it is wise to support those who shoot for the stars by softening the blow of failure, ensuring that the fall will not be too harsh.

Likewise, because we realize that the accidents of birth—physical or mental impairments as well as social disadvantage—can mean that any of us might face harder obstacles in the pursuit of happiness, we would be wise to provide extra support to those for whom such support can make a difference in achieving success.

These observations suggest to us three necessary characteristics for a just society: (1) a safety net to protect people who dare to dream, and (2) remedial supports to offset the unfairly hard prospects some face, to encourage them to try. Social philosophers tell us that when a society provides for basic safety and remedial support, it has set up a system that makes it reasonable for its members to play by the rules. The final requirement of a just society, then, is (3) that the rules themselves be fair in the way they are devised and even-handed in the way they are applied. This means that the rules apply equally to everybody and do not create an advantage to some members of society over others. A society lacking any of these three elements of social justice—safety net, remedial supports, and equitable laws—will find large numbers of its members disinterested in playing by the rules.

In any society, however, some will disobey the law. A sense of a lack of social justice may contribute to the willingness of some to disobey the law, but even in just societies, some will transgress. What happens when people fail to live within a society's rules? How do we promote justice when some refuse to obey the laws that the rest of the citizens respect? The traditional response of the criminal justice system to rule breaking is adversarial. This approach accuses suspects, tries defendants, and punishes offenders. The idea of justice in the community is that punishing the guilty ought not be the final objective of the justice system. The emerging community justice perspective, because it recognizes the central importance of social justice, holds that traditional criminal justice responses are not enough.

Instead, community justice holds as an ideal the promotion of quality of community life for all parties involved—offender, victim, and community. In the face of crime, this means there are three key elements of community justice—**sanctioning, problem solving,** and **restoration.** Let us first summarize each of these elements of community justice, before we explore them in greater detail.

Justice as a Sanction

Criminal conduct cannot be allowed to stand without a response from the community, a response that makes a public statement that the behavior is wrong. Justice requires that criminal offenders receive a sanction. The sanction symbolizes the community's condemnation of the offender for the misconduct, and it proclaims the community's resolve that this conduct shall not be permitted.

A sanction can take many forms. For all practical purposes, every sanction is a restriction upon the freedom of the law violator. Incarceration, of course, is a very extreme restriction, but it is not the only form that such restrictions may take. Curfews, home detention, compulsory community service, official reporting, and a host of routine conditions all restrict the choices of offenders. In so doing, they impose a sanction. The question from the correctional standpoint is, What type of sanction is called for with this offender for this crime?

Justice as Problem Solving

Crime stems from problems and it causes problems. A range of problems help to produce crime; for example, inadequate schools, neighborhood disorder, drug addiction, and unemployment would make everyone's list of criminogenic factors. The range of problems caused by crime is nearly as broad: declining housing values, empty public places, property loss, and emotional hardship, for example.

Because these problems occur at multiple levels, they must be solved at multiple levels. Problems in community life, such as empty streets or neighborhood disorder, require organized action on the part of community groups. Justice officials can facilitate this sort of action. More personal problems require services for those affected by crime.

Justice as Restoration of Community Life

At its most basic level, crime damages community life. It does so by creating the sorts of problems described above, but it also damages the capacity of victims and offenders alike to take rightful places as fully responsible citizens. It also leads community members who are neither victim nor offender to develop a sense of distrust of community life, a doubt of the capacity of the community to provide a safe and wholesome environment.

The end result of justice in the community is restoration of community life. For victims, this means having the losses suffered as a result of the crime ameliorated. For offenders, restoration follows making amends for the offense and taking steps to make sure it will not recur. For the community, restoration means renewal of a kind of confidence in community life and a faith in its potential. The issue faced by justice officials is how to put into motion a mechanism for achieving this level of restoration.

As we see from our discussion, community justice is quite different from traditional criminal justice in three important ways: It is based on the neighborhood rather than on the legal jurisdiction, it is problem solving rather than adversarial, and it is restorative rather than retributive. For a more specific list of the differences between the restorative and retributive (traditional) paradigms of justice see Table 9.1.

TABLE 9.1   RETRIBUTIVE VERSUS RESTORATIVE JUSTICE

Old Paradigm Retributive Justice	New Paradigm Restorative Justice
1. Crime defined as violation of the state	1. Crime defined as violation of one person by another
2. Focus on establishing blame, on guilt, on past (did he/she do it?)	2. Focus on problem-solving, on liabilities and obligations, on future (what should be done?)
3. Adversarial relationships and process normative	3. Dialogue and negotiation normative
4. Imposition of pain to punish and deter/prevent	4. Restitution as a means of restoring both parties; reconciliation/restoration as goal
5. Justice defined by intent and by process: right rules	5. Justice defined as right relationships; judged by the outcome
6. Interpersonal, conflictual nature of crime obscured, repressed; conflict seen as individual vs. state	6. Crime recognized as interpersonal conflict; value of conflict recognized
7. One social injury replaced by another	7. Focus on repair of social injury
8. Community on sideline, represented abstractly by state	8. Community as facilitator in restorative process
9. Encouragement of competitive, individualistic values	9. Encouragement of mutuality
10. Action directed from state to offender: • victim ignored • offender passive	10. Victim and offender's roles recognized in both problem and solution: • victim rights/needs recognized • offender encouraged to take responsibility
11. Offender accountability defined as taking punishment	11. Offender accountability defined as understanding impact of action and helping decide how to make things right
12. Offense defined in purely legal terms, devoid of moral, social, economic, political dimensions	12. Offense understood in whole context—moral, social, economic, political
13. "Debt" owed to state and society in the abstract	13. Debt/liability to victim recognized
14. Response focused on offender's past behavior	14. Response focused on harmful consequences of offender's behavior
15. Stigma of crime unremovable	15. Stigma of crime removable through restorative action
16. No encouragement for repentance and forgiveness	16. Possibilities for repentance and forgiveness
17. Dependence upon proxy professionals	17. Direct involvement by participants

Source: Howard Zehr, "Restorative Justice." *IARCA Journal,* March 1991, p. 7. Reprinted by permission.

THE VICTIM AND COMMUNITY JUSTICE

In the retributive justice paradigm, crime is viewed as a "violation of the state." But the newer restorative justice paradigm recognizes that crime is also a violation of one person by another. In this way, the restorative and community justice ideas are similar to those that support the victims' rights movement. This is not a coincidence. As mentioned earlier, both restorative and community justice are linked to the victims' rights movement. Like victims' programs, restorative and community justice are rooted in offender accountability and victim reparation. Included in this are mechanisms that foster financial compensation for victims.

The victims' movement began in the 1970s when it was realized that the concerns of victims in the criminal justice system were often forgotten. A significant factor for change in the status of victims in the criminal justice system came in 1982 when the President's Task Force on Victims of Crime explicated the problems of victims in the system and suggested ways to improve the situation. The task force recommended sixty-eight programmatic and legislative initiatives for states and citizens to pursue to support victims of crime, among the most notable, the expansion of various victims' assistance programs.[11] In the 1990s, the victims' movement grew to such proportions that advocacy groups called for an amendment to the U.S. Constitution to address the issues that would assist crime victims. Although the amendment was never passed into law, the lawmakers in individual states responded. Today, all fifty states have passed legislation that provides some financial support to crime victims. Many of the community justice and restorative justice programs presently have some component that provides victims financial or psychological assistance.

A COMMUNITY CORRECTIONS VIEW OF JUSTICE

How is justice advanced by community correctional mechanisms? Our discussion of the elements of justice suggests that justice in the community requires the development of crime-response mechanisms for sanctioning, problem solving, and restoration. In today's community justice movement, these approaches are being developed.

Sanctioning Systems

A *system of sanctions* is a way of making criminal penalties fit into a rational framework. In a sanctioning system, each criminal offense is associated with a designated penalty or range of penalties. The obvious benefit of a system of sanctions is that penalties are predictable, and there is a measure of equity between the crime and the punishment. Sanctioning systems are used because they are thought to prevent sentencing disparity by assisting different judges to select similar penalties for different defendants and at different times.

The most important requirement of a rational framework for sentencing is that the more severe punishments be reserved for the more serious offenses. Since a purpose of the penalty is to restrict freedom, the severity of a penalty is typically understood in terms of the amount of loss of freedom suffered as a consequence of the penalty. The severity of a penalty is calibrated according to the degree to which it restricts an offender's freedoms. Sentences to incarceration have an easy time meeting with calibration: It is readily apparent that a three-year sentence is more severe than a two-year sentence, for example.

When we compare two sentences to prison, we rapidly know which one will be more severe, and we assume that one of the reasons is that the crime was more serious.

This is not as easy to do for sentences to community supervision. Three years on probation is less onerous than five years on probation. But it is not immediately obvious how much of a difference the extra two years makes in the loss of freedom, since we assume that the degree of probation supervision wanes over time. Moreover, there is no easy way to take into account the conditions of community supervision, such as compulsory drug treatment or community service. Because the losses of freedom that are incurred under community penalties are so difficult to calibrate, it often seems as though community supervision sentences are not punitive at all.

The inability to calibrate the severity of sentences to community supervision has been a significant difficulty for those who want to make these penalties more widely used. If there is no simple way to compare different community supervision penalties or to equate them to terms of incarceration, then community supervision will never become a mainstream penalty in the minds of offenders or, more important, the citizenry. To rectify this problem, recent reformers have developed two new concepts to describe the relationship between community supervision penalties and other criminal sanctions: sanction units and interchangeability.[12] These new ideas are used to provide a basis for calibrating community penalties, making them comparable to each other and to institutional penalties.

Sanction units express the penalty deserved from each crime in the form of "units" of punishment. The more serious the crime, the more units it deserves. Penalties are assigned sanction unit values as well: A year in prison might be valued at 20 sanction units; a year on probation as 4 sanction units; a six-month, residential drug treatment program might be 12 sanction units. **Interchangeability** is the idea that as long as the sanction units add up to the total amount deserved, any combination of penalties may be selected by the sentencing authority.

A great advantage of the sanction unit approach is that different forms of sanctions may be given values in the calibration system. This gives the sentencing authority a means for comparing community penalties with the more typical form of punishment—incarceration. The chart on the next page provides an illustration. It shows that the greatest impact of incarceration, as a sanction, occurs during the first year. Each additional year provides declining sanction impact. It also shows that compulsory treatment programs have sanction value— in fact, they represent significant incursions into the freedom of the offender. Under this hypothetical model, a three-year sentence to incarceration is worth 47 sanction units. This would be a typical sentence for a robbery, say, or for a recidivist burglary (that is, a sanctioning system might establish that a robbery or repeat burglary deserved 40–50 sanction units of punishment).

Under principles of interchangeability, a judge could develop a community-based penalty that involved the following formula:

• Six months of intensive supervision	4 units
• Five years of regular probation	15 units
• 80 hours of community service	4 units
• Six months of residential drug treatment	12 units
• Three months of home detention	3 units
• 20 days of day fine	8 units
Sanction total	46 units

This would amount to a community penalty that was similar, in onerousness, to the incarcerative term, since the sanction units would be nearly the same. In theory, the sentencing authority could impose such a penalty interchangeably with a straight incarcerative term of three years. The real test of such a system, of course, is how it works out in practice. We might all agree that we would rather be required to perform the full package of community penalty requirements listed above than to go to prison for a three-year sentence (minus time off for good behavior, of course). In this sense, it might seem that the community penalty is a more lenient option, despite the equivalent sanction units.

The next step in the development of a system that would account for incarceration and community sanction units is proposed below.

Punishment Type	Sanction Units
First year of incarceration	20 units
Second year of incarceration	15 units
Each additional year of incarceration	12 units
Six months of intensive supervision	4 units
One year of regular probation	3 units
Forty hours of community service	2 units
Six months of residential drug treatment	12 units
Three months of home detention	3 units
Five days of day fine	2 units
Full restitution to the victim	5 units

It is true, of course, that exact equivalence is not established in this example. While some might prefer the community penalty, it is not altogether clear that a three-year sentence with no additional personal losses other than the significant loss of time free on the streets is worse than five years under community supervision, with intensive supervision and home detention requirements, treatment program requirements, community service requirements, and financial obligations. The community penalty begins to emerge as intrusive in its own right when it is expressed as sanction units. Indeed, one study found that jail inmates, offered an opportunity to be released onto strict supervision, but for a longer period than the jail term, opted to stay locked up and finish the sentence rather than be subjected to the tight supervision implied in the alternative.[13]

The sanctioning system has three advantages over traditional sentencing approaches. First, it enables very different forms of sanctions to be expressed in units that symbolize one of the intentions of a sanction—to penalize the law violator by restricting freedom. Second, the sanction units can be devised to recognize how treatment programs can be included in the calculus of the total penalty instead of simply added onto a penalty. Third, the sanction unit method can provide a basis for choosing a community penalty that is not merely "giving a break."

Why, then, would a sentencing judge choose a community penalty? Some of the reasons have to do with the effectiveness of the sanction—a few studies have suggested that all else being equal, treatment programs offered in community settings are more effective than those offered in institutional settings.[14] Undoubtedly, however, one of the most significant incentives is a concern for social justice.

Social justice becomes important because so many of the people sentenced by courts begin with a strike against them. Many judges recognize that adding incarceration to the mix of an offender's problems can do little to promote a long-term adjustment for that offender. Equally important, judges know of the formidable problems of street life in the neighborhoods where those who are about to be sentenced live. Sympathetic judges can envisage how difficult it is to live in those environments, and they can well understand that a couple of years in prison will make it no easier for that offender to learn how to make it in the difficult circumstances that will await him or her upon release from prison. In the short run, a prison sentence may seem logical. But in the long run, a sentence that holds promise of preparing the offender to deal more successfully with the kinds of community problems faced in those environments will seem both wiser and more just.

Problem Solving in Community Justice

The community setting provides a superior location for problem solving around criminal behavior. After all, it is the problems within communities that lead to crime, and it is among those who live in high-crime communities that the problems caused by crime are felt. We consider the role of community-based correctional work in dealing with problems resulting from crime in the following section. Here, we investigate the way problems that cause crime can be addressed under community justice methods.

Figure 9.2 proposes two sets of circumstances that lead to criminal behavior: the problem set and the opportunity set. The **problem set** contains traditional factors that are known to affect risk systematically: age, sex, competency (intelligence, education, etc.). Within the problem set is a series of personal variables: thrill-seeking desires; prior experiences as a victim, with other victims, and with

FIGURE 9.2   RISK ASSESSMENT FOR INTERVENTION

Source: Todd R. Clear and David R. Karp, *The Community Justice Ideal: Preventing Crime and Achieving Justice* (Boulder, CO: Westview Press, 1999).

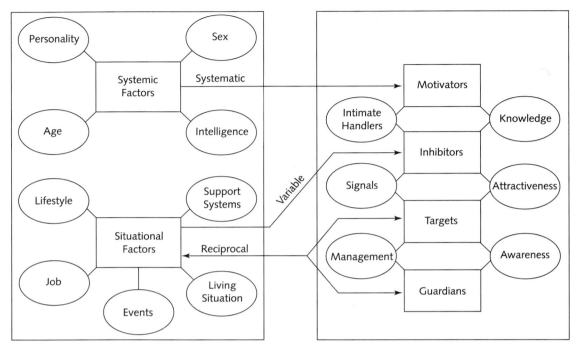

Problem Set   Opportunity Set

the justice system. A wide range of treatment programs are used to deal with these types of factors, from education/training programs to anger management and victim sensitivity programs. Risk factors such as those in the problem set can be addressed by programs offered either in the community or while the offender is in custody.

This is not the case for factors identified by the **opportunity set.** This set of problems includes situational components of risk, borrowed from routine activities theory.[15] **Routine activities theory** states that crimes will occur in any given situation, so long as two elements are present and two are absent. Present in the situation must be (1) an offender who is motivated to commit an offense, and (2) a suitable target for that offense; absent must be (1) an effective guardian of the suitable target, and (2) an intimate or loved one whose involvement in the offender's life might prevent the decision to commit the offense. According to routine activities theory, crimes occur as a part of everyday life, when in the course of events motivated offenders encounter suitable targets where there are no effective guardians nor intimates to detract from the temptation of the crime.

Each of these elements of the opportunity set may be addressed by a community-based correctional program. The offender's motivation level may be reduced by developing techniques for controlling temptation (anger management or relaxation methods). The presence of intimates may also act on motivation levels by strengthening inhibitors. Targets may be "hardened" in traditional ways by locks or streetlights, but when targets are individual community members, they may be hardened by informing them of what to look for as precursors of reoffending, or by providing potential guardians more access to knowledge of the offender and possible targets.

The opportunity set shows just how essential the community is to solving the problems that contribute to crime. While a variety of treatment programs may be provided in custodial settings, those factors listed here as falling within the opportunity set—many of which are far more instrumental in the problems of crime—may only be addressed in community-based strategies.

Two types of strategies are suggested by this analysis. One set of strategies focuses on the offender within a network of relationships. These strategies involve first identifying the most significant persons in the offender's life, and then finding ways to enlist them as supports for the offender's law-abiding behavior.

To use key intimates as sources for strengthening the offender's law-abiding conduct is a rational idea for several reasons. Research has shown that as offenders begin to enjoy stronger relationships with family members, especially spouses or children, they reduce their involvement with pro-criminal associates and begin to refrain from new criminal activity.[16] Intimate associates can also act as surrogate guardians, since they can be trained to look for trouble signs that suggest new criminal conduct is imminent, and intervene before the crimes occur. Or offenders can learn how to avoid situations that may pose temptations, situations where desirable targets might occur—for example, sex offenders can be trained to avoid socializing in bars where possible targets might occur under inebriated states. Finally, potential victims—especially those who have been victims of crime before—can be trained to engage in safety techniques that make crime less likely. All of this is consistent with community-based justice approaches.

A second version of community-based, crime problem-solving approaches includes **situational crime prevention** strategies.[17] These strategies are based upon studies of where the crimes are occurring at the highest rate. Typically, it is found that in a high-crime area, as much as 60 percent of crime occurs in very specific locations. Situational crime prevention proceeds by analyzing what it is about those locations that promotes the high rates of crime, and then trying to alter the underlying dynamics that are found. For example, an abandoned building might promote gang behavior or drug activity; proximate bars and midnight food stores may lead to higher rates of robbery. The solution might be to tear down the abandoned structures, or to change the hours of the food stores. Studies of situational crime prevention strategies find that they can reduce crime rates by as much as 40 percent—a result that has led to increasing popularity of these approaches.

Situational crime prevention strategies and opportunity set strategies have different levels at which they are focused. The former are concerned with locations, the latter with people. But they have in common the fact that crime problems can be diagnosed and solutions can be developed that prevent crime. However, this can occur only when the justice system shifts its focus away from merely incarcerating offenders, toward working with offenders and their networks of relationships in the community contexts where crime rates are so high.

Restoration of the Community

One ideal of community justice is that the community may recover from costs of crime. This ideal includes recovery for everyone affected by the crime. To achieve this aim, there must be a restorative process that is quite different from the traditional approach built around blame and punishment.

The restorative process is not adversarial like a criminal trial. A trial is designed to establish guilt or innocence of an accused, with appropriate protections for the rights of the accused. These rights are protected through a series of restrictions on what may be considered "evidence" of the defendant's guilt. The goal of a trial is a verdict. By contrast, the restorative process is designed to evaluate a broad range of information relating to the problem itself—in this case, how to deal with the consequences of the crime. There are fewer rules of evidence, and there is a flexible approach to testimony and decision making. The objective is to arrive at a plan that all parties in the process agree holds promise of resolving the problems caused by the crime.

Who are the parties? Here, again, a restorative process differs from the traditional adversarial approach. In the traditional justice model, the citizen is in a "contest" with the state—as implied by the title, *Smith* v. *Arkansas.* The defendant is represented by a defense attorney; the state is represented by a prosecutor. Recently, reformers have pointed out that this approach does not represent, formally, the interests of the victims of the crime or the community in which the offender and victim live. A restorative process attempts a more open approach in which the offender, the victim, and the community may all express their interests and expectations, toward a plan of action. This is illustrated by Figure 9.3, which shows that three parties are intertwined in a set of tasks. Let us describe those tasks.

The Tasks of the Offender. The offender's first task is to take responsibility for the offense. This admission is the offender's concession that the act was wrong and that the community's normative standards are affirmed. One related and recently revived theme in acceptance of guilt and sentencing is the centuries-old philosophy that emphasizes "shame as punishment". In Puritan

FIGURE 9.3 CORE RESPONSIBILITIES OF PARTIES IN THE
SANCTIONING PROCESS

Source: Todd R. Clear and David R. Karp, *The Community Justice Ideal: Preventing Crime and Achieving Justice* (Boulder, CO: Westview Press, 1999).

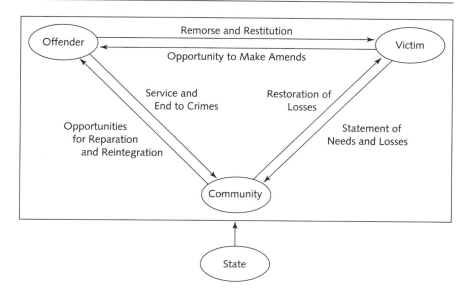

times, **shaming** was a strategy based on the idea that sentences should punish and deter offenders through the show of strong public humiliation. The idea has regained acceptance in the current correctional climate because of prison overcrowding, high incarceration costs, and the concommitant calls for retribution. Australian criminologist John Braithwaite, the main advocate for shaming, has found it to be successful with some kinds of offenders because it holds the potential to enhance moral awareness among offenders, thereby building conscience and self-control.[18]

The second task for the offender is to take responsibility for undoing the effects of the offense on the victim and on the community. The tangible costs borne by the victim may be reimbursed through financial or labor restitution. The less tangible costs—for example, emotional strains and loss of a sense of safety—are harder for the offender to restore. Responsibility for these effects can be taken through symbolic acts of restitution to the community, such as community service.

The offender's third task is to assure the community that such criminal behavior will not occur again. This is done through affirmative acts that give the community reason for confidence: involvement in risk reduction treatment programs, compliance with restriction on behavior, and educational or job-training programs.

Promoting Justice in the Community   **327**

This list of tasks is consistent with a study recently completed by the Vermont Department of Corrections. They commissioned a series of focus groups to learn what "ordinary citizens" want to have as the consequences of penalties imposed on offenders. The list provided by citizens included the following:

- For the offender to take responsibility for the crime
- For the offender to make restitution to the victim
- For the offender to contribute something back to the community as a symbol of remorse
- For the offender to take steps to ensure that the crime won't happen again
- For the offender to learn something from the experience[19]

The Tasks of the Victim. The victim naturally has less burdensome tasks than the offender. Restoration of the victim begins with the ability to state the scope of losses, tangible and intangible, that have resulted from the crime. Then the victim must determine the types of resources, financial and otherwise, that would be necessary to restore, as much as possible, the losses suffered. Finally, the victim must lay out the conditions under which any fear of or resentment toward the offender may be diminished.

These are tasks that prove, for many victims, enormously difficult. They may also be so complex that a simple statement is impossible. Thus, the victim is not always required to achieve these ends, but instead is asked to participate in the process with an aim of eventual restoration. Whether that process will be successful is dependent not just upon the strengths of the victim, but also upon both offender and community responses to the process.

The Tasks of the Community. The community is represented by the myriad institutions encompassed by it—from family and friendship networks to voluntary organizations and social welfare agencies. These institutions have a responsibility to the victim to recognize the importance of losses resulting from victimization and to provide supports necessary for the victim to achieve the optimal recovery. The community's responsibility to the offender includes providing an opportunity for the offender to perform reparative tasks for the victim and the community and to obtain the assistance, supervision, and supports—including treatment intervention programs—necessary to live in the community crime-free.

Thus, the obligations of the community are to its members—to provide the possibility of recovery and restoration for victims and offenders alike. By building and maintaining the supports necessary for victims and offenders to carry out their tasks, the community creates the foundation for restoring community quality of life after criminal events.

An interest in restoration is perhaps the most dramatic difference between a community justice ideal and the traditional, adversarial justice model. It is also its greatest challenge. Just as adversarial justice can result in failure—an innocent person can be convicted, the guilty acquitted, or an unfair penalty imposed—community justice can fail to achieve restoration. Because the social justice aim of restoration is more complicated than the simple criminal justice aim of punishment, there are more ways that community justice can fail. Offenders will become reinvolved in crime; community members will resist an offender's reintegration; victims will be unable or unwilling to be open to restoration. When this happens, the backup approach of adversarial justice is invoked, with an emphasis on retribution instead of restoration.

Despite the likelihood of failure, those who hold high a vision of justice in the community are willing to take the chance. When they compare the current system to an alternative approach that emphasizes sanctioning, problem solving, and restoration, they argue that the risk is worth the return.

ISSUES IN THE PURSUIT OF JUSTICE IN THE COMMUNITY

Most would recognize that the model of justice in the community presented above is ambitious. Some do not agree that the model is desirable. Those who feel that the community provides a better setting for achieving justice make three important arguments in their behalf.

Three Arguments in Favor of Community Justice

The arguments in support of a community justice model stem from important differences between it and the traditional adversarial approach that emphasizes confinement as a penalty. These are differences that advocates of community justice believe make it preferable to a system centered on incarceration. Three of the more important differences are problem solving, citizen involvement, and cost-effectiveness.

Community Justice Deals with the Problem of Crime, Not Its Symptoms.
One of the most common complaints about contemporary criminal justice is that it operates as a "revolving door." Picture a group of men in prison garb, walking in circles through the turning door, into a courthouse, and back out again. The revolving door is a powerful image, for it portrays the justice system as an ineffectual, rapid-fire processing system, where offenders are shuttled through without much happening to them.

This revolving-door complaint has been used to argue for a tougher criminal justice system. But no matter how tough the contemporary justice system gets—within reason—it is destined to operate as something of a revolving door by its very nature. So long as the justice system seeks primarily to convict the guilty and then punish them for their crimes, and little else, it is a system that makes no promise about more ambitious objectives. Even as offenders serve longer periods of time behind bars, as has been the case over the last decade, the overwhelming majority are eventually released. And upon their release, their victims and their neighbors wonder about the revolving door through which they seem to have walked. Evidence for this is provided by the fact that while prison sentences have been growing, citizens have remained skeptical about the operations of the justice system.

For this reason, community justice advocates assert that developing a community-oriented approach that gives priority to problem solving is an attractive alternative. The desirability of a problem-solving model comes from two of its main characteristics: It seeks to identify the sources of crime so that they may be altered and future crimes prevented; and it takes into account the human tragedies that arise as a result of crimes, seeking to ameliorate them.

The problem-solving metaphor in community-based justice resonates well with the American psyche. Government in the United States is typically asked to be pragmatic. Americans are an idealistic people, but they seem to want a government that is practical and can solve real-life problems. When it comes to crime, Americans want offenders to be punished, but they want even more for crime to be prevented.

Former Wisconsin Corrections Commissioner Walter Dickey, now a law school professor, tells a story about an infamous street corner in Milwaukee, Wisconsin: 9th and Cortland. In one six-month period, he says, police made a total of ninety-four arrests on that street corner alone. That is an average of one arrest every two days. Most of the arrests involved drugs, and perhaps half of them resulted in prison sentences. Dickey asks, "What did the citizens of Wisconsin get for this effort? Did the corner of 9th and Cortland get any safer?" His answer is ironic: The police in Milwaukee admit that the corner remains one of the most unsafe locations in the city. Dickey's point is that it is hard to imagine a more concentrated effort from traditional criminal justice than was made on this street corner—multiple arrests each week and thousands of months of imprisonment. And yet the street corner remains no better than it was when the effort started.

Stories such as this bolster the claim that a problem-solving approach would make a lot more sense. Such an approach would attack the problems of 9th and Cortland in Milwaukee from a different perspective than simply making arrests there. On one level, the community justice approach would seek to deal with the issues of the people who are being arrested there—in this case, mostly for drug-related crimes—by confronting their personal problems that promote their drug criminality: addiction, joblessness, and so forth. On the other hand, the specific attributes of that street corner that make it a popular place for drug crime—abandoned buildings, physical isolation, proximity to bars, and so forth—would also be addressed. Finally, the collateral effects of so much criminal behavior for nearby properties and residents would also be of concern. The goal would be not merely to make arrests but to leave the street corner better off after the justice system's involvement there.

Not all problems are solvable, of course, and community-oriented justice is not a panacea. What is different about this approach is that it recognizes that what makes crime such a harmful part of modern life is the many problems that it causes for victims and the many problems that create high crime rates. Bringing those problems into the picture, even though they may not be easy to address, is an advantage some proclaim for a community justice orientation.

Community Justice Involves Victims and the Community in the Justice Process. The traditional justice system operates as a contest between the state and the accused. It is a system operated by professionals—attorneys and judges—under a restrictive set of procedural rules. Even though many people are affected by a crime—the victim, the community, the offender's family— the current system makes little provision for involvement of any of these principles in the sanctioning process.

In recent years, the victims' rights movement has made inroads in the isolated way the justice process works. Probation officers investigate the impact of the offense on the victim and report this information to the sentencing judge. At the sentencing hearing, the victim may join the offender in speaking regarding the penalty. But most victims leave the process with a sense of having been a side issue in their own criminalization. It can lead to a deep feeling of abandonment by the system.

A sentencing hearing can be a surreal event. Sobbing members of the offender's family will beg the court for leniency; victims, perhaps equally grieving, will implore the court to be stern. In some unusual cases, there may be an expert or two testifying as to the offender's suitability for treatment programs. It is a postconviction revisitation to the contest between the state and the offender, with the former nearly always pressing for the toughest possible sentence, the latter trying to avoid that sentence, and not much common ground between the two.

This process is not well designed to produce a penalty that either the victim or the offender thinks makes sense. It continues to reinforce an ethic that the offender should be expected to try to avoid the consequences of the criminal act, and it does not enable the victim to have any sense of involvement in the selection of a penalty. The result is a sentence that typically leaves the offender feeling even more attacked by the system, strikes the victim as inadequate, and leaves the sentencing judge with little confidence it will work as an effective sanction. It is of little surprise that this approach does not seem to lead to much that people can feel good about.

Attempts to carve out a different strategy, in which community members, victims, and the offender work together to develop a sanction that addresses the problems each of them faces, when they are successful, often result in sanctions that each party feels are more effective, and victims in particular find more satisfactory.[20] There is also some preliminary evidence to suggest that the requirements contained within the sanctions developed under these guidelines are more likely to be successfully adhered to by the offender.

Involving citizens—victims, community members, and others—in the sanctioning process has another advantage. It opens them up to the possibility of deeper involvement in crime prevention activity. Either as community volunteers working with offenders, or as a part of groups implementing crime prevention strategies, citizens who have a sense of involvement in the justice process become more responsible for a broader range of public safety concerns where they live. The result is that the responsibility for dealing with crime will lie not just with a group of hired professionals, but with all of us.

Community Justice Is Cost-Effective. Today's justice process is an expensive public service. Let us return to the example cited earlier by Professor Dickey, where ninety-four arrests were made in a six-month period, and ask how much money might have been spent on those cases. Of course, the cost in salaries of police officers, judges, attorneys, and so on, is not easily estimated. But we can say that if one-half of these offenders were sentenced to prison, and served an average of two years in prison, then prison costs will be significant: At $20,000 per year for forty-seven people to serve two years in prison, for example, the total bill would be over $1.8 million, not counting the salaries of the law enforcement and court officials. That is a lot to spend on a street corner for six months of criminal justice. It is especially a lot to spend if the street remains just as unsafe after the money is gone.

The amount of money now spent on justice is astounding—for example, the state budgets of correctional agencies in 1998 ranged from $17.1 million in North Dakota to $4.0 billion in California.[21] The argument of community-based justice advocates is that this money can be invested far more wisely in other ways, particularly in trying to address the problems that afflict high-crime communities.

This can be illustrated in a simple way. Let us say a twenty-five-year-old man is found guilty of a third serious felony, and, according to a three-strikes law, is sentenced to life without parole. If he lives to the age of seventy-five—a reasonable expectation—and each year in prison costs $20,000, then this sentence, in effect, costs $1 million for this single offender. Community justice advocates say that it is possible to imagine a large number of alternatives that would be a better investment for a million taxpayer dollars. For example, the areas where many offenders come from have numerous needs—after-school projects, public health for newborns, security for public housing, jobs, recreational alternatives for youth, and so on. There are so many needs, and there is so little money to spend on those needs.

The reason, say community justice advocates, is that we are spending the money on offenders, not on crime prevention. If our sanctioning priority were not simply to punish, but to make crime less likely, these advocates say that a very different crime policy would follow, and we would reap valuable results from it. The math is straightforward. A year in prison costs $20,000 or more, but that same year on probation costs 5 percent of that amount, or less. The difference is money that can be invested in other crime prevention priorities.

The key, of course, is whether the offender can be dealt with in a way that does not leave the community unduly at risk. Community justice requires that equal attention be paid to selecting only those offenders whose risk can be adequately managed in community contexts, and to developing and monitoring risk management approaches that are practical and effective.

Yet, there are never any guarantees. Offenders are, by nature, a risk to the community, but many offenders will stay crime-free despite the risk they represent. How much of a risk will the community tolerate? The question is answered partly by the alternative. If a community is able to use otherwise unavailable funds in order to improve quality of life by reducing crime in other ways, then it might make sense to take the risk. This, at least, is the viewpoint of the community justice advocate.

Three Concerns About Community Justice

It should not be surprising that community-oriented justice, despite the arguments above, is not to everyone's taste. There are two important reasons. Community justice is a new idea, and while its arguments are appealing to some, much of its value has yet to be conclusively proven. Perhaps more important, the contemporary justice system has a long, deeply ingrained tradition in the United States. Many have a strong commitment to the status quo, and not only because of vested interests—the Western justice tradition is one of the great advances of democratic governance. Because community justice is new, observers have raised a number of important questions about its prospects. Three central concerns are individual rights, social inequality, and increased costs. Any attempts to embrace community justice will inevitably be forced to face these issues.

Community Justice and Individual Rights. In a community justice model, different communities will vary in the ways they pursue public safety and improved quality of life. For example, if localities are allowed to determine justice (and crime) priorities, then it follows that services such as policing and prosecution may operate with differences in resource allocation and even practical action, even though they operate under identical criminal codes. How far may these differences go before they violate our belief in equality under the law? To what extent may a locality exert its unique vision of social control without infringing on freedoms of "deviant" members who are in the minority? Will a neighborhood justice movement take some characteristics of vigilantism; if not, what will stop that trend?

As citizens become more active in various aspects of the justice process, the state's role in presiding over that process is undercut. The adversarial ideal assumes that the state accuses a citizen and brings to bear evidence that supports the accusation. The dispute is between the state and the accused. Inserting other citizens—neighbors and residents—into that arrangement muddies the water by creating a third party to the dispute. It is unclear precisely what ought to be the role of the third party—observational, participatory, advisory, or even advocacy? Whatever the role, the presence of that party means that the state and its adversary can no longer be concerned only about each other. The concern for rights protections extends beyond those of the accused to the rights of victims and, indirectly, to affected community members. The question is, *What does the growth of interest in the community mean for the rights of criminal suspects?* And since some research has shown that individual characteristics promote serious delinquency more than community characteristics, some people wonder if a focus on communities will lead us to ignore individuals' problems that need to be addressed.[22]

We must be uneasy about the implications of any developments that undermine the protection of rights. Perhaps the finest contribution of Western civilization to modern life is the idea of the sanctity and dignity of the individual. This idea is given life in the form of legal rights, in which citizens stand equal to one another as well as to the state. Any movement toward community justice taken at the expense of this priceless heritage would impose a cultural cost of profound dimensions. Community justice ideals *will* alter established practices of substantive and procedural criminal law. The test will be to devise the changes in such a way that our precious civil liberties will be protected.

Community Justice and Social Inequality. Neighborhoods differ not only in their crime control priorities but also in their capacities, resources, and resilience in meeting crime problems. The same inequality that characterizes the United States at the individual level plays out as a community dynamic. The justice system really operates as two different systems, one for people with financial resources and another for the poor. *Is there any assurance that the same kind of inequality will not come to characterize community justice?*

This is not a small concern. Research shows that the higher victimization rates of African Americans and Latinos is due, almost completely, to the fact that they live in disadvantaged places where violence persists.[23] Research also shows that poor communities, particularly those hit hard by crime, also tend to lack resources to regulate neighborhood problems and pursue social control.[24] These communities do not come together to solve problems, and they have low rates of citizen participation in official business. One lesson of community policing has been that in troubled neighborhoods, it is often difficult to get citizens to take responsible action in response to their crime problems.

More prosperous localities will also have disproportionate political influence in many city and county governments. They will be better at organizing to influence the crime priorities, directing the funding decisions, and protecting their residents from negative impacts of change. A community justice model that enables localities to pursue interests and preferences will inevitably raise the potential for these more successful communities to strengthen their position in relation to other localities.

Community justice cannot treat all communities as of equal importance or as independent from one another. Studies show that the most effective community organizations tend to be "neighborhood associations" that advance the needs of identifiable sections of a city.[25] But these are most likely to be lacking in the poorest communities. Therefore, we must recognize that communities exist within larger social and political systems, and local problems and public policies to address them must be understood within this broader context.

Inequality breeds crime. It would be a dismal irony if community justice, advanced to help places deal more effectively with their crime problems, contributed to the very dynamics that make those problems worse. If the problem of inequality is to be avoided, some local areas will likely require differential resource investment to take advantage of the promise of community justice.

Community Justice and Increasing Criminal Justice Costs. We spend nearly $100 billion on the criminal justice system every year. The cost of justice is increasing, and the burden it places on local areas through taxes interferes with the capacity to fund schools, provide child health care, and maintain basic services. A community justice model calls for criminal justice organizations to augment current services. *How will these services be paid for?*

The disparity between community resources and crime rates means that local revenues cannot be the basis for funding community justice. As indicated, the very communities that most suffer from crime are least able to pay to combat it. Some mechanism for shifting financial resources from affluent communities to impoverished ones will be needed. This will obviously raise sensitive political issues because taxpayers are leery of spending for services from which they do not directly benefit.

In addition, some way of shifting costs *within* the existing justice budget will be needed. New money for new programs is scarce, and a proposal to greatly increase funding of justice work will be met with skepticism. Community justice programs that shift the onus for crime fighting to the community without providing resources to do it are doomed to fail.[26]

Instead, community justice needs to be based on a shifting of resources within existing justice functions. The overall dollar costs of justice cannot be expected to rise too much; what can occur is a change in the allocation of justice dollars to provide support for new activities in place of previous functions. Community justice calls for collaboration between criminal justice agencies and other governmental and community social welfare agencies and services. Coordinated efforts will enhance effectiveness by combining the resources of different agencies using similar strategies to obtain different ends. For example, while one agency's objective may be increasing employment within a neighborhood, this goal may also reduce criminal activity.

PERSPECTIVES ON COMMUNITY JUSTICE

Systems

Community justice is an idea that has developed as a method for overcoming the weaknesses of the formal criminal justice system. In this respect, it is a challenge to the vested interests of traditional justice agencies. For example, community justice strategies hope to redirect criminal justice funding that has been devoted to incarceration away from the corrections system and toward community-level needs, such as housing, drug treatment, and employment development. We can imagine that criminal justice agencies might not be enthusiastic about having their funding go elsewhere.

On the other hand, most of the important community justice innovation has come about because criminal justice agencies have realized that the traditional way of doing business was not working, and they have led the way to many of the new community justice programs. So even though community justice may be seen as posing a threat to criminal justice, some of the most ardent proponents of community justice are practitioners within the criminal justice system.

The question is, What will happen if community justice continues to grow? Will it begin to serve as a threat to traditional criminal justice operations? Will traditional criminal justice organizations themselves change to incorporate more of the community justice model?

There is, of course, an alternative scenario: Community justice may be a kind of "fad." The criminal justice system has strong roots and deeply established traditions, and it may be that community justice concepts will pass, and the future will look back on this as one in a series of new ideas, soon replaced by the next innovation.

Evidence

Community justice is a very new approach, and there is, as yet, little evidence one way or another regarding the basic strategies of community justice.

That does not mean there are no "community justice" facts. To the contrary, community justice is an idea that has grown out of an impressive

The Implementation of Community Corrections

empirical foundation showing how important "place" is for crime and justice. Some of these studies showed that although crime occurs everywhere, it is concentrated in certain neighborhoods where the poor and disadvantaged live. Some of these studies showed that community factors affect the way individuals adjust to community life—when ex-prisoners are released to poor and crime-infested neighborhoods, they find it far harder to succeed. Some studies showed that community-based initiatives were successful in combating crime.

The experience of criminal justice officials also proved important in the development of community justice. The first agency to realize how important it was to have community support for justice initiatives was the police. Later, the courts and then correctional agencies joined in that realization. A national movement developed that sought ways to encourage greater citizen participation in and support for the efforts of criminal justice.

Advocates of community justice have a great deal of optimism about their approach, but they do not have an equal amount of evidence to back it up. One of the major cycles in criminal justice is that highly vaunted reforms, once evaluated, turn out to have disappointing results. Will this be the fate of community justice?

People

Community justice orientations place a heavy emphasis on people—especially ordinary citizens who get involved with the criminal justice system. By opening its doors to the public for involvement, the community justice model creates a variety of roles for citizens to play in the criminal justice and correctional system. People can volunteer as mentors or counselors, they can join advisory boards or work on particular justice projects, and they can attend community meetings and let their voices be heard.

It takes a different kind of criminal justice professional to appreciate this new, open door for citizens. Many criminal justice workers have professional training and expect to be able to perform their jobs without a great deal of outside influence. But community justice accepts the influence of nonprofessionals—outsiders to the system—as an important aspect of effective services. Many criminal justice workers find this a change that is difficult to make.

Community justice becomes most "personal," though, when it adjusts its practices to fit particular communities. Informally, it has often been the case that justice practices differed from one place to another. But community justice embraces those differences as being an essential aspect of effectiveness, and so the community justice worker has to learn how to be sensitive to and interested in the nuances of the place in which the work is being done.

Is this a good idea? Is it an attractive part of community justice, or does it detract from the professionalism of the system? Will people find it fair? Will it ever be able to become a standard aspect of practice?

Bureaucracy

Community justice is antibureaucracy—and therein lies one of the biggest challenges for the approach. Bureaucracies develop for a reason, usually having in part to do with the need to regularize actions, reduce unpredictability of services, and create the capacity for accountability. It will not be possible for community justice orientations to be in operation for very long without regularity of procedures, predictability of services, and accountability for actions.

It is not just that the everyday needs of organizations require these bureaucratic elements. The clients of these organizations need them, too—including the communities that are the clients of community justice. If organizations are irregular in their practices, unpredictable in their policies, or unaccountable for their work, clients are among the first to object. Imagine, for example, trying to make use of a community center that has no established hours and no predetermined programs.

The question facing community justice leaders is how to create innovative programs that have the aspects needed by bureaucratic organizations without the liabilities of bureaucracy. How do community justice managers maintain a spirit of innovation and creativity without neglecting the needs of clients for stable programs and dependable practices? The answer to this question will, in large part, tell us what the long-term prospects are for community justice as a new way of doing business.

THE FUTURE OF COMMUNITY JUSTICE

Community justice is a new idea. It has proved very popular, but the important question to ask about any new idea in correctional work is whether it has staying power. We might wonder whether the community justice movement will be a brief aspect of today's justice politics or, as its advocates intend, a long-term force in the reform of the justice system.

The popularity of community justice derives in part from deep dissatisfactions with contemporary justice politics. Many have become alarmed by the trends described in earlier chapters such as the increased use of surveillance and the ever growing size of correctional populations. Because it embraces community safety without the emphasis on "toughness" or surveillance, community justice provides an attractive alternative for many who are disillusioned with existing strategies.

In some ways, community justice is a throwback. Those who promote more local, informal, and citizen-supported responses to crime seem to have an image of the way communities traditionally dealt with misbehavior in the past—by collective effort to overcome it. If community justice is desirable because it calls us to a nostalgic past, it is likely to be short-lived. Modern problems call for modern solutions, not fuzzy history. The way we dealt with deviance in the past was often harsh, and far too frequently dehumanizing of fellow citizens. If the call for community justice is not much more than a call for return to the past, it will not last long.

But if the community justice movement is successful in developing and demonstrating a true alternative to traditional criminal justice—with local, problem-solving, restorative solutions to crime problems—then it will be traditional bureaucratic justice that will someday be a thing of the past.

SUMMARY

In a time when our society and the problems we face are becoming more diverse, it is an appropriate time to also think of solutions that are different or "outside of the box" from our myopic perspective. In criminal justice, we need to widen our view of the punishment of offenders from the traditional retributive model of deterrence and severe punishment to the emerging view of community justice. Community justice is not a simple idea that can be easily explained. It is at once a *philosophy* of justice, a *strategy* of justice, and a series of justice *programs*. Community justice differs from traditional criminal justice in that it is neighborhood based, problem solving, and restorative, rather than jurisdiction based, case processing, and adversarial. Community justice holds that sanctioning, problem solving, and restoration for all parties involved should be essential elements of the criminal justice system.

There are at least three arguments in favor of the community justice approach: It addresses the roots of crime problems, it involves the victim and the community in the process, and it is cost-effective. Yet many questions remain unanswered about the community justice movement. Problems with community justice include the need to protect individual rights, the problem of social inequality, and the immense cost of the justice system. The future of community justice will lie in the degree to which its programs can deliver a safer community without exacerbating the problems of the justice system.

| DISCUSSION QUESTIONS |

1. What are the limits of developing a correctional system that would utilize the concepts of community justice?

2. What factors in society would possibly obstruct the implementation of opportunity set or routine activities theory?

3. Based on the concepts proposed in this chapter, how would having an intimate partner or loved one reduce the chance of crime commission for some offenders? Why?

4. Who do you believe has the responsibility to restore justice in the community after the commission of a crime?

5. At the core of the community justice approach is the idea that crime does not happen in a vacuum, but is created by a plethora of community issues. Based on this idea, how would you eliminate a crime problem in your community such as drugs or juvenile delinquency?

┤ SUGGESTED READINGS ├

Bazemore, G. "Balanced and Restorative Justice for Juvenile Offenders: An Overview of New OJJDP Initiatives" (Monograph). Washington, DC: U.S. Department of Justice, Office of Juvenile Delinquency Prevention, 1993. Although this document is directed for use with restorative justice for juveniles, it still has much helpful information about main concepts of restorative justice.

Clear, Todd R., and Karp, David R. *The Community Justice Idea: Promoting Safety and Achieving Justice.* Boulder, CO: Westview Press, 1999. Provides an argument for community justice as a philosophy and strategy.

McCold, P. *Restorative Justice: An Annotated Bibliography.* Monsey, NY: Criminal Justice Press and Willow Tree Press, 1997. Offers an invaluable resource for information about restorative justice. Over 500 entries provide a comprehensive overview of the literature on the topic.

Van Ness, D. W., and Heetderks Strong, Karen. *Restorative Justice.* Cincinnati, OH: Anderson, 1997. Provides theory, principles for application, and steps for implementation of the restorative justice concept.

Zehr, Howard. *Changing Lenses.* Scottdale, PA: Herald Press, 1990. Considered one of the "classics" and among the first books written about restorative justice.

┤ WEB SITES ├

Web site for information on juvenile justice and restorative justice
www.ncjrs.org/juvenilejustice.asp

Web site for articles on restorative justice available through Campaign for Equity and Restorative Justice
www.cerj.org

Web site for the Vermont Department of Corrections reparative program
www.doc.state.vt.us/gw2/media.htm

Web site for a bibliography on restorative justice
http://fresno.edu/pacs/links.shtml

Web site for the National Restorative Justice Institute
www.cerj.org

Web site for a series of community crime prevention strategies in practice
http://midget.towson.edu:8001/MDCP.html

1. These and other community justice projects are described in Todd R. Clear and David R. Karp, *The Community Justice Ideal: Preventing Crime and Achieving Justice* (Boulder, CO: Westview Press, 1999).

2. Scott Decker and Barrick Van Winkle, *Life in the Gang: Family, Friends and Violence* (New York: Cambridge University Press, 1996).

3. Marc Mauer, *African American Males and the Criminal Justice System* (Washington, DC: The Sentencing Project, 1996).

4. B. Galaway and J. Hudson, eds., *Criminal Justice, Restitution, and Reconciliation* (Monsey, NY: Willow Tree Press, 1990).

5. Todd R. Clear and David R. Karp, "Toward the Ideal of Community Justice," *NIJ Journal* (October 2000) (Washington, DC: U.S. Department of Justice, National Institute of Justice, NCJ 184447).

6. Robert J. Sampson, Stephen W. Raudenbush, and Felton Earles, "Neighborhoods and Violent Crime: A Multilevel Study of Collective Efficacy," *Science* 277 (August 15, 1997): 1–7.

7. T. Armstrong, D. Maloney, and D. Romig, "The Balanced Approach in Juvenile Probation: Principles, Issues and Application," *Perspectives* (Winter 1990).

8. K. Pranis, "Restorative Justice: Back to the Future in Criminal Justice" (Working Paper) (Minneapolis: Minnesota Citizens Council, 1993).

9. P. Freivalds, *Balanced and Restorative Justice Project (BARJ)* (Washington, DC: Government Printing Office, 1996).

10. M. Umbreit and H. Zehr, "Restorative Family Group Conferences: Differing Models and Guidelines for Practice," *Federal Probation* 60:3 (September 1996): 24–30.

11. *President's Task Force on Victims of Crime, Final Report* (Washington, DC: Government Printing Office, 1982).

12. See Norval Morris and Michael Tonry, *Between Prison and Probation: Intermediate Punishments in a Rational Sentencing System* (New York: Oxford University Press, 1990).

13. William Spelman, *Criminal Incapacitation* (New York: Plenum, 1994).

14. Don Andrews, "The Psychology of Criminal Conduct and Effective Treatment," in *What Works: Reducing Criminal Offending*, ed. James McGuire (Chichester: Wiley, 1995).

15. Lawrence Cohen and Marcus Felson, "Social Change and Crime Rate Trends: A Routine Activities Approach," *American Sociological Review* 44 (1979): 588–608.

16. Robert Sampson and John Laub, *Crime in the Making: Pathways and Turning Points Through Life* (Cambridge: Harvard University Press, 1993).

17. Ronald V. Clarke and Marcus Felson, eds., *Routine Activity and Rational Choice: Advances in Criminological Theory* (New Brunswick: Transaction Press, 1993).

18. John Braithwaite, *Crime, Shame, and Reintegration* (Cambridge University Press, 1989).

19. John Perry and John Gorzcyk, "Restructuring Corrections: Using Market Research in Vermont," *Corrections Management Quarterly* 1:3 (1997): 26–35.

20. Gordon Bazemore, "Restorative Justice and Earned Redemption: Victims, Communities and Offender Reintegration," *American Behavioral Science* 768 (March 1998).

21. *The 1998 Corrections Yearbook* (Middletown, CT: Criminal Justice Institute), p. 87.

22. Olaf Wikstrom and Rolf Loeber, "Do Disadvantaged Neighborhoods Cause Well-Adjusted Children to Become Adolescent Delinquents? A Study of Male Juvenile Serious Offending, Individual Risk and Protective Factors, and Neighborhood Context," *Criminology* 38:4 (November 2000): 1109–1143. Characteristics of disadvantage in neighborhoods do not seem to increase the impact of risk factors or reduce the impact of protective factors (at the individual level) of serious delinquency.

23. Janet L. Lauritsen and Norman A. White, "Putting Violence in Its Place: The Influence of Race, Ethnicity, Gender, and Place on the Risk of Violence," *Criminology and Public Policy* 1:1 (November 2001): 37–60.

24. Robert J. Bursick, Jr., and Harold G. Grasmick, *Neighborhoods and Crime: The Dimensions of Effective Community Control* (New York: Lexington Books, 1993).

25. Kente Portney and Jeffrey Berry, "Mobilizing Minority Communities: Social Capital and Participation in Urban Neighborhoods, *American Behavioral Scientist* 40:5 (March 1997): 632–644.

26. Nancy Jurik, Joel Blumenthal, Brian Smith, and Edwardo Portillos, "Organizational Co-optation or Social Change? A Critical Perspective on Community-Criminal Justice Partnerships," *Journal of Contemporary Criminal Justice* 16:3 (August 2000): 292–320.

Chapter 10

Parole

Photo: Anne Marie Reynolds, 64, talks with members of the state Parole Board, in December 2000, after winning her release. Reynolds, of Jackson, N.H., had been imprisoned since killing her husband nearly sixteen years ago. At the hearing Reynolds described the years of emotional, physical, and sexual abuse she endured before shooting her husband in 1985. AP/Wide World Photos

An African American minister active in party politics, a retired corporate executive, a man who owns a small business, and a woman interested in civic affairs sit as a parole board to consider the lengths of the sentences of Maurice Williams and nineteen other inmates. Convicted of first-degree robbery, Williams is serving his first major sentence, five to ten years. As he enters the hearing room at the maximum security prison, he seems relaxed and confident, more sure of himself than most inmates at parole hearings. His time in prison has been productive: He has earned a high school general equivalency diploma, he has received a good report from the director of the drug treatment program and a supporting report from the prison psychiatrist, and his brother has written that he will give him a job in his grocery store in the old neighborhood. Still, he is a bit nervous. He has never been before the parole board before, and he wonders about the people he is facing. Who are they? What do they know about him? How will they react to his file?

The minister asks Williams about his plans for the future. Williams answers that he will live with his brother and work in the store. The woman wants to know if he will be hanging out with his old buddies. Williams tries to assure her that although many still live nearby, he will avoid them. "I've learned my lesson. I'm gonna keep away from those guys." After a few more minutes, during which the members shuffle through the papers in his file, Williams is told that he can return to his cell and that he will learn the board's decision by evening.

In the discussion that follows Williams's departure, several panel members express skepticism about his prison performance and wonder if he is merely a con artist who will do anything to earn early release. The businessman predicts that Williams will fall back into trouble soon after he hits the streets: "I know that neighborhood. It will be impossible for him to stay away from those influences." Eventually they compromise and decide to grant Williams an extended parole—that is, he will be paroled, but not on the date he first becomes eligible. One member has already started to study another of the files stacked before him. It is 9:20 A.M. One case down on a typical hearing day and nineteen to go.

Maurice Williams's hearing was typical of federal and state release procedures used from 1920 to 1973 when there was a nationwide sentencing and release policy. Under this approach, all states and the federal government used indeterminate sentencing, authorized discretionary release by parole boards, and supervised prisoners after release, all in the interest of the rehabilitation of offenders.[1] Today scenes similar to the one above still occur, but fewer states maintain parole boards or allow boards the wide discretion they had in the past.

GETTING OUT OF PRISON

It is hard to imagine a more enormous change than going to prison—unless it is coming home from prison. The person who goes to prison enters a tightly controlled world of depersonalization and indignity. But the person returning from prison enters a world that cares little about the embittering prison life left behind and how it may have damaged self-esteem and robbed confidence.

The released offender faces a daily pace and array of choices so different from the world of the prison that it may at first seem an alien culture. Everyone in prison seems to want out, but once given that chance too many ex-offenders cannot cope, and they end up back in prison where they started.

Each year, upwards of 600,000 inmates are released from prison. They go back to their prior environs filled with hope and perhaps also a bit wary of how they will be received. Many try to find work, housing, and friends who will help them stay out of trouble. Others are eager to rejoin in the thrills and intrigues that got them into trouble in the first place. At best it is a struggle, at worst an impossible challenge. Within a year, as many as one in five will be back in the prisons they left, faced with the brutal fact of their inability to live on the streets without getting afoul of the law. The cycle of recidivism—going to prison and getting out only to return again all too soon—is a puzzling but undeniable fact for many offenders.

Nearly 95 percent of those who enter prison will leave; 80 percent will be released to parole supervision. (See Figure 10.1) In 2000, there were 725,527 people on parole in the United States.[2] What is interesting is the threefold increase in the number of parolees over the twenty years since 1980, when there were 220,438 persons assigned to parole. Parole is the fastest growing of the four major components of corrections, and with the massive incarcerations of the past decade, the number on parole is likely to reach 1 million in the next five years.

FIGURE 10.1 NUMBER OF ADULTS UNDER PAROLE SUPERVISION, 1980–2000

Source: U.S. Department of Justice, Bureau of Justice Statistics, "Nation's Correctional Population Reaches New High," Press Release, August 26, 2001.

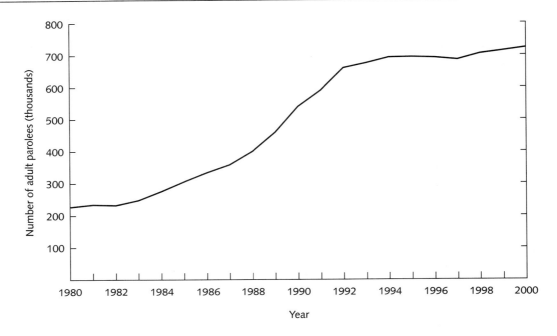

PAROLE RELEASE

For decades, parole was available in almost every state in the United States, but a twenty-year period of sentencing reform has severely restricted parole eligibility. The first state to abolish parole release was Maine, in 1976. As of January 1, 2001, fifteen states had abolished parole (Arizona, Delaware, Florida, Illinois, Indiana, Kansas, Maine, Minnesota, Mississippi, North Carolina, Ohio, Oregon, Virginia, Washington, and Wisconsin).

Among the remaining states that allow prisoners to be released by the parole process, many of those states restrict parole to certain offenders under certain circumstances. For example, four states (Alaska, Louisiana, New York, and Tennessee) have abolished discretionary parole for certain violent offenders.[3] Those states that deny or restrict the possibility for *release* by a parole board usually provide for *supervision* by parole officers for offenders released by other mechanisms. Thus, it is important to distinguish between the release functions of parole, which are waning in popularity, and the supervision functions of parole, which seem to remain as popular as ever.

Parole has customarily been defined as the conditional release of a prisoner from incarceration but not from the legal custody and supervision of the state.

Offenders who subsequently comply with the conditions of parole and do not come into further conflict with the law generally receive an absolute discharge from supervision at the end of their sentences. If parolees break a rule, parole may be revoked and they must return to a correctional facility.

Parole, then, rests on three concepts:

- *Grace or privilege:* The prisoner could be kept incarcerated, but the government extends the privilege of release.
- *Contract or consent:* The government enters into an agreement with the prisoner whereby the prisoner promises to abide by certain conditions in exchange for being released.
- *Custody:* Even though the offender is released from prison, he or she is still a responsibility of the government. Parole is an extension of correctional programs into the community.

Advocates of parole debate among themselves which of these three models is most appropriate. Tough-minded parole experts argue that parolees have very few rights and are fortunate to have been extended the opportunity to serve a portion of the sentence on the streets. They say that parolees should be thought of as prisoners who happened to be classified as "community" level of custody, allowing them to reside in the community. Thus, they see parole as a type of custody, and they see the granting of parole as an offering of the privilege—a chance to show what the offender can do if allowed some freedom.

Other parole advocates see parole release as a more standard function of the corrections systems that employ parole boards. They point out that making parole available is not an act of mercy, but rather it is a policy that serves the interest of the state. If the prisoner abides by the rules and shows evidence of dealing with the problems that led to criminality, then the state has agreed to allow the prisoner a chance to try the streets before the sentence is fully served. They see the parole system as a kind of agreement, like a contract, between the prisoner and the state to find a way to meet the needs of both parties—the state gets to see if the offender will become a law-abiding citizen; the prisoner gets to leave the prison early. If both parties keep their promises, then parole is a win-win situation.

In this chapter, we review the background of parole, the process of leaving prison, trying to make it on the streets, and, for some, ending up back in. We show that there are numerous ways to get out of prison and almost as many ways to go back. The struggles facing offenders released from prison are easy enough to understand, and they are usually made even more complicated by the fact that most releasees are not free citizens. They have served their time, but they still have to report to agents of the state, usually parole officers. Given all the obstacles facing releasees, we can begin to understand why so many of them do not take advantage of their freedom, but instead continue to fail.

PAROLE SUPERVISION

Parole supervision varies greatly in the United States. In North Dakota there are 246 former inmates on parole, whereas in California over 117,000 require parole supervision.[4] Even with the increase in the number of offenders on parole, there has not been an increase in the number of parole officers. In the 1970s, the average caseload size was around forty-five. Today caseloads of seventy are common.

Research has shown that most parolees have less than two fifteen-minute face-to-face contacts with their parole officer each month.[5] This would explain why in California it was reported that parole officers "lost track" of about one-fifth of the parolees they were assigned to in 1999.[6]

ORIGINS OF PAROLE

Parole is formally defined as the release of an offender from a correctional institution after he or she has served a portion of the sentence with conditions of good behavior and supervision in the community. The word *parole* comes from the French term *parole d'honneur,* which means "word of honor." Parole was used during time of war as a means of releasing prisoners with the promise that they would not resume arms in a current conflict.

Parole in the United States evolved during the nineteenth century out of such English, Australian, and Irish practices as conditional pardon, apprenticeship by indenture, and "tickets-of-leave" or licenses. These methods had as their common denominator the movement of criminals out of prison (usually in response to overcrowding), the need for labor, and the cost of incarceration, rather than any rationale linked to the goal of the criminal sanction. Until the middle of the nineteenth century, England relied on transportation as one of the major sanctions. When America gained independence, Australia and other Pacific colonies became the outlets for England's overcrowded prisons; offenders were given conditional pardons known as **tickets-of-leave** and sent to those outposts of the empire.

The extension of the parole idea in the United States was linked to the indeterminate sentence. As states adopted indeterminate sentencing, parole followed. By 1900, twenty states had parole systems and by 1925, forty-six states did; Mississippi and Virginia finally followed suit in 1942. Beginning in 1910, each federal prison had its own parole board made up of the warden, the medical officer, and the superintendent of prisons of the Department of Justice. The boards made release suggestions to the attorney general. In 1930 Congress created the U.S. Board of Parole, which replaced the separate boards. Today, all jurisdictions have some mechanism for releasing felons into the community under supervision, although parole is no longer as common as it used to be.

STATE OF NEW YORK EXECUTIVE DEPARTMENT— DIVISION OF PAROLE

GENERAL RULES GOVERNING PAROLE

When an inmate of a correctional institution is approved for parole or conditional release, he or she must agree to the following conditions of parole which are made a part of the release agreement: I will voluntarily accept Parole supervision. I fully understand that my person, residence and property are subject to search and inspection. I understand that parole supervision is defined by these Conditions of Release and all other conditions that may be imposed upon me by the Board or its representatives.

I understand that my violation of these conditions may result in the revocation of my release.

Conditions of Release

1. I will proceed directly to the area to which I have been released and, within twenty-four hours of my release, make my arrival report to that Office of the Division of Parole unless other instructions are designated on my release agreement.
2. I will make office and/or written reports as directed.
3. I will not leave the State of New York or any other State to which I am released or transferred, or any area defined in writing by my Parole Officer without permission.
4. I will permit my Parole Officer to visit me at my residence and/or place of employment and I will permit the search and inspection of my person, residence and property. I will discuss any proposed changes in my residence, employment or program status with my Parole Officer. I understand that I have an immediate and continuing duty to notify my Parole Officer of any changes in my residence, employment or program status when circumstances beyond my control make prior discussion impossible.
5. I will reply promptly, fully and truthfully to any inquiry of or communication by my Parole Officer or other representative of the Division of Parole.
6. I will notify my Parole Officer immediately any time I am in contact with or arrested by any law enforcement agency. I understand that I have a continuing duty to notify my Parole Officer of such contact or arrest.
7. I will not be in the company of or fraternize with any person I know to have a criminal record or whom I know to have been adjudicated a Youthful Offender except for accidental encounters in public places, work, school or in any other instance with the permission of my Parole Officer.

8. I will not behave in such manner as to violate the provisions of any law to which I am subject which provide for a penalty of imprisonment, nor will my behavior threaten the safety or well-being of myself or others.

9. I will not own, possess, or purchase any shotgun, rifle or firearm of any type without the written permission of my Parole Officer. I will not own, possess or purchase any deadly weapon as defined in the Penal Law or any dangerous knife, dirk, razor, stiletto or imitation pistol. In addition, I will not own, possess or purchase any instrument readily capable of causing physical injury without a satisfactory explanation for ownership, possession or purchase.

10. In the event that I leave the jurisdiction of the State of New York, I hereby waive my right to resist extradition to the State of New York from any state in the Union and from any territory or country outside the United States. This waiver shall be in full force and effect until I am discharged from Parole or Conditional Release. I fully understand that I have the right under the Constitution of the United States and under law to contest any effort to extradite me from another state and return me to New York, and I freely and knowingly waive this right as a condition of my Parole or Conditional Release.

11. I will not use or possess any drug paraphernalia or use or possess any controlled substance without proper medical authorization.

12. Special Conditions:

13. I will fully comply with the instructions of my Parole Officer and obey such special additional written conditions as he, a Member of the Board of Parole or an authorized representative of the Division of Parole, may impose.

DIFFERENT KINDS OF PAROLE RELEASE

Except for the small number who die in prison, all inmates will eventually be released to live in the community. With the critique of rehabilitation, the move to determinate sentencing, and the public's view that the system was "soft" on criminals, parole boards have been abolished in fifteen states.[7] Three states—Colorado, Connecticut, and Florida—first abolished, then reestablished the equivalent of parole boards after finding that actual time served was not increased, because crowding became so great that inmates had to be released early.[8] Even in states that retained parole, some boards have been reluctant to grant it. In Texas, for example, 57 percent of all cases considered for parole release in 1988 were approved; by 1998 that figure had dropped to just 20 percent.[9]

FIGURE 10.2 METHODS OF RELEASE FROM STATE PRISON

Felons are released from prison to the community, usually under parole supervision, through various means depending upon the law.

Source: Jeremy Travis and Joan Petersilia, "Reentry Reconsidered," *Crime and Delinquency* 47 (July 2001): 295.

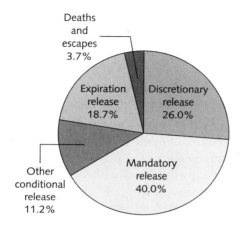

There are now four basic mechanisms for persons to be released from prison: (1) discretionary release, (2) mandatory release, (3) expiration release, and (4) other conditional release. Figure 10.2 shows the percentage of felons released by the various mechanisms.

Discretionary Release

Discretionary release is when an inmate is released as the result of decisions made by parole boards or commissions. Until the mid-1970s, all states and the federal government had systems of discretionary release by which the **parole board** (or its equivalent) determined the exact date for an inmate to enter the community. Discretionary release is tied to the indeterminate sentencing method, in which a minimum and maximum term of incarceration are specified by the judge, allowing the parole board to determine the release date within these limits. This approach also is tied to the rehabilitation model and the idea that parole decisions should be guided by the offender's past, the nature of the offense committed, and the inmate's behavior and participation in rehabilitative programs, as well as the prognosis for a crime-free future.

Parole boards in states with indeterminate sentences have the discretion to release offenders to the community within the boundaries set by the sentence and the penal law. Members must follow certain procedures and are expected to base their decisions on formally stated release criteria, yet inmates know

FIGURE 10.3   PAROLE ELIGIBILITY CALCULATION FOR MAURICE WILLIAMS

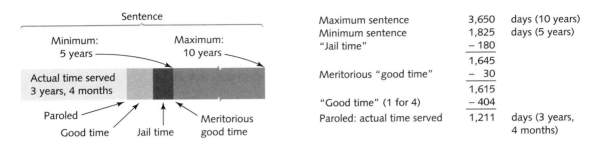

Maximum sentence	3,650	days (10 years)
Minimum sentence	1,825	days (5 years)
"Jail time"	− 180	
	1,645	
Meritorious "good time"	− 30	
	1,615	
"Good time" (1 for 4)	− 404	
Paroled: actual time served	1,211	days (3 years, 4 months)

how they should present themselves so as to win parole. The consequences of discretionary release have an impact beyond the individual case.

Figure 10.3 shows the calculations involved in computing parole eligibility for Maurice Williams, who was given a five- to ten-year sentence for the crime of first-degree robbery. At the time of sentencing, he had been held in jail for six months awaiting trial and disposition of his case. Williams did well in the maximum security prison to which he was sent. He stayed out of trouble and thus was able to amass good-time credit at the rate of one day for every four that he spent on good behavior. In addition, he was given thirty days' meritorious credit when he completed his high school equivalency test after attending the prison school for two years. After serving three years and four months of his sentence, he appeared before the parole board and was granted extended parole. He will be released into the community on the date set by the board. Although the formal release decision is granted by the board acting as a whole, in most states this power is delegated to panels of two or three members sitting at the parole-granting hearings. In several states the responsibility is further delegated to a hearing examiner, usually a correctional staff member, who conducts the actual interview with the inmate and makes a recommendation to the full board.

During the past two decades, the procedures used by discretionary release boards have undergone major changes. Most states have taken measures to ensure due process at the release hearing; about half the states now allow counsel to be present and witnesses to be called and keep verbatim transcripts.

In addition, most parole authorities now immediately provide the inmate with both a written and an oral explanation of the decision. This is a far cry from the earlier practices, when the inmate went alone into a "roomful of strangers," spent about five minutes before the board, and later was informed in writing only that parole had been "granted" or "denied." Yet even now most inmates do not have access to their files and so are unable to determine the primary reason for denial or approval. And although the Supreme Court has issued due process rules for revocation hearings, it has not extended these procedures to the release interview.[10]

Mandatory Release

Mandatory release occurs after an inmate has served time equal to the total sentence minus good time, if any, or to a certain percentage of the total sentence as specified by law. Mandatory release is found in federal jurisdictions and states with determinate sentences and good-time provisions. Without a parole board to decide whether the offender is ready for release and has ties to the community, such as family or a job, mandatory release is a matter of bookkeeping to check the correct amount of good time and to make sure the sentence has been accurately interpreted. The prisoner is released conditionally to parole supervision for the rest of the sentence.

This seems straightforward enough, but like much else in this field, it is more complicated than it seems. A prison sentence can sound like a discrete time—say, five years. But the "mandatory release date"—the date at which the prisoner must be released—has to be calculated, and this can be complicated. A simple five-year term can lead to a complicated calculation of maximum release date, based on accumulation of earned good time (sometimes referred to as credit time). Different scenarios are complicated by the inmate's classification, institutional behavior, and program participation. Each affect the actual time to be served. The bottom line is that if an inmate cannot be held longer than five years, longer sentences will require either new charges or additional court hearings. But after that truism, an inmate, through the way he or she behaves in prison, often has a great deal of impact on the eventual time that has to be served.

Good time is when inmates can accumulate days, months, and years off their maximum sentence by behaving well in prison. This behavior usually entails avoiding institutional infractions and participating in prison programs. In all states but Hawaii and Utah, a provision is made for good time.[11] The first good-time statute was passed in New York in 1817 in order to solve the crowding problem at Newgate prison in Greenwich Village. The statute permitted a sentence reduction of up to 25 percent for first-time inmates. Currently, good-time deductions usually range up to one-third of the maximum sentence, which often means an inmate can gain up to ten days per month off his or her sentence. In some states, good time is subtracted from the minimum sentence. As a result, some inmates are eligible for parole before the minimum sentence is served. Good time is often added with *meritorious time*—time received for special achievement such as education or program completion—to significantly reduce a sentence.

In recent years, there has been controversy about good time. The pressures in favor of increasing the amount of good time a prisoner can earn come from overcrowded prison populations and court decrees ordering states to place limits on prisoners. It is relatively straightforward for a legislature to shave days off the prisoner's sentence by increasing good-time credits that can be earned, and this type of reform avoids the negative publicity that can accompany a parole release. But when the good-time credits lead to very early "mandatory" releases, the same kinds of criticisms that are applied to parole boards begin to affect the good-time laws.

In the past twenty-five years, there has been a shift in the use of discretionary and mandatory release. Inmates used to be more likely to be released using the discretionary model. Whereas 71.8 percent of state prisoners left prison in 1977 through the discretionary decision of a parole board, as of 2001 the number had been reduced to 26 percent. Conversely, mandatory releases from state prisons increased from about 6 percent of all releases in 1977 to 40 percent.[12] In some states, like Maine, various determinate sentencing laws have formally abolished parole supervision. As a consequence, inmates are given what are called expiration releases.

Expiration Release

An increasing percentage of prisoners are given an **expiration release.** These inmates receive an unconditional release from incarceration when their terms expire, minus good time, without parole supervision. As a result, they cannot be returned to prison for their current offense. These offenders have "maxed out." Another term used to describe this kind of release is **flat time.**

In the wake of the "tough on crime" policies of the last two decades, the percentage of inmates released to parole supervision, among all releasees, has dropped. For example, Massachusetts saw the percentage of male releasees to supervision halved between 1990 and 1999. Even when eligible for parole, many prisoners have bypassed the board and the controlled, supervised release it provides; instead, they have decided to "stick it out" until the expiration of their sentence and be released to the community without supervision. This has been particularly true, and worrisome, in light of the threefold increase in the percentage of male inmates' expiration releases directly from maximum security prisons without the benefit of parole supervision and support.[13]

OTHER KINDS OF PRISON RELEASE PROGRAMS

In addition to the formal mechanism of parole, there are at least two groups of ways in which prison inmates can be released into the community. One group of release programs is under the guise of clemency. Clemency is a merciful or lenient act by a judge, governor, or president. Clemency is also a policy that states that executive or legislative action can reduce the severity of the punishment, waive the legal punishment of one or more individuals, or even exempt individuals from prosecution for certain actions. Among the most common reasons for clemency are postconviction evidence of a prisoner's innocence, illness, and providing evidence for other crimes.[14] Four forms of clemency are

FIGURE 10.4 CLEMENCIES AND PARDONS GRANTED TO INMATES (1991–1999)*

Source: *The 1996 Corrections Yearbook* (South Salem, NY: Criminal Justice Institute, 1997); and *The 2000 Corrections Yearbook* (Middletown CT: Criminal Justice Institute, 2000).

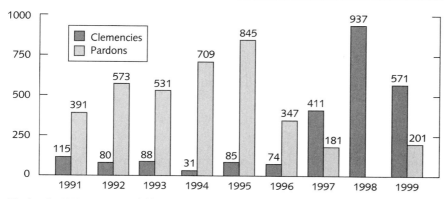

*Pardons for 1998 were not available at time of publication.

pardons, amnesties, commutations, and reprieves. A summary of the recent use of clemency and pardons is included in Figure 10.4.

Pardon

A **pardon** is when a government official restores to an individual all rights and privileges of a citizen. Contemporary pardons serve three main purposes: (1) to remedy a miscarriage of justice, (2) to remove the stigma of a conviction, and (3) to mitigate a penalty. Full pardons for miscarriages of justice are rare but do occur. For example, you may have read of an individual released from prison after the discovery that the crime had been committed by someone else. Pardons are most commonly given to expunge (erase) the criminal records of first-time offenders. But in most states, pardons are given infrequently, only a handful each year.

For the accused, pardons prevent the further progression of criminal justice proceedings. More than likely, pardons involve those already incarcerated and can mean early release. There are two kinds of pardons. The *absolute pardon* fully restores to an individual all the rights and privileges of a citizen. A *conditional pardon* requires some condition(s) to be met before the pardon can be officially granted. The U.S. Constitution gives the president full pardoning power in federal cases.

The mechanisms and conditions for obtaining a pardon vary greatly among the states. In many cases, the governor retains the full power to pardon. In others, the governor must share pardon powers with the state senate or a pardons board. For example, in Utah the Board of Pardons has absolute pardoning authority. In New York, the only way one can receive a pardon is if evidence is provided that determines a person did not commit the offense for which he or she was convicted. Other states have unique variations such as placing time restrictions on pardons. In these states, a pardon is granted only if an inmate has no further convictions for five or ten years after completing the sentence.

Due to the victims' rights movement, the war on drugs, and the public's general sentiment to be "tough" on crime, it is increasingly difficult to obtain a pardon. The pardon process is likely to remain as a highly publicized and controversial issue that will be subject to shifts in ideology among elected officials.[15]

Amnesty

Amnesty is a variation of the pardon during which release may be granted to a group or class of offenders. President Jimmy Carter granted amnesty to Vietnam-era draft evaders, many of whom had fled to Canada. In other areas around the world, amnesty has been used by revolutionary governments to release political dissidents.

Commutation

Commutation is a shortening of the sentence originally ordered by a court of law by either the governor or a board of pardons. As with pardons, the laws concerning commutation vary greatly from state to state. Commutation might be offered when an inmate has a terminal illness such as cancer or AIDS, or is having a baby, or when an inmate cooperates with correctional officials. Inmate cooperation may come during the investigation of a criminal act or during the commission of a prison riot. In each of these cases, the inmate might receive early release into the community. Another instance in which we hear of commutations is when an offender's sentence is changed from the death penalty to life imprisonment. It is also common for a governor or pardoning board to grant a few commutations at Christmastime.

President Clinton created considerable controversy when during the last two hours before he left office in 2001 he issued 140 pardons and commuted 36 sentences—a final-day fury unmatched by any other departing president. However, in comparison, President Clinton ranks only fifteenth of the eighteen presidents in the twentieth century in the total number of pardons and commutations.

Reprieve

A reprieve is the temporary postponement of the execution of a sentence, usually in order for an appeal to be brought before a court of law. The most common use of reprieve is in death penalty cases. In these cases, the governor or even the president can grant a "stay of execution" for an inmate to provide additional

---

┤ 🚶🚶🚶 ├

INTERSTATE COMPACTS

The Interstate Compact for parole is an agreement among the fifty states, Puerto Rico, the Virgin Islands, and the District of Columbia that allows individuals paroled by one state to be supervised in another state. The basic authority for the Interstate Compact is contained in federal legislation originally passed in 1934.

Similar compacts have been developed between jurisdictions to allow for reciprocity of probation supervision.

---

time for legal action. In some states, like Georgia, the Board of Pardons and Paroles may grant a reprieve that lasts a few hours or a few days. This situation would arise when an offender requests to visit a critically ill family member or to attend a family funeral. An inmate can also receive a reprieve if he or she needs medical treatment outside the prison system. A reprieve does not usually result in permanent release from a correctional institution.

In addition to the different forms of clemency, there are other kinds of parole release programs that are instituted by various correctional agencies. These include furloughs, work and study release, emergency release, halfway houses, and shock parole.

Furlough

Many states have laws that permit inmates to leave prison for short periods of time. The leaves are called **furloughs,** and they are used for preparing the inmate for parole release or for some specific reason approved by the correctional authorities. Inmates can use furloughs to visit family members who are ill or to attend funerals, visit community residential centers, or search for employment opportunities. Furloughs are usually given to inmates in one- to three-day intervals. In 1999, there were almost 86,000 furloughs granted in the United States.[16] Not all inmates are allowed furloughs. Restrictions are placed on inmates who have life sentences or who have committed sex offenses.

A special kind of furlough program is employed by the federal correctional system. The Federal Bureau of Prisons requires almost every offender nearing release from confinement to reside in a community residential center (CRC) as prerelease furloughers. The purpose is to achieve closer surveillance of the offender by requiring a transitional period of up to 120 days in a CRC. In most jurisdictions, those furloughed are legally still inmates and can be more easily returned to confinement if they commit technical violations or a new offense.

THE USE OF FURLOUGHS IN GERMAN CORRECTIONS

The German correctional system is primarily driven by a federal law named the *Code on the Execution of Prison Sentences and Measures Involving the Deprivation of Liberty,* also called the *Prison Act of 1976.* One of the aspects of the law states each inmate is allowed up to 21 days of home leave per year. Inmates with this privilege are allowed to leave the prison for 1–2 days to live with family or close friends. All inmates can receive home leave as long as they have not lost the privilege through poor prison behavior. Even serious criminals and those with a "life" sentence can receive this privilege. (More that 15 years is a life sentence in Germany, but it is rare that an inmate will serve more than 17–18 years). If an inmate is a "lifer" he can receive a home leave after 10–12 years if he follows the following criteria. First, the inmate's in-prison behavior must be positive. No serious discipline reports can be present, especially in the areas of violence or drug involvement. Second, during the home leave the inmate must be accompanied by a social worker, chaplain, or correctional officer. It is generally believed that home leaves are an essential part of the inmates' rehabilitative process because it allows inmates to maintain family and community ties.

Source: Harry R. Dammer, "The Practice of Rehabilitation in German Prisons," *Journal of Offender Rehabilitation* 24:1/2 (1996): 6.

Work and Study Release

Work release is a prison program in which inmates are temporarily released into the community in order to meet job responsibilities. In effect, the beginning of work release came about with the original ticket-of-leave practices of the Irish system and Sir Walter Crofton. However, the formation of work release as we know it today in the United States began in 1913 when the state of Wisconsin passed the first work release legislation, called the Huber law, which allowed counties to release inmates during working hours. Work release serves at least two purposes. It helps inmates ease into the transition of release into the community, and it helps inmates gain employment and a skill before release. These programs also can provide an economic benefit for the local or state correctional system. Offenders who are on work release are often required to pay room and board to the state, and they may be asked to begin to provide financial support for their families.

Work release programs were the precursor to study release programs—whereby inmates attend local colleges and technical schools. Study release is sometimes used in states where education beyond the high school (GED) level is not available in the prison system. Relatively few offenders choose the study release option over work release. Unless the offender is able to obtain some form of financial assistance, most are unable to afford the cost of a college education. This is unfortunate because a significant body of research has determined that educating criminal offenders is clearly one of the most effective methods of reducing recidivism and is far less expensive than incarceration.[17] Work release and/or study release programs are common in forty-four states. In 1999, over 44,000 inmates were involved in either work or study release, with over 90 percent dedicated to work release.[18]

Emergency Release

It may be necessary at certain times to allow a group of inmates to be released from incarceration earlier than usual. For example, in states that have developed serious prison crowding problems, there may be a court order from a judge or legislative mandate to reduce the prison population to a certain level. Some states have addressed this issue by forming policies to systematically make inmates eligible for release from prison. Others may deal with the problem on a more ad hoc basis, but the results are the same—inmates are released earlier than originally planned.

Halfway House

Offenders are often released into the community and allowed to reside in a halfway house. The **halfway house,** also called a work release center or community correctional center, was another result of the 1913 Huber law, which let prisoners work in gainful occupations outside the prison as long as they returned to their cells at night. The idea underlying the halfway house is straightforward: Return to the community after institutionalization requires an adjustment, and a relatively controlled environment improves adjustment. Because studies indicate that the highest failure rates of parolees occur in the early months of parole, this idea seems plausible. Recently, halfway houses have become more than mere stopping points for prisoners released from custody; they now employ direct treatment methods (such as therapeutic community techniques) to help offenders confront the problems they face when they return to the community.

Shock Parole

In at least nine states, **shock parole** is a decision made by a paroling authority whereby an inmate is released early from his or her sentence after a brief period of incarceration. It is used for first-time offenders with the hope that

CONNECTICUT HALFWAY HOUSES, INC.: A NONPROFIT CORRECTIONS AGENCY

In 1962 Connecticut Halfway Houses, Inc. (CHHI), a private, nonprofit, community-based corrections agency, was founded by a group of concerned citizens with a grant from the Watkinson Foundation. Since 1966 CHHI has been delivering supervision, treatment, and comprehensive individualized services to sentenced offenders and those determined to be at risk of involvement with the criminal justice system, who have been referred under contract by agencies such as the Federal Bureau of Prisons, Federal Probation, the Connecticut Department of Corrections, and the Connecticut Office of Adult Probation. Out-client alternatives to incarceration as well as residential and aftercare services are provided to over 2,200 clients annually in fifteen programs and residential facilities located throughout the state. CHHI operates with an annual budget of over $3.5 million and a staff of 150.

Specialized services encompass case management, individual and group counseling, education, substance abuse services, AIDS education, relapse prevention, anger management, employment readiness training, literacy, life skills training, money management, and community service. A principal goal of the agency is to enhance the opportunities available to these individuals to become productive, contributing members of their families and communities.

Five residential programs serving a total of 126 adult males, adult females, and youthful offenders are operated by CHHI. Residential work release programs provide services to offenders who are either on pretrial status, on probation, approaching their sentence discharge date, or presently on supervised home release. Aftercare programs are offered as part of the discharge planning process and incorporate training in the use of community support services. Each residential facility provides professional services and counseling to enhance ex-offenders' rehabilitation and reintegration into the community.

Substance abuse counseling programs are offered to clients who have been incarcerated or placed on probation because of behaviors influenced by their drug use (committing crimes to support a habit, possession or distribution of drugs). Services include in-depth assessment and evaluation of their drug/alcohol status and history, supervision, urine screening, and case management.

As part of Connecticut's commitment to intermediate sanctions, alternative incarceration centers have been established. The programs accept predominantly court-referred clients as part of a pretrial diversion program, as well as probation and supervised home prerelease violators. Clients are required to have daily contact with the centers, including providing an itinerary of their daily activities. Preapproved destinations, including places of employment, are spot-checked by telephone and with random site visits on an ongoing basis. Clients are required to submit to regular drug testing, participate in substance abuse counseling, and receive support services designed to meet their individual needs. Participation in community service work projects, designed to benefit the communities located near the centers, is viewed as an important program component and assists in developing community support. Supervised work crews provide labor to cities, towns, and charitable organizations. While these projects have proved both a beneficial and cost-effective source of productive labor, more importantly they provide clients with an opportunity to give something back to their communities.

Connecticut Halfway Houses, Inc., was awarded a certificate of merit for its community service projects by President George Bush in 1991. With the statewide growth in intermediate sanctions programs, the size of the annual budget and staff has recently tripled. CHHI is currently investigating the development of new programs to serve the future needs of the criminal justice system.

this brief exposure to prison will "shock" the offender to change his or her ways in a positive direction and that the offender will be released before he or she becomes too familiar with the prison culture. A typical program will allow shock parolees to be released from prison if the following criteria are met:

1. The offense for which the prisoner is incarcerated was not murder or aggravated assault.
2. The prisoner has not served at least thirty days for a prior felony conviction in any federal or state reformatory or prison.
3. The prisoner is not a psychopathic offender.
4. Further confinement for purposes of rehabilitation or correction is not needed.
5. There is a strong possibility that the offender will respond positively to early parole and is not likely to commit another crime.[19]

Another release program that has been used in conjunction with house arrest and electronic monitoring, and allows inmates to be released into the community after a period of incarceration, is *home release*. Although used sparingly (such as in the state of Arizona), home release allows for nondangerous inmates to return to their residence to serve the remainder of their sentence. Inmates who are elderly, terminally ill, or who can support the case for their ability to remain crime-free while living at home, are good candidates for this kind of release.

HOW PAROLE WORKS

Although there is disagreement about the basis for the parole system, there is agreement about the goals of a parole decision. In its original development, the idea of parole was to support (or reward) the prisoner's rehabilitation. In 1933, the American Prison Association asserted that the prisoner's fitness for reentry into the community should depend on the answers to the following questions:

- Has the institution accomplished all that it can for the offender?
- Are the offender's attitude and adjustment such that further incarceration will be harmful?
- Does a suitable environment await the offender on the outside?[20]

These and other questions that parole boards ask are, by their very nature, subjective interpretations, and parole boards began to be criticized as "arbitrary and capricious" in their release decisions. For one thing, critics charged that it was impossible for anyone to know with any degree of certainty whether a prisoner had been rehabilitated. In practice, it seemed that different parole decision makers paid attention to different factors in arriving at their parole recommendations.

Criticism of the arbitrariness of parole has led to attempts to structure the release decision by specifying precisely the factors to be considered in a parole decision and the weight those factors would be given. Called "parole guidelines," these systems do not eliminate discretion, but they provide a blueprint for the decision makers to use in considering each parole applicant. Parole guidelines were first developed and adopted in the 1970s by the U.S. Parole Commission. It was hoped that they would help "achieve a balance between the evils of completely unstructured discretion and those of a totally fixed and mechanical approach."[21] The guidelines developed by the Parole Commission were based on research that showed parole decisions could be predicted based on specific variables. In particular, three variables were found to best explain a large number of parole decisions:

- Seriousness of the offense
- Institutional record of the inmate
- Risk for future recidivism

Based on these variables, the Parole Commission developed an instrument called the **salient factor score (SFS)**.[22] The SFS is an actuarial device that measures six offender characteristics and assigns a score to each. The scores are then combined with a set of guidelines that helps to determine the sentence that would best predict parole prognosis. In recent years, several states have used the SFS as a model to develop their own guidelines with the intention of formalizing the parole decision-making process.

Parole guidelines systems vary somewhat, but they always include specific factors from three areas that parole boards consider.

1. They have substantially observed the rules of the institution in which they have been confined.
2. Their release will not depreciate the seriousness of the offense or promote disrespect for the law.
3. Their release will not jeopardize the public welfare.

Consideration of these factors points to how the parole release decision has shifted away from the reliance upon an assessment of the prisoner's progress toward rehabilitation, and toward a greater emphasis on equity, justice, and public safety.

Parole guidelines can be justified on the basis that they require the board to focus its deliberations on criteria that are reasonable and lead toward decisions that treat similar cases similarly. Advocates of parole guidelines say that perhaps the most important functions of parole are, first, to even out the effects of judicial sentencing disparity and, second, to support the integrity of institutional programs. The first aim is achieved by setting a **presumptive parole date.** The presumptive parole date is given to the offender soon after entering prison. It is a date by which the inmate can expect to be released if there are no disciplinary or other problems during incarceration. It takes into account the offense and other conduct, and not just the judge's sentence. Harsh sentences can be adjusted downward by earlier parole; lenient sentences can be adjusted by delaying parole. The integrity of the institutional programs is supported by favoring release when offenders do well in these programs and delaying release when inmates' disciplinary misconduct record indicates they were a problem to the administration.

There are some critics of parole guidelines. The guidelines make assumptions about the future behavior of offenders seeking parole based on certain factors about the offense and the offender. In short, they serve to *predict* the likelihood of parole success. Prediction of any kind of human behavior is tricky business. It cannot be accomplished without uncertainty and error.

Two things can go wrong with predicting the behavior of offenders seeking parole. One is overprediction. In this case, an inmate is denied parole because he or she may be a risk to society. Overprediction occurs when the offender, if given the chance, would not have committed a violent act. The second is underprediction. When it is believed that an inmate is a good parole risk, and the inmate is released and then commits another serious crime, the parole decision was faulty based on underprediction. Each prediction issue poses its own set of problems for the criminal justice system. Overprediction creates injustice for the offender and unnecessary imprisonment costs for the system. Underprediction can create a new set of victims, cause disrespect for the parole system, and develop political problems for the parole board and connected politicians. This creates a no-win situation for those making parole decisions. In the end, the decisions must be made based on what is the least dangerous or most-likely-to-be-successful alternative. It is a difficult task for all concerned.

Parole Eligibility

Eligibility for a parole hearing varies greatly from state to state. In prison films and novels, inmates say they are going to "apply" for parole. In fact, one does not apply. Eligibility to appear before the parole board is determined by statute. Usually, the eligibility is a proportion of the sentence—sometimes the minimum term but more often the maximum. Typically, however, the inmate is credited for some form of good time—time off the sentence for "good behavior"—and sometimes this can result in an earlier eligibility.

The prisoner might not be released at the first parole hearing before a parole board. Parole boards, also called parole commissions, decide when an offender is ready for conditional release and may function as the body that evokes revocation of parole. Nationally, parole rates vary dramatically from state to state. Much of the variability depends on how early the initial hearing is allowed by law. In states that allow prisoners to come before the parole board quite early in their sentence, rates of granting parole at these hearings can be quite low, as little as 15 percent. In states that make inmates wait longer to see the parole board, granting rates are more liberal, though they seldom exceed two-thirds of all initial hearings.

When a person is denied parole, the parole board sets a new date for another hearing. Often these are prescribed by law—annually, for example. But to prevent overloading the parole hearing docket and to be fair to prisoners for whom parole hearings are perhaps the most stressful experience of the prison term, some parole boards set up a "parole contract." They specify a date for the next hearing based on a review of the case and what the offender needs to accomplish in prison to earn parole. If the inmate does his or her part—completing a program and staying free of serious rules violations—parole will be an expected result.

The Preparole Investigation

The preparole investigation has the same function as a PSI for the sentencing judge—it provides the decision maker with information on which to base the release decision. The parole plan is prepared by institutional staff (often, parole officers assigned to the prison) who interview the inmate and other people who will be affected if the inmate is released. There are two particularly important documents most parole boards want to know about: the release plan and the victim impact statement.

The most common reason a parole board denies parole is that the parole release plan is not acceptable. Release plans describe what the inmate will do if granted release—a complete release plan involves a promise by an employer of a job, an acceptable place to live, and entry into treatment programs for any existing problems such as drug abuse or uncontrollable anger. The plan, which will be verified by the officer writing the report, will let the board know what the inmate's life will look like if they grant release, and it will help the board decide if the circumstances of the release will put the public at risk or give the inmate a chance to make it. Parole plans are fragile, however, and a promised job may disappear between the writing and the release date. So boards press the inmate about the elements of the plan, because they want to be sure it is reliable.

Even if a plan makes sense, the board may not grant parole. The most common reason for denying parole when there is a reasonable plan is that the inmate has not served enough time, given the seriousness of the crime. Often, the vehicle for this conclusion is provided by the **victim impact statement,** which details the impact of the crime on the victim and describes how a release will affect the victim emotionally and materially. Victim impact statements are a relatively new practice of parole boards, often required by law.

Parole staff contact the victim, document how the crime has affected the victim's life, and ask the victim's opinion about the possibility of release. The advent of victim impact statements has increased the accountability of parole decisions to the victim. Critics say this has occurred at the cost of unequal treatment—offenders whose victims were able to get their lives together after the crime are more likely to be released than offenders whose victims continue to suffer, even though they have been convicted of the same crime.

The Parole Hearing

During the past decade, parole hearings have undergone major changes. Most states have taken measures to ensure due process at the release hearing; about half the states now allow counsel to be present and witnesses to be called, and they keep verbatim transcripts.

Because hearings can be complicated and time-consuming, most parole boards reserve them for the most difficult cases to decide. The majority of cases involving routine matters are determined by hearing officers. A parole hearing officer operates as an agent of the board, reviewing cases and applying established board policy to decide whether a case warrants a full-blown hearing. In cases with a good parole plan and a neutral victim impact statement, where the inmate has already served a substantial proportion of the sentence and has good institutional adjustment, the granting of a parole may be fairly straightforward. When parole boards set specific-enough guidelines that enable this kind of decision, the hearing officer can decide in the name of the board for many of the cases in the system. When a hearing officer uncovers some troubling aspect to a case, such as a victim deeply opposed to release, the case can be scheduled for the full board to review in a formal hearing.

NEW YORK STATE PAROLE PREPARATION PLAN

Community Prep

Bureau/Area: _____

Alias: _____

True Name: _____

SSN: _____

Co-defendants: _____

_____

_____

Case Name: _____

NYSID: _____

Sentence: _____ AND DT: _____

Offense: _____

Institution: _____

DOB: _____ ME DT: _____

Board DT: _____ CR DT: _____

Approved Residence Program

Address _____
      Number   Street   City   Apt#   Telephone#

Rent/Mortgage $ _____ Pvt House _____ Apt. _____ Furnished Room _____ Other _____

Persons in Household:

Name (Primary Tenant)	Name	Relationship
Name	Name	Relationship
Person Contacted	Date	Time	Method

Approved Employment/Program

Name: _____ Type of Business: _____

Address: _____
      Number   Street   City   Telephone#

Position

Offered: _____ Salary: _____

_____ Duty Description: _____

Person Contacted	Date	Time	Method

Comments/Supervision Plan: _____

_____

_____

_____

Parole Officer	Signature	Date:
Senior Parole Officer	Signature	Date:
Area Supervisor	Signature	Date:

Controversy exists regarding what should occur in a parole hearing—who should be allowed to testify and what topics should be covered. Some parole boards prohibit the inmate from appearing, and instead allow only testimony of family members, friends, and the parole officer who will handle the case.

Other boards schedule their hearings at the prison itself, so the inmate can appear and make a case for release. The answer to the question of who should attend the parole hearing determines where the hearing will be held. Hearings that take place in the prison are usually convenient only for the inmate involved, and testimony of others interested in the case is taken in writing. Parole boards that want to hear from citizens and victims schedule public hearings in large cities within their jurisdiction, to make that kind of participation possible.

A recent addition to the parole hearing has been the role of the victim. Most parole boards now provide for representation by the victim of the crime, either in person or through a victim advocate. In the latter case, there is often an official state agency that interviews the victim and makes the results known to the board at the hearing.

In the end, one is left to wonder how much the hearing shapes the parole decision. Most parole boards have established release policies that they follow—some in the form of guidelines—and these, far more than the events of the hearing, determine the parole decision of the board. Because hearings are of reduced importance to the parole process, many states allow parole boards to make decisions without a formal hearing—and in these states, the parole board is more of a release policy body than a group that decides individual cases.

Preparing for Release

Knowledge of the date of an offender's release exerts a powerful influence on all aspects of incarceration. With release to community supervision, the final phase of the offender's ties to corrections begins. At least it is hoped that this will be the final phase, and that the inmate will not reenter the criminal justice system.

In most states, the goal is to prepare the offender for reentry into society through the gradual allocation of freedoms and responsibilities during the period of incarceration. Prisoners are placed at a high level of custody when they enter the institution and are periodically evaluated. As they progress, the level of custody is lowered so they can reestablish family ties and begin to heal the damage done by their crime and subsequent incarceration. Furloughs and increased visitation privileges are often arranged. Toward the latter part of the sentence, the offender may be placed on work release, transferred to a halfway house, or given other opportunities to live in the community.

In some correctional systems, release planning begins as much as a year in advance of the targeted release date; in others, it begins only after the parole board has set that date. In California, for example, a three-week, full-time training program is given to inmates who are within fifteen to forty-five days of release. Inmates are given training in the attitudes needed to get and keep a job, communication skills, family roles, money management, and community and parole resources. The prisoners and their needs are evaluated. Each prisoner is then given a list of five objectives to be achieved within thirty days of being paroled, and the names and addresses of five public or private agencies that can be called upon for assistance. During the training program, each prisoner participates in at least one mock job interview and acquires a California driver's license.

A similar program in North Carolina includes transfer of the participating inmates to a housing unit reserved for prereleasees. One week of the four-week period is devoted to family readjustment training. With the emphasis on reintegration and community supervision, offenders are no longer confined to one cell in one institution for the duration of their terms; they move about a great deal from one security level to another and from one institution to another as they prepare for the day when they will be released.

The Parole Board

Membership on a parole board is always a political appointment. But the politics of being named to a parole board vary greatly from one state to another. Most states set some standards for being named to the board, often requiring some professional expertise such as training in psychology or experience in the criminal justice system. These states want parole decisions to reflect some learned expertise about crime and justice—and human behavior. In other states, the ideal parole board member is thought to be an average private citizen, someone who can represent the values of the community and whose common sense will help ensure reasonable decisions.

Sometimes, being a parole board member is considered a full-time responsibility, and salaries are competitive with other professions. But parole board members are sometimes "volunteers" who work part-time and receive only expenses and a small honorarium. In either case, it is not obvious why someone would want to be a member of a parole board. The hours can be long, with frequent travel to remote locations for hearings—and stacks and stacks of parole files to read before each hearing. The job can also be thankless—an inmate's family will blame the board when parole is denied but will feel no gratitude when parole is granted, thinking it was deserved. And whenever a parolee fails and commits a new offense, someone will inevitably look over the board members' shoulders to see reasons why parole never should have been granted in the first place.

As a result, parole board members tend to be an unusual breed. They are often motivated by a strong sense of public duty and a deeply felt commitment to the safety of the communities they represent and the life chances of the inmates they review. The rewards of the job come when a prisoner "makes it" and the board members feel a sense of personal accomplishment in having taken a chance.

THE ORGANIZATION OF RELEASING AUTHORITIES

By the statutes they enact, legislatures either grant authority to parole boards to release prisoners or stipulate the conditions for mandatory release from a determinate sentence. Historically such power rested in the hands of the governor, who as recently as 1939 remained the only paroling authority in sixteen states. The governor no longer has that power, though in most states he or she appoints most of the members of the parole board.

The structuring of a releasing authority raises certain fundamental questions. For example, should it be autonomous or consolidated with the corrections authority? How should field services be administered? Should the parole board sit full-time or part-time? And how should board members be appointed? Over the past decade, states have tended to create strong links between the paroling authority and the department of corrections, emphasizing professionalization of parole board personnel.

Autonomous Versus Consolidated

A board may be either independent from the correctional institutions (**autonomous model**) or an independent decision-making body within the department of corrections (consolidation model). The states divide about equally in this regard. Proponents of the autonomous model argue that independence from correctional personnel promotes more objective parole decisions. The board should not be influenced, they say, by such considerations as the institution's wish to reduce its population or to punish prison rules violators.

Critics counter that the autonomous parole board can become unresponsive to the needs and programs of corrections and is too far removed from the daily activities of the institutions to appreciate the subtleties of individual cases. This problem is exacerbated by the fact that autonomous boards depend on others for the information on which they base their decisions. When the decision-making process is fragmented, the institutional staff and the parole board may work at cross-purposes. Parole boards often are critical of the information they are given to help them make crucial decisions. Frequently, the facts are fitted into a stereotyped format and the individual aspects of a given case are lost, resulting in potentially arbitrary, unfair, and undesirable decisions. Many prisoners would rather have the releasing decision made by institutional personnel who know them personally than by an outside board. Other critics say that persons with little knowledge of or experience with the correctional process often are appointed to autonomous boards.

In response to these criticisms, parole activities have tended recently to be located within the department of corrections or in a multifunctional department of human services. Under this model, the board retains its independent decision-making authority but is organizationally close enough to the department to be sensitive to institutional and correctional needs. When parole decisions are made by people closely connected with corrections, they are more likely to be based on individual offenders' suitability for release.

But we must remember that no matter what the formal organizational structure, the paroling authority does not exist in a vacuum, immune to political and organizational influences. The autonomous parole board may develop conflicts with correctional authorities so that the information needed for decision making may be "unavailable" or biased. The **consolidated board** runs the risk of being viewed by prisoners and the general public as merely a rubber stamp for the corrections department. Boards of both types have to operate under the pressure of public opinion. Parole board members understand that they have to be very cautious in releasing prisoners because if parolees commit further offenses, the news media always zero in on the board for having let them out.

Field Services

Questions similar to those concerning the organization of the releasing authority surround the organization of field services. Should community supervision be administered by the paroling authority, or should it be part of the department of corrections? When the parole board administers field services, proponents of this model say, consistent policies can be developed with regard to parole, release, and supervision. During the past decade, however, there has been a movement to make the transition from prison to the community more gradual, and most departments have instituted such preparole programs as work release and educational release. Therefore, it is argued, the institutional staff and the parole board must be coordinated—an objective more easily attained if they are in the same department.

Full-Time Versus Part-Time

A third set of questions concerns full-time versus part-time boards. Because of the increased complexity of corrections, many people, in both discretionary and mandatory release states, hold that administration of parole should be a full-time enterprise. The type of person who is able to serve full-time on a parole board differs considerably from one who serves part-time. Membership on a board that meets full-time requires one to devote all of one's energies to the job. Full-time boards attract criminal justice professionals, who usually are well paid. However, members of part-time boards, paid on a per diem basis, are thought to better represent the community because they have other careers and are independent of the criminal justice system.

Appointment

Members of the paroling authority may be appointed by the governor or by the head of the corrections department. Some people believe that gubernatorial selection insulates the members from the department, provides "better" members, and permits greater responsiveness to public concerns. Others believe that the parole mechanism should be apolitical and that it should be operated by people who really know something about corrections.

Selection of members of parole boards is often based on the assumption that people with training in the behavioral sciences are able to discern which candidates have been rehabilitated and are ready to return to society. However, in many states political considerations dictate that members should include representatives of specific racial groups or geographic areas. For example, the Mississippi board recently consisted of a contractor, a businessman, a farmer, and a clerk; the Florida board included a newspaperman, an attorney, and a man with experience in both business and probation; the Washington State board had persons with training and experience in sociology, government and law, the ministry, and juvenile rehabilitation. As you might imagine, boards as disparate as these turn out widely varied release decisions.

Parole Board and Officer Liability

When a parole board releases a convicted criminal, it is because they believe justice has been served, the offender has been rehabilitated, or more simply, because the prison is overcrowded. Unfortunately, parole release is not an exact science and there are some mistakes made in prediction. When a parolee is released and commits another crime, public outcry is significant and there is often a call for action. Sometimes, the public calls to hold government officials and the parole board legally accountable for the new crime. Most courts have ruled that parole boards enjoy judicial immunity when making decisions to release or not to release an inmate. This means that parole boards perform judicial functions like judges and are generally exempt from lawsuits.[23] The case of *Martinez* v. *California* was very important in deciding legal issues related to parole board members. In this case, a parolee named Thomas was convicted of attempted rape and murder of fifteen-year-old Mary Martinez.

Thomas had been released from prison for five months. During the trial, it was determined that during his parole process a number of sentencing and correctional officials recommended that Thomas not be released by the parole board. But after serving five years of a one- to two-hundred-year sentence, he was paroled. The parents of Mary Martinez sued, arguing that parole officials subjected their daughter to deprivation of life without due process of law.

Because state law provided legal immunity for parole board members, the state of California argued that they were not liable in this case. The case led to an important ruling by the U.S. Supreme Court. The Court ruled in a unanimous decision that statutes made by government officials to provide civil (tort) immunity for parole officials were constitutional.[24]

Parole and probation officers do not enjoy the same level of legal immunity as parole boards. During the commission of their legally prescribed duties, parole and probation officers are generally allowed what is called qualified or quasi-immunity. Qualified immunity provides legal protection from lawsuits unless the parole or probation officer violates any clearly established constitutional right of any person of which a reasonable person would have known.

Another important legal issue relative to parole and probation officers is whether they are liable to individuals for actions of their clients. For example, when an ex-offender on parole commits another crime that harms another, should the parole officer be held liable for failure to protect the third party? Courts on the state and federal levels have not reached any consensus on this issue. In some cases, it has been ruled that the immunity is reduced when it can be shown that parole officials displayed negligent and reckless behavior.[25]

However, generally it has been held by the courts that according to what is called the *public duty doctrine,* officers are protected from liability for crimes committed by probationers and parolees. The public duty doctrine in tort law states that

> no liability may be imposed for a public official's negligent conduct unless it is shown that "the duty breached was owed the injured person as an individual and was not merely the breech of an obligation owed to the public in general. . . ."[26]

This means that parole and probation officers, like other public officials, have the duty to protect the public in general, but not any specific person in particular. The public duty doctrine, then, generally shields officers from liability for crimes committed by probationers or parolees.[27]

TRUTH IN SENTENCING

By the late 1970s, most state correctional systems were severely overcrowded, with a chronic shortfall in prison space. The urgency of overcrowded prison facilities created pressures for early release of prisoners to make room for those arriving at the front door. But the newly arriving inmates were facing even longer sentences than those released, and so trying to manage prison populations through accelerated release programs was like trying to bail a sinking rowboat with a teaspoon. Correctional administrators found themselves caught in a policy vise: Increasing sentencing lengths produced inflexible increases in prison populations of newly sentenced offenders, while severe levels of overcrowding demanded that some prisoners be released to reduce population pressures. Even the most aggressive building programs proved incapable of lessening the populations of prisons straining at the seams.

Early release of prisoners was a short-term solution that came at a long-term cost. The specter of revolving-door justice, always a public relations problem for the justice system, grew even more dramatic. By 1994, the proportion of the sentence served nationwide had dropped to 44 percent.[28] Many elected officials became alarmed by this trend. They saw themselves as working hard to toughen criminal penalties, only to be thwarted by correctional prison release policies. The dropping proportion of the sentence served led to an impression that the system was becoming more lenient.

This impression may not have been completely accurate. Some studies showed that time served was stable or higher, despite the changes in release policy. Nonetheless, elected officials felt their legislative changes needed to be bolstered by eliminating the early release of offenders, and a nationwide "truth in sentencing" movement gained popularity in the mid-1990s, presented as a way to solve the problem of prison releases.

Many different versions of **truth in sentencing** were proposed, but they all have in common the basic idea that offenders will serve all or most of the sentence imposed by the court. The most common target for time served is the one established by the federal sentencing guidelines—85 percent of the sentence. A truth-in-sentencing approach, then, restricts the release decision dramatically, requiring offenders to serve nearly all of the sentence before release eligibility, regardless of good time, clemency, or any other consideration.

Truth in sentencing sounds as though it strengthens the role of the sentencing judge in the sentencing process, but this is not fully accurate. In most states that have "truth in sentencing," judges have very little discretion over the sentences they impose. In fact, the reform strengthens the role of the legislature, which writes the penal code with far less discretion than that allowed by any justice system official. North Carolina's statutes, which many believe are the best example of the approach, illustrate how the "truth" model places most of the control over the sentencing decision in the hands of legislators.

POSTRELEASE SUPERVISION

Returning to the streets after years behind bars is a shock; the most normal, unremarkable events seem to take on overwhelming significance. Max, an inmate who was in prison for six years, described his experience to a team of researchers:

> The first few days out were a flash. That's all I can say, man. There's cars and dogs and trees and people, you know, and you walk down the street and there's mailboxes and there's houses and screen doors. And it all comes back to you.
>
> Things that you'd wanted to do, places that you'd wanted to go, things you wanted to see. It's all there, and you try to get them all at once. That's one reason

why a lot of people are going back, man, because they're trying to do everything at once. I'm still flashing. Sometimes I think I'm back in the joint, man. I say, "Wow, where am I? I'm free. I'm here. I'm doing fine."[29]

The popular notion is that once offenders have completed their prison sentences, they have paid their "debt" and are ready to start life anew. The reality is that the vast majority of offenders released from prison remain subject to correctional authority for some time. For many offenders, this authority is represented by the parole officer; for others, it is the staff of a halfway house or work release center. The "freedom" of release is constrained: The whereabouts of offenders are monitored, and their associations and daily activities are checked.

The freedom of offenders who are released outright—either because they have completed their maximum term (the maximum sentence minus good time) or because there is no parole supervision—is also less complete than it may seem. The former inmate still has many serious handicaps to face: long absence from family and friends, legal and practical limitations on employment possibilities, the suspicion and uneasiness of acquaintances, even the strangeness of everyday living. The outside can seem alien and unpredictable after even a short time in the artificial environment behind bars.

No matter what the intentions of others, the former inmate always faces the cold fact that no truly "clean start" is possible. The change in status is from convict to former convict; the new status is nearly as stigmatizing as the old, and in many ways it is more frustrating. In the former convict's mind, he or she is "free." Yes, the crime was a big mistake, but the prison time has paid for it and now there is a chance to turn over a new leaf. Yet most people look at the parolee askance and treat him or her as though there is still something to prove. The experience can be more than disappointing: It can be embittering.

The period after a person is released from prison is about "making it," the struggle of the former inmate not to return to prison. Many fail; about half of all released offenders return to prison within six years. From another perspective, though, the number of offenders who succeed is impressive. Most are under the scrutiny of agents of the state; all are faced with significant legal, familial, and social strains. How many of us would be vulnerable to misconduct under such pressures? Released offenders are playing with what seems to be a stacked deck; that so many make it is testimony to their perseverance.

THE STRANGENESS OF REENTRY

Although release can be euphoric, it can also be a letdown, particularly for parolees who return after two, three, or more years away. In their minds, families and friends have been snapshots in time, but now everyone is changed (and the parolee has changed): moved, taken a new job, or, perhaps most disturbing, become almost a stranger. The first attempts to restore old ties can be threatening experiences and can deeply disappoint. How many relationships—with spouses, children, and even dear friends—can survive the strain of long separation unscarred? As if reestablishing old relationships were not difficult enough, it has to be done in an unfamiliar environment. In the prison, every aspect of life is programmed: waking, eating, relaxing, talking, sleeping. One effect of institutionalization is that routine decision-making skills atrophy. The decisions about one's daily life are made by others. There are plenty of sad-funny stories of parolees looking at a menu for the first time in years and panicking at the prospect of choosing a meal and ordering it. Compare this simple task to the more important tasks of finding a job and finding housing. The rule of prison is dependence. The rule on the outside is independence, and this takes a shifting of mental gears.

THE PROBLEM OF UNMET PERSONAL NEEDS

Parolees are aware that they have critical needs, problems they must face if they are to make it on the streets. As one parolee has said:

> The first few days I was out were about the roughest days of this entire period . . . no money, no transportation, no job, and no place to live. Now these things have a way of working themselves out in time, but you have to contact the right people, and sometimes it's hard to find the right people. I was lucky enough to make a contact with a fellow at the Service Center and he gave me enough money to tide me over out of a fund that they had. I'd say the first week was rough.[30]

When asked to name their needs, parolees have very practical concerns: education, money, and job tend to top the list. Yet they are not always realistic in their thinking about how to meet their needs. Many parolees are unable to identify the specific things to avoid doing in order to stay out of trouble.

BARRIERS TO SUCCESS

Soon after release, offenders learn that they have achieved an in-between status: They are back in society but not totally free. Ex-offenders soon find out that life is not so easy on the outside. In many cases, the difficulty in living outside the institution is caused by a number of barriers to success. The most common are barriers to employment, being stigmatized, and statutory limitation stemming from a common-law tradition that persons who are incarcerated are "civilly dead" and have lost all civil rights.

Employment

Barriers to employment are both formal and informal. Employers hesitate to hire parolees because they view a conviction as evidence of untrustworthiness. To the cumulative effect of statutory and informal discrimination must be added many offenders' unrealistic expectations for employment.

> Contrary to my prison expectations, finding employment was not an easy task. In fact, it took me over six weeks to find my first job, even though, at least for the first month, I made a conscientious and continuing effort to find employment. I quickly found that I had no marketable skills. My three years' experience working for a railroad before I was imprisoned provided me with no work skills transferable to other forms of employment. Nor did my prison assignments in the tag shop (making license plates and street signs), in the soap shop (making soap), or as a cellhouse worker prove to be of any assistance. The only job openings available to me were nonskilled factory work and employment in service-oriented businesses. Finally, after six weeks, I found employment mixing chemicals in vats for placement later in spray cans. After two weeks, the personnel manager told me that he had to discharge me because I had lied about my criminal history (I had). Even though my foreman spoke up for me, supposedly company policy had to be followed.[31]

The legal barriers to employment are perhaps the most frustrating because they constitute an insurmountable wall between the offender and job opportunities. Three major studies of such statutes have been done. One found 307 occupations that required licenses in one or more states, licenses that were denied to former offenders merely on the basis of a prior conviction. Some statutes were very specific, barring people convicted of certain offenses from particular jobs (convicted child molesters from employment in day-care centers, for instance). Other statutes were much broader, barring from employment in some fields any person who gave evidence of moral turpitude or a lack of good moral character—characteristics that many people attribute to persons convicted of crimes.[32]

Such statutes bar employment in some job areas that are most important to former offenders. All of the states, for instance, restrict former offenders from employment as barbers (even though many prisons provide training programs in barbering), beauticians, and nurses. Jobs that pay well tend to be reserved for people with no criminal records. It is not unusual for newly released offenders to find themselves legally barred from jobs they held before they were incarcerated.

A study of restrictions on government positions found that most states bar or restrict the employment of former offenders through either civil service regulations or special statutes. Even a prior arrest for a felony without a conviction can lead to rejection. Cities and counties have more restrictions than do state governments. A prior arrest, even as a juvenile, is an absolute bar to employment in a criminal justice occupation in one-fifth of the jurisdictions studied, though criminal justice agencies that have hired former convicts rate their job performance equal to, or better than, that of the average employee.[33]

Stigmatization

The stigma of conviction stays with the former felon throughout his or her lifetime. No matter what former offenders do with the remaining days of life, they will always be referred to as an "ex-con." When people find out a person has served time in a correctional institution, it is common for them to think, "Is he dangerous?" or "What could she have possibly done to wind up in prison?" During the job application process, the ex-offender may find it difficult to obtain employment because of the stigma attached to being a former inmate. This could impact his or her parole status when meaningful employment is a parole requirement. When trying to develop new relationships after release, ex-offenders may be placed in an ethical quandary. Should they reveal that they have served time in prison? If they are truthful they may be spurned, untrusted, or treated with indignation. To feel fulfilled and good about themselves, all humans need some form of acceptance from peers or loved ones.

Many ex-offenders, because of stigmatization, feel a lack of acceptance from the general public. In some cases, the only place they can turn for support is to their criminal peer group. This can lead to further legal problems and additional imprisonment.

In the juvenile system (see Chapter 12), the terminology used to describe the offender and the process implemented is slightly different from that used for the adult offender. This is because it is believed that juveniles have the opportunity for change, and to label them as criminal so early in life may limit future success. We have not accepted this philosophy with adult offenders.

Conversely, we have adopted the "scarlet letter" approach of forever branding offenders with their misdeeds. It appears that the concepts of forgiveness and *tabula rasa*—to start anew and with a clean slate—have been neglected in our society.

Civil Disabilities

In many jurisdictions, former offenders lose a number of civil rights that belong to a typical person simply because of citizenship. The right to vote and to hold public office are two civil rights that are generally limited upon conviction. Only three states (Maine, Massachusetts, and Vermont) allow convicted felons to vote. In forty-eight states and the District of Columbia a person in prison cannot vote. In thirty-two states offenders cannot vote if on parole, and in twenty-nine they cannot vote if on probation. In ten states felons are disenfranchised for life.[34] Twenty-one states return the right to hold public office to felony offenders following discharge from probation, parole, or prison; nineteen states permanently restrict that right except for pardoned felons. Other civil rights, such as serving on juries and holding positions of public trust (such as most government jobs), are denied felons in many states. A summary of civil rights restrictions for felony offenders is found in Table 10.1.

TABLE 10.1   RESTRICTIONS OF FELONY OFFENDERS' CIVIL RIGHTS

Jurisdiction	Voting Permanently Lost vs. Restorable	Parental Rights Yes vs. No	Divorce Permanently Yes vs. No	Public Employment Permanently Lost vs. Restorable	Juror Permanently Lost vs. Restorable	Holding Office Permanently Lost vs. Restorable	Firearm "Violent" Felony vs. "Any" Felony	Criminal Registration Yes vs. No	Civil Death Yes vs. No
Alabama	X	X	X	X	X	X		X	
Alaska			X		X		X		
Arizona		X					X	X	
Arkansas	X		X		X	X	X		
California		X			X	X[1]	X	X	
Colorado		X							
Connecticut			X				X		
Delaware				X	X	X	X		
D.C.			X		X	X[1]	X		
Florida	X				X	X	X	X	
Georgia			X		X	X	X		
Hawaii					X		X		
Idaho			X		X				X
Illinois			X				X		
Indiana		X	X		X		X		
Iowa	X			X	X	X	X		
Kansas		X					X		
Kentucky	X				X	X	X		
Louisiana			X						
Maine						X[1]	X		
Maryland			X		X				
Massachusetts		X				X[1]	X		
Michigan		X					X		
Minnesota			X						
Mississippi	X	X	X	X		X	X	X	X
Missouri					X				
Montana					X		X		
Nebraska					X		X		
Nevada	X	X			X	X	X	X	

(continues)

TABLE 10.1 (CONTINUED)

	Voting Permanently Lost vs. Restorable	Parental Rights Yes vs. No	Divorce Permanently Yes vs. No	Public Employment Permanently Lost vs. Restorable	Juror Permanently Lost vs. Restorable	Holding Office Permanently Lost vs. Restorable	Firearm "Violent" Felony vs. "Any" Felony	Criminal Registration Yes vs. No	Civil Death Yes vs. No
Jurisdiction									
New Hampshire			X				X		
New Jersey			X		X	X			
New Mexico	X				X	X	X		
New York			X		X	X	X		X
North Carolina									
North Dakota			X						
Ohio			X		X	X			
Oklahoma			X		X		X		
Oregon		X					X		
Pennsylvania			X		X		X		
Rhode Island	X	X	X	X	X	X			X
South Carolina				X	X	X			
South Dakota		X	X						
Tennessee	X	X	X		X	X		X	
Texas			X		X	X	X		
Utah			X		X			X	
Vermont			X						
Virginia	X		X		X	X			
Washington									
West Virginia			X				X		
Wisconsin		X				X	X		
Wyoming		X			X				

X = right is restricted or jeopardized

[1] = right is restricted for specific offenses

Source: Velmer Burton, Francis Cullen, and Lawrence Travis, "The Collateral Consequences of a Felony Conviction," *Federal Probation* 51 (1987): 55.

In addition to the main restrictions mentioned above, offenders are also often subjected to other disabilities within society. These have been called *collateral consequences of conviction.* Collateral consequences of conviction are restrictions or disabilities that are not directly imposed by a sentencing authority but stem from the fact of conviction. They have been dictated onto offenders by licensing bodies and private individuals because it is perceived that the ex-offender lacks "good moral character." Examples of these collateral consequences are ownership, control, or possession of firearms; suspension or revocation of a driver's license; dishonorable discharge from the armed forces; and as mentioned, restrictions on practicing certain occupations.[35]

Thus, offenders must have certain misgivings about reentry: adjustment to a strange environment; stigmatization; the unavoidable need for job training, employment, money, and support; and limitations on opportunity. If offenders believe that the cards are stacked against them, they have reason for thinking so.

RESTORING THE RIGHTS OF EX-OFFENDERS

Restrictions and liabilities of rights of the ex-offender are removed in a variety of ways. In all but eight states, at least some civil rights are automatically restored upon completion of sentence. Twenty states provide automatic restoration of all civil rights upon completion of sentence, while the remaining twenty-two restore one or more of the rights lost by conviction.[36]

Another method is when a state provides the offender with a special document called a Certificate of Relief from Disabilities. This certificate states that the offender has completed his or her sentence. The purpose of this document is to relieve the ex-offender of the collateral consequences of conviction, to facilitate acquiring job opportunities, and to assist in getting any license that may be necessary for employment.

Probably the only real solution for restoring the rights of ex-offenders is **expungement** of their criminal records. Formally, expungement means the removal (or erasure) of a conviction from state records. In practice, while offenders whose records have been expunged may legally say that they have never been convicted, records of the convictions are kept and can be made available upon inquiry. The problem with expungement is that it does not automatically restore rights. Although at least twenty-eight states have some method of restoring civil rights through expungement, the states expunge only certain kinds of offenders. For example, limits are placed on offenders who are second-time offenders, not on probation, violent offenders, and those with firearm offenses. Moreover, the practicalities of expungement legislation are generally both cumbersome and inadequate. Although expungement is often thought to overcome the deleterious personal effect of a criminal record, it really provides little true relief from the consequences of imprisonment.

AFTERCARE

Because of the many needs of offenders after parole release, many jurisdictions have begun to experiment with innovative postrelease and supervision programs that go beyond traditional parole supervision. These are called "aftercare" programs. **Aftercare** is a term that is more common in the addictions treatment area than in corrections. It is linked more closely with rehabilitation than with current correctional ideologies. Aftercare programs make an effort to deal with the offender's problems and have at their base community-based treatment, continuity of care, offender assessment and classification, and case management. These programs may be as simple as helping ex-offenders construct a resume or prepare for a job interview. Others may be more extensive and deal with job assessment, developing job skills, and dealing with addiction or family problems. Some efforts have been made by isolated programs to attach comprehensive aftercare to the postincarceration experience. But that idea has not flourished because of the "get tough" attitude of citizens and politicians, the lack of resources for such programs, and the legal restrictions placed on forced treatment.[37]

The fact that aftercare is an afterthought is troubling because prior research and common sense tell us that those who spend time in prison often have a difficult time adjusting to life in free society. More confusing is the fact that correctional research has recently shown that surveillance programs combined with rehabilitation efforts are more likely to be effective in reducing addiction and subsequent criminal activity.[38]

The box "Project Return" describes one example of an aftercare program that attempts to deal with some of the already stated problems of parolees.

PROJECT RETURN

Project Return was developed by Dr. Robert E. Roberts, with the assistance of the Tulane University School of Public Health and Tropical Medicine.

The program has been created to work with former offenders and assist their efforts to reintegrate into free society.

A. Goals and Objectives

1. To provide an integrated delivery network aimed at reducing the high rate of recidivism of former offenders, which includes: substance abuse treatment and family counseling, GED education and academic enhancement, job training, and placement assistance.
2. To provide more appropriate intervention for youthful offenders.
3. To implement a cost-effective working model that reduces the amount of tax revenues presently spent to reincarcerate 75 percent of all those released from prison in Louisiana.
4. To contribute to the restoration of public safety in New Orleans by preventing crime otherwise committed by repeat offenders.

Target groups of Project Return are former offenders released or paroled from prison. Approximately 85 percent of this population in Louisiana is

African American; 75 percent is male; 92 percent are high school dropouts with average reading skill at fifth or sixth grade levels; and 100 percent are convicted felons.

B. Program Components

Each week participants spend approximately 12 hours in GED/academic coursework, 8.5 hours in Addictions Education, 6.5 hours in hands-on computer training, 4.5 hours in Employability Skills training, 4 hours in Communication Skills, and 2 hours in Community Building. A stipend of $2.50 per hour is paid to each participant during the sixty to ninety days he or she is in the program prior to job placement.

C. Performance Measures

The most important performance measure of Project Return is the rate of recidivism, which currently is less than 5 percent for our participants. In addition, data is maintained on participants obtaining and sustaining a steady employment pattern by means of follow-up questionnaires.

D. Accomplishments to Date

Among the 20 classes Project Return has graduated since 1994, roughly $2/3$ of the 1,000 convicted felons who participated are currently employed.

This exceeds the U.S. Department of Labor projected outcome for this population by 227 percent. The Bureau of Justice Assistance's Division of Correctional Options has called Project Return the most successful prison aftercare program in the nation. It offers another way of thinking about this part of our population, hopefully a more practical, realistic, respectful, and forwardthinking approach that stresses the rebuilding of lives and the reclaiming of human resources.

Concentrating its efforts on those at highest risk of committing more crimes and returning to prison, this unique program has proven that it can break the cycles of criminal behavior that have consistently drained our economy and destroyed the safety of our neighborhoods. Furthermore, it can transform that behavior into a productive work force of tax paying citizens contributing to the local economy rather than depending on welfare, selling of drugs, or armed robbery as a means of support.

Of the 1,000 former offenders who have participated in the program, less than 100 have been reincarcerated, representing a recidivism rate of less than 10 percent. Compared to Louisiana's average of 37.5 percent within the first six months following release and 75 percent over the next five years, this represents a return on investment of $80 to $100 million to potential victims of crime according to a U.S. Department of Justice Statistics report on the costs of crime.

This report found that the average offender who returns to prison will do so in four years and will create $100,000 of damage per year to his/her victims.

The cost per participant in Project Return is $3,800 plus $1,200 in training wages. Every 90 days a new class of 50 convicted felons is accepted into the program while 200 to 300 on the waiting list are turned away.

Source: www.projectreturn.com/body.html

REVOCATION OF PAROLE

When people fail on parole, their parolee status is revoked and they are returned to prison to continue serving their sentences. Like probation, parole can be revoked for two reasons: (1) commission of a new crime or (2) violation of the conditions of supervision (a "technical violation"). Technical violations are controversial because they involve conduct that is not criminal, such as failure to report an address change to the parole officer. Critics of parole argue that it is improper to reimprison a parolee for such minor infractions. In practice, revocations seldom result from a single rules violation—prisons are far too crowded to make this kind of strictness a common practice. To be returned to prison on a technical violation, a parolee usually has to demonstrate a persistent pattern of noncompliance or else give the parole officer reason to believe he or she has returned to crime. Observers believe that most revocations occur only when the parolee is arrested on a serious charge or cannot be located by the officer.

Perspectives on the parolee's status in the community have changed over the years. Early reformers saw parole decisions as grace dispensed out of the goodwill of the correctional authority. According to this notion, parole could be revoked at any time and for any reason. Subsequently, reformers began to view parole as a privilege, earned through good behavior in prison and retained through adherence to the conditions of parole. More recently, some commentators have begun to describe parole as a right of prisoners who have served enough time in prison, and they urge that technical violations be eliminated as a basis for return to prison. The "rights" view does not now prevail officially in any parole system, although the state of Washington places strict limits on the penalties that may be imposed on technical violators.

If parole is a privilege, as many people argue, its revocation is not subject to due process or rules of evidence. In some states, liberal policies of granting parole have been justified on the grounds that revocation can be swiftly imposed whenever the offender violates the parole rules. Under the New York statute, for example, if a parole officer has reason to believe that a parolee has lapsed or is about to lapse into criminal conduct or into the company of criminals, or has violated any important condition of parole, the officer may rearrest the parolee. The officer's power to recommend revocation because the parolee is "slipping" seems to hang over the parolee like the proverbial sword of Damocles, suspended by a hair.

When the parole officer alleges that a technical violation of parole has occurred, the U.S. Supreme Court requires that a two-stage revocation proceeding be held. Although the Court has exempted the revocation proceeding from the normal requirements of a criminal trial, it has held in the case *Morrissey* v. *Brewer* (1972) that many due process rights must be accorded the parolee. In the first stage, the parole board determines whether there is probable cause that a violation has occurred. The parolee then has the right to be notified of the charges, to be informed of evidence, to be heard, to present witnesses, and to confront the parole board's witnesses (providing no witness would be endangered by such a confrontation). In the second stage, the parole board determines whether the violation is sufficiently severe to warrant returning the parolee to prison.[39]

The number of parole revocations is difficult to determine. A combined revocation and recommitment rate of approximately 25 percent within three years of release has been reported for years; these data, however, do not distinguish between persons returned to prison for technical violations and those returned for new criminal offenses. Recent studies using standard definitions of revocation rates have put this figure higher in some jurisdictions, but they also have disclosed that the total failure rate varies dramatically, from 25 percent to over 50 percent. In addition, recent studies show that state prison dischargees appear to be improving in their rates of successful completion of their parole terms.

The degree to which these rates reflect technical rules violations varies among states as well. Overall, about 35 percent of all new prison admissions were parole violators in 1999. Only 20 percent of those returning to prison were for a new conviction.[40]

Although parole failures tend to occur early in the release period, they also continue throughout supervision. A study completed several years ago showed that federal parolees born in the same year (a cohort) continued to be arrested up to thirty years after release.[41] In short, failure is an ominous probability for parolees.

Information on the typical length of reconfinement for a technical parole violation indicates that those whose original charges are the most serious can expect to serve the most time for their violation. The guidelines of the Federal Parole Commission recommend up to eight months for revoked parolees who do not have a history of violations and a longer period (eight to sixteen months) for persistent violators, those whose violations occur less than eight months after release, and those found to have a negative employment/school record during supervision. Most states do not have such guidelines. Potentially, the offender whose parole is revoked may be required to serve the remainder of the unexpired sentence.

CALIFORNIA: LEADING THE NATION IN THE REVOCATION OF EX-PRISONERS

When it comes to supervising parolees, something is going on in California that is vastly different from other states. The numbers are stunning. Less than one-fourth of California's prison releasees succeed on parole, a rate lower than any other state but Hawaii. Overall, parolees in the United States succeed on parole 42 percent of the time, but California parolees perform so badly that when they are removed from the calculations, the national rate jumps to 53 percent. And over two-thirds of those who enter the California prison system are going to prison because they failed on community supervision. Why is it so difficult to make it on parole in California?

The most important difference between California and the rest of the United States is that those who supervise offenders in the community—especially parole officers—are known for their strict enforcement of the rules. Parolees in California are relentlessly tested for drug use, closely monitored in curfews and associations, and strictly required to work and pay their fines, restitution, and other justice fees. The toughness shows in the statistics: compared to other parolees around the country, California parolees are nearly 50 percent more likely to be revoked for a failed drug test, and nearly one-third more likely to be revoked for other rules violations. While 70 percent of parolees nationally are returned for new felony arrests, only 60 percent of California's returnees are cited for that failure.

Some Californians think this is good news. They say that proven risks to the community are being watched much more closely in California than anywhere else in the country, and the minute a problem arises they are dealt with quickly and strictly.

But critics are not so sure California's approach is wise. They point out that growing prison populations are expensive, especially in California, where a year in prison costs in excess of $21,000 per offender. Money tends to be shifted from public education and welfare to pay for the punishments of these offenders, and when so many of them are rules violators rather than repeat felons, critics wonder if this is a wise investment. The real cynics point out that the prison guards union, which has consistently pressed for tough sentencing laws and close enforcement policies with parolees, benefits from the growth in the prison population with increased influence on public policy makers and pressure for more officers with higher salaries.

Source: U.S. Department of Justice, Bureau of Justice Statistics, *Bulletin* (October 2001): 11.

STREET TIME

When it comes time to revoke parole, it must be decided how much time an offender will serve. In cases that involve a technical violation, some states employ what is called **street time.** Street time is when an inmate is returned to an institution for a technical violation and he or she receives credit for time spent under supervision before the violation. For example, if an inmate is placed on parole for two years, and one year into his parole he commits a technical violation, he would then be returned to the correctional institution for no longer than one year.

ADVANTAGES OF PAROLE

Lower Cost

The proper use of parole can reduce the period of incarceration. The cost to incarcerate a single offender varies greatly in the United States, but the conservative average is estimated at over $20,000 per year. This does not include the original cost of building prisons, which has been stated to be $100,000 to build one prison cell. In some jurisdictions, parolees can actually provide monies to local governments. For example, in New York parolees are required to pay $30 per month, in check or money order, to the state's official banking institution. Parole provides supervision in the community for only a small percentage of what it costs to incarcerate.

Controls the Prison Population

If you asked correctional officials if they wished to eliminate parole, they would undoubtedly reply a loud NO! Imagine trying to control over 1,000 inmates who have shown themselves to be "socially unacceptable." The possibility of parole provides inmates with motivation to behave while incarcerated. At least one recent study supports the contention that parole can act as a deterrent to institutional misbehavior. The study showed lower rates of postreview misconduct for offenders denied parole compared to offenders granted parole hearings.[41]

Mitigates Harshness of Sentencing Codes

When a serious crime is committed, citizens want justice served by long-term imprisonment. They are angry about the offense and may seek retribution. They may be afraid that the offender will soon be released only to commit another crime. The result in this case is that an offender will receive a very strict sentence by either the sentencing judge or by the various mandatory sentencing laws passed by state and federal legislatures in recent years. At the time of the commission of a heinous crime, this reaction is very understandable.

However, after the passage of time judges and correctional officials, removed from the emotions of the event, are sometimes able make a rational choice as to what is best for the society, the offender, and the criminal justice system. Parole can help serve this purpose.

Restitution

In some cases, offenders are required by the court to pay restitution to victims or institutions they have harmed. Parole can provide an opportunity for an offender to repay his or her financial debt to society.

Rehabilitation

Parole and other forms of conditional release are a better alternative than releasing an offender to total freedom. Because they are supervised and provided assistance with personal problems, former inmates have a better chance of being successful in the community if on parole.

DISADVANTAGES OF PAROLE

Increased Risk to the Community

Whenever a parole board releases an inmate, there is the chance that he or she will reoffend. When this occurs, the news media is sure to publicize the matter and the public is sure to be outraged. Correctional authorities are criticized for the decision, and the validity of parole is questioned. To many people, the committing of a new and especially a violent crime by a parolee cannot be tolerated, even if it may be an infrequent occurrence.

Justice Is Not Served

Critics of parole argue that when inmates are released prior to the date to which they were sentenced, they "cheat" the system. If an offender is sentenced to ten years in prison, critics feel the term should be completed.

Rehabilitation Is Not Working

Based on the "Nothing works" argument of Robert Martinson, many feel that rehabilitation is a farce. Also, because inmates know that if they show they are "rehabilitated" they will have a better chance to be released, it is common for them to learn to beat or manipulate the system in order to secure early parole release.

Abuse of Discretion

Those who sit on parole boards and act as parole officers make important decisions on a daily basis about the release of offenders into the community. These persons are human, and even with the best intentions, humans are prone to follow their own prejudices and predilections. The abuse of discretion is one of the major concerns of those who believe parole release decisions are made without any scientific foundation and leads to arbitrary and often discriminatory release patterns.[42]

SHOULD PAROLE BE ELIMINATED?

Many people think parole is an anachronism and needs to be eliminated. In fact, we are now in the second major antiparole movement of the last fifty years. In the 1970s, several states abolished their parole boards, and a similar jump in abolition occurred in the mid-1990s. This movement reflects a national disquiet about parole. Citizens are uneasy when offenders are released from prison, and this discomfort is magnified when a highly publicized case of parole results in serious crimes by the parolee. People think that streets would be safer if parole were abolished and prisoners had to stay in prison and finish their sentences.

This view has been criticized as naive, for three reasons. First, it is not feasible under current resources to have every offender serve all or most of the sentence. U.S. judges are often said to give the longest prison sentences in the Western world, and the prison population would explode if there were no mechanism to reduce these long sentences. One of the important features of parole is that it allows an administrative body to alter a judge's pronouncement at sentencing. In states that have abolished parole, prison population growth has been a severe problem that must be countered by other ways of reducing judges' sentences.

Second, most parolees are not a violent risk to the community. It is true that failure rates of offenders on parole are high, but only a small proportion of those failures involve a violent crime. The more common case is that a parolee fails because of inability to abide by the rules or an arrest for a less serious offense. The raw truth is that under any system of sentencing, the vast majority of offenders will be released into the community. Some will commit crimes. The question is less "how" does an inmate get released than "when." The evidence is equivocal on the impact of having parole on the timing of release—some parole states have shorter time-served than national averages, but others have longer.

A third argument has been advanced to support discretionary release, such as parole: There is a need for separate review of sentencing decisions and occasional repair when sentences imposed by the court are too severe. The criminal law does not provide for a systematic review of sentencing decisions, other than by a parole board or similar organization. Supporters of the parole concept point out that an independent review of judicial decisions can improve the fairness of sentences by adjusting sentences that are unfair when compared to other sentences.

Many feel that eliminating parole is another way to be "tough on crime." Interestingly, eliminating parole may be a bad idea relative to public safety. If parole is eliminated, then an inmate's release actually becomes automatic at the end of a set term. In this way, it has been argued, you actually decrease the ability to keep very dangerous offenders in prison. One example is the convicted kidnapper Richard Allen Davis, who was rejected for parole six times in California. When the state passed a law ending parole, he was released automatically because he had served a sufficient amount of time. A few months later he murdered twelve-year-old Polly Klaas.[43]

THE EFFECTIVENESS OF PAROLE

The effectiveness of corrections is usually measured by rates of recidivism, the percentage of former offenders who return to criminal behavior after release. One of the problems with statistics on recidivism is that the concept means different things to different people. The rates reported vary from 5 to 70 percent, depending on how one counts three things: (1) the event (arrest, conviction, parole revocation), (2) the duration of the period in which the measurement is made, and (3) the seriousness of the behavior counted. Typically, an analysis of recidivism is based on rearrest or reimprisonment for either another felony conviction or a parole violation for up to three years after release.

In 2000, approximately 43 percent of parolees successfully completed parole, while about 42 percent were returned to prison for parole violations or new offenses. Others were transferred to new jurisdictions, absconded, or died. Of first-time releasees in 1999, 63 percent completed parole successfully as compared to 56 percent in 1990.[44]

It is hard to know how much of this success results from parole work and how much reflects the sheer determination of the parolee. When Howard Sacks and Charles Logan compared a group of court-ordered releasees with a similar group under parole supervision, they found that those discharged without supervision recidivated—as measured by having a new conviction for any crime—at a faster rate, especially during their first year of freedom. By the third year, 77 percent of the parole group had recidivated, compared with 85 percent of those discharged directly to the street.[45]

The effectiveness of traditional parole work has been questioned based on studies of small parole caseloads. These studies find that the assumptions underlying attempts to reduce caseload size are incorrect. When parole case-loads are reduced to between thirty and thirty-five clients per officer, the officers do not spend more total time with clients (instead, they improve on the quality of paperwork), nor do the offenders become more likely to succeed.

Officers may well be overburdened with cases, but the evidence is scant that simply unburdening them is the answer. On the other hand, a growing body of evidence suggests that parole supervision can be effective if it is structured to achieve certain aims. For example, behavioral treatment programs combined with close surveillance and sporadic urine testing for drug addicts on parole can significantly reduce rates of new addiction, new crime, and drug-related death.[46] One of the most important new strategies for improving supervision effectiveness is to increase the structure placed on the discretion of parole officers and to focus that structure on approaches that are likely to be successful. In a recent Texas parole study, traditional supervision methods were compared to a structured strategy including a standardized intake interview, a carefully monitored classification and case-planning system, and a systematic program of officer performance appraisal. Parolees supervised under the new, more structured approach fared better in terms of criminal behavior and social adjustment (as measured by such factors as employment).[47]

The effectiveness of parole supervision has earned mixed reviews. Yet, because parolees who remain crime-free for two years often succeed thereafter, correctional administrators continue to seek to revise parole practices in ways that will help offenders make it.

PERSPECTIVES ON PAROLE

Systems

Parole and early release programs are "inventions" of the system, and so it is not surprising that these programs are supported because of the benefits they provide to the system. The main systems benefits used to explain the value of these release programs have shifted over the years. When these programs first developed, they were presented as ways to reward prisoners whose behavior in prison was positive. This was seen as a way to support the authority of those who administer prisons by giving prisoners an incentive to comply with the rules and not be problems for those in charge. It was also seen as a way that the ideals of rehabilitation could be supported through prison administration.

Today, those arguments remain, but they have been overshadowed by a different argument. Parole and early release are advocated as a way to keep prison populations under control. Prison administrators, faced with daunting prison crowding, see them as a "release value" that can open the back door when they cannot control the flow through the front door.

These systems functions often mean that the support for parole and early release programs is weak. They are not argued for as positive contributions, but as necessary arrangements. And whenever a prisoner who is given parole or early release gets arrested for a crime, the systems benefits come to be weighed against the interests of pubic safety.

People

The most important dynamic facing those who are involved in systems of parole and early release is that the stakes are high and the issues are difficult. These programs are faced with making decisions about people who are incarcerated, and these offenders tend to have the longest criminal involvement and the greatest sense of risk to the community. The difference in costs to the system are huge: A prisoner will cost upwards of $25,000 a year, but an ex-prisoner under community supervision will cost no more than $1,000 a year. This trade-off is sufficiently tempting that parole and early release programs remain in operation in every state of the nation, even though they have received substantial criticism over the years.

The criticisms stem from the trade-off between system costs and public safety. Parole and early release programs place in the community convicted felons who would otherwise have been incarcerated. Inevitably, some of those ex-prisoners commit crimes, and when they do, the decision to place them in the community seems to have been unwise. The entire system then can be brought under intense scrutiny by a single offender's actions.

Because of this, correctional workers in the parole process feel a pressure to be conservative in their decision making. They are reluctant to take risks with offenders who seem to present a problem for the system, and they are quick to react to any problems that early releasees have while under their authority in the community. This conservatism seems to have grown in recent years. The proportion of prison intake that comes not from new crimes but from failures under community supervision seems to be growing, almost doubling in the last decade. Some of this is due to the slowing down of new prison commitments for felonies, because crime has been dropping. But some of it is due to the increasing unwillingness of people in the parole and early release process to take risks: Behavior by ex-convicts that may have been overlooked ten years ago now places that offender under scrutiny and may result in recommitments to prison.

Evidence

How effective are parole and early release programs? This is a complicated question, because a great deal of the answer hangs on the question, "compared to what?"

There is no question that parole and other early release programs can be superior to incarceration. Of first-time prison releasees—those who are exiting a prison for the first time in their lives—the vast majority will not return to prison within three years after their release. But for those who do not make it, those who return to prison and face a second release, the prospects in subsequent releases are poor: As many as two-thirds or more will end up back in prison yet again. So getting the good risks out of prison and adjusting to the community is a wise correctional practice, and keeping the first-time releases from going back is also good practice.

The problem is that no proven way exists for identifying the best risks so they can be released and keeping released offenders who get into trouble from having to return. For at least ninety years, criminologists have been searching for better release criteria with little success.[48]

Inevitably, parole and early release systems are forced to compare their effects with those of prison, and prison seems to be a completely effective way of preventing crime, according to the critics of early release. Of course, this is the conundrum: The more we use prison, the worse the risk of those who are released from prison—and the more likely that we will be pressured to rely on prison instead of release. It is a spiral that increasingly emphasizes prison over community supervision, even when we know that community supervision is the more desirable option overall.

Bureaucracy

Parole and early release bureaucracies are dominated by the pressures of failure. When an offender under community supervision of parole or early release fails, the wisdom of the system can come under scrutiny. Therefore, early release bureaucracies tend to be conservative. Like all bureaucracies, these programs develop rules and procedures to regularize the practices of the early release approach. But these rules are dominated by the overall conservative posture of the early release function. In order to protect itself against the inevitable criticism that comes when an offender under early release fails—especially when a particularly heinous crime is committed—the system develops a strict way of handling any problems that ex-prisoners represent: loss of a job, relapse to drug use, conflict with a spouse, difficulty getting along with others. In hindsight, any of these problems will look like a "signal" of impending trouble, should an offender who has had adjustment problems end up committing a serous crime. So these kinds of misbehaviors are taken seriously, and specific rules are developed for how they are to be handled.

The existence of "procedures" can seem to handcuff staff as they try to work through the problems many offenders face when adjusting to the community after a period of confinement. But when it comes to flexibility with offenders, the system's need for certainty in procedures overrules.

SUMMARY

The idea of release on parole originated with Captain Alexander Maconochie and Sir Walter Crofton, who sought to reform the prison system by giving convicts an opportunity to demonstrate they had reformed, and thereby earn their release. Today, well over 90 percent of all offenders sentenced to prison are released, and parole is the most well established form of release. In recent years, however, a wave of sentencing reform has resulted in a greater variety of forms of release from prison. Most reform has had the effect of making the offender serve a higher percentage of the judge's sentence. In many states, this has been accomplished by abolishing the parole release system, but even in these states, there is typically a period of supervision after the offender is released into the community.

Offenders who are released into the community face significant barriers in their effort to avoid return to prison. From problems getting jobs to difficulties in adjusting to the new freedom, ex-offenders typically face a difficult period of adjustment when they first hit the streets. Offenders also face restrictions on their legal rights in a variety of ways.

Although it is difficult to determine the exact number of parole revocations, it is clear that revocation is a far too likely occurrence for many offenders. Revocation in many instances is unrelated to the commission of a new offense. Although there are many advantages to parole, the disadvantages have prompted many states and the federal government to eliminate parole. Some factors that impact the effectiveness of parole are whether someone is a first-time offender, whether the offender stays out of trouble in the two-year period subsequent to release, and whether quality aftercare is provided. It is unclear what direction parole will take in future years because it is always embroiled in economic, political, and social controversy.

DISCUSSION QUESTIONS

1. Imagine that you have just been released from prison after a five-year term. What are the first things you will do? What problems can you expect to face?
2. How effective is parole?
3. What are the arguments for and against the elimination of parole?
4. Should those on parole have their legal rights restored? Why or why not? If so, what specific rights should be restored?
5. What factors should a parole board consider when it evaluates a prisoner for release?
6. Suppose, as a parole board member, you are confronted by a man who has served six years of a ten- to twenty-year sentence for murder. He has a good institutional record, and you do not believe him to be a threat to community safety. Would you release him to parole supervision at this time? Why or why not?
7. Given the current public attitude toward criminals, what do you see as the likely future of parole release?

⊣ SUGGESTED READINGS ⊢

Glaser, Daniel. *The Effectiveness of a Prison and Parole System.* New York: Bobbs-Merrill, 1964. Represents a classic study of the links between incarceration and parole.

Maruna, Shadd. *Making Good: How Ex-Convicts Reform and Rebuild their Lives.* Washington, DC: American Psychological Association, 2001.

Rhine, Edward E., Smith, William R., and Jackson, Ronald W. *Paroling Authorities: Recent History and Current Practice.* Laurel, MD: American Correctional Association, 1991. Reports the results of a national survey conducted by the ACA Task Force on Parole.

Simon, Jonathan. *Poor Discipline: Parole and the Social Control of the Underclass 1890–1990.*

Chicago: University of Chicago Press, 1993. Explores the use of parole to control poor and disadvantaged members of society.

Sull, Errol Craig, *Makin' It: A Parole and Probation Survival Guide.* Lanham, MD: American Correctional Association, 1999. A list of "survival tips" for ex-offenders under community supervision that gives a glimpse of what it takes to "make it."

Zamble, Edward, and Quinsey, Vernon. *The Criminal Recidivism Process.* Cambridge, England: Cambridge University Press, 1997. Presents research on what makes offenders fail to adjust to the community.

⊣ WEB SITES ⊢

Web site for Bureau of Justice Statistics (BJS) on parole
    http://ojp.usdoj.gov/bjs/pandp.htm
Web site for U.S. Parole Commission, which still handles parole for those federal prisoners whose offense was committed prior to November 1, 1987
    www.usdoj.gov/uspc
Web site with information on various services offered to parolees
    www.cdc.state.ca.us/program/parole.htm

Web site where crime victims may access resources for opposing release of an inmate
    http://home.sprynet.com/~statnisle/todo.htm
Web site for the American Probation and Parole Association
    www.appa_net.org

⊣ NOTES ⊢

1. Jeremy Travis and Joan Petersilia, "Reentry Reconsidered: A New Look at an Old Question," *Crime and Delinquency* 47 (July 2001): 291–313.

2. U.S. Department of Justice, Bureau of Justice Statistics, "Nation's Correctional Population Reaches New High," Press Release, August 26, 2001.

3. U.S. Bureau of Statistics, *Trends In Parole: 1990–2000,* NCJ 184735 (Washington, DC, September 2001).

4. Camille Camp and George Camp, eds., *The 2000 Corrections Yearbook* (Middletown, CT: Criminal Justice Institute, 2000), p. 167.

5. Joan Petersilia, "Parole and Prisoner Reentry in the United States," in *Prisons,* ed. Michael Tonry and Joan Petersilia, vol. II (Chicago: University of Chicago Press, 1999), p. 505.

6. *Los Angeles Times,* quoted in "State Agencies Lost Track of Parolees," *Santa Barbara News Press,* August 27, 1999.

7. Petersilia, "Parole and Prisoner Reentry in the United States," p. 480.

8. Fox Butterfield, "Eliminating Parole Boards Isn't a Cure-All Experts Say," *New York Times,* January 10, 1999, p. 12.

9. Tony Fabelo, *Biennial Report to the 76th Texas Legislature* (Austin, TX: Criminal Justice Policy Council, 1999).

10. *Morrissey* v. *Brewer,* 408 U.S. 471, 92 S.Ct. 2593, 33 L. Ed. 2nd 484 (1972).

11. James Austin, "Sentencing Guidelines: A State Perspective," *NIJ Journal* (March 1998).

12. Jeremy Travis and Joan Petersilia, "Reentry Reconsidered," *Crime and Delinquency* 47 (July 2001): 295.

13. Katharine Bradley and R. B. Michael Oliver, "The Role of Parole," *Policy Brief* (July 2001) (Boston, MA: Community Resources for Justice).

14. George E. Rush, ed., *The Dictionary of Criminal Justice,* 4th ed. (Guilford, CT: Duskin, 1994).

15. Clifford Dorne and Kenneth Gewerth, "Mercy in a Climate of Retributive Justice: Interpretations from a National Survey of Executive Clemency Procedures," *New England Journal on Criminal and Civil Confinement* 25:2: 413–468.

16. Camp and Camp, *The Corrections Yearbook,* p. 129.

17. For a brief summary of this research, see "Educating Offenders" by Dennis J. Stevens, *Forum on Corrections Research* 10:1 (January 1998): 33–36.

18. Camp and Camp, *The Corrections Yearbook,* p. 126.

19. Diane Vaughn et al., "Shock Probation and Shock Parole: The Impact of Changing Correctional Ideology," in *Corrections: Problems and Prospects,* ed. D. Peterson and C. Thomas (Englewood Cliffs, NJ: Prentice Hall, 1980), pp. 216–237.

20. Cited in Edwin H. Sutherland, Donald R. Cressey, and David F. Luckenbill, *Principles of Criminology,* 11th ed. (Dix Hills, NJ: General Hall, 1992), p. 560.

21. D. M. Gottfredson, L. T. Wilkins, and P. Hoffman, *Guidelines for Parole and Sentencing* (Lexington, MA: Heath, 1978), p. 37.

22. U.S. Parole Commission, *Rules and Procedures Manual* (Washington, DC: U.S. Department of Justice, 1997), p. 58.

23. R. V. DelCarmen and J. A. Pilant, "The Scope of Judicial Immunity for Probation and Parole Officers," *Perspectives* (Summer 1994): 14–21. Published by the American Probation and Parole Association.

24. *Martinez* v. *California,* 444 U.S. 277, 1980.

25. *Grim* v. *Arizona Board of Pardons,* 564 P. and 1227 (1997); *Donahoo* v. *Alabama,* 479 So. 2nd 1188 (1985); *Grantham* v. *Mississippi Dept. of Corrections,* 522 So. 2nd 219 (1988).

26. *Taggart* v. *State,* 822 P. 2nd 243 (WA. 1992).

27. For more information about civil liabilities and other legal issues for probation and parole officers and supervisors, see a document published by the National Institute of Corrections at www.nicic.org/pubs/2001/017068.pdf

28. Bureau of Justice Statistics, *Prison Sentences and Time Served for Violence* (Rockville, MD: Bureau of Justice Statistics, 1995).

29. Rosemary J. Erickson, Waymon J. Crow, Louis Zurcher, and Archie V. Connet, *Paroled but Not Free* (New York: Human Sciences Press, 1973), p. 15.

30. Gordon Waldo and Ted G. Chiricos, "Work Release and Recidivism: An Empirical Evaluation of Social Policy," *Evaluation Quarterly* 1 (1986): 87–108.

31. Robert M. Grooms, "Recidivist," *Crime and Delinquency* 28 (October 1982): 542–543.

32. S. J. Burton, F. Cullen, and L. Travis, III, "The Collateral Consequences of a Felony Conviction: A National Study of State Statutes," *Federal Probation* 51:3 (July 1986): 52–60.

33. Herbert S. Miller, *The Closed Door* (Washington, DC: Georgetown University Law Center, 1972), pp. 95–99.

34. J. Fellner and M. Mauer, *Losing the Vote: The Impact of Felony Disenfranchisement Laws in the United States* (Washington, DC: The Sentencing Project, 1998).

35. P. F. Cromwell and G. G. Killinger, *Community-Based Corrections: Probation, Parole and Intermediate Sanctions,* 3rd ed. (Minneapolis, MN: West, 1994), p. 314.

36. V. S. Burton, Jr., L. F. Travis, III, and F. T. Cullen, "Reducing the Legal Consequences of a Felony Conviction: A National Survey of State Statutes," *International Journal of Comparative and Applied Criminal Justice* 12:1 (Spring 1988): 106.

37. Thomas C. Castellano, "Aftercare," *Corrections Today* 57:5 (August 1995): 80–88.

38. P. Gendreau, F. T. Cullen, and J. Bonta, "Intensive Rehabilitation Supervision: The Next Generation in Community Corrections?" *Federal Probation* 58:1: 72–78; and J. Petersilia and S. Turner, *Evaluating Intensive Supervision of Probation and Parole: Results of a Nationwide Experiment,* National Institute of Justice Research in Brief (Washington, DC: U.S. Department of Justice, 1994).

39. *Morrissey* v. *Brewer,* 408 U.S. 471, 92 S.Ct. 2593, 33 L. Ed. 2nd 484 (1972).

40. U.S. Bureau of Statistics, *Trends in Parole: 1990–2000.*

41. Jon Proctor and Michael Pease, "Parole as Institutional Control: A Test of Specific Deterrence and Offender Misconduct," *Prison Journal* 80:1 (March 2000): 39–56.

42. David J. Rothman, *Conscience and Convenience: The Asylum and Its Alternatives in Progressive America* (Boston: Little, Brown, 1980); and Jonathan Simon, *Poor Discipline: Parole and the Social Control of the Underclass 1890–1990.* (Chicago: University of Chicago Press, 1993).

43. Fox Butterfield, "Eliminating Parole Boards Isn't a Cure-All Experts Say," p. 12.

44. U.S. Bureau of Statistics, *Trends in Parole: 1990–2000.*

45. H. R. Sacks and C. H. Logan, "Does Parole Make a (Lasting) Difference?" in *Criminal Justice: Law and Politics,* 4th ed., ed. George F. Cole (Pacific Grove, CA: Brooks/Cole, 1984), pp. 362–378.

46. D. M. Anglin, "What Works with Substance Abusing Offenders" (paper presented to the IARCA Conference on What Works, Seattle, November 3, 1994).

47. Greg Markey and Michael Eisenberg, *Follow-Up Study of Texas Parole Case Management Project* (Austin: Texas Board of Pardons and Parolees, 1987).

48. Samuel Walker, *Popular Justice: A History of American Criminal Justice,* 2nd rev. ed. (New York: Oxford University Press, 1998).

Chapter 11

Special Offenders in the Community

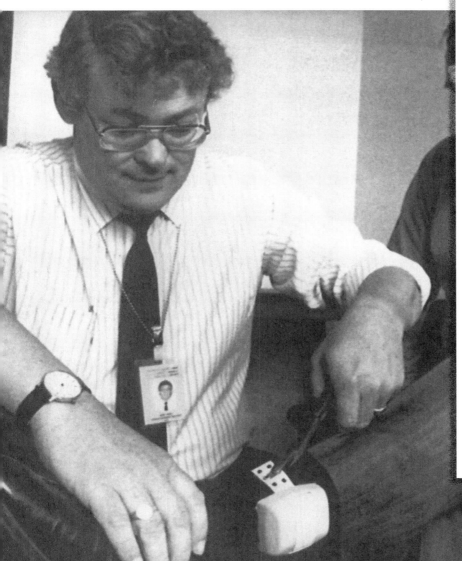

| KEY TERMS AND CONCEPTS |
---

alcohol abuser   mentally handicapped offender

career criminal   mentally ill offender

deinstitutionalization   relapse prevention

drug abuser   sex offender

drug court   specialized supervision

mental health court   therapeutic jurisprudence

Pete is a fifty-year-old parolee who has been out of prison for six years. During that time, he stayed free from drugs and crime, went to school, worked, and was active in community service. He voulunteered hundreds of hours of his time to educate the public about prison issues and the death penalty laws in his state. Last month, while depressed over the terminal illness of his brother, he again began to use cocaine. This month, he tested positive for cocaine during his parolee visit and is now in jail.

Nevin was forced to have oral sex with a man when he was about five years old. Now he is forty-nine and serving a five- to ten-year term for sexual assault of a ten-year-old boy. Nevin has confronted correctional authorities with a problem. He has filed a lawsuit to force the state to provide treatment for him after his release from prison. He has no money to pay for treatment, and he says flatly that he will never be able to resist the attraction he feels toward young boys.

Ron, a thirty-three-year-old man who functions at the level of a ten-year-old, was sentenced to a five-year prison term for bank robbery. He was easily identified by the police because he signed his name on the note he gave to the teller demanding money.

Offenders with problems such as those described above present tremendous challenges to the criminal justice system. In many cases, these offenders have needs that cannot be addressed within the current resources available in the community. The public response to the release of these offenders into probation or parole supervision is often controversial and sometimes results in open display of social disapproval. Community-based correctional agencies are always at the center of the storm. They are responsible for taking care of the offender and guiding him or her to a better life and at the same time are responsible for the safety of the public and must take action when it is jeopardized. For correctional agencies, the supervison of offenders with special needs is a juggling act. They must find the time and resources to supervise these high-maintenance offenders, while not neglecting the remainder of their caseloads, which may include even more serious offenders. How is this accomplished within a correc-

Photo: An electronic monitor is attached to a remand prisoner as part of an experiment in England. © Eric Shaw Topham-PA/ The Image Works

tional climate that often calls for "get tough" approaches and for the demise of rehabilitation? This is certainly not an easy task. The initial step toward the efficient supervision of those with special needs is the identification of who needs what kind of supervision. Finding the available resources and placing the offender follows. Then comes what may be the hardest part—supervision. In this chapter, we will address the different kinds of "special" offenders and review some ways to effectively supervise these offenders in the community.

TYPES OF OFFENDERS AND THEIR PROBLEMS

In some respects, every offender assigned to correctional supervision is unique; no two are exactly alike. Thus, in referring to "types" of offenders, individuals may be grouped together because they share an important characteristic (such as type of offense) even when they differ in some other vital characteristic (such as prior record, social class, or intelligence).

Any attempt to describe groups of offenders reflects a decision to generalize about people while potentially sacrificing individualism. For example, we tend to talk about "sex offenders" or "lifestyle criminals" as though they all behaved in the past (and will behave in the future) in the same way. This approach simplifies policymaking and correctional programming, but it bears little resemblance to reality. Therein lies the peril of grouping offenders: We forget that the grouping is done only to enable correctional officials to take action and may inevitably distort portraits of individual offenders.

To be honest, then, our discussion of criminal categories will contain disputable statements about groups of offenders with whom corrections must work. Keep this in mind as you read about types of offenders. Whether drug or sex offender, some individuals will fit into a group nicely; others will be more difficult to place; and all individuals within a group will vary in some respects. The groupings are made for our convenience, to help us understand the types of people corrections manages and the ways in which their characteristics influence the work of corrections.

THE SUBSTANCE ABUSER

Substance abuse and addiction has a fundamental influence on the nature of the correctional population. As noted by the National Center for Addiction and Substance Abuse, crime and alcohol and drug abuse in the United States are joined at the hip. Four out of five jail and prison inmates "had been high when they committed their crimes, had stolen to support their habit or had a history of drug and alcohol abuse that led them to commit crime."[1]

Criminal law typically distinguishes between the use of illegal drugs and the illegal use of alcohol. In the case of drugs, any unauthorized possession of a controlled substance is prohibited. Laws against mere possession of some drugs are so strict that in the federal system as well as in many states, prison terms are mandatory for these offenders. In contrast, possession of alcohol is prohibited only for minors. The criminal justice system becomes involved in alcohol offenders' lives primarily because of their conduct under the influence of alcohol. The difference between these two types of offenders is important for correctional policy, so we discuss them separately.

THE DRUG ABUSER

Our culture is a drug-using culture, from aspirin and caffeine to marijuana and cocaine. Not surprisingly, then, substance abuse figures prominently in criminal behavior. A national survey of state prison inmates found that almost 30 percent of those serving time for violent offenses admitted they were under the influence of an illegal drug when they committed the crime.[2] A similar survey of local jails found that nearly one in four were there for drug crimes.[3] In over one-third of all violent criminal victimizations, the victim perceives the offender as under the influence of drugs or alcohol.[4] As Figure 11.1 shows, from 31 to 81 percent of offenders arrested in twenty-one U.S. cities tested positive for an illegal drug at the time of their arrest.[5]

The street addict's life is structured by the need to get money to support the habit, and that need often leads to property crime. Studies of the relationship between drugs and crime have found that although much of the money for supporting a drug habit may be legitimately obtained, a high proportion of drug users admit engaging in income-generating crimes. Even if an addict supports only a small fraction of the habit's cost through crime, this can translate into a considerable amount of crime.

Habits costing $50–$150 a day are not uncommon. Because stolen goods are fenced at much less than their market value, an addict must steal goods worth several times the cost of the drug just to support the habit. Figure 11.2 shows some of the crimes committed to support a drug habit. Robbery is more directly lucrative than theft but also more chancy: There is always a risk of violence, and the victim may have little cash.

Treatment programs for people who compulsively or habitually use drugs do not have high success rates, and some are controversial. As the social movement against heroin grew in the 1950s and 1960s, support for clinical treatment of addiction also grew, and special drug treatment facilities were opened to house addicts as a special population of incarcerated offenders. Civil commitment procedures were often used to send convicted offenders to such facilities, where their incarceration term frequently exceeded what they would otherwise have received. Evaluations of these programs showed dismal results. For example, the first long-term follow-up of 100 releasees from one program

FIGURE 11.1 DRUG USE BY BOOKED ARRESTEES IN TWENTY-ONE U.S. CITIES

A large proportion of felony arrestees are under the influence of drugs at the time of their arrest.

Source: U.S. Department of Justice, National Institute of Justice, *ADAM: 1999 Annual Report* (Washington, DC: Government Printing Office, 2000).

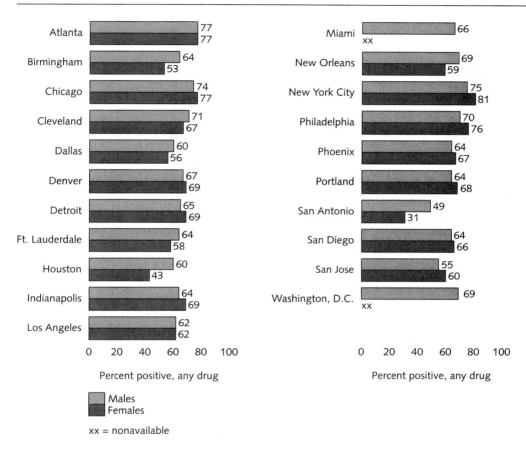

City	Males	Females
Atlanta	77	77
Birmingham	64	53
Chicago	74	77
Cleveland	71	67
Dallas	60	56
Denver	67	69
Detroit	65	69
Ft. Lauderdale	64	58
Houston	60	43
Indianapolis	64	69
Los Angeles	62	62
Miami	66	xx
New Orleans	69	59
New York City	75	81
Philadelphia	70	76
Phoenix	64	67
Portland	64	68
San Antonio	49	31
San Diego	64	66
San Jose	55	60
Washington, D.C.	69	xx

Percent positive, any drug

■ Males
■ Females

xx = nonavailable

found only 10 instances of 5 or more consecutive years of abstinence following hospitalization.[6]

Since the 1980s, federal policies have sought to combat drug abuse by providing tougher criminal sanctions. Punishments for drug possession and sales were made considerably harsher, especially in the federal courts, where sentences of ten years or longer became routine. At the same time, there has been a renewed emphasis on treatment for drug addiction for criminal offenders based on research showing that treatment for drug-abusing offenders can reduce substance use, criminal behavior, and recidivism whether the offender enters treatment voluntarily or under coercion[7] and that drug treatment programs can be at least as effective as other forms of correctional rehabilitation.[8] An even more important and convincing study completed in 1996 by the Rand Corporation stated that

FIGURE 11.2 PERCENTAGE OF CONVICTED JAIL INMATES WHO COMMITTED THEIR OFFENSES TO SUPPORT A DRUG HABIT

Drugs and crime are closely connected for addicts.

Source: U.S. Department of Justice, Bureau of Justice Statistics, *Profile of Jail Inmates, 1996* (April 1998) and *Drug Use, Testing and Treatment in Jails* (May 2000).

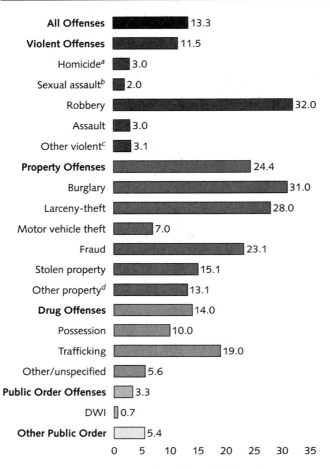

^{a} Includes murder, nonnegligent manslaughter, and negligent manslaughter
^{b} Includes rape
^{c} Includes kidnapping
^{d} Includes arson

in cases involving substance abuse (specifically cocaine) and addiction, the use of rehabilitation and treatment outside of prison is approximately seven times more effective than extended (mandatory minimum) sentences, and two to three times more effective than "traditional" shorter prison sentences.[9]

DEALING WITH DRUG OFFENDERS
IN THE COMMUNITY

The **drug abuser** presents both treatment and management problems for corrections. Although the mere act of drug abuse is not considered a serious offense, the collateral acts of predatory crime and violence are considered very serious. Thus correctional personnel must address the effects of drug dependency while the client is in detention, on probation, in prison, or on parole. The drug abuser also represents a potential control problem for community corrections because of a high likelihood of rearrest. Most are compulsive about their substance abuse, and they will be driven to deceive in order to avoid detection of continuing use. For many drug offenders, recovery is in reality periods of abstinence, sometimes lasting months, that are interrupted by "slips" in which drug use recurs. These periods of active drug use can be very short or last for months. Thus, even when drug-using offenders are doing well, there is always a potential for relapse. The correctional staff must be constantly vigilant about supporting the offender when things are going well, but they must react immediately when there is evidence of a return to drug use.

The stakes can be quite high. Research shows that drug offenders commit far more crimes when they are using drugs than when they are straight. So keeping drug offenders sober is not merely a matter of helping them maintain an acceptable lifestyle: Community safety is often at stake. Most drug-using offenders represent little criminal risk to anybody when they are not using, but that can change dramatically—all because of a relapse.

The community supervision of drug-using offenders can be characterized by four words: treatment, testing, consequences, and progress.

Few drug-involved offenders can become clean on their own; nearly all need some form of drug *treatment*. The type of treatment depends on the degree and seriousness of the drug dependency. Users who are caught early in their drug-using careers can often do well after a series of drug education sessions followed by supervision. However, those who have a well-established dependence will need detoxification and a period of residential drug treatment. Thirty days is a minimum amount of residency for effective drug treatment, but experts recommend periods far longer for deeply addicted offenders: 90 to 180 days is often thought necessary.[10] Unless a person gets physically completely clean and mentally prepared for the daily struggle after residential care ends, the prospects for abstinence are very poor.

Hand in hand with treatment goes drug *testing*. Many drug offenders will deny their drug dependence, and because they will also hide any dabbling, the correctional supervisor must have a way to be certain the offender is remaining clean. The answer is drug testing. Most drug-testing systems begin with very frequent (weekly or more) drug tests. After the offender has been clean for a period of time, say three months, the frequency of testing is reduced.

Eventually, an offender who has remained clean can expect only sporadic, though random, drug tests to be employed. But as long as the person is under correctional supervision, there will always be drug tests—for a severely drug-involved offender relapse can occur even after years of sobriety.

When the person turns in a dirty drug test, there must be *consequences*. Usually, graduated sanctions will be used. The initial dirty urine will result in curfews; later failed drug tests will lead to detention. The offender must know that any dabbling in drugs will be detected, and detection of drugs will result in hardship.

Some people are inclined to impose very heavy sanctions after the first drug failure—they want to say "zero tolerance." This makes for good rhetoric, but with drug offenders it is a mistake, for two reasons. First, no matter how hard an offender is trying to stay clean, it is only reasonable that failures will occur in a population of drug offenders. Second, if the policy is really one of zero tolerance, by far most drug offenders will fail, many of whom would eventually make it under a more workable policy. What drug specialists learn to look for is *progress:* Is the offender staying involved in treatment? Are the slips short and minor in nature? Is the length of sobriety between slips increasing? These are the signs that show a drug-involved offender is improving, and although these offenders will always struggle with their urges, progress is a good sign that they can eventually get sober for the long term.

The development of the Arrestee Drug Abuse Monitoring program (ADAM) has assisted law enforcement, correctional officials, and social service providers in learning more about the drug tendencies of offenders. The "Arrestee Drug Abuse Monitoring Program" box explains more about this important information resource. The remainder of this section on dealing with drug offenders will include descriptions of programs that serve drug offenders in the community. They serve as time-tested examples of what can be done to reduce the reliance on incarceration and provide support for the continuing trend to increase and improve drug treatment options for offenders in the community.

The TASC Program

One of the common programs for drug-abusing offenders is the Treatment Alternatives to Street Crime program (TASC). Many local and state drug treatment programs have implemented at least some elements of the TASC model. Created in 1972, the main idea behind TASC is that there are many drug-using offenders who could benefit from being diverted from incarceration and who would not, under appropriate levels of supervision, present a serious risk to the community. TASC can be implemented prior to adjudication, as an alternative to incarceration, or as a condition of parole release.

TASC provides case management for drug-abusing defendants and offenders, serving as a bridge between criminal justice agencies (courts and probation) and treatment providers. Currently, there are more than 180 TASC projects in

ARRESTEE DRUG ABUSE MONITORING PROGRAM (ADAM)

The National Institute of Justice's Arrestee Drug Abuse Monitoring Program (ADAM) was initiated in 1998 to track trends in the prevalence and types of drug use among booked arrestees in urban areas. The multi-site information network provided by ADAM plays an integral role in understanding the links between drug use and crime.

ADAM collects data at thirty-five sites under a centralized system that includes rigorously standardized procedures, minimum requirements for interviewers, and ongoing accountability at all data collection sites. At each ADAM site, trained interviewers collect voluntary and anonymous interviews and urine specimens from adult male, juvenile male, and juvenile female booked arrestees. Arrestees are approached within forty-eight hours of arrest and asked to participate. The questions asked of the arrestees have recently been expanded to include issues related to firearms, methamphetamine use, gang activity, HIV-related behavior, and domestic violence.

Source: www.adam-nij.net

twenty-seven states and two territories. They provide screening, assessment, treatment planning, monitoring, urinalysis, and court liaison functions.

The concept of TASC emerged from research showing that treatment is more effective in settings in which legal sanctions and close supervision provide incentives for clients to conform with treatment program protocols and objectives. Longer duration of treatment is consistently associated with better treatment outcome, and clients who are under legal coercion generally stay in treatment longer than those who are not.

Case management, through TASC, incorporates support, staff training, data collection, client identification based on eligibility criteria, assessment and referral, urinalysis, and monitoring. TASC clients remain in treatment six to seven weeks longer than other criminal justice clients, whether referred to residential or outpatient programs.[11]

La Bodega de la Familia

In 1996, the Vera Institute of Justice in New York City launched La Bodega de la Familia. La Bodega ("the family grocery") is located within Manhattan's Lower East Side and serves a densely populated twenty-four-square-block area called Loisaida. It is designed to respond to the substance abuse problem that impacts forty to fifty families who have been referred by police, probation or parole, local residents, or community organizations. La Bodega uses the family case management approach (FCM). In this approach, the entire family, not just the drug abuser, is involved in the rehabilitation process. Prevention and treatment are conducted with the hope that the needs of the abuser and

PETER YOUNG HOUSING, INDUSTRIES AND TREATMENT

Alcohol and drug addiction rehabilitation, training and housing, the "Glidepath to Recovery" system

"Rehabilitate, don't incarcerate!" is the longtime slogan of Father Peter Young, a Catholic priest who has spent over forty-three years working with men and women struggling to stay out of prison and free themselves from addiction. His conviction is simple: Despite millions spent on building and maintenance prisons, jails don't work; recovery and rehabilitation do.

His programs make proficient use of "wounded healers," those who have themselves successfully gone through recovery and are therefore best able to help those who are addicted.

Working out of the Albany, N.Y., area, Father Young has helped thousands of addicted people reclaim their lives and futures by means of his "glidepath" philosophy.

The "glidepath" has three components: recovery, housing, and jobs. Joined seamlessly together, these offer addicted men and women a fighting chance to become healthy, employed, taxpaying citizens with careers, families, friendships, and futures.

What is "glidepath"? Too often, those suffering from addictions have problems that go beyond physical dependencies. They often do not have jobs or shelter. Without basic living needs, treatment often fails.

A pilot who lands his plane on an aircraft carrier follows a glidepath that includes critical direction from the support team. PYHIT is that glidepath for the addicted. It provides clients with comfortable housing, a place that they can take pride in. Training them with valuable job skills in one of PYHIT's own industries like the Schuyler Inn and LeMoyne Manor. And the alcoholism and substance abuse services as well as medical attention and support they need to fully treat their dependencies through Office of Alcoholism and Substance Abuse certified programs.

Peter Young Housing, Industries and Treatment (PYHIT) is one of the most respected programs serving those with addictions. This success is based on the "glidepath" theory that Father Young has applied in his ministries for decades.

Source: Peter Young Shelter Services, Inc., Box 1338, Albany, NY 12201. Used with permission.

the family will be addressed. The program provides twenty-four-hour support services for families in the program in situations such as domestic violence, drug abuse relapse, and contact with police agencies.[12]

Drug Courts

In addition to the supervision of drug offenders in the community after they have been placed on probation or parole, the past eleven years have seen the birth and astronomical growth of a special and far-reaching program created to deal with drug offenders prior to adjudication. This program is the **drug court.**

The first drug court was implemented in 1989 in Miami, Florida, when Judge Herbert M. Klien became frustrated with the impact of drug offenses on the county court system. He was determined to "solve the problem of larger numbers of people on drugs," and the drug court movement was born. The drug court idea gained formal acceptance and financial support when in 1994 Title V of the Violent Crime Control Law Enforcement Act (P.L. 103-322) was passed by Congress. The law provided grant money to local courts, state courts, units of government, and Indian tribal governments to develop community drug courts.

The purpose of the drug courts was to provide nonviolent, substance-abusing adults and juveniles with sanctions and services necessary to change their deviant behaviors. Drug courts have been formally defined by the National Association of Drug Court Professionals as "special courts designed to handle cases involving drug-addicted offenders through an extensive supervision and treatment program." The drug court movement has paved the way for the **therapeutic jurisprudence** approach toward dealing with criminal offenders. This approach looks to deal with a wide range of social problems through treatment rather than full immersion (i.e., prosecution, adjudication, and incarceration) into the criminal justice system. Special courts dealing with domestic violence, driving while intoxicated, and mental health offenders have developed from this model.

The specifics of how drug courts actually work vary from program to program, yet in general they follow a simple formula. A nonviolent drug offender is brought before a judge during the preliminary hearing or sentencing stage. Offenders are given a choice whether to participate in the drug court program or continue with typical processing. In many cases, such processing would result in incarceration. The offender is then given a set of rules to follow by the judge that may include abstaining from drugs, attending drug treatment sessions, taking drug tests, or appearing before a probation officer on a regular basis. The offender's performance is directly communicated to the judge who then rewards for good behavior, or admonishes or provides an alternative sanction for noncompliance. The drug court provides offenders with a clear choice whether to take control of their own recovery or subject themselves to further contact with the criminal justice system.[13]

The growth of drug courts has been extraordinary. By December 2000, nearly 600 drug courts were operating in all 50 states, the District of Columbia, Puerto

Rico, Guam, and 2 federal districts. Another 450 are in the planning stages.[14] There are three reasons for the tremendous growth of drug courts. First, in the late 1980s, a growing body of research surfaced establishing treatment as a viable way to reduce crime.[15] This research also showed that compelled treatment was as effective as voluntary treatment.[16] Prior to this time, it was believed that rehabilitation of criminal offenders, especially those who were unwilling to seek help, was ineffective and that only strict punishment could deter criminal activity. Second, although the early evaluations of drug courts were mostly anecdotal, many believed in their efficacy and that they achieved their aims.[17] When the National Association of Drug Court Professionals (NADCP) was founded in 1994, there were less than fifteen drug court members. By 1999, the NADCP held a convention that included 3,000 participants.[18]

Finally, and for many the bottom line, it is believed that drug courts save money. It has been stated by the National Association of Drug Court Professionals that incarceration of drug offenders costs between $20,000 and $50,000 per person per year, with the capital costs of building a prison cell at around $80,000. In contrast, the typical drug court system costs less than $2,500 per year.[19]

In recent years, there has been an attempt to seriously evaluate the effectiveness of drug courts. A study sponsored by the National Institute of Justice of the nation's first drug court in Miami, Florida, showed a 33 percent reduction in rearrests for drug court graduates compared with non–drug court offenders. In evaluations of other drug courts by American University in Washington, D.C., it was determined that recidivism rates of drug court program graduates range from 0 to 20 percent.[20]

Yet, drug courts are not without their critics. Some feel that drug courts may be a good idea but are concerned that without planning and the necessary support resources, their effectiveness will be minimal. Identification and eligibility criteria must be formed, social service providers must be cultivated and financially supported, and supervision systems need to be firmly in place. Even if fully supported, drug courts can be exploited by offenders who see addiction as an excuse or "a way out" of being incarcerated. This could lead to even more crime or at least the overuse of the drug court system. Also, some feel that drug courts are too "soft" on criminals and that placing more emphasis on treatment rather than punishment is a waste of time and money. In spite of detractors, it appears that drug courts are firmly entrenched as part of the criminal justice landscape for years to come.

THE ALCOHOL ABUSER

Unlike marijuana, heroin, and other controlled substances, alcohol is widely available and relatively inexpensive, and its consumption is an integral part of life in the United States. Only when alcohol leads to problems such as unemployment, family disorganization, and crime does society become concerned.

The alcohol abuser's problem translates into crime much less directly than that of the drug user. Because alcohol is legal for adults, no criminal subculture surrounds its use. Whereas many addicts must engage in a criminal act just to get the drug of their choice, the alcoholic need only go to the corner store. However, alcoholics may produce far more disastrous consequences than heroin addicts do. According to estimates, alcohol use contributes to almost 100,000 deaths annually, five times the total number of homicides reported to the police. Alcohol is more closely associated with crimes of violence than any illegal drug. Moreover, many automobile injuries and personal offenses are at least partly caused by intoxication. Alcohol use impairs coordination and judgment, reduces inhibitions, and confuses understanding; criminal acts can easily follow. Thus a drunk's drive home may become vehicular homicide, a domestic dispute may become aggravated assault, a political debate or quarrel over money may become disorderly conduct, and a night of drinking may lead to burglary or auto theft.

Although research on alcoholic offenders has focused on the incarcerated, these offenders appear in other correctional environments as well. One survey found that offenders convicted of driving while intoxicated (DWI) made up 14 percent of probationers, 7 percent of jail inmates, and 2 percent of state prisoners.[21]

Like drug abusers, **alcohol abusers** present problems for probation officers, community treatment providers, and parole officers. Because some alcoholics become assaultive when they drink, dealing with them is neither pleasant nor safe.

Other problems are also related to the treatment of alcohol abusers. To some extent, the problems stem from Americans' generally ambivalent attitude toward alcohol use—it is seen as recreational behavior rather than deviance. Consequently, treatment programs seem to work best when they focus on getting people to recognize the nature of their own patterns of alcohol use rather than on alcohol use per se. This is one reason the program of Alcoholics Anonymous (AA) has consistently proved the most successful of alcohol treatment methods: It provides intensive peer support to help people face their own personal inability to manage alcohol use.

Despite its general success, AA may be of limited usefulness to criminal offenders, many of whom come from lower social classes that appear less responsive to AA's middle-class orientation. Moreover, AA views itself as a strictly voluntary treatment program; individuals must want to help themselves to subscribe to it. This characteristic often clashes with the coercive nature of treatment in corrections, which may require attendance at AA meetings as a condition of the sentence. The poor fit between AA's voluntary peer group structure and the involuntariness of corrections may explain why studies find these programs somewhat ineffective with offenders convicted of public drunkenness.

Special Offenders in the Community

SEX OFFENDERS

There are many kinds of **sex offenders.** It is important to know the distinctions among the different types of sex offenders in order to develop a supervision approach that works. The three basic types of sex offenders are (1) rapists (sexual assaulters), (2) child molesters (pedophiles), and (3) prostitutes. Each subclass of sex offender has a variety of economic, psychological, and situational motivations, and for each the correctional response is deeply influenced by prevailing public opinion about the crimes themselves.

Unfortunately, many sex offenders are recidivists because treatment is often not successful. In recent years, sixteen states have enacted "sexually violent predator" statutes. These laws are based on the belief that society needs a way to keep potentially dangerous "perverts" off the streets after their sentences have been served. Many states are placing released sex offenders under longer terms of intense supervision; others have imposed tougher sentencing measures. All states now have laws requiring public notification when sex offenders are paroled.

Some states have civil commitment procedures extending the terms of those judged to be sexual predators. In 1997, the U.S. Supreme Court in *Kansas* v. *Hendricks* upheld that state's Sexually Violent Predator Act. As in other states with these laws, Kansas developed commitment procedures allowing a court to determine whether a sexual predator was still dangerous and should remain incarcerated and treated indefinitely. There are now more than 900 sex offenders locked away for indefinite terms.[22]

The Rapist

With the resurgence of feminism in the 1960s and 1970s, the justice system's response to rape became a major political issue. Indeed, to discuss rape under the heading of "sex offenses" risks ignoring that it is primarily an act of violence against women. In her classic study *Against Our Will,* Susan Brownmiller persuasively argued that rape needs to be reconceptualized; it is not a sex crime but a brutal personal assault: "To a woman the definition of rape is fairly simple. . . . A deliberate violation of emotional, physical and rational integrity and . . . [a] hostile, degrading act of violence. . . ."[23] When rape is placed where it truly belongs, within the context of modern criminal violence and not within the purview of archaic masculine codes, the crime retains its unique dimensions, taking its place with armed robbery and aggravated assault. The link between lethal violence and sexual assault is illustrated by the fact that about half of all murders of women committed by acquaintances and two-thirds of those by strangers occurred in the process of sexual assaults.[24]

The widespread recognition that rape is not sexually motivated, but represents a physical intrusion fueled by a desire for violent coercion, led to two broad shifts in criminal justice. The first was a move to redefine the crime of "rape" as a gender-neutral "sexual assault" or even as a special case of the general crime of assault. The second was a trend toward harsher sentences for convicted rapists.

The Child Molester

Few offenses are so uniformly reviled or have so great a stigma attached to the act as child molestation. However, only in recent years, with more open discussion of sexual issues, has significant scholarly attention been given to convicted child molesters.

The picture of the child molester that emerges is more tragic than disgusting. Estimates are that as many as 90 percent of child molesters were themselves molested as children, and studies show that sex offenders are about twice as likely as other offenders to report being sexually victimized as a child.[25] Child molestation is a complex crime involving many factors; it ordinarily stems from deep feelings of personal inadequacy on the part of the offender. As many as 20 percent of child molesters are over fifty years old, and many cases involve ambivalent feelings of attachment between adults and children that gradually become converted into sexual contact.

Many victims of molestation are confused by the crime and feel guilty about it because their emotional attachment to their molesters is quite real. They usually are aware that the act is "wrong" or "bad." And if the act arouses pleasurable feelings, the situation is further complicated.

The Prostitute

Prostitution is more an economic crime than a sexual crime; that is, it is an illegal business transaction between a service provider and a customer. Public opinion about prostitution is ambivalent; public policy seems to fluctuate between "reform" legislation designed to legalize and regulate prostitution and wholesale police roundups of hookers and pimps to "clean up" the streets. The AIDS epidemic has fueled renewed concern that prostitutes are major transmission agents for the disease. In response, some courts have ordered infected prostitutes to refrain from practicing their trade. In any event, prostitution exists (even flourishes) in virtually every section of the country, and when prostitutes or their pimps are punished, the sentence generally is probation or a fine.

A study of female street prostitutes in the Los Angeles County Jail found that many began their work at age fifteen, and one-third got started through family or friends. Seventy percent had children but 90 percent of these do not have custody of them. The study found that street prostitutes tend to be children of dysfunctional families, brought up in an absence of parents and in an atmosphere of drugs and sexual assault.[26]

Because prostitution is an economic crime, correctional caseworkers are forced to find a substitute vocation for offenders. This is not easy, for many prostitutes lack education and marketable skills, and many are addicted to drugs. Further, many attempt to leave the trade but few are successful until age, illness, or a disability renders them less productive. Because prostitution is more a public nuisance than a public threat, caseworkers are likely to accord such cases low priority, as are the courts and prosecutors. Therefore, prostitution is a crime that often receives marginal enforcement of laws and indifferent punishment.

DEALING WITH SEX OFFENDERS IN THE COMMUNITY

The most widely used strategy with sex offenders is **relapse prevention.** Relapse prevention is based on the assumption that many sex offenders are compulsive. For them, prevention of new sexual criminality is a constant struggle. The relapse prevention method recognizes the struggle and builds supports for the offender in facing the sexual compulsion. It involves three key elements: knowledge, signal detection, and multiple sources of contact.

The *knowledge* dimension of sex offender treatment involves getting the offender to understand the wrongfulness of criminal sexual deviance. Rapists will often see women as "asking" for the sexual assault; child sex offenders will describe themselves as "teaching" the children or "loving" them. The offender must come to see these kinds of sentiments as the rationalizations that they are. One of the benefits of the penalty—nearly all serious sex offenders are given some period of confinement as an aspect of their sentence—is that it conveys society's disapproval of the conduct in no uncertain terms.

The offender's knowledge of the symptoms of reoffending will also play an important role in treatment, through monitoring *signals* of relapse. Generally, when a sex offender is on the verge of reoffending, there are "signals" of impending problems. These include substance abuse, erratic behavior, changes in routines, missing work, buying sex magazines, and a variety of other actions that indicate instability in the offender's situation.

The question is, what should the corrections system do when it encounters these signals? With the exception of illicit drug use, none of these activities is illegal, and certainly they are common occurrences in everyday life. But to a corrections professional assigned the responsibility for supervising a former sex offender who displays these "signals," the choices are not easy. If the signal is a false alarm, the offender's adjustment can be interrupted or even impeded by the alarm of an investigation. On the other hand, if the offender is headed toward relapse, the consequences of failure to react can be ominous for a new victim of a crime.

The key, then, is *contact*. The correctional caseworker needs to maintain regular and broad-based contact, not just with the offender, but with the offender's family, employers, neighbors, and everyday acquaintances. The contact with the offender has as its purpose a kind of sensitive surveillance of the offender's moods and reactions to events in his life. The contact with other persons in the offender's life is to get information and perspectives not coming through direct contact with the offender himself. Family members, coworkers, and neighbors often know the answers to such questions as "Is the offender showing any evidence of erratic behavior?" "Is the offender acting evasive or otherwise secretive?" and "Has he been keeping odd hours?"

This kind of intensive surveillance bothers people who are concerned about the offender's rights and the intrusion of the state into the lives of citizens who have not committed crimes. It makes us all uncomfortable to have law enforcement professionals working their way so deeply into the lives of private citizens, watching family members and neighbors so closely. Yet the alternative, trusting that the offender will make it successfully without the reinforcements of monitoring and rapid response to signals of new problems, invites tragedy.

THE MENTALLY ILL OFFENDER

Few images disturb people more than that of the "crazy," violence-prone criminal whose acts seem random, senseless, or even "psychopathic." To understand such people better, others often roughly classify them as "disturbed" or **mentally ill offenders**—people whose rational processes do not seem to operate in a normal way. Mentally ill offenders are less able to think realistically about their conduct, including criminal conduct. Not all mentally ill offenders are violent or psychopathic. Recent studies show that only 3 percent of the violent behavior in the United States is attributable to mental disorder, and people with mental illness are more likely to be victims of crime than perpetrators of violence.[27] Yet those citizens whose mental disorders translate into criminality present significant problems for corrections.[28] Nationwide, almost 300,000 inmates in prisons and jails suffer from schizophrenia, manic depression, or major depression. In addition, about 550,000 probationers have a mental condition or have stayed overnight in a mental hospital at some point in their life.[29]

It is now recognized that the classification of most violent offenders as "mentally ill" is both an overgeneralization and a social issue. For one thing, not all violent offenders are demonstrably mentally ill. For another, the decision to apply the label "sick" (which the term *psychopath* or *sociopath* implies, *-path* meaning "ill person") makes the person seem somehow less whole and makes it easier to justify extreme correctional measures.

The central problem with the mental health model of criminality is that the mind cannot be observed; a person's inner feelings and thoughts can only be inferred from behavior. When we see people behaving in outrageous or bizarre ways, we are tempted to infer that their mind or emotions work in strange ways. We call these people "sick" or "emotionally ill" even when there is no evidence of an illness, in the sense of the flu or any other physical disease. In earlier times, deities, witches, and instincts were considered to cause a variety of odd or criminal behaviors. As Thomas Szasz has argued, today we use the term *mental illness* to explain behaviors we do not understand, even if the behavior is not caused by a "disease of the brain."[30]

Our need to explain some criminal behavior as "mental illness" can easily lead us to overgeneralize and ascribe mental illness to all criminals. The National Commission on the Causes and Prevention of Violence recognized the problem when it concluded that (1) the popular idea that the mentally ill are overrepresented in the population of violent criminals is not supported by research evidence, and (2) people identified as mentally ill generally pose no greater risk of committing violent crimes than does the population as a whole.[31]

This conclusion underscores the problem for corrections represented by mentally ill offenders: Their mental illness is often a separate issue from their criminality, and dealing with their criminality may not require treatment of their mental illness. In other words, the fact that a person has mental or emotional problems and is an offender does not necessarily mean that he or she will continue to offend until the mental or emotional problems are resolved.

The general public links mental illness, crime, and the insanity defense because of a handful of highly publicized trials, such as that of John Hinckley, the would-be assassin of Ronald Reagan. But only about 8 percent of convicted or accused persons in mental hospitals are there because they were found not guilty by reason of insanity. Another 6 percent are in hospitals because they have been judged mentally disordered sex offenders, and 32 percent have been found incompetent to stand trial. The largest group (54 percent), and the group of greatest concern to corrections, consists of offenders who became mentally ill after having been imprisoned.[32]

In the coming decades, community corrections will face an increased number of mentally ill clients. Much of the increase is related to a major policy shift in the mental health field: **deinstitutionalization** or the shift to decarcerate and release those with mental issues into community care. With the availability of drugs that inhibit aberrant behavior, it has become possible to release a multitude of mental patients to the community. Unfortunately, undersupervised or even unsupervised former patients often fail to take their medication and then commit deviant or criminal acts. Because of their behavior, some are shuttled back and forth between the mental hospital and jail or prison.[33] Mentally ill offenders have high rates of homelessness, unemployment, alcohol and drug use, and physical and sexual abuse prior to their current arrest.

The main problem these offenders pose is managerial: Their behavior may be erratic, and they often have trouble adjusting to regular community life. For many of these offenders, the rules of community supervision—regular reporting, curfews, and gainful employment—are not easy to sustain. Sometimes, their behavior is difficult for community supervision staff to understand, and they may seem resistant to supervision—though often this is merely a manifestation of their own mental health difficulties and not their attitude toward being under correctional control.

Reducing the criminality of mentally ill offenders involves working closely with mental health treatment agencies. The working relationship between mental health and correctional agencies is mutually supportive. Correctional staff provide these agencies with more client contact than they can ordinarily expect with traditional mental health services. Community corrections can serve as a source of information about direct observation of work and leisure behavior, and the correctional agency can interview employers, family members, and others about the client's behavior in ways that mental health agencies ordinarily cannot do. On the other hand, the mental health treatment provider can prescribe drugs, grant access to residential treatment services, and engage in a professional level of psychotherapy—all of these are approaches that correctional staff do not use.

DEALING WITH MENTALLY ILL OFFENDERS IN THE COMMUNITY

As we just discussed, the key element of supervising mentally ill offenders in the community is gaining cooperation and working with mental health agencies that provide services to these offenders. Relative to actual probation or parole supervision, however, there is a broad range of procedures and practices that can be useful to help those who are mentally ill become successful in community supervision.

First, it is important to provide early *identification* and *classification* procedures. Not all offenders need the same level of mental health services, nor do they all need the same level of supervision. Being able to decipher levels of need is essential for effective delivery of service community supervision. This will also help courts and correctional agencies determine whether services should be tied into community supervision.

Persons with mental illness may also be assigned to *specialized caseloads*. Probation and parole departments often provide specialized caseloads for sex offenders, juveniles, or drug offenders but rarely for those with mental health issues. Offenders with mental illness on probation may find it difficult to negotiate the social service bureacracy and find the services they need. From a parole perspective, those with mental health issues have at least the same needs as other offenders when it comes to adjusting to community living after incarceration. In addition to specialized caseloads, *intensive supervision* might be needed to monitor high-risk offenders with mental issues. This may be especially important immediately after release from jail or prison or with high-risk mentally ill offenders.

Relapse prevention techniques, like those used with sex offenders, also can help improve the supervision of mentally ill offenders. Close supervision, continuous information sharing, and identification of early signs of stress or failure are key ingredients in this process. And finally, *progressive sanctions* for technical violation of probation or parole supervision is another strategy that can be used in combination with others to reduce recidivism. Because mental illness is often a cyclical process, these offenders may drift in and out of deviant behavior and criminality. Progressive sanctions allow correctional staff some flexibility to be responsive to the changing needs and circumstances of mentally ill offenders without immediately returning them to jail or prison. In the end, the effectiveness of supervision of mentally ill offenders is closely linked to the degree to which a treatment regime is established and followed. So long as these offenders are succeeding in treatment, they will do well under community supervision.

THE MENTALLY HANDICAPPED OFFENDER

The forty-three-year-old man entered the Dunkin' Donuts shop, approached the counter, and demanded, "All your money and a dozen doughnuts." With his finger pointed inside his pocket, he announced that he had a gun and would use it. When the police arrived, they found the man standing outside the shop eating the doughnuts—just as they had found him after several previous holdups. The man's name is Eddie; he has an IQ of 61. He has served prison sentences for this type of offense, but almost immediately upon release he commits another such crime.

Charlie, who has an IQ of 85, set fire to a trash barrel in the hallway of his apartment building. A psychotic woman tenant, panicked by the smoke, jumped out of the window and was killed by the fall. Charlie is awaiting trial for murder.

These cases point to another problematic type of person for the correctional system: the **mentally handicapped offender,** often referred to as mentally retarded or developmentally disabled. An estimated 2 to 3 percent of the U.S. population is mentally handicapped (having IQs below 70). Among the incarcerated population, about 5 percent (50,000) are in this category, and a much higher percentage of those are on probation or under juvenile care. In California alone, correctional agencies handle 22,000 adults and juveniles who are classified as mentally retarded.[34]

Like other Americans, mentally handicapped people commit crimes, but there is no proven link between their disability and a propensity for criminal behavior. Their criminality may result from the fact that they do not know how to obtain what they want without breaking the law. It may also result from the fact that they are easily duped by persons who think deviant behavior is a joke or who use them to illicitly secure something for themselves. Mentally handicapped people also are disproportionately poor, so if they need or want something, they may commit a crime to get it. And because they cannot think quickly, they get caught more often than other criminals do. As a Los Angeles police officer told researcher Joan Petersilia, "They are the last to leave the scene, the first to get arrested, and the first to confess."[35]

The majority of the offenses committed by mentally handicapped people are classified as property or public order crimes. This is not to say that they do not also commit serious violent crimes; among the incarcerated, a higher proportion of mentally handicapped offenders than others have been convicted of homicide and other crimes against persons.

Deinstitutionalization has also been a recent focus of programs to deal with mentally handicapped individuals. Like the mentally ill, the mentally handicapped have been returned to the community, where they are expected to live, work, and care for themselves with minimal supervision. Because they have difficulty adjusting to the rules of the community, they often come to the attention of the criminal justice system.

Some observers believe that mentally handicapped offenders are less criminals than misfits who lack training in how to live in a complex society; they belong not in prison but in a treatment facility where they could learn rudimentary survival skills. Criminal justice practitioners often argue that mentally handicapped offenders constitute a mental health problem, but because they have committed crimes, mental health agencies do not want them. Thus, they are shunned by both camps and get little help from either.

There is a need for the development of appropriate correctional programs for mentally ill and mentally handicapped offenders. In many prisons and jails, such inmates are segregated with others who have special needs. This strategy has been criticized because some of these offenders are preyed upon by others in the unit. While incarcerated, they are often the butts of practical jokes and exploited as scapegoats or sexual objects. Recent litigation has called attention to the fact that these offenders require special programs, and the Americans with Disabilities Act (ADA) provides federal oversight to local correctional programs for those suffering from mental disabilities.

What can community corrections do for or with this special category of offender? Obviously, the usual routines of probation, diversion, incarceration, and community service will not work. Mentally handicapped individuals typically are not comfortable with change, are difficult to employ outside of sheltered workshops, and are not likely to improve significantly in terms of mental condition or social habits. And so they violate probation or break prison rules and are further penalized.

In several states, such as Massachusetts and Texas, programs within probation and parole provide additional assistance and services to mentally retarded offenders. Day reporting centers are used in some states as well as halfway houses. The goal of these programs is to help mentally disabled offenders to gain the skills and discipline they need to live independent and crime-free lives.[36]

THE LOW-INTELLIGENCE OFFENDER

It has been estimated that over one-third of prisoners, probationers, and parolees have lower-than-normal intellectual functioning.[37] Some of the same issues that face offenders with mental illness also face those with low intelligence: erratic behavior, difficulties in following instructions and obeying rules, and unsettled personal and social interactions. The reasons for these problems are somewhat different, however. Low-intelligence offenders have trouble understanding how to comply with supervision requirements and how to communicate with the correctional worker who is in charge. These offenders are typically easily led, and so they may fall under the influence of others who might reinvolve them in criminal conduct. The problem for low-intelligence offenders is often that they are not naturally inclined to criminal behavior, but because they want to please the person they are talking to, they cannot always sustain their attention to pro-social behavior. Supervision of those with low intelligence must be carried out very deliberately. These offenders will often be cooperative with supervision requirements, but they may have trouble following complicated or long-term supervision plans. Supervision goals must be simple and short-term. When they are accomplished, recognition and other rewards will reinforce the low-intelligence offender's progress and overall cooperation. In the end, this offender will typically do well under supervision, so long as the supervision effort is tailored to the special needs that exist for those offenders who have limited intellectual functioning.

MENTAL HEALTH COURTS

A recent innovation in criminal justice that seems to be most helpful in dealing with offenders with a wide range of mental problems is the **mental health court.** Mental health courts are treatment courts that provide an alternative to traditional criminal justice system processing for those who volunteer to participate. They provide pretrial treatment options that attempt to tailor to the individual needs of defendants. Modeled after drug courts, mental health courts also create alternatives for courts, law enforcement, and correctional agencies when dealing with nonviolent, mentally ill offenders.

The first mental health court was developed in Broward County, Florida, in 1997 after local officials became frustrated with the county's handling of defendants suffering from mental disorders. The original mission of the mental health court was to "address the unique needs of the mentally ill in our criminal justice system." The box "Goals and Guiding Principles of Mental Health Court" lists the goals and guiding principles of the Broward County Court. The court has served as a model for the development of similar courts throughout the United States including three programs that began soon after Broward County in Anchorage, Alaska (1998), King County, Washington (1999), and San Bernardino, California, (1999).[38]

In November 2000, the mental health court movement received a considerable boost when President Clinton signed into law legislation that created a mental health courts system (America's Law Enforcement and Mental Health Project Act). The legislation established a grant to create 100 pilot mental health courts for dealing with mentally ill detainees. Each of these courts was to provide separate dockets that handle only cases involving mentally ill offenders, specialized training for law enforcement and court personnel, centralized case management, and standards that would ensure volunteerism, judicial monitoring, and services for all nonviolent mentally ill or retarded offenders.[39] Time and quality evaluation research will determine whether the mental health court movement is a success, but based on the numbers of participants that enter these courts it appears that they were long in waiting.

GOALS AND GUIDING PRINCIPLES OF MENTAL HEALTH COURT BROWARD COUNTY, FLORIDA

Goals

- Create effective interactions between the criminal justice and mental health systems
- Ensure legal advocacy for the mentally ill defendant
- Ensure that mentally ill defendants do not languish in jail because of their mental illness
- Balance the rights of the defendant and the public safety by recommending the least restrictive, most appropriate, and most workable disposition
- Increase access for the mentally ill defendant to community mental health services by creating centralized services
- Divert mentally ill defendants with minor criminal charges to community-based mental health services

- Reduce the contact of the mentally ill defendant with the criminal justice system by creating a bridge between the criminal justice system and the mental health system
- Monitor the delivery and receipt of mental health services and treatment
- Solicit participation from consumers and family members in court decisions

Guiding Principles

- The INVOLVEMENT of consumers and family members should be encouraged for all persons with mental illness.
- ACCESS to appropriate and flexible mental health services should be ensured for all persons with mental illness.
- The jail is a COMMUNITY institution, and the mentally ill inmate is a community concern.
- CREATIVE use of existing resources can encourage and inspire many needed changes without the massive infusion of new resources.
- Mental health services targeting the COEXISTING DISORDERS of mental illness and substance abuse should be a priority.
- CROSS TRAINING of law enforcement, mental health, and corrections personnel is crucial.

Source: www.co.broward.fl.us

LIFESTYLE OFFENDERS

The most difficult supervision challenge is provided by those who are committed to criminal lifestyles. These criminals are referred to as **career criminals.** When criminologist Walter Reckless first developed the idea of the career criminal, he had in mind a specific set of attributes:

1. Crime is his way of earning a living, his main occupation.
2. He develops technical skills useful to the commission of his crimes.
3. He started as a delinquent child and progressed toward criminality.
4. He expects to do some time in prison as a "cost" of doing this type of work.
5. He is psychologically normal.[40]

Reckless attributed these characteristics to a small, more or less undifferentiated group of offenders who worked at crime, including organized crime figures, white-collar criminals, and professional criminals who worked continuously at an illegal occupation. However, given research ranging from studies of a group of men born in Philadelphia in 1958 to interviews with convicted and imprisoned adults in California, Texas, and Michigan, scholars in the 1980s concluded that a small group of active criminals commits a majority of all crimes.[41] This led to a significant shift in thinking about career criminals. Instead of applying the term to someone whose work is crime, policymakers began to use it to refer to any offender with several convictions or arrests. Thus, a person with as few as three or four convictions now is commonly labeled a "career criminal." This may seem a bit odd to most of us; we would hardly call our own jobs a career if we had been seen at work only three or four times.

Of course, many individuals who are repeatedly convicted actually do admit to more crimes, sometimes many more than the handful for which they are being punished. Peter Greenwood's famous study of robbers, for example, found that as many as half of those with multiple convictions for robbery admitted to having committed a large number of robberies for which they were not caught.[42] Undeniably, this small minority made something of a career out of that crime. Still, many repeaters—almost half of Greenwood's sample, for example—are not high-rate offenders. That is, the mere existence of multiple convictions does not mean that the person is working at crime as a career as Reckless defined it; the person may simply be a frequent offender (have committed several crimes in the past few years) who shifts from one type of crime to another.

Why, then, this recent trend to paint the picture of the career criminal with such a broad brush? The answer has to do partly with political pressures. With the devaluation of rehabilitation in the 1970s came renewed confidence in incapacitation as the appropriate correctional course. But if incapacitation was the political catchword, what group would be the target? Previous studies had unearthed so few career criminals that this notion was not promising for crime control hard-liners. Yet, if the career criminal concept could be expanded to include virtually all multiple repeaters, then the target group for this newly popular policy would be large indeed.

Corrections has borne the cost of this conceptual shift. Much as in the case of violent situational criminals, pressure has grown to keep repeaters in prison longer to prevent them from pursuing their predatory "careers." Yet these criteria result in nonprofessional but intermittent offenders being misclassified as career criminals. One result is that they contribute to prison overcrowding.

Without question, our prisons hold some career criminals—professional offenders committed to lives of crime. But we must examine the accuracy of the overall label and recognize that any decision to classify offenders has social and political significance.

GANGS IN THE COMMUNITY

The prototypical lifestyle offender is the *gang member*. This kind of offender has affiliated with others who break the law, and usually there are more antisocial influences in this offender's life than pro-social influences. Supervision focuses on counteracting the antisocial forces while strengthening the pro-social forces.

Most of the antisocial forces are the associates—gang members and others involved in crime. Typically, a supervision condition requires these offenders to have no contact with known gang members. Since the gang members may be the primary means of personal support, and the offender may feel that these gang members are a source of protection from other gangs, complying with a "no-contact" condition is difficult. Enforcing the condition is also problematic because community supervision agents have limited sources of information to confirm or deny the offender's associations. From a handful of contacts a month, it is not easy to get the full story of what is going on.

With lifestyle offenders, then, the most effective way of reducing risk is to change the lifestyle. Even for gang members, this strategy has promise, because as exciting as the gangster life may be, it is fraught with danger and strains. For most youngsters, it eventually grows old. All but the most committed gangsters eventually tire of the high-risk lifestyle, and by their early twenties, many want a way out. Community supervision efforts can help them by providing exits from gang life: new jobs, new locations, supports for family relationships, and so on. The aim of reducing risk for lifestyle offenders also involves strengthening the role of pro-social supports, since these supports will form the strength from which the offenders leave the lifestyle.

In the end, the effectiveness of approaches to lifestyle offenders depends on the creation of viable, new lifestyle options for them. Many want a job, a home, and a family, but they see no way to obtain these goals, so they exchange the legitimate aims for more accessible, but less conventional, gang rewards. When these decisions have run their course, most lifestyle offenders will want a chance for a more conventional life. Community supervision is most effective when it capitalizes on these desires and helps these offenders develop the pro-social supports they need.

The image of the committed criminal—the career criminal—is a disturbing one, and many of our toughest laws and strictest supervision practices are designed with this offender in mind. But career criminals are atypical in a community supervision caseload. Nonetheless, there is a great deal at stake in the way they adjust to the community, and so the way they are supervised is a matter of some priority in most community supervision agencies.

SPECIAL SUPERVISION PROGRAMS

The needs of probationers vary dramatically. Sex offenders require different supervision strategies than do cocaine addicts; mentally ill offenders must be handled differently than embezzlers. With caseloads often exceeding 100 probationers per officer, it is unrealistic to expect the probation officer to tailor the supervision effort to fit each person on the caseload. Instead, there has been a growing emphasis on specializing probation caseloads. Specialization groups probationers with similar problems into a single caseload. It allows the probation officer to develop better expertise in handling that problem, and it promotes a concentrated supervision effort to deal with that problem.

Studies of **specialized supervision** show this approach has promise. A program of employment counseling and support services failed to reduce recidivism, but it did have a positive effect on the employment status of its participants. Specialized treatment programs operated by probation agencies have reduced recidivism for sex offenders.[43] In general, targeted, specialized services have been found to be more effective than traditional services.

Recent interest in the problem of substance abuse has increased the attention given to offenders on probation who have problems with drugs and alcohol. Several special programs have been tried to combat the use of drugs by probationers. These programs typically take advantage of new techniques for drug surveillance and treatment. Urinalysis is used to determine whether an offender is continuing to use drugs. Antabuse, a drug that stimulates nausea when combined with alcohol, is used to inhibit alcohol use. Methadone, a drug that overcomes the craving for heroin, is used to allow addicts to avoid withdrawal symptoms. These approaches are often combined with close surveillance to reinforce abstinence on the part of probationers.

Another new special program, discussed in Chapter 8, is to pair the probation officer more closely with street police officers. Officers who work in tandem with the police are often given caseloads of especially tough probationers. The special police liaison enables more effective searches and arrests and allows probation to take advantage of information available to the police about probationers.

The difficulty with special supervision programs is what to do with the "ordinary" offender who is slated for traditional services. There is often a feeling that "regular" probation is a less attractive function, and conflict among the specialized units can become a serious management problem. As a consequence, specialized service programs in probation, even when successful, require extensive managerial support.

SUMMARY

Some offenders who live in the community have special needs that can only be met with proper identification and unique supervision techniques. In this chapter, we discussed these offenders as well as the different ways to effectively supervise them. Substance abusers, both alcohol and drug, are particularly troublesome for the criminal justice system because of the volume of crime associated with addictive behavior. A number of promising programs, including drug courts, have recently been shown to be effective in reducing crime among this offender population.

Sex offenders are a controversial population that requires relapse prevention techniques involving knowledge, signal detection, and multiple sources of contact. Mentally ill, mentally handicapped, and low-intelligence offenders are a growing problem in criminal justice because of the deinstitutionalization movement that occurred since the 1970s. Mental health courts have recently tried to address some of the needs of these special offenders. Lifestyle offenders, especially gangs, can also pose unique challenges for correctional officials, and they require additional kinds of risk prevention techniques. Finally, special supervision programs such as intensive probation supervision and specialized caseloads that focus on problem aspects such as drug use can be effective tools for community supervision personnel.

--------| **DISCUSSION QUESTIONS** |--------

1. What is the "success rate" for reducing the criminality of those with alcohol or drug problems? What can we do to increase the rate?
2. Find out the location of the nearest drug court. Invite a judge or court representative to class to ask them about program components. How effective is the program?
3. What makes sex offenders such a difficult population to supervise in the community?
4. What strategies do you feel would be most effective for the supervision of offenders with mental health issues?
5. What role should public opinion play in punishing various offenders?

--------| **SUGGESTED READINGS** |--------

Flanagan, Timothy (ed.). *Long-Term Imprisonment: Policy, Science and Correctional Practice.* Thousand Oaks, CA: Sage, 1995. Provides a selection of papers and studies on offenders who serve long sentences.

Hobbs, Richard. *Bad Business.* New York: Oxford University Press, 1995. Studies professional criminals using interviews to understand their motivations for crime and methods of work.

McCarthy, Belinda, and Langworthy, Robert. *Older Offenders.* New York: Praeger, 1988. Summarizes studies of the needs and problems of elderly offenders.

Nolan, James, L. (ed.) *Drug Courts in Theory and Practice.* Hawthorne, NY: Aldine de Gruyter, 2002. Edited book provides eleven articles about the implementation and assessment of drug courts.

Schwartz, Barbara K., and Cellini, Henry P. *The Sex Offender: Corrections, Treatment, and Legal Practice.* Kingston, NJ: Civil Research Institute, 1995. Collected papers dealing with all aspects of sex offenders in corrections, from psychodynamics to treatment and management in the community.

--------| **WEB SITES** |--------

Web site that describes the Arrestee Drug Abuse Monitoring (ADAM) program
www.adam-nij.net

Web site that provides extensive resources, facts, and figures about drug courts
www.ncjrs.org/drug_courts/facts.html

Web site for the drug court of New South Wales,
Australia
www.lawlink.nsw.gov.au/drugcrt/drugcrt.nsf/
pages/index
Web site about the Mary Magdalene Project, an
organization providing sanctuary for prostitutes
www.prostitution-recovery.org

Web site for the National Association of Drug
Court Professionals
www.nadcp.org/index.html

| NOTES |

1. *Behind Bars: Substance Abuse and America's
   Prison Population* (New York: National Center
   for Addiction and Substance Abuse, 1997);
   New York Times, January 9, 1998, p. A1.
2. U.S. Department of Justice, Bureau of Justice
   Statistics, *Bulletin,* January 1999, p. 3.
3. U.S. Department of Justice, Bureau of Justice
   Statistics, *Bulletin,* May 2000, p. 2.
4. Lawrence A. Greenfeld, *Alcohol and Crime: An
   Analysis of National Data on the Prevalence of
   Alcohol Involvement in Crime* (Washington, DC:
   U.S. Department of Justice, 1998), p. 9.
5. U.S. Department of Justice, National Institute
   of Justice, *ADAM: 1997 Annual Report on Adult
   and Juvenile Arrestees* (Washington, DC: Government Printing Office, 1998), p. 9.
6. George E. Vaillant, "A 20-Year Follow-up of
   New York Narcotic Addicts," *Archives of General Psychiatry* 29 (August 1973): 237–241.
7. D. Farabee, M. Prendergast, and M. D. Anglin,
   "Effectiveness of Coerced Treatment of Drug-
   Abusing Offenders," *Federal Probation* 62:1
   (June 1998): 3–10.
8. M. L. Prendergast, M. D. Anglin, J. Wellisch,
   R. P. Corbett, Jr., and M. K. Harris, "Treatment for Drug-Abusing Offenders," in *Federal
   Probation,* 59:4 (December 1995): 66–76.
9. J. P. Caukins, C. P. Rydell, W. L. Schwabe, and
   James Chiesa, "Mandatory Minimum Drug
   Sentences: Throw Away the Key or Taxpayers'
   Money?" 1997, Rand, Santa Monica: CA.
   www.rand.org/publications/
10. James A. Inciardi, Dorothy Lockwood, and
    Robert M. Hooper, "Delaware Treatment Pro-
    gram Presents Promising Results," *Corrections
    Today* (February 1994): 34–40.
11. D. S. Lipton, "The Effectiveness of Treatment
    for Drug Abusers Under Criminal Justice
    Supervision," National Institute of Justice
    Research Report, November 1995.
12. Carol Shapiro, *La Bodega de las Familia:
    Reaching Out to the Forgotten Victims of Sub-
    stance Abuse,* NCJ 170595 (Washington, DC.
    Bureau of Justice Assistance, 1998). Also see
    www.familyjusticeinc.org/labodega
13. www.ojp.usdoj.gov/dcpo/Define/intro.htm
14. www.ncjrs.org/drug_courts/facts.html
15. Robert L. Hubbard et al., "Criminal Justice
    Client in Drug Abuse Treatment," in *Com-
    pulsory Treatment of Drug Abuse: Research
    and Clinical Practice* (NIDA Research Mono-
    graph 86), ed. C. G. Leukfield and F. M.
    Tims (Washington, DC: U.S. Department of
    Health and Human Services, National Insti-
    tute of Drug Abuse, 1988): p. 66. Also see
    M. D. Anglin and T. H. Maugh, Ensuring
    Success in Interventions with Drug-Using
    Offenders, *Annals of the American Academy
    of Political and Social Sciences* 521 (1992):
    66–90; and G. P. Falkin, D. S. Lipton, and
    H. K. Wexler, "Drug Treatment in State
    Prisons," in *Treating Drug Problems,* vol. 2,
    ed. D. R. Gerstein and H. H. Harwood
    (Washington, DC: National Academy Press,
    1992), pp. 89–131.
16. Farabee, Prendergast, and Anglin, "Effectiveness
    of Coerced Treatment of Drug-Abusing
    Offenders."
17. Dale Sechrest, "Determinates of Graduation
    from a Day Treatment Drug Court in Califor-
    nia: A Preliminary Study," *Journal of Drug Issues*
    31:1 (2001): 129–146.

18. Richard S. Gebelein, "The Rebirth of Rehabilitation: Promise and Perils of Drug Courts," in *Sentencing and Corrections: Issues for the 21st Century,* No. 6, U.S. Department of Justice, Office of Justice Programs, May 2000.

19. See the NCJRS Web page at www.ncjrs.org/drug_courts/drug_courts.html

20. www.usdoj.gov/dcpo/hello.htm Also see more recent evaluations: C. Spohn, "Drug Courts and Recidivism: The Results of an Evaluation Using Two Comparison Groups and Multiple Indicators of Recidivism," *Journal of Drug Issues* 31:1 (2001): 149–173; and "Drug War Facts." www.drugwarfacts.org/drugcour.htm

21. U.S. Department of Justice, Bureau of Justice Statistics, *Special Report,* June 1999, p. 1.

22. *New York Times,* April 22, 2001, p. A1.

23. Susan Brownmiller, *Against Our Will* (New York: Simon & Schuster, 1975), pp. 376–377.

24. Lawrence A. Greenwood, *Sex Offenses and Offenders: An Analysis of Data on Rape and Sexual Assault* (Washington, DC: Government Printing Office, 1997).

25. Ibid., p. 23.

26. Mary Magdalene Project, Beyond 2000: Research Report on Street Prostitution. www.prostitution-recovery.org

27. John Monahan, "Mental Illness and Violent Crime," *Research in Review* (Washington, DC: National Institute of Justice, October 1996).

28. Robert D. Hare, "Psychopathy: A Clinical Construct Whose Time Has Come," *Criminal Justice and Behavior* 23:1 (March 1996): 25–54.

29. U.S. Department of Justice, Bureau of Justice Statistics, *Special Report,* July 1999.

30. Thomas S. Szasz, *Law, Liberty, and Psychiatry* (New York: Macmillan, 1963), p. 12.

31. U.S. National Commission on the Causes and Prevention of Violence, *Crimes of Violence* (Washington, DC: Government Printing Office, 1969), p. 444.

32. U.S. Department of Justice, Bureau of Justice Statistics, *Report to the Nation on Crime and Justice* (Washington, DC: Government Printing Office, 1983), p. 68.

33. Bruce A. Arrigo, "Transcarceration: A Constitutive Ethnography of Mentally Ill Offenders," *Prison Journal,* 81(2): 162–186.

34. Joan Petersilia, "Justice for All? Offenders with Mental Retardation and the Criminal Justice System," *Prison Journal* 77:4 (December 1997): 358–380.

35. Joan Petersilia, *Doing Justice? Criminal Offenders with Developmental Disabilities* (Berkeley: California Policy Research Center, University of California, 2000), p. 5.

36. Ibid., p. 45.

37. Sheilagh Hodgins, "The Criminality of Mentally Disordered Persons," in *Mental Disorder and Crime,* ed. Sheilagh Hodgins (Newbury Park: Sage, 1993), pp. 3–22.

38. Bureau of Justice Statistics, *Emerging Judicial Strategies for the Mentally Ill in the Criminal Caseload: Mental Health Courts in Ft. Lauderdale, Seattle, San Bernardino, and Anchorage,* U.S. Department of Justice, Office of Justice Programs, Monograph NCJ 182504, April 2000.

39. Pete V. Domenici, Senator, "Mental Health Courts Bill Signed into Law," FDHC Press Release, November 15, 2000.

40. Walter C. Reckless, *The Crime Problem* (New York: Appleton-Century-Crofts, 1961), pp. 153–177.

41. Alfred Blumstein, Jacqueline Cohen, Jeffrey Roth, and Christy Visher, *Criminal Careers and "Career Criminals"* (Washington, DC: National Academy of Sciences, 1986).

42. Peter Greenwood, *Selective Incapacitation* (Santa Monica, CA: Rand Corporation, 1982).

43. *This Works: Community Sanctions and Services for Special Offenders* (LaCrosse: IARCA, 1994).

Chapter 12

The Juvenile Offender in the Community

⊣ OBJECTIVES ⊢

The reader should be able to

1. Explain the reasons why we should treat juvenile offenders differently than adult offenders.

2. Discuss the rationale for lowering the criminal age of responsibility.

3. Describe how we deal with juvenile offenders whose crimes do not fit the definition of normal juvenile behavior.

4. Examine the history of juvenile court, and the main principle guiding it—parens patriae.

5. Understand the difference in terminology used in the juvenile and adult criminal justice systems.

6. Explore the special community correctional programs available to juveniles such as diversion, aftercare, intermediate sanctions, school, and volunteer probation programs.

7. Speculate about the future of juvenile corrections in the twenty-first century.

Remember when you were fourteen years old? How did you get along with adults? What did you think of your teachers? Your friends? What were your attitudes toward conventional values such as "obeying the law" and "planning for your future"? In what ways are you different, now, from the way you were back then? If you are like most people, you have changed a lot since you were fourteen years old. You are more mature, have a different view of the rest of the world, and think of yourself in different terms. You are no longer an old child; you are an adult.

To some extent, everyone who goes through this metamorphosis from adolescence to adulthood faces the same experiences: the hopes and fears that go with preadolescence; the emotional highs and lows of the teenage years; the powerful and troubling peer associations that dominate those parts of our lives. Developmental psychologists tell us that there are predictable patterns to the growing-up processes that play themselves out in everyone's lifetime. Yet we also know that some young people face different hardships as they go through these processes. Among the differences that affect how one person grows up compared to another are forces such as poverty, the effectiveness of the parents, and personal intellectual and emotional strengths. If every child must travel through the jungle of adolescence to get to adulthood, each child's journey follows a unique pathway, defined in part by forces out of the child's control.

Even the question of what is in the young person's "control" sparks dispute. No one can control the circumstances of birth—from the basics such as sex or physical gifts to social factors such as the wealth or (even) the number of one's parents. These forces, over which a person has no power, work as powerful constraints on later life choices. So, while we might all hold adults responsible for their choices later in life, it would be unrealistic to think of five-, six-, or seven-year-olds as responsible for their destinies. And yet, the world a twelve-, thirteen-, or fourteen-year-old encounters is very much a product of events that occurred those seven years earlier. Likewise, the young adult of nineteen, twenty, or twenty-one must live with many of the consequences of actions taken seven years earlier—and those actions were shaped by events seven years before then.

Photo: Juvenile offenders work with severely disabled children as part of their jail time and rehabilitation program.
© Tony Savino/The Image Works

At what age can we start holding people responsible for their conduct? This fundamental question of legal philosophy is made complicated by the reality of human development. There is not a magic birthday on which people change from products of their circumstances to creators of their own destiny.

The change from childhood to adulthood is gradual, and each of us goes at a personal pace that depends on our surrounding circumstances—our family structure, our socioeconomic status, and our personal capacities—and is not dictated solely by the calendar. We would all agree that seven-year-olds bear a different moral responsibility for what they do than eighteen-year-olds, but exactly where, in between, do we draw the line? Since everyone is a bit different, it may seem that drawing such a line is unrealistic. But since we all agree that we want to treat the very young differently from the not-so-young, we must draw a line somewhere. Or perhaps we must draw two lines, one at which we begin to hold people partially responsible for their actions, and another at which we hold them fully responsible.

Perhaps we would think of the first line as the "age of responsibility" and the second line as the "age of adulthood." This is, essentially, the reason for a juvenile code. It reflects the commonsense belief that children are different from adults, and that simple justice would ask us to treat them differently. As we discuss below, there is today some controversy about this simple, seemingly commonsense idea. Some people think that in trying to draw these age distinctions, we do juveniles a disfavor.

Others think that failing to hold young people accountable for their conduct encourages them to be irresponsible. For these critics, the justice system would be better if age were not a legal factor in the jurisdiction of an offender, but rather were a consideration in the penalty applied after a conviction is obtained.

There is probably at least some truth to these complaints about the juvenile justice system. But even with these concerns, most contemporary justice advocates are against collapsing the juvenile system into the adult system and making no distinction about the age of the defendant. In today's justice system, we expect to treat the very young offender differently than the older accomplice, and we expect to take different issues into account when considering the appropriate response to misdeeds on the part of each. In particular, we take a different approach to dealing with juvenile offenders in the community. What is the rationale for these differences?

IMPORTANT DIFFERENCES BETWEEN ADULT AND JUVENILE OFFENDERS

In thinking about juvenile offenders under community supervision, it is useful to begin by thinking about how juveniles are different from young adults. These differences, it is thought, justify having a separate correctional system to deal with juvenile offenders in the community. In reviewing this list, we should remember that every offender is different. For every case that illustrates the differences juveniles represent to correctional authorities, there will be a case in which the differences are not as sharp. Moreover, juvenile offenders range in age from ten, eleven, and twelve, to sixteen and seventeen, and older juvenile offenders will look more like adults than their younger counterparts. But on average, juveniles represent a different set of challenges to correctional authorities, differences that are reflected in the operations of the justice system for juveniles.

These are the most important differences between adults and juveniles under correctional supervision in the community:

- Juveniles are young and may easily change.
- Juveniles have a high rate of desistance from crime.
- Juveniles' families are an important part of their lives.
- Juveniles are easily influenced by their peers.
- Juveniles have little responsibility for anyone other than themselves.

Juveniles Are Young and May Easily Change

The very youthfulness of juvenile offenders is thought to be an advantage by correctional caseworkers. Juvenile offenders do not have a long history of commitment to criminal behavior. Most correctional professionals believe this makes the juvenile offender more susceptible to the influence of correctional programs. Young offenders can be molded by good role models and timely supervision.

The youthfulness of juvenile offenders is a double-edged sword. Younger offenders are not as entrenched in negative peer associations, nor do they have the deep penetration into criminal activity that is a characteristic of more experienced offenders. In this way, their habits are less well formed and may be more easily altered. But age is also a predictor of recidivism: The younger the juvenile offender—and the more serious the misconduct—the more likely it is that the offender will be arrested again. As a consequence, the general experience of correctional workers that younger offenders make more malleable clients is countered by the fact that so many of the very young will find it hard to stay out of trouble with the law.

The youthful age has a marked effect on intervention strategies, since age affects the way a person learns and changes. Young people learn from involvement-oriented activities, such as interaction that is recreational and entertaining. This is more true with younger offenders; the supervision effort involves playing games, going on outings, and engaging in enjoyable activities with the youth and the correctional worker together. The use of enjoyable activities allows a bond to develop between the professional staff and the juvenile offender, and through that bond may come the influence that enables the young offender to find satisfying alternatives to criminal activity.

There are, of course, other kinds of interaction with young offenders—as described below, programs of supervision and control apply to them as well. But the feeling is that young offenders need, first and foremost, to be seen as young: easily led, anxious for acceptance and love, and dependent on adults for self-concept and insights into life choices. Correctional professionals try to provide those adult role models, either themselves or through "mentors."

Juveniles Have a High Rate of Desistance from Crime

It is true that, all else being equal, age is the best predictor of recidivism: The younger the offender, the more likely that offender will fail under community supervision. But as important as that statistic is, it can be misleading. For it is also true that juvenile offenders, as a group, have lower failure rates than adults. How can this seeming contradiction be explained? It is not uncommon for youth to get arrested, but most juveniles who get into trouble with the law once never get arrested again. This is the key—most juvenile offenders find a way to stay out of trouble a second time. That is why correctional professionals are often so positive about the prospects of juvenile offenders, and many juvenile offenders are indeed good prospects. Age is, thus, a positive factor in correctional work. Yet among the minority who fail, the failure rate increases as the age of first involvement in juvenile crime decreases. Despite the high success rate of juveniles, even the very young, a look at those who fail will turn up large numbers of those whose criminality began at a very early age.

This is double good news for community supervision. First, it means that juveniles, as a group, do not present an unreasonable risk to the community. Giving them a chance to make it will often pay off. At the same time the risks are reasonable, the potential gains are considerable, since every juvenile whose delinquent career is interrupted represents an adult criminal career that is prevented. The exception to this general rule applies to very young offenders—age thirteen and under, for example—who commit sophisticated, serious offenses.

When children commit adult-style crimes, they are at special risk to repeat these or more serious offenses. It is important to remember that many child offenders convicted of heinous offenses are able to avoid new crimes, but we also must remember that the cards are stacked in their disfavor. Because of the special risks associated with children who engage in adult criminality, community supervision must be undertaken with the utmost care.

Juveniles' Families Are an Important Part of Their Lives

One of the more common community supervision strategies is to involve key members of the offender's life in the supervision effort. With adult offenders, for example, there are often family members who will take a hand in helping to monitor the offender's adjustment, serving as a support to the supervision effort. Family members can be very influential in supervision. They can reinforce the importance of attending treatment programs and help support the offender's attempts to make changes in lifestyle, and they are even sources of information about the offender's adjustment to the community. When an adult is under community supervision, corrections professionals may try to find a key influence on the offender and enlist that person's help in the supervision tasks.

Of course, all participation by outsiders in the supervision of adult offenders is completely voluntary on their part—they are, after all, under no legal obligation to do anything except obey the laws themselves. Correctional workers will look for opportunities to recruit the cooperation of potential supportive outsiders, but they are unable to compel anyone to help.

For juvenile offenders, it is different. The role of family is not merely useful, it is critical to the success of the supervision effort. This is true because the juvenile is, by virtue of age, deeply connected to the immediate family system (parents, siblings, and extended family) in ways that do not happen for adults. Under most juvenile law, for example, the juvenile actually becomes a ward (dependant) of the state, and the legal parent and the court (usually through probation officers) accept joint responsibility for the formal supervision of the young offender. Under the law, then, the court system is a copartner to the family in the supervision effort. It is thought reasonable to take this approach, because the child's delinquency is taken as evidence the parents are not capable of effective supervision without support from the court.

It sounds good to have a connection between family and professionals, but experienced caseworkers know that the family is often one of the more serious problems that contributes to the delinquent behavior. There may be inadequate parental supervision, leaving the child free to get into trouble. Or conflicts between the child and adults may promote delinquency as the child's way of "getting back" or even unintentionally calling attention to the conflict. Abuse, alcoholism or drug addiction, or even mental illness on the part of key adults who are supposed to be the parents to the child may all contribute to problems that end in delinquency. When this happens, it is not uncommon for the adults in the situation to resist taking a positive role in the supervision effort. They may be hostile to the efforts of the correctional worker, or they may excuse the child's misbehavior or even condone it.

It is complicated enough when people not under the formal authority of the justice system are involved in the correctional process, but when the offender is a legal minor, the court's interest in the activities of key adults in that offender's life becomes amplified. If adult misconduct is contributing to the juvenile's tendency to disobey the law, the court may compel the adult to remedy the situation—sometimes the parent will be ordered into treatment programs or parental skills training programs. In particularly problematic situations, the adult will lose parental rights with the child.

In some cases, the adults in the juvenile's life do not include a logical, effective parent. When the father is not present and the mother is incapable of sufficient parenting due to personal problems such as substance abuse or even incarceration, the community supervision effort will focus on locating a substitute parental figure. On a part-time basis, this will include "big brothers" or "big sisters"—volunteer adults who spend concentrated time with the juvenile and represent role models for the young person to emulate. In extreme cases, the juvenile will be "placed"—removed from the home and relocated with new adults who will provide the necessary parenting missing from the original home.

No matter how difficult the parental situation, the young person's family situation is a factor in all juveniles' community supervision. The parental function is seen as the most significant ally to the work of the correctional authorities when it is strong, or, when it is weak, the most crucial problem to be solved. Sibling activity is also important, when there is an older youth who might be a negative influence, or when there is a younger child whose social development is put at risk by the delinquent's influence. Whatever the complexities of the juvenile offender's family life—and there are as many stories as there are families—addressing them takes center stage in juvenile community corrections.

Juveniles Are Easily Influenced by Their Peers

Very few juvenile offenders commit crimes alone. With isolated exceptions, juvenile crime is a group phenomenon. Young people, in groups, gather to socialize, and a common part of the social behavior involves testing boundaries and challenging each other to try new things. We often associate with "gangs" the criminal behavior that may arise from young groups' social activity, but all studies of young people in groups find that group criminality can arise even when what we think of as "gangs" are not involved. Young people are learning how to be social, and confronting the rules of adult conduct is a part of that learning.

This social aspect of youth criminality is a reflection of the fact that peer relationships are the most important influences on normal youth during their preadolescent and teenage years. When we are in those volatile years, what our friends think of us is very important—it will often become more important than the opinions of our parents or other adults. When the pressures of youth group social behavior include some delinquent acts, it is not easy (or common) for youth to be able to effectively resist the pressure.

Thus, some crime is a more or less normal part of youth group social life. Perhaps this is one of the reasons that youth have such high rates of desistance—being caught engaging in group delinquency may be all the reason that most youth need to resist the pressure in the future. But we must also recognize that much of this adolescent delinquency is not what we think of as serious, interpersonal crime. Though serious consequences can arise from adolescent drinking and fighting, we do not think of these events with the same concern that we have for selling drugs, carrying weapons, or stealing others' property. We are inclined to think of the former as "normal growing up" and the latter as serious trouble.

The problem is that delinquents can drift from the everyday rule breaking of truancy, fighting, and drinking into far more serious crime. This can happen especially when the group behavior gets escalated by continuing pressure for ever greater risk taking. While we might all remember instances of violating curfews, drinking alcohol, and other group delinquency that seemed merely "fun," many of the most serious forms of delinquency begin with just this sort of misbehavior. And while we should not equate the everyday delinquent acts that often go along with adolescence with serious crimes that make a person a candidate for incarceration, we should recognize that studies consistently find very high rates of self-reported serious delinquency among samples of older teenagers. For all juvenile misbehavior, from the trivial to the serious, the group seems to be a ubiquitous influence.

From the standpoint of community supervision, the question is how to incorporate the reality of juveniles' peer-focus into supervision strategies. Correctional professionals know that it is unrealistic to think that a juvenile might sever ties to important peers entirely—though in extreme cases, these peers are so problematic that just such a requirement is established by the court. These court-ordered breaks between delinquents and these peers are difficult to enforce, and they have limited prospects for success unless the juvenile under supervision wants to avoid the peer influences, too. The more common approach is to make an assessment of the strengths and weaknesses of various peer relations for a juvenile under supervision, then try to strengthen the positive peer contacts while reducing the negative. This can involve concentrated use of recreational programs, which place peers in contact with each other under adult supervision, and may involve other structured peer experiences such as camps and adult-supervised outdoor activities.

The key to the problem of peer relations lies in recognizing that strong peer associations are going to exist for normal preadolescents and teenagers under any circumstances. What correctional workers try to do is to shape those peer relations, replacing the negative with the positive. The objective, then, is not to eliminate peer associations, but to use them to improve the juvenile's adjustment. Replacing delinquent peer relations with new peers who reinforce decisions not to break the law contains the potential for a double benefit.

Juveniles Have Little Responsibility for Anyone Other Than Themselves

A final difference between juvenile offenders and their adult counterparts is that the plans for supervising the latter must take into account the formal responsibilities of an adult, including employment, spousal relationships, offspring, and so forth. For an adult, a fully successful adjustment to the community involves taking on these roles productively. Juveniles, by contrast, will eventually be expected to take on these roles—and much of the supervision strategy may be devoted to preparing the young person for adult life including these roles—but there need not be as immediate a concern for these aspects of the juvenile's adjustment.

Responsibility, for a juvenile, will typically require considerations in other arenas: school performance and behavior, compliance with a curfew, and developing interpersonal skills, for example. A key difference between these juvenile roles and adult roles is that the juvenile typically has no formal responsibility for anyone else's well-being. The juvenile's community supervision plan, thus, can take the appearance of a self-absorbed schedule. The supervision plan may include specified recreational activities after school, leisure time with a "big brother" or "big sister," tutoring support for academic progress, rewards for achieving improved grades in school, and so on. The supervision plan is about the juvenile's progress toward mature adulthood.

Under normal circumstances, community supervision may be concerned about the effect of various adults on the juvenile's behavior and adjustment, but it will not need to pay as much attention to the effect of the juvenile on others. In this sense, community supervision of juvenile offenders is a more uncomplicated matter than for adults.

There are two obvious exceptions to the offender focus of juvenile supervision. Many juveniles will be required to pay restitution to the victim of the crime. This will mean getting a job to earn the repayment, and structuring the repayment so that the requirement can be met in a reasonable time. The other exception has to do with juveniles who themselves have children. When very young offenders are parents, the child's daily care often falls on adults connected to the juvenile—parents or grandparents, aunts or uncles. The community supervision plan will often provide for rudimentary support by the juvenile to his or her child, in preparation for assuming a larger responsibility for child care in later adulthood.

THE PROBLEM OF YOUTH CRIME

It disturbs us to think of a child as "dangerous" or "sinister," but we are forced by daily news to consider the unpleasant truth that some young people commit serious crimes. Each year, about 1,400 youths under the age of 18 are arrested for homicide, 5,000 for forcible rape, and a troubling 69,600 for aggravated assault.[1]

Many of these cases become local or national news stories. Particularly troubling were the nine highly publicized stories that occurred between February 1997 and April 1999 in which teenagers shot and killed their teachers and fellow students. The events in Alaska, Arkansas, California, Colorado, Kentucky, Mississippi, Oregon, Pennsylvania, and Tennessee were lead stories in the news for weeks. The horrific conduct, and the way it forced itself onto the public agenda, led to fundamental reform of juvenile justice.[2] Predictable calls came for "getting tough" with serious offenders, as well as demands for actions to strengthen families, control guns, and reduce youth alienation.

But in fact, the juvenile crime incidents just described are rare. In a nation with 75 million people 18 years of age or younger, there were 2.5 million arrests of juveniles in 1999, only 104,000 of which (about 4 percent) were for violent crimes.[3] After rising from 1988 to 1994, the juvenile violent crime rate has dropped 36 percent since 1994 to the lowest level since 1988.[4] Yet when Americans are asked to identify the two or three most serious problems facing children, they cite drugs and crime. Why is juvenile crime such a major concern despite the fact that juvenile crime is actually declining?

We are particularly unsettled by juvenile crime for reasons beyond the numbers. Young people represent our future. We expect them to be busy growing up, learning how to become productive citizens and developing skills for a satisfying life. We do not expect them to be committing crimes that damage the quality of community life. And because they are starting criminal behavior at such a young age, we worry about the future—how long before a young person's criminal career fades? How much damage will be left in its wake? And finally, what should we do with juveniles who commit such heinous crimes?

JUVENILES WHO DO NOT FIT THE USUAL PATTERN OF JUVENILE BEHAVIOR

Because of the differences between juveniles and adults, and the circumstances that flow from them, it is thought reasonable to have a separate correctional process for juvenile offenders. Yet we must understand that although these characteristics are true in general about juvenile offenders, there are many exceptions; and for every juvenile, some of these factors are more accurate than others. What does it mean when a given juvenile's circumstances do not fit these general observations?

The juvenile justice system is predicated upon what we might call "normal" juvenile delinquency. It may seem like a contradiction in terms—"normal" delinquency—but the words call attention to the fact that delinquent behavior is not uncommon in teenage years, and certainly for young males in difficult living situations, delinquency will be an expected aspect of adolescence.

There is no textbook rule about what is "normal"; rather, it is a feeling we have about what kind of misbehavior is often associated with growing up. Because some level of delinquency is, in this sense, normal, we might think it is reasonable to react to it with less alarm than we might feel in response to similar misbehavior by adults. Our reasoning is that juveniles require not a punitive correctional response, but a developmental one, because their behavior is a part of a common developmental pattern.

We would be naive to think that the juvenile justice paradigm applies equally to every juvenile who breaks the law. In our discussion above, we saw that for each of the differences between adults and juveniles we enumerated, there were well-known cases where the distinction did not apply. Some juveniles are already hardened in their ways and are unlikely to change; some will continue their criminality well into adulthood; some lack meaningful families who can help with supervision; some are loners, unaffected by peer influences; and some are already acting in adult roles, with jobs, spouses, and children to support.

What should we do when a youthful offender does not act as we would expect a juvenile to act? One of the most important considerations appears to be the age of the juvenile and whether the behavior is age-appropriate. There are big differences in what we find "normal" between the ages of, say, fourteen and seventeen, even though in terms of time alone this is less than three years. A fourteen-year-old boy might sometimes be angry and engage in hostile and irrational behavior and be thought only "troubled," but the same behavior by a seventeen-year-old will be seen as immature. In the same way, when a very young juvenile—for example, a preteen—engages in an extremely violent act, we are alarmed by the very antisocialness of a young person who should be undergoing socialization. It is clear that our criteria for "normalcy" in delinquency is the degree to which the misbehavior seems to fit the juvenile's age and the developmental issues that normally go along with that age.

Likewise, we expect misbehavior to be social. It does not surprise us or unduly alarm us to learn that so much of delinquency occurs in adolescent groups, where youngsters who are learning how to be socially connected to one another will occasionally resort to delinquency as a means of becoming socially accepted by their group. Gangs are, of course, an extreme example of this phenomenon, but even them we can understand—though we have trouble with impersonal gang violence and broad-scale gang criminality. When a juvenile who gets into trouble is without these social connections, we see this as abnormal. The lone child who commits crime for personal pleasure rather than social acceptance is comparatively rare, and we have trouble understanding this as "normal" in a young person's development.

We also find it hard to understand when a child or near-child engages in what seems to be gratuitous violence. Some children will engage in petty property offenses, stealing things they want or vandalizing places they resent. A few will get into fights. But when we encounter children who kill each other or plot to hurt someone, we are deeply unsettled. The label "delinquent" seems far too weak to characterize this kind of person and these kinds of crimes.

The existence of unusual juvenile criminality has been one of the reasons some observers question the wisdom of having a separate juvenile justice system. They say we ought to treat all criminal acts with the seriousness they deserve, regardless of the perpetrator's age. To the extent the person's age contributed to the gravity of the act, it could be taken as an aggravating or mitigating factor in sentencing. And certainly, age would also be a consideration in the design and management of correctional programs. Offenders could be assigned to programs based partly on classifications as to age and maturity level. But critics of juvenile justice argue that we should do away with the separate system of justice, because there are so many exceptions to the stereotypes on which the juvenile justice system is based.

Under current practice, in the most extreme exceptions when juveniles commit serious crimes, they are transferred from juvenile to adult court. The main mechanism for transferring juvenile offenders to adult court jurisdiction is called a **waiver** (sometimes called certification). There are at least four types of waivers: judicial, legislative, prosecutorial, and demand.[5]

In the judicial waiver, the transfer to adult criminal court comes as a result of the decision of a judge. This is the most common kind of waiver, and because it comes from the discretion of the judge, it is sometimes called a discretionary waiver. In the legislative waiver, the juvenile is automatically transferred to adult court jurisdiction because the legislature has predetermined that some crimes and age groups are to be tried in adult courts. Prosecutorial waiver takes place after the offender is referred into juvenile court, when the prosecutor conducts interviews and feels the case is serious enough to warrant adult court jurisdiction. In the demand waiver, the juvenile actually initiates the transfer to adult court. This would be beneficial when the juvenile wants a jury trial—a privilege that is not granted in many juvenile courts.

Forty-nine states have the discretion to transfer juveniles to adult courts, but the procedures to invoke waiver vary greatly. In the state of Vermont, the age for transferring a juvenile to adult court is as low as ten. In most states, the age of transfer is fourteen. Figure 12.1 explains the youngest age for which juveniles may be transferred to adult court. Most studies of waiver seem to find that the rate of waiver is very small, with estimates around 1 percent of all formally handled juvenile court cases nationally.[6]

It appears the number of juveniles being transferred to adult courts is increasing. With the rise in juvenile violent crime in the late 1980s and early 1990s, many jurisdictions looked to change their transfer procedures. Between 1992 and 1995, forty states and the District of Columbia changed their procedures to make it easier to transfer a juvenile case to adult court. Some states lowered the age of responsibility for certain crimes, and others mandated transfer for juvenile offenders with criminal histories.[7]

However, the very low *rate* of waivers suggests that abolition of the juvenile justice system might not change things as much as we would expect. If proponents of abolition are correct in saying that the offender's age would still be taken into consideration in the handling of a case, then very low rates of waiver indicate that for the most part, we would want to treat juveniles as requiring special handling due to their tender age. The vast majority who now go into programs designed to take account of juveniles' age and family circumstances—the differences we described above—would still require such programs. The small minority who are now waived to adult court would,

FIGURE 12.1 THE YOUNGEST AGE AT WHICH JUVENILES MAY BE TRANSFERRED TO ADULT CRIMINAL COURT

Source: U.S. Department of Justice, Office of Juvenile Justice and Delinquency Prevention, *Trying Juveniles as Adults in Criminal Court* (Washington, DC: Government Printing Office, 1998), pp. 14–15.

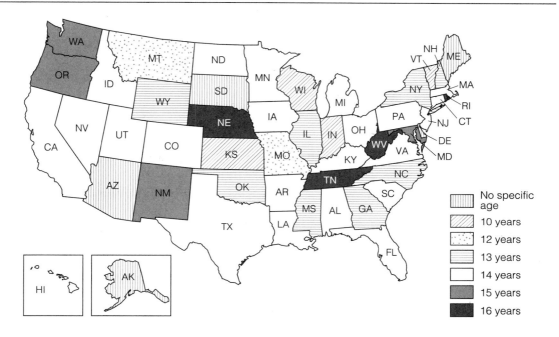

without juvenile justice, be treated as adults anyway. As a consequence, perhaps little would change.

Although there are many proposals for reform of juvenile justice, there is, to date, no nationwide movement to abolish the juvenile court that seems strong enough to prevail in any of the states. Thus, in discussing juvenile offenders in the community, we are left with today's most common approaches in community corrections for juveniles. We turn to a description and analysis of these programs in the sections below. But before describing the different kinds of community corrections programs for juveniles, we will briefly discuss the historical context of juvenile court and juvenile community corrections.

THE DEVELOPMENT OF THE JUVENILE COURT

Until the early nineteenth century, juveniles over the age of seven who committed crime were treated as adults if the state could show they knew the difference between right and wrong. Because of this, children were often treated very brutally for acts of mischief. They were sent to workhouses, confined with adults, and subjected to harassment or sexual exploitation by other prisoners.

But this kind of treatment for juveniles was to change after 1838 and the court case *Ex parte Crouse.* In the case, a father objected to his daughter's commitment to the Philadelphia House of Refuge. But the Supreme Court of the Commonwealth of Pennsylvania approved the commitment based on the doctrine of **parens patriae.** This doctrine, literally translated as "the state as the father," is interpreted to mean that the state can act in the child's best interest by taking over the role of parent if the parents are unable or unwilling to provide the proper treatment for the child at home. Because of this doctrine, a child can be removed from the home and placed in an alternative setting, not for punishment but for his or her personal betterment.

Parens patriae was later to be used as the foundation for the development of the first juvenile court in Cook County (Chicago), Illinois, in 1899. Established by the Illinois legislature and guided by the leadership of Judge Julian Mack (1866–1943), the court dealt with neglected and abused children, runaways, school dropouts, and juveniles who had committed crimes. Juveniles were seen not as criminals but as wards of the state. By 1925, all but two states had adopted this model, and by 1945, every state had a complete juvenile code.

Under the guise of parens patriae, young persons are not considered criminals but are called juvenile delinquents. Additional differences in terminology have been introduced over the years to separate the behavior of juveniles from that of adults. (See the box "Adult Justice Versus Juvenile Justice Terminology.")

Juveniles are not "found guilty"; they are "adjudicated." After a youth has been adjudicated, the judge does not impose a sentence; rather, a "disposition"

ADULT JUSTICE VERSUS JUVENILE JUSTICE TERMINOLOGY

Arrested	Detained (police contact)
Criminal	Delinquent
Crime	Delinquent act
Charged	Held
Indictment	Petition
Trial	Adjudication hearing
Beyond a reasonable doubt	Preponderance of the evidence
Convicted	Adjudicated (as responsible)
Sentence	Disposition
Incarcerated	Committed or Placed
Prison	Training school
Parole	Aftercare

is made. The report the judge uses to make a disposition is called a "social history." These differences in terms reflect the important conceptual difference on which the juvenile court is founded—that being parens patriae. Juveniles, by virtue of their young age, are thought not capable of being guilty in the same way as adults, for they lack the capacity to form the criminal intent (*mens rea*) on which adult criminal responsibility relies. Because they will not be found guilty, they will not be punished. But if they are found to have engaged in the alleged wrongdoing—adjudicated as responsible for the act—it will be assumed that the misconduct reflects problems in the juvenile's situation that need to be addressed. The disposition (in adult jargon, the sentence) is the court's order about the ways those problems will be addressed.

In addition to being able to be charged with criminal offenses and being labeled a "delinquent," juveniles can also be charged with being a **status offender.** A status offense is when a young person is subject to state authority because of conduct that is illegal only because the child is under a certain age. Examples of status offenses are running away, disobeying parents, truancy, and curfew violations. Until the 1970s, juvenile courts treated status offenders like juvenile delinquent cases. But that formally changed in 1974 when the Federal Juvenile Justice and Delinquency Prevention Act (JJDP Act) legislated that status offenders need to be handled differently than delinquents. More specifically, the JJDP Act mandated that, with certain exceptions, status offenders should be deinstitutionalized and required that they be removed from secure confinement facilities. Since then, the attitude has shifted to viewing status offenders as less dangerous and having different needs than serious juvenile delinquents. This has led some jurisdictions to develop special categories of young offenders called **CHINS** (children in need of supervision). Other jurisdictions have developed similar acronyms to describe juveniles, such as PINS, MINS, and JINS. These terms reflect persons, minors, or juveniles in need of supervision.

Over the past thirty years, there have been two developments that have weakened the ideas of parens patriae. First, in the 1970s a number of due process challenges brought before the courts led to more legal protections for juveniles. Because of these legal protections, juveniles are no longer viewed as having limited legal rights in the name of doing what was "best" for their development. Two cases that illustrate that emphasis toward due process for juveniles are *Kent* v. *United States* and *In re Gault.*

In 1966, the U.S. Supreme Court ruled in *Kent* v. *United States*[8] that when juveniles are to be waived to adult court, they are entitled to a waiver hearing, a statement of reasons for the waiver, and assistance of counsel. Prior to this case, juvenile court judges had considerable discretion when deciding whether to transfer cases to adult court. In the case *In re Gault,*[9] the Supreme Court ruled that juveniles are entitled to certain due process rights—specifically, notice of charges, right to remain silent, and right to counsel in proceedings that may lead to commitment to an institution. Further, the decision to send a juvenile to a state institution cannot be made without sworn testimony subject to cross-examination. In short, the key elements of the Fifth and Sixth Amendments to the U.S. Constitution were applicable to the juvenile justice system. See the box "Major Decisions by the U.S. Supreme Court" for a series of decisions by the U.S. Supreme Court extending due process rights to juveniles.

The second development that has apparently weakened parens patriae has occurred since 1980. During the 1980s and into the 1990s, the push to get more "tough" on crime and criminals has also permeated to juvenile offenders. Laws that lower the age of criminal responsibility, increase the punitive nature of sentences, and reduce rehabilitation programs reflect the shift from the idea that juveniles are not as responsible for their indiscretions because they are immature or mistreated. Individual responsibility and strict punishment is the current trend.

Today, juvenile courts and juvenile correctional systems that operate under a legal code separate from adults are present in all fifty states. The **age of**

MAJOR DECISIONS BY THE U.S. SUPREME COURT REGARDING THE RIGHTS OF JUVENILES

Since the mid-1960s, the Supreme Court has gradually expanded the rights of juveniles but has continued to recognize that the logic of a separate system for juvenile offenders justifies differences from some adult rights.

Kent v. *United States* (1966) Requires "essentials of due process" for juvenile offenders.

In re Gault (1967) Specifies the "essentials" of due process required by notice, hearing, counsel, and cross-examination.

In re Winship (1970) Requires a standard of "beyond a doubt" for delinquency matters.

McKeiver v. *Pennsylvania* (1971) Holds that jury trials are not required for juvenile court hearings.

Breed v. *Jones* (1975) Waiver to adult court following adjudication in juvenile court violates the constitutional guarantee against double jeopardy.

Smith v. *Daily Mail Publishing Co.* (1979) The press may report certain aspects of juvenile court cases and matters.

Eddings v. *Oklahoma* (1982) The age of a defendant must be considered as a mitigating factor in capital crimes.

Schall v. *Martin* (1984) Preventive pretrial detention is allowed for juvenile defendants who are found "dangerous."

Stanford v. *Kentucky* (1989) Set minimum age for capital punishment at sixteen.

TABLE 12.1 THE UPPER AGE OF JUVENILE COURT JURISDICTION IN DELINQUENCY MATTERS AS DEFINED BY STATE STATUTE

Oldest age for original juvenile court jurisdiction in delinquency matters				
15	**16**	**17**		
Connecticut	Georgia	Alabama	Kentucky	Oklahoma
New York	Illinois	Alaska	Maine	Oregon
North Carolina	Louisiana	Arizona	Maryland	Pennsylvania
	Massachusetts	Arkansas	Minnesota	Rhode Island
	Michigan	California	Mississippi	South Dakota
	Missouri	Colorado	Montana	Tennessee
	South Carolina	Delaware	Nebraska	Utah
	Texas	District of Columbia	Nevada	Vermont*
		Florida	New Hampshire	Virginia
		Hawaii	New Jersey	Washington
		Idaho	New Mexico	West Virginia
		Indiana	North Dakota	Wisconsin
		Iowa	Ohio	Wyoming
		Kansas		

- Many states have higher upper ages of juvenile court jurisdiction in status offense, abuse, neglect, or dependency matters—often through age 20.
- In many states the juvenile court has jurisdiction over young adults who committed offenses while juveniles.
- Several states also have minimum ages of juvenile court jurisdiction in delinquency matters—ranging from 6 to 12.
- Many states exclude married or otherwise emancipated juveniles from juvenile court jurisdiction.

*In Vermont the juvenile and criminal courts have concurrent jurisdiction over all 16- and 17-year-olds.

Source: L. Szymanski, *Upper Age of Juvenile Court Jurisdiction Statutes Analyses* (1994 update) (Pittsburgh, PA: National Center for Juvenile Justice, 1995).

(majority) responsibility, which is the age at which the juvenile code ceases to apply and the offender is subject to the adult criminal code, differs among the states, from a low of fifteen years old in three states to a high of seventeen years old in twenty-six states.[10] (See Table 12.1.) The administrative authority for juvenile corrections takes two forms. In a majority of states, there is a separate juvenile justice authority that handles correctional matters. In others, the correctional function of juvenile justice is operated as a division of the same agency that handles adult corrections.

Even though the reforms of recent decades have changed the procedures and to a lesser extent the practices of the juvenile justice system, in many respects the underlying philosophy of the juvenile court remains very much as these original reformers intended. Juveniles receive a different version of treatment by their justice system, one that places less emphasis on punishment and more emphasis on individualized treatment. The rationale for this difference was described above in the ways that juveniles differ from adults, ways that ought to be considered in the way the law works.

JUVENILE COMMUNITY CORRECTIONS

Although juvenile community corrections is generally perceived to have developed with the foundation of juvenile court in Illinois in 1899, the fact is, dealing with juveniles in the community began much earlier in the nineteenth century. In England, as early as 1820, legal guardians were appointed to children who were without proper supervision. During the years 1866 through 1871, an unofficial probation officer called a "beadle" was employed in London to supervise juveniles.[11]

In the United States, the first form of community corrections for juveniles was also probation, and it was developed in Massachusetts in 1869 when an act was passed by the state legislature allowing a board of charities to find homes for troubled youths and to visit them periodically. These services grew, and by 1890 became a regular part of the state court system.[12]

Much of our discussion of corrections in the community in earlier chapters applies to juvenile community corrections. Yet there are some themes specific to juvenile corrections that apply across jurisdictions. In the discussion below, we develop some of those themes.

Juvenile Probation

In more than half (53 percent) of cases, the juvenile delinquent is placed on probation and released to the custody of a parent or guardian. Often the judge orders the delinquent to undergo some form of education or counseling. The delinquent can also be required to pay a fine or make restitution while on probation.

Juvenile probation is similar to adult probation in that the offender, in this case a juvenile, is placed under the supervision of an officer of the court. If that offender wishes to remain living in the community, he or she must abide by certain rules and conditions. Juvenile probation is also a disposition by the court that is less punitive than incarceration and emphasizes treatment and rehabilitation of the juvenile. How juvenile probation is administered varies considerably across the United States. In most states and the District of Columbia, juvenile probation is administered by the local judicial system, usually the county court. In other states, a variety of administrative methods are used, such as state/judicial, state/executive, and combinations thereof (see Table 12.2). There are on average some 500,000 juveniles on probation at any one time.[13]

There are also different types of juvenile probation supervision. With **informal juvenile probation,** the juvenile will receive supervision by an officer of the court and is required to follow certain rules. But with informal probation, the court has not made a formal determination that the child is under its jurisdiction, nor has the child been formally adjudicated as a delinquent or

TABLE 12.2 JUVENILE PROBATION SUPERVISION IN THE
UNITED STATES

State Administration		Local Administration	
Judicial Branch	**Executive Branch**	**Judicial Branch**	**Executive Branch**
Connecticut	Alaska	Alabama	**California**
Hawaii	**Arkansas**	Arizona	**Idaho**
Iowa	Delaware	**Arkansas**	**Minnesota**
Kentucky	Florida	**California**	**Mississippi**
Nebraska	**Georgia**	Colorado	New York
North Carolina	**Idaho**	District of Columbia	Oregon
North Dakota	**Kentucky**	**Georgia**	**Washington**
South Dakota	**Louisiana**	Illinois	**Wisconsin**
Utah	Maine	Indiana	
West Virginia	Maryland	Kansas	
	Minnesota	**Kentucky**	
	Mississippi	Louisiana	
	New Hampshire	Massachusetts	
	New Mexico	Michigan	
	North Dakota	**Minnesota**	
	Oklahoma	Missouri	
	Rhode Island	Montana	
	South Carolina	Nevada	
	Tennessee	New Jersey	
	Vermont	Ohio	
	Virginia	**Oklahoma**	
	West Virginia	Pennsylvania	
	Wyoming	**Tennessee**	
		Texas	
		Virginia	
		Washington	
		Wisconsin	
		Wyoming	

Note: States in **boldface** indicate that probation is provided by a combination of agencies. Often larger, urban counties operate local probation departments, while the state administers probation in smaller counties.

Source: H. Hurst and P. Torbet, *Organization and Administration of Juvenile Services: Probation, Aftercare, and State Institutions for Delinquent Youth* (Washington, DC: Government Printing Office, 1993).

status offender. Informal probation is voluntary, and both parties know ahead of time that future adjudication is possible if the informal status is unsuccessful. In **formal juvenile probation,** the youth has been adjudicated to be a delinquent or a status offender and will be subject to rules of probation supervision similar to those of adult probation.

From a distance, juvenile probation appears not very different from adult probation: Professional probation officers carry caseloads of juveniles on probation, they see these probationers in their offices and in "the field" (at school or in the home), and they monitor the juvenile's adjustment to the community and compliance with the orders of the court. Referrals may be made to local community services, and regular progress reports are made to the court.

The differences between adult and juvenile probation are subtle, and they stem from the differences between adult and juvenile offenders described in the first section of this chapter. Juvenile probation officers will often try to develop personal relationships with their clients, something that is discouraged for adult probation officers. To achieve this bond, juvenile probation officers will often engage in recreational activities with their clients, or they will accompany them to social activities. It is through this bond that juvenile probation officers seek the youngster's trust, which they hope will form the basis for long-lasting change in the offender's behavior. Sometimes, juvenile probation officers will mix the child on probation with other young people who are not under court supervision, with the aim of furthering the youth's reintegration into more socially acceptable peer relationships.

In carrying out supervision of the juvenile probationer, the probation officer will need to work closely with social service agencies in the community that have an involvement in the life of the juvenile and the family. Probation officers will spend time in the schools, talk to teachers and guidance counselors, and learn about school programs for troubled youth. This will especially include recreational programs and youth counseling programs.

Probation officers will also be in close contact with family service agencies, welfare providers, and programs that support young mothers and provide substitutes for missing fathers. In some respects, the probation officer will serve the role of linchpin for the array of services available in a community that might be used to help a young person stay out of trouble. In this way, the probation officer is viewed as a resource manager who has as his or her primary responsibility to help identify probationers' needs and connect them with available services.

Although the ideals of rehabilitation and reintegration are important in all community supervision, they receive special emphasis among juvenile probation workers. It is important to recognize, however, that juvenile probation is changing. A sense of unease about how juvenile probation handles serious offending among youth has led to a new interest in the techniques and practices of adult supervision: surveillance and control.

Privatized Juvenile Probation

In recent years, there has been a movement in juvenile probation to allow private companies and institutions to provide services to youthful offenders. The impetus behind privatization is that many juvenile probation programs are unable to afford and provide services for the large number of juveniles under their care. With privatization, outside companies and institutions are contracted to provide various services to different groups of juveniles. The types of programs that have been developed include intensive probation supervision, supervision of status offenders, and even weekend adventure programs. Privatization can provide more diverse types of programs for juveniles at a much lower cost than can public probation systems. However, questions relative to effectiveness and ethics may cause some concern. Will a private company in charge of supervising juveniles, with the bottom line being cost-benefit concerns, provide the same quality of care as those who have been publicly entrusted to pursue this task? Should the government delegate the duty of social control of juveniles to private companies? How does this idea fulfill the ideals of parens patriae? These questions are unanswered because the issue of privatization of probation for juveniles has not been carefully studied. These issues will surely become more of a concern as more jurisdictions turn to privatization of juvenile probation services.

Because of the difference in legal philosophy, terminology, and supervision, juvenile probation caseloads are seldom combined with adult probation. The adult probation system places an emphasis on surveillance and law enforcement that is often downplayed by juvenile probation policies. Supervision policies are more formalized with adult offenders, with a specified number of office reports, drug tests, and other measures of control. Even though juvenile probation shows the first glimmer of these structured approaches, it still remains a less routinized form of correctional supervision, with much room for creativity and individuality in the probation officer's approach to the job.

Juvenile Aftercare

Throughout the United States, juveniles who are released from correctional institutions receive some form of aftercare that is administered by state, local or private agencies.[14] The term **aftercare** refers to the services provided to juveniles after they have been *placed*—removed from their home and put under some form of custodial care. Aftercare operates in a way similar to adult parole. It receives juveniles who have been under some form of custody—typically the state's training school, but sometimes a foster home or residential placement—and provides supervision and support during the period of readjustment to community life. The importance of aftercare rests on the fact that youth face significant obstacles of adjustment after they have been away from their homes, and the chances of failure for such youth are quite high.

Most aftercare services are provided by agencies that are independent of adult correctional functions and distinct from the other juvenile correctional services. When this is true, the aftercare agency is usually quite small in terms of staffing and is responsible for a small number of clients compared to other social services. The smallness of the aftercare function has enabled some aftercare systems to escape the close scrutiny that other correctional agencies receive routinely. At the same time, concerns about the inefficiency of such a small, but statewide, agency lead to periodic attempts to restructure aftercare services by placing them under more efficient, large, social service agencies. In several states, juvenile aftercare has been folded into juvenile probation to save money.

Aftercare caseloads are typically (though not always) much smaller than adult parole caseloads, and are even smaller than juvenile probation caseloads. This general pattern derives both from the comparatively small number of aftercare clients in a given state and from a recognition of the difficulties faced by juveniles just after they are released from a residential placement, training school, or reformatory. The most difficult time period—and that of greatest recidivism risk—is the period immediately following a juvenile's release to the community. Caseloads are kept low in order to enable a concentrated effort on behalf of these youth.

Aftercare workers know that youth who have been returned from confinement face significant adjustment problems and require substantial attention and support. First of all, a youth who has been placed in a custodial setting by the court has either engaged in some form of serious criminal behavior or has exhibited a pattern of persistent disobedience of less serious laws and of court-ordered rules of behavior. In either case, there is a potential for trouble. The serious offender will have committed a frightening crime and will face a fearful community, a family that may not welcome the return, and a school system that doubts the juvenile's readiness to behave. The persistent delinquent will have been the source of trouble to family, neighbors, school officials, and others, and will not be received with open arms. It is up to the aftercare worker to negotiate the young person's return to the community by helping the juvenile understand the community's apprehensions, while showing the community evidence that the juvenile deserves a second chance.

The aftercare worker also must closely follow the juvenile's adjustment, even while advocating for the juvenile. The risk of recidivism is sufficiently high that the community has a stake in the effectiveness of aftercare scrutiny. There is a recognition by all involved in the aftercare system that a careful balance is needed between support and control, for these juveniles include the most serious cases in the juvenile justice system. By the same token, much is to be gained. When an aftercare worker is able to successfully negotiate a juvenile through the first months of return to the community, it can mean that a lifetime of crime will be avoided.

There has recently been some promising news about the effectiveness of aftercare programs for juveniles. In Pennsylvania, an evaluation of an intensive supervision aftercare program for serious juvenile offenders was shown to reduce rearrests compared to putting offenders on probation.[15] A similar program for minor offenders in North Carolina was shown to reduce future offending.[16] Because of the success of aftercare programs, and the realization that institutionalization does not accomplish reductions in recidivism, the number of aftercare programs has increased in recent years

Intermediate Sanctions for Juveniles

Some would say the complaint that few sanctioning options exist between traditional probation and custodial dispositions is as true in juvenile justice as it is in adult criminal justice. The pressure for the development of effective intermediate sanctions in juvenile justice has been somewhat later to arrive than its adult counterpart, but it is now a very strong trend.

One of the reasons for the slowness of development of intermediate sanctions in juvenile corrections is that some of what intermediate sanctions offer resembles the traditional forms of juvenile corrections. Adult probation is interested in intensive probation supervision as an intermediate sanction, but adult IPS caseloads are often of about the same size as many traditional juvenile caseloads—numbering in the twenties or thirties. The adult system is developing electronically monitored home detention, but the juvenile system has made routine use of curfews that restrict a youth to the home except during school hours. Community service and restitution have been standard aspects of juvenile court dispositions for many years. It has seemed to some that the intermediate sanctions movement in adult corrections has had little to distinguish it from business as usual in juvenile corrections.

It is true that the extremes of juvenile corrections were never as far apart as the extremes of adult corrections. Juvenile probation has never reached the level of bureaucratic paper-shuffling that is represented by some versions of adult probation. Certainly, the time limit on custodial placements—that they not exceed the youth's attainment of the age of majority—makes juvenile institutional dispositions less extreme than many adult prison terms. But even with these caveats, the logic of intermediate sanctions applies well to juvenile correctional policy.

The advent of intermediate sanctions in juvenile justice has meant that judges have wider choices in making dispositions. When a juvenile persistently disobeys court rules but is not engaged in serious crime, punitive options are now available that are not as extreme as the training school, which results in time away from the regular school system and puts the youth at risk of developing hardened attitudes through exposure to committed delinquents in those facilities. Moving away from simple community supervision, and toward intermediate sanctions, juvenile corrections systems have developed work-based community service programs, restitution centers where young people work to pay back the victim, and after-school assignments that keep the youth's free time to a minimum. Under intermediate sanctioning approaches, juveniles will be required to complete training programs on awareness of the impact of crimes on victims, and they will be sent to summer camps that require community service labor cleaning parks and other public

INTERVENTION MODEL FOR JUVENILE INTENSIVE AFTERCARE

Source: David M. Altschuler and Troy L. Armstrong, *Intensive Aftercare for High-Risk Juveniles: Policies and Procedures* (Washington, DC: Office of Juvenile Justice and Delinquency Prevention, 1994), p. 3.

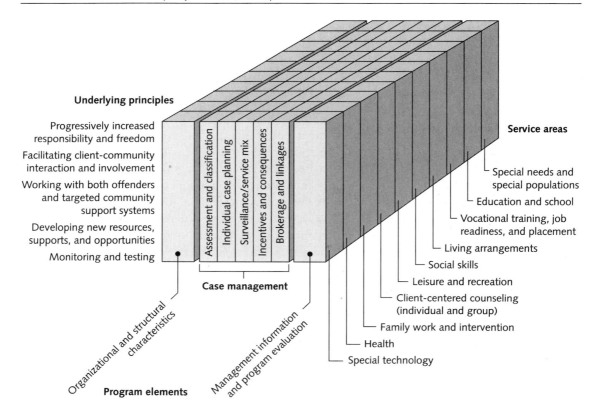

AN AFTERCARE PROGRAM

The Intensive Aftercare Program (IAP) model has been developed to integrate different criminological theories for guiding intensive supervision of chronic juvenile offenders. This model focuses on reintegrating the offender into the community while applying social control theory, strain theory, and social learning theories. The figure above depicts the program elements of IAP.

places. The intermediate sanctions movement in juvenile corrections may take different forms than the adult counterpart, but the objectives are very similar: Provide a dispositional option more stringent than regular probation but less onerous than custody, provide a better chance for the offender to change his or her behavior, and provide a less costly, more reasonable sanction that fits misbehavior of intermediate seriousness.

JUVENILE COMMUNITY CORRECTIONS ACTS

As we indicated in Chapter 4, the first community corrections act in the United States, the Probation Subsidy Act, was passed in California and also applied to juvenile offenders. The act was designed to encourage counties in California to retain their juveniles at home instead of sending them to the state training institution. As an incentive for keeping the offenders at home, the act provided for a fee of $4,000 to be given to the counties for each juvenile offender retained within the county. At one point, over forty-seven counties were receiving over $22 million dollars to develop community programs.[17]

However, as described in Chapter 4, an evaluation of the Probation Subsidy Act turned up results that were not considered wholly positive by its advocates. On the one hand, the financial incentives worked. Juvenile offenders who had been previously sent to the state's training school—at substantial expense to the state—were retained locally at reduced cost. But studies showed they did not necessarily get better treatment locally. Many were retained in local custodial facilities that did not provide the kinds of rehabilitation programs available in the state training school. Those who misbehaved under community supervision were immediately sent to state facilities, negating any savings. On average, the juveniles were under closer control and had more severe intrusions into their lives after the law was passed than before.

More recently, community corrections acts have been passed in a number of states and many have included provisions for juveniles. The state of Minnesota has become a model for many juvenile community corrections acts. The state provides a subsidy to any county or group of counties that develops its own community corrections programs. If a youth in Minnesota is adjudicated to be delinquent and requires institutional (training school) care by the state, the cost is subtracted from the subsidy. The result of the act has been a reluctance by individual counties to send youth to training school and the concommitant establishment of a wide variety of residential or day treatment programs.

Another example is a program in Ohio, gaining national acclaim, that seeks to return funds to communities that retain juvenile offenders rather than send them to state-run schools. RECLAIM Ohio—Reasoned and Equitable Community and Local Alternatives—provides a significant payback to county leaders who can show that juveniles who might have been sent to training schools

JUVENILE JUSTICE IN NEW ZEALAND

In New Zealand, the juvenile justice system is concerned with the well-being of the youth, as well as encouraging the family and victim to be involved in the process. In this way, the New Zealand system is based on the restorative justice approach, which tries to restore the offender, victim, and community after a crime has been committed. (Restorative justice is discussed in more detail in Chapters 2 and 9.) One way this approach is implemented in New Zealand is through the development of a unique process called Family Group Conferencing (FGC). Family Group Conferencing is used for all types of crimes committed by juveniles (under seventeen years of age) in New Zealand. In less serious matters in which formal juvenile justice system intervention may not be necessary, a police youth justice coordinator, the victim, the juvenile, and his or her family get together and develop a plan to handle the matter. If the juvenile agrees to and completes the plan, the case is not referred formally to the court. If agreement is not reached on a plan, if the youth fails to complete the plan, or if the youth denies the charge, then the case is handled formally by the juvenile court. But when the youth is eventually found responsible for the offense, the FGC is again convened and a recommendation is made to the court before official sentencing. Therefore, the FGC plays an active role at many different levels of the juvenile system in New Zealand. A typical FGC proceeds in the following manner:

- Introduction
- Explanation of the procedure by FGC coordinator
- Summary statement provided by police
- Offender comments on accuracy of police statement
- Victim (or representative) presents views on offense
- Discussion of possible outcomes
- Discussion of possible outcomes by family members
- Development of a plan by offender and family
- Presentation of plan and negotiation
- Agreement from the police and victim
- Recording of plan and close of meeting

Source: Adapted from G. Maxwell and A. Morris, *Family, Victims and Culture: Youth Justice in New Zealand* (Wellington, New Zealand: Social Policy Agency and Victoria University of Wellington, Institute of Criminology, 1993).

paid by state taxes are instead being kept in local, innovative programs designed especially for local needs. The program has proven popular because it appeals to conservative ideals of cost-effective public policy and local control, while appealing to liberal beliefs in rehabilitation of juvenile offenders.[18]

The interest in juvenile community corrections acts appears to be growing. There are two main reasons for this interest. First, most people realize that removing a young person from the community is an extreme solution, useful only in the most extreme cases. Disrupting the juvenile's community ties and family relationships can interfere with the youth's long-term prospects for successful adjustment by damaging these already fragile supports that will be necessary for the youth to make it in the community. Second, and just as compelling, for most youth the institutional stay will be short—six months to a year in custody is a very common sanction. Eventually the youth returns to the community, where the real work of successfully adjusting to community life occurs. Advocates of community corrections ask, "Why wait?"

There are some additional advantages to community corrections for juveniles. The cost of custody in a juvenile training school is usually at least double that for an adult in prison, which means there is more money to work with in creating incentives to keep offenders and in designing and implementing effective alternatives in the community. Moreover, public opinion toward youthful offenders is not as harsh as that toward adult offenders, so it is easier to obtain public support for juvenile community corrections. Finally, because youth incarceration numbers are smaller than the adult numbers, it is easier to show success in saving money by diverting offenders to local programs.

Because very few of those who are sent to juvenile institutions are the youngest of juvenile offenders, community corrections acts tend to specify the older juvenile offender as a target for services. This is a high-risk, high-payoff youth. Caught between the ages of minor offending and an adult crime, the youthful offender is closer to an adult in behavior and attitude than most juvenile offenders. Many are on the verge of adult criminal careers and have engaged in lawbreaking that resembles adult criminality; thus, they are considered high risk. The payoff is also high: If their movement into adult criminal lifestyles can be prevented, they, their family, and the community are saved enormous financial and personal costs in crime and punishment.

SPECIAL JUVENILE CORRECTIONAL PROGRAMS

In addition to the traditional probation and aftercare programs, a number of community-based programs are available for juveniles today, many of which are similar to those used in adult community corrections. Described below are

ONE EXAMPLE OF DEINSTITUTIONALIZATION

Under the leadership of the then-commissioner of Youth Services Jerome Miller, most of the juvenile institutions/training schools in the state of Massachusetts were closed during the early 1970s. After visiting a number of institutions Miller, a professor of social work, believed that the juvenile correctional system in Massachusetts was filled with problems such as harsh punishments, violence, and ineffectiveness for long-term change. After an incident of brutality at one of the training schools, Miller closed the school. Because he received little opposition, he quickly moved to close all the institutions.

Miller believed that a new system was needed and before it was to be developed, the old one had to be eliminated. He was successful in closing the institutions, the last one in 1972. In the place of training schools, Miller created a network of state-funded, privately owned community-based facilities.

Evaluations of the Massachusetts experience by the Harvard University Center for Criminal Justice concluded that it was a success. Even today, Massachusetts has the lowest rate in the United States of juveniles placed in public facilities. However, due to increased criticism and increase in the fear of crime, by 1975 Massachusetts began to reopen juvenile correctional facilities for serious juvenile offenders. Jerome Miller received considerable notoriety and some harsh criticism for his efforts. He remains a staunch advocate of the deinstitutionalization movement of adult and juvenile offenders.

Source: Jerome G. Miller, *Last One over the Wall: The Massachusetts Experience in Closing Reform Schools* (Columbus: Ohio State University Press, 1991).

some of these programs, including a mention of only a few of the more recent ideas that have been implemented in juvenile community corrections.

Diversion

Although we discussed diversion in detail in Chapter 6, it is important to highlight it again here because of its importance for juvenile corrections. The idea behind juvenile diversion is much the same as it is for adults: Juveniles in trouble need help, not stigmatization. Diversion means juveniles who are picked up by police are not taken into custody but referred to community agencies for assistance with their problems. The problems might be poor relationships with family, poor school performance, or chemical abuse issues.

With diversion, the juvenile has the responsibility to fulfill an obligation (counseling, school attendance, curfew) so as to avoid having his or her case handled formally in the court.

Diversion can take two major forms. The most direct form is simply to stop processing the case, in the expectation that the main objectives of the justice process have been achieved—the juvenile has realized the wrongness of the conduct and has shown a convincing willingness to refrain from it in the future. This form of diversion is seldom final—if the young person returns to court on a new referral, the old charges may be considered again with the new one.

Increasingly, juveniles are diverted to specific programs. This option may be selected when the court determines that the young person's delinquency is a result of certain problems in the child's life that may best be addressed by a program designed to help the juvenile, and the finding of delinquency would not be helpful. These diversion programs often deal with developmental issues such as the child's social skills or response to frustration in school performance. Diversion to mental health treatment for emotionally disturbed youth is also commonly preferred to formal processing.

The logic of diversion is based on the developmental pattern of delinquency. It is thought that most juveniles drift into delinquent behavior as a gradual part of growing up. As their misconduct becomes more serious, they "signal" a need for help to get out of the pathway to delinquency. The diversion strategy tries to provide that help as early as possible. For example, recent studies show that misbehaviors such as stubbornness, resistance to authority, and interpersonal aggressiveness, when they are exhibited at the early, preadolescent ages, are indicative of a risk of later delinquency.[19] Other studies find that truancy is a predictor of later delinquency.[20] That is why diversion programs to help disruptive children learn to cope and to retain children in school are considered important aspects of delinquency prevention, not requiring formal juvenile processing of every child referred to court.

In the late 1960s, youth service bureaus (YSBs) were developed in many states to promote the aims of diversion. The idea was that juvenile cases that were deemed nonserious would be sent to the YSB for screening. The screening would divert status offenders (truants, runaways) out of the formal juvenile justice system and refer the remaining less serious delinquency cases to community agencies for assistance.

The major criticism of diversion and YSBs is that the main purposes of these programs have not been fully realized. Youths who would otherwise be released to parents or given a verbal reprimand have been incorporated into the system because of these programs—an obvious example of net widening. When juveniles are brought into diversion and YSB programs, there is also doubt as to whether stigmatization has been avoided. It is unlikely, and probably unwise, to expect these programs to be eliminated. But improvements are needed, such as to formalize the procedures and rights of young people who appear in juvenile court or participate in pretrial diversion.[21]

Alternative Courts for Juveniles

In the attempt to extend the diversion idea and keep juveniles from immersion into the criminal justice system, two kinds of special courts have developed. **Juvenile drug courts** have been established within juvenile courts to provide intensive treatment for eligible drug-involved youth and their families. More than 140 of these courts have been developed since 1995 with more than 100 more being planned. The drug courts provide intensive court supervision and the delivery of services for a wide range of personal and family problems.[22] Because of their newness, extensive evaluation of the drug courts is unavailable at this juncture. But it appears that drug courts hold considerable promise for the increase of educational achievement and the reduction of recidivism and drug use.[23] The box "Goals of the Juvenile Drug Court" provides a list of the common goals of juvenile drug courts.

Teen courts, also called youth courts, first originated in Ithaca, New York, in the early 1960s. They are a growing alternative to traditional juvenile court involvement for younger juveniles, those with no prior arrests, and those charged with less serious law violations. Over 675 teen courts are now in operation in the United States. Teen courts are administered by juvenile courts,

GOALS OF THE JUVENILE DRUG COURT

- Provide immediate intervention, treatment, and structure in the lives of juveniles using drugs through the ongoing, active oversight and monitoring by the drug court judge.
- Improve juveniles' level of functioning in their environment, address problems that may be contributing to their use of drugs, and develop/strengthen their ability to lead crime- and drug-free lives.
- Provide juveniles with skills that will aid them in leading productive substance-free and crime-free lives, including skills relating to their educational development, sense of self-worth, and capacity to develop positive relationships in the community.
- Strengthen the families of drug-involved youth by improving the capacity of families to provide structure and guidance to their children.
- Improve system capacity to promote accountability for both juvenile offenders and the services they are provided.

Source: Caroline S. Cooper, "Juvenile Drug Court Programs," *JAIBG Bulletin,* U.S. Department of Justice, Office of Juvenile Justice and Delinquency Prevention, May 2001, p. 7; and M. Roberts, J. Brophy, and C. Cooper, "The Juvenile Drug Court Movement," Fact Sheet (Washington, DC: U.S. Department of Justice, Office of Juvenile Justice and Delinquency Prevention, 1997).

FIGURE 12.2 SANCTIONS IMPOSED BY TEEN COURTS

Source: The Urban Institute, Washington, DC, National Survey of Youth Courts and Teen Courts, 1998.

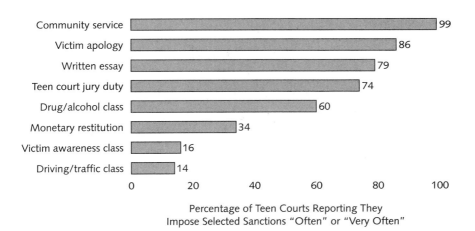

Percentage of Teen Courts Reporting They
Impose Selected Sanctions "Often" or "Very Often"

probation departments, schools, and some religious organizations. They differ from adult courts in that young persons are responsible for most of the process and determine the disposition.

There are two teen court models. The first are trial models that have an adult as judge, although a few permit juveniles to act as judge. The second is a peer jury model that directly questions the offenders. Teen courts mostly handle cases of theft, minor alcohol and drug offenses, vandalism, and disorderly conduct. For a graphic description of the kinds of sentences handed out by teen courts, see Figure 12.2.

Adults are also involved as court administrators, and they supervise courtroom activities. In some teen courts, adults act as judges while youth serve as lawyers and jurors. Although some research has shown that teen courts may be associated with low recidivism rates, improved youth attitudes toward authority, and increased knowledge of the justice system, more research must be completed before teen court effectiveness can be substantiated.[24]

Restitution and Community Service

The use of restitution and community service programs has grown considerably in recent years. By the mid-1980s, more than 35 states and over 400 jurisdictions had developed some form of monetary or community service.[25] In financial restitution programs, the juvenile is required to pay a fee to the victim or a community organization. Because fewer juveniles are employed, the use of community service is more commonplace. In community service programs, juveniles are ordered to work a certain number of hours, usually at a nonprofit or government agency. Typical places of work are YMCAs, public parks, nursing homes, community centers, and local streets.[26]

Although net widening may also be an issue with the implementation of these programs, evidence has shown that restitution can serve the dual purpose of getting juveniles to pay their debts and reducing recidivism.[27]

Intensive Probation Supervision for Juveniles

Some juvenile probation agencies have begun to develop intensive supervision approaches for juveniles (also called JIPS). In some cases, the requirements of the JIPS programs exceed by far the intensiveness of adult IPSs. A juvenile IPS officer might carry fifteen cases or fewer, and might well see each client almost on a daily basis—more than once a day if necessary. Police–probation partnerships have been used to further strengthen the intensity of juvenile intensive supervision, since the police can add a component of surveillance to the probation services. Similar to the research about the results of adult IPS programs, it appears that the effectiveness of JIPS programs has yet to be substantiated.

One study by Richard Weibush examined the recidivism rate of juvenile offenders placed into a JIPS program. He determined that increased community supervision of juveniles can be an effective alternative to incarceration.[28]

Others have indicated less-than-optimistic reports stating that "neither the possible effectiveness nor the possible ineffectiveness of these programs has been carefully examined."[29] More and better-quality research is surely needed in this area.

Home Confinement and Electronic Monitoring

Although not used nearly as extensively with juveniles as with adults, electronic monitoring and home confinement (house arrest) are also a community-based sentencing option for youthful offenders. Home confinement (HC) is when the offender is restricted to home during specified periods of time. He or she is randomly checked by phone calls or visits by a court officer. The limiting of hours for young people to be out of the house is nothing unusual; parents have always tried to provide such discipline. But having the court intervene and assist the family in providing these restrictions is a more recent phenomenon.

As a supplement to HC, courts have tried to impose electronic monitoring (EM) on juveniles. EM is applied through fitting the offender with an unremovable device that emits a signal that is received by a computer and then transmitted to the probation department to determine if the offender has left his or her court-ordered location.

Because so few juvenile EM programs are available, the research about their implementation and effectiveness is limited. One survey indicated that as of the late 1980s, only eleven programs of the type existed.[30] Because of the benefits that EM/HC can provide for the juvenile corrections system, notably reducing costs through limiting incarceration, it will most likely grow as a sentencing option in the years to come.

Balanced Probation

In **balanced probation (BP),** the goal is to combine the philosophical ideals of both conservative and liberal crime control models. This idea attempts to blend the recent call to "get tough" on juvenile offenders with the traditional ideas of parens patriae and rehabilitation for juveniles. The juvenile is to be responsible for his or her actions and fulfill all personal obligations, while at the same time being supported with rehabilitation programs. More specifically, the balanced approach tries to follow the principles of (1) accountability, (2) community protection, and (3) competency development.[31] To implement BP, juvenile offenders attend some treatment-oriented program while being required to pay restitution or provide community service to victims.

Although balanced probation is a relatively new concept in juvenile community corrections, the idea has developed as an extension of the restorative justice approach. As discussed in Chapter 9, this approach calls for active participation by the juvenile, the system, and the community when dealing with delinquency. Balanced probation and restorative justice hold much promise for juvenile corrections because they are less punitive than the adult court, while promoting individual responsibility on the part of the juvenile.[32] Perhaps more important, because they combine the components of two different theoretical (and political) approaches, they may be able to gain considerable financial support—a necessity for long-term viability.

School Probation Programs

In some jurisdictions, juvenile probation officers (JPOs) are stationed in high schools instead of in the local county probation office. Their purpose is to work closely with the schools and juveniles under probation supervision. In addition to supervising those on probation, JPOs may transport students for court hearings, watch attendance patterns, chaperone extracurricular activities, and give classroom presentations about crime, drugs, and the juvenile justice system. It is hoped that having a JPO on the school grounds will improve school attendance and behavior, which will in the long term reduce juvenile delinquency and institutional placement.

Community Volunteers

A common program for juveniles in the community is the community volunteer program. Over 2,000 programs of the type are in operation today, using unpaid volunteers to assist probation officers in a number of functions.

Volunteer probation officers can provide a positive role model for young people by acting responsibly and within the legal boundaries of society. They can act as a confidant, advocate, and friend while supporting the goals and policies of the probation department. Volunteers can also assist the regular court-appointed probation officers in supervision duties such as checking on school attendance, curfew, and work responsibilities.

It is possible that volunteers can create harm for juvenile offenders and problems for probation departments. Ethical and legal complications could arise. For example, if the volunteer harms the juvenile in any way—such as using physical means to discipline the youth or by providing unsound moral advice—the local authorities could be held legally responsible. But with proper screening and training, volunteers can do much to improve the quality of life for many young people and reduce the workload of probation officers.

VOLUNTEERS IN PROBATION PROGRAM

More than 500 people assist the Orange County Probation Department by serving as volunteers through the Volunteers in Probation (VIP) program. Because probation officers have large numbers on their caseloads, typically ranging from 80 to 120 per officer, volunteers play an important role in supporting the work of probation officers and likewise are valuable mentors and assistants at the five juvenile institutions run by the Probation Department.

Among the typical duties of VIPs are:

- Serving as a case aide, to assist a Deputy Probation Officer with a caseload of probationers by doing drug testing, checking school attendance, or driving probationers to counseling sessions.
- Being a "big brother" or "big sister" to a young probationer, by tutoring, participating in recreational activities, or teaching the young person a skill.
- Providing translation for Spanish-speaking or Vietnamese-speaking probationers or family members (and, to a lesser degree, translations in other Asian languages besides Vietnamese).
- Visiting youths in juvenile institutions as a religious volunteer, to cut hair, to teach skills, to tutor, or to coordinate recreational activities and arts-and-crafts projects.

Volunteers must be at least 18 years old and pass criminal and motor vehicle background checks. (Having a prior criminal record *does not* automatically exclude a person from volunteering, but needs to be discussed with the volunteer coordinator.)

Source: http://ocnet.oc.ca.gov/probation/vip.htm

THE SPECIAL PROBLEM OF GANGS

No discussion of juvenile justice would be complete without a comment on the special problem of gangs. It is estimated that the United States has over 840,000 gang members operating in over 31,000 gangs,[33] and that these young offenders are involved in over half a million serious crimes.[34] Studies show that gangs vary widely in makeup, and it is important to bear in mind that most gangs are not violent and many gang members engage in positive as well as negative social behaviors. An important distinction must also be made between traditional street gangs that provide the social connections that many adolescents need and that engage in varieties of criminal conduct, and drug gangs that are organized into cohesive business structures and often use violence as a method of doing business.

Gangs permeate the work of correctional officials. In custodial facilities, they offer a profound challenge to control the population and to manage the potential for intergang conflict. In community settings, gangs provide hostile competition to the prosocial programs developed by correctional leaders. For the community, gangs are a primary source of fear and peril. Especially where gang members are armed, the presence of the gang can be a central destabilizing force in neighborhood life.

Recent initiatives have shown some success with gangs. One of the most impressive has been the Boston Gun Project, described in the box "Operation Ceasefire and Operation Nite Lite."[35] This project involved a coordinated effort of prosecutors, probation officers, street gang workers, and police to target gun use by gang members. They focused on "getting the message out" that gun violence would not be tolerated, and they backed it up by prosecuting fully any gang member found involved in a gun crime. Within the first year, homicides went down from weekly events to near zero.

OPERATION CEASEFIRE AND OPERATION NITE LITE

One night, Boston probation officers Bill Stewart and Rick Skinner accepted an offer from their friends, police officers Bob Merner and Bob Fratalia, to spend Saturday evening in the backseat of a squad car touring the streets of Dorchester, a troubled inner-city area. Merner and Fratalia were members of the police department's gang unit who had been collaborating with probation officers in efforts to deal with a growing problem of gang violence in another troubled neighborhood, Roxbury.

A few hours into the evening, the cruising police car got an emergency call reporting a gunshot victim in a nearby street. Arriving at the scene, the four saw a crowd of about twenty-five residents—mostly young men—milling around a face-down body, dead from a bullet to the head. This was a familiar scene to the police, but the presence of the probation officers gave it a new twist. Stewart and Skinner recognized many of the bystanders as young men on probation and under curfew orders, who were out on the town. The victim also turned out to be one of Stewart's probationers. In all, perhaps a dozen curfew-violating probationers were at the scene. As Stewart recalls, "They were amazed to see me out there at night with the cops. They tried to cover their faces. They knew that, unlike the cops, I could recognize them." Officer Fratalia was also amazed. Bystanders at a crime scene normally claim to have seen nothing, but Stewart was able to elicit information from the young people who faced having their probation revoked for curfew breaking.

Out of this experience, Operation Nite Lite—the simple idea of enforcing juvenile probation curfews—was born. Operation Nite Lite brings probation into the field and aims probation services at juvenile gang members with guns. Where gang violence is a serious problem, there can be no higher priority than reducing gang street violence.

Operation Nite Lite is part of a broader effort in Boston known as Operation Ceasefire, a coordinated attempt to end gang gun violence. Ceasefire is based on the knowledge that a few offenders account for a substantial proportion of all crime and that these offenders are often concentrated in particular city neighborhoods.

Operation Ceasefire uses two strategies. First, interagency collaboration identifies individuals and gangs at risk for committing violence. A task force of federal, state, and municipal criminal justice and social service agencies regularly meet to share information, identify gang members to be targeted, discuss tactics to increase investigation effectiveness, and develop a repertoire of interventions and strategies.

A second strategy is aimed at increasing deterrence through swift and certain sanctioning. When a violent act is committed, the various agencies can at their discretion not only arrest suspects but also shut down drug markets, strictly enforce probation restrictions, make disorder arrests, deal more strictly with cases in adjudication, deploy federal enforcement power, and so on.

Operation Ceasefire develops in gang members a new set of expectations regarding violent behavior. When gang members seek rehabilitative services, the program assists them. But when they persist in violent activity, the coordinated agencies hit them with undesirable sanctions until the violence stops.

The Boston program has been going strong since late 1992 and has had unexpected success. Firearm homicides have dropped from 65 per year to 21. Firearm homicides by juveniles have dropped from 10 to an astounding 0 for two years running. National attention has been focused on Boston's success story.

Source: Todd R. Clear and David R. Karp, *Community Justice: Preventing Crime and Achieving Justice, Report to the National Institute of Justice* (Tallahassee: Florida State University, 1999).

THE PROSPECTS OF SUPERVISING
JUVENILES IN THE COMMUNITY

The policy and practice of community supervision of juvenile offenders is undergoing change. Juvenile corrections has, for many years, taken a backseat to adult corrections in the limelight of public awareness. The front page of the newspaper seems always to contain a story about an adult parolee or probationer, or an adult career criminal. Juveniles' crimes, until very recently, were reserved for the back pages. High-profile gang criminality and the recent spate of school shootings has ended the anonymity of juvenile correctional work.

Public policymakers are turning their attention to the juvenile justice system, and there is reason to think that the decades of reform in adult corrections since the 1970s will be replayed in the juvenile justice arena. What will this mean? The public climate is today enamored of "get-tough" measures, and we are already beginning to see the influence of this thinking on juvenile justice.

There is more pressure to increase the waiver of serious juveniles to the adult court, where their sentences may be longer and their punishments harsher. Local political leaders call for a tougher brand of probation, and the populations within training schools are beginning to grow. These are all the familiar echos of changes in the adult criminal justice system, and few are surprised to see them arising again in respect to juveniles, now that the public spotlight has landed there.

It is not so likely, however, that the reform process for juveniles will exactly reproduce that for adults. No matter how the extreme case is portrayed in the papers, the everyday juvenile offender remains unsophisticated and susceptible to change, under appropriate programs. Most juvenile crime is still a minor kind of misbehavior, not at all like the highly charged cases of serious violence that dominate the news. To paint all juvenile offenders with a broad, adult criminal brush would not only be unwise, it would be inaccurate.

So some middle ground will be found. The relative anonymity of the juvenile justice system is a thing of the past. Scrutiny will apply to juvenile justice policy and practice, and juvenile justice professionals will face pressure to conform their programs to the more strict models that exist in the adult system.

Few observers will note the irony that even as the pressure mounts to toughen juvenile justice, dissatisfaction with the adult model toward which they are moving remains high. In the end, it will fall to the workers who carry out the tasks of the system and the visionaries who chart its course through politically charged waters to make it all work. As in all cycles of reform, eventually the focus will shift elsewhere.

SUMMARY

Since the late 1800s, the juvenile court has been rooted in the principles of parens patriae. Creation of the juvenile court in 1899 established a separate juvenile justice system dealing with delinquency, neglected children, and dependent children. The philosophy of juvenile justice is based on the assumption that decisions should be in the best interest of the child. This requires that police officers, judges, and correctional workers be granted discretion so as to tailor decisions that best meet this goal. However, under some circumstances judges may waive jurisdiction, and a juvenile may be dealt with in the adult criminal justice system.

The juvenile justice system operates its own agencies for institutional and community correctional functions. The differences between juveniles and adults are reflected in the practices of juvenile justice agencies, as the main objective is to move these errant children toward responsible adulthood. While the ideals of rehabilitation and reintegration are important in all community supervision, they receive special emphasis among juvenile probation workers. This is because of the differences in the characteristics of juvenile and adult offenders in the community. Programs in juvenile justice have not always been effective in achieving this goal. In this country, the juvenile justice system has been criticized both for being too lenient and for insufficiently protecting juveniles' rights.

Currently, the public is enamored with "get tough" measures, and this thinking is permeating to juvenile justice policy. As a result, juvenile corrections and more specifically probation is in the midst of change. There is pressure to increase waivers to adult court where sentences are longer and punishments harsher. A sense of unease about how juvenile probation handles serious offending among youth has led to a new interest in the techniques and practices of adult supervision. Among those practices are stricter forms of probation and parole supervision, as well as increased use of incarceration. At the same time, there are a number of newer programs that appear promising as alternatives to incarceration. Many of these are untested, but they appear to be cheaper and are no less effective than traditional juvenile justice methods.

DISCUSSION QUESTIONS

1. At what age should juveniles be treated as adults in the eyes of the law?
2. Do we really need a separate court system for juveniles accused and convicted of crimes? What would be an alternative system?
3. Which juvenile corrections programs do you feel best reflect the original ideals of juvenile court and of parens patriae?
4. Who should administer probation and aftercare services for juveniles? Private or public agencies?

County or state? Some other agency? Explain your position.

5. Based on the current attitude toward juvenile offenders, what do you predict juvenile corrections will look like in the next century?

| SUGGESTED READINGS |

Clapp, Elizabeth J. *Mothers of All Children.* University Park: Pennsylvania State University Press, 1998. Describes the role of the Chicago Woman's Club and women of the Progressive Movement who developed and promoted the juvenile court movement.

Feld, Barry C. *Bad Kids: Race and the Transformation of the Juvenile Court.* New York: Oxford University Press,1999. Examination of the recent shift in policies regarding youth crime and the juvenile justice system in the context of the importance of race in American society.

Finckenauer, J. O. *Scared Straight! and the Panacea Phenomenon.* Englewood Cliffs, NJ: Prentice Hall, 1982. The author explains that many of the causes and effects of juvenile crime have been created by our search for a cure-all. One example is the advent of "Scared Straight" programs, which have questionable effectiveness.

Miller, Jerome. *Last One over the Wall: The Massachusetts Experience in Closing Reform Schools.* Columbus: Ohio State University Press, 1991. Describes the context, process, and impact of the only attempt to fully deinstitutionalize one juvenile correctional system.

Puntz, Patricia, and Scali, Mary Ann. *Beyond the Walls: Improving Conditions of Confinement for Youth in Custody.* Washington, DC: Office of Juvenile Justice and Delinquency Prevention, January 1998. Discusses attempts to develop innovative and effective treatment programs in juvenile institutions.

Schwartz, Ira M. *Justice for Juveniles: Rethinking the Best Interests of the Child.* Lexington, MA: Lexington Books, 1989. Schwartz argues that when it comes to our current juvenile justice system, the efforts we make in the "best interest" of children often go awry.

| WEB SITES |

Web site for general information on juvenile probation
www.ccjrs.org

Web site for juvenile justice correctional information by states
www.yopb.ca.gov

Web site for information about National Youth Court Center
www.youthcourt.net

Web site for National Youth Gang Center, which provides a volume of information about youth gangs and effective responses to them
www.iir.com/nygc

Web site for National Criminal Justice Reference Service, which provides information on many juvenile justice issues such as corrections, courts, and gangs
www.ncjrs.org

| NOTES |

1. Howard N. Snyder, "Juvenile Arrests 1999," *Juvenile Justice Bulletin* (Washington, DC: U.S. Department of Justice, 2000), p. 3.

2. Peter Benekos, "Juvenile Crime and Public Policy: From Panic to Punishment," Research in Brief, *Corrections Now* (ACJS Corrections Section Newsletter) 3:1 (November 1998).

3. Snyder, "Juvenile Arrests 1999."

4. *New York Times,* December 15, 2000, p. A22.

5. Technically, only the judicial waiver actually involves the transfer of a juvenile from the juvenile court to the adult criminal court. In the other three types, the juvenile never actually enters the juvenile court system.

6. A. L. Stahl, "Delinquency Cases Waived to Criminal Court, 1987–1996" (FS-9999), OJJDP Fact Sheet (Washington, DC: Office of Juvenile Justice and Delinquency Prevention, 1999).

7. "Office of Juvenile Justice and Delinquency Prevention Research Report 2000," U.S. Department of Justice, Office of Justice Programs, Washington, DC, May 2001.

8. *Kent* v. *United States,* 383 U.S. 541, 550 (1966).

9. *In re Gault,* 387 U.S. 1 (1967).

10. L. Szymanski, *Upper Age of Juvenile Court Jurisdiction Analysis, 1994 Update* (Pittsburgh, PA: National Center for Juvenile Justice, 1995).

11. P. F. Cromwell and G. C. Killinger, *Community-Based Corrections: Probation, Parole, and Intermediate Sanctions,* 3rd ed. (St. Paul, MN: West, 1994).

12. National Advisory Commission on Criminal Justice Standards and Goals, *Corrections* (Washington, DC: Government Printing Office, 1983), p. 75.

13. Ronald P. Corbett, Jr., "Juvenile Probation on the Eve of the New Millennium," *Federal Probation* 58:2 (December 1999): 78–87.

14. Howard Snyder and Melissa Sickmund, *Juvenile Offenders and Victims: A National Report* (Washington, DC: Office of Juvenile Justice and Delinquency Prevention, 1995), p. 90.

15. Harry Sontheimer and L. Goodstein, "Evaluation of Juvenile Intensive After-Care Probation: After-Care Versus System Response Effects," *Justice Quarterly* 10 (1993): 197–227.

16. Kenneth Land, P. L. McCall, and J. R. Williams, "Something That Works in Juvenile Justice: An Evaluation of North Carolina Counselor's Intensive Protection Supervision Randomized Experimental Project, 1987–1989," *Evaluation Review* 14: 574–606.

17. E. M. Lemert and F. Dill, *Offenders in the Community* (Lexington, MA: Heath, 1978).

18. Melissa M. Moon, Brandon K. Applegate, and Edward J. Latessa, "RECLAIM Ohio: A Politically Viable Alternative to Treating Youthful Felony Offenders," *Crime and Delinquency* (October 1997): 438–456.

19. Barbara Tatem Kelley, Rolph Loeber, Kate Keenan, and Mary DeLamatre, "Developmental Pathways in Boys' Disruptive and Delinquent Behavior," Office of Juvenile Justice and Delinquency Prevention, U.S. Department of Justice, Washington, DC, December 1997.

20. Eileen M. Gary, "Truancy: First Step to a Lifetime of Problems," Office of Juvenile Justice and Delinquency Prevention, U.S. Department of Justice, Washington DC, October 1996.

21. J. Wass and R. Marks, "Youth Offenders Act Revamps Juvenile Justice in Canada," *Corrections Today* 54:8 (December 1992): 88.

22. Caroline S. Cooper, "Juvenile Drug Court Programs," *JAIBG Bulletin,* U.S. Department of Justice, Office of Juvenile Justice and Delinquency Prevention, May 2001, p. 1. Also see Robin J. Kimbrough, "Treating Substance Abuse: The Promise of Juvenile Drug Courts," *Juvenile Justice: Prevention Works.* OJJDP, U.S. Department of Justice, Office of Juvenile Justice and Delinquency Prevention, 5:2 (December 1998): 11–19.

23. Cooper, "Juvenile Drug Court Programs," p. 13.

24. Jeffrey A. Butts and Janeen Buck, "Teen Courts: A Focus on Research," Office of Juvenile Justice and Delinquency Prevention, U.S. Department of Justice, Washington, DC, October 2000, p. 9.

25. Anne Schneider, "Restitution and Recidivism Rates of Juvenile Offenders: Results from Four Experimental Studies," *Criminology* 24 (1986): 533–552.

26. Albert R. Roberts, *Juvenile Justice: Policies, Programs and Services* (Chicago: Dorsey Press, 1989).

27. Schneider, "Restitution and Recidivism Rates of Juvenile Offenders."

28. Richard G. Weibush, "Juvenile Intensive Supervision: The Impact on Felony Offenders Diverted from Institutional Placement," *Crime and Delinquency* 39 (1993): 68–89.

29. Ted Palmer, *The Re-Emergence of Correctional Intervention* (Newbury Park, CA: Sage, 1992), p. 82.

30. Joseph B. Vaughn, "A Survey of Juvenile Electronic Monitoring and Home Confinement Programs," *Juvenile and Family Court Journal* 40 (1989): 4.

31. G. Bazemore and M. S. Umbreit, *Balanced and Restorative Justice* (Washington, DC: Office of Juvenile Justice and Delinquency Prevention, U.S. Department of Justice, October 1994).

32. For a more comprehensive discussion of the use of restorative justice for juveniles, see "Balanced and Restorative Justice for Juveniles: A Framework for Juvenile Justice in the 21st Century," OJJDP, Balanced and Resorative Justice Project, August 1997.

33. James C. Howell, "Youth Gangs: An Overview," Office of Juvenile Justice and Delinquency Prevention, U.S. Department of Justice, Washington, DC, August 1998.

34. G. David Curry, Richard A. Ball, and Scott H. Decker, "Estimating the National Scope of Gang Crime from Law Enforcement Data," National Institute of Justice, U.S. Department of Justice, Washington, DC, August 1996.

35. David M. Kennedy, Anne M. Piehl, and Anthony A. Braga, "Youth Violence in Boston: Gun Markets, Serious Youth Offenders, and a Use-Reduction Strategy," *Law and Contemporary Problems* 59:1 (1996): 147–184.

Chapter 13

The Future of the Offender in the Community

Nobody can tell the future. Perhaps that is one of the things that makes speculating about the future so interesting. In a way, we all have equal access to the future, and so when it comes to the game of "thinking about the future," we can all play.

Not that all visions of the future are equally valid. Someone who invents a future scenario based on the disappearance of gravity from the earth, for example, is painting a pretty unlikely picture, one that flies in the face of physical science. Still, such a speculation might be interesting; it might expose for us how deeply imbedded is the force of gravity into our every movement. But the scenario, no matter how thought provoking, would do little to prepare us for the future.

When we think about the future, we first must ask ourselves, "What changes are likely to occur?" It is here, in this question, that we face the biggest challenge, for who can know what events will occur? Some events are predictable: There will be a presidential election in the year 2004 (though who can say with authority who will win?); there will be hurricanes, tornadoes, floods, and vast fires along our countryside (though precisely where, who can say?); and the economy will affect all our lives (though how, we cannot know for certain).

Alongside the predictable forces will come the unpredictable, and herein lies our greatest uncertainty. The scope of our uncertainty about the future is illustrated by a few recent events: In 1975, who would have predicted the fall of communism? In 1985, who would have predicted the near-decade growth in the economy? Or, in 1965, who would have predicted a 500 percent increase in the prison population in twenty-five years? Or that in 1995, crime would begin to drop and continue to drop by the year 2001 to lows not seen since the 1970s? So when it comes to thinking about the future, we engage in a kind of "informed speculation." It will be, by definition, impossible to predict with any accuracy the unforeseen events, such as the startling fall of communism or the unprecedented rise in the size and scope of the apparatus of punishment.

Of course, after these events have occurred, we will all benefit from 20/20 hindsight: We will see clearly the clues we should have paid more attention to, and here and there will be a lonely spectator who will say, "I told you so!" But the unforeseen event will have to happen with little preparation on our part. What we can do is think about the directions being suggested by the more predictable forces at play in community supervision, and ask ourselves the more provocative questions about key choices that face us today in this area.

Below we describe four important forces that will, one way or another, shape the progress of the field of community supervision of offenders. Although we cannot know with certainty how any of those forces will play out in the future, we can make some educated guesses. After exploring those forces, we turn our attention to six provocative questions. Within the answers to these questions will be contained much of the road map to a vision for the future.

Photo: John Walters, director of the White House Office of National Drug Control Policy, third from right, speaks to recovering addicts and counselors at Central City Concern, a drug rehabilitation facility in Portland, Oregon. AP/Wide World Photos

FOUR FORCES THAT WILL
SHAPE THE FUTURE

This part of "the future" is easy. We know that, no matter what the future holds, it will have been shaped to a great extent by a handful of critical forces. The list of important forces is arbitrary, but there are not that many forces on the list. Here we will discuss four, and we will leave it to the reader to think of others and consider their importance.

Politics

One of the biggest changes in crime policy has been the arrival of hardball politics as a force in policy formation. It may be difficult for people of college age today to believe that politics and crime policy were not always so closely intertwined, but the pressure of electoral politics on crime legislation is a relatively recent phenomenon. "Crime in our streets" was a euphemism that stood for the unrest surrounding the civil rights and antiwar protests in the 1960s, and by the 1970s, getting tougher on crime was a part of every political candidate's package of promises. No example is more starkly apparent than George H. W. Bush's use of the "Willie Horton" ads, which hit hard against the release of the violent recidivist under Michael Dukakis's administration as governor of Massachusetts. Public relations polling showed that voters responded viscerally to the image of Horton's hard-looking mug shot, followed by photographs of the innocent victims of his brutal crimes, after he was let out. Critics pointed out that the ads appealed not just to safety but also to racist fears, since Horton was black and his victims were white, but that is a matter of some debate.

In today's political world, the get-tough rhetoric has become a monotone. It seems as though every politician, regardless of his or her views on other issues, paints a tough, uncompromising picture with regard to crime. It does not stretch reality much to say that there is no meaningful political debate, really, about crime—there is only the (increasingly ironic) tendency of everyone to try to find a new, viscerally appealing way to show how tough we should be about it.

So the question is, where is this headed? On the one hand, no political career can survive long without a few choice phrases about getting serious about crime. On the other hand, as the political parties begin to sound ever more alike on these issues, the substance gives way to a kind of mind-numbing symbolism. If every political aspirant is equally against crime in tough, no-nonsense ways, then will crime as a political issue begin to disappear? What will happen with the politics of crime policy in the future? If we are being optimistic, we could surmise that there will be a swing back to more treatment-based approaches to dealing with drug offenders. This appears to be happening more readily as states are seeing the economic benefits of treating rather than incarcerating drug offenders.

Strongly related to politics is the media's impact on community attitudes toward crime and justice as well as the political reaction that it causes. Crime continues to be a staple of all news programming. In fact, even though the number and seriousness of crimes committed have diminished in recent years, the number of television news shows depicting crime-related topics continues to grow each year. Whenever there is a violent crime committed by an ex-offender on parole, there is often extensive media coverage that calls for an "investigation of the system" or the elimination of parole. How will the media depict crime in the future? Can and will the media be used to spread the word about programs that have been shown to be effective in the fight against crime? How might such programming impact politics and the way resources are allocated for criminal justice?

Technology

America is a technical nation; our wealth was built by the productive use of machinery, and we have a deeply held belief in the importance of "building a better mousetrap": finding better ways to get things done. How will this affect community supervision of offenders? There are three areas in which the technical capacity of community supervision has accelerated in recent years: risk assessment, control techniques, and risk reduction methods. Each of these areas will continue to be developed, but the question is whether any big advances are around the corner in any of them. After all, each of these techniques is designed to deal with the pervasiveness of what we have called human "uncertainty"—the lack of predictability about human behavior—and we can be fairly certain that humans are not going to become less uncertain in the way they act.

Risk assessment methods have been perhaps the most widely spread in the field of community corrections since the late 1970s. Back then, only a handful of probation agencies used standardized risk checkoff forms to classify offenders for supervision priority. Today, just about every agency uses one form or another of this approach. But still, the rates of prediction error are sufficiently high that they must be a serious consideration in the formulation of supervision policy. Every agency that assesses risk must take into account the certainty that some of those assessments will be wrong. Improvements in the ability to assess risk would be a major breakthrough in supervision policy, but is this likely? There are no indications today that such a big leap forward in prediction technology is just beyond the horizon; we will probably have to be satisfied with small improvements over time.

With the advent of electronic monitoring and the increased reliance on drugs that control behavior, community supervision has entered a new age of behavior monitoring and management. Advances in satellite technologies and the use of local kiosks have made probation supervision more accessible.

What are the next steps? Are there any new and formidable control techniques that will be developed and marketed? To answer this question, we would first be reminded that the great groundswell of excitement and concern that accompanied the first implementation of electronic monitors has proven overstated on both accounts. The doomsday scenario has not occurred; monitors are used comparatively sparingly, and with no appreciable impact on staffing levels or personal freedoms for us all. At the same time, these devices have their own failure rate, and the more persistent offenders have found ways to get around even these controls. The same might be said about drug-based behavior controls.

The attractiveness of gadgets and chemicals is so deeply imbedded in our national consciousness that we will probably stay interested in these developments and test new forms of technical controls when they are invented. But we will not find any magic bullets through machinery.

The rebirth of an interest in rehabilitative programming was one of the surprises of the 1990s—everybody seemed to think rehabilitation was "dead." There has been an excitement in the field for new studies that show promising results for "appropriate" treatment programs. To the extent these initial studies are confirmed by continuing evaluations, treatment programs will receive a new life. But there can be no mistaking the fact that even in the best of programs, many offenders fail. And these failures will continue to test the credibility and viability of treatment programming technologies.

There can be no question that technologies of community supervision will continue to evolve into ever more effective strategies for behavior prediction, control, and change. But the advances will be at the margins.

Economy

After two decades of struggle, the biggest American story of the 1990s was that the economy was booming for nearly a half decade. This has meant that jobs were created, unemployment was down, and economic hope increased. What did this mean for corrections? The immediate impact was felt in the loosening of the governmental fiscal belt a bit. For years, the corrections system occupied an enviable position among the government services—it grew while other services shrunk. Politicians ran on platforms of getting tough on crime, and when they got elected they had to pay the tab: Between 1975 and 1990, the budgets of corrections agencies grew 1,000 percent. The impact of this growth can be illustrated by comparing it to the many government services that were forced to downsize in order to make do with stable budgets, or even to cut costs and absorb shrinking allocations. Tax reform increased the pressure by reducing the rate of tax revenues available for distribution among the competing services.

During this time, something of a resentment developed between the agencies that were forced to absorb the cuts and corrections, whose budget grew every year. A premium began to be placed on programs that promised to reduce the pace of correctional budgetary growth—this was a major impetus for the intermediate sanctions movement. We might say that fiscal constraints of the 1970s and 1980s forced a certain degree of innovation.

But all that seemed to change in the year 2001. The economy slowed, the stock market sank, and these conditions were exacerbated by the tragic events of September 11, 2001. Although the long-term economic impact of the terrorist attacks and the subsequent "war on terrorism" are yet to be determined, it is clear that the free spending on corrections that the system enjoyed in the 1980s and 1990s is now being questioned. It is certain that corrections will be under pressure to keep its costs down. How much pressure is an interesting issue—will government services that have benefited from the economic growth in the 1990s be resistant to the correctional juggernaut, when money becomes tighter? How will this pressure feed back into politics, as those seeking election try to establish platforms of public services for which new funds must be found?

Crime

Here, the recent news has been very good indeed. Depending on the way one counts, crime has been dropping for between seven and ten consecutive years, and there has been a steady decline since 1994. In some of our major cities, rates of homicide are down to levels not experienced since the early 1970s. This news is a surprise to us all, but a welcome relief.

This is not to say that crime rates are acceptable. Even with these enormous drops in crime, the rate of violence in the United States is closer to that of developing, Third World nations than to that of mature, Western democracies. Our property crime rate is not that unusual, compared to similar nations, but we have far too much violent crime.

The role of the changing crime rate provides fascinating speculation. What if crime continues to fall? Will its prominence on the screen of public opinion also begin to wane? If that is the case, then how will the politics of crime policy adjust to a context in which rhetoric about punishment no longer carries such a powerful punch? Or, if the power of crime politics continues unabated, how will that be possible under conditions of regular reports of dropping crime? Another, less attractive, line of speculation is provided by the possibility that the drop in crime will end, and we will see a new increase in violence. We have no hard data to predict this outcome (or any other, for that matter), but if the drop in crime ends, then surely the public response will affect correctional policy. The question is, how?

SIX QUESTIONS TO PONDER ABOUT THE SUPERVISION OF OFFENDERS IN THE COMMUNITY

These four trends set the groundwork for us to ponder a few questions about the future of correctional policy concerning offenders in the community. Many questions could be asked; here are six:

1. What will it mean as community supervision becomes increasingly professionalized?

One subtle, but important, change in community supervision has been professionalization. What was previously a field in which any preparation sufficed (and lack of success in other endeavors was often a motivator), there is now an expectation that correctional workers, particularly those in the community, will have a degree of professional preparation and continuing education to inform their work. The evidence for a greater professional expectation is supported by the enormous growth in the membership and participation of the American Probation and Parole Association (APPA), the professional organization for community corrections workers. The large number of undergraduates who finish their education as criminal justice majors helps feed that professionalism.

In other fields, professional development is accompanied by standards of practice, accreditation of programs, and processes of internal accountability. It will be interesting to see how much of this also occurs in community supervision. There are already indications of movement in this area. The APPA offers "continuing education" credit for attendance at its conferences and training programs. A group at the University of Cincinnati has undertaken to develop an assessment package that will tell program managers whether their programs conform to the known standards for the most effective strategies. Civil liability suits have pressed the field to articulate its standards for contacts and supervision, especially in the case of misbehavior.

As the field gets more "professionalized," we might wonder if it will lose some of the attraction it has held in the past to certain types of workers. In practice, probation and parole officers have been used to vast amounts of discretion in the way they carry out their work. They also tended to mold the job to fit their preferences—seeing whom they wanted, when they wanted, how they wanted. At the same time, they worked with very little guidance and got used to a great deal of second-guessing. This aspect of the job is changing, and we can think about how these changes will affect the day-to-day realities of the work, and its satisfactions for those who do the job.

2. What directions will the field take in response to arguments about costs?

An increasing emphasis on government fiscal responsibility will influence all types of government services, including corrections. At the policy level, correctional priorities will be assessed to show whether they are fiscally sound. At the practice level, a given approach will be compared to its alternatives, in terms of cost-effectiveness. Whenever we hear a debate about the "optimal" caseload size on probation or parole, we are hearing a discussion of cost-effectiveness without the use of that term.

Two recent reports illustrate the manner in which these analyses will proceed.

A study by a team of economists has found that the "social" costs of crime far outweigh the "financial" costs of crime.[1] Their work suggests that preventing a crime has much more social payoff than we have previously thought, and that to the degree tough measures prevent crimes, they may be cost-effective even if they are expensive. A prison term that costs $25,000 a year may pay for itself in crimes prevented. But what of other alternatives to prison? A study by Rand researchers estimates that early treatment programs save $7 for every dollar they cost, in terms of crimes prevented. This is an even better ratio than the prison cost-savings others have promoted.

The debate about cost-effectiveness is illustrated by the use of "technical revocations"—the return to prison of those who break the rules under community supervision. Does this cost more money than it saves? The question comes down to how much crime is prevented by the revocation—a matter about which very little is known. But what we do know is that the problem is not a small one: In several states, more than half the prison admissions every year are due to revocations on probation and parole, many of which are "technical" in nature.

3. Will the reemergence of rehabilitation be a long-term force?

If there is anything we have learned about supervision methods, it is that the old debate, "treatment versus punishment," is misleading. We have been used to thinking that the two approaches were diametrically opposed, and so we must choose between them. In fact, recent work has shown us that these can be mutually reinforcing strategies. For example, treatment approaches can be used to teach offenders new behaviors, surveillance strategies can help correctional staff know if the change strategies are working, and punishment (or, more likely, reward) approaches reinforce changes that have occurred. The astronomical growth of drug courts is evidence of this new attitude.

We can wonder how long the new emphasis on rehabilitation will last. Its popularity remains high among correctional staff, and every poll of citizens finds they want offenders to be rehabilitated. But the degree of support in the middle—by political leaders and public opinion makers—remains quite limited. This is a nation that has grown used to thinking punitively about crime.

At stake is what it feels like to be a community supervision worker. If the main tasks of community supervision are punitive—if the job consists of carrying out the painful consequences of criminal conviction—then it is hard to see how it will remain very satisfying for very many people, in the long run.

But if the job continues to embrace the ideal of change, the noble idea that some importance is placed on helping offenders make a new life for themselves, then its appeal for the professional will probably remain strong.

4. Will community supervision be asked to play a role as the prison population ages?

The prison population is aging. This is partly because the general population is aging, but even in today's world of AARP-influenced political interests, crime remains a young person's game. The main reason the prison population is aging is that prison sentences are growing longer—in some cases, much longer.

Two aspects of this aging prison population are problematic. First, it is very costly. Health care among prisoners is very expensive, and it drives up the costs of the prison system far more than mere growth in populations alone. Second, aged prisoners represent a very small risk to the public. Keeping people locked up into their fifties, sixties, and seventies, is, on average, not good public safety policy.

It may turn out that, as the furor about crime abates under reduced levels of crime, and as concern about the costs of punishment grows, we will begin to see proposals for the release of some of the most aged prisoners in the system.

Community supervision agencies will be asked to develop new programs to supervise those offenders. If so, it is interesting to ask what those programs will look like, and how they will operate. After all, the offenders handled by these programs will be socially damaged by decades of incarceration; many of them will not recall what it was like to be free, and those who do will recall a world very different from the one into which they are released. It is also interesting to speculate on what will happen the first time one of these aged releasees commits a serious offense.

5. What role will parole supervision play as discretionary release gradually evaporates?

The dominant trend today in sentencing is the extreme reduction or elimination altogether of discretionary release of offenders from incarceration. If this trend continues, there will be very few parole boards in operation, and most offenders will know about when they are due for release on the day they enter the prison system.

This does not mean that parole supervision will end. In every case where a state has eliminated parole release, it has seen fit to retain the supervision function. Few reformers think it is advisable to have offenders released from prison without any supervision whatsoever. But this is a new status for a prisoner—released but not free.

What kind of parole will emerge from this change? There are many possibilities. For example, a new parole system could be built on an ethic of surveillance. People who carry out this type of work could be a part of the police function—much as were the original parole officers under the ticket-of-leave system in the 1800s. Or these parole officers could be the other extreme—adjustment counselors. This role would encompass a range of problem-solving responsibilities, in which parole officers would work cooperatively with the recent releasee to determine the best way to solve problems the former inmate faces making it in the community. Which of these two versions of the job seems more interesting?

6. Will "community justice" continue to emerge as a new, competing paradigm for justice?

In an earlier chapter, we made an argument for a new vision of supervision of the offender in the community—we called it "community justice." There is a growing interest in this idea. Much of the interest stems from what people perceive to be the failures of the traditional approach to "doing justice" in the community. The arrest-conviction-punishment model has provided little in the way of real satisfaction to the public or the professionals, despite its continuing visceral appeal to us all. A new model, built on problem solving and cooperation, is seen by some as the natural alternative.

There is much experimentation going on with the "community justice" concept, all around the country. Prosecution and policing are increasingly being located in community areas, and the courts are beginning to follow. As corrections move in that direction, it will be interesting to see how it changes to reflect a more determined public that is concerned about a set of problems in its own backyard.

It is too early to tell how important the idea of "community justice" really will be. In fact, its precise meaning still remains fuzzy, even to its proponents: Is it primarily restorative? Preventive? Or merely local? What does it mean for the victim of crime? These questions, and others, will be the subject matter of the community justice movement. Where will it lead and how long will it last?

THE OFFENDER IN THE COMMUNITY: AN OPPORTUNITY

We are used to thinking of the offender in the community as a threat. But let us close our study of this topic by thinking about how this represents an opportunity.

We began this book by pointing out how many offenders there are in the community, and how normal it is for offenders to be living in their communities. Most of the discussion that followed this observation was devoted to describing, analyzing, and assessing the agencies, practices, and policies that have arisen due to the existence of offenders in our midst. But this phenomenon also provides three important opportunities.

It provides an opportunity for safer communities. If we can find ways to assist, cajole, control, or otherwise influence these fellow citizens to refrain from crime, then we all benefit. We have seen that the idea of a community completely free of offenders is unrealistic. But we have also seen that there are myriad programs, policies, and practices that each contribute toward those citizens' successful adjustment to crime-free life in our neighborhoods. We can, by advocating those approaches that work, and by supporting their continuation, help build a safer society, person by person.

We are also provided an opportunity to improve justice. Most of those who get involved in the criminal justice system have faced significant disadvantages in their life circumstances. This does not excuse their behavior; many who come from similar circumstances are able to avoid this kind of trouble, and the accidents of birth are not a type of permission to make up a different set of rules. But it is also basically honest to recognize that few of us would trade places with where the vast majority of those in prison or jail, on probation or parole, started out. We can build a better social justice system by committing ourselves to a policy of not discarding fellow citizens when they run afoul of the law.

This is, as well, an opportunity for you, the reader. Having read about community supervision of offenders, having studied the issues and waded through the complexities, you will now see why this is such an important area of study, one to which you might well wish to devote your life's work.

⊣ NOTES ⊢

1. Mark A. Cohen, Ted R. Miller, and Brian Wiersema, *Victim Costs and Consequences, The Costs of Crime* (Washington, DC: U.S. Department of Justice, 1996).

Glossary

absconders Offenders who, while under some form of community supervision, flee the jurisdiction within which they are required to stay.

aftercare Programs that make an effort to deal with the offender's problems and have as their base community-based treatment, continuity of care, offender assessment and classification, and case management.

age of (majority) responsibility The age at which the juvenile code ceases to apply and the offender is subject to the adult criminal code.

aggregate assessment approach Takes into account a local jurisdiction's sentencing history and/or current practice to determine the amount a local jurisdiction will be reimbursed for its CCA programs.

alcohol abuser A person whose use of alcohol is difficult to control, disrupting normal living patterns and frequently leading to violations of the law while under the influence of alcohol or in attempting to secure it.

assessment process The procedures by which an offender is reviewed for possible placement in a correctional program.

Augustus, John A Boston bootmaker who was the first to stand bail for defendants under authority of the Boston Police Court. He thereby is called the father of probation.

autonomous model A parole board model that is independent from the correctional institute.

bail Pretrial release program that requires personal or financial guarantee of future appearance in court.

balanced justice Justice is best served when the community, victim, and youth are viewed as equal participants in the system who all need attention and individualization.

balanced probation (BP) The idea developed as an extension of the restorative justice approach that calls for active participation by the juvenile, the system, and the community when dealing with an offender.

base rate Overall failure rate.

benefit of clergy When a criminal could receive refuge from prosecution through seeking repentance for the crime and claim the protection of the church.

boot camp Short-term institutional sentence, usually followed by probation, that puts the offender through a physical regimen designed to develop discipline and respect for authority.

broken windows probation One example of a performance-based supervision model that calls for probation services to embrace new problem-solving and partnership strategies that have proven successful for law enforcement.

capital punishment Death penalty for crime.

career criminal A person who sees crime as a way of earning a living, who has numerous contacts with the criminal justice system over time, and who may view the criminal sanction as a normal part of life.

case-by-case assessment approach Asks sentencing authorities to decide if they would have used prison for a given case, had the CCA program been unavailable.

case management Any system that provides for the organized and client-specific supervision of offenders.

chemical controls One of the main strategies for controlling human behavior.

CHINS Children in need of supervision. Some jurisdictions have developed similar acronyms to describe juveniles, such as PINS, MINS, and JINS (persons, minors, or juveniles in need of supervision).

classification system Standardized criteria by which offenders are placed into groups for purposes of assignment to appropriate correctional programs.

cognitive therapies General therapies that deal with the broad spectrum of offenders under correctional supervision.

community corrections Nonincarcerative programs for offenders who remain within the community while serving their sentences.

community corrections acts (CCAs) Provide states with opportunities to return some of their revenues to local correctional authorities if they elect to keep offenders locally rather than sentence them to state prison.

community corrections centers Facilities operated in the community by federal, state, local, or private entities that provide rehabilitation, treatment programs, and/or residential living opportunities to offenders. These facilities are nonconfining and allow offenders to leave daily to use community resources.

community justice Recent trend to include victims, the community, and the offender in the process of justice.

community service Unpaid service to the public to symbolically atone for the harm done by the crime.

commutation Shortening of the sentence originally ordered by a court of law by either the governor or a board of pardons.

conditions of supervision Rules of conduct with which offenders under community supervision must comply in order to remain in the community.

conscience collective A collective social sentiment in favor of community norms and values.

consolidated board Parole board acting as an independent decision-making body within the department of corrections.

continuous signaling device Type of electronic monitoring that is active in that it sends continuous signals that are picked up by a receiver.

continuum of sanctions A range of correctional strategies that vary in terms of level of intrusiveness and control.

corporal punishment Punishment inflicted on the body of the offender with whips or other devices that cause pain.

corrections A component of the larger criminal justice system that includes the various programs, services, facilities, and organizations responsible for the management of individuals who have been accused or convicted of crime.

crime control model A model based on the assumption that criminal behavior can be controlled by more incarceration and other forms of strict supervision in the community.

criminal justice system A term used to explain and understand all of the agencies whose goal it is to control crime. The main components of the system are the police, courts, and corrections.

criminogenic needs Offender needs that, if unresolved, might tend to lead toward more criminality.

criteria of eligibility Factors that an offender's situation must have in order for him or her to be eligible for a correctional program.

day fine Criminal penalty based on the amount of income an offender earns for a day's work.

day reporting centers (DRCs) Offenders on pretrial release, probation, or parole are required to appear at a certain location on a regular basis to receive supervision or participate in rehabilitation programs.

deinstitutionalization The release of mental patients from mental hospitals and their return to the community.

determinate sentencing Penalty to be served by the offender is "fixed" at the time of sentencing, based on the penalty imposed by the judge.

deterrence To punish a person so that the entire population might be discouraged to commit crime.

discretion The opportunity to make a personal decision.

discretionary release Inmate is released as a result of decisions made by parole boards or commissions within the boundaries set by the sentence and the penal law.

diversion A strategy that seeks to avoid formal processing of the offender by the criminal justice system.

drug abuser A person whose use of illegal chemical substances disrupts normal living patterns to the extent that social problems develop, often leading to criminal behavior.

drug court Special court designed to handle cases involving drug-addicted offenders through an extensive supervision and treatment program.

dynamic risk factors Factors that can be changed by planned and sustained programs; can change due to an event in the offender's life or due to purposeful correctional programs.

early release The release of a prisoner prior to the completion of the prison sentence.

electronic monitoring (EM) Type of intermediate punishment used to expand the surveillance capacity of supervision while in the community.

expiration release Unconditional release from incarceration when an offender's term expires, minus good time.

expungement The removal (or erasure) of an offender's conviction from state records.

false negatives Wrongful predictions that a person will not recidivate.

false positives Wrongful predictions that a person will recidivate.

felony probation Probation used for serious offenders.

flat time Expiration of full sentence.

formal juvenile probation When a juvenile has been adjudicated to be a delinquent or a status offender and will be subject to rules of probation supervision similar to those on adult probation.

funding sources for CCAs Fiscal incentives needed to fund local correctional options and to encourage local sentencing authorities to use them in preference to state prison.

furloughs Policy that permits inmates to leave prison for short periods of time with the goal being to prepare an offender for parole release.

galley slavery When criminals were forced to power ships by rowing.

good time Provision that enables inmates to accumulate days, months, and years off their maximum sentence by behaving well in prison.

halfway house An agency-administered or contract facility located in the community designed to transition inmates nearing the end of their sentences from prison life to community living; also called a community treatment center.

house arrest/home confinement Offenders are sentenced to terms of incarceration, but they serve those terms in their own homes.

imprisonment A sentence imposed upon the conviction of a crime that is the deprivation of liberty in a penal institution.

incapacitation Incarcerating an offender to reduce the capacity to commit crime.

indeterminate sentencing The judge imposes a minimum and/or maximum sentence, within which the prisoner is eligible for release on parole.

inevitability of error No strategy will guarantee success in handling offenders in the community.

informal juvenile probation When the juvenile receives supervision by an officer of the court and is required to follow certain rules, but the court has not made a formal determination that the child is under its jurisdiction nor has the child been formally adjudicated as a delinquent or status offender.

intensive probation supervision (IPS) Offender receives probation as an alternative to incarceration under the conditions of strict reporting and frequent face-to-face contacts with a probation officer who has a limited caseload.

intermediate sanctions Correctional strategies that are less severe than prison but provide more control than probation.

jails Facilities authorized to hold pretrial detainees and sentenced misdemeanants for periods usually no longer than one year.

judicial reprieve When a judge grants the request of a convicted offender, that his or her sentence be suspended for a specified length of time, on condition of good behavior.

juvenile drug courts A court diversion project that provides intensive treatment for eligible drug-involved youth and their families.

mandatory release Inmate serves the required amount of time to be released.

mandatory sentencing Sentences stipulating some minimum period of incarceration that must be served by persons convicted of selected crimes; the judge has no discretion and is not allowed to suspend the sentence.

mark system A prison leave system developed by Maconochie whereby prisoners could enter stages of increasing responsibility that led to freedom.

mental health court Modeled after drug courts, the mental health court handles cases dealing with nonviolent, mentally ill offenders.

mentally handicapped offender A person whose limited mental development prevents adjustment to the rules of society.

mentally ill offender A "disturbed" person whose criminal behavior may be traced to diminished or otherwise abnormal capacity to think or reason as a result of psychological or neurological disturbance.

meta-analysis Adds together a large number of diverse studies, each of which might be too small to justify firm conclusions, and then searches through the aggregate for statistical patterns.

mixed sentence Sentence that requires an offender to serve some period of time in a correctional facility (usually weekends) while being on probation supervision in the community.

needs criteria Factors in a case that indicate problems related to criminal behavior.

net widening When some program or form of social control is given to an individual who otherwise would not be part of the system.

new offense violation The offender on probation is involved with a new crime, which is a violation of the law.

NIMBY A term that means "Not In My Back Yard." It is applied in corrections when citizens do not want correctional facilities built and managed in their neighborhoods.

opportunity set Set of problems that includes situational components of risk; borrowed from routine activities theory.

paper reporting Level of supervision in which the contacts are by mail or telephone only, and occur once per month; reserved for the lowest-risk offender and used in order to provide supervision to the lowest-risk cases with a minimal requirement of resources.

pardon When a government official restores to an individual all rights and privileges of a citizen.

parens patriae Literally translated as "the state of the father" and interpreted to mean that the state can act in the child's best interest by taking over the role of parent if the parents are unable or unwilling to provide the proper treatment for the child at home.

parole Release of a prisoner to community supervision in which surveillance and services are used to improve the prisoner's adjustment to the community.

parole board Determines which inmates in a correctional facility may be released on parole, when the release takes place, and under what conditions the parole is granted.

payback formula Formula to determine how much the state might spend on incarcerating certain offenders, whereby a portion of those costs are designated for return to the localities for keeping offenders from those target groups in local programs.

performance-based supervision An administrative strategy in probation supervision that calls for a shift in the focus of supervision from the activities of supervision to the results of supervision.

presumptive parole date The date by which an inmate can expect to be released if there are no disciplinary or other problems during incarceration.

pretrial release Person receives diversion from prosecution but must fulfill certain conditions or face the charges.

principle of interchangeability The concept that different forms of intermediate sanctions can be calibrated to make them equivalent as punishments despite their differences in approach.

prisons Facilities reserved for the confinement of persons convicted of serious crimes.

probabilistic classification A concept that describes decisions made by correctional officials based on statistical analysis of past behavior to predict future chances of the same behavior.

probation A sentence and a status; people placed on probation are allowed to remain in the community so long as they obey probation rules and refrain from committing new crimes.

problem set Contains traditional factors that are known to affect risk.

problem solving in community justice Problems in community life require organized action on the part of community groups.

program salience The determination as to whether a correctional treatment is appropriate or suitable to the needs and situation of the offender.

programmed contact device Type of electronic monitoring involving a passive monitor that responds only to inquiries.

PSI Presentence investigation typically ordered by the court following the offender's conviction.

recidivism An additional arrest, conviction, or violation of community supervision requirements by a person who has already been convicted of at least one offense.

recidivism in probation Measured in at least four different ways—violations of the conditions of probation, arrests for new offenses committed by probationers, convictions for new offenses, and revocations of probation.

recidivism risk factors Variables that tend to increase risk.

rehabilitation Process of restoring a convicted offender to a constructive place in society through some form of treatment.

reintegration A model that emphasizes the maintenance of the offender's ties to family and the community as a method of reform, in recognition of the fact that the offender will eventually be returning to the community.

relapse prevention Recognizes the struggle and builds supports for the sex offender in facing the sexual compulsion.

release on own recognizance (ROR) The accused promises to appear in court on a specified date and time in exchange for release from custody; no cash or property bond is required; allows for the defendant's release so long as a list of conditions are met.

restitution Payment by the offender to the victim to reimburse some or all of the costs of the crime.

restoration in community justice For victims, having the losses suffered as a result of the crime ameliorated; for offenders, making amends for the offense and taking steps to promise it will not recur; and for the community, renewal of confidence in community life and a faith in its potential.

restorative justice The belief that a penal sanction should seek to restore the victim's losses and allow the offender to be restored to the community.

retribution Punishment inflicted on a person because he or she deserves to be penalized to a degree commensurate with the crime.

revocation When an offender fails on probation or parole to fulfill the obligations of supervision and is returned to the court for resentencing or is incarcerated to continue serving sentence.

risk assessment Use of a series of risk factors to determine the overall likelihood that a given offender will reoffend.

risk control Application of restrictions such that the offender is less likely to be able to engage in criminal behavior.

risk criteria Factors in a case that indicate the likelihood of a new offense.

risk management Philosophy that correctional officials must allocate correctional resources according to the risk represented by correctional clients.

risk reduction The use of treatment programs to change the offender's basic level of risk, resulting in a lower overall probability of new offenses among high-risk offenders.

routine activities theory Crimes occur as a part of everyday life, when in the course of events motivated offenders encounter suitable targets where there are no effective guardians nor intimates to detract from the temptation of the crime.

salience of treatments Correctional treatment program that asks not "What works?" but instead asks "What works with whom under what conditions?"

salient factor score (SFS) Guidelines developed by the U.S. Parole Commission to assist in making parole decisions. It has served as the model for parole guidelines developed throughout the United States.

sanction units in community justice Express the penalty deserved for each crime in the form of "units" of punishment; the more serious the crime, the more units it deserves.

sanctioning in community justice Symbolizes the community's condemnation of the offender for the misconduct, and proclaims the community's resolve that this conduct shall not be permitted.

secular law The law of the civil society, as distinguished from church law.

self-report studies Surveys that ask respondents to report on their own recent criminal activity.

sentence disparity When divergent penalties are given to offenders with similar backgrounds, who have committed the same offense, with no clear justification.

sentencing guidelines A set of "suggested" standards the judge must consider in selecting a sentence.

seriousness scales Rankings of crimes, composed from a survey of a sample of respondents.

sex offender A person who has committed a sexual act prohibited by law, such as rape, child molestation, or prostitution, for economic, psychological, or even situational reasons.

shaming The centuries-old strategy based on the idea that criminal sentences should punish and deter offenders through the show of strong public humiliation.

shock incarceration An offender sentenced to incarceration is released after a period of time in confinement (the shock) and resentenced to probation.

shock parole Decision made by a paroling authority whereby an inmate is released early from his or her sentence after a brief period of incarceration.

shock probation Practice of sentencing offenders to prison, allowing them to apply for probationary release, and then releasing and resentencing to probation.

situational crime prevention Analyzing what it is about locations that promotes the high rates of crime,

and then trying to alter the underlying dynamics that are found.

special conditions of probation Conditions of probation applied to a particular case by the judge due to special circumstances of the offender.

special needs of women offenders Child care responsibilities, economic independence, and substance abuse.

specialized supervision Groups probationers with similar problems into a single caseload, allows the probation officer to develop better expertise in handling that problem, and promotes a concentrated supervision effort to deal with that problem.

split sentence A sentence that includes both time in an institution and a period of time in the community under supervision.

stakes The likelihood that a program failure will create credibility problems for the program.

static risk factors Factors that cannot be changed by external forces, but can change naturally.

status offender A young person who is subject to state authority because of conduct that is illegal only because the child is under a certain age.

street time When an inmate is returned to an institution for a technical violation and he or she receives credit for time spent under supervision before the violation.

structured differential supervision Different offenders receive different types of supervision from staff, based on the problems they represent.

structured enforcement Creates some flexibility in the responses of the system to both enforce the rules of conduct and conserve the valuable time of staff and administrators for the most serious violations.

subsystems of criminal justice Police, courts, and corrections agencies that act within the larger system.

supervision continuum A range of supervision levels is established, and offenders are classified to begin at a level appropriate to their risk, and move upward or downward depending on their behavior.

surveillance Keeping an awareness of the whereabouts and activities of an offender under community supervision, usually through close monitoring.

target group for CCA   A set of offenders who meet specified criteria—usually offense and prior record—that would ordinarily lead them to be sentenced to state prison, but that make state officials want them to be kept locally.

technical violation   An infraction of one of the conditions of probation but not involving violation of law.

teen courts   A method of diversion for juveniles whereby young persons act as court personnel and determine dispositions for minor offenses.

therapeutic jurisprudence   A court-developed approach that looks to deal with a wide range of social problems through treatment rather than full immersion (i.e., prosecution, adjudication, and incarceration) into the criminal justice system.

ticket-of-leave   Also known as the Irish or intermediate system. After a period of strict imprisonment, offenders were transferred to an intermediate prison where they could accumulate marks based on work performance, behavior, and educational improvement. Eventually they would be given tickets-of-leave and released under supervision.

tourniquet sentencing   An approach in which the sentencing judge increases and tightens the amount and conditions of punishment based on offender performance.

transportation   The practice of removing offenders from the community to another land, often a penal colony.

true diversions   When a program actually prevents a person from being incarcerated or immersed into the criminal justice system. Some programs claim to be diversionary but actually increase an offender's contact with the criminal justice system.

truth in sentencing   Offenders will serve all or most of the sentence imposed by the court.

Type I error   Classifying a case as low risk of failure, and the person turns out to fail.

Type II error   Classifying the case as high risk of failure, and the person turns out to succeed.

unit fine   Fine based on a week's income rather than a day's income.

victim impact statement   Details the impact of the crime on the victim and describes how a release will affect the victim emotionally and materially.

violation   Failure to comply with a condition of supervision.

volunteer probation officer   Unpaid volunteer used to assist regular probation officers in a number of court-related functions.

waiver to adult court   The mechanism for transferring juvenile offenders to adult court jurisdiction; also called transfer or certification.

war on crime   Term first used by President Richard Nixon that employed a "get tough" rhetoric and image of dealing with criminals.

war on drugs   A series of policies and laws that adopted the strict criminalization and enforcement of drug sales.

wergild   Punishment that required offenders to recompense the families of their victims, and thus helped reduce the amount of violent, retaliatory bloodshed.

work release   Prison program in which inmates are temporarily released into the community in order to meet job responsibilities.

workload formula   Represents the agency's estimate of whether its staff resources are sufficient to carry out its case management system; total time required for all cases in the agency is calculated by summing the amount of time for each classification level and multiplying by the number of cases in that level.

Index

Netherlands, The, 200
New Jersey, 71, 72
New offense violations, 278
New York, 87, 178, 181, 212, 217, 218,
245, 307, 346, 349–350, 366,
383–384, 405–407
New Zealand, 312, 452
Nicholson, Jack, 140
NIMBY mindset, 106
Nixon, Richard, 51, 270
Nonviolent *versus* violent crimes, 69–71,
74–75
North Carolina, 90–92, 346
North Dakota, 87, 332

Offenders. *See also* Drug use; Juvenile
offenders
career, 420–421
characteristics, 75–76
civil rights of, 377–380
classification of, 61–67, 76–78,
126–129
and crime prevention, 66–67
and criminogenic needs, 64–65,
145–146
distinctions in needs of, 78
and diversion programs, 185–189
electronic monitoring of, 132–133,
206, 222–224, 458–459, 472
and employment, 376–377
freedom of movement of, 131
and gangs, 421–422
influences on corrections and, 44–51
and intermediate sanctions, 16, 52,
204–205, 233–234
legal rights of, 162
lifestyle, 420–421
living in the community, 32–33,
474–478
low-intelligence, 418
mentally handicapped, 416–418
mentally ill, 47, 413–415
and the need/responsivity principle,
149–150
overlap and ambiguity in classification
of, 77
placement in community corrections,
73–76
prevalence of, 3–5
on probation, 280–281
problems in classifying, 76–78
public opinion of, 32–33, 89, 105–106
restoration tasks of, 326–328
restoring rights of ex-, 380
and risk assessments, 63–64, 75–76,
112–113, 117–119, 126–129

and the risk principle, 147–148
and the sanction principle, 148–149
and the setting principle, 148
sex, 282–284, 410–413
and structured enforcement, 123–124
and suitability for treatment, 65–66
and supervision continuum, 122–123
supervision levels for, •21–122
surveillance of, 130
target group and community
corrections, 88–92, 233
types of, 399–412
women, 284–286
Offenses
classifying, 67–73
drug, 4, 71–72
and exclusions from community
corrections, 74–75
seriousness scales, 68–69
sex, 72–73
violent *versus* nonviolent, 69–71
Office of National Drug Control Policy,
50
Ohio, 225, 346, 451
Oklahoma, 97
O'Leary, Vincent, 45, 112
One Flew Over the Cuckoo's Nest, 140
Operation Ceasefire, 461–462
Operation Nite Lite, 461–462
Oregon, 97, 164, 212, 305, 346

Packer, Herbert, 50
Pardons, 355–356
Parens patriae, 440–442
Parole, 16–17, 91, 476–477. *See also*
Probation; Supervision
and abuse of discretion, 387
advantages of, 386–387
aftercare, 380–383
and appointment to boards, 371
and autonomous *versus* consolidated
parole boards, 369–370
barriers to successful, 375–377
boards, 368–369, 368–372
bureaucracy, 392
and civil rights, 377–380
combined with probation, 251–253
and conditions of release, 349–350
as a contract or consent, 347
and corrections systems, 390–391
costs, 23f, 386
as custody, 347
different kinds of, 350–354
disadvantages of, 387–388
and discretionary release, 351–352
effectiveness of, 389–390, 391–392

eligibility, 364
elimination of, 388–389
in England, 39–40, 348
evidence on, 391–392
and expiration release, 354
field services, 370
and finding employment, 376–377
and full-time *versus* part-time parole
boards, 370–371
as a grace or privilege, 347
guidelines, 362–369
hearings, 344–345, 365–367
history of, 346–347
and interstate compacts, 357
in Japan, 268–269
leniency of, 48–49
and mandatory release, 353–354
officer and board liability, 371–372
and organization of releasing
authorities, 369–372
origins of, 39–41, 348
and postrelease supervision, 373–374
and preparing offenders for release,
367–368
and preparole investigation, 364–365
and the problem of unmet personal
needs, 375
and recidivism, 6
and rehabilitation, 387
in the reintegration era, 47–48
and restitution, 387
revocation of, 383–385
and risk to the community, 387
and the Salient Factor Score (SFS),
112, 362
and sentencing guidelines, 386–387
shock, 359–361
statistics, 5f, 346f, 384
and stigmatization, 377–380
and the strangeness of reentry into the
community, 374–375
and street time, 386
supervision, 348
and truth in sentencing, 372–373
and the war on crime era, 48–49
Patuxent Institution, 77
Payback formula, 88, 93, 94–95
Peers and juvenile offenders, 433–434
Penn, William, 95
Pennsylvania, 226, 420, 440
People perspective of community
corrections, 26–27
Performance-based supervision,
286–287
Peter Young Housing, Industries and
Treatment (PYHIT), 406
Petersilia, Joan, 219, 417